# CRICKET YEAR

# CRICKET YEAR

### TWENTY-SIXTH EDITION
September 2006 to September 2007


Edited by JONATHAN AGNEW

with additional contributions by
Mark Baldwin
Tony Cozier
Pat Gibson
Jim Maxwell
Derek Underwood

A & C Black • London

Edited by Jonathan Agnew
Assistant editing by Mark Baldwin
with additional contributions by
Tony Cozier
John Etheridge
Gulu Ezekiel
Pat Gibson
Haydn Gill
Andrew Hignell
Jim Maxwell
Mark Pennell
Bruce Talbot
Derek Underwood
Paul Weaver
Tim Wellock
With special thanks to the NAB Group and to the England & Wales Cricket Board

The publishers would also like to thank *The Times* for their kind permission to
reproduce the photograph of Mark Baldwin on page 32.

First published in 2007 by
A & C Black Ltd
38 Soho Square
London W1D 3HB

www.acblack.com

Copyright © 2007 Jonathan Agnew

A copy of the CIP entry for this book is available from the British Library.

ISBN: 978-0-7136-8728-6

10 9 8 7 6 5 4 3 2 1

A & C Black uses paper produced with elemental chlorine-free pulp, harvested
from managed sustainable forests.

Project editor: Julian Flanders at Butler and Tanner
Design: Kathie Wilson at Butler and Tanner
Project manager: Nicky Thompson
Statistics and County information: Press Association
Pictures © PA Photos, except page 9 © Peter Baxter &
page 145 © IS Sport (photo Ian Smith)

Printed and bound in Great Britain
by Butler and Tanner, Frome and London

# CONTENTS

6 Aggers' View
*by Jonathan Agnew*

10 ICC WORLD TWENTY20

15 Mahendra Dhoni *by Paul Weaver*

16 ENGLAND

16 West Indies in England
*by Jonathan Agnew*

21 NatWest Series v. West Indies
*by Jonathan Agnew*

22 Monty Panesar *by Derek Underwood*

24 India in England
*by Jonathan Agnew*

28 NatWest Series v. India
*by Jonathan Agnew*

30 Kevin Pietersen *by John Etheridge*

32 ENGLISH DOMESTIC SEASON
Introduction *by Mark Baldwin*

33 MCC v. Sussex

34 LV County Championship
*by Mark Baldwin*

58 Rain Stops Play *by Andrew Hignell*

82 Robert Croft *by Mark Baldwin*

92 Sussex: LV County Champions
*by Bruce Talbot*

98 First-Class County Form Charts

134 NatWest Pro40 *by Mark Baldwin*

144 Worcestershire: NatWest Pro40 Champions
*by Pat Gibson*

146 Twenty20 Cup *by Mark Baldwin*

154 Kent: Twenty20 Cup Winners
*by Mark Pennell*

156 Friends Provident Trophy *by Mark Baldwin*

170 Durham: Friends Provident Trophy Winners
*by Tim Wellock*

172 AUSTRALIA

172 England in Australia *by Jonathan Agnew*

182 Australia Report *by Jim Maxwell*

184 BANGLADESH

187 INDIA *by Gulu Ezekiel*

190 NEW ZEALAND

194 PAKISTAN

198 SOUTH AFRICA

205 SRI LANKA

208 ICC WORLD CUP *by Haydn Gill*

216 WEST INDIES *by Tony Cozier*

218 ZIMBABWE

220 Other International Matches

# AGGERS' VIEW

### by Jonathan Agnew

I vividly remember sitting at this very desk exactly a year ago looking back on the 2006 summer, but scarcely able to contain my excitement at the forthcoming prospect of flying to Australia to watch the most anticipated Ashes series for decades.

The pain of the crushing disappointment that followed has eased now, and a lot of water has since flowed under the bridge. Duncan Fletcher, the England coach, found his position became increasingly untenable the more he claimed that his was the best-prepared team ever to take on Australia. That simply was not true: England's build-up was an embarrassment to all who witnessed the early weeks of the tour, to the extent that the players seemed genuinely surprised by the ferocity of the Australian juggernaut that demolished them at Brisbane.

One outcome of that debacle is that the coach, now Peter Moores, will be managed – strictly, we hope – by Hugh Morris, England's new managing director. Fletcher had no such check or balance, and therefore no one appeared to question his decisions.

It is true that Fletcher did a great deal for English cricket, and every coach does have a shelf life, but it was the fault of the England and Wales Cricket Board that he was able to plan such a controversial

Does the body language say it all? Duncan Fletcher's long-awaited autobiography included serious criticism of Andrew Flintoff's off-field behaviour during the Ashes tour and World Cup. Fletcher enjoyed excellent relationships with his first two England captains, Nasser Hussain and Michael Vaughan, during his seven-and-a-half-year reign as head coach. Freddie, however, proved to be a pedalo too far.

preparation for that most high profile of sporting events without anybody – apart from the English and Australian media – apparently raising so much as an eyebrow.

It was clear, come last January and the 5-0 Ashes defeat, that only an outstanding World Cup could save Fletcher and, as has become their habit in that tournament, England were anything but. Hobbling through the early stages, the players seemed nervous and unwilling to take the sort of free-spirited risk one associates with the likes of Herschelle Gibbs, Yuvraj Singh or Andrew Symonds.

A drunken Andrew Flintoff, the vice-captain, meanwhile capsized a pedalo in the early hours of the morning between games at St Lucia. He was suspended and fined, but the real damage, according to Michael Vaughan, was inflicted on the morale of the team. The fact was that England were already finding it tough enough competing out of their depth, without distractions such as the 'Fredalo' incident.

Sadly, Flintoff made little impact on the year. He underwent two further operations – that makes four in all – on his troublesome left ankle, and he does not expect to feature again until the summer of 2008.

It seems unlikely that he will ever be the force he once was with the ball, not through lack of effort, pace or bounce, but simply because the ankle will not stand a day-to-day pounding. There have been suggestions made that Flintoff might become solely a one-day cricketer – an interesting reversal of the usual trend which is to pursue a Test career as long as possible – and in his case it has merit.

**Above** Australia's Nathan Bracken clean bowls South Africa captain Graeme Smith as Australia's advance on the World Cup trophy continues in St Lucia.

**Below** West Indies captain Brian Lara is applauded by the England players as he walks out to bat in his last match before retiring during the World Cup Super Eights in Barbados on 21 April.

**Above** Crowds at the ICC World Twenty20 were enthusiastic, large and clearly having a good time. Satisfied spectators were, however, just one aspect of a hugely successful event.

**Below** Indian opener Gautam Gambhir digs out an Umar Gul yorker during the ICC World Twenty20 final against Pakistan in Johannesburg.

Peter Baxter, *Test Match Special*'s long-serving producer, bowed out in style during the programme's 50th-anniversary year.

The World Cup itself was a disgrace – and a tedious, protracted one at that. Once again, the main thrust of the tournament was all about making as much money as possible, with little consideration given to the game and its supporters. It will be remembered for empty grounds (in Guyana, for example, locals were charged a month's salary to watch South Africa versus Sri Lanka), for a chaotic and badly administered final and for the sad and untimely death of an immensely popular man, Bob Woolmer. At least the murder charge – which no one in the cricketing world seriously believed – has been revoked, and the stress and likely repercussions of Pakistan's early exit appear to have been too much for him to bear.

So dreadful was the World Cup, indeed, that all eyes were firmly focused on the first ICC World Twenty20 tournament, which was staged in South Africa in September. And, thank goodness, the administrators this time got it right. Spectators were encouraged by tickets costing as little as £1.50, they were not searched repeatedly every few yards and they could bring in flags of their own choosing – and even drink bottled water.

Let us hope that the message has sunk in: that these world tournaments are cricket's global shop window. Admittance fees are an irrelevant pittance when compared to the money generated by television and advertising revenue, and the grounds must be full of people having a good time. The players fed off the atmosphere in South Africa and produced some tremendous, innovative cricket in a format of the game that endears itself to all generations. It is not, in my view (and the players' too, for that matter) the future of cricket, but it is an important part of the future of the game. Hopefully it will replace the unpopular and wholly unnecessary Champions Trophy.

But then we cannot expect the ICC to have a firm handle on the game it controls. After all, they were exposed as a bunch of nincompoops at Darrell Hair's unsuccessful tribunal. The nadir arrived splendidly when the President of the West Indies Cricket Board did not know that umpire Billy Doctrove – one of the central figures in the case – is a West Indian. It bordered on the hilarious, but actually it beggars belief that cricket is still capable of being run by incompetents such as that.

The year 2007 will also be remembered as marking the 50th anniversary of BBC Radio's *Test Match Special* programme and, more significantly perhaps, the retirement of its long-standing and long-suffering producer, Peter Baxter.

Peter always had a gentle hand on the tiller, but little more than that, and his genial approach – combined with the broadcasting of brilliant commentators like John Arlott and Brian Johnston – have made the programme what it is today. I will miss Peter enormously as a colleague, but particularly as a friend during the long months away from home every winter, and I know that everyone still involved with every aspect of *TMS* will strive to build on the platform that Peter so carefully and meticulously built over his 34 years at the helm.

*Jonathan Agnew*
*Leicestershire, October 2007*

# ICC WORLD TWENTY20

## by Jonathan Agnew

After the horrible hash that the ICC made of the Cricket World Cup earlier in 2007, the game desperately needed its next global tournament to be a success.

Happily, the ICC World Twenty20 came along just at the right time… and happy is a word I think most suits the memory of it. It was short, sweet, action-packed, well organised, sensibly priced, and magnificently well attended by fervent supporters. For everyone involved – players, administrators, fans and the media – it was a happy tournament.

It is a complicated and sometimes difficult job to report and comment on it, of course. You never know what's going to happen next, and when it does it all happens so fast. But the fact that the Twenty20 game changes so quickly, and that it is so new in international terms that there seem to be no accepted rules of how to approach it, makes it even more exciting to watch.

There were a lot of thrilling moments in the tournament, too, though England's far greater experience of the format (there have been five domestic Twenty20 Cups now since 2003) didn't do very much for them in the end.

Tactically, there were different approaches from different teams. India, the eventual winners, liked to bat first and get the runs on the board and this method clearly worked well for them. England, under Paul Collingwood, also started out in the tournament wanting to bat first – but then they switched around to putting the opposition in. People were plainly learning on the hoof, but then that made things even more gloriously unpredictable.

The Australian attitude, coming into the tournament, was interesting. At first, it looked as if they were treating it all as a bit of a giggle, but then they had their backsides kicked in their first game against Zimbabwe and that seemed not just to wake them up but everyone else too.

Upsets are obviously more possible in a shorter form of the game but, unlike the World Cup six months earlier, if there was a one-sided affair then it was all over more quickly. There was no lingering over the defeat of an outgunned side. It was like watching a mercy killing, I suppose, if one team got well ahead of another.

And – as the games flowed, one after another in double-quick time – the cricket was always highly entertaining, and always of an excellent standard. The thousands upon thousands who came to watch, and who were not ridiculously overcharged for the privilege or had their flags and banners confiscated, went away again thrilled by what they had seen. Everyone had a great time at the grounds, and the party atmosphere was entirely genuine and never contrived.

Well, there were some who didn't always enjoy the experience: the poor old bowlers. A lot of bowlers copped a load of flak – and not just Stuart Broad in that incredible over when Yuvraj Singh clobbered him for six sixes. As a former professional bowler myself, it often looked extremely painful.

But, then again, some bowlers did come through with reputations intact, and in some cases enhanced. Umar Gul's yorkers were consistently effective and Daniel Vettori was well worth his status as the tournament's most economical bowler, conceding fewer than six runs per over which is a superb effort.

Young Broad, meanwhile, is a feisty sort of lad and I don't think the Yuvraj onslaught will be of major damage to his future career. In the atmosphere of Twenty20, moreover, with crowds baying and the springy bats of today seemingly able to propel the ball ever further into the stands (and often over them), anything can happen – and often did.

Vettori's bowling, however, bears a little further study because it is evidence of how a clever spinner – varying his pace and flight and using all his experience to keep the batsman guessing – can be as effective, or more

**Opposite** Daniel Vettori, the New Zealand left-arm spinner, was the most economical bowler in the highly successful ICC World Twenty20 tournament.

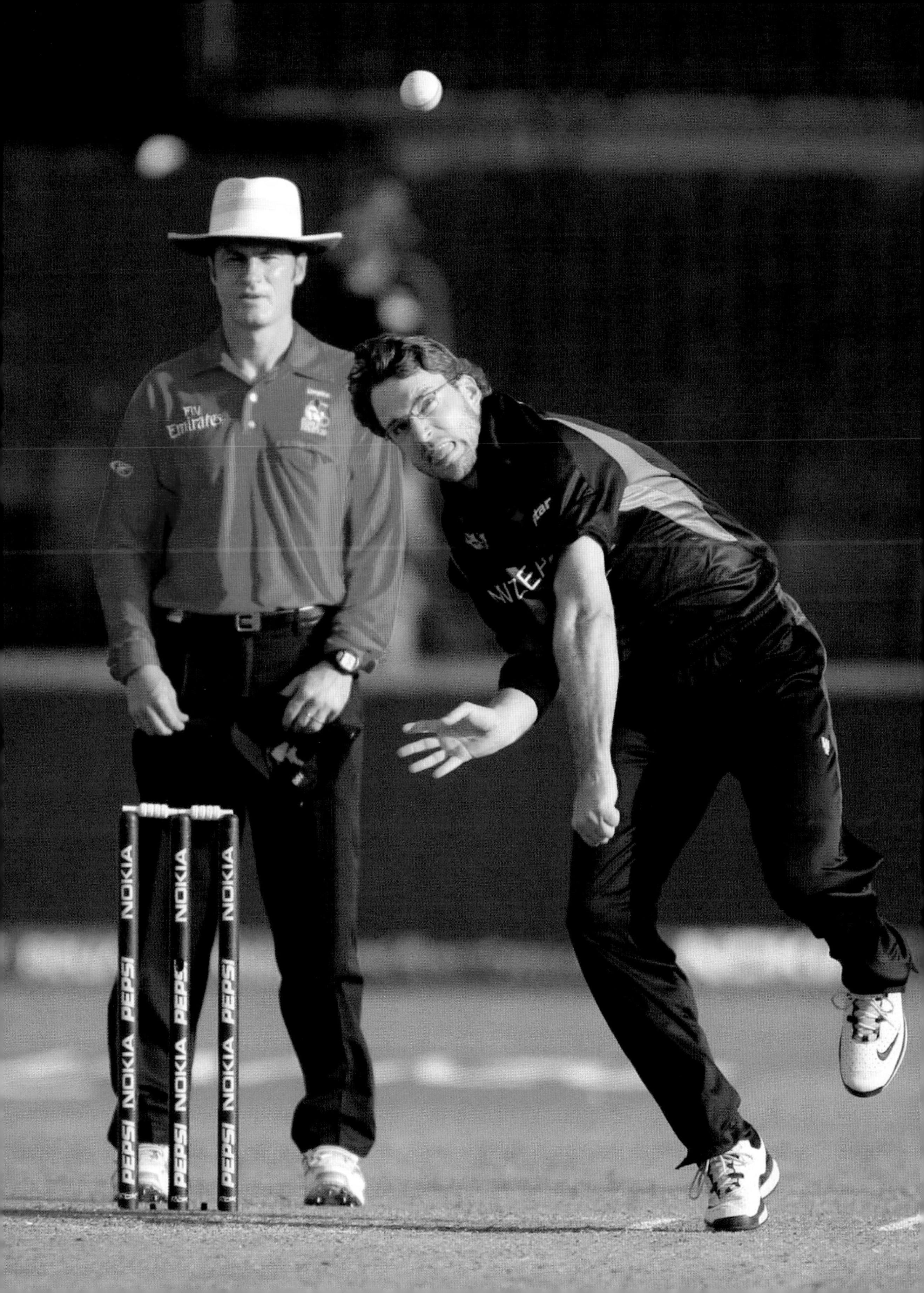

effective, than the fastest and nastiest bowler. Even more so than with conventional one-day cricket, it was imagined that Twenty20 would be the death of spinners, but New Zealand's slow left-armer and new captain showed just how the opposite is true.

The fielding, of course, took modern-day collective and individual brilliance to new levels, and the overall tone for the tournament was set right from the amazing opening match between South Africa and the West Indies. Not that the West Indians' appalling fielding and bowling was representative, you understand, only the thrilling spectacle and the way batsmen constantly manufactured shots and mixed awesome power with placement to score runs at jaw-dropping speed.

I bumped into Jonty Rhodes on the airport bus the day after the match in which South Africa eventually triumphed despite Chris Gayle's incredible initial onslaught, and as he was involved with the South African team management I asked him if my eyes had not deceived me and that – at the height of Gayle's assault – there had been three changes of tactics in the field in the space of three balls.

No, said Jonty, I was wrong. It had been FOUR changes of tactics in FOUR balls – that's how hard South Africa were working in desperation to keep the lid on things.

It was fascinating, indeed, to watch for the remainder of the tournament as captains and bowlers tried their best to maintain some sort of control in the field. They tried packed offside fields, packed legside fields, long off back, long off in, fine leg back, fine leg up inside the circle, bowlers coming over the wicket, bowlers coming around the wicket… you name it, they tried it.

Batsmen, on the other hand, were always trying

to manufacture shots to areas unguarded by boundary fielders, and the flip to fine leg – when fine leg was up – seemed to me to be clearly an area where most batsmen thought they could gain huge dividends.

Switch-hitting, too, is something I reckon will take off even more as batsmen seek to make field-setting a truly impossible task but, in this superb first World Twenty20, it was perhaps fitting that the fateful final shot of the whole event should be yet another attempt to propel the ball to or over the fine-leg boundary.

With the match teetering on a knife-edge in the final over, and the pressure immense, Pakistan batsman Misbah-ul-Haq opted for just such a stroke off a clearly nervous Joginder Singh. Misbah had all but snatched the match away from India with a truly brilliant innings, but he couldn't quite find just one more shot of genius.

As Sreesanth took the catch at short fine leg, and the whole of India erupted in joy, I couldn't help but feel sorry for Misbah. Was that the right or wrong shot to play, and was it the right or wrong time to play it?

I just don't know. Poor Misbah. But what a moment, what a finish and what a heart-stopping spectacle.

If ICC don't abandon their unloved Champions Trophy tournament right now, and replace it with the World Twenty20, they will be mad.

Poor Misbah-ul-Haq looks on in despair as India's players celebrate their victory against Pakistan in the ICC World Twenty20 final at the Wanderers, Johannesburg.

**Group A** – 11 September 2007 at Johannesburg
**West Indies** 205 for 6 (20 overs) (CH Gayle 117)
**South Africa** 208 for 2 (17.4 overs) (HH Gibbs 90*)
*South Africa (2pts) won by 8 wickets*

13 September 2007 at Johannesburg
**West Indies** 164 for 8 (20 overs) (DS Smith 51,
Shakib Al Hasan 4 for 34)
**Bangladesh** 165 for 4 (18 overs) (Aftab Ahmed 62*,
Mohammad Ashraful 61)
*Bangladesh (2pts) won by 6 wickets*

15 September 2007 at Cape Town
**Bangladesh** 144 all out (19.3 overs)
**South Africa** 146 for 3 (18.5 overs)
*South Africa (2pts) won by 7 wickets*

|              | P | W | L | T | NR | RR    | Pts |
|--------------|---|---|---|---|----|-------|-----|
| South Africa | 2 | 2 | 0 | 0 | 0  | 0.97  | 4   |
| Bangladesh   | 2 | 1 | 1 | 0 | 0  | 0.15  | 2   |
| West Indies  | 2 | 0 | 2 | 0 | 0  | -1.23 | 0   |

**Group B** – 12 September 2007 at Cape Town
**Australia** 138 for 9 (20 overs)
**Zimbabwe** 139 for 5 (19.5 overs) (BRM Taylor 60*)
*Zimbabwe (2pts) won by 5 wickets*

13 September 2007 at Cape Town
**England** 188 for 9 (20 overs) (KP Pietersen 79,
E Chigumbura 4 for 31)
**Zimbabwe** 138 for 7 (20 overs)
*England (2pts) won by 50 runs*

14 September 2007 at Cape Town
**England** 135 all out (20 overs)
**Australia** 136 for 2 (14.5 overs) (ML Hayden 67*)
*Australia (2pts) won by 8 wickets*

|           | P | W | L | T | NR | RR    | Pts |
|-----------|---|---|---|---|----|-------|-----|
| Australia | 2 | 1 | 1 | 0 | 0  | 0.97  | 2   |
| England   | 2 | 1 | 1 | 0 | 0  | 0.15  | 2   |
| Zimbabwe  | 2 | 1 | 1 | 0 | 0  | -1.20 | 2   |

**Group C** – 12 September 2007 at Durban
**Kenya** 73 all out (16.5 overs) (MR Gillespie 4 for 7)
**New Zealand** 74 for 1 (7.4 overs)
*New Zealand (2pts) won by 9 wickets*

14 September 2007 at Johannesburg
**Sri Lanka** 260 for 6 (20 overs) (ST Jayasuriya 88,
DPMD Jayawardene 65)
**Kenya** 88 for 9 (19.3 overs)
*Sri Lanka (2pts) won by 172 runs*

15 September 2007 at Johannesburg
**New Zealand** 164 for 7 (20 overs) (RL Taylor 62)
**Sri Lanka** 168 for 3 (18.5 overs) (ST Jayasuriya 61)
*Sri Lanka (2pts) won by 7 wickets*

|             | P | W | L | T | NR | RR    | Pts |
|-------------|---|---|---|---|----|-------|-----|
| Sri Lanka   | 2 | 2 | 0 | 0 | 0  | 4.72  | 4   |
| New Zealand | 2 | 1 | 1 | 0 | 0  | 2.40  | 2   |
| Kenya       | 2 | 0 | 2 | 0 | 0  | -8.05 | 0   |

**Group D** – 12 September 2007 at Durban
**Pakistan** 171 for 9 (20 overs)
**Scotland** 120 all out (19.5 overs) (Shahid Afridi 4 for 19,
Umar Gul 4 for 25)
*Pakistan (2pts) won by 51 runs*

13 September 2007 at Durban
**India** v. **Scotland**
*Match abandoned – 1pt each*

14 September 2007 at Durban
**India** 141 for 9 (20 overs) (AR Uthappa 50,
Mohammad Asif 4 for 18)
**Pakistan** 141 for 7 (20 overs) (Misbah-ul-Haq 53)
*Match tied – India (2pts) won 3-0 on bowl-out*

|          | P | W | L | T | NR | RR    | Pts |
|----------|---|---|---|---|----|-------|-----|
| India    | 2 | 0 | 0 | 1 | 1  | 0.00  | 3   |
| Pakistan | 2 | 1 | 0 | 1 | 0  | 1.27  | 2   |
| Scotland | 2 | 0 | 1 | 0 | 1  | -2.55 | 1   |

## Super Eights

**Group E** – 16 September 2007 at Johannesburg
**New Zealand** 190 all out (20 overs)
**India** 180 for 9 (20 overs) (G Gambhir 51, DL Vettori 4 for 20)
*New Zealand (2pts) won by 10 runs*

at Cape Town
**South Africa** 154 for 8 (20 overs)
**England** 135 for 7 (20 overs)
*South Africa (2pts) won by 19 runs*

18 September 2007 at Durban
**New Zealand** 164 for 9 (20 overs) (CD McMillan 57)
**England** 159 for 8 (20 overs) (DL Maddy 50)
*New Zealand (2pts) won by 5 runs*

19 September 2007 at Durban
**New Zealand** 153 for 8 (20 overs) (M Morkel 4 for 17)
**South Africa** 158 for 4 (19.1 overs) (JM Kemp 89*)
*South Africa (2pts) won by 6 wickets*

at Durban
**India** 218 for 4 (20 overs) (V Sehwag 68, G Gambhir 58, Yuvraj Singh 58)
**England** 200 for 6 (20 overs)
*India (2pts) won by 18 runs*

20 September 2007 at Durban
**India** 153 for 5 (20 overs) (RP Sharma 50*)
**South Africa** 116 for 9 (20 overs) (RP Singh 4 for 13)
*India (2pts) won by 37 runs*

|  | P | W | L | T | NR | RR | Pts |
|---|---|---|---|---|---|---|---|
| India | 3 | 2 | 1 | 0 | 0 | 0.75 | 4 |
| New Zealand | 3 | 2 | 1 | 0 | 0 | 0.05 | 4 |
| South Africa | 3 | 2 | 1 | 0 | 0 | -0.12 | 4 |
| England | 3 | 0 | 3 | 0 | 0 | -0.70 | 0 |

**Group F** – 16 September 2007 at Cape Town
**Bangladesh** 123 for 8 (20 overs)
**Australia** 124 for 1 (13.5 overs) (ML Hayden 73*)
*Australia (2pts) won by 9 wickets*

17 September 2007 Day/Night at Johannesburg
**Pakistan** 189 for 6 (20 overs) (Shoaib Malik 57, Younus Khan 51)
**Sri Lanka** 156 for 9 (20 overs)
*Pakistan (2pts) won by 33 runs*

18 September 2007 at Johannesburg
**Australia** 164 for 7 (20 overs)
**Pakistan** 165 for 4 (19.1 overs) (Misbah-ul-Haq 66*, Shoaib Malik 52*)
*Pakistan (2pts) won by 6 wickets*

Day/Night at Johannesburg
**Sri Lanka** 147 for 5 (20 overs)
**Bangladesh** 83 all out (15.5 overs)
*Sri Lanka (2pts) won by 64 runs*

20 September 2007 at Cape Town
**Sri Lanka** 101 all out (19.3 overs) (SR Clark 4 for 20)
**Australia** 102 for 0 (10.2 overs) (ML Hayden 58*)
*Australia (2pts) won by 10 wickets*

at Cape Town
**Bangladesh** 140 all out (19.4 overs) (Junaid Siddique 71)
**Pakistan** 141 for 6 (19 overs)
*Pakistan (2pts) won by 4 wickets*

|  | P | W | L | T | NR | RR | Pts |
|---|---|---|---|---|---|---|---|
| Pakistan | 3 | 3 | 0 | 0 | 0 | 0.84 | 6 |
| Australia | 3 | 2 | 1 | 0 | 0 | 2.26 | 4 |
| Sri Lanka | 3 | 1 | 2 | 0 | 0 | -0.70 | 2 |
| Bangladesh | 3 | 0 | 3 | 0 | 0 | -2.03 | 0 |

## Semi-Finals

22 September 2007 at Cape Town
**New Zealand** 143 for 8 (20 overs)
**Pakistan** 147 for 4 (18.5 overs) (Imran Nazir 59)
*Pakistan won by 6 wickets*

at Durban
**India** 188 for 5 (20 overs) (Yuvraj Singh 70)
**Australia** 173 for 7 (20 overs) (ML Hayden 62)
*India won by 15 runs*

## FINAL – PAKISTAN v. INDIA
### 24 September 2007 at Johannesburg

### INDIA

| | | |
|---|---|---|
| G Gambhir | c Mohammad Asif b Umar Gul | 75 |
| Y Pathan | c Shoaib Malik b Mohammad Asif | 15 |
| AR Uthappa | c Shahid Afridi b Sohail Tanvir | 8 |
| Yuvraj Singh | c & b Umar Gul | 14 |
| *MS Dhoni (capt) | b Umar Gul | 6 |
| RP Sharma | not out | 30 |
| IK Pathan | not out | 3 |
| Harbhajan Singh | | |
| Joginder Sharma | | |
| S Sreesanth | | |
| RP Singh | | |
| Extras | lb 1, w 4, nb 1 | 6 |
| | (5 wkts 20 overs) | **157** |

| | O | M | R | W |
|---|---|---|---|---|
| Mohammad Asif | 3 | 0 | 25 | 1 |
| Sohail Tanvir | 4 | 0 | 29 | 1 |
| Shahid Afridi | 4 | 0 | 30 | 0 |
| Mohammad Hafeez | 3 | 0 | 25 | 0 |
| Umar Gul | 4 | 0 | 28 | 3 |
| Yasir Arafat | 2 | 0 | 19 | 0 |

**Fall of Wickets:**
1-25, 2-40, 3-103, 4-111, 5-130

### PAKISTAN

| | | |
|---|---|---|
| Mohammad Hafeez | c Uthappa b Singh RP | 1 |
| Imran Nazir | run out | 33 |
| *Kamran Akmal | b Singh RP | 0 |
| Younus Khan | c Pathan Y b Joginder Sharma | 24 |
| Shoaib Malik (capt) | c Sharma b Pathan IK | 8 |
| Misbah-ul-Haq | c Sreesanth b Joginder Sharma | 43 |
| Shahid Afridi | c Sreesanth b Pathan IK | 0 |
| Yasir Arafat | b Pathan IK | 15 |
| Sohail Tanvir | b Sreesanth | 12 |
| Umar Gul | b Singh | 0 |
| Mohammad Asif | not out | 4 |
| Extras | b 1, lb 4, w 6, nb 1 | 12 |
| | (all out 19.3 overs) | **152** |

| | O | M | R | W |
|---|---|---|---|---|
| Singh RP | 4 | 0 | 26 | 3 |
| Sreesanth | 4 | 1 | 44 | 1 |
| Joginder Sharma | 3.3 | 0 | 20 | 2 |
| Pathan Y | 1 | 0 | 5 | 0 |
| Pathan IK | 4 | 0 | 16 | 3 |
| Harbhajan Singh | 3 | 0 | 36 | 0 |

**Fall of Wickets:**
1-2, 2-26, 3-53, 4-65, 5-76, 6-77, 7-104, 8-138, 9-141

Umpires: MR Benson (England) & SJA Taufel (Australia)
Toss: India
Twenty20 debut: Y Pathan
Man of the Match: IK Pathan
Man of the Series: Shahid Afridi

## India won by 5 runs

# MAHENDRA DHONI

Paul Weaver, of the *Guardian*, meets a player who looks like being the next huge star of India.

M ahendra Singh Dhoni has the potential to become the richest, most adored cricketer the game has ever seen. In India, cricket's wealthiest and most passionate land, Sachin Tendulkar still currently holds those titles. But Dhoni, 26, with his handsome features and explosive game, is the new big thing in Indian cricket.

Already massively popular, he achieved true god-like status in late September 2007 by leading India, even without Tendulkar, Ganguly and Dravid, to their wildly dramatic ICC World Twenty20 final victory. The sky, indeed, is Dhoni's only limit.

He arrived at the top table of Indian cricket from the small town of Ranchi in the backwaters of Jharkhand and, in Tests as well as limited-overs cricket, has brought new life to an ageing side. But he is more than merely a gifted all-round cricketer. Dhoni endorses 17 products, including clothing, motorbikes, soap and a bank, and his image can be seen on giant advertising hoardings all over the subcontinent.

Crowds, indeed, gather wherever he goes and whenever he comes out to bat there is a frenzy of anticipation. He has played for his country for just over three years but his impact has been profound. He scored 40 and 68 not out when he made his first-class debut in 1999–2000 but it is in the shorter game where his aggressive talent has come into its own.

In just his fifth one-day international he scored 148 from 123 balls against Pakistan and six months later he made 183 not out from 145 balls against Sri Lanka hitting 15 fours and ten sixes and breaking Adam Gilchrist's record for a wicketkeeper in an ODI. He has found Test cricket a little more difficult but still managed 148 at Faisalabad in only his fifth game.

But, as he explained to me, the truth is he could have been lost to football. 'When I was 12 or 13 years old there used to be a football training camp near where I lived and at that age I was quite inclined towards football and goalkeeping, so I went along. I practised for a couple of years. Then my school cricket team needed a wicketkeeper. We used to play canvas ball cricket, which is a version played with a tennis ball on an 18-yard pitch. My games teacher told me that the basics were the same for wicketkeeping as for goalkeeping in that you moved to one side or the other and you had to catch the ball. So that's how it started.

'I played canvas ball cricket for about a year and after that I started playing for the school team. But I still love football. I support Manchester United.' Zinedine Zidane was his favourite

Looks, charisma and a major prize-winner: Mahendra Singh Dhoni is fast emerging as one of the new superstars of world cricket.

footballer but now it is Cristiano Ronaldo. During last summer's tour of England, his first lengthy visit to the country, he enjoyed what in effect amounted to anonymity – especially compared to the situation at home.

'In India I cannot go anywhere. Cricket there is something more than an obsession. I have to be careful. There are places where I will get mobbed but there is no security risk.'

Even so, five armed policemen were called after one female supporter breached security at Eden Gardens, Calcutta.

The man called 'Mahi' found life in England a little more peaceful. 'I can go everywhere there and no one recognises me. I can walk the streets and sit in McDonald's.'

Overall, though, besides being an idol in a country where cricket is the most important thing in the world, he is a person mature enough and intelligent enough to see the reality behind his superstar status. 'I am only three years old in international cricket terms and I am still learning,' he says.

There is, clearly, still so much more to come.

# ENGLAND

## WEST INDIES IN ENGLAND
### by Jonathan Agnew

After the interminable World Cup – in which self-interest and financial reward were considered more important than anything else – cricket lovers hoped for some entertainment and excitement from the Test series against the West Indies which followed almost immediately after England's players returned from the Caribbean.

Sadly, however, this must rank as one of the dullest, most predictable and low-quality Test series ever played between two senior international teams. The West Indies were simply dreadful and it could be argued that this accounted – in part, at least – for England's atrocious bowling.

None of this was helped by the weather. And whoever devised the itinerary, which after Lord's then took in the northernmost grounds at Leeds, Manchester and Chester-le-Street, must have had a wicked sense of humour. The bitter cold only relented when it rained – which it did for most of the time. The cricket was as gloomy as the weather, and it was clear to see that most of the West Indians were not enjoying themselves one bit.

Ryan Sidebottom took eight West Indies wickets on a highly successful Test comeback at Headingley, after a six-year absence, including this second-innings scalp of Devon Smith – caught by Andrew Strauss at second slip.

Alastair Cook scored his fifth Test century on the first day of the series, and he was joined on the second by Paul Collingwood, Ian Bell and – appearing in his first Test – Matt Prior, who appeared to resolve the wicketkeeping debate once and for all by playing belligerently for his 126 not out.

England posted a massive 553 for 5 but the West Indies – led by Shiv Chanderpaul and helped by an injury to Matthew Hoggard – made a fight of their first innings having been reduced to an ominous 83 for 2. Monty Panesar claimed five lbws in his best figures of 6 for 129 as England took a first-innings lead of 116. Kevin Pietersen then scored 109 to keep England well in control. West Indies needed 401 to win, and entered the final day with all ten wickets standing only for rain and bad light to allow only 20 overs to be bowled.

At Leeds, England rattled up another huge score – 570 for 7 – and this time the West Indies crumbled under the pressure in the absence of their most experienced batsmen, Ramnaresh Sarwan – injured while fielding and who missed the rest of the series – and Chanderpaul.

Pietersen added a double-hundred to his ton at Lord's but the most pleasing aspect of England's innings was the return to the team after 18 months of Michael Vaughan. He responded typically with his 16th Test hundred, and then savoured a remarkable recall by his former Yorkshire team-mate, Ryan Sidebottom.

It had seemed inevitable that both father (Arnie) and son would share the distinction of forming a 'one cap wonder' group of their own, but having made his only previous appearance in 2001 – and apparently not having had a haircut since – Ryan claimed 4 for 42 in ideal swing-bowling conditions to bundle the sorry West Indies out for just 146. He then took four more to finish with 8 for 86 in the game as the tourists were dispatched for 141 in their second innings to complete their heaviest defeat in Test cricket – the small matter of an innings and 283 runs.

So to Old Trafford, with Daren Ganga now at the helm and England distracted by some indiscreet comments by Vaughan about Andrew Flintoff's 'Fredalo' incident in the World Cup. Flintoff, who had undergone his third ankle operation, came to the Test, and the two kissed and made up before England completed their second victory of the four-match series.

England batted first again and scored 370 by lunch on the second day. Bell came within three runs of a century while Andrew Strauss's form was beginning to give rise to concern. In the West Indies first innings the bowling of Liam Plunkett and Steve Harmison reached its nadir. Can there ever have been such grotesquely wide bowling in a Test match? Yet West Indies spinelessly contrived to lose their last six wickets for 13 runs to complete a

## FIRST TEST – ENGLAND v. WEST INDIES
### 17–21 May 2007 at Lord's

### ENGLAND

| | First Innings | | | Second Innings | | |
|---|---|---|---|---|---|---|
| AJ Strauss (capt) | c Smith b Powell | 33 | | c Morton b Collymore | 24 | |
| AN Cook | c Bravo b Taylor | 105 | | c Ramdin b Collymore | 65 | |
| OA Shah | c Smith b Powell | 6 | | c Ramdin b Collymore | 4 | |
| KP Pietersen | c Smith b Collymore | 26 | | lbw b Gayle | 109 | |
| PD Collingwood | b Bravo | 111 | | c Morton b Bravo | 34 | |
| IR Bell | not out | 109 | | c Ganga b Bravo | 3 | |
| *MJ Prior | not out | 126 | | c Bravo b Gayle | 21 | |
| LE Plunkett | | | | st Ramdin b Gayle | 0 | |
| SJ Harmison | | | | not out | 11 | |
| MS Panesar | | | | not out | 3 | |
| MJ Hoggard | | | | | | |
| Extras | b 8, lb 17, w 9, nb 3 | 37 | | b 1, lb 3, w 1, nb 5 | 10 | |
| | (5 wkts dec 142 overs) | 553 | | (8 wkts dec 66.5 overs) | 284 | |

| | First Innings | | | | Second Innings | | | |
|---|---|---|---|---|---|---|---|---|
| | O | M | R | W | O | M | R | W |
| Powell | 37 | 9 | 113 | 2 | 9 | 0 | 44 | 0 |
| Taylor | 24 | 4 | 114 | 1 | 4 | 0 | 21 | 0 |
| Collymore | 32 | 5 | 110 | 1 | 15 | 1 | 58 | 3 |
| Bravo | 32 | 8 | 106 | 1 | 18 | 2 | 91 | 2 |
| Gayle | 10 | 0 | 48 | 0 | 20.5 | 4 | 66 | 3 |
| Morton | 1 | 0 | 4 | 0 | - | - | - | - |
| Sarwan | 6 | 0 | 33 | 0 | - | - | - | - |

**Fall of Wickets**
1-88, 2-103, 3-162, 4-219, 5-363
1-35, 2-51, 3-139, 4-241, 5-248, 6-264, 7-264, 8-271

### WEST INDIES

| | First Innings | | | Second Innings | | |
|---|---|---|---|---|---|---|
| CH Gayle | b Plunkett | 30 | | not out | 47 | |
| D Ganga | lbw b Panesar | 49 | | not out | 31 | |
| DS Smith | b Panesar | 21 | | | | |
| RR Sarwan (capt) | lbw b Panesar | 35 | | | | |
| S Chanderpaul | lbw b Panesar | 74 | | | | |
| RS Morton | lbw b Panesar | 14 | | | | |
| DJ Bravo | c Cook b Collingwood | 56 | | | | |
| *D Ramdin | c Collingwood b Plunkett | 60 | | | | |
| DB Powell | not out | 36 | | | | |
| JE Taylor | c sub b Harmison | 21 | | | | |
| CD Collymore | lbw b Panesar | 1 | | | | |
| Extras | b 4, lb 17, w 16, nb 3 | 40 | | b 4, lb 3, w 3, nb 1 | 11 | |
| | (all out 116.1 overs) | 437 | | (0 wkts 22 overs) | 89 | |

| | First Innings | | | | Second Innings | | | |
|---|---|---|---|---|---|---|---|---|
| | O | M | R | W | O | M | R | W |
| Hoggard | 10.1 | 3 | 29 | 0 | - | - | - | - |
| Harmison | 28 | 2 | 117 | 1 | 8 | 1 | 21 | 0 |
| Plunkett | 30 | 7 | 107 | 2 | 11 | 1 | 48 | 0 |
| Collingwood | 11.5 | 3 | 34 | 1 | - | - | - | - |
| Panesar | 36.1 | 3 | 129 | 6 | 3 | 0 | 13 | 0 |

**Fall of Wickets**
1-38, 2-83, 3-151, 4-165, 5-187, 6-279, 7-362, 8-387, 9-424

Umpires: Asad Rauf (Pakistan) & RE Koertzen (South Africa)
Toss: West Indies
Test debut: MN Prior
Man of the Match: AN Cook

## Match drawn

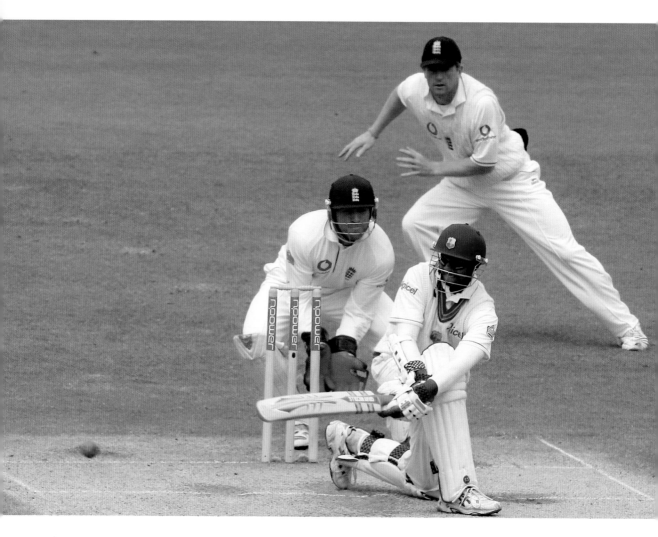

Shivnarine Chanderpaul sweeps during the Fourth Test at the Riverside, in which he scored 206 runs to take his series tally to 446 in five innings at an average of 148.66.

desperate day and enable England to build a match-winning lead once again.

At least there was some interest along the way as Darren Sammy, the first St Lucian to play Test cricket, claimed an unlikely 7 for 66 with his gentle medium pace. He then twanged a hamstring, and was not seen again in the series. Chanderpaul was badly missed by Panesar at mid off on 18, and he held England up again with an unbeaten 116, but West Indies were packing their bags halfway through the final day and heading for Chester-le-Street two down with one Test to play.

Of all their defeats, the West Indian effort at the Riverside was comfortably the worst. So much time was lost in the course of the game that they really should have forced a draw, but morale had ebbed away and the

weather was appalling. Sidebottom took his first five-wicket haul (5 for 88) in the first innings, but Chanderpaul showed what application and determination could achieve by clinging unspectacularly to the crease for six and three-quarter hours to score an unbeaten 136 out of 287.

Strauss made a heartening, but unconvincing 77, while Collingwood scored his first Test hundred on his home ground and with Prior impressing again with 62, England reached exactly 400 to post a lead of 113. West Indies only had to bat out the final day to save the game, but they crumbled feebly as Harmison bowled with great fire and Panesar took 5 for 46. England needed 110 to win from 52 overs, and after Vaughan sealed it with 48 not out he announced that he was stepping down as one-day captain in favour of Paul Collingwood.

## SECOND TEST – ENGLAND v. WEST INDIES
### 25–28 May 2007 at Headingley

### ENGLAND

| | First Innings | | |
|---|---|---|---|
| AJ Strauss | c Ramdin b Powell | 15 | |
| AN Cook | lbw b Gayle | 42 | |
| MP Vaughan (capt) | c Morton b Taylor | 103 | |
| KP Pietersen | c Taylor b Bravo | 226 | |
| PD Collingwood | c Gayle b Collymore | 29 | |
| IR Bell | c Ramdin b Collymore | 5 | |
| *MJ Prior | b Powell | 75 | |
| LE Plunkett | not out | 44 | |
| RJ Sidebottom | | | |
| SJ Harmison | | | |
| MS Panesar | | | |
| Extras | b 1, lb 15, w 9, nb 6 | 31 | |
| | (7 wkts dec 122.3 overs) | **570** | |

| | First Innings | | | |
|---|---|---|---|---|
| | O | M | R | W |
| Powell | 33 | 5 | 153 | 2 |
| Collymore | 29 | 1 | 110 | 2 |
| Taylor | 22 | 4 | 116 | 1 |
| Bravo | 24.3 | 3 | 97 | 1 |
| Gayle | 14 | 1 | 78 | 1 |

**Fall of Wickets**
1-38, 2-91, 3-254, 4-316, 5-329, 6-489, 7-570

### WEST INDIES

| | First Innings | | Second Innings (following on) | |
|---|---|---|---|---|
| CH Gayle | lbw b Sidebottom | 11 | c Prior b Plunkett | 13 |
| D Ganga | lbw b Sidebottom | 5 | lbw b Sidebottom | 9 |
| DS Smith | c Cook b Plunkett | 26 | (4) c Strauss b Sidebottom | 16 |
| SC Joseph | c Strauss b Harmison | 13 | (5) lbw b Sidebottom | 1 |
| RS Morton | c Prior b Harmison | 5 | (6) c Prior b Harmison | 25 |
| DJ Bravo | b Sidebottom | 23 | (7) c Plunkett b Panesar | 52 |
| *D Ramdin | c Prior b Plunkett | 6 | (8) lbw b Harmison | 5 |
| DB Powell | c Collingwood b Plunkett | 8 | (3) lbw b Sidebottom | 0 |
| JE Taylor | not out | 23 | b Harmison | 0 |
| CD Collymore | c Strauss b Sidebottom | 3 | not out | 0 |
| RR Sarwan (capt) | absent hurt | | absent hurt | |
| Extras | lb 13, w 3, nb 7 | 23 | b 1, lb 14, nb 5 | 20 |
| | (all out 37 overs) | 146 | (all out 42.1 overs) | 141 |

| | First Innings | | | | Second Innings | | | |
|---|---|---|---|---|---|---|---|---|
| | O | M | R | W | O | M | R | W |
| Sidebottom | 12 | 2 | 42 | 4 | 15 | 4 | 44 | 4 |
| Harmison | 12 | 0 | 55 | 2 | 13.1 | 3 | 37 | 3 |
| Plunkett | 12 | 1 | 35 | 3 | 8 | 2 | 25 | 1 |
| Panesar | 1 | 0 | 1 | 0 | 6 | 1 | 20 | 1 |

**Fall of Wickets**
1-17, 2-23, 3-68, 4-74, 5-82, 6-94, 7-114, 8-124, 9-146
1-20, 2-22, 3-30, 4-47, 5-57, 6-120, 7-141, 8-141, 9-141

Umpires: Asad Rauf (Pakistan) & RE Koertzen (South Africa)
Toss: England
Man of the Match: KP Pietersen

## England won by an innings and 283 runs

## THIRD TEST – ENGLAND v. WEST INDIES
### 7–11 June 2007 at Old Trafford

### ENGLAND

| | First Innings | | Second Innings | |
|---|---|---|---|---|
| AJ Strauss | lbw b Taylor | 6 | lbw b Edwards | 0 |
| AN Cook | c Bravo b Sammy | 60 | lbw b Gayle | 106 |
| MP Vaughan (capt) | b Collymore | 41 | c & b Sammy | 40 |
| KP Pietersen | c Bravo b Collymore | 9 | hit wkt b Bravo | 68 |
| PD Collingwood | lbw b Taylor | 10 | c Ganga b Sammy | 42 |
| IR Bell | c Ramdin b Collymore | 97 | c Ramdin b Sammy | 2 |
| *MJ Prior | c Morton b Bravo | 40 | c Ramdin b Sammy | 0 |
| LE Plunkett | b Edwards | 13 | c Bravo b Sammy | 0 |
| SJ Harmison | c Ramdin b Edwards | 18 | c Morton b Sammy | 16 |
| RJ Sidebottom | b Edwards | 15 | not out | 8 |
| MS Panesar | not out | 14 | c Gayle b Sammy | 0 |
| Extras | b 15, lb 8, w 6, nb 18 | 47 | b 2, lb 6, w 6, nb 12, p 5 | 31 |
| | (all out 105.1 overs) | 370 | (all out 85.3 overs) | 313 |

| | First Innings | | | | Second Innings | | | |
|---|---|---|---|---|---|---|---|---|
| | O | M | R | W | O | M | R | W |
| Taylor | 20 | 1 | 67 | 2 | 10 | 0 | 42 | 0 |
| Edwards | 20.1 | 2 | 94 | 3 | 12 | 0 | 54 | 1 |
| Collymore | 25 | 5 | 60 | 3 | 7 | 2 | 24 | 0 |
| Bravo | 23 | 4 | 94 | 1 | 8 | 2 | 14 | 1 |
| Sammy | 17 | 7 | 32 | 1 | 21.3 | 2 | 66 | 7 |
| Chanderpaul | - | - | - | - | 11 | 1 | 43 | 0 |
| Gayle | - | - | - | - | 16 | 0 | 57 | 1 |

**Fall of Wickets**
1-13, 2-117, 3-132, 4-132, 5-166, 6-264, 7-285, 8-324, 9-338
1-1, 2-99, 3-221, 4-265, 5-272, 6-272, 7-272, 8-300, 9-313

### WEST INDIES

| | First Innings | | Second Innings | |
|---|---|---|---|---|
| CH Gayle | c Cook b Plunkett | 23 | c Collingwood b Harmison | 16 |
| D Ganga (capt) | lbw b Harmison | 5 | lbw b Harmison | 0 |
| DS Smith | c Bell b Panesar | 40 | c Cook b Panesar | 42 |
| RS Morton | c Strauss b Harmison | 35 | lbw b Panesar | 54 |
| S Chanderpaul | c Pietersen b Panesar | 50 | not out | 116 |
| DJ Bravo | c Prior b Sidebottom | 24 | c Cook b Panesar | 49 |
| *D Ramdin | c Pietersen b Sidebottom | 5 | c Collingwood b Panesar | 34 |
| DJG Sammy | c Collingwood b Panesar | 1 | c & b Panesar | 25 |
| JE Taylor | c Strauss b Panesar | 0 | c Cook b Harmison | 11 |
| CD Collymore | c Collingwood b Panesar | 4 | (11) c Bell b Panesar | 0 |
| FH Edwards | not out | 0 | (10) c Bell b Harmison | 0 |
| Extras | b 20, lb 10, w 9, nb 3 | 42 | b 14, lb 21, w 8, nb 4 | 47 |
| | (all out 52.4 overs) | 229 | (all out 132.5 overs) | 394 |

| | First Innings | | | | Second Innings | | | |
|---|---|---|---|---|---|---|---|---|
| | O | M | R | W | O | M | R | W |
| Sidebottom | 12 | 3 | 48 | 3 | 27 | 8 | 53 | 0 |
| Harmison | 11 | 2 | 53 | 2 | 33 | 8 | 95 | 4 |
| Plunkett | 12 | 0 | 43 | 1 | 16 | 2 | 57 | 0 |
| Panesar | 16.4 | 5 | 50 | 4 | 51.5 | 13 | 137 | 6 |
| Collingwood | 1 | 0 | 5 | 0 | - | - | - | - |
| Pietersen | - | - | - | - | 5 | 2 | 17 | 0 |

**Fall of Wickets**
1-17, 2-49, 3-116, 4-157, 5-216, 6-224, 7-225, 8-225, 9-225
1-4, 2-35, 3-88, 4-161, 5-249, 6-311, 7-348, 8-385, 9-385

Umpires: BF Bowden (New Zealand) & Aleem Dar (Pakistan)
Toss: England
Test debut: DJG Sammy
Man of the Match: MS Panesar

## England won by 60 runs

## FOURTH TEST – ENGLAND v. WEST INDIES
### 15-19 June 2007 at the Riverside

## SERIES AVERAGES
### England v. West Indies

### WEST INDIES

| | First Innings | | Second Innings | |
|---|---|---|---|---|
| D Ganga (capt) | c Cook b Sidebottom | 0 | (3) c Prior b Hoggard | 6 |
| CH Gayle | lbw b Hoggard | 28 | (1) c Prior b Hoggard | 52 |
| DS Smith | b Sidebottom | 4 | (2) lbw b Hoggard | 0 |
| RS Morton | c Sidebottom b Harmison | 6 | b Panesar | 7 |
| S Chanderpaul | not out | 136 | b Panesar | 70 |
| DJ Bravo | b Hoggard | 44 | c Sidebottom b Panesar | 43 |
| MN Samuels | b Sidebottom | 19 | c Collingwood b Panesar | 2 |
| *D Ramdin | c Collingwood b Sidebottom | 13 | b Panesar | 4 |
| DB Powell | c Prior b Harmison | 1 | c Vaughan b Harmison | 4 |
| FH Edwards | b Sidebottom | 5 | b Harmison | 0 |
| CD Collymore | lbw b Panesar | 13 | not out | 16 |
| Extras | b 4, lb 13, nb 1 | 18 | b 1, lb 12, w 2, nb 3 | 18 |
| | (all out 97.1 overs) | 287 | (all out 64 overs) | 222 |

| | First Innings | | | | Second Innings | | | |
|---|---|---|---|---|---|---|---|---|
| | O | M | R | W | O | M | R | W |
| Sidebottom | 29 | 10 | 88 | 5 | 15 | 4 | 40 | 0 |
| Hoggard | 26 | 8 | 58 | 2 | 11 | 4 | 28 | 3 |
| Harmison | 25 | 4 | 78 | 2 | 20 | 2 | 92 | 2 |
| Panesar | 13.1 | 2 | 34 | 1 | 16 | 2 | 46 | 5 |
| Collingwood | 4 | 1 | 12 | 0 | - | - | - | - |
| Pietersen | - | - | - | - | 2 | 0 | 3 | 0 |

**Fall of Wickets**
1-0, 2-32, 3-34, 4-55, 5-141, 6-199, 7-219, 8-220, 9-229
1-7, 2-15, 3-38, 4-94, 5-162, 6-169, 7-175, 8-188, 9-194

### ENGLAND

| | First Innings | | Second Innings | |
|---|---|---|---|---|
| AJ Strauss | c Ramdin b Edwards | 77 | b Powell | 13 |
| AN Cook | c Ramdin b Edwards | 13 | c Bravo b Powell | 7 |
| MP Vaughan (capt) | c Bravo b Edwards | 19 | not out | 48 |
| MJ Hoggard | c Gayle b Collymore | 0 | | |
| KP Pietersen | c Ramdin b Edwards | 0 | (4) c Samuels b Gayle | 28 |
| PD Collingwood | b Collymore | 128 | (5) not out | 5 |
| IR Bell | c Morton b Powell | 11 | | |
| *MJ Prior | c Smith b Edwards | 62 | | |
| SJ Harmison | c Ganga b Powell | 9 | | |
| RJ Sidebottom | not out | 26 | | |
| MS Panesar | b Powell | 4 | | |
| Extras | b 5, lb 8, w 15, nb 23 | 51 | b 4, nb 6 | 10 |
| | (all out 100 overs) | 400 | (3 wkts 21.4 overs) | 111 |

| | First Innings | | | | Second Innings | | | |
|---|---|---|---|---|---|---|---|---|
| | O | M | R | W | O | M | R | W |
| Edwards | 23 | 1 | 112 | 5 | 7 | 0 | 46 | 0 |
| Powell | 32 | 6 | 89 | 3 | 7 | 0 | 38 | 2 |
| Collymore | 29 | 5 | 116 | 2 | - | - | - | - |
| Gayle | 9 | 3 | 25 | 0 | 3.4 | 0 | 11 | 1 |
| Bravo | 2 | 0 | 10 | 0 | - | - | - | - |
| Samuels | 5 | 0 | 35 | 0 | 4 | 0 | 12 | 0 |

**Fall of Wickets**
1-37, 2-110, 3-119, 4-121, 5-133, 6-165, 7-334, 8-369, 9-369
1-16, 2-29, 3-105

Umpires: BF Bowden (New Zealand) & Aleem Dar (Pakistan)
Toss: England
Man of the Match: S Chanderpaul
Man of the Series: S Chanderpaul

## England won by 7 wickets

### ENGLAND

| Batting | M | Inns | NO | Runs | HS | Av | 100 | 50 | c/st |
|---|---|---|---|---|---|---|---|---|---|
| KP Pietersen | 4 | 7 | 0 | 466 | 226 | 66.57 | 2 | 1 | 2/- |
| MJ Prior | 4 | 6 | 1 | 324 | 126* | 64.80 | 1 | 2 | 8/- |
| MP Vaughan | 3 | 5 | 1 | 251 | 103 | 62.75 | 1 | - | 1/- |
| PD Collingwood | 4 | 7 | 1 | 359 | 128 | 59.83 | 2 | - | 8/- |
| AN Cook | 4 | 7 | 0 | 398 | 106 | 56.85 | 2 | 2 | 7/- |
| RJ Sidebottom | 3 | 3 | 2 | 49 | 26* | 49.00 | - | - | 2/- |
| IR Bell | 4 | 6 | 1 | 227 | 109* | 45.40 | 1 | 1 | 3/- |
| AJ Strauss | 4 | 7 | 0 | 168 | 77 | 24.00 | - | 1 | 5/- |
| LE Plunkett | 3 | 4 | 1 | 57 | 44* | 19.00 | - | - | 1/- |
| SJ Harmison | 4 | 4 | 1 | 54 | 18 | 18.00 | - | - | -/- |
| MS Panesar | 4 | 4 | 2 | 21 | 14* | 10.50 | - | - | 1/- |
| OA Shah | 1 | 2 | 0 | 10 | 6 | 5.00 | - | - | -/- |
| MJ Hoggard | 2 | 1 | 0 | 0 | 0 | 0.00 | - | - | -/- |

| Bowling | Overs | Mds | Runs | Wkts | Av | Best | 5/inn | 10m |
|---|---|---|---|---|---|---|---|---|
| MS Panesar | 143.5 | 26 | 430 | 23 | 18.69 | 6-129 | 3 | 1 |
| RJ Sidebottom | 110 | 31 | 315 | 16 | 19.68 | 5-88 | 1 | - |
| MJ Hoggard | 47.1 | 15 | 115 | 5 | 23.00 | 3-28 | - | - |
| SJ Harmison | 150.1 | 22 | 548 | 16 | 34.25 | 4-95 | - | - |
| LE Plunkett | 89 | 13 | 315 | 7 | 45.00 | 3-35 | - | - |
| PD Collingwood | 16.5 | 4 | 51 | 1 | 51.00 | 1-34 | - | - |

Also bowled: KP Pietersen 7-2-20-0.

### WEST INDIES

| Batting | M | Inns | NO | Runs | HS | Av | 100 | 50 | c/st |
|---|---|---|---|---|---|---|---|---|---|
| S Chanderpaul | 3 | 5 | 2 | 446 | 136* | 148.66 | 2 | 3 | 1/- |
| DJ Bravo | 4 | 7 | 0 | 291 | 56 | 41.57 | - | 2 | 7/- |
| RR Sarwan | 2 | 1 | 0 | 35 | 35 | 35.00 | - | - | -/- |
| CH Gayle | 4 | 8 | 1 | 220 | 52 | 31.42 | - | 1 | 3/- |
| DS Smith | 4 | 7 | 0 | 149 | 42 | 21.28 | - | - | 4/- |
| RS Morton | 4 | 7 | 0 | 146 | 54 | 20.85 | - | 1 | 6/- |
| D Ramdin | 4 | 7 | 0 | 127 | 60 | 18.14 | - | 1 | 11/1 |
| D Ganga | 4 | 8 | 1 | 105 | 49 | 15.00 | - | - | 3/- |
| JE Taylor | 3 | 5 | 1 | 55 | 23* | 13.75 | - | - | 1/- |
| DJG Sammy | 1 | 2 | 0 | 26 | 25 | 13.00 | - | - | 1/- |
| DB Powell | 3 | 5 | 1 | 49 | 36* | 12.25 | - | - | 1/- |
| MN Samuels | 1 | 2 | 0 | 21 | 19 | 10.50 | - | - | 1/- |
| CD Collymore | 4 | 7 | 2 | 37 | 16* | 7.40 | - | - | -/- |
| SC Joseph | 1 | 2 | 0 | 14 | 13 | 7.00 | - | - | -/- |
| FH Edwards | 2 | 4 | 1 | 5 | 5 | 1.66 | - | - | -/- |

| Bowling | Overs | Mds | Runs | Wkts | Av | Best | 5/inn | 10m |
|---|---|---|---|---|---|---|---|---|
| DJG Sammy | 38.3 | 9 | 98 | 8 | 12.25 | 7-66 | 1 | - |
| FH Edwards | 62.1 | 3 | 306 | 9 | 34.00 | 5-112 | 1 | - |
| CD Collymore | 137 | 19 | 478 | 11 | 43.45 | 3-58 | - | - |
| CH Gayle | 73.3 | 8 | 285 | 6 | 47.50 | 3-66 | - | - |
| DB Powell | 118 | 20 | 437 | 9 | 48.55 | 3-89 | - | - |
| DJ Bravo | 107.3 | 19 | 412 | 6 | 68.66 | 2-91 | - | - |
| JE Taylor | 80 | 9 | 360 | 4 | 90.00 | 2-67 | - | - |

Also bowled: RS Morton 1-0-4-0, RR Sarwan 6-0-33-0, S Chanderpaul 11-1-43-0, MN Samuels 9-0-47-0.

## NATWEST SERIES v. West Indies
### by Jonathan Agnew

Having been so critical of the West Indies' effort in the Test series, it is only right to recognise a great change of heart in the one-day games that followed. Chris Gayle had been noticeably underwhelmed by the English weather, but given the captaincy, he was revitalised to the extent of being a new man.

The teams shared the two-match Twenty20 challenge which kicked off the pyjama-fest, and England had a convincing win in the first 50-overs game at Lord's where only three West Indians – Chanderpaul, Bravo and Rampaul – reached double figures.

But, in the form of his life, Chanderpaul scored his seventh one-day hundred at Edgbaston and Marlon Samuels hit 77 as the tourists posted 278 for 5. This was comfortably too many for England who never got going, and were bundled out for 217.

The third and final game at Trent Bridge was thus a decider, and Gayle made England pay for two missed chances by hammering 82. Runako Morton hit 82 not out from just 89 balls, and added 92 with Bravo from only 49 deliveries as 116 runs came from the last ten overs. Shah made 51 and Collingwood 44, but when England slumped to 144 for 5, the game was up.

## TWENTY20 INTERNATIONALS

**Match One**
28 June 2007 at The Oval
**West Indies** 208 for 8 (20 overs) (DS Smith 61, MN Samuels 51)
**England** 193 for 7 (20 overs) (PD Collingwood 80)
*West Indies won by 15 runs*

**Match Two**
29 June 2007 at The Oval
**West Indies** 169 for 7 (20 overs) (CH Gayle 61)
**England** 173 for 5 (19.3 overs) (OA Shah 55*)
*England won by 5 wickets*

**Series drawn**

## ONE-DAY INTERNATIONALS

**Match One**
1 July 2007 at Lord's
**England** 225 all out (49.5 overs) (IR Bell 56, FH Edwards 5 for 45)
**West Indies** 146 all out (39.5 overs) (S Chanderpaul 53*)
*England won by 79 runs*

**Match Two**
4 July 2007 at Edgbaston
**West Indies** 278 for 5 (50 overs) (S Chanderpaul 116*, MN Samuels 77)
**England** 217 all out (46 overs) (MJ Prior 52, R Rampaul 4 for 41)
*West Indies won by 61 runs*

**Match Three**
7 July 2007 at Trent Bridge
**West Indies** 289 for 5 (50 overs) (CH Gayle 82, RS Morton 82*)
**England** 196 all out (44.2 overs) (OA Shah 51, DB Powell 4 for 40)
*West Indies won by 93 runs*

**West Indies won the series 2–1**

Another boundary for the extraordinary Shivnarine Chanderpaul, who followed up his Test series heroics with more important runs as the West Indies bounced back in the one-day arena.

# MONTY PANESAR

Derek Underwood, former Kent and England left-arm spinner, gives his appreciation
of Monty Panesar's dramatic emergence at International level during the past two years.

I first met Monty Panesar at the Evening of Spin dinner in London in September 2006, which was organised by the Lord's Taverners and Surrey as part of the 50th anniversary celebrations of Jim Laker's 19-wicket Test haul against the 1956 Australians. A host of former and current international spinners were invited along, including Shane Warne.

The chance to chat with both Monty and Shane was a real privilege for me. Warne, in my view, is the best spinner there has ever been, while England and English cricket is very fortunate indeed to have Panesar. I was struck by how very polite and nice he is, and although he is obviously a naturally shy person I really warmed to him on that first meeting. I think the public have also quickly recognised how likeable he is, judging by the reception he gets everywhere he goes.

Monty is also a bowler I really want to watch. I've been fortunate to see him bowl live, as it were, both in this country and last winter in Australia, but when a Test match is on the television at home and he comes on to bowl then I want to stop what I'm doing and sit down to see what happens.

He wants wickets, and he bowls to get wickets, and without wishing to slight other slow left-arm spinners who opt to come over the wicket, it is very nice indeed to see one bowling around the wicket and in an attacking manner.

Monty had a fine series against the West Indies last summer, and he would have enjoyed the pitches giving him a bit of assistance, but what I really liked about him was something I witnessed at first hand in Perth last winter.

He had bowled beautifully to take five wickets in Australia's first innings in that third Ashes Test, but in their second innings Adam Gilchrist got going and was hitting the England bowlers, Monty included, to all parts. But Monty was still skipping up from the outfield looking to bowl his next over, and his body language of intense disappointment when the captain, Andrew Flintoff, told him he was taking him off spoke volumes to me.

One of the best ways of assessing a slow bowler is to see how often he drops one short outside the off stump, especially when he is under pressure from a batsman going well. Psychologically, it is easy to pitch it short if the batsman is hitting you through extra cover or over the top. But Monty rarely gets cut, and that's a good sign. Bishan Bedi was rarely cut, too. It is better to err on the side of pitching too far up, because top batsmen at Test level will hit you for four every time if you drop short.

Monty, like all of us, will have to endure the lean spells if he is to prosper long-term in Test match cricket. What will help him is if England remain successful for long periods, and keep putting big totals on the board. Then he can really get to work, and he has shown already in his relatively short Test career that he loves to bowl and can bowl sides out.

He has a very good, rhythmical action and maintaining that rhythm is very important. Monty's enthusiasm for bowling is also very evident, and so far he seems to have the fortunate knack of often getting an early wicket. Believe you me, the difference between having 1 for 30 and 0 for 30 is a big one.

As for the future, I wish only the best for Monty. And, as he gains more experience of playing in different conditions, he will become a better all-round bowler.

The best piece of advice I was ever given was that it is vital to realise that for every pitch you bowl on there is a pace to bowl. Sometimes it's right to push it through, as Monty can do, and at other times you must give it more air and look to get more turn that way. In fact, you are forever learning, and whenever I bowled I was always using the first two or three overs to make up my mind about the right pace to bowl.

You sense, meanwhile, with Monty, that he is in his element bowling in Test match cricket and that he will be around for a long time to come. I certainly hope so.

*Derek Underwood took 297 wickets in 86 Tests, between 1966 and 1982, at an average of 25.83.*

## ICC PLAYER RANKINGS

| Top Ten Test Bowlers (as at 1 July 2007) | | |
|---|---|---|
| 1 | Muttiah Muralitharan | Sri Lanka |
| 2 | Makhaya Ntini | South Africa |
| 3= | Shaun Pollock | South Africa |
| 3= | Anil Kumble | India |
| 5 | Shane Bond | New Zealand |
| 6= | Monty Panesar | England |
| 6= | Matthew Hoggard | England |
| 8 | Stuart Clark | Australia |
| 9 | Mohammad Asif | Pakistan |
| 10 | Shoaib Akhtar | Pakistan |

In 2007 Monty Panesar became the first England spinner to be ranked in the top ten Test listings since Derek Underwood 30 years ago.

| Top Ten Test Bowlers (as at 1 July 1977) | | |
|---|---|---|
| 1 | Dennis Lillee | Australia |
| 2 | Bishan Bedi | India |
| 3 | Jeff Thomson | Australia |
| 4 | Derek Underwood | England |
| 5 | Andy Roberts | West Indies |
| 6 | Michael Holding | West Indies |
| 7 | Max Walker | Australia |
| 8 | BS Chandrasekhar | India |
| 9= | Bob Willis | England |
| 9= | Imran Khan | Pakistan |

Derek Underwood had already been ranked at number one in the world from late August 1969 until early August 1973.

**Opposite** The 'Sikh of Tweak', England's Monty Panesar, gives another ball a real rip. He has not looked back since claiming his hero, Sachin Tendulkar, as his first Test wicket in Nagpur in March 2006.

## INDIA IN ENGLAND
### by Jonathan Agnew

Happily, the three-match Test series against India lifted the summer. Tough, competitive cricket was to the fore, and climaxed at The Oval where Rahul Dravid became only the third Indian captain to win a series in England. The defeat ended Michael Vaughan's unbeaten run, and produced England's first home defeat of this century to anyone other than Australia.

After a great deal of public analysis of his poor technique, Strauss appeared to be on his way to turning his fortunes around on the first day at Lord's. Dropped horribly by Dinesh Karthik on 43, Strauss reached 96 before suffering an apparent attack of nerves. Advancing down the pitch to Anil Kumble, the left-hander steered a sharp catch to Dravid at slip to end a stand of 142 with his old opening partner, Vaughan.

Sri Sreesanth wrapped up the lower order to dismiss England for a disappointing 298 – they lost 9 for 80 – but India then fell foul of the swinging ball. James Anderson and Sidebottom moved the ball in every direction, taking nine of the ten wickets between them, and bundled India out for only 201.

The prospect of a brilliant finish was set up when England were bowled out for 282 on the fourth day, to leave India with a difficult – but not impossible – 380 to win. Unfortunately, bad light descended just before tea, and having given England a fair chance to claim the one wicket they needed to win, the umpires quite rightly abandoned play with India still 98 runs short.

Something stirred up the players from both teams before they met again at Trent Bridge, in what became one of the most petulant and bad-tempered matches we have seen for a long time. Sreesanth was the main protagonist on the Indian side, bowling what he claimed was an unintentional – but devastatingly straight – beamer at Pietersen, and then running well through the crease to fire a bouncer from round the wicket at Collingwood. England, for their part, were little better with Prior's constant, boorish and childish sledging from behind the wicket being particularly tedious.

**Opposite** James Anderson, the Lancashire seam and swing bowler, picked up seven wickets at Lord's as England all but won the opening Test of their series against India.

### FIRST TEST – ENGLAND v. INDIA
19–23 July 2007 at Lord's

#### ENGLAND

| | First Innings | | Second Innings | |
|---|---|---|---|---|
| AJ Strauss | c Dravid b Kumble | 96 | c Tendulkar b Khan | 18 |
| AN Cook | lbw b Ganguly | 36 | lbw b Khan | 17 |
| MP Vaughan (capt) | c Dhoni b Singh | 79 | b Singh | 30 |
| KP Pietersen | c Dhoni b Khan | 37 | b Singh | 134 |
| PD Collingwood | lbw b Kumble | 0 | c Laxman b Singh | 4 |
| RJ Sidebottom | b Singh | 1 | (9) c Dravid b Kumble | 9 |
| IR Bell | b Khan | 20 | (6) b Singh | 9 |
| *MJ Prior | lbw b Sreesanth | 1 | (7) c Dhoni b Khan | 42 |
| CT Tremlett | lbw b Sreesanth | 0 | (8) b Khan | 0 |
| MS Panesar | lbw b Sreesanth | 0 | lbw b Singh | 3 |
| JM Anderson | not out | 0 | not out | 4 |
| Extras | b 9, lb 10, w 7, nb 2 | 28 | b 9, lb 1, w 2 | 12 |
| | (all out 91.2 overs) | 298 | (all out 78.3 overs) | 282 |

| | First Innings | | | | Second Innings | | | |
|---|---|---|---|---|---|---|---|---|
| | O | M | R | W | O | M | R | W |
| Khan | 18.2 | 4 | 62 | 2 | 28 | 6 | 79 | 4 |
| Sreesanth | 22 | 8 | 67 | 3 | 16 | 3 | 62 | 0 |
| Singh | 17 | 6 | 58 | 2 | 16.3 | 3 | 59 | 5 |
| Ganguly | 9 | 3 | 24 | 1 | - | - | - | - |
| Kumble | 23 | 2 | 60 | 2 | 17 | 3 | 70 | 1 |
| Tendulkar | 2 | 0 | 8 | 0 | 1 | 0 | 2 | 0 |

**Fall of Wickets**
1-76, 2-218, 3-252, 4-255, 5-272, 6-286, 7-287, 8-287, 9-297
1-40, 2-43, 3-102, 4-114, 5-132, 6-251, 7-251, 8-266, 9-275

#### INDIA

| | First Innings | | Second Innings | |
|---|---|---|---|---|
| KD Karthik | lbw b Sidebottom | 5 | (2) c Collingwood b Anderson | 60 |
| W Jaffer | c & b Tremlett | 58 | (1) c Pietersen b Anderson | 8 |
| R Dravid (capt) | c Prior b Anderson | 2 | lbw b Tremlett | 9 |
| SR Tendulkar | lbw b Anderson | 37 | lbw b Panesar | 16 |
| SC Ganguly | b Anderson | 34 | lbw b Sidebottom | 40 |
| RP Singh | c Anderson b Sidebottom | 17 | (10) b Panesar | 2 |
| VVS Laxman | c Prior b Sidebottom | 15 | (6) b Tremlett | 39 |
| *MS Dhoni | c Bell b Anderson | 0 | (7) not out | 76 |
| A Kumble | lbw b Sidebottom | 11 | (8) lbw b Sidebottom | 3 |
| Z Khan | c Strauss b Anderson | 7 | (9) c Prior b Tremlett | 0 |
| S Sreesanth | not out | 0 | not out | 4 |
| Extras | b 4, lb 7, nb 4 | 15 | b 13, lb 5, w 6, nb 1 | 25 |
| | (all out 77.2 overs) | 201 | (9 wkts 96 overs) | 282 |

| | First Innings | | | | Second Innings | | | |
|---|---|---|---|---|---|---|---|---|
| | O | M | R | W | O | M | R | W |
| Sidebottom | 22 | 5 | 65 | 4 | 19 | 4 | 42 | 2 |
| Anderson | 24.2 | 8 | 42 | 5 | 25 | 4 | 83 | 2 |
| Tremlett | 20 | 8 | 52 | 1 | 21 | 5 | 52 | 3 |
| Collingwood | 3 | 1 | 9 | 0 | 1 | 0 | 6 | 0 |
| Panesar | 8 | 3 | 22 | 0 | 26 | 7 | 63 | 2 |
| Vaughan | - | - | - | - | 4 | 0 | 18 | 0 |

**Fall of Wickets**
1-18, 2-27, 3-106, 4-134, 5-155, 6-173, 7-175, 8-192, 9-197
1-38, 2-55, 3-84, 4-143, 5-145, 6-231, 7-247, 8-254, 9-263

Umpires: SA Bucknor (West Indies) & SJA Taufel (Australia)
Toss: England
Test debut: CT Tremlett
Man of the Match: KP Pietersen

### Match drawn

Matters came to a head when Zaheer Khan complained that jelly beans had been scattered about the crease as he batted, and England's top flight – who we are often reminded by the captain play 'tough cricket' – were suddenly made to look embarrassingly infantile.

But it was a good game, nonetheless, dominated by Zaheer's brilliant left-arm swing bowling. England fell well short of a competitive total in the first innings, although conditions were perfect for bowling. Zaheer took four wickets as England made 198 and India then replied with 481 as Sachin Tendulkar – who missed out at Lord's – compiled a masterly 91. Karthik, Ganguly and Laxman all chipped in to post a lead of 283, which always looked to be a match winner.

Vaughan batted beautifully for his 124, watching bemused from the non-striker's end as Sreesanth lost the plot (including a deliberate shoulder barge on the captain for which he was fined) and Collingwood fought hard for his 63. But as he has done so often, Kumble nipped out the tail and Zaheer took 5 for 75 to finish with nine wickets in the game. England's lead of 73 was then knocked off in just over 20 overs.

England had to win at The Oval to save the series, and defend their captain's record, but the moment Dravid won the toss and batted on a typically flat Oval pitch, the odds were stacked against them.

India cashed in spectacularly, posting the small matter of 664: their highest Test score against England, despite some appalling umpiring decisions by the South African, Ian Howell. Curiously, the only century of the innings – and India's only centurion of the series – was posted by Kumble who, in his 118th Test, became the oldest Indian to score his first hundred, and the most experienced in the world in terms of matches played.

Prior conceded a record number of byes for a specialist keeper, and his world quickly fell apart when he dropped not only Tendulkar, but also

*No one has played more Tests before recording a maiden Test hundred than Anil Kumble, the veteran India leg spinner, who scored 110 not out at The Oval.*

Laxman to boot. Having seemed so secure at the start of the summer, Prior subsequently found himself without a central contract. Every Indian made double figures – the 11th occasion of that particular feat in Tests and, all in all, it added up to an insurmountable challenge.

Apart from Strauss and Vaughan, England's top order all made starts, but there was the pressure of the clock ticking away in the background to add to the tension. Bowled out for 345, India had a lead of 319 and Dravid betrayed his conservative inclinations by deciding against enforcing the follow-on. It was a decision that almost backfired when, before lunch on the fourth day, India were 11 for 3 with Jaffer, Karthik and Tendulkar all dismissed.

But Sidebottom was out of the attack through injury and, painstakingly, Dravid refused to yield. He faced 96 balls for his 12, but took enough time out of the day to ensure that his team was not embarrassed. Finally, with 20 overs remaining, he declared and England entered the final day needing to score 444 with all ten wickets remaining.

Pietersen made a hundred but, as seems so often to be the case, got himself out immediately afterwards, and Bell scored 67, but Dravid always had the option of setting the field back if he needed to. England were left to rue the bad weather which denied them at Lord's and which otherwise would have left an excellent series on level terms.

## SECOND TEST – ENGLAND v. INDIA
### 27–31 July 2007 at Trent Bridge

### ENGLAND

| | First Innings | | Second Innings | |
|---|---|---|---|---|
| AJ Strauss | c Tendulkar b Khan | 4 | c Dhoni b Khan | 55 |
| AN Cook | lbw b Ganguly | 43 | lbw b Khan | 23 |
| MP Vaughan (capt) | c Tendulkar b Khan | 9 | b Khan | 124 |
| KP Pietersen | lbw b Singh | 13 | lbw b Singh | 19 |
| PD Collingwood | b Sreesanth | 28 | c Karthik b Khan | 63 |
| IR Bell | lbw b Khan | 31 | lbw b Khan | 0 |
| *MJ Prior | c Dravid b Kumble | 11 | b Singh | 7 |
| CT Tremlett | b Kumble | 20 | c Singh b Kumble | 5 |
| RJ Sidebottom | not out | 18 | not out | 25 |
| MS Panesar | c Laxman b Khan | 1 | c Karthik b Kumble | 4 |
| JM Anderson | b Kumble | 1 | b Kumble | 1 |
| Extras | b 8, lb 7, w 1, nb 3 | 19 | b 6, lb 7, w 9, nb 7 | 29 |
| | (all out 65.3 overs) | 198 | (all out 104 overs) | 355 |

| | First Innings | | | | Second Innings | | | |
|---|---|---|---|---|---|---|---|---|
| | O | M | R | W | O | M | R | W |
| Khan | 21 | 5 | 59 | 4 | 27 | 10 | 75 | 5 |
| Sreesanth | 12 | 7 | 16 | 1 | 21 | 2 | 60 | 0 |
| Singh | 10 | 1 | 56 | 1 | 18 | 5 | 52 | 2 |
| Ganguly | 8 | 4 | 11 | 1 | 6 | 0 | 22 | 0 |
| Kumble | 12.3 | 2 | 32 | 3 | 25 | 2 | 104 | 3 |
| Tendulkar | 2 | 0 | 9 | 0 | 7 | 0 | 29 | 0 |

**Fall of Wickets**
1-4, 2-24, 3-47, 4-101, 5-109, 6-147, 7-157, 8-186, 9-195
1-49, 2-130, 3-175, 4-287, 5-287, 6-304, 7-323, 8-329, 9-333

### INDIA

| | First Innings | | Second Innings | |
|---|---|---|---|---|
| KD Karthik | c Cook b Panesar | 77 | c Prior b Tremlett | 22 |
| W Jaffer | c Prior b Tremlett | 62 | c Pietersen b Tremlett | 22 |
| R Dravid (capt) | c Bell b Panesar | 37 | not out | 11 |
| SR Tendulkar | lbw b Collingwood | 91 | c Cook b Tremlett | 1 |
| SC Ganguly | c Prior b Anderson | 79 | not out | 2 |
| VVS Laxman | c Prior b Tremlett | 54 | | |
| *MS Dhoni | c Prior b Sidebottom | 5 | | |
| A Kumble | c Prior b Tremlett | 30 | | |
| Z Khan | not out | 10 | | |
| RP Singh | lbw b Panesar | 0 | | |
| S Sreesanth | lbw b Panesar | 2 | | |
| Extras | b 16, lb 16, w 1, nb 1 | 34 | b 4, lb 6, w 2, nb 3 | 15 |
| | (all out 158.5 overs) | 481 | (3 wkts 24.1 overs) | 73 |

| | First Innings | | | | Second Innings | | | |
|---|---|---|---|---|---|---|---|---|
| | O | M | R | W | O | M | R | W |
| Sidebottom | 36 | 11 | 75 | 1 | 8 | 0 | 28 | 0 |
| Anderson | 33 | 4 | 134 | 1 | 9 | 2 | 23 | 0 |
| Tremlett | 40 | 13 | 80 | 3 | 7.1 | 2 | 12 | 3 |
| Collingwood | 16 | 3 | 59 | 1 | - | - | - | - |
| Panesar | 33.5 | 8 | 101 | 4 | - | - | - | - |

**Fall of Wickets**
1-147, 2-149, 3-246, 4-342, 5-409, 6-414, 7-464, 8-473, 9-474
1-47, 2-55, 3-62

Umpires: IL Howell (South Africa) & SJA Taufel (Australia)
Toss: India
Man of the Match: Z Khan

## India won by 7 wickets

## THIRD TEST – ENGLAND v. INDIA
### 9-13 August 2007 at The Oval

### INDIA

| | First Innings | | Second Innings | |
|---|---|---|---|---|
| KD Karthik | c Prior b Sidebottom | 91 | c Collingwood b Tremlett | 8 |
| W Jaffer | c Pietersen b Anderson | 35 | lbw b Anderson | 0 |
| R Dravid (capt) | b Anderson | 55 | c Strauss b Collingwood | 12 |
| SR Tendulkar | c Strauss b Anderson | 82 | b Anderson | 1 |
| SC Ganguly | lbw b Collingwood | 37 | c Strauss b Collingwood | 57 |
| VVS Laxman | c Prior b Tremlett | 51 | not out | 46 |
| *MS Dhoni | c Cook b Pietersen | 92 | c Prior b Tremlett | 36 |
| A Kumble | not out | 110 | not out | 8 |
| Z Khan | c Anderson b Panesar | 11 | | |
| RP Singh | c Bell b Anderson | 11 | | |
| S Sreesanth | c Vaughan b Panesar | 35 | | |
| Extras | b 33, lb 13, w 2, nb 6 | 54 | b 1, lb 5, nb 6 | 12 |
| | (all out 170 overs) | 664 | (6 wkts dec 58 overs) | 180 |

| | First Innings | | | | Second Innings | | | |
|---|---|---|---|---|---|---|---|---|
| | O | M | R | W | O | M | R | W |
| Sidebottom | 32 | 8 | 93 | 1 | - | - | - | - |
| Anderson | 40 | 5 | 182 | 4 | 15 | 8 | 34 | 2 |
| Tremlett | 40 | 6 | 132 | 1 | 15 | 2 | 58 | 2 |
| Panesar | 45 | 5 | 159 | 2 | 18 | 1 | 58 | 0 |
| Collingwood | 7 | 1 | 11 | 1 | 10 | 1 | 24 | 2 |
| Pietersen | 6 | 0 | 41 | 1 | - | - | - | - |

**Fall of Wickets**
1-62, 2-189, 3-199, 4-276, 5-354, 6-417, 7-508, 8-570, 9-591
1-10, 2-10, 3-11, 4-76, 5-89, 6-158

### ENGLAND

| | First Innings | | Second Innings | |
|---|---|---|---|---|
| AJ Strauss | c Sreesanth b Khan | 6 | c Laxman b Singh | 32 |
| AN Cook | c Singh b Kumble | 61 | c Laxman b Kumble | 43 |
| JM Anderson | lbw b Singh | 16 | | |
| MP Vaughan (capt) | c & b Kumble | 11 | (3) c Dhoni b Sreesanth | 42 |
| KP Pietersen | c Dravid b Tendulkar | 41 | (4) c Karthik b Sreesanth | 101 |
| PD Collingwood | lbw b Sreesanth | 62 | (5) lbw b Sreesanth | 40 |
| IR Bell | c Dhoni b Khan | 63 | (6) lbw b Kumble | 67 |
| *MJ Prior | c Tendulkar b Sreesanth | 0 | (7) not out | 12 |
| RJ Sidebottom | c & b Khan | 2 | (8) not out | 3 |
| CT Tremlett | not out | 25 | | |
| MS Panesar | lbw b Kumble | 9 | | |
| Extras | b 16, lb 12, w 10, nb 11 | 49 | b 2, lb 4, w 9, nb 14 | 29 |
| | (all out 103.1 overs) | 345 | (6 wkts 110 overs) | 369 |

| | First Innings | | | | Second Innings | | | |
|---|---|---|---|---|---|---|---|---|
| | O | M | R | W | O | M | R | W |
| Khan | 22 | 13 | 32 | 3 | 20 | 3 | 59 | 0 |
| Sreesanth | 21 | 2 | 80 | 2 | 21 | 7 | 53 | 3 |
| Kumble | 29.1 | 7 | 94 | 3 | 37 | 9 | 123 | 2 |
| Singh | 18 | 3 | 72 | 1 | 13 | 2 | 50 | 1 |
| Ganguly | 5 | 1 | 8 | 0 | - | - | - | - |
| Tendulkar | 7 | 0 | 26 | 1 | 19 | 0 | 78 | 0 |
| Laxman | 1 | 0 | 5 | 0 | - | - | - | - |

**Fall of Wickets**
1-12, 2-78, 3-119, 4-124, 5-202, 6-288, 7-303, 8-305, 9-305
1-79, 2-86, 3-152, 4-266, 5-289, 6-363

Umpires: SA Bucknor (West Indies) & IL Howell (South Africa)
Toss: India
Man of the Match: A Kumble
Men of the Series: JM Anderson and Z Khan

## Match drawn

## SERIES AVERAGES
England v. India

### ENGLAND

| Batting | M | Inns | NO | Runs | HS | Av | 100 | 50 | c/st |
|---|---|---|---|---|---|---|---|---|---|
| KP Pietersen | 3 | 6 | 0 | 345 | 134 | 57.50 | 2 | – | 3/– |
| MP Vaughan | 3 | 6 | 0 | 295 | 124 | 49.16 | 1 | 1 | 1/– |
| AN Cook | 3 | 6 | 0 | 223 | 61 | 37.16 | – | 1 | 3/– |
| AJ Strauss | 3 | 6 | 0 | 211 | 96 | 35.16 | – | 2 | 4/– |
| PD Collingwood | 3 | 6 | 0 | 197 | 63 | 32.83 | – | 2 | 2/– |
| IR Bell | 3 | 6 | 0 | 190 | 67 | 31.66 | – | 2 | 2/– |
| RJ Sidebottom | 3 | 6 | 3 | 58 | 25* | 19.33 | – | – | –/– |
| MJ Prior | 3 | 6 | 1 | 73 | 42 | 14.60 | – | – | 12/– |
| CT Tremlett | 3 | 5 | 1 | 50 | 25* | 12.50 | – | – | 1/– |
| JM Anderson | 3 | 5 | 2 | 22 | 16 | 7.33 | – | – | 3/– |
| MS Panesar | 3 | 5 | 0 | 17 | 9 | 3.40 | – | – | –/– |

| Bowling | Overs | Mds | Runs | Wkts | Av | Best | 5/inn | 10m |
|---|---|---|---|---|---|---|---|---|
| PD Collingwood | 37 | 6 | 109 | 4 | 27.25 | 2-24 | – | – |
| CT Tremlett | 143.1 | 36 | 386 | 13 | 29.69 | 3-12 | – | – |
| JM Anderson | 146.2 | 31 | 498 | 14 | 35.57 | 5-42 | 1 | – |
| RJ Sidebottom | 117 | 28 | 303 | 8 | 37.87 | 4-65 | – | – |
| KP Pietersen | 6 | 0 | 41 | 1 | 41.00 | 1-41 | – | – |
| MS Panesar | 130.5 | 24 | 403 | 8 | 50.37 | 4-101 | – | – |

Also bowled: MP Vaughan 4-0-18-0.

### INDIA

| Batting | M | Inns | NO | Runs | HS | Av | 100 | 50 | c/st |
|---|---|---|---|---|---|---|---|---|---|
| A Kumble | 3 | 5 | 2 | 162 | 110* | 54.00 | 1 | – | 1/– |
| MS Dhoni | 3 | 5 | 1 | 209 | 92 | 52.25 | – | 2 | 6/– |
| VVS Laxman | 3 | 5 | 1 | 205 | 54 | 51.25 | – | 2 | 4/– |
| SC Ganguly | 3 | 6 | 1 | 249 | 79 | 49.80 | – | 2 | –/– |
| KD Karthik | 3 | 6 | 0 | 263 | 91 | 43.83 | – | 3 | 3/– |
| SR Tendulkar | 3 | 6 | 0 | 228 | 91 | 38.00 | – | 2 | 4/– |
| W Jaffer | 3 | 6 | 0 | 185 | 62 | 30.83 | – | 2 | –/– |
| R Dravid | 3 | 6 | 1 | 126 | 55 | 25.20 | – | 1 | 4/– |
| S Sreesanth | 3 | 4 | 2 | 41 | 35 | 20.50 | – | – | 1/– |
| Z Khan | 3 | 4 | 1 | 28 | 11 | 9.33 | – | – | 1/– |
| RP Singh | 3 | 4 | 0 | 30 | 17 | 7.50 | – | – | 2/– |

| Bowling | Overs | Mds | Runs | Wkts | Av | Best | 5/inn | 10m |
|---|---|---|---|---|---|---|---|---|
| Z Khan | 136.2 | 41 | 366 | 18 | 20.33 | 5-75 | 1 | – |
| RP Singh | 92.3 | 20 | 347 | 12 | 28.91 | 5-59 | 1 | – |
| SC Ganguly | 28 | 8 | 65 | 2 | 32.50 | 1-11 | – | – |
| A Kumble | 143.4 | 25 | 483 | 14 | 34.50 | 3-32 | – | – |
| S Sreesanth | 113 | 29 | 338 | 9 | 37.55 | 3-53 | – | – |
| SR Tendulkar | 38 | 0 | 152 | 1 | 152.00 | 1-26 | – | – |

Also bowled: VVS Laxman 1-0-5-0.

## NATWEST SERIES v. India
## by Jonathan Agnew

The small matter of seven one-day internationals brought the summer to a close – what a shame that an extra Test could not have been staged instead of at least three of them – but despite an overwhelming feeling of weariness, the series surpassed expectation.

England comfortably won the opener at the Rose Bowl with Cook and Bell scoring hundreds. Most of the crowd had dispersed long before the end, and this was not the most promising of starts. But one-day cricket is nothing if not unpredictable, and the second game was clinched by India by just nine runs after Tendulkar made a beautiful 99 and Dravid 92 not out from just 92 balls. Flintoff, back in the fray once again, took his first five-wicket haul in one-day internationals.

England's fielding proved to be the difference in the third game – India were looking very slow in the circle – and a close encounter at Old Trafford was won by England by three wickets to take a 3-1 lead in the series.

India rattled up a mighty 324 for 6 at Headingley with Tendulkar and Yuvraj Singh in spectacular form. This was reduced to 280 from 39 overs by Duckworth/Lewis, but that was still a total well beyond England, for whom Flintoff had returned to the sidelines.

A brilliant game at The Oval levelled the series. Dimitri Mascarenhas remarkably clubbed the last five balls of the innings from Yuvraj for sixes and Shah scored an outstanding hundred, but India got home with two balls and two wickets to spare thanks to Robin Uthappa's 47 from 33 balls.

Sadly, the 'final' at Lord's failed to live up to its billing as India were skittled for just 187, despite 50 from Dhoni. England found themselves 11 for 2 with both openers out for ducks, but were steered home with 12 overs to spare by determined half-centuries from Pietersen and Collingwood.

## ONE-DAY INTERNATIONALS

**Match One**
21 August 2007 at The Rose Bowl
**England** 288 for 2 (50 overs) (IR Bell 126*, AN Cook 102)
**India** 184 all out (50 overs) (JM Anderson 4 for 23)
*England won by 104 runs*

**Match Two**
24 August 2007 at Bristol
**India** 329 for 7 (50 overs) (SR Tendulkar 99, R Dravid 92*, A Flintoff 5 for 56)
**England** 320 for 8 (50 overs) (IR Bell 64, AD Mascarenhas 52)
*India won by 9 runs*

### Match Three

27 August 2007 at Edgbaston
**England** 281 for 8 (50 overs) (IR Bell 79)
**India** 239 all out (48.1 overs) (SC Ganguly 72, R Dravid 56)
*England won by 42 runs*

### Match Four

30 August 2007 at Old Trafford
**India** 212 all out (49.4 overs) (Yuvraj Singh 71,
SR Tendulkar 55, SCJ Broad 4 for 51)
**England** 213 for 7 (48 overs) (AB Agarkar 4 for 60)
*England won by 3 wickets*

### Match Five

2 September 2007 at Headingley
**India** 324 for 6 (50 overs) (Yuvraj Singh 72, SR Tendulkar 71,
SC Ganguly 59, G Gambhir 51)
**England** 242 for 8 (39 overs) (PD Collingwood 91*)
*India won by 38 runs – DL Method: target 280 from 39 overs*

### Match Six

5 September 2007 at The Oval
**England** 316 for 6 (50 overs) (OA Shah 107*,
KP Pietersen 53, LJ Wright 50)
**India** 317 for 8 (49.4 overs) (SR Tendulkar 94,
SC Ganguly 53)
*India won by 2 wickets*

### Match Seven

8 September 2007 at Lord's
**India** 187 all out (47.3 overs) (MS Dhoni 50)
**England** 188 for 3 (36.2 overs) (KP Pietersen 71*,
PD Collingwood 64*)
*England won by 7 wickets*

**England won the series 4–3**

Owais Shah (right) congratulates his batting partner,
Dimitri Mascarenhas, after the Hampshire all-rounder
had finished off England's innings at The Oval in
remarkable style by hitting the left-arm spin of India's
Yuvraj Singh for five successive sixes.

# KEVIN PIETERSEN

John Etheridge, the long-serving cricket correspondent of *The Sun*, believes
Kevin Pietersen is already out of sight as England's best-ever one-day batsman.

Kevin Pietersen has nailed the argument. This man is England's finest one-day batsman of all time and has reached that lofty pinnacle in less than three years. Case closed.

In fact, the statistics and overwhelming force of Pietersen's batting suggest the contest is not even close. Pietersen is miles ahead of his nearest challenger as his country's most brilliant limited-overs willow wielder.

Forget Gooch, forget Lamb, forget Fairbrother, forget Knight, KP's the boy. Before the NatWest Series against West Indies in the summer of 2007, Pietersen's career one-day batting average was 56.28 and his strike rate an electric 91.47. Although those figures had fallen slightly to 49.77 and 88.28 by the end of his 66th ODI in Sri Lanka in mid-October, they are still mighty impressive. He is also the fastest man in history to score 2,000 runs in one-day internationals.

These are extraordinary numbers and explain why he was ranked the No.1 ODI batsman in the world in June and July 2006 (he was also third in the Test list at the time). He remains highly placed in both ICC rankings, and no other England batsman comes close.

Yet it is not simply the figures that elevate Pietersen ahead of the rest. It is the dazzling and dynamic style with which he plunders his runs. KP hits the ball to parts of the field that the coaching manual and geometry insist are nigh on impossible. He propels balls through mid wicket or square leg or even fine leg when logic says it should be patted to extra cover. Of course, he is just as likely to hit the same ball to the boundary with a reverse sweep.

This is a result of Pietersen's lightning eye, exquisite timing and soaring confidence. Hitting the ball to unexpected areas is a priceless asset in one-day batting.

Pietersen adopts a modest public stance when discussing his stellar career as a one-day performer. For instance, he claimed that being rated No.1 in the world distorts the reality of who is actually the best. Whether one believes him is another matter, of course, because fragile self-belief has never been a problem for Pietersen.

He says, 'I know there are better players than me. Ricky Ponting, Matthew Hayden – people like that are better than me. It was great to be No.1 but it doesn't mean much when you're not winning trophies. My priority is to try to help England become as successful in one-day cricket as we are in Test cricket.'

Pietersen strutted on to the one-day international stage before he played Test cricket and he arrived like a hurricane. His bravado was as compelling as his batting. After averaging 104 in three matches against Zimbabwe in late 2004, he scored three centuries in six innings against South Africa the following spring.

That's South Africa, the country where he was born and raised to an English mother and South African father, and then departed because he disagreed with the quota system that seeks to promote non-white cricketers.

His first one-day innings in England was a pulverising 91 not out from 65 balls against Australia at Bristol in June 2005 which captain Michael Vaughan described as 'genius-like'.

Among England batsmen, Nick Knight has the next-highest one-day average of 40.29 but his strike rate is in a different parish at 71.32. Former opening batsman Chris Broad (now an ICC match referee and father of seam bowler Stuart) averaged 40.03 but he scored his runs at an almost inconceivably slow 55.62 per 100 balls.

So the list continues – several splendid batsmen, but all distantly trailing Pietersen. How about Neil Fairbrother, the unorthodox left-handed 'finisher' of the 1980s and 1990s? Not close. His figures are 39.47 and 72.06. Allan Lamb? Nope. He averaged 39.31 with a strike rate of 75.69.

And these batsmen are not just chosen at random – Knight, Broad, Fairbrother and Lamb are the next four highest-averaging one-day batsmen for England behind Pietersen.

OK, so boundaries have shrunk in recent years and bat technology as well as increased fielding restrictions during the power plays have all aided quick scoring, but they do not distort statistics that much.

Pietersen is box office, a star whose fascination transcends cricket. But do not be fooled. Pietersen is a single-minded cricketer whose ambition has long been to become the best batsman in the world – and he is pretty damn close to achieving it already. Then he wants to stay at the top of the pile.

Few work harder in the nets or have a more lucid game plan. He does not walk out to bat and improvise – he has a clear method and knows exactly where he wants to score runs off each bowler.

He insists, 'When I first came into the England team, I was only 24 and I was growing up and enjoying myself. I was single and having fun, like every youngster should. But now I'm not really interested in all that malarkey. I just want to play good cricket and I will never take on any work off the field which disturbs my preparation or focus for a match.'

# ENGLISH DOMESTIC SEASON

## INTRODUCTION
**by Mark Baldwin**

There has never been a better time to watch county cricket. It is a golden age for the English domestic game, and if you didn't get to see much of it in 2007 then I would strongly advise you to start making plans to get to a county ground near you in 2008.

And that is not just because of the cricketing talent now on view at the 18 county venues, and the rich mix of entertainment on show. For a start, the weather simply has to improve next summer…

But, even with unprecedented levels of rain interruption – especially in the LV County Championship and the Twenty20 Cup – many regard last season as a classic for county cricket. It had the closest and most exciting Championship finish for many years, with the title eventually claimed for the third time in five years by an exceptional Sussex side, it saw a major breakthrough in terms of trophy-winning by Durham – until 1992, it must be remembered, a minor county – while in Kent and Worcestershire there emerged two more winners with vivid 'behind the success' stories to tell.

Yet it is the overall health of the county game, in terms of the abilities of the hundreds of players who play it, the increasing numbers of people who watch it, the facilities offered by the grounds that stage it, and the competitive standard and attractiveness of the cricket itself, which leads me to call this a golden age.

Given a fair deal in 2008 with regards to hours of sunshine, more people should also cotton on to the fact that county cricket offers more genuine star performers per pound spent at the gate than any other major sport. By my calculation, no fewer than 141 international cricketers represented the 18 first-class counties in 2007.

With county administrators recognising more and more, too, the benefits of staging matches in genuinely characterful and pleasant settings such as Arundel, Oakham, Tunbridge Wells, Chesterfield, Scarborough and Liverpool, attending county cricket matches is something to be enjoyed (and afforded) as a family or group. Yes, I know that the 2007 weather washed away the entire Cheltenham Festival, for so long a jewel in the county game's crown, as well as whole matches at lovely venues such as Abergavenny and – of course – Worcester, but in 2008 these will be back.

Also back, thankfully, will be many of the global stars who enriched county cricket last season. In 2007, indeed, there were seven of the elite members of the 100 Test cap club who graced the Championship: Warne, Langer, Chanderpaul, Fleming, Inzamam-ul-Haq, Muralitharan and Jayasuriya.

These are giants of the game, due to be joined with a century of Test caps this winter by Chaminda Vaas, who played for Middlesex. And, among the supporting cast of last summer's regular county players who also have more than 50 Test appearances to their name, are many who dominated the upper reaches of either the batting or bowling lists: Harbhajan Singh, Mark Ramprakash, Mushtaq Ahmed, Younus Khan, VVS Laxman, Marcus Trescothick, Andrew Caddick, Darren Gough and Graeme Hick.

Of current England players, meanwhile, only Kevin Pietersen failed to appear in at least one Championship match, and thankfully the early stages of the Peter Moores regime has revealed a new willingness (indeed, desire) to allow centrally contracted players to play more for their counties than they did under Duncan Fletcher's control.

The general uproar that greeted Warwickshire's unfathomable decision not to include the specially released Ian Bell in their Friends Provident Trophy semi-final against Hampshire – for whom Pietersen played – illustrated how much they were swimming against a turning tide.

Proposals for a revised county format for the 2009 season, meanwhile, drawn up by Hugh Morris's domestic review group, should lead at last to a more uniform and easy-to-understand fixture schedule, but officials will tamper radically with the present set-up at their peril. The 40-over game, though popular with the public and with county treasurers, somewhat dilutes a powerful mix of four-day, 50-over and 20-over cricket, and should probably be pruned at least.

Yet my only serious reservation about what is to come first, in 2008, is that counties can now field only one official overseas player instead of two. This, to my mind, is a big mistake as all the evidence points to a clear rising of standards beneficial to young English talent in recent seasons, and counties will simply retaliate by signing on yet more Kolpak players.

Two Kolpaks per county XI, plus two official overseas cricketers would provide the ideal balance, although many counties often had more than four non-England qualified cricketers in their line-ups last season and it doesn't seem to have stopped a strong line of new, young English players of genuine talent coming through a robust system.

To end, here are three composite XIs, of players who appeared in Championship cricket in 2007, to illustrate the great good health of the English domestic game – and our good fortune to be witnessing it:

County Championship XI:
Trescothick, Langer, Sangakkara, Ramprakash, D Hussey, Shah, Flintoff, Warne (capt), Clark, Harmison, Muralitharan.

Over-35 XI (age at end of season in brackets):
Langer (36), Crawley (36), Ramprakash (38), S Law (38), Hick (41), Nixon (36), Gibson (38), Warne (38), Mushtaq Ahmed (37), Gough (37), Caddick (38). (The top six all averaged more than 39, and 58.52 between them, and the five bowlers took 332 wickets.)

England Under-21 XI (county and age at end of season in brackets): B Godleman (Middlesex, 18), J Denly (Kent, 21), T Westley (Essex, 18), B Wright (Glamorgan, 19), A Wakely (Northamptonshire, 18), A Rashid (Yorkshire, 19), S Davies (Worcestershire, 21), C Jordan (Surrey, 18), J Harris (Glamorgan, 17), D Evans (Middlesex, 20), S Finn (Middlesex, 18). (The above played a total of 106 first-class matches between them in the 2007 season.)

*Mark Baldwin, a former cricket correspondent of the Press Association, has covered county cricket for* The Times *since 1998.*

## MCC v. SUSSEX
### 13–16 April at Lord's

Alastair Cook, unwanted by England at the World Cup in the Caribbean, instead opened up the new domestic season by taking 142 off the County Champions, Sussex, in the traditional curtain-raiser at Lord's. Chosen to captain the MCC, Cook royally entertained a 2,000-strong opening-day crowd basking in the warm April sunshine with a 225-ball innings that was his first since the Ashes were lost in Australia.

Sussex replied strongly through Murray Goodwin and Mike Yardy, with Goodwin taking only 176 balls to score 134, but Yardy had to retire hurt one run short of his own hundred when he was struck on the left index finger by a lifter from Steve Harmison armed with the second new ball. X-rays later revealed a fracture.

An unbeaten 120 from Owais Shah then added to MCC's small halfway advantage, although there was a farcical 75-minute delay at the start of the final day – one of the warmest April days on record – after a malfunctioning sprinkler on the edge of the square sent water trickling down the Lord's slope on to the pitch rather than the outfield.

The match itself petered out into a draw, after Cook had set Sussex the purely notional target of 368 in 49 overs.

**MCC** 425 all out (23.4 overs) (AN Cook 142, RJ Kirtley 4 for 31) & 327 for 5 dec (99 overs) (OA Shah 120*, APR Gidman 56)
**Sussex** 385 all out (104.4 overs) (MH Yardy 99 retired hurt, MW Goodwin 134) & 121 for 4 (34 overs) *Match drawn*

Alastair Cook cover drives at Lord's to reach his century.

# LV COUNTY CHAMPIONSHIP

## by Mark Baldwin

### Round One: 18–21 April 2007

It did not take long for Mushtaq Ahmed to remind English cricket of his continued presence as one of the most effective and consistent match-winners the historic County Championship has ever seen. The Pakistani leg-spinner, little more than two months away from his 37th birthday, took 6 for 74 on the opening day of the new season as Sussex, the champions, bowled out Kent for 216 at Hove. That, in effect, was good enough to set them up for a convincing victory, achieved early on day four, although Richard Montgomerie also deserves much of the credit as he battled through nine and a half hours to kick off his benefit season with an epic 175. His effort was largely responsible for Sussex topping 500, and Mushtaq then teased out another four second-innings victims as he and Rana Naved-ul-Hasan worked their way through the Kent batting.

A dramatic game of cricket on an excellent Oval pitch ended with Yorkshire's new captain, Darren Gough, who had opted not to enforce the follow-on, celebrating his strategy as he, Matthew Hoggard and Adil Rashid

Darren Gough proved to be an instant inspiration after moving back home from Essex during the close season to take on the challenge of captaining a Yorkshire team in some disarray following a winter of discontent in the Broad Acres.

combined to bowl out Surrey for just 170 on the final day. It was Yorkshire's first Championship victory at The Oval since 1978 and was 'an awesome win', said Gough. He and Rashid, the 19-year-old leg-spinning prodigy, had shared seven first innings wickets too – while Rashid's batting skills had also been showcased in an 86 sandwiched between the controversial new Kolpak signing Jacques Rudolph's 122 on debut and a remarkable ninth-wicket stand of 246 between Tim Bresnan and Jason Gillespie against an increasingly ragged Surrey attack belying the fact that it contained four bowlers with Test experience. Both Bresnan and Gillespie hit hundreds, and it was the fifth-highest ninth-wicket stand in first-class history.

Mark Ramprakash's 88th first-class hundred, and a fluent 124 from Scott Newman, then took Surrey to 221 for 1 in reply to Yorkshire's huge first innings total but Rashid induced a collapse and Craig White's 131-ball 117 – including seven sixes all off Nayan Doshi – sped Yorkshire to a second-innings declaration. When White reached three figures, it was the first time Surrey had ever had four centuries made against them in a Championship match.

There was also early woe for Worcestershire, beaten on their home ground by Durham, for whom Steve Harmison took a five-wicket haul and Michael Di Venuto carried his bat on his county debut before adding a second-innings 83 to that first-innings unbeaten 155.

In the second division, Nottinghamshire made an early statement of intent by overwhelming Leicestershire at Trent Bridge, while Derbyshire could not force a win against a depleted Essex. At Taunton, however, a

shirtfront pitch reduced Somerset's meeting with Middlesex to a run-soaked and fairly pointless draw. Justin Langer, with 315 in Somerset's record total of 850 for 7 declared – in reply to Middlesex's own 600 for 4 declared – scored his second triple-hundred in

## Round One: 18–21 April Division One

### SUSSEX v. KENT – at Hove

| KENT | First Innings | | Second Innings | |
|---|---|---|---|---|
| JL Denly | c Mgomerie b Mushtaq Ahmed | 37 | c Hopkinson b Mushtaq Ahmed | 63 |
| RWT Key (capt) | lbw b Lewry | 6 | c Kirtley b Lewry | 0 |
| M van Jaarsveld | lbw b Lewry | 0 | c Kirtley b Naved-ul-Hasan | 26 |
| MJ Walker | c Prior b Kirtley | 21 | c Goodwin b Mushtaq Ahmed | 59 |
| DI Stevens | c Kirtley b Naved-ul-Hasan | 35 | c Wright b Mushtaq Ahmed | 19 |
| *GO Jones | b Mushtaq Ahmed | 2 | c Prior b Wright | 9 |
| Yasir Arafat | lbw b Mushtaq Ahmed | 33 | c Prior b Naved-ul-Hasan | 40 |
| R McLaren | st Prior b Mushtaq Ahmed | 44 | c Prior b Naved-ul-Hasan | 29 |
| SJ Cook | b Mushtaq Ahmed | 3 | b Naved-ul-Hasan | 5 |
| MM Patel | st Prior b Mushtaq Ahmed | 15 | c Lewry b Mushtaq Ahmed | 52 |
| RH Joseph | not out | 11 | not out | 36 |
| Extras | b 4, lb 5 | 9 | b 5, lb 6 | 11 |
| | (all out 59.2 overs) | 216 | (all out 88.1 overs) | 349 |

Bowling
Naved-ul-Hasan 15.5-1-64-1. Lewry 8-4-23-2. Mushtaq Ahmed 21.3-2-74-6. Kirtley 14-2-46-1.
Naved-ul-Hasan 24-2-106-4. Lewry 9.1-2-35-1. Mushtaq Ahmed 41.1-4-145-4. Kirtley 10-2-30-0. Wright 3.5-2-13-1.
Fall of Wickets: 1-26, 2-26, 3-57, 4-73, 5-76, 6-132, 7-160, 8-153, 9-181
1-2, 2-48, 3-148, 4-157, 5-175, 6-177, 7-245, 8-252, 9-263

| SUSSEX | First Innings | | Second Innings | |
|---|---|---|---|---|
| CD Hopkinson | c Cook b Joseph | 13 | (2) lbw b Patel | 11 |
| RR Montgomerie | c Jones b Yasir Arafat | 175 | (1) not out | 33 |
| CD Nash | lbw b Joseph | 50 | lbw b Yasir Arafat | 1 |
| MW Goodwin | c & b Cook | 23 | not out | 7 |
| CJ Adams (capt) | c Jones b Cook | 0 | | |
| *MJ Prior | lbw b Stevens | 14 | | |
| LJ Wright | c Patel b Joseph | 7 | | |
| Naved-ul-Hasan | c McLaren b Stevens | 75 | | |
| RJ Kirtley | c Jones b McLaren | 51 | | |
| Mushtaq Ahmed | b Yasir Arafat | 27 | | |
| JD Lewry | not out | 13 | | |
| Extras | b 11, lb 12, w 13, nb 26 | 62 | w 1, nb 4 | 5 |
| | (all out 156.2 overs) | 510 | (2 wkts 18.1 overs) | 57 |

Bowling
Joseph 22-2-78-3. McLaren 28-6-95-1. Yasir Arafat 28.2-5-104-2. Cook 23-5-61-2. Stevens 24-5-42-2. Patel 25-4-90-0. Denly 6-3-17-0.
Joseph 6-1-16-0. McLaren 1-0-2-0. Cook 2-0-12-0. Patel 6-0-17-1. Yasir Arafat 3.1-1-10-1.
Fall of Wickets: 1-26, 2-159, 3-195, 4-195, 5-232, 6-254, 7-371, 8-465, 9-479
1-35, 2-40

*Sussex won by 8 wickets – Sussex (22pts), Kent (3pts)*

### SURREY v. YORKSHIRE – at The Oval

| YORKSHIRE | First Innings | | Second Innings | |
|---|---|---|---|---|
| C White | c Ramprakash b Ormond | 7 | c Brown b Doshi | 117 |
| JJ Sayers | c Batty b Clarke | 26 | c Ramprakash b Doshi | 57 |
| A McGrath | c Batty b Azhar Mahmood | 20 | c Clarke b Doshi | 2 |
| Younus Khan | b Clarke | 4 | c Batty b Clarke | 12 |
| JA Rudolph | c Ramprakash b Magoffin | 122 | c Ramprakash b Schofield | 28 |
| *GL Brophy | lbw b Magoffin | 22 | b Doshi | 12 |
| AU Rashid | b Azhar Mahmood | 86 | b Doshi | 19 |
| TT Bresnan | st Batty b Doshi | 116 | not out | 4 |
| D Gough (capt) | c Newman b Azhar Mahmood | 23 | | |
| JN Gillespie | not out | 123 | | |
| MJ Hoggard | | | | |
| Extras | b 12, lb 7, w 6, nb 20 | 45 | b 4, lb 8, w 1, nb 2 | 15 |
| | (9 wkts dec 154 overs) | 594 | (7 wkts dec 58.1 overs) | 266 |

Bowling
Ormond 24-6-101-1. Magoffin 24-8-73-2. Azhar Mahmood 27-4-73-3. Clarke 16-3-71-2. Doshi 35-10-118-1. Schofield 23-1-114-0. Benning 5-0-25-0. Ormond 8-2-24-0. Azhar Mahmood 7-0-27-0. Magoffin 6-1-21-0. Doshi 21.1-3-111-6. Schofield 16-1-71-1.
Fall of Wickets: 1-35, 2-69, 3-73, 4-73, 5-127, 6-317, 7-319, 8-348, 9-594
1-163, 2-169, 3-187, 4-221, 5-231, 6-253, 7-266

| SURREY | First Innings | | Second Innings | |
|---|---|---|---|---|
| SA Newman | c Gillespie b Hoggard | 124 | c Brophy b Hoggard | 89 |
| *JN Batty | c McGrath b Hoggard | 5 | c White b Rashid | 14 |
| MR Ramprakash | c Brophy b Gillespie | 115 | lbw b Rashid | 24 |
| JGE Benning | lbw b Rashid | 0 | (6) c Sayers b Hoggard | 7 |
| ND Doshi | st Brophy b Rashid | 1 | (10) c Younus Khan b Rashid | 15 |
| AD Brown | c McGrath b Rashid | 4 | (5) lbw b Hoggard | 7 |
| R Clarke | c Brophy b Gough | 42 | b Rashid | 3 |
| Azhar Mahmood | c Brophy b Hoggard | 32 | (7) c Rudolph b Hoggard | 0 |
| CP Schofield | not out | 0 | (8) b Rashid | 11 |
| J Ormond | c Brophy b Gough | 0 | (9) c Brophy b Gough | 1 |
| SJ Magoffin | b Gough | 6 | not out | 9 |
| Extras | b 4, lb 6, w 1, nb 4 | 15 | lb 5, nb 4 | 9 |
| | (all out 84 overs) | 344 | (all out 50.3 overs) | 170 |

Bowling
Hoggard 13-4-48-2. Gough 8-1-28-3. Gillespie 10-3-23-1. Rashid 24-3-105-4. Younus Khan 9-2-41-0. Bresnan 13-3-64-0. McGrath 2-0-15-0. Rudolph 1-1-25-0. Hoggard 12-4-34-4. Gough 11-2-50-3. Rashid 17.3-2-64-3. Gillespie 2-0-7-0. Bresnan 5-2-10-0.
Fall of Wickets: 1-25, 2-221, 3-231, 4-233, 5-237, 6-265, 7-334, 8-338, 9-338
1-47, 2-58, 3-78, 4-102, 5-124, 6-124, 7-133, 8-145, 9-149

*Yorkshire won by 346 runs – Surrey (5pts), Yorkshire (22pts)*

### WARWICKSHIRE v. LANCASHIRE – at Edgbaston

| WARWICKSHIRE | First Innings | | Second Innings | |
|---|---|---|---|---|
| IJ Westwood | c Cork b Keedy | 33 | c Sutcliffe b Keedy | 32 |
| DL Maddy | c Sutcliffe b Newby | 71 | b Newby | 14 |
| UL Trott | c Law b Newby | 0 | b Newby | 0 |
| JO Troughton | b Chapple | 100 | c Law b Keedy | 25 |
| AGR Loudon | c Sutton b Newby | 104 | c Horton b Keedy | 3 |
| *TR Ambrose | c Cork b Chapple | 30 | not out | 51 |
| JE Anyon | c Sutcliffe b Keedy | 37 | | |
| HH Streak (capt) | not out | 55 | (7) c Law b Keedy | 4 |
| TD Groenewald | c Loye b Keedy | 16 | (8) c Horton b Newby | 30 |
| N Tahir | lbw b Keedy | 12 | | |
| DW Steyn | c Chilton b Keedy | 9 | (9) not out | 17 |
| Extras | b 2, lb 5, nb 16 | 23 | b 4, lb 7, nb 2 | 13 |
| | (all out 159.3 overs) | 490 | (7 wkts dec 56 overs) | 189 |

Bowling
Cork 32-14-93-0. Chapple 29-6-88-2. Hogg 27-2-58-0. Newby 24-5-85-3. Keedy 52.3-12-159-5.
Cork 9-3-24-0. Chapple 12-4-22-0. Keedy 22-2-73-4. Newby 11-1-52-3. Hogg 2-0-7-0.
Fall of Wickets: 1-79, 2-80, 3-181, 4-255, 5-330, 6-381, 7-403, 8-443, 9-462
1-34, 2-34, 3-62, 4-74, 5-87, 6-95, 7-162

| LANCASHIRE | First Innings | | Second Innings | |
|---|---|---|---|---|
| MJ Chilton (capt) | c Groenewald b Streak | 14 | (2) c Trott b Loudon | 14 |
| IJ Sutcliffe | b Streak | 4 | (1) c Troughton b Loudon | 51 |
| MB Loye | c Westwood b Steyn | 14 | not out | 105 |
| SG Law | b Steyn | 21 | run out | 38 |
| PJ Horton | c Ambrose b Groenewald | 76 | not out | 8 |
| *LD Sutton | c Ambrose b Anyon | 111 | | |
| G Chapple | c Ambrose b Steyn | 30 | | |
| KW Hogg | b Steyn | 29 | | |
| DG Cork | b Anyon | 12 | | |
| OJ Newby | c Maddy b Anyon | 0 | | |
| G Keedy | not out | 1 | | |
| Extras | b 1, lb 7, w 3, nb 20 | 31 | b 6, lb 6, w 3 | 15 |
| | (all out 110.1 overs) | 333 | (3 wkts 66 overs) | 189 |

Bowling
Steyn 25-5-70-4. Streak 22-6-53-2. Groenewald 11-3-37-1. Tahir 21-3-50-0. Anyon 15.1-2-85-3. Maddy 3-1-2-0. Loudon 10-2-17-0. Troughton 3-0-11-0. Steyn 8-1-30-0. Streak 5-3-5-0. Loudon 23-2-64-2. Troughton 14-0-33-0. Tahir 4-1-9-0. Anyon 7-1-32-0. Maddy 1-0-1-0. Groenewald 4-2-3-0.
Fall of Wickets: 1-12, 2-23, 3-23, 4-71, 5-218, 6-265, 7-310, 8-321, 9-322
1-14, 2-82, 3-173

*Match drawn – Warwickshire (12pts), Lancashire (9pts)*

### WORCESTERSHIRE v. DURHAM – at Worcester

| DURHAM | First Innings | | Second Innings | |
|---|---|---|---|---|
| MJ Di Venuto | not out | 155 | (2) lbw b Batty | 83 |
| WR Smith | lbw b Bollinger | 5 | (1) lbw b Kabir Ali | 22 |
| GJ Muchall | c Davies b Bollinger | 6 | run out | 29 |
| DM B'enstein (capt) | c Davies b Malik | 10 | not out | 103 |
| BW Harmison | b Malik | 6 | lbw b Batty | 0 |
| *P Mustard | lbw b Kabir Ali | 23 | c Kabir Ali b Sillence | 38 |
| GR Breese | c Hick b Batty | 3 | lbw b Bollinger | 53 |
| OD Gibson | st Davies b Batty | 25 | c Davies b Batty | 19 |
| CD Thorp | lbw b Bollinger | 1 | c Hick b Batty | 9 |
| G Onions | b Sillence | 16 | b Kabir Ali | 19 |
| SJ Harmison | c Hick b Batty | 30 | lbw b Kabir Ali | 6 |
| Extras | b 4, lb 15, w 2, nb 12 | 33 | b 9, lb 12, nb 14 | 35 |
| | (all out 74.2 overs) | 313 | (all out 110.3 overs) | 416 |

Bowling
Bollinger 14-3-60-3. Kabir Ali 15-0-76-1. Malik 13-0-70-2. Sillence 13-2-52-1. Batty 19.2-5-36-3.
Bollinger 19-2-94-1. Kabir Ali 19.3-5-65-3. Malik 10-0-56-0. Batty 37-7-123-4. Sillence 16-4-74-1. Solanki 2-0-3-0.
Fall of Wickets: 1-33, 2-43, 3-80, 4-98, 5-164, 6-183, 7-229, 8-232, 9-270
1-35, 2-141, 3-161, 4-161, 5-232, 6-323, 7-365, 8-383, 9-408

| WORCS | First Innings | | Second Innings | |
|---|---|---|---|---|
| PA Jaques | c Mustard b Onions | 19 | b Harmison SJ | 97 |
| SC Moore | c Breese b Gibson | 46 | lbw b Harmison SJ | 0 |
| VS Solanki (capt) | b Gibson | 24 | run out | 67 |
| BF Smith | c Mustard b Thorp | 0 | c Breese b Harmison SJ | 2 |
| Kabir Ali | b Gibson | 2 | (9) lbw b Thorp | 19 |
| GA Hick | c Onions b Harmison SJ | 35 | c Mustard b Onions | 35 |
| *SM Davies | b Onions | 14 | (6) c Mustard b Harmison SJ | 4 |
| GJ Batty | lbw b Harmison SJ | 20 | (7) c Harmison B/W b Harmison SJ | 47 |
| RJ Sillence | lbw b Harmison SJ | 0 | (8) lbw b Thorp | 6 |
| DE Bollinger | c Mustard b Onions | 21 | c Breese b Thorp | 2 |
| MN Malik | not out | 13 | not out | 5 |
| Extras | lb 12, w 1, nb 4 | 17 | b 2, lb 9 | 11 |
| | (all out 57 overs) | 191 | (all out 78.4 overs) | 297 |

Bowling
Onions 15-5-47-3. Harmison SJ 19-6-52-3. Thorp 10-2-43-1. Gibson 13-3-37-3. Onions 13-1-46-1. Harmison SJ 24-5-63-5. Gibson 14-2-29-0. Breese 14-1-82-0. Thorp 12.4-1-51-3. Smith 3-0-15-0.
Fall of Wickets: 1-43, 2-87, 3-94, 4-104, 5-105, 6-131, 7-135, 8-135, 9-164
1-4, 2-131, 3-168, 4-175, 5-183, 6-242, 7-263, 8-271, 9-290

*Durham won by 241 runs – Worcestershire (3pts), Durham (20pts)*

## Round One: 18–21 April Division Two

### SOMERSET v. MIDDLESEX – at Taunton

| MIDDLESEX | First Innings | | Second Innings | |
|---|---|---|---|---|
| BL Hutton | lbw b Jones | 17 | b Blackwell | 10 |
| NRD Compton | c Spurway b Blackwell | 67 | b Caddick | 15 |
| OA Shah | lbw b Trego | 193 | not out | 72 |
| ET Smith (capt) | run out | 68 | not out | 103 |
| BA Godleman | not out | 113 | | |
| *DC Nash | not out | 100 | | |
| TJ Murtagh | | | | |
| RL Johnson | | | | |
| M Kartik | | | | |
| CEW Silverwood | | | | |
| A Richardson | | | | |
| Extras | b 18, lb 15, w 3, nb 6 | 42 | lb 1, w 6, nb 2 | 9 |
| | (4 wkts dec 157 overs) | **600** | (2 wkts 52 overs) | **209** |

**Bowling**
Caddick 34-7-127-0. Willoughby 30-6-89-0. Jones 27-5-109-1. Trego 18-6-48-1. Blackwell 24-4-88-1. White 21-0-79-0. Hildreth 3-0-27-0.
Caddick 10-1-54-1. Blackwell 18-7-27-1. Willoughby 10-2-38-0. White 6-0-42-0. Jones 8-1-47-0.
**Fall of Wickets:** 1-39, 2-170, 3-327, 4-407
1-25, 2-25

| SOMERSET | First Innings | |
|---|---|---|
| ME Trescothick | c Godleman b Kartik | 70 |
| NJ Edwards | c Richardson b Silverwood | 9 |
| JL Langer (capt) | b Murtagh | 315 |
| JC Hildreth | c Compton b Silverwood | 116 |
| CL White | st Nash b Kartik | 114 |
| ID Blackwell | c sub b Kartik | 6 |
| PD Trego | b Kartik | 130 |
| *SHP Spurway | not out | 44 |
| PS Jones | not out | 1 |
| AR Caddick | | |
| CM Willoughby | | |
| Extras | b 14, lb 17, w 2, nb 12 | 45 |
| | (7 wkts dec 178.3 overs) | **850** |

**Bowling**
Silverwood 30-4-125-2. Johnson 27.3-1-142-0. Richardson 26-0-127-0. Murtagh 25-1-147-1. Kartik 50-8-168-4. Shah 16-0-90-0. Compton 4-0-20-0.
**Fall of Wickets:** 1-25, 2-120, 3-362, 4-589, 5-611, 6-719, 7-845

*Match drawn – Somerset (10pts), Middlesex (10pts)*

### NOTTINGHAMSHIRE v. LEICESTERSHIRE – at Trent Bridge

| LEICESTERSHIRE | First Innings | | Second Innings | |
|---|---|---|---|---|
| DDJ Robinson (capt) | c Shafayat b Swann | 50 | lbw b Ealham | 37 |
| JK Maunders | c Read b Franks | 82 | run out | 31 |
| HD Ackerman | b Shreck | 18 | c Ealham b Swann | 112 |
| JL Sadler | c Read b Franks | 18 | c Shafayat b Ealham | 0 |
| J Allenby | lbw b Ealham | 14 | c Franks b Ealham | 3 |
| *TJ New | c Hussey b Sidebottom | 16 | c Hussey b Ealham | 57 |
| Mansoor Amjad | st Read b Swann | 5 | c Read b Sidebottom | 20 |
| CW Henderson | c Gallian b Franks | 47 | c Hussey b Sidebottom | 10 |
| DD Masters | b Shreck | 1 | c Read b Shreck | 9 |
| RP Singh | b Swann | 25 | c Read b Sidebottom | 0 |
| NGE Walker | not out | 0 | not out | 0 |
| Extras | b 3, lb 13, w 1, nb 6 | 23 | b 13, lb 10, w 1, nb 8 | 32 |
| | (all out 102.1 overs) | **299** | (all out 89.5 overs) | **311** |

**Bowling**
Sidebottom 24-9-43-1. Shreck 24-3-98-2. Ealham 21-8-63-1. Franks 20.1-6-49-3. Swann 13-6-30-3.
Sidebottom 20-3-49-3. Shreck 20.5-2-84-1. Ealham 17-7-43-4. Franks 12-1-41-0. Swann 20-6-71-1.
**Fall of Wickets:** 1-124, 2-155, 3-167, 4-194, 5-203, 6-208, 7-246, 8-251, 9-299
1-76, 2-82, 3-82, 4-94, 5-268, 6-268, 7-290, 8-309, 9-309

| NOTTS | First Innings | | Second Innings | |
|---|---|---|---|---|
| JER Gallian | c New b Masters | 150 | c Robinson b Henderson | 37 |
| BM Shafayat | lbw b Walker | 0 | not out | 41 |
| MA Wagh | c Maunders b Walker | 74 | not out | 30 |
| DJ Hussey (capt) | c Walker b Henderson | 105 | | |
| SR Patel | c Ackerman b Walker | 6 | | |
| *CMW Read | run out | 36 | | |
| MA Ealham | b Singh | 2 | | |
| PJ Franks | c Ackerman b Masters | 32 | | |
| GP Swann | c Ackerman b Singh | 46 | | |
| RJ Sidebottom | b Singh | 0 | | |
| CE Shreck | not out | 1 | | |
| Extras | b 10, lb 11, w 7, nb 20 | 48 | lb 1, w 1, nb 2 | 4 |
| | (all out 129.4 overs) | **500** | (1 wkt 26.3 overs) | **112** |

**Bowling**
Singh 25.4-6-106-3. Walker 28-4-106-3. Masters 34-8-101-2. Henderson 21-5-64-1. Allenby 6-0-26-0. Amjad 15-0-76-0.
Walker 2-0-10-0. Singh 4-1-12-0. Amjad 7.3-1-28-0. Henderson 9-0-50-1. Masters 4-1-11-0.
**Fall of Wickets:** 1-14, 2-190, 3-339, 4-358, 5-370, 6-379, 7-425, 8-465, 9-467
1-55

*Nottinghamshire won by 9 wickets – Nottinghamshire (22pts), Leicestershire (5pts)*

### ESSEX v. DERBYSHIRE – at Chelmsford

| DERBYSHIRE | First Innings | | Second Innings | |
|---|---|---|---|---|
| SD Stubbings | c Chopra b Danish Kaneria | 33 | lbw b ten Doeschate | 9 |
| WPC Weston | c Foster b ten Doeschate | 21 | | |
| CR Taylor | c Pettini b Danish Kaneria | 55 | (2) c Cook b Danish Kaneria | 96 |
| SM Katich (capt) | b Danish Kaneria | 50 | (3) not out | 88 |
| Hassan Adnan | b Phillips | 33 | (4) run out | 33 |
| IJ Harvey | c Foster b Tudor | 136 | (5) not out | 0 |
| AG Botha | c Irani b Danish Kaneria | 8 | | |
| *DJ Pipe | not out | 133 | | |
| GG Wagg | c Pettini b Middlebrook | 51 | | |
| T Lungley | lbw b Middlebrook | 3 | | |
| KJ Dean | c Pettini b Danish Kaneria | 10 | | |
| Extras | b 1, lb 8, w 3, nb 6 | 18 | b 5 | 5 |
| | (all out 143.3 overs) | **551** | (3 wkts dec 61 overs) | **231** |

**Bowling**
Tudor 19-5-66-1. Westfield 13-1-64-0. ten Doeschate 19-2-98-1. Danish Kaneria 52.3-8-152-5. Middlebrook 22-3-77-2. Phillips 17-2-79-1. Cook 1-0-6-0.
Tudor 8-2-22-0. ten Doeschate 6-1-24-1. Danish Kaneria 21-0-76-1. Middlebrook 19-0-84-0. Phillips 7-0-20-0.
**Fall of Wickets:** 1-56, 2-62, 3-123, 4-191, 5-259, 6-285, 7-425, 8-528, 9-538
1-23, 2-154, 3-224

| ESSEX | First Innings | | Second Innings | |
|---|---|---|---|---|
| ML Pettini | c Botha b Dean | 0 | (2) c Pipe b Dean | 2 |
| AN Cook | lbw b Dean | 100 | (1) c Harvey b Botha | 21 |
| V Chopra | c Stubbings b Dean | 10 | c Taylor b Harvey | 69 |
| RC Irani (capt) | c Harvey b Botha | 144 | not out | 28 |
| *JS Foster | b Lungley | 61 | not out | 4 |
| RN ten Doeschate | lbw b Lungley | 2 | | |
| TJ Phillips | c Taylor b Wagg | 20 | | |
| JD Middlebrook | c Katich b Botha | 19 | | |
| AJ Tudor | c Harvey b Botha | 3 | | |
| MS Westfield | not out | 4 | | |
| Danish Kaneria | c sub b Lungley | 5 | | |
| Extras | b 10, lb 9, w 4, nb 16 | 39 | lb 2, w 3, nb 2 | 7 |
| | (all out 124.3 overs) | **407** | (3 wkts 58 overs) | **131** |

**Bowling**
Dean 24-7-65-3. Lungley 22.3-7-69-3. Harvey 12-0-47-0. Wagg 26-6-70-1. Botha 35-13-108-3. Katich 5-0-29-0.
Dean 11-7-13-1. Lungley 13-4-37-0. Botha 18-5-30-1. Wagg 6-1-16-0. Katich 4-0-19-0. Harvey 6-1-14-1.
**Fall of Wickets:** 1-10, 2-39, 3-193, 4-317, 5-321, 6-375, 7-375, 8-379, 9-402
1-15, 2-36, 3-119

*Match drawn – Essex (11pts), Derbyshire (12pts)*

## Round Two: 25–28 April Division One

### YORKSHIRE v. DURHAM – at Headingley

| DURHAM | First Innings | | Second Innings | |
|---|---|---|---|---|
| WR Smith | c Bresnan b Shahzad | 34 | (2) b Hoggard | 11 |
| MJ Di Venuto | c Brophy b Bresnan | 27 | (1) b Gough | 1 |
| GJ Muchall | lbw b Rashid | 17 | c sub b Hoggard | 1 |
| DM B'kenstein (capt) | c Rudolph b Rashid | 83 | c Younus Khan b Hoggard | 3 |
| BW Harmison | c Younus Khan b Gough | 6 | b Hoggard | 0 |
| *P Mustard | lbw b Rashid | 10 | c sub b Bresnan | 32 |
| GR Breese | lbw b Bresnan | 19 | lbw b Shahzad | 21 |
| OD Gibson | c Gale b Rashid | 38 | c sub b Bresnan | 0 |
| CD Thorp | c Brophy b Rashid | 0 | not out | 30 |
| G Onions | c Brophy b Gough | 24 | st sub b Rashid | 41 |
| SJ Harmison | not out | 2 | lbw b Hoggard | 23 |
| Extras | b 4, lb 8, nb 2 | 14 | b 4, lb 2 | 6 |
| | (all out 75.4 overs) | **274** | (all out 39.1 overs) | **169** |

**Bowling**
Hoggard 14-3-33-0. Gough 14-3-46-2. Shahzad 10-0-44-1. Bresnan 17-3-51-2. Rashid 20.4-3-88-5.
Hoggard 11.1-2-32-5. Gough 12-2-34-1. Shahzad 7-1-22-1. Bresnan 5-1-36-2. Rashid 4-0-39-1.
**Fall of Wickets:** 1-55, 2-73, 3-94, 4-117, 5-152, 6-203, 7-207, 8-207, 9-264
1-1, 2-2, 3-14, 4-14, 5-17, 6-72, 7-73, 8-78, 9-138

| YORKSHIRE | First Innings | | Second Innings | |
|---|---|---|---|---|
| C White | c Mustard b Harmison SJ | 3 | c Mustard b Harmison SJ | 8 |
| JJ Sayers | not out | 149 | not out | 10 |
| JA Rudolph | c Mustard b Thorp | 9 | not out | 10 |
| Younus Khan | lbw b Thorp | 42 | | |
| AW Gale | lbw b Harmison SJ | 36 | | |
| *GL Brophy | hit wkt b Harmison SJ | 80 | | |
| AU Rashid | b Gibson | 1 | | |
| TT Bresnan | c Breese b Harmison SJ | 0 | | |
| D Gough (capt) | c Mustard b Harmison SJ | 50 | | |
| A Shahzad | c Smith b Onions | 2 | | |
| MJ Hoggard | c Mustard b Harmison SJ | 1 | | |
| Extras | b 10, lb 15, w 2, nb 14 | 41 | lb 1, w 1 | 2 |
| | (all out 142.3 overs) | **414** | (1 wkt 6.3 overs) | **30** |

**Bowling**
Onions 27-9-58-1. Harmison SJ 37.3-9-87-6. Gibson 27-7-88-1. Thorp 25-7-69-2. Breese 19-3-59-0. Harmison BW 3-0-22-0. Benkenstein 4-2-6-0.
Onions 3.3-0-22-0. Harmison SJ 3-1-7-1.
**Fall of Wickets:** 1-12, 2-27, 3-93, 4-186, 5-316, 6-317, 7-318, 8-400, 9-413
1-10

*Yorkshire won by 9 wickets – Yorkshire (21pts), Durham (4pts)*

### WARWICKSHIRE v. SUSSEX – at Edgbaston

| WARWICKSHIRE | First Innings | |
|---|---|---|
| IJ Westwood | lbw b Mushtaq Ahmed | 82 |
| DL Maddy (capt) | c Goodwin b Naved-ul-Hasan | 2 |
| IJL Trott | c Hopkinson b Mushtaq Ahmed | 84 |
| JO Troughton | lbw b Naved-ul-Hasan | 26 |
| AGR Loudon | b Naved-ul-Hasan | 32 |
| *TR Ambrose | b Mushtaq Ahmed | 72 |
| LC Parker | lbw b Mushtaq Ahmed | 0 |
| TD Groenewald | c Adams b Naved-ul-Hasan | 20 |
| N Tahir | c Prior b Naved-ul-Hasan | 7 |
| DW Steyn | not out | 31 |
| JE Anyon | run out | 0 |
| Extras | b 8, lb 16, w 5, nb 6 | 35 |
| | (all out 128.3 overs) | **391** |

**Bowling**
Naved-ul-Hasan 37-7-123-5. Kirtley 21-8-51-0. Martin-Jenkins 12-3-26-0. Liddle 17-5-43-0. Mushtaq Ahmed 41.3-7-124-4.
**Fall of Wickets:** 1-13, 2-174, 3-175, 4-216, 5-268, 6-269, 7-334, 8-346, 9-386

| SUSSEX | First Innings | | Second Innings (following on) | |
|---|---|---|---|---|
| CD Hopkinson | c Trott b Maddy | 47 | (2) c Trott b Anyon | 55 |
| RR Montgomerie | c Trott b Steyn | 0 | (1) c Groenewald b Anyon | 6 |
| CD Nash | lbw b Anyon | 0 | c Trott b Maddy | 24 |
| MW Goodwin | c Maddy b Anyon | 8 | lbw b Anyon | 31 |
| CJ Adams (capt) | c & b Maddy | 41 | c Ambrose b Anyon | 27 |
| *MJ Prior | lbw b Groenewald | 3 | c Trott b Maddy | 18 |
| RSC Martin-Jenkins | lbw b Groenewald | 20 | lbw b Tahir | 8 |
| Naved-ul-Hasan | b Maddy | 4 | c Trott b Tahir | 0 |
| RJ Kirtley | not out | 13 | not out | 2 |
| Mushtaq Ahmed | b Steyn | 4 | c Maddy b Tahir | 0 |
| CJ Liddle | lbw b Steyn | 4 | lbw b Tahir | 15 |
| Extras | lb 5, nb 2 | 7 | lb 12, nb 8 | 20 |
| | (all out 42.5 overs) | **151** | (all out 64.3 overs) | **206** |

**Bowling**
Steyn 10.5-2-36-3. Anyon 9-1-41-2. Tahir 5-3-11-0. Maddy 10-5-18-3. Groenewald 8-0-40-2.
Steyn 14-3-31-0. Anyon 17-4-55-4. Tahir 14.3-5-47-4. Maddy 11-4-31-2. Groenewald 4-2-17-0. Trott 4-1-13-0.
**Fall of Wickets:** 1-1, 2-2, 3-14, 4-99, 5-106, 6-114, 7-130, 8-134, 9-141
1-7, 2-51, 3-111, 4-132, 5-165, 6-182, 7-186, 8-186, 9-186

*Warwickshire won by an innings and 34 runs – Warwickshire (21pts), Sussex (3pts)*

### SURREY v. HAMPSHIRE – at The Oval

| HAMPSHIRE | First Innings | | Second Innings | |
|---|---|---|---|---|
| JHK Adams | c Butcher b Salisbury | 86 | c Butcher b Salisbury | 29 |
| MJ Brown | c Batty b Akram | 42 | not out | 115 |
| JP Crawley | lbw b Akram | 7 | not out | 66 |
| MJ Lumb | c Batty b Salisbury | 49 | | |
| CC Benham | c Butcher b Clarke | 76 | | |
| *N Pothas | not out | 85 | | |
| AD Mascarenhas | c Azhar Mahmood b Salisbury | 18 | | |
| SK Warne (capt) | c Ramprakash b Ormond | 48 | | |
| SD Udal | lbw b Salisbury | 2 | | |
| JTA Bruce | c Azhar Mahmood b Doshi | 32 | | |
| JA Tomlinson | | | | |
| Extras | b 2, lb 25, w 3, nb 6 | 36 | lb 10, w 2, nb 2 | 14 |
| | (9 wkts dec 126.4 overs) | **481** | (1 wkt dec 47 overs) | **224** |

**Bowling**
Ormond 24-8-78-1. Akram 16-2-71-2. Azhar Mahmood 22-7-66-0. Clarke 15-1-57-1. Salisbury 31-3-121-4. Doshi 18.4-2-61-1.
Ormond 3-0-13-0. Akram 6-0-25-0. Doshi 18-0-80-0. Azhar Mahmood 5-0-20-0. Salisbury 15-0-76-1.
**Fall of Wickets:** 1-82, 2-99, 3-178, 4-214, 5-313, 6-344, 7-413, 8-416, 9-481
1-86

| SURREY | First Innings | | Second Innings | |
|---|---|---|---|---|
| SA Newman | c Lumb b Mascarenhas | 0 | c Adams b Bruce | 3 |
| *JN Batty | c Pothas b Bruce | 2 | c Pothas b Udal | 121 |
| MR Ramprakash | not out | 107 | st Pothas b Udal | 43 |
| MA Butcher (capt) | c Pothas b Warne | 50 | (5) c Crawley b Udal | 72 |
| AD Brown | c Pothas b Warne | 0 | (6) c Pothas b Warne | 24 |
| R Clarke | lbw b Tomlinson | 8 | (7) c Adams b Udal | 0 |
| Azhar Mahmood | lbw b Warne | 5 | (8) c & b Tomlinson | 69 |
| IDK Salisbury | b Tomlinson | 18 | (9) st Pothas b Warne | 103 |
| J Ormond | c Benham b Warne | 0 | (4) c Pothas b Warne | 0 |
| ND Doshi | c Adams b Bruce | 0 | not out | 2 |
| Mohammad Akram | lbw b Warne | 0 | b Tomlinson | 4 |
| Extras | b 4, lb 4, w 1, nb 4 | 13 | b 6, lb 7, w 2, nb 11 | 26 |
| | (all out 60 overs) | **203** | (all out 133.3 overs) | **467** |

**Bowling**
Mascarenhas 13-4-39-1. Bruce 9-0-48-2. Tomlinson 20-7-53-2. Udal 3-0-10-0. Warne 15-2-45-5.
Mascarenhas 9-4-25-0. Bruce 17-2-81-1. Tomlinson 19.2-4-76-2. Warne 44-13-128-3. Adams 4-2-6-0. Udal 40.1-6-138-4.
**Fall of Wickets:** 1-0, 2-8, 3-133, 4-133, 5-150, 6-157, 7-192, 8-195, 9-200
1-8, 2-102, 3-113, 4-242, 5-277, 6-277, 7-283, 8-460, 9-462

*Hampshire won by 35 runs – Surrey (4pts), Hampshire (22pts)*

successive matches for the county, following his 342 at Guildford the previous July. Earlier, the 18-year-old Billy Godleman had made an unbeaten century for Middlesex on his Championship debut.

## Round Two: 25–28 April

A quite thrilling match at The Oval saw Surrey come within 35 runs of making the highest successful fourth-innings run-chase in Championship history against Shane Warne's Hampshire. In the end, it was the remarkable Warne who found himself coming out on top just when it seemed that even his magic powers were being forced under the spell of a magnificent 177-run eighth-wicket stand between Ian Salisbury and Azhar Mahmood. But, with 43 needed from nine overs and three wickets still intact, Azhar saw James Tomlinson cling on to a fierce straight drive and, soon after, Salisbury was tempted down the pitch by Warne and stumped for a brave 123-ball 103 which featured two sixes and 16 fours. James Ormond was then yorked and Hampshire, handicapped by the loss of Shaun Udal and Dimitri Mascarenhas with injuries, had finally managed to win a game they had dominated from the outset. Indeed, on the first three days, it was only Mark Ramprakash's 107 not out – more than half of Surrey's first-innings total – which provided any resistance as Warne recorded the 65th five-wicket return of his great career. But then came the

astonishing final day, which Surrey began on 105 for 2, and a great effort built on Jon Batty's 121 and Mark Butcher's 72.

Darren Maddy, chosen by Warwickshire to succeed Heath Streak as captain when the Zimbabwean stood

## Round Two: 25–28 April Division Two

### LEICESTERSHIRE v. SOMERSET – at Leicester

| SOMERSET | First Innings | | Second Innings | |
|---|---|---|---|---|
| ME Trescothick | c Robinson b Masters | 77 | lbw b Masters | 17 |
| NJ Edwards | c Amjad b Masters | 4 | c New b Singh | 79 |
| JL Langer (capt) | lbw b Masters | 14 | c Amjad b Singh | 92 |
| JC Hildreth | c New b Masters | 0 | c Ackerman b Singh | 9 |
| CL White | c New b Singh | 11 | c Singh b Henderson | 69 |
| ID Blackwell | c New b Singh | 0 | lbw b Henderson | 29 |
| PD Trego | c New b Henderson | 50 | b Amjad | 6 |
| *SHP Spurway | b Henderson | 0 | c Henderson | 1 |
| PS Jones | b Masters | 114 | b Amjad | 19 |
| AR Caddick | c Singh b Masters | 51 | st New b Amjad | 1 |
| CM Willoughby | not out | 4 | not out | 1 |
| Extras | b 1, lb 15, w 3, nb 4 | 23 | b 14, lb 19, nb 20 | 53 |
| | (all out 84.4 overs) | 357 | (all out 86.4 overs) | 376 |

Bowling
Masters 20.4-6-60-6. Walker 19-2-99-0. Singh 17.4-4-70-2. Maunders 13-2-51-0. Henderson 15-1-61-2.
Masters 9-4-21-1. Singh 14-3-62-3. Henderson 30-5-111-3. Walker 9-0-69-0. Amjad 17.4-1-52-3. Maunders 7-0-28-0.
Fall of Wickets: 1-33, 2-49, 3-49, 4-71, 5-71, 6-165, 7-182, 8-201, 9-347 1-30, 2-205, 3-219, 4-234, 5-296, 6-307, 7-316, 8-363, 9-375

| LEICESTERSHIRE | First Innings | | Second Innings | |
|---|---|---|---|---|
| JK Maunders | b Willoughby | 26 | (2) lbw b Caddick | 10 |
| DDJ Robinson (capt) | b Blackwell | 122 | (1) b Caddick | 10 |
| HD Ackerman | lbw b Willoughby | 1 | c Spurway b Blackwell | 17 |
| JL Sadler | c Spurway b Willoughby | 3 | b White | 22 |
| DD Masters | c Langer b Willoughby | 9 | (9) c Trescothick b Trego | 7 |
| J Allenby | lbw b Trego | 77 | lbw b Trego | 1 |
| *TJ New | c Hildreth b Trego | 53 | c Edwards b White | 54 |
| Mansoor Amjad | c Trego b Willoughby | 67 | c Trescothick b White | 1 |
| CW Henderson | lbw b Trego | 4 | (5) c Edwards b White | 1 |
| RP Singh | c Spurway b Trego | 1 | b Trego | 2 |
| NGE Walker | not out | 2 | not out | 9 |
| Extras | lb 11, w 4, nb 5 | 20 | b 1, lb 7, w 1, nb 6 | 15 |
| | (all out 110.4 overs) | 385 | (all out 38.1 overs) | 150 |

Bowling
Caddick 22-4-83-0. Trego 20.4-3-72-4. Willoughby 28-9-97-5. Jones 17-3-79-0. Blackwell 23-6-43-1.
Caddick 10-3-29-2. Willoughby 3-0-15-0. Jones 3-1-5-0. Blackwell 4-3-2-1. White 9.1-0-42-3. Trego 9-2-49-4.
Fall of Wickets: 1-42, 2-44, 3-48, 4-55, 5-249, 6-261, 7-378, 8-378, 9-380 1-15, 2-35, 3-53, 4-56, 5-71, 6-71, 7-74, 8-116, 9-122

*Somerset won by 198 runs – Leicestershire (7pts), Somerset (21pts)*

### ESSEX v. GLAMORGAN – at Chelmsford

| ESSEX | First Innings | |
|---|---|---|
| ML Pettini | st Wallace b Croft | 86 |
| AN Cook | c Waters b Wharf | 0 |
| V Chopra | c Wallace b Waters | 86 |
| RC Irani (capt) | b Waters | 218 |
| *JS Foster | st Wallace b Croft | 7 |
| RN ten Doeschate | c Croft b Wright | 148 |
| TJ Phillips | lbw b Croft | 0 |
| JD Middlebrook | not out | 13 |
| AJ Tudor | not out | 10 |
| Danish Kaneria | | |
| AC McGarry | | |
| Extras | b 1, lb 6, w 1, nb 4 | 16 |
| | (7 wkts dec 167 overs) | 584 |

Bowling
Davies 31-3-138-0. Wharf 31-2-110-1. Waters 30-5-117-2. Watkins 17-5-52-0. Croft 54-6-142-3. Wright 4-0-14-1.
Fall of Wickets: 1-2, 169, 3-189, 4-214, 5-527, 6-533, 7-570

| GLAMORGAN | First Innings | | Second Innings (following on) | |
|---|---|---|---|---|
| MTG Elliott | run out | 95 | (2) c Pettini b Danish Kaneria | 75 |
| DD Cherry | c Foster b Danish Kaneria | 48 | (1) b Danish Kaneria | 0 |
| HT Waters | c Foster b Danish Kaneria | 33 | (11) c ten Doeschate b D Kaneria | 0 |
| *MA Wallace | lbw b Tudor | 13 | (3) b Danish Kaneria | 10 |
| MJ Powell | c Pettini b Phillips | 64 | (4) st Foster b Danish Kaneria | 8 |
| DL Hemp (capt) | b Danish Kaneria | 5 | (5) lbw b Middlebrook | 4 |
| BJ Wright | c Foster b Danish Kaneria | 11 | (5) lbw b Middlebrook | 4 |
| RE Watkins | lbw b Danish Kaneria | 29 | c Pettini b Danish Kaneria | 2 |
| AG Wharf | b Danish Kaneria | 38 | (7) c Foster b Middlebrook | 2 |
| RDB Croft | lbw b Danish Kaneria | 0 | (9) not out | 42 |
| AP Davies | not out | 24 | (10) c Pettini b Phillips | 12 |
| Extras | b 8, lb 10, w 2, nb 6 | 26 | b 4, lb 2, nb 2 | 8 |
| | (all out 145.4 overs) | 394 | (all out 69.5 overs) | 183 |

Bowling
Tudor 21-6-48-1. McGarry 15-3-52-0. Danish Kaneria 47.4-16-105-7.
ten Doeschate 1-1-47-0. Middlebrook 32-9-61-0. Phillips 20-3-58-1. Chopra 1-0-5-0.
McGarry 7-3-20-0. Middlebrook 34-8-76-3. Danish Kaneria 25.5-4-76-6. Phillips 3-2-5-1.
Fall of Wickets: 1-139, 2-153, 3-170, 4-253, 5-266, 6-281, 7-312, 8-323, 9-323 1-52, 2-64, 3-82, 4-89, 5-92, 6-102, 7-109, 8-144, 9-178

*Essex won by an innings and 7 runs – Essex (22pts), Glamorgan (4pts)*

### MIDDLESEX v. NORTHAMPTONSHIRE – at Lord's

| MIDDLESEX | First Innings | | Second Innings | |
|---|---|---|---|---|
| BL Hutton | b van der Wath | 6 | c Wessels b Klusener | 37 |
| NRD Compton | b van der Wath | 12 | lbw b van der Wath | 8 |
| OA Shah | c Peters b Klusener | 41 | c Wessels b Wigley | 24 |
| ET Smith (capt) | c Sales b van der Wath | 25 | (5) run out | 38 |
| BA Godleman | c Wessels b van der Wath | 77 | (6) lbw b Brown | 40 |
| *DC Nash | c Sales b Crook | 10 | (7) not out | 44 |
| TJ Murtagh | c Wessels b van der Wath | 40 | (8) c Wessels b van der Wath | 34 |
| RL Johnson | c Wessels b van der Wath | 0 | (9) c Klusener b Wigley | 9 |
| M Kartik | c Wessels b Brown | 25 | (4) c Sales b van der Wath | 5 |
| CEW Silverwood | c Crook b Klusener | 4 | c Rogers b Brown | 30 |
| A Richardson | not out | 0 | b Wigley | 0 |
| Extras | b 5, lb 6, w 1, nb 6 | 18 | b 18, lb 6, w 2, nb 8 | 34 |
| | (all out 81.3 overs) | 258 | (all out 115 overs) | 362 |

Bowling
van der Wath 18.3-6-49-6. Crook 13-2-58-1. Wigley 16-3-52-0. Klusener 16-2-59-2. Brown 16-6-29-1.
van der Wath 26-7-102-3. Crook 25-5-91-0. Klusener 13-5-21-1. Wigley 19-3-65-3. Brown 30-12-54-2. Afzaal 2-0-5-0.
Fall of Wickets: 1-10, 2-39, 3-74, 4-97, 5-127, 6-201, 7-203, 8-243, 9-254 1-13, 2-47, 3-58, 4-110, 5-138, 6-196, 7-267, 8-297, 9-350

| NORTHANTS | First Innings | | Second Innings | |
|---|---|---|---|---|
| SD Peters | c Nash b Johnson | 8 | (2) b Richardson | 0 |
| CJL Rogers | c Hutton b Silverwood | 12 | (1) c Nash b Johnson | 8 |
| *MH Wessels | c Nash b Murtagh | 16 | (4) c Godleman b Kartik | 58 |
| DJG Sales (capt) | c Nash b Richardson | 14 | (5) c Smith b Kartik | 4 |
| U Afzaal | c Nash b Richardson | 39 | (3) c Kartik b Silverwood | 16 |
| DH Wigley | c Godleman b Richardson | 23 | (10) lbw b Richardson | 4 |
| RA White | c Compton b Kartik | 16 | (6) c Hutton b Kartik | 0 |
| L Klusener | not out | 44 | (7) c Godleman b Silverwood | 20 |
| JJ van der Wath | c Hutton b Richardson | 0 | (8) c Smith b Richardson | 5 |
| SP Crook | c Godleman b Silverwood | 11 | (9) not out | 8 |
| JF Brown | c Shah b Johnson | 2 | c & b Richardson | 8 |
| Extras | lb 13, w 1, nb 6 | 20 | b 1, lb 10, w 7, nb 8 | 26 |
| | (all out 51.4 overs) | 211 | (all out 87 overs) | 255 |

Bowling
Silverwood 13-1-55-2. Johnson 13-4-2-69-2. Richardson 13-2-44-4.
Murtagh 7-2-17-1. Kartik 5-2-13-1.
Richardson 20-4-55-4. Silverwood 19-3-50-2. Johnson 13-1-45-1. Kartik 28-6-76-3. Murtagh 7-3-13-0.
Fall of Wickets: 1-12, 2-30, 3-48, 4-68, 5-123, 6-132, 7-160, 8-162, 9-192 1-6, 2-31, 3-53, 4-182, 5-196, 6-211, 7-234, 8-238, 9-247

*Middlesex won by 154 runs – Middlesex (19pts), Northamptonshire (4pts)*

### GLOUCESTERSHIRE v. NOTTINGHAMSHIRE – at Bristol

| NOTTS | First Innings | | Second Innings | |
|---|---|---|---|---|
| JER Gallian | c Adshead b Lewis | 10 | lbw b Noffke | 0 |
| BM Shafayat | c Spearman b Noffke | 79 | c Taylor b Noffke | 0 |
| MA Wagh | b Noffke | 71 | c Adshead b Noffke | 12 |
| DJ Hussey (capt) | c Hardinges b Kirby | 21 | c Taylor b Hardinges | 77 |
| SR Patel | c Adshead b Noffke | 89 | c Adshead b North | 176 |
| *CMW Read | b Hardinges | 7 | not out | 43 |
| MA Ealham | c Adshead b Noffke | 27 | not out | 5 |
| PJ Franks | b Kirby | 26 | | |
| GP Swann | c Gidman b Noffke | 0 | | |
| RJ Sidebottom | not out | 8 | | |
| AJ Harris | c Adshead b Noffke | 0 | | |
| Extras | b 15, lb 12, w 6, nb 28 | 61 | b 7, lb 2, nb 11 | 20 |
| | (all out 111.1 overs) | 399 | (5 wkts dec 80 overs) | 333 |

Bowling
Lewis 21-4-65-1. Noffke 24.1-6-68-6. Kirby 27-8-75-2. Hardinges 20-4-93-1. Gidman 8-0-34-0. North 14-2-37-0.
Noffke 15-5-45-3. Kirby 17-5-44-0. Hardinges 15-1-80-1. Lewis 6-3-12-0. Gidman 8-0-67-0. North 11-1-46-1. Taylor 5-0-28-0.
Fall of Wickets: 1-34, 2-196, 3-203, 4-240, 5-258, 6-299, 7-383, 8-384, 9-395 1-0, 2-17, 3-24, 4-200, 5-314

| GLOS | First Innings | | Second Innings | |
|---|---|---|---|---|
| Kadeer Ali | b Harris | 48 | (2) c Shafayat b Harris | 9 |
| CM Spearman | c Hussey b Sidebottom | 100 | (1) c Hussey b Swann | 85 |
| GP Hodnett | b Franks | 25 | c Hussey b Franks | 61 |
| MJ North | c Hussey b Harris | 24 | b Sidebottom | 22 |
| APR Gidman | c Gallian b Franks | 17 | c Patel b Swann | 88 |
| CG Taylor | b Franks | 0 | c Gallian b Swann | 5 |
| *SJ Adshead | b Swann | 21 | lbw b Franks | 0 |
| MA Hardinges | b Harris | 31 | not out | 18 |
| AA Noffke | b Sidebottom | 16 | c Shafayat b Franks | 15 |
| J Lewis (capt) | not out | 42 | c Read b Ealham | 15 |
| SP Kirby | c Hussey b Sidebottom | 16 | c Read b Ealham | 0 |
| Extras | lb 5, nb 4 | 9 | b 4, lb 4, w 9, nb 12 | 29 |
| | (all out 85.4 overs) | 328 | (all out 94.5 overs) | 353 |

Bowling
Sidebottom 24.4-4-72-3. Harris 23-2-120-3. Franks 14-3-53-3. Ealham 13-3-47-0. Swann 11-2-31-1.
Sidebottom 20-5-43-1. Swann 18.2-6-53-2. Harris 10-2-35-1. Franks 20.3-4-89-3. Swann 24-0-122-3. Patel 2-0-3-0.
Fall of Wickets: 1-146, 2-154, 3-169, 4-240, 5-253, 6-302, 7-320, 8-343, 9-353 1-12, 2-172, 3-180, 4-246, 5-253, 6-302, 7-320, 8-343, 9-353

*Nottinghamshire won by 51 runs – Gloucestershire (6pts), Nottinghamshire (21pts)*

Darren Maddy, who had moved from Leicestershire to Warwickshire, soon found himself captaining his new team-mates after the resignation of Heath Streak.

down from the job just before the game, responded by leading the county to a innings win against Sussex, whose batting fell away alarmingly. 'It's just been one of the most amazing weeks of my life,' said Maddy. 'I've made my debut for a new county, been given my cap and been made captain, and now I've led the team to victory against the champions.' Yorkshire, meanwhile, maintained their flying start to the season by crushing Durham, despite a six-wicket haul for Steve Harmison. The leg-spin of Adil Rashid claimed five more prime wickets in Durham's first innings, and Matthew Hoggard cleaned up after Joe Sayers had laboured 417 balls to carry his bat for 149 and earn Yorkshire a match-winning lead.

Ronnie Irani hit an authoritative 218 from 347 balls, adding 313 for the fifth wicket with Ryan ten Doeschate, whose 148 occupied only 200 balls, but Essex's innings victory against Glamorgan owed even more to Danish Kaneria's 13 wickets in the match. The Welsh county's first innings featured an incredible show of defiance from nightwatchman Huw Waters, who came in at 139 for 1 on the second evening and lasted five hours and 265 balls for a mere 33 before being seventh out at 312.

Flags were at half-mast at Bristol as a mark of respect for former England double-international Arthur Milton, who died on the day before Gloucestershire's match against Nottinghamshire, but the county's modern-day players had no answer to the power of Samit Patel's strokeplay. The 22-year-old hit 89 and then a career-best 176, from just 203 balls with three sixes and 28 fours, to prove to be the difference between the sides.

Young Billy Godleman impressed again for Middlesex by compiling a skilful and mature first-innings 77 as they ground out an attritional win against Northamptonshire at Lord's, with Alan Richardson proving his return to full fitness following an injury-ravaged 2006 by picking up four wickets in each innings. There was an important eight-wicket match haul, too, for the born-again Peter Trego at Grace Road as Somerset overpowered Leicestershire following the first day boost of an unlikely ninth-wicket stand of 146 between Steffan Jones, who made a career-best 114, and Andrew Caddick.

## Round Three: 2–5 May

The sudden downturn in fortunes of Sussex, the defending champions, reached crisis proportions at

Canterbury as Kent walloped them inside two days following combative hundreds from Matthew Walker and Yasir Arafat. The seam of Ryan McLaren, Arafat – against his former county – and Simon Cook then shocked the Sussex batsman into tame defeat. And, at Old Trafford, Surrey's early-season problems were exacerbated as Lancashire, given a slender first-innings lead by Stuart Law's 76th first-class century, sent their opponents crashing to a fatal second-innings 34 for 6 by the close of the second day. From that there was no escape.

Warwickshire's graph continued its sharp upward turn, however, under Darren Maddy's leadership, as Worcestershire were trounced by an innings at New Road. Jim Troughton's 162 was a vital innings for the victors, but most plaudits were won by Tim Ambrose, at 24 a possible future England wicketkeeper, who propelled Warwickshire beyond 600 with a superb 325-ball innings of 251 not out, featuring 34 fours. After that Graeme Hick made 91 but no one else put up much of a fight as Naqqash Tahir picked up six wickets in the match and the speedy Dale Steyn took eight, including a second-innings 5 for 49.

Hampshire held out determinedly for a draw at the Rose Bowl against a Yorkshire side intent on a third successive victory. Nic Pothas played the match-saving innings, but much of the attention over the four days had been on Younus Khan, who added 202 not out to his first innings 106, and England captain Michael

Vaughan who scored a fine 72 at the start of only his 11th Championship appearance in six seasons but then suffered a cracked finger in Yorkshire's second innings – an injury which was to prevent him from playing in

## Round Three: 2–5 May Division One

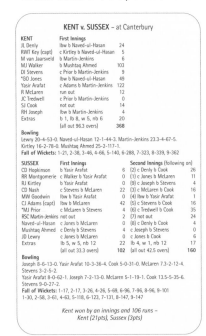

**KENT v. SUSSEX – at Canterbury**

**KENT** First Innings
| | | |
|---|---|---|
| JL Denly | lbw b Naved-ul-Hasan | 24 |
| RWT Key (capt) | c Kirtley b Naved-ul-Hasan | 5 |
| M van Jaarsveld | b Martin-Jenkins | 6 |
| MJ Walker | b Mushtaq Ahmed | 103 |
| DI Stevens | c Prior b Martin-Jenkins | 9 |
| *GO Jones | lbw b Naved-ul-Hasan | 49 |
| Yasir Arafat | c Adams b Martin-Jenkins | 122 |
| R McLaren | run out | 12 |
| JC Tredwell | c Prior b Martin-Jenkins | 0 |
| SJ Cook | not out | 14 |
| RH Joseph | lbw b Martin-Jenkins | 4 |
| Extras | b 1, lb 8, w 5, nb 6 | 20 |
| | (all out 96.3 overs) | **368** |

Bowling
Lewry 20-4-53-0. Naved-ul-Hasan 12-1-44-3. Martin-Jenkins 23.3-4-67-5. Kirtley 16-2-78-0. Mushtaq Ahmed 25-2-117-1.
Fall of Wickets: 1-21, 2-38, 3-46, 4-66, 5-140, 6-288, 7-323, 8-339, 9-362

**SUSSEX** First Innings / Second Innings (following on)
| | First Innings | | Second Innings | |
|---|---|---|---|---|
| CD Hopkinson | b Yasir Arafat | 6 | (2) c Denly b Cook | 26 |
| RR Montgomerie | c Walker b Yasir Arafat | 0 | (1) c Jones b McLaren | 11 |
| RJ Kirtley | b Yasir Arafat | 0 | (9) c Joseph b Stevens | 4 |
| CD Nash | c Stevens b McLaren | 22 | (3) c Stevens b Cook | 16 |
| MW Goodwin | lbw b Yasir Arafat | 0 | (4) lbw b Yasir Arafat | 1 |
| CJ Adams (capt) | lbw b McLaren | 42 | (5) c Stevens b Cook | 16 |
| *MJ Prior | c McLaren b Stevens | 4 | (6) c Tredwell b Cook | 35 |
| RSC Martin-Jenkins | not out | 2 | (7) not out | 24 |
| Naved-ul-Hasan | c Jones b McLaren | 4 | (8) c Denly b Cook | 4 |
| Mushtaq Ahmed | c Denly b Stevens | 4 | c Joseph b Stevens | 0 |
| JD Lewry | c Jones b McLaren | 0 | c Jones b Cook | 6 |
| Extras | lb 4, w 5, nb 12 | 22 | lb 4, w 5, nb 2 | 15 |
| | (all out 33.3 overs) | **102** | (all out 42.5 overs) | **160** |

Bowling
Joseph 8-6-13-0. Yasir Arafat 10.3-3-36-4. Cook 5-0-31-0. McLaren 7.3-2-12-4. Stevens 3-2-5-2.
Yasir Arafat 8-0-62-1. Joseph 7-2-13-0. McLaren 5-1-19-1. Cook 13.5-5-35-6. Stevens 9-0-27-2.
Fall of Wickets: 1-17, 2-17, 3-26, 4-26, 5-69, 6-96, 7-96, 8-96, 9-101
1-30, 2-58, 3-61, 4-63, 5-118, 6-123, 7-131, 8-147, 9-147

*Kent won by an innings and 106 runs –*
*Kent (21pts), Sussex (3pts)*

---

**LANCASHIRE v. SURREY – at Old Trafford**

**SURREY** First Innings / Second Innings
| | First Innings | | Second Innings | |
|---|---|---|---|---|
| SA Newman | c Keedy b Cork | 60 | lbw b Chapple | 0 |
| *JN Batty | c Horton b Smith | 70 | run out | 0 |
| MR Ramprakash | c Sutton b Newby | 13 | c Chapple b Cork | 7 |
| MA Butcher (capt) | b Newby | 9 | c Chilton b Chapple | 32 |
| AD Brown | b Smith | 69 | lbw b Cork | 0 |
| R Clarke | lbw b Keedy | 19 | b Chapple | 1 |
| JGE Benning | lbw b Keedy | 13 | (8) b Smith | 36 |
| IDK Salisbury | b Newby | 4 | (9) c Horton b Chapple | 0 |
| NC Saker | c Sutcliffe b Keedy | 8 | (7) c Sutton b Cork | 1 |
| J Ormond | not out | 4 | b Newby | 20 |
| Mohammad Akram | lbw b Keedy | 1 | not out | 8 |
| Extras | b 5, lb 7, nb 2 | 14 | b 1, lb 10 | 11 |
| | (all out 93.3 overs) | **284** | (all out 35 overs) | **120** |

Bowling
Chapple 16-1-51-0. Cork 15-3-59-1. Newby 18-1-44-3. Smith 20-5-56-2.
Keedy 22.3-6-57-4. Chilton 2-0-5-0.
Chapple 15-4-40-4. Cork 14-3-39-3. Smith 3-0-17-1. Newby 3-1-13-1.
Fall of Wickets: 1-117, 2-136, 3-156, 4-158, 5-209, 6-236, 7-251, 8-278, 9-280
1-0, 2-0, 3-20, 4-20, 5-31, 6-32, 7-74, 8-80, 9-104

**LANCASHIRE** First Innings / Second Innings
| | First Innings | | Second Innings | |
|---|---|---|---|---|
| MJ Chilton (capt) | c Batty b Akram | 31 | (2) not out | 34 |
| IJ Sutcliffe | lbw b Saker | 2 | (1) lbw b Saker | 3 |
| G Keedy | b Saker | 9 | | |
| MB Loye | lbw b Ormond | 35 | (3) c Newman b Akram | 1 |
| SG Law | lbw b Clarke | 120 | (4) c Salisbury b Akram | 1 |
| PJ Horton | c Batty b Saker | 36 | (5) not out | 49 |
| *LD Sutton | c Newman b Saker | 0 | | |
| G Chapple | c Salisbury b Saker | 9 | | |
| DG Cork | c Clarke b Ormond | 17 | | |
| TC Smith | not out | 26 | | |
| OJ Newby | lbw b Salisbury | 7 | | |
| Extras | lb 11, nb 12 | 23 | lb 2 | 2 |
| | (all out 96.2 overs) | **315** | (3 wkts 21.2 overs) | **90** |

Bowling
Akram 16-7-37-1. Saker 20-4-76-5. Clarke 16-2-62-1. Ormond 20-5-52-2.
Salisbury 24.2-4-59-1. Benning 4-0-18-0.
Akram 8-3-22-2. Saker 4-1-24-1. Ormond 4-0-18-0. Salisbury 3-0-12-0.
Clarke 2.2-0-12-0.
Fall of Wickets: 1-2, 2-22, 3-78, 4-92, 5-210, 6-210, 7-224, 8-265, 9-307
1-3, 2-4, 3-8

*Lancashire won by 7 wickets –*
*Lancashire (20pts), Surrey (5pts)*

---

**WORCESTERSHIRE v. WARWICKSHIRE – at Worcester**

**WARWICKSHIRE** First Innings
| | | |
|---|---|---|
| IJ Westwood | lbw b Kabir Ali | 2 |
| DL Maddy (capt) | c Davies b Kabir Ali | 0 |
| IJL Trott | b Jones | 39 |
| JO Troughton | c Davies b Batty | 162 |
| AGR Loudon | c Davies b Sillence | 45 |
| *TR Ambrose | not out | 251 |
| HH Streak | c Hick b Solanki | 66 |
| TD Groenewald | not out | 13 |
| N Tahir | | |
| DW Steyn | | |
| JE Anyon | | |
| Extras | b 10, lb 3, w 13, nb 6 | 32 |
| | (6 wkts dec 163 overs) | **610** |

Bowling
Kabir Ali 34-7-122-2. Malik 24-8-102-0. Sillence 31-4-130-1. Batty 42-10-107-1.
Jones 15-2-82-1. Solanki 17-0-54-1.
Fall of Wickets: 1-2, 2-3, 3-82, 4-195, 5-349, 6-575

**WORCS** First Innings / Second Innings (following on)
| | First Innings | | Second Innings | |
|---|---|---|---|---|
| SC Moore | c Loudon b Anyon | 47 | (2) c Ambrose b Tahir | 0 |
| PA Jaques | c Maddy b Steyn | 0 | (1) lbw b Steyn | 2 |
| VS Solanki (capt) | c Ambrose b Streak | 35 | c Loudon b Steyn | 4 |
| BF Smith | lbw b Streak | 50 | lbw b Steyn | 65 |
| GA Hick | c Trott b Tahir | 91 | c Loudon b Tahir | 66 |
| *SM Davies | c Groenewald b Tahir | 1 | c Groenewald b Tahir | 0 |
| GJ Batty | c Westwood b Troughton | 10 | lbw b Streak | 14 |
| RJ Sillence | not out | 29 | c Maddy b Steyn | 1 |
| Kabir Ali | c Ambrose b Tahir | 0 | lbw b Steyn | 4 |
| RA Jones | lbw b Steyn | 1 | not out | 11 |
| MN Malik | c Maddy b Steyn | 0 | c Westwood b Streak | 4 |
| Extras | lb 7, w 7, nb 10 | 24 | b 1, lb 15, w 1, nb 20 | 37 |
| | (all out 101.4 overs) | **288** | (all out 61.4 overs) | **209** |

Bowling
Steyn 20.4-7-56-3. Anyon 13-3-44-1. Tahir 10-3-37-3. Streak 14-2-33-2.
Groenewald 14-4-28-0. Maddy 5-0-10-0. Loudon 15-2-39-0. Troughton 10-0-34-1.
Maddy 4-1-9-0. Groenewald 6-3-11-0. Loudon 5-0-24-0.
Steyn 12-1-49-5. Tahir 16-3-31-3. Streak 9.4-4-29-2. Anyon 9-1-40-0.
Fall of Wickets: 1-1, 2-68, 3-121, 4-180, 5-183, 6-236, 7-279, 8-279, 9-288
1-2, 2-2, 3-9, 4-159, 5-161, 6-168, 7-179, 8-193, 9-205

*Warwickshire won by an innings and 113 runs –*
*Worcestershire (3pts), Warwickshire (22pts)*

---

**HAMPSHIRE v. YORKSHIRE – at the Rose Bowl**

**YORKSHIRE** First Innings / Second Innings
| | First Innings | | Second Innings | |
|---|---|---|---|---|
| JJ Sayers | c Lumb b Ervine | 17 | lbw b Clark | 6 |
| MP Vaughan | run out | 72 | retired hurt | 16 |
| A McGrath | c Brown b Warne | 7 | c Pothas b Clark | 7 |
| Younus Khan | lbw b Bruce | 106 | not out | 202 |
| JA Rudolph | c Pothas b Clark | 3 | (6) c Pothas b Clark | 22 |
| *GL Brophy | c Pothas b Bruce | 13 | (7) not out | 100 |
| AU Rashid | c Bruce b Tomlinson | 54 | | |
| TT Bresnan | c Warne b Tomlinson | 5 | | |
| JN Gillespie | c Benham b Bruce | 2 | | |
| D Gough (capt) | b Bruce | 4 | | |
| MJ Hoggard | not out | 4 | (5) c Ervine b Warne | 61 |
| Extras | b 4, lb 4, nb 4 | 12 | b 10, lb 4, w 5, nb 2 | 25 |
| | (all out 93.4 overs) | **299** | (4 wkts dec 106.5 overs) | **439** |

Bowling
Clark 12-3-37-1. Bruce 20-2-56-4. Tomlinson 20.4-2-68-2. Ervine 14-3-42-1.
Warne 18-1-63-1. Adams 9-2-25-0.
Clark 22.5-0-83-3. Bruce 17-7-44-0. Tomlinson 15-1-78-0. Ervine 21-3-86-0.
Warne 29-2-114-1. Adams 2-0-16-0.
Fall of Wickets: 1-57, 2-77, 3-134, 4-149, 5-183, 6-282, 7-284, 8-289, 9-293
1-29, 2-34, 3-186, 4-245

**HAMPSHIRE** First Innings / Second Innings
| | First Innings | | Second Innings | |
|---|---|---|---|---|
| JHK Adams | c Brophy b Bresnan | 22 | c McGrath b Younus Khan | 90 |
| MJ Brown | lbw b Bresnan | 105 | c Brophy b Gillespie | 8 |
| JP Crawley | c Brophy b Bresnan | 32 | (4) c Rudolph b Younus Khan | 50 |
| MJ Lumb | c Brophy b Bresnan | 5 | (5) c Rudolph b Younus Khan | 57 |
| CC Benham | c Rudolph b Rashid | 2 | (6) c McGrath b Younus Khan | 0 |
| *N Pothas | not out | 70 | (7) not out | 76 |
| SM Ervine | c Brophy b Gillespie | 14 | (8) c Rudolph b Rashid | 14 |
| SK Warne (capt) | c McGrath b Gillespie | 10 | (9) c Rudolph b Gillespie | 33 |
| SR Clark | c Brophy b Gillespie | 3 | (10) not out | 4 |
| JTA Bruce | c Rashid b Hoggard | 7 | (3) b Gillespie | 4 |
| JA Tomlinson | b Rashid | 1 | | |
| Extras | lb 7, w 4, nb 12 | 23 | b 9, lb 7, nb 10 | 26 |
| | (all out 95.3 overs) | **296** | (8 wkts 105 overs) | **366** |

Bowling
Hoggard 19-2-52-1. Gough 9-2-40-0. Rashid 26.3-2-79-2. Bresnan 22-6-65-4.
Gillespie 14-4-40-3. Younus Khan 3-0-17-0. Rudolph 3-1-4-0.
Hoggard 11-2-30-0. Gillespie 14-3-44-3. Rashid 33-4-126-1. Bresnan 7-1-42-0.
Gough 15-4-33-0. McGrath 6-2-15-0. Rudolph 1-0-8-0. Younus Khan 18-4-52-4.
Fall of Wickets: 1-68, 2-158, 3-166, 4-169, 5-181, 6-218, 7-228, 8-232, 9-275
1-12, 2-22, 3-116, 4-198, 5-208, 6-265, 7-286, 8-336

*Match drawn – Hampshire (9pts), Yorkshire (9pts)*

the opening Test match of the summer against the West Indies at Lord's.

Jason Gallian's 178 and another blazing hundred from Samit Patel was the basis of Nottinghamshire's innings rout of Glamorgan, for whom the only

**Opposite** Kent's Yasir Arafat appeals successfully for lbw against his former Sussex team-mate Murray Goodwin during his side's innings victory at Canterbury.

consolations were Ben Wright's unbeaten 66 in the face of Charlie Shreck's six-wicket demolition job and fellow teenager James Harris becoming, at 16 years and 351 days, the youngest Glamorgan bowler to take a Championship wicket. Northamptonshire were the second division's other winners in this round, Johan van der Wath leading a recovery from 217 for 7 that eventually proved decisive against an Essex side who earlier could not stop a horrible slide from 240 for 1 to 334 all out following the dismissal of Alastair Cook for 136.

There were more mountainous totals at Taunton, with Somerset holding out comfortably for the draw after Derbyshire had equalled the highest total ever made by a visiting team to the County Ground – 801 (the same total run up by Lancashire in the 1895 match made famous by Archie MacLaren's then world record 424). And Gloucestershire's game against Leicestershire at Bristol was also drawn, on a lifeless pitch, with the visitors more than happy to avoid defeat after losing David Masters with injury and also having to play the last three days without Claude Henderson, their left-arm spinner, who flew to South Africa to be with his mother Susan, who was seriously ill with cancer.

## Round Three: 2–5 May Division Two

### NOTTINGHAMSHIRE v. GLAMORGAN – at Trent Bridge

**NOTTS** — First Innings
| | | |
|---|---|---|
| JER Gallian | c sub b Wharf | 178 |
| BM Shafayat | c Elliott b Harris | 2 |
| MA Wagh | c Wallace b Waters | 3 |
| DJ Hussey (capt) | c Wallace b Watkins | 81 |
| SR Patel | c Hemp b Wright | 108 |
| *CMW Read | c Wallace b Wharf | 34 |
| MA Ealham | c Cherry b Harris | 12 |
| PJ Franks | c Wright b Wharf | 4 |
| GP Swann | c Cherry b Waters | 25 |
| RJ Sidebottom | b Wharf | 18 |
| CE Shreck | not out | 0 |
| Extras | lb 3, w 1, nb 6 | 10 |
| | (all out 122.4 overs) | 475 |

Bowling
Harris 25-7-86-2. Waters 20.4-2-73-2. Wharf 21-1-97-4. Watkins 16-2-78-1. Croft 21-1-101-0. Wright 11-0-37-1.

Fall of Wickets: 1-7, 2-12, 3-148, 4-329, 5-411, 6-428, 7-428, 8-435, 9-461

**GLAMORGAN** — First Innings / Second Innings (following on)
| | | | | | |
|---|---|---|---|---|---|
| DD Cherry | c Read b Sidebottom | 0 | (2) lbw b Shreck | | 0 |
| *MA Wallace | c Swann b Sidebottom | 7 | (3) lbw b Shreck | | 6 |
| RE Watkins | c Read b Sidebottom | 4 | (8) c Hussey b Swann | | 20 |
| MJ Powell | b Ealham | 53 | (5) c Ealham b Shreck | | 0 |
| DL Hemp (capt) | c Read b Ealham | 54 | (6) c Gallian b Shreck | | 47 |
| BJ Wright | c Hussey b Ealham | 10 | (7) not out | | 66 |
| MTG Elliott | c Read b Ealham | 47 | (1) c Read b Shreck | | 30 |
| AG Wharf | c Read b Swann | 0 | (9) lbw b Sidebottom | | 0 |
| RDB Croft | c Shafayat b Swann | 17 | (10) c Shafayat b Franks | | 9 |
| JAR Harris | lbw b Patel | 21 | (4) c Wagh b Shreck | | 11 |
| HT Waters | not out | 6 | run out | | 2 |
| Extras | b 8, lb 14, nb 2 | 24 | b 4, lb 6, nb 4 | | 14 |
| | (all out 70.4 overs) | 262 | (all out 76 overs) | | 205 |

Bowling
Sidebottom 14-0-54-3. Shreck 18-3-73-0. Franks 14-4-41-0. Ealham 14-5-37-4. Swann 10-2-35-2. Patel 0.4-0-0-1.
Sidebottom 21-7-43-1. Shreck 22-4-62-6. Franks 11-3-34-1. Ealham 6-2-25-0. Swann 15-5-30-1. Patel 1-0-1-0.

Fall of Wickets: 1-0, 2-11, 3-22, 4-128, 5-133, 6-148, 7-200, 8-215, 9-234
1-2, 2-14, 3-50, 4-50, 5-57, 6-128, 7-165, 8-170, 9-192

*Nottinghamshire won by an innings and 8 runs – Nottinghamshire (22pts), Glamorgan (5pts)*

### NORTHAMPTONSHIRE v. ESSEX – at Northampton

**ESSEX** — First Innings / Second Innings
| | | | | | |
|---|---|---|---|---|---|
| ML Pettini | b Brown | 67 | c Wessels b Crook | | 50 |
| AN Cook | c O'Brien b Panesar | 136 | lbw b van der Wath | | 37 |
| V Chopra | lbw b Wigley | 38 | lbw b Panesar | | 9 |
| RS Bopara | c Wessels b Crook | 26 | c Peters b Brown | | 12 |
| RC Irani (capt) | not out | 34 | lbw b Klusener | | 1 |
| *JS Foster | c O'Brien b Crook | 0 | lbw b Brown | | 17 |
| RN ten Doeschate | lbw b Crook | 0 | not out | | 33 |
| JD Middlebrook | b Crook | 0 | b Brown | | 0 |
| AJ Tudor | lbw b Klusener | 0 | b Brown | | 0 |
| A Nel | c Panesar b Klusener | 0 | (11) c O'Brien b Crook | | 1 |
| Danish Kaneria | c Panesar b Wigley | 21 | (10) b Crook | | 12 |
| Extras | b 1, lb 4, w 7 | 12 | lb 12, w 4, nb 2 | | 18 |
| | (all out 104.5 overs) | 334 | (all out 64 overs) | | 190 |

Bowling
van der Wath 3-1-6-0. Wigley 15.5-1-91-2. Crook 18-4-56-4. Klusener 25-9-54-2. Panesar 18-2-72-1. Brown 25-8-50-1.
van der Wath 11-4-32-1. Wigley 4-0-27-0. Crook 13-3-40-3. Panesar 13-4-24-1. Klusener 10-2-29-1. Brown 13-3-26-4.

Fall of Wickets: 1-190, 2-240, 3-266, 4-289, 5-289, 6-289, 7-289, 8-303, 9-307
1-43, 2-69, 3-111, 4-112, 5-137, 6-161, 7-163, 8-167, 9-186

**NORTHANTS** — First Innings / Second Innings
| | | | | | |
|---|---|---|---|---|---|
| SD Peters | c Irani b Tudor | 39 | c Irani b Bopara | | 5 |
| U Afzaal | lbw b Middlebrook | 66 | c sub b Danish Kaneria | | 39 |
| MH Wessels | c Foster b Tudor | 0 | lbw b Nel | | 0 |
| DJG Sales (capt) | c Cook b Nel | 35 | c Irani b Danish Kaneria | | 37 |
| *NJO'Brien | lbw b Danish Kaneria | 3 | not out | | 13 |
| L Klusener | c Foster b Nel | 8 | not out | | 12 |
| SP Crook | lbw b Danish Kaneria | 53 | | | |
| JJ van der Wath | b Nel | 94 | | | |
| MS Panesar | b Danish Kaneria | 33 | | | |
| DH Wigley | b Danish Kaneria | 53 | | | |
| JF Brown | not out | 0 | | | |
| Extras | b 8, lb 13, w 1, nb 10 | 32 | lb 2, w 2 | | 4 |
| | (all out 136.2 overs) | 416 | (4 wkts 29.3 overs) | | 110 |

Bowling
Nel 26.2-5-62-3. Tudor 18-5-55-2. Bopara 19-1-73-0. ten Doeschate 8-1-35-0.
Danish Kaneria 41-9-108-4. Middlebrook 24-5-62-1.
Nel 12-7-20-1. Bopara 3-0-15-1. Danish Kaneria 12-1-61-2.
ten Doeschate 2.3-2-12-0.

Fall of Wickets: 1-14, 2-72, 3-83, 4-96, 5-113, 6-217, 7-217, 8-306, 9-416
1-10, 2-45, 3-47, 4-93

*Northamptonshire won by 6 wickets – Northamptonshire (22pts), Essex (5pts)*

### SOMERSET v. DERBYSHIRE – at Taunton

**DERBYSHIRE** — First Innings
| | | |
|---|---|---|
| WPC Weston | lbw b Caddick | 0 |
| SD Stubbings | c Kieswetter b Turner | 58 |
| CR Taylor | run out | 21 |
| SM Katich (capt) | lbw b Willoughby | 221 |
| Hassan Adnan | run out | 21 |
| IJ Harvey | lbw b Trego | 153 |
| AG Botha | lbw b Caddick | 101 |
| *DJ Pipe | c White b Hildreth | 106 |
| GG Wagg | not out | 55 |
| T Lungley | not out | 30 |
| KJ Dean | | |
| Extras | b 14, lb 19, w 3, nb 20 | 56 |
| | (8 wkts dec 181.3 overs) | 801 |

Bowling
Caddick 35-10-150-3. Willoughby 31-7-85-1. Turner 26-1-126-1. Trego 24-1-113-1. Hildreth 13-2-62-1. Durston 24-1-117-0. White 28-3-0-115-0.

Fall of Wickets: 1-0, 2-0, 3-150, 4-207, 5-459, 6-488, 7-688, 8-712

**SOMERSET** — First Innings / Second Innings (following on)
| | | | | | |
|---|---|---|---|---|---|
| ME Trescothick | b Wagg | 32 | c & b Wagg | | 24 |
| NJ Edwards | b Dean | 5 | st Pipe b Wagg | | 81 |
| JL Langer (capt) | c Taylor b Dean | 4 | not out | | 136 |
| JC Hildreth | c Botha b Wagg | 45 | b Lungley | | 32 |
| *C Kieswetter | c Taylor b Wagg | 63 | | | |
| CL White | c Katich b Botha | 138 | (5) lbw b Lungley | | 6 |
| WJ Durston | c Pipe b Dean | 50 | (6) not out | | 15 |
| PD Trego | c Weston b Wagg | 67 | | | |
| AR Caddick | c Pipe b Harvey | 2 | | | |
| ML Turner | c Harvey b Wagg | 57 | | | |
| CM Willoughby | not out | 23 | | | |
| Extras | b 4, lb 12, w 2, nb 26 | 44 | b 2, lb 5, nb 8 | | 15 |
| | (all out 136.4 overs) | 530 | (4 wkts 68 overs) | | 309 |

Bowling
Dean 29-9-64-3. Lungley 28-7-99-0. Botha 37-6-178-1. Wagg 34.4-1-148-5. Harvey 4-0-25-1.
Dean 14-1-59-0. Lungley 14-1-85-2. Harvey 4-0-30-0. Wagg 16-3-45-2. Botha 16-2-66-0. Katich 4-0-17-0.

Fall of Wickets: 1-13, 2-17, 3-89, 4-104, 5-262, 6-367, 7-392, 8-409, 9-463
1-60, 2-161, 3-235, 4-257

*Match drawn – Somerset (11pts), Derbyshire (12pts)*

### GLOUCESTERSHIRE v. LEICESTERSHIRE – at Bristol

**GLOS** — First Innings / Second Innings
| | | | | | |
|---|---|---|---|---|---|
| CM Spearman | c Sadler b Masters | 38 | (2) c Rosenberg b Broad | | 26 |
| Kadeer Ali | lbw b Allenby | 92 | (1) c New b Allenby | | 43 |
| GP Hodnett | run out | 67 | run out | | 55 |
| MJ North | c Rosenberg b Broad | 86 | c Allenby b Robinson | | 106 |
| APR Gidman (capt) | c New b Allenby | 17 | not out | | 0 |
| CG Taylor | b Broad | 8 | | | |
| *SJ Adshead | b Allenby | 81 | | | |
| MA Hardinges | c Allenby b Broad | 36 | | | |
| AA Noffke | c Sadler b Allenby | 2 | | | |
| SP Kirby | b Allenby | 22 | | | |
| AJ Ireland | not out | 4 | | | |
| Extras | b 10, lb 31, w 5, nb 8 | 54 | b 6, lb 3, w 4, nb 6 | | 19 |
| | (all out 143.2 overs) | 507 | (4 wkts dec 51.2 overs) | | 249 |

Bowling
Broad 33-6-111-3. Langeveldt 35-8-97-0. Masters 17-3-62-1. Allenby 34.2-6-125-5. Henderson 7-2-49-0. Robinson 1-0-2-0.
Langeveldt 14-1-53-0. Broad 7-1-23-1. Allenby 14-3-71-1. Rosenberg 9.2-1-45-0. Robinson 7-0-48-1.

Fall of Wickets: 1-59, 2-197, 3-249, 4-273, 5-330, 6-337, 7-446, 8-457, 9-482
1-45, 2-107, 3-248, 4-249

**LEICESTERSHIRE** — First Innings / Second Innings
| | | | | | |
|---|---|---|---|---|---|
| TJ New | c Kadeer Ali b North | 98 | b Kirby | | 16 |
| DDJ Robinson (capt) | lbw b Noffke | 14 | c Adshead b Ireland | | 36 |
| HD Ackerman | c Adshead b North | 59 | lbw b Ireland | | 28 |
| JL Sadler | c Noffke b Gidman | 45 | c Spearman b Taylor | | 32 |
| *PA Nixon | c Adshead b Kirby | 17 | lbw b Ireland | | 15 |
| J Allenby | c Spearman b Kirby | 0 | not out | | 47 |
| MC Rosenberg | run out | 64 | c Taylor b Noffke | | 17 |
| SCJ Broad | c Hodnett b Noffke | 22 | c Ireland b Hardinges | | 9 |
| DD Masters | c Gidman b North | 0 | not out | | 5 |
| CK Langeveldt | c Taylor b Kirby | 9 | | | |
| CW Henderson | absent hurt | | | | |
| Extras | b 19, lb 4, lb 4, w 1, nb 4 | 35 | b 14, lb 6, w 13 | | 13 |
| | (9 wkts 127.3 overs) | 376 | (7 wkts 79.5 overs) | | 218 |

Bowling
Noffke 32-10-94-2. Kirby 28.3-9-75-3. Ireland 19-1-71-0. Hardinges 16-5-54-0. North 26-3-64. Gidman 6-2-41-1.
Noffke 21-5-66-1. Kirby 20.5-5-56-1. Hardinges 7-1-21-1. Ireland 14-4-39-3. North 6-1-15-0. Taylor 11-6-13-1.

Fall of Wickets: 1-32, 2-131, 3-232, 4-240, 5-245, 6-316, 7-357, 8-358, 9-376
1-22, 2-77, 3-100, 4-122, 5-140, 6-177, 7-199

*Match drawn – Gloucestershire (12pts), Leicestershire (10pts)*

## Round Four: 8–12 May

Yorkshire went back to the top of the Championship table by crushing Worcestershire by an innings and 260 runs at Headingley. They were in command right from the off, Craig White and Joe Sayers putting on 177 for

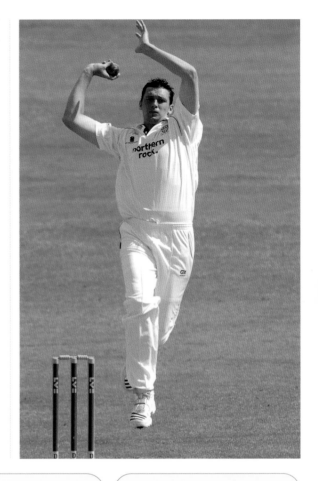

### Round Four: 8–12 May Division One

**YORKSHIRE v. WORCESTERSHIRE – at Headingley**

| YORKSHIRE | First Innings | |
|---|---|---|
| C White | c Davies b Sillence | 97 |
| JJ Sayers | c Moore b Nel | 123 |
| A McGrath | lbw b Nel | 19 |
| Younus Khan | b Malik | 12 |
| JA Rudolph | not out | 129 |
| *GL Brophy | lbw b Nel | 44 |
| AU Rashid | b Nel | 5 |
| TT Bresnan | c Moore b Sillence | 33 |
| D Gough (capt) | not out | 22 |
| JN Gillespie | | |
| MJ Hoggard | | |
| Extras | b 3, lb 21, w 5, nb 8 | 37 |
| | (7 wkts dec 153 overs) | 521 |

**Bowling**
Kabir Ali 31-8-81-0. Malik 27-4-98-1. Nel 27-5-74-4. Sillence 34-7-120-2. Batty 29.5-5-100-0. Moore 5-0-24-0.
**Fall of Wickets:** 1-177, 2-227, 3-257, 4-298, 5-402, 6-408, 7-486

| WORCS | First Innings | | Second Innings (following on) | |
|---|---|---|---|---|
| SC Moore | c Rudolph b Hoggard | 0 | (2) c Rudolph b Gough | 9 |
| PA Jaques | c Gough b Hoggard | 38 | (1) c Rashid b Bresnan | 21 |
| VS Solanki (capt) | b Gillespie | 5 | c Rudolph b Rashid | 19 |
| Kabir Ali | c McGrath b Hoggard | 12 | (9) c Sayers b Younus Khan | 15 |
| BF Smith | c Rudolph b Gough | 0 | (4) b Bresnan | 0 |
| GA Hick | lbw b Hoggard | 11 | (5) c Younus Khan b Bresnan | 0 |
| *SM Davies | c Rashid b Hoggard | 0 | (6) b Rashid | 38 |
| GJ Batty | c Gillespie b Rashid | 24 | (7) c White b Bresnan | 10 |
| RJ Sillence | c Rashid b Gillespie | 22 | (8) c McGrath b Rashid | 6 |
| JD Nel | c Brophy b Gillespie | 8 | (11) not out | 7 |
| MN Malik | not out | 1 | (10) c Younus Khan b Rashid | 0 |
| Extras | b 1, lb 5, nb 2 | 8 | lb 2, w 1, nb 4 | 7 |
| | (all out 42.5 overs) | 129 | (all out 55 overs) | 132 |

**Bowling**
Hoggard 14-5-34-5. Gillespie 13.5-2-56-3. Rashid 8-2-14-1. Gough 7-2-19-1.
Hoggard 9-4-16-0. Gough 10-6-10-4. McGrath 1-1-0-0. Bresnan 10-6-10-4.
Rashid 17-4-47-4. Gillespie 7-1-24-0. Younus Khan 2-0-6-1.
**Fall of Wickets:** 1-12, 2-39, 3-57, 4-58, 5-71, 6-71, 7-72, 8-102, 9-122
1-14, 2-49, 3-49, 4-49, 5-58, 6-75, 7-89, 8-120, 9-120

*Yorkshire won by an innings and 260 runs –*
*Yorkshire (22pts), Worcestershire (2pts)*

---

**HAMPSHIRE v. LANCASHIRE – at the Rose Bowl**

| LANCASHIRE | FIRST INNINGS | |
|---|---|---|
| MJ Chilton (capt) | c Pothas b Bruce | 9 |
| PJ Horton | c Brown b Bruce | 3 |
| MB Loye | c Benham b Clark | 13 |
| BJ Hodge | c Lumb b Clark | 4 |
| SG Law | lbw b Clark | 61 |
| A Flintoff | lbw b Warne | 61 |
| *LD Sutton | b Clark | 37 |
| G Chapple | c Pothas b Clark | 17 |
| SI Mahmood | lbw b Clark | 13 |
| JM Anderson | c Warne b Clark | 0 |
| G Keedy | not out | 4 |
| Extras | b 4, lb 16, nb 6 | 26 |
| | (all out 62.3 overs) | 207 |

**Bowling**
Clark 23.3-6-82-7. Bruce 18-4-63-2. Mascarenhas 10-3-21-0. Tremlett 8-3-10-0. Warne 3-0-11-1.
**Fall of Wickets:** 1-6, 2-21, 3-28, 4-31, 5-92, 6-158, 7-181, 8-190, 9-190

| HAMPSHIRE | First Innings | |
|---|---|---|
| JHK Adams | c Loye b Mahmood | 16 |
| MJ Brown | b Anderson | 18 |
| JP Crawley | lbw b Anderson | 40 |
| MJ Lumb | lbw b Mahmood | 3 |
| CC Benham | c Flintoff b Mahmood | 46 |
| *N Pothas | c Sutton b Chapple | 0 |
| AD Mascarenhas | c Hodge b Anderson | 74 |
| SK Warne (capt) | b Chapple | 12 |
| SR Clark | c Horton b Chapple | 12 |
| JTA Bruce | b Keedy | 16 |
| CT Tremlett | not out | 14 |
| Extras | b 4, lb 4, w 1, nb 12 | 21 |
| | (all out 63.3 overs) | 272 |

**Bowling**
Anderson 16-0-83-3. Chapple 20-2-65-3. Mahmood 14-0-69-3. Flintoff 9-1-25-0. Keedy 4.3-2-22-1.
**Fall of Wickets:** 1-28, 2-57, 3-61, 4-107, 5-108, 6-156, 7-199, 8-219, 9-247

*Match drawn – Hampshire (9pts),*
*Lancashire (8pts)*

---

**SURREY v. WARWICKSHIRE – at The Oval**

| WARWICKSHIRE | First Innings | | Second Innings | |
|---|---|---|---|---|
| IJ Westwood | c Butcher b Saker | 24 | not out | 4 |
| DL Maddy (capt) | c Newman b Nicholson | 134 | not out | 1 |
| IR Bell | lbw b Saker | 9 | | |
| IJL Trott | c Schofield b Doshi | 20 | | |
| JO Troughton | c Batty b Saker | 24 | | |
| AGR Loudon | c Batty b Nicholson | 0 | | |
| *TR Ambrose | c Brown b Saker | 14 | | |
| HH Streak | b Nicholson | 21 | | |
| N Tahir | c Butcher b Clarke | 6 | | |
| DW Steyn | c Brown b Schofield | 51 | | |
| JE Anyon | not out | 5 | | |
| Extras | lb 7, w 2, nb 12 | 21 | | 0 |
| | (all out 87 overs) | 329 | (0 wkts 2 overs) | 5 |

**Bowling**
Nicholson 26-5-68-3. Saker 19-3-98-4. Clarke 15-4-60-1. Benning 4-0-20-0. Doshi 16-3-56-1. Schofield 7-2-20-1.
Clarke 1-0-4-0. Brown 1-0-1-0.
**Fall of Wickets:** 1-64, 2-88, 3-165, 4-208, 5-221, 6-236, 7-236, 8-263, 9-273

| SURREY | First Innings | |
|---|---|---|
| SA Newman | c Ambrose b Steyn | 73 |
| *JN Batty | not out | 154 |
| MR Ramprakash | not out | 120 |
| MA Butcher (capt) | | |
| AD Brown | | |
| R Clarke | | |
| JGE Benning | | |
| CP Schofield | | |
| MJ Nicholson | | |
| NC Saker | | |
| ND Doshi | | |
| Extras | b 6, lb 16, w 7, nb 24 | 53 |
| | (1 wkt dec 117.3 overs) | 400 |

**Bowling**
Steyn 24-6-75-1. Tahir 19-5-35-0. Anyon 24.3-4-111-0. Streak 16-1-68-0. Maddy 7-4-6-0. Trott 10-3-27-0. Loudon 13-2-45-0. Troughton 4-1-11-0.
**Fall of Wickets:** 1-117

*Match drawn – Surrey (12pts),*
*Warwickshire (7pts)*

---

**DURHAM v. KENT – at the Riverside**

| DURHAM | First Innings | | Second Innings | |
|---|---|---|---|---|
| MJ Di Venuto | not out | 204 | (2) lbw b Hall | 58 |
| WR Smith | lbw b Yasir Arafat | 13 | (1) lbw b Hall | 21 |
| PD Collingwood | c Jones b Yasir Arafat | 0 | b Yasir Arafat | 58 |
| KJ Coetzer | c Tredwell | 74 | b Hall | 3 |
| DM Blenstein (capt) | c McLaren b Tredwell | 2 | not out | 77 |
| *P Mustard | b McLaren | 23 | lbw b Yasir Arafat | 5 |
| GT Park | lbw b McLaren | 0 | c Jones b Hall | 61 |
| GR Breese | b McLaren | 5 | not out | 0 |
| LE Plunkett | c Jones b Tredwell | 35 | | |
| G Onions | c & b Tredwell | 4 | | |
| SJ Harmison | c Jones b McLaren | 5 | | |
| Extras | b 9, lb 9, w 6, nb 18 | 42 | b 7, lb 9, nb 20 | 36 |
| | (all out 86.5 overs) | 407 | (6 wkts dec 72.5 overs) | 319 |

**Bowling**
Yasir Arafat 17-2-85-2. Joseph 8-0-62-0. McLaren 19.5-2-91-4. Hall 10-0-48-0.
Tredwell 27-2-88-4. Stevens 5-1-15-0.
Yasir Arafat 19.5-3-85-2. Hall 17-3-68-4. McLaren 10-2-33-0. Joseph 6-0-51-0. Tredwell 13-1-47-0. Stevens 7-3-19-0.
**Fall of Wickets:** 1-46, 2-46, 3-227, 4-243, 5-286, 6-290, 7-296, 8-359, 9-367
1-49, 2-144, 3-148, 4-150, 5-173, 6-318

| KENT | First Innings | | Second Innings | |
|---|---|---|---|---|
| JL Denly | c Mustard b Harmison | 17 | c Mustard b Harmison | 92 |
| RWT Key (capt) | lbw b Onions | 169 | c Plunkett b Harmison | 11 |
| M van Jaarsveld | lbw b Plunkett | 10 | c Mustard b Harmison | 0 |
| MJ Walker | c Mustard b Plunkett | 72 | c Plunkett b Harmison | 1 |
| DI Stevens | b Plunkett | 10 | c Mustard b Plunkett | 35 |
| *GO Jones | b Harmison | 0 | lbw b Onions | 1 |
| AJ Hall | c Mustard b Plunkett | 42 | c Collingwood b Plunkett | 3 |
| Yasir Arafat | b Harmison | 17 | c Mustard b Plunkett | 6 |
| R McLaren | b Plunkett | 1 | not out | 6 |
| JC Tredwell | c Mustard b Harmison | 25 | c Smith b Harmison | 0 |
| RH Joseph | not out | 7 | retired hurt | 2 |
| Extras | b 7, lb 17, w 1, nb 4 | 29 | lb 4, nb 8 | 12 |
| | (all out 113.3 overs) | 400 | (all out 50.3 overs) | 169 |

**Bowling**
Onions 23-1-92-1. Harmison 24.3-3-75-4. Plunkett 32-5-105-5.
Collingwood 14-3-27-0. Breese 14-0-55-0. Benkenstein 6-1-22-0.
Plunkett 20-7-54-3. Harmison 19.3-3-61-5. Onions 8-0-38-1. Collingwood 3-1-12-0.
**Fall of Wickets:** 1-45, 2-74, 3-247, 4-282, 5-283, 6-318, 7-362, 8-363, 9-385
1-26, 2-27, 3-55, 4-131, 5-134, 6-137, 7-157, 8-161, 9-161

*Durham won by 157 runs – Durham (22pts), Kent (8pts)*

**Opposite** Steve Harmison boosted Durham's early-season Championship performances with his pace and bounce.

the first wicket. White was out for 97, but Sayers went on to reach three figures and the in-form Jacques Rudolph then scored 129 not out himself to guide Yorkshire past 500. Then the home side's multi-talented bowling attack got to work: Matthew Hoggard and Jason Gillespie doing the damage in Worcestershire's first-innings capitulation and Tim Bresnan and Adil Rashid sharing eight wickets when they followed on.

Rain ruined the prospect of positive results at both the Rose Bowl and The Oval, where Mark Ramprakash scored yet another hundred, but Durham emerged smiling from a fiercely fought contest at the Riverside against Kent. Michael Di Venuto carried his bat again for 204, from 248 balls, but Kent replied with a major innings from Rob Key and Durham had to work hard again in their second innings to gain the advantage. In a tense final session, and after Kent's resistance had been stiffened by a highly promising 92 from young Joe Denly, with a six and 14 fours, the high pace and bounce of Steve Harmison – well-supported by Liam Plunkett – finally won the day. Indeed, with time running out, it was a nasty lifter from Harmison that struck Rob Joseph on the helmet and forced him to leave the field – thus clinching the win for Durham.

Tom Lungley took nine wickets in the match, including a magnificent second-innings 5 for 20, as Derbyshire earned themselves a satisfying win against Leicestershire, but bad weather helped both Middlesex and Northamptonshire to emerge with draws. Middlesex had to follow on against Nottinghamshire at Trent Bridge, where Charlie Shreck once more terrorised their batsmen with first-innings figures of 6 for 79. In 2006 the giant Shreck had taken 8 for 31 when Middlesex had been shot out for just 49 on the same ground, before later in the season grabbing a hat-trick in another six-wicket haul at Lord's.

But at least Middlesex made a better fist of things second time around, largely thanks to Andrew Strauss's 120 from 152 balls, with three sixes and 14 fours, and an excellent 80 from Billy Godleman. Northants, meanwhile, also had to follow on at Wantage Road but by then the game was over as a contest deep into the final day after David Sales's 150, with two sixes and 20 fours, had provided some sort of home answer to the power of Marcus Trescothick. The Somerset opener dominated the first day and a half, striking four sixes and 36 fours in a career-best 284 from 379 balls and even cutting England spinner Monty Panesar down to size in the process. Justin Langer and James Hildreth also contributed significantly to Somerset's huge total, as did Ian Blackwell in a typically violent 81 from 47 balls, with four sixes and 11 fours.

## Round Four: 8–12 May Division Two

### NORTHAMPTONSHIRE v. SOMERSET – at Northampton

**SOMERSET** First Innings

| | | |
|---|---|---|
| ME Trescothick | c Sales b Klusener | 284 |
| NJ Edwards | b Panesar | 28 |
| JL Langer (capt) | c Brown b Panesar | 86 |
| JC Hildreth | c White b Brown | 111 |
| CL White | c Wessels b Brown | 1 |
| ID Blackwell | c Peters b Panesar | 81 |
| PD Trego | not out | 32 |
| *C Kieswetter | not out | 0 |
| AR Caddick | | |
| PS Jones | | |
| CM Willoughby | | |
| Extras | b 8, lb 4, w 2, nb 4 | 18 |
| | (6 wkts dec 146.4 overs) | 641 |

**Bowling**
van der Wath 22-3-71-0. Crook 23-3-109-0. Klusener 27-7-99-1. Brown 39-5-184-2. Panesar 32.4-3-149-3. White 3-0-17-0.
**Fall of Wickets:** 1-96, 2-292, 3-519, 4-522, 5-528, 6-641

**NORTHANTS** First Innings / Second Innings (following on)

| | First Innings | | Second Innings (following on) | |
|---|---|---|---|---|
| SD Peters | b Caddick | 2 | lbw b Caddick | 4 |
| DJ Jacobs | c Langer b Caddick | 32 | lbw b Caddick | 3 |
| MH Wessels | c Kieswetter b Caddick | 45 | not out | 7 |
| DJG Sales (capt) | not out | 150 | not out | 18 |
| RA White | c Langer b Caddick | 45 | | |
| L Klusener | c Langer b Trego | 36 | | |
| *NJ O'Brien | c Kieswetter b Trego | 4 | | |
| SP Crook | c Kieswetter b Trego | 11 | | |
| JJ van der Wath | not out | 53 | | |
| MS Panesar | | | | |
| JF Brown | | | | |
| Extras | lb 11, nb 6, p 5 | 22 | | 0 |
| | (7 wkts dec 98.1 overs) | 400 | (2 wkts 8.2 overs) | 32 |

**Bowling**
Caddick 23.1-3-105-4. Willoughby 21-4-77-0. Jones 20-2-90-0. Trego 18-1-71-3. Blackwell 16-5-41-0.
Caddick 4.2-0-18-2. Trego 4-0-14-0.
**Fall of Wickets:** 1-30, 2-35, 3-125, 4-206, 5-270, 6-280, 7-300
1-4, 2-11

*Match drawn – Northamptonshire (9pts), Somerset (11pts)*

### NOTTINGHAMSHIRE v. MIDDLESEX – at Trent Bridge

**NOTTS** First Innings

| | | |
|---|---|---|
| JER Gallian | c Nash b Johnson | 17 |
| BM Shafayat | c Strauss b Dalrymple | 67 |
| MA Wagh | c Nash b Murtagh | 10 |
| DJ Hussey (capt) | c Strauss b Murtagh | 48 |
| SR Patel | c Nash b Murtagh | 0 |
| *CMW Read | c sub b Richardson | 20 |
| MA Ealham | c sub b Murtagh | 1 |
| PJ Franks | c Johnson b Richardson | 92 |
| GP Swann | c Dalrymple b Murtagh | 47 |
| RJ Sidebottom | c Smith b Murtagh | 15 |
| CE Shreck | not out | 0 |
| Extras | lb 11, w 6, nb 2 | 19 |
| | (all out 113.5 overs) | 336 |

**Bowling**
Murtagh 38-16-87-6. Richardson 31.5-10-34-3. Franks 12-2-50-1.
Joyce 3-0-18-0. Dalrymple 14-2-47-1.
**Fall of Wickets:** 1-39, 2-56, 3-135, 4-135, 5-160, 6-161, 7-177, 8-275, 9-332

**MIDDLESEX** First Innings / Second Innings (following on)

| | First Innings | | Second Innings (following on) | |
|---|---|---|---|---|
| AJ Strauss | c Hussey b Shreck | 4 | b Swann | 120 |
| BA Godleman | lbw b Ealham | 6 | c Shafayat b Sidebottom | 80 |
| OA Shah | b Shreck | 29 | not out | 21 |
| EC Joyce | c Gallian b Shreck | 36 | not out | 1 |
| ET Smith (capt) | c Read b Ealham | 38 | | |
| *DC Nash | c Read b Ealham | 21 | | |
| JWM Dalrymple | lbw b Franks | 8 | | |
| TJ Murtagh | c Franks b Shreck | 5 | | |
| RL Johnson | c Patel b Shreck | 0 | | |
| A Richardson | c Hussey b Shreck | 0 | | |
| M Kartik | not out | 0 | | |
| Extras | b 4, lb 9, nb 16 | 29 | lb 1, w 6, nb 14 | 21 |
| | (all out 60.5 overs) | 176 | (2 wkts 71 overs) | 243 |

**Bowling**
Shreck 27-8-79-6. Ealham 21-5-10-34-3. Franks 12-2-50-1.
Shreck 18-3-78-0. Ealham 7-2-32-0. Franks 13-1-44-0. Sidebottom 14-4-39-1.
Swann 17-2-44-1. Patel 4-1-5-0.
**Fall of Wickets:** 1-14, 2-14, 3-50, 4-126, 5-126, 6-143, 7-160, 8-162, 9-176
1-185, 2-242

*Match drawn – Nottinghamshire (10pts), Middlesex (7pts)*

### DERBYSHIRE v. LEICESTERSHIRE – at Derby

**LEICESTERSHIRE** First Innings / Second Innings

| | First Innings | | Second Innings | |
|---|---|---|---|---|
| DDJ Robinson (capt) | c Rankin b Wagg | 19 | (2) c Stubbings b Lungley | 14 |
| JK Maunders | c Botha b Wagg | 15 | (6) c Botha b Lungley | 5 |
| TJ New | b Wagg | 0 | (1) c Stubbings b Rankin | 4 |
| HD Ackerman | c Pipe b Lungley | 1 | (3) b Wagg | 27 |
| J Allenby | lbw b Dean | 36 | (4) lbw b Lungley | 0 |
| JL Sadler | b Lungley | 1 | (5) c Pipe b Wagg | 5 |
| *PA Nixon | lbw b Lungley | 40 | b Lungley | 42 |
| Mansoor Amjad | c Pipe b Wagg | 41 | c Pipe b Wagg | 6 |
| NGE Walker | c Katich b Botha | 24 | c Pipe b Rankin | 16 |
| RAO Cummins | lbw b Dean | 5 | c Pipe b Lungley | 2 |
| CK Langeveldt | not out | 3 | not out | 1 |
| Extras | lb 9, w 1, nb 4 | 24 | lb 9, w 1, nb 4 | 14 |
| | (all out 66.4 overs) | 209 | (all out 57.3 overs) | 137 |

**Bowling**
Dean 22-6-54-2. Rankin 13-1-58-0. Lungley 20-3-54-4. Wagg 10-3-28-3.
Botha 1.4-0-8-1.
Dean 9-2-16-0. Rankin 13-0-46-2. Wagg 15-3-39-3. Lungley 15.3-9-20-5.
Botha 5-3-7-0.
**Fall of Wickets:** 1-35, 2-35, 3-36, 4-46, 5-83, 6-83, 7-168, 8-177, 9-188
1-5, 2-42, 3-42, 4-52, 5-57, 6-57, 7-67, 8-115, 9-134

**DERBYSHIRE** First Innings / Second Innings

| | First Innings | | Second Innings | |
|---|---|---|---|---|
| SD Stubbings | c Allenby b Langeveldt | 63 | (2) c B b Amjad | 16 |
| WPC Weston | lbw b Walker | 5 | (1) lbw b Amjad | 8 |
| CR Taylor | c Nixon b Langeveldt | 4 | | |
| SM Katich (capt) | lbw b Allenby | 94 | (3) not out | 45 |
| TR Birt | c Ackerman b Walker | 25 | (4) c Nixon b Langeveldt | 1 |
| AG Botha | lbw b Walker | 4 | | |
| *DJ Pipe | b Amjad | 36 | (5) not out | 10 |
| GG Wagg | c Walker b Amjad | 4 | | |
| T Lungley | c Allenby b Langeveldt | 0 | | |
| KJ Dean | st Nixon b Amjad | 0 | | |
| WB Rankin | not out | 0 | | |
| Extras | b 4, lb 8, nb 16 | 28 | lb 2, nb 6 | 8 |
| | (all out 83.4 overs) | 259 | (3 wkts 17.3 overs) | 88 |

**Bowling**
Langeveldt 23-9-64-3. Walker 19-3-67-3. Amjad 7.4-1-16-3. Cummins 15-3-45-0.
Allenby 14-6-23-1. Maunders 5-0-30-0.
Langeveldt 7-1-40-1. Walker 5-1-24-0. Amjad 5.3-1-22-2.
**Fall of Wickets:** 1-16, 2-27, 3-116, 4-180, 5-186, 6-253, 7-258, 8-259, 9-259
1-27, 2-44, 3-61

*Derbyshire won by 7 wickets – Derbyshire (19pts), Leicestershire (4pts)*

## Round Five: 15–19 May Division One

### SUSSEX v. SURREY – at Hove

**SURREY** First Innings
| | | |
|---|---|---|
| SA Newman | c Martin-Jenkins b Wright | 38 |
| *JN Batty | c Kirtley b Naved-ul-Hasan | 39 |
| MR Ramprakash | not out | 266 |
| MA Butcher (capt) | b Mushtaq Ahmed | 179 |
| AD Brown | not out | 50 |
| R Clarke | | |
| RS Clinton | | |
| IDK Salisbury | | |
| MJ Nicholson | | |
| NC Saker | | |
| ND Doshi | | |
| Extras | b 4, lb 18, w 6, nb 26 | 54 |
| | (3 wkts dec 146.4 overs) | **626** |

**Bowling**
Naved-ul-Hasan 26-4-103-1. Kirtley 27-5-89-0. Martin-Jenkins 28-6-97-0. Mushtaq Ahmed 35-2-178-1. Wright 24-0-107-1. Adams 4-0-9-0. Hopkinson 2-0-16-0. Nash 0.4-0-5-0.
**Fall of Wickets:** 1-83, 2-112, 3-515

**SUSSEX** First Innings / Second Innings (following on)
| | First Innings | | Second Innings (following on) | |
|---|---|---|---|---|
| CD Hopkinson | lbw b Nicholson | 0 | c Batty b Nicholson | 8 |
| RR Montgomerie | c Batty b Clarke | 78 | c Ramprakash b Nicholson | 3 |
| CD Nash | b Nicholson | 53 | c Salisbury b Doshi | 46 |
| MW Goodwin | c Batty b Nicholson | 119 | not out | 205 |
| CJ Adams (capt) | c Doshi b Nicholson | 32 | not out | 102 |
| *AJ Hodd | c Brown b Clarke | 43 | | |
| RSC Martin-Jenkins | c Batty b Clarke | 4 | | |
| LJ Wright | not out | 14 | | |
| Naved-ul-Hasan | c Brown b Nicholson | 0 | | |
| Mushtaq Ahmed | b Doshi | 14 | | |
| RJ Kirtley | c Salisbury b Doshi | 0 | | |
| Extras | b 4, lb 18, w 6, nb 2 | 5 | b 2, lb 5, w 1 | 8 |
| | (all out 118.3 overs) | **365** | (3 wkts 96 overs) | **372** |

**Bowling**
Nicholson 29-7-89-5. Saker 23-7-71-0. Clinton 14-3-38-0. Clarke 16-4-57-3. Doshi 23.3-6-60-2. Salisbury 12-0-44-0. Butcher 1-1-0-0. Nicholson 19-3-73-2. Saker 15-5-50-0. Doshi 22-0-88-1. Clarke 10-0-39-0. Salisbury 24-3-81-0. Clinton 3-0-17-0. Brown 3-0-17-0.
**Fall of Wickets:** 1-0, 2-110, 3-170, 4-230, 5-313, 6-329, 7-342, 8-342, 9-365 1-13, 2-16, 3-119

*Match drawn – Sussex (9pts),*
*Surrey (12pts)*

### WARWICKSHIRE v. DURHAM – at Edgbaston

**WARWICKSHIRE** First Innings
| | | |
|---|---|---|
| IJ Westwood | lbw b Gibson | 0 |
| DL Maddy (capt) | lbw b Onions | 0 |
| KC Sangakkara | c Mustard b Onions | 149 |
| IJL Trott | c Gibson b Onions | 3 |
| JO Troughton | c Mustard b Onions | 1 |
| AGR Loudon | c Di Venuto b Benkenstein | 105 |
| JE Anyon | c Mustard b Onions | 34 |
| *TR Ambrose | c Mustard b Onions | 15 |
| HH Streak | not out | 16 |
| TD Groenewald | c Benkenstein b Onions | 0 |
| DW Steyn | c Mustard b Onions | 0 |
| Extras | lb 8, nb 4 | 12 |
| | (all out 94.2 overs) | **335** |

**Bowling**
Onions 26.2-8-101-8. Gibson 21-6-78-1. Davies 19-6-45-0. Killeen 18-2-69-0. Benkenstein 8-4-24-1. Smith 2-0-10-0.
**Fall of Wickets:** 1-1, 2-1, 3-19, 4-23, 5-252, 6-303, 7-304, 8-329, 9-335

**DURHAM** First Innings
| | | |
|---|---|---|
| WR Smith | b Anyon | 38 |
| MJ Di Venuto | c Ambrose b Steyn | 9 |
| GJ Muchall | c Trott b Maddy | 30 |
| KJ Coetzer | c Loudon b Steyn | 46 |
| DM B'kenstein (capt) | not out | 93 |
| *P Mustard | c Maddy b Loudon | 16 |
| GT Park | b Steyn | 15 |
| OD Gibson | not out | 14 |
| M Davies | | |
| N Killeen | | |
| G Onions | | |
| Extras | b 2, lb 2, w 1, nb 8 | 13 |
| | (6 wkts 96.3 overs) | **274** |

**Bowling**
Steyn 21-1-85-3. Anyon 20.3-4-62-1. Streak 18-5-43-0. Maddy 8-3-19-1. Groenewald 15-6-39-0. Trott 2-1-5-0. Loudon 12-2-17-1.
**Fall of Wickets:** 1-21, 2-80, 3-82, 4-159, 5-195, 6-236

*Match drawn – Warwickshire (9pts),*
*Durham (9pts)*

### LANCASHIRE v. WORCESTERSHIRE – at Old Trafford

**LANCASHIRE** First Innings / Second Innings
| | First Innings | | Second Innings | |
|---|---|---|---|---|
| MJ Chilton (capt) | b Kabir Ali | 6 | (2) c Moore b Batty | 59 |
| PJ Horton | lbw b Kabir Ali | 10 | (1) lbw b Nel | 139 |
| MB Loye | lbw b Kabir Ali | 5 | lbw b Malik | 35 |
| BJ Hodge | c Smith b Sillence | 49 | b Sillence | 10 |
| SJ Croft | c Davies b Sillence | 21 | c Davies b Sillence | 1 |
| *LD Sutton | c Sillence b Kabir Ali | 25 | b Kabir Ali | 14 |
| G Chapple | c Davies b Kabir Ali | 5 | c Hick b Kabir Ali | 2 |
| DG Cork | c Hick b Kabir Ali | 14 | not out | 11 |
| SI Mahmood | c Davies b Kabir Ali | 13 | not out | 4 |
| JM Anderson† | b Kabir Ali | 0 | | |
| M Muralitharan | not out | 1 | | |
| TC Smith | | | | |
| Extras | lb 6, nb 6 | 12 | b 2, lb 3, w 1, nb 15 | 21 |
| | (all out 49 overs) | **161** | (7 wkts 88 overs) | **296** |

**Bowling**
Kabir Ali 16-3-50-8. Malik 11-2-30-0. Nel 7-2-21-0. Sillence 11-1-48-2. Batty 4-1-6-0.
Kabir Ali 19-5-52-2. Malik 23-4-72-1. Nel 11-3-27-1. Sillence 14-3-53-2. Batty 20-3-82-1. Solanki 1-0-5-0.
**Fall of Wickets:** 1-14, 2-23, 3-24, 4-48, 5-126, 6-130, 7-141, 8-146, 9-146 1-165, 2-244, 3-261, 4-263, 5-263, 6-272, 7-291
† Replaced by TC Smith

**WORCS** First Innings
| | | |
|---|---|---|
| PA Jaques | b Anderson | 21 |
| SC Moore | c Chilton b Mahmood | 29 |
| VS Solanki (capt) | c Chapple b Muralitharan | 54 |
| BF Smith | c Horton b Cork | 1 |
| GA Hick | c Loye b Muralitharan | 110 |
| *SM Davies | lbw b Muralitharan | 43 |
| GJ Batty | lbw b Muralitharan | 1 |
| RJ Sillence | b Chapple | 0 |
| Kabir Ali | lbw b Muralitharan | 39 |
| MN Malik | lbw b Muralitharan | 3 |
| JD Nel | not out | 0 |
| Extras | b 9, lb 10, w 5, nb 2 | 26 |
| | (all out 97.3 overs) | **327** |

**Bowling**
Anderson 12-0-62-1. Cork 19-1-61-1. Chapple 16-2-57-1. Muralitharan 33.3-9-72-6. Mahmood 16-3-52-1. Smith 1-0-4-0.
**Fall of Wickets:** 1-28, 2-94, 3-103, 4-130, 5-244, 6-250, 7-255, 8-319, 9-324

*Match drawn – Lancashire (7pts), Worcestershire (10pts)*

## Round Five: 15–19 May Division Two

### GLOUCESTERSHIRE v. GLAMORGAN – at Bristol

**GLAMORGAN** First Innings
| | | |
|---|---|---|
| MTG Elliott | c Hardinges b Noffke | 4 |
| DD Cherry | c Adshead b Ireland | 0 |
| *MA Wallace | c Hardinges b Noffke | 128 |
| MJ Powell | b Hardinges | 16 |
| DL Hemp (capt) | c Rudge b Hardinges | 15 |
| BJ Wright | c Hodnett b Hardinges | 19 |
| RE Watkins | c Adshead b Fisher | 17 |
| AG Wharf | not out | 128 |
| RDB Croft | c & b Ireland | 11 |
| JAR Harris | c Hardinges b North | 7 |
| SP Jones | c Fisher b Noffke | 5 |
| Extras | b 10, lb 10, w 4, nb 18 | 42 |
| | (all out 147.3 overs) | **392** |

**Bowling**
Noffke 29.3-8-62-3. Ireland 31-8-92-2. Rudge 12-2-40-0. Hardinges 27-11-59-3. Gidman 12-4-31-0. Fisher 20-4-58-1. North 16-4-30-1.
**Fall of Wickets:** 1-4, 2-4, 3-51, 4-79, 5-154, 6-199, 7-310, 8-332, 9-379

**GLOS** First Innings / Second Innings (following on)
| | First Innings | | Second Innings (following on) | |
|---|---|---|---|---|
| Kadeer Ali | c & b Harris | 13 | (2) lbw b Croft | 102 |
| ID Fisher | b Harris | 6 | (1) lbw b Wharf | 0 |
| GP Hodnett | c Elliott b Harris | 8 | lbw b Harris | 21 |
| MJ North | c Wallace b Harris | 94 | c Elliott b Croft | 13 |
| APR Gidman (capt) | b Watkins | 8 | c Wright b Croft | 0 |
| CG Taylor | c Powell b Croft | 10 | c Wallace b Harris | 31 |
| *SJ Adshead | c Wallace b Harris | 19 | b Harris | 3 |
| MA Hardinges | lbw b Harris | 19 | c Wallace b Harris | 68 |
| AA Noffke | c Wallace b Wharf | 15 | lbw b Harris | 61 |
| WD Rudge | c Wallace b Croft | 0 | not out | 4 |
| AJ Ireland | not out | 10 | not out | 4 |
| Extras | b 6, lb 4, w 3, nb 4 | 17 | b 8, lb 4, w 2, nb 8 | 22 |
| | (all out 71.4 overs) | **219** | (9 wkts dec 95 overs) | **328** |

**Bowling**
Harris 22-6-66-7. Wharf 9.4-2-18-1. Jones 18-4-61-0. Croft 15-4-42-1. Watkins 7-2-22-1.
Wharf 19-0-75-1. Watkins 5-1-15-0. Croft 28-3-94-3. Jones 19-4-51-0. Harris19-6-52-5. Wright 3-0-24-0. Cherry 2-0-5-0.
**Fall of Wickets:** 1-10, 2-21, 3-48, 4-71, 5-96, 6-140, 7-186, 8-193, 9-193 1-1, 2-45, 3-87, 4-91, 5-140, 6-146, 7-194, 8-315, 9-322

*Match drawn – Gloucestershire (7pts),*
*Glamorgan (10pts)*

### LEICESTERSHIRE v. ESSEX – at Leicester

**LEICESTERSHIRE** First Innings / Second Innings
| | First Innings | | Second Innings | |
|---|---|---|---|---|
| DDJ Robinson (capt) | c Pettini b Nel | 43 | not out | 41 |
| TJ New | lbw b Napier | 4 | not out | 14 |
| HD Ackerman | c Chopra b Napier | 20 | | |
| J Allenby | c Middlebrook b Napier | 21 | | |
| *PA Nixon | lbw b Danish Kaneria | 85 | | |
| MC Rosenberg | c Pettini b Nel | 0 | | |
| JL Sadler | c Napier b McGarry | 15 | | |
| Mansoor Amjad | c Pettini b McGarry | 9 | | |
| DT Rowe | b ten Doeschate | 85 | | |
| NGE Walker | b Napier | 31 | | |
| CK Langeveldt | not out | 10 | | |
| Extras | b 6, lb 4, w 2, nb 4 | 16 | b 1 | 1 |
| | (all out 79.1 overs) | **335** | (0 wkts dec 17.1 overs) | **56** |

**Bowling**
Nel 15-4-58-2. Napier 19.1-6-55-3. McGarry 15-3-62-2. Bopara 14-3-39-1. ten Doeschate 10-0-63-1. Danish Kaneria 6-1-48-1.
Nel 3-1-17-0. Napier 3-0-23-0. Middlebrook 6-1-9-0. Phillips 5.1-1-6-0.
**Fall of Wickets:** 1-4, 2-33, 3-67, 4-122, 5-122, 6-153, 7-177, 8-283, 9-311

**ESSEX** First Innings
| | | |
|---|---|---|
| V Chopra | lbw b Walker | 4 |
| *ML Pettini | c Ackerman b Walker | 1 |
| RS Bopara | lbw b Langeveldt | 3 |
| RC Irani (capt) | c Nixon b Langeveldt | 40 |
| TJ Phillips | c & b Walker | 4 |
| RN ten Doeschate | c Ackerman b Langeveldt | 3 |
| JD Middlebrook | c New b Rowe | 12 |
| GR Napier | not out | 72 |
| Danish Kaneria | c Sadler b Rowe | 18 |
| A Nel | lbw b Allenby | 10 |
| AC McGarry | b Langeveldt | 10 |
| Extras | b 8, lb 8, w 3, nb 6 | 25 |
| | (all out 59.4 overs) | **201** |

**Bowling**
Walker 17-5-55-3. Langeveldt 22.4-8-41-4. Amjad 8-2-32-0. Rowe 5-1-27-2. Allenby 5-0-30-1.
**Fall of Wickets:** 1-4, 2-7, 3-7, 4-48, 5-55, 6-66, 7-80, 8-104, 9-140

*Match drawn – Leicestershire (10pts),*
*Essex (8pts)*

### DERBYSHIRE v. MIDDLESEX – at Derby

**MIDDLESEX** First Innings / Second Innings
| | First Innings | | Second Innings | |
|---|---|---|---|---|
| BA Godleman | c Pipe b Wagg | 23 | c Pipe b Lungley | 57 |
| NRD Compton | c Pipe b Rankin | 51 | lbw b Wagg | 30 |
| BL Hutton | lbw b Wagg | 10 | (8) not out | 32 |
| EC Joyce | lbw b Lungley | 21 | (5) c Hassan Adnan b Rankin | 8 |
| ET Smith (capt) | b Lungley | 28 | (3) c Hassan Adnan b Botha | 8 |
| *DC Nash | lbw b Dean | 21 | (7) c Birt b Rankin | 6 |
| JWM Dalrymple | c Pipe b Lungley | 2 | (6) c Wagg b Rankin | 4 |
| WPUJC Vaas | not out | 56 | (9) lbw b Wagg | 10 |
| TJ Murtagh | c Birt b Rankin | 1 | (10) c sub b Rankin | 2 |
| CEW Silverwood | c Katich b Rankin | 10 | (11) c Rankin b Botha | 14 |
| A Richardson | c Weston b Rankin | 9 | (4) lbw b Lungley | 2 |
| Extras | b 1, lb 7, w 2, nb 6 | 16 | b 5, lb 5, w 1, nb 4 | 14 |
| | (all out 91.3 overs) | **248** | (all out 72 overs) | **180** |

**Bowling**
Dean 20-6-59-1. Rankin 23.3-7-80-4. Wagg 25-6-71-2. Lungley 15-7-20-3. Botha 8-3-10-0.
Rankin 15-3-41-4. Wagg 23-8-46-2. Lungley 17-7-30-2. Botha 17-5-54-2.
**Fall of Wickets:** 1-56, 2-57, 3-64, 4-84, 5-100, 6-112, 7-121, 8-136, 9-157
1-56, 2-57, 3-64, 4-84, 5-100, 6-112, 7-121, 8-136, 9-157

**DERBYSHIRE** First Innings / Second Innings
| | First Innings | | Second Innings | |
|---|---|---|---|---|
| SD Stubbings | c Nash b Richardson | 23 | (2) not out | 21 |
| WPC Weston | lbw b Vaas | 14 | (1) c Godleman b Vaas | 12 |
| Hassan Adnan | lbw b Silverwood | 29 | not out | 12 |
| SM Katich (capt) | b Richardson | 28 | | |
| TR Birt | c Hutton b Richardson | 59 | | |
| AG Botha | c & b Silverwood | 9 | | |
| *DJ Pipe | b Richardson | 11 | | |
| GG Wagg | b Richardson | 40 | | |
| T Lungley | c Smith b Silverwood | 0 | | |
| KJ Dean | not out | 2 | | |
| WB Rankin | c Nash b Vaas | 3 | | |
| Extras | b 1, lb 4, w 2 | 7 | b 4, lb 4 | 8 |
| | (all out 80.2 overs) | **225** | (1 wkt 29 overs) | **53** |

**Bowling**
Vaas 20.2-5-49-2. Silverwood 22.1-6-65-3. Richardson 23-9-50-5. Murtagh 1.5-0-1-0. Dalrymple 9-1-34-0. Hutton 4-1-21-0.
Vaas 8-3-14-1. Silverwood 6-1-10-0. Richardson 7-4-4-0. Hutton 4-1-7-0. Dalrymple 4-0-10-0.
**Fall of Wickets:** 1-28, 2-46, 3-96, 4-157, 5-160, 6-174, 7-196, 8-196, 9-220 1-27

*Match drawn – Derbyshire (8pts), Middlesex (8pts)*

## Round Five: 15–19 May

Three draws in Division One meant little change in the table, but while the weather interfered with things at Old Trafford and Edgbaston it took an excellent rearguard action by Sussex to save the Champions' skin at Hove against a Surrey side in which Mark Ramprakash was at his awesome best.

Quite how Ramprakash was continuing to be ignored by the England selectors was hard to fathom. He took on a Sussex attack based on the considerable Test-class skills of Mushtaq Ahmed and Naved-ul-Hasan, and backed up by James Kirtley and the in-form Robin Martin-Jenkins, and utterly dominated it during an epic innings of 266 not out. It was his 91st first-class hundred, his 13th score above 200, and it took his season's run tally to 676. He had made eight hundreds in 2006, of course, but here was a fourth ton of the new campaign barely a month into it. His total command was such that he faced only 332 balls, hitting three sixes and 31 fours.

His third-wicket partnership of 403 in 91 overs with Mark Butcher, the Surrey captain, was the highest made against Sussex in the Championship and, indeed, only bettered at Hove by the 428 added by Warwick Armstrong and Monty Noble for the 1905 Australians. Yet Sussex, forced to follow on despite totalling 365, held on with some comfort on a final day they began on a distinctly edgy 35 for 2; Murray Goodwin was the main home hero, adding an unbeaten 205 to his first innings 119, while Chris Adams also fought hard for his 102 not out.

The remarkable achievements of James Harris, who turned 17 on the first day of the match, lit up Glamorgan's draw with Gloucestershire at Bristol. Slightly-built, but strong and wiry and generating deceptive pace from a whippy, natural action, Harris became the youngest-ever player to claim seven wickets in a Championship innings as Gloucestershire were forced to follow on in the face of a Glamorgan total also featuring career-best hundreds from Mark Wallace and Alex Wharf. By following up his 7 for 66 with 5 for 52, moreover, the Gorseinon College student – who was due to take exams the following week – then became the youngest cricketer to claim more than ten wickets in a match. Despite Harris's heroics, however, the game was drawn.

Time lost to weather denied Derbyshire the chance of victory against Middlesex, after Irish fast bowler Boyd Rankin had picked up eight wickets in the match, and washouts on both days one and two at Grace Road also condemned Leicestershire's meeting with Essex to a draw.

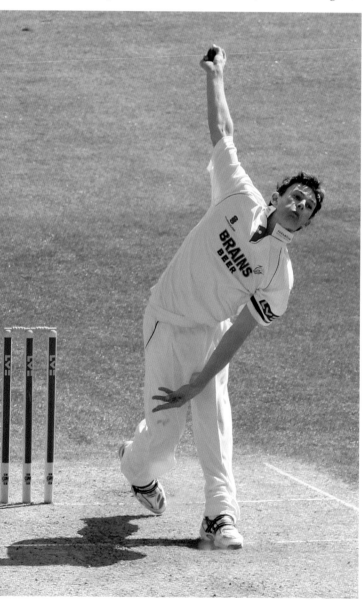

An early sighting of one of the most exciting young players to emerge in the county game during 2007 – Glamorgan's James Harris, who was still 16 when he made his first-class debut.

## Round Six: 23–27 May

Durham went into second place in the Championship race after a fine six-wicket win over Yorkshire at the Riverside, while Sussex ended a difficult period by thrashing Worcestershire by an innings at New Road. Shane Warne and Hampshire, meanwhile, were left frustrated by Kent's decision to delay a second-innings declaration at Canterbury. Warne was in trouble, too, for shouting obscenities after being given out lbw on the second afternoon; he later apologised to the umpires.

Ottis Gibson's all-round abilities lay behind Durham's triumph, adding 71 to his earlier 7 for 81 to help to earn his team a handy halfway lead. Graham Onions then did the second-innings damage to Yorkshire, despite half-centuries from Anthony McGrath and Jacques Rudolph, who added 79 to his assured first-innings 111, and Michael Di Venuto's 53 then guided Durham to their modest victory target.

Mushtaq Ahmed, much tormented by the death of Bob Woolmer at the World Cup (he was Woolmer's assistant coach within the Pakistan team set-up) suddenly found form again as Sussex bowled out Worcestershire for just 100 in reply to their own 512 for 8 declared, in which Carl Hopkinson made a career-best 83 and Murray Goodwin struck a third successive hundred. Mushtaq then followed up his first innings 5 for 22 by taking three

more scalps, although Graeme Hick's 134th first-class century, and sixth-wicket stand of 124 with Gareth Batty, did hold up the Champions awhile.

At the St Lawrence Ground, meanwhile, a feisty contest began with Joe Denly carrying his bat as well as keeping Kent afloat with a maiden Championship hundred, before Hampshire recovered strongly from an initial slide to 85 for 6. As conditions eased, further Kentish hundreds from Rob Key, Martin van Jaarsveld and Darren Stevens tortured Warne, who finished with rare bruised figures of 1 for 142. Six dropped catches by Kent, however, clearly saved his Hampshire team from further grief as they battled through their second innings to earn a draw.

Stephen Peters's 107, and a subsequent first-innings lead of 205, set up Northamptonshire's win against Derbyshire, and there were also comfortable victories for Somerset in the West Country derby at Taunton and for Nottinghamshire over Essex at Trent Bridge. Middlesex, meanwhile, slaughtered Glamorgan by an innings after dismissing them for a mere 60 on the opening morning. And the Welsh county were also docked eight points for producing a 'poor' pitch at Swansea.

Charl Willoughby and Andrew Caddick both performed beautifully to bowl out Gloucestershire for 202 on yet another excellent Taunton surface, and Cameron White's commanding 241, featuring three

## Round Six: 23–27 May Division One

### DURHAM v. YORKSHIRE – at the Riverside

| YORKSHIRE | First Innings | | Second Innings | |
|---|---|---|---|---|
| C White | b Gibson | 64 | b Onions | 0 |
| JJ Sayers | c Mustard b Gibson | 4 | c Mustard b Gibson | 3 |
| A McGrath | c Coetzer b Davies | 7 | c Coetzer b Wiseman | 62 |
| Younus Khan | b Gibson | 49 | b Onions | 5 |
| JA Rudolph | b Gibson | 111 | c Benkenstein b Gibson | 79 |
| AU Rashid | c Mustard b Davies | 30 | c Di Venuto b Gibson | 0 |
| TT Bresnan | c Muchall b Gibson | 27 | b Onions | 0 |
| *SM Guy | c Mustard b Gibson | 25 | c Mustard b Claydon | 28 |
| D Gough (capt) | c Mustard b Gibson | 17 | (10) c Di Venuto b Onions | 0 |
| JN Gillespie | b Onions | 15 | (9) not out | 23 |
| GJ Kruis | not out | 0 | b Onions | 7 |
| Extras | b 4, lb 2, w 2, nb 36 | 44 | lb 7, nb 4 | 11 |
| | (all out 115 overs) | 393 | (all out 59.2 overs) | 218 |

**Bowling**
Onions 26-6-99-1. Claydon 17-0-94-0. Gibson 28-8-81-7. Davies 18-5-44-2. Wiseman 19-6-43-0. Benkenstein 7-0-26-0.
Onions 15.2-3-53-5. Gibson 11-5-63-3. Claydon 10-0-45-1. Davies 14-3-49-0. Wiseman 4-3-1-1.
**Fall of Wickets:** 1-24, 2-35, 3-145, 4-158, 5-233, 6-294, 7-359, 8-360, 9-387
1-0, 2-6, 3-17, 4-104, 5-107, 6-116, 7-176, 8-199, 9-200

| DURHAM | First Innings | | Second Innings | |
|---|---|---|---|---|
| MJ Di Venuto | c Guy b Gillespie | 11 | (2) c Guy b Gillespie | 53 |
| WR Smith | b Gough | 6 | (1) lbw b Gough | 3 |
| GJ Muchall | lbw b Gillespie | 48 | c Guy b Gough | 6 |
| KJ Coetzer | b McGrath | 91 | c Guy b Bresnan | 6 |
| DM Benkenstein (capt) | b Gough | 68 | not out | 32 |
| *P Mustard | c Guy b Gillespie | 59 | not out | 22 |
| OD Gibson | c Guy b Bresnan | 71 | | |
| PJ Wiseman | c Guy b Kruis | 27 | | |
| M Davies | lbw b Gough | 21 | | |
| G Onions | lbw b Bresnan | 21 | | |
| ME Claydon | not out | 14 | | |
| Extras | b 3, lb 22, nb 14, p 5 | 44 | b 1, lb 4, nb 4 | 9 |
| | (all out 126.5 overs) | 481 | (4 wkts 33.5 overs) | 131 |

**Bowling**
Gough 20.5-5-76-3. Gillespie 25-6-73-3. Bresnan 30-6-94-2. Kruis 19-4-85-1. Rashid 24-4-90-0. McGrath 8-1-33-1.
Gough 9-1-18-2. Gillespie 7-0-29-1. Bresnan 10-2-25-1. Kruis 5-0-34-0. Rashid 2.5-0-20-0.
**Fall of Wickets:** 1-17, 2-17, 3-83, 4-214, 5-304, 6-322, 7-390, 8-426, 9-448
1-10, 2-22, 3-35, 4-77

*Durham won by 6 wickets – Durham (22pts), Yorkshire (7pts)*

### WORCESTERSHIRE v. SUSSEX – at Worcester

| SUSSEX | First Innings | |
|---|---|---|
| CD Hopkinson | c Davies b Malik | 83 |
| RR Montgomerie | c Davies b Kabir Ali | 9 |
| CD Nash | c Davies b Malik | 16 |
| MW Goodwin | lbw b Kabir Ali | 112 |
| CJ Adams (capt) | c Batty b Kabir Ali | 91 |
| *AJ Hodd | c Davies b Batty | 72 |
| RSC Martin-Jenkins | c Davies b Malik | 17 |
| LJ Wright | not out | 55 |
| Naved-ul-Hasan | c Solanki b Batty | 26 |
| Mushtaq Ahmed | | |
| JD Lewry | | |
| Extras | b 4, lb 14, w 3, nb 10 | 31 |
| | (8 wkts dec 130.5 overs) | 512 |

**Bowling**
Kabir Ali 27-6-77-3. Bollinger 21-5-78-0. Malik 23-4-94-3. Nel 25-3-105-0. Batty 34.5-2-140-2.
**Fall of Wickets:** 1-25, 2-71, 3-190, 4-305, 5-362, 6-404, 7-464, 8-512

| WORCS | First Innings | | Second Innings (following on) | |
|---|---|---|---|---|
| PA Jaques | c Hodd b Lewry | 5 | lbw b Naved-ul-Hasan | 0 |
| SC Moore | c M'gomerie b Mushtaq Ahmed | 47 | c Goodwin b Martin-Jenkins | 22 |
| VS Solanki (capt) | c Nash b Naved-ul-Hasan | 13 | c Wright b Martin-Jenkins | 17 |
| BF Smith | c Montgomerie b Lewry | 0 | b Martin-Jenkins | 5 |
| GA Hick | c Hopkinson b Mushtaq Ahmed | 15 | c M'gomerie b Mushtaq Ahmed | 108 |
| *SM Davies | c Hopkinson b Mushtaq Ahmed | 0 | c Adams b Wright | 40 |
| GJ Batty | b Wright | 0 | lbw b Mushtaq Ahmed | 64 |
| Kabir Ali | c M'gomerie b Mushtaq Ahmed | 9 | c Adams b Naved-ul-Hasan | 6 |
| DE Bollinger | b Mushtaq Ahmed | 0 | lbw b Naved-ul-Hasan | 4 |
| MN Malik | b Wright | 1 | not out | 4 |
| JD Nel | not out | 2 | c Ett b Mushtaq Ahmed | 4 |
| Extras | b 6, nb 2 | 8 | b 8, lb 8, w 1, nb 10 | 27 |
| | (all out 27.2 overs) | 100 | (all out 71 overs) | 303 |

**Bowling**
Lewry 6-1-21-2. Naved-ul-Hasan 5-2-17-1. Wright 8.2-0-34-2. Mushtaq Ahmed 8-3-22-5.
Lewry 13-3-47-0. Naved-ul-Hasan 12-0-63-3. Mushtaq Ahmed 31-2-117-3. Martin-Jenkins 7-5-17-3. Wright 8-0-43-1.
**Fall of Wickets:** 1-6, 2-25, 3-28, 4-78, 5-80, 6-85, 7-93, 8-93, 9-98
1-3, 2-40, 3-45, 4-50, 5-134, 6-258, 7-279, 8-285, 9-289

*Sussex won by an innings and 109 runs – Worcestershire (2pts), Sussex (22pts)*

### KENT v. HAMPSHIRE – at Canterbury

| KENT | First Innings | | Second Innings | |
|---|---|---|---|---|
| JL Denly | not out | 115 | c Mascarenhas b Clark | 0 |
| RWT Key | lbw b Clark | 0 | lbw b Mascarenhas | 120 |
| M van Jaarsveld | c Warne b Clark | 12 | c Burrows b Tremlett | 109 |
| MJ Walker | b Clark | 4 | c Ervine b Clark | 46 |
| DI Stevens | c Brown b Mascarenhas | 11 | b Adams | 105 |
| *GO Jones | c Burrows b Mascarenhas | 0 | b Clark | 4 |
| AJ Hall | b Warne | 1 | c Brown b Warne | 48 |
| Yasir Arafat | c Burrows b Warne | 7 | c Warne b Adams | 19 |
| R McLaren | c Burrows b Clark | 4 | not out | 25 |
| JC Tredwell | b Warne | 17 | not out | 27 |
| SJ Cook | c Warne b Tremlett | 8 | | |
| Extras | b 10, lb 2, nb 8 | 20 | b 7, lb 5, w 2, nb 16 | 30 |
| | (all out 58.4 overs) | 199 | (8 wkts dec 149 overs) | 533 |

**Bowling**
Clark 14-1-48-4. Mascarenhas 15-6-29-2. Tremlett 9.4-0-54-1. Ervine 6-3-14-0.
Warne 14-2-42-3.
Clark 28-5-80-3. Tremlett 30-4-76-1. Mascarenhas 20-3-76-1. Warne 37-2-142-1. Carberry 2-0-6-0. Ervine 20-3-95-0. Adams 11-1-37-2. Crawley 1-0-9-0.
**Fall of Wickets:** 1-1, 2-43, 3-55, 4-72, 5-74, 6-98, 7-110, 8-129, 9-182
1-0, 2-223, 3-268, 4-344, 5-350, 6-433, 7-466, 8-483

| HAMPSHIRE | First Innings | | Second Innings | |
|---|---|---|---|---|
| JHK Adams | c Jones b Yasir Arafat | 31 | b Yasir Arafat | 31 |
| MJ Brown | lbw b Yasir Arafat | 0 | c Jones b Yasir Arafat | 24 |
| JP Crawley | c van Jaarsveld b Cook | 16 | c Denly b Yasir Arafat | 38 |
| MJ Lumb | c Walker b Yasir Arafat | 0 | c Jones b Hall | 48 |
| MA Carberry | lbw b McLaren | 7 | c Hall b Yasir Arafat | 6 |
| SM Ervine | lbw b Cook | 22 | not out | 56 |
| AD Mascarenhas | lbw b Yasir Arafat | 90 | not out | 33 |
| *TG Burrows | run out | 35 | | |
| SK Warne (capt) | lbw b McLaren | 19 | | |
| CT Tremlett | not out | 11 | | |
| SR Clark | c Walker b Yasir Arafat | 14 | | |
| Extras | b 10, lb 8, w 1, nb 18 | 37 | b 10, lb 5, w 2, nb 22 | 39 |
| | (all out 84.3 overs) | 272 | (5 wkts 89 overs) | 275 |

**Bowling**
Yasir Arafat 21.3-4-63-5. Hall 15-3-49-0. Cook 14-4-56-2. McLaren 14-4-61-2. Tredwell 11-1-26-0.
Yasir Arafat 23-4-90-4. Hall 16-4-47-1. Tredwell 19-3-53-0. Cook 13-7-13-0. McLaren 13-5-41-0. Denly 5-2-16-0.
**Fall of Wickets:** 1-5, 2-52, 3-52, 4-52, 5-83, 6-85, 7-188, 8-224, 9-252
1-58, 2-77, 3-151, 4-165, 5-184

*Match drawn – Kent (7pts), Hampshire (9pts)*

The ageless Andy Caddick is pictured flowing into his delivery stride during yet another significant and committed spell for his beloved Somerset.

## Round Six: 23–27 May Division Two

### NORTHAMPTONSHIRE v. DERBYSHIRE – at Northampton

| DERBYSHIRE | First Innings | | Second Innings | |
|---|---|---|---|---|
| WPC Weston | c O'Brien b Crook | 13 | absent hurt | |
| SD Stubbings | c Peters b Klusener | 36 | lbw b van der Wath | 104 |
| Hassan Adnan | lbw b Crook | 15 | c Peters b van der Wath | 7 |
| SM Katich (capt) | c White b Crook | 0 | c Afzaal b White | 85 |
| TR Birt | b Brown | 5 | (1) b van der Wath | 37 |
| GM Smith | c O'Brien b Brown | 8 | (5) c Sales b Wigley | 17 |
| AG Botha | not out | 53 | (6) c Afzaal b van der Wath | 4 |
| *DJ Pipe | c Sales b van der Wath | 4 | (7) c Jacobs b Wigley | 0 |
| GG Wagg | c Peters b Wigley | 11 | (8) b Crook | 8 |
| T Lungley | b Wigley | 0 | not out | 0 |
| WA White | c O'Brien b van der Wath | 10 | (9) c O'Brien b Wigley | 4 |
| Extras | b 1, lb 2, w 2 | 5 | b 1, lb 4, w 6, nb 6 | 17 |
| | (all out 60 overs) | 160 | (all out 94.3 overs) | 283 |

**Bowling**
van der Wath 17-5-41-2. Wigley 7-1-41-2. Klusener 14-6-31-1. Crook 15-6-34-3. Brown 7-2-10-2.
van der Wath 23-6-67-4. Crook 14-3-40-1. Brown 22-7-48-0. Klusener 19-5-55-0. Wigley 10.3-1-33-3. White 6-1-35-1.
**Fall of Wickets:** 1-49, 2-61, 3-61, 4-70, 5-78, 6-83, 7-94, 8-110, 9-110 1-87, 2-97, 3-240, 4-251, 5-257, 6-259, 7-278, 8-280, 9-283

| NORTHANTS | First Innings | | Second Innings | |
|---|---|---|---|---|
| SD Peters | b Pipe b White | 107 | not out | 28 |
| DJ Jacobs | lbw b White | 56 | c Pipe b White | 1 |
| U Afzaal | c Pipe b Smith | 54 | c Pipe b Wagg | 4 |
| DJG Sales (capt) | c Birt b Smith | 4 | (5) lbw b Wagg | 2 |
| RA White | c Birt b Botha | 0 | (6) not out | 43 |
| L Klusener | c Botha b White | 32 | | |
| *NJO'Brien | not out | 49 | | |
| JJ van der Wath | c Birt b White | 2 | | |
| SP Crook | c Birt b White | 33 | | |
| DH Wigley | c Birt b Botha | 0 | (4) lbw b Wagg | 0 |
| JF Brown | c Katich b Botha | 21 | w 2 | 2 |
| Extras | b 1, lb 5, w 9, nb 6 | | | |
| | (all out 120.5 overs) | 365 | (4 wkts 17.3 overs) | 80 |

**Bowling**
Wagg 28-3-120-0. White 27-8-87-5. Lungley 5-3-9-0. Smith 30-14-84-2. Botha 30.5-11-59-3.
White 7-0-34-1. Wagg 8-1-26-3. Smith 1-0-13-0. Botha 1-0-3-0. Birt 0.3-0-4-0.
**Fall of Wickets:** 1-91, 2-202, 3-206, 4-223, 5-276, 6-277, 7-291, 8-364, 9-365 1-8, 2-13, 3-13, 4-23

*Northamptonshire won by 6 wickets –
Northamptonshire (21pts), Derbyshire (3pts)*

### GLAMORGAN v. MIDDLESEX – at Swansea

| GLAMORGAN | First Innings | | Second Innings | |
|---|---|---|---|---|
| DD Cherry | b Wright | 10 | (2) c Godleman b Peploe | 15 |
| JP Maher | c Nash b Silverwood | 3 | (1) lbw b Richardson | 3 |
| *MA Wallace | c Nash b Richardson | 4 | (4) lbw b Dalrymple | 7 |
| MJ Powell | c Nash b Richardson | 0 | (5) not out | 39 |
| DL Hemp (capt) | c Peploe b Silverwood | 7 | (6) lbw b Peploe | 13 |
| BJ Wright | c Godleman b Peploe | 5 | (7) c & b Dalrymple | 3 |
| AG Wharf | b Wright | 14 | (8) run out | 15 |
| RDB Croft | c Shah b Richardson | 11 | (9) c Nash b Richardson | 5 |
| DG Wright | lbw b Peploe | 0 | (10) lbw b Richardson | 1 |
| DA Cosker | b Richardson | 4 | (11) c Shah b Richardson | 10 |
| HT Waters | not out | 8 | (3) st Nash b Peploe | 19 |
| Extras | lb 2, w 2, nb 4 | 8 | b 17, w 6, nb 6 | 29 |
| | (all out 34 overs) | 60 | (all out 65.5 overs) | 159 |

**Bowling**
Silverwood 11-3-23-2. Richardson 11-7-7-4. Wright 8-2-21-2. Peploe 4-0-7-2.
Silverwood 7-2-10-0. Richardson 13.5-6-23-4. Wright 5-2-7-0. Peploe 21-5-58-3. Dalrymple 19-3-44-2.
**Fall of Wickets:** 1-3, 2-14, 3-14, 4-16, 5-30, 6-46, 7-46, 8-47, 9-54 1-7, 2-40, 3-53, 4-55, 5-78, 6-81, 7-120, 8-138, 9-140

| MIDDLESEX | First Innings | |
|---|---|---|
| BA Godleman | c Cherry b Waters | 15 |
| NRD Compton | c Powell b Wharf | 29 |
| OA Shah | c Waters b Wharf | 15 |
| EC Joyce | b Wright DG | 58 |
| ET Smith (capt) | lbw b Wright DG | 29 |
| *DC Nash | c Wright DG b Cosker | 10 |
| JWM Dalrymple | c Wallace b Wright DG | 0 |
| CT Peploe | b Cosker | 13 |
| CJC Wright | c Wright BJ b Cosker | 3 |
| CEW Silverwood | not out | 25 |
| A Richardson | b Cosker | 9 |
| Extras | b 1, lb 1, w 1, nb 12 | 15 |
| | (all out 62.3 overs) | 221 |

**Bowling**
Wharf 16-1-82-2. Wright DG 16-4-60-3. Waters 8-1-22-1. Wright BJ 2-0-4-0. Croft 10-1-30-0. Cosker 10.3-0-21-4.
**Fall of Wickets:** 1-39, 2-55, 3-74, 4-150, 5-153, 6-153, 7-170, 8-178, 9-185

*Middlesex won by an innings and 2 runs –
Glamorgan (3pts), Middlesex (18pts)*

### SOMERSET v. GLOUCESTERSHIRE – at Taunton

| SOMERSET | First Innings | | Second Innings | |
|---|---|---|---|---|
| ME Trescothick | c North b Ireland | 17 | | |
| NJ Edwards | c Marshall b Hardinges | 21 | c Snell b Greenidge | 44 |
| JL Langer (capt) | c Snell b Greenidge | 18 | (1) b Greenidge | 41 |
| JC Hildreth | b Hardinges | 60 | (3) not out | 51 |
| CL White | b Banerjee | 241 | (4) not out | 16 |
| ID Blackwell | c Taylor b Greenidge | 2 | | |
| PD Trego | c North b Greenidge | 48 | | |
| *C Kieswetter | c Snell b Greenidge | 30 | | |
| ML Turner | c Snell b Hardinges | 5 | | |
| AR Caddick | c Snell b Greenidge | 25 | | |
| CM Willoughby | not out | 0 | | |
| Extras | b 10, lb 4, w 5, nb 10 | 29 | b 4, lb 10, w 6 | 20 |
| | (all out 123.3 overs) | 496 | (2 wkts 32 overs) | 172 |

**Bowling**
Greenidge 29-2-143-4. Ireland 23-2-112-2. Hardinges 26-5-101-3. Gidman 8-3-25-0. Banerjee 27.3-6-74-1. North 5-0-17-0. Marshall 5-0-10-0.
Greenidge 8-0-57-2. Ireland 9-0-49-0. North 8-0-29-0.
**Fall of Wickets:** 1-29, 2-53, 3-65, 4-188, 5-203, 6-360, 7-427, 8-436, 9-490 1-84, 2-105

| GLOS | First Innings | | Second Innings (following on) | |
|---|---|---|---|---|
| GP Hodnett | c Hildreth b Caddick | 32 | (2) run out | 108 |
| Kadeer Ali | c Hildreth b Caddick | 7 | (1) c Turner b Blackwell | 95 |
| HJH Marshall | lbw b Willoughby | 86 | lbw b Caddick | 20 |
| MJ North | c Kieswetter b Caddick | 4 | c Kieswetter b Willoughby | 106 |
| APR Gidman (capt) | c Trescothick b White | 22 | lbw b Caddick | 13 |
| CG Taylor | c Caddick b Willoughby | 21 | not out | 101 |
| *SD Snell | c White b Willoughby | 6 | c Kieswetter b Caddick | 6 |
| MA Hardinges | b Willoughby | 0 | lbw b Caddick | 0 |
| CG Greenidge | lbw b Willoughby | 6 | lbw b Caddick | 0 |
| V Banerjee | not out | 4 | c Kieswetter b Willoughby | 1 |
| AJ Ireland | c Trescothick b Turner | 3 | c Edwards b Caddick | 0 |
| Extras | b 2, lb 1, nb 8 | 11 | lb 6, w 1, nb 8 | 15 |
| | (all out 54.1 overs) | 202 | (all out 152.5 overs) | 465 |

**Bowling**
Caddick 9-0-50-3. Willoughby 14-6-33-5. Turner 7.1-2-30-1. Trego 9-2-40-0. White 15-0-46-1.
Caddick 36.5-7-111-6. Willoughby 28-8-76-2. Turner 23-2-84-0. Blackwell 36-11-79-1. Trego 19-1-73-0. White 10-0-36-0.
**Fall of Wickets:** 1-31, 2-54, 3-66, 4-123, 5-163, 6-171, 7-173, 8-187, 9-188 1-165, 2-203, 3-291, 4-317, 5-397, 6-426, 7-428, 8-428, 9-462

*Somerset won by 8 wickets – Somerset (22pts),
Gloucestershire (4pts)*

### NOTTINGHAMSHIRE v. ESSEX – at Trent Bridge

| ESSEX | First Innings | | Second Innings | |
|---|---|---|---|---|
| V Chopra | c Read b Footitt | 32 | c Read b Ealham | 1 |
| ML Pettini (capt) | c Ealham b Shreck | 0 | c Read b Shreck | 1 |
| RS Bopara | c Shreck b Franks | 1 | b Franks | 50 |
| TJ Phillips | c Read b Franks | 1 | c Read b Ealham | 0 |
| *JS Foster | c Hussey b Footitt | 7 | c Fleming b Ealham | 12 |
| RN ten Doeschate | c Fleming b Ealham | 33 | c Ealham b Franks | 102 |
| JD Middlebrook | c Franks b Footitt | 81 | c Swann b Shreck | 4 |
| GR Napier | c Hussey b Swann | 40 | c Franks b Ealham | 37 |
| Danish Kaneria | c Shreck b Footitt | 65 | b Franks | 4 |
| A Nel | lbw b Footitt | 8 | not out | 0 |
| AC McGarry | not out | 5 | absent hurt | |
| Extras | b 5, lb 8, w 9, nb 22 | 44 | b 4, lb 7, w 1, nb 12 | 24 |
| | (all out 73.4 overs) | 317 | (all out 59.2 overs) | 235 |

**Bowling**
Shreck 24-8-84-1. Ealham 18-4-66-1. Franks 11-0-75-2. Footitt 15.4-3-59-5. Swann 5-1-20-1.
Shreck 18-6-48-2. Ealham 18.2-5-47-4. Footitt 7-0-51-0. Franks 7-0-42-3. Swann 7-1-28-0. Hussey 2-0-8-0.
**Fall of Wickets:** 1-3, 2-29, 3-41, 4-43, 5-85, 6-94, 7-197, 8-286, 9-298 1-1, 2-11, 3-15, 4-35, 5-80, 6-99, 7-229, 8-235, 9-235

| NOTTS | First Innings | |
|---|---|---|
| JER Gallian | c Phillips b Nel | 0 |
| BM Shafayat | lbw b Bopara | 67 |
| MA Wagh | c Middlebrook b Nel | 68 |
| SP Fleming (capt) | c Pettini b Danish Kaneria | 32 |
| DJ Hussey | b Bopara | 275 |
| *CMW Read | not out | 165 |
| MA Ealham | lbw b Danish Kaneria | 2 |
| PJ Franks | c Pettini b Danish Kaneria | 1 |
| GP Swann | not out | 6 |
| MHA Footitt | | |
| CE Shreck | | |
| Extras | b 6, lb 14, w 8, nb 20 | 48 |
| | (7 wkts dec 134 overs) | 664 |

**Bowling**
Nel 31-8-103-2. Napier 23-3-128-0. McGarry 2.1-0-8-0. Bopara 22.5-5-98-2. Danish Kaneria 29-2-131-3. ten Doeschate 11-1-63-0. Middlebrook 7-0-54-0. Phillips 7-0-48-0. Chopra 1-0-11-0.
**Fall of Wickets:** 1-0, 2-145, 3-149, 4-236, 5-595, 6-626, 7-648

*Nottinghamshire won by an innings and 112 runs –
Nottinghamshire (22pts), Essex (5pts)*

sixes and 32 fours, then set up the win. Somerset, though, had to fight hard to achieve it – with Caddick again outstanding with 6 for 111 – as a maiden century by Grant Hodnett, a 90-over 95 by Kadeer Ali and further hundreds from Marcus North and Chris Taylor took the visitors to 465 themselves second time around.

At Nottingham there was a county record fifth-wicket stand of 359 between David Hussey and Chris Read as Essex were overwhelmed despite resistance from James Middlebrook and Ryan ten Doeschate. After Mark Footitt's 5 for 59, Notts were put into an impregnable position by Hussey's 275 from just 227 balls, including an astonishing 14 sixes and 27 fours, and Read's unbeaten 165 from 201 balls, with five sixes and 12 fours. Both innings were career-bests.

## Round Seven: 30 May–4 June

One of the great wins in Gloucestershire's history lit up a crazy piece of administrative scheduling, which forced them to play eight consecutive days of Championship cricket. At 6.18 pm on the fourth day, after an astonishing finish to their game against Northamptonshire at Archdeacon Meadow in Gloucester, they were celebrating a four-run win clinched by taking three wickets in the final over. Less than 17 hours later, they were facing another day in the field at Derby.

For three days of the match against Northants, indeed, it seemed as if Gloucestershire were heading for a routine win. Hundreds from Marcus North, who had a fine all-round game, and Alex Gidman had earned them a sizeable first-innings lead, and 23-year-old slow left-arm Vikram Banerjee had bowled promisingly in conditions offering little help. Gidman's second century of the match enabled the home side to declare on the third evening, but Northants batted confidently after starting the final day on 49 without loss and 99 from David Sales and a 148-ball 111 from Lance Klusener took them to within sight of a famous victory themselves.

But then Klusener holed out and, amid huge tension, Northants lost their last four wickets for six runs. Eight was required from the last over, bowled by the impressive Carl Greenidge, and Gloucestershire sniffed an improbable win when Niall O'Brien was run out attempting a suicidal single to Gidman from the first ball. Steven Crook slogged a two but was dismissed by the third ball and, after a single, Monty Panesar mis-hit the next ball to extra cover to seal his side's fate.

Ravi Bopara hit a beautifully paced 147 not out, from 217 balls with 14 fours, to guide Essex to what had seemed a stiffish victory target against Glamorgan, for whom Gareth Rees, 22, had earlier scored a maiden

## Round Seven: 30 May–4 June Division One

### SURREY v. KENT – at Whitgift School

| SURREY | First Innings | | Second Innings | |
|---|---|---|---|---|
| SA Newman | lbw b Hall | 9 | run out | 20 |
| *JN Batty | c Jones b Hall | 9 | c Hall b Yasir Arafat | 25 |
| MR Ramprakash | c Jones b Yasir Arafat | 35 | c sub b Tredwell | 108 |
| MA Butcher (capt) | c van Jaarsveld b Hall | 4 | c van Jaarsveld b Yasir Arafat | 4 |
| AD Brown | b Hall | 18 | b Tredwell | 68 |
| R Clarke | b Yasir Arafat | 3 | (7) lbw b McLaren | 0 |
| IDK Salisbury | c Jones b Yasir Arafat | 6 | (6) b McLaren | 16 |
| MJ Nicholson | not out | 48 | c McLaren b Tredwell | 13 |
| NC Saker | c Tredwell b McLaren | 6 | c Hall b McLaren | 13 |
| ND Doshi | c Tredwell b Stevens | 13 | c van Jaarsveld b Cook | 11 |
| Mohammad Akram | c Tredwell b Hall | 4 | not out | 0 |
| Extras | lb 8, w 1, nb 4 | 13 | b 11, lb 10, w 2, nb 18 | 41 |
| | (all out 43.5 overs) | 166 | (all out 92.1 overs) | 319 |

**Bowling**
Yasir Arafat 15.5-4-49-3. Hall 17-4-59-5. Cook 3-0-19-0. McLaren 6-0-26-1. Stevens 2-1-5-1.
Yasir Arafat 25-6-62-2. Hall 19-4-76-0. McLaren 23-4-86-3. Cook 7-2-15-1. Tredwell 16.1-3-53-3. Stevens 2-0-6-0.
**Fall of Wickets:** 1-13, 2-50, 3-62, 4-76, 5-82, 6-86, 7-88, 8-118, 9-149 1-48, 2-69, 3-81, 4-210, 5-227, 6-227, 7-248, 8-283, 9-319

| KENT | First Innings | |
|---|---|---|
| JL Denly | b Clarke | 85 |
| RWT Key (capt) | c Batty b Nicholson | 6 |
| M van Jaarsveld | c Saker b Akram | 166 |
| JC Tredwell | st Batty b Doshi | 17 |
| DI Stevens | b Salisbury | 174 |
| *GO Jones | not out | 106 |
| MJ Walker | | |
| AJ Hall | | |
| Yasir Arafat | | |
| R McLaren | | |
| SJ Cook | | |
| Extras | lb 9, w 1 | 10 |
| | (5 wkts dec 123.2 overs) | 564 |

**Bowling**
Akram 27-8-81-1. Nicholson 30-2-134-1. Saker 14-1-71-0. Clarke 5.3-2-16-1. Salisbury 21.2-2-102-1. Doshi 20-2-123-1. Butcher 5-0-28-0.
**Fall of Wickets:** 1-18, 2-179, 3-218, 4-354, 5-564

*Kent won by an innings and 79 runs –*
*Surrey (1pt), Kent (22pts)*

### WARWICKSHIRE v. HAMPSHIRE – at Edgbaston

| HAMPSHIRE | First Innings | | Second Innings | |
|---|---|---|---|---|
| JHK Adams | c Maddy b Anyon | 1 | c Trott b Anyon | 11 |
| MJ Brown | b Groenewald | 39 | c Ambrose b Tahir | 21 |
| JP Crawley | c Groenewald b Anyon | 18 | c Ambrose b Maddy | 73 |
| MJ Lumb | c Loudon b Groenewald | 5 | c Ambrose b Steyn | 16 |
| MA Carberry | c Loudon b Groenewald | 52 | c Ambrose b Anyon | 2 |
| *N Pothas | c Trott b Maddy | 22 | not out | 126 |
| AD Mascarenhas | b Tahir | 8 | b Tahir | 20 |
| SK Warne (capt) | c Sangakkara b Tahir | 4 | c Groenewald b Tahir | 0 |
| CT Tremlett | run out | 6 | not out | 30 |
| SR Clark | not out | 0 | | |
| JTA Bruce | lbw b Tahir | 0 | | |
| Extras | b 2, lb 8, w 2, nb 2 | 14 | b 4, lb 1, nb 8 | 13 |
| | (all out 67.1 overs) | 169 | (7 wkts 93 overs) | 312 |

**Bowling**
Steyn 17-6-32-0. Anyon 16-4-47-2. Tahir 18.1-6-41-3. Groenewald 12-5-26-3. Maddy 2-1-8-1. Loudon 2-0-5-0.
Steyn 23-4-72-1. Anyon 16-5-72-2. Tahir 15-4-33-3. Groenewald 13-3-37-0. Loudon 12-3-37-0. Maddy 5-1-22-1. Troughton 7-3-11-0. Trott 2-0-3-0.
**Fall of Wickets:** 1-15, 2-52, 3-69, 4-74, 5-116, 6-133, 7-147, 8-169, 9-169 1-11, 2-44, 3-71, 4-85, 5-206, 6-263, 7-263

| WARWICKSHIRE | First Innings | |
|---|---|---|
| IJ Westwood | c Clark b Mascarenhas | 51 |
| DL Maddy (capt) | c Pothas b Clark | 24 |
| KC Sangakkara | c & b Clark | 5 |
| IJL Trott | lbw b Bruce | 3 |
| JO Troughton | c Lumb b Bruce | 18 |
| AGR Loudon | st Pothas b Warne | 103 |
| *TR Ambrose | c Clark b Mascarenhas | 0 |
| TD Groenewald | c Lumb b Clark | 10 |
| N Tahir | c Adams b Warne | 5 |
| DW Steyn | c Mascarenhas b Tremlett | 26 |
| JE Anyon | not out | 14 |
| Extras | lb 1, nb 2 | 3 |
| | (all out 66.2 overs) | 262 |

**Bowling**
Clark 15-3-65-3. Bruce 11-3-38-2. Mascarenhas 13-3-40-2. Tremlett 17-3-71-1. Warne 10.2-1-47-2.
**Fall of Wickets:** 1-25, 2-30, 3-52, 4-126, 5-134, 6-161, 7-179, 8-184, 9-217

*Match drawn – Warwickshire (9pts),*
*Hampshire (7pts)*

### SUSSEX v. LANCASHIRE – at Hove

| LANCASHIRE | First Innings | | Second Innings | |
|---|---|---|---|---|
| MJ Chilton (capt) | c Adams b Martin-Jenkins | 26 | (2) c Wright b Mushtaq Ahmed | 23 |
| PJ Horton | c Hodd b Naved-ul-Hasan | 20 | (1) c Adams b Naved-ul-Hasan | 4 |
| BJ Hodge | c Montgomerie b Lewry | 43 | lbw b Lewry | 15 |
| SG Law | c Hodd b Naved-ul-Hasan | 5 | c Ambrose b Lewry | 12 |
| SJ Croft | c M'gomerie b Mushtaq Ahmed | 9 | c Adams b Lewry | 65 |
| TC Smith | c Hodd b Wright | 19 | st Hodd b Mushtaq Ahmed | 44 |
| *LD Sutton | lbw b Naved-ul-Hasan | 40 | (8) c Hodd b Wright | 35 |
| DG Cork | st Hodd b Nash | 17 | (7) c Naved-ul-Hasan b Lewry | 8 |
| SI Mahmood | lbw b Mushtaq Ahmed | 8 | not out | 5 |
| JM Anderson | lbw b Nash | 1 | | |
| M Muralitharan | not out | 1 | (10) not out | 8 |
| Extras | lb 9, nb 18 | 27 | b 8, lb 4 | 16 |
| | (all out 103.3 overs) | 330 | (8 wkts dec 56 overs) | 206 |

**Bowling**
Lewry 20-6-49-1. Naved-ul-Hasan 22-3-94-3. Wright 15-0-53-1.
Martin-Jenkins 12-4-36-1. Mushtaq Ahmed 32-6-88-2. Nash 1.3-1-1-2.
Lewry 18-3-81-3. Naved-ul-Hasan 9-2-36-1. Mushtaq Ahmed 23-4-58-2.
Martin-Jenkins 4-2-9-1. Wright 2-0-10-1.
**Fall of Wickets:** 1-26, 2-89, 3-116, 4-139, 5-187, 6-274, 7-305, 8-328, 9-329 1-25, 2-25, 3-49, 4-129, 5-137, 6-186, 7-191, 8-197

| SUSSEX | First Innings | | Second Innings | |
|---|---|---|---|---|
| CD Nash | c Sutton b Mahmood | 47 | lbw b Muralitharan | 35 |
| RR Montgomerie | c Smith b Mahmood | 28 | c Sutton b Anderson | 50 |
| MH Yardy | c Sutton b Muralitharan | 42 | c Horton b Muralitharan | 4 |
| MW Goodwin | lbw b Muralitharan | 0 | c Horton b Muralitharan | 23 |
| CJ Adams (capt) | lbw b Muralitharan | 40 | c Sutton b Muralitharan | 1 |
| *AJ Hodd | lbw b Cork | 9 | not out | 16 |
| RSC Martin-Jenkins | lbw b Muralitharan | 7 | not out | 4 |
| LJ Wright | not out | 32 | | |
| Naved-ul-Hasan | st Sutton b Muralitharan | 15 | | |
| Mushtaq Ahmed | c Chilton b Muralitharan | 1 | | |
| JD Lewry | c Smith b Cork | 0 | | |
| Extras | b 1, lb 2, w 1 | 4 | b 14, lb 1, w 1 | 16 |
| | (all out 75.4 overs) | 235 | (5 wkts 63 overs) | 145 |

**Bowling**
Anderson 11-5-46-0. Cork 11.4-2-37-2. Smith 14-4-44-1. Mahmood 15-5-32-2. Muralitharan 23-8-73-5.
Anderson 12-1-42-1. Cork 7-2-15-0. Mahmood 12-1-38-0. Muralitharan 26-13-25-4. Croft 2-0-5-0. Smith 3-2-4-0. Hodge 1-0-1-0.
**Fall of Wickets:** 1-78, 2-91, 3-91, 4-164, 5-166, 6-177, 7-208, 8-227, 9-235 1-93, 2-93, 3-97, 4-108, 5-135

*Match drawn – Sussex (8pts), Lancashire (10pts)*

Championship hundred, while after a rained-off first day Leicestershire and Nottinghamshire enjoyed an exciting draw at Oakham School.

The other second division victory of the round went to Middlesex, who downed Somerset at Lord's after catching them on a seam-friendly pitch at the start, reducing them to 36 for 4 in the 17 overs possible on day one and then following that up so well the next morning that Justin Langer gambled on declaring with two wickets still to fall. Chris Silverwood's second-

innings 6 for 49 made sure Somerset could not escape, despite a fighting rearguard action thereafter.

In the first division, Sussex held out determinedly against Muttiah Muralitharan at Hove, Warwickshire drew with Hampshire after a first day washout at Edgbaston, and Kent thumped Surrey at Whitgift School after Andrew Hall's five wickets had destroyed their first innings. A stand of 161 between Joe Denly and Martin van Jaarsveld then put Kent in total command and Darren Stevens' 202-ball 174, with five sixes and 25 fours, and Geraint Jones's

One of the most remarkable matches of the LV County Championship is finally over, and Gloucestershire's players quite rightly celebrate wildly after their four-run win against Northamptonshire at Gloucester.

first hundred since the Headingley Test against New Zealand in 2004 – from just 94 balls – left the home side with nowhere to go. Mark Ramprakash's 39th century for Surrey came in his 91st match for the county; it took Peter May 202 games to score the same number.

### Round Seven: 30 May–4 June Division Two

**GLOUCESTERSHIRE v. NORTHAMPTONSHIRE – at Gloucester**

| GLOS | First Innings | | Second Innings | |
|---|---|---|---|---|
| GP Hodnett | b Crook | 60 | (2) lbw b Wigley | 11 |
| Kadeer Ali | b van der Wath | 0 | (1) c Sales b Crook | 2 |
| HJH Marshall | c van der Wath b Wigley | 30 | b Klusener | 38 |
| MJ North | c O'Brien b Klusener | 109 | b Crook | 1 |
| APR Gidman (capt) | lbw b Klusener | 130 | not out | 105 |
| CG Taylor | c O'Brien b Panesar | 36 | run out | 46 |
| DO Brown | lbw b Klusener | 5 | c Jacobs b Panesar | 10 |
| MA Hardinges | c O'Brien b Panesar | 2 | c White b Afzaal | 20 |
| *SD Snell | b Crook | 10 | st O'Brien b Panesar | 6 |
| CG Greenidge | c Sales b Crook | 2 | | |
| V Banerjee | not out | 0 | | |
| Extras | b 5, lb 1, w 1, nb 2 | 9 | lb 3, w 2 | 5 |
| | (all out 120 overs) | 394 | (8 wkts dec 56 overs) | 244 |

Bowling
van der Wath 6-1-34-1. Crook 19-1-71-3. Wigley 18-1-77-1. Klusener 31-7-85-3. Panesar 35-12-84-2. White 11-0-37-0.
Crook 12-3-40-2. Wigley 10-0-67-1. Panesar 19-3-75-2. Klusener 8-3-22-1. White 5-0-29-0. Sales 1-0-3-0. Afzaal 1-0-5-1.
Fall of Wickets: 1-1, 2-51, 3-125, 4-299, 5-352, 6-358, 7-367, 8-384, 9-393
1-8, 2-33, 3-44, 4-61, 5-160, 6-184, 7-233, 8-244

| NORTHANTS | First Innings | | Second Innings | |
|---|---|---|---|---|
| SD Peters | c North b Gidman | 31 | b North | 46 |
| DJ Jacobs | b Hardinges | 4 | b Greenidge | 27 |
| U Afzaal | c Hardinges b North | 24 | c Greenidge b North | 37 |
| DJG Sales (capt) | lbw b Brown | 4 | b Greenidge | 99 |
| RA White | c Taylor b Banerjee | 0 | c North b Gidman | 35 |
| L Klusener | lbw b Banerjee | 96 | c Gidman b Banerjee | 111 |
| *NJO'Brien | b Banerjee | 2 | (8) run out | 18 |
| SP Crook | lbw b Banerjee | 7 | (9) b Greenidge | 2 |
| MS Panesar | c Snell b North | 20 | (10) c Gidman b Greenidge | 2 |
| JJ van der Wath | c Kadeer Ali b Brown | 25 | (7) c & b Banerjee | 9 |
| DH Wigley | not out | 5 | not out | 1 |
| Extras | lb 7, nb 4 | 11 | lb 8, lb 7, w 2, nb 4, p 5 | 26 |
| | (all out 99.5 overs) | 223 | (all out 109.5 overs) | 411 |

Bowling
Greenidge 14-2-54-0. Hardinges 19-7-49-1. Gidman 19-7-81-1. Brown 10-3-25-2.
Banerjee 24.5-6-38-4. North 18-3-23-2.
Greenidge 10.5-2-32-4. Hardinges 15-4-32-0. North 26-3-109-2.
Banerjee 35-5-140-2. Gidman 16-4-57-1. Brown 7-2-21-0.
Fall of Wickets: 1-6, 2-56, 3-63, 4-64, 5-66, 6-73, 7-167, 8-147, 9-208
1-58, 2-123, 3-124, 4-191, 5-343, 6-368, 7-405, 8-408, 9-410

*Gloucestershire won by 4 runs –*
*Gloucestershire (21pts), Northamptonshire (4pts)*

### Round Eight: 5–9 June

Sussex's revival picked up pace when they beat Hampshire by 166 runs at Arundel, while Yorkshire's title challenge stuttered somewhat when they failed to beat Kent at Tunbridge Wells after enforcing the follow-on. Elsewhere in Division One, there were heroic rearguard actions by Durham and Surrey to deny Lancashire and Worcestershire respectively.

Mushtaq Ahmed came out on top in his battle of the leg spinners with Shane Warne, despite the Australian maestro taking a first-innings 5 for 91. The contest actually turned Sussex's way when Mushtaq and Luke Wright were belting belligerent fifties to boost a home first innings struggling at 233 for 8, but then 'Mushy' picked up 7 for 72 to rout Hampshire for 202 in reply. A 95-ball unbeaten 103 by Sussex captain Chris Adams further strengthened his own hand, and Hampshire's second-innings resistance was eventually broken.

An unfortunate hand injury to Darren Gough, their inspirational new captain, probably cost Yorkshire victory at the Nevill Ground. Gough was in the middle of a burst of three wickets for 14 runs with the second new ball when he suffered a broken bone in his right hand attempting a sharp caught and bowled chance and, although he carried on for a while and picked up another wicket, he soon had to leave the field as the pain intensified. Gough's 6 for 47 was his best return for Yorkshire since September 1996, and he did re-emerge dramatically on the final day – after ice treatment and

---

**LEICESTERSHIRE v. NOTTINGHAMSHIRE – at Oakham School**

| LEICESTERSHIRE | First Innings | | Second Innings | |
|---|---|---|---|---|
| TJ New | c Ealham b Franks | 51 | c Hussey b Footitt | 14 |
| DDJ Robinson (capt) | lbw b Ealham | 0 | c Shreck b Franks | 7 |
| HD Ackerman | c Read b Shreck | 14 | b Franks | 20 |
| A Jacobs | lbw b Shreck | 0 | not out | 39 |
| *PA Nixon | c Read b Shreck | 98 | not out | 20 |
| J Allenby | c Shafayat b Footitt | 93 | | |
| Mansoor Amjad | st Read b Swann | 4 | | |
| CW Henderson | c Swann b Shreck | 32 | | |
| DT Rowe | c Swann b Franks | 12 | | |
| GJP Kruger | c Fleming b Shreck | 4 | | |
| NGE Walker | not out | 0 | | |
| Extras | b 6, lb 12, w 4, nb 34 | 56 | lb 2, w 4, nb 8 | 14 |
| | (all out 98.3 overs) | 364 | (3 wkts dec 20 overs) | 114 |

Bowling
Shreck 26.3-5-97-5. Ealham 29-4-84-1. Footitt 11-3-32-1. Swann 17-1-65-1. Franks 15-1-68-2.
Footitt 8-0-39-1. Franks 6-0-36-2. Shafayat 4-0-20-0. Gallian 2-0-17-0.
Fall of Wickets: 1-4, 2-40, 3-44, 4-114, 5-286, 6-293, 7-331, 8-360, 9-364
1-26, 2-26, 3-67

| NOTTS | First Innings | | Second Innings | |
|---|---|---|---|---|
| JER Gallian | c Walker b Kruger | 19 | c Jacobs b Walker | 60 |
| BM Shafayat | lbw b Ealham | 17 | c Kruger b Amjad | 45 |
| MA Wagh | b Rowe | 4 | c Nixon b Amjad | 78 |
| SP Fleming (capt) | not out | 32 | c Amjad b Henderson | 72 |
| DJ Hussey | not out | 11 | c Nixon b Rowe | 79 |
| *CMW Read | | | not out | 17 |
| MA Ealham | | | c sub b Walker | 9 |
| PJ Franks | | | lbw b Walker | 11 |
| GP Swann | | | c Robinson b Walker | 11 |
| CE Shreck | | | not out | 0 |
| MHA Footitt | | | | |
| Extras | lb 2, nb 17 | 19 | b 6, lb 8, w 2, nb 20 | 36 |
| | (3 wkts dec 27 overs) | 102 | (8 wkts 91 overs) | 363 |

Bowling
Kruger 9-1-32-2. Walker 6-1-24-0. Henderson 7-2-18-0. Rowe 5-1-26-1.
Kruger 11-2-38-0. Walker 18-4-70-4. Rowe 10-1-62-1. Allenby 19-4-48-0.
Amjad 24-1-76-2. Henderson 9-1-55-1.
Fall of Wickets: 1-43, 2-46, 3-71
1-123, 2-130, 3-185, 4-311, 5-312, 6-329, 7-347, 8-361

*Match drawn – Leicestershire (9pts),*
*Nottinghamshire (7pts)*

---

**GLAMORGAN v. ESSEX – at Swansea**

| GLAMORGAN | First Innings | | Second Innings | |
|---|---|---|---|---|
| GP Rees | c Flower b Danish Kaneria | 107 | lbw b Danish Kaneria | 14 |
| N Peng | c Napier b Palladino | 13 | b Danish Kaneria | 20 |
| JP Maher | c Foster b Palladino | 4 | lbw b Middlebrook | 19 |
| MJ Powell | c ten Doeschate b D Kaneria | 62 | not out | 12 |
| DL Hemp (capt) | c Flower b Danish Kaneria | 53 | b Middlebrook | 36 |
| *MA Wallace | c Pettini b Phillips | 34 | lbw b Danish Kaneria | 5 |
| AG Wharf | lbw b Danish Kaneria | 18 | not out | 22 |
| RDB Croft | c Chopra b Phillips | 8 | | |
| JAR Harris | lbw b Danish Kaneria | 1 | | |
| DA Cosker | b Phillips | 0 | | |
| HT Waters | not out | 5 | | |
| Extras | b 8, lb 8, w 3, nb 18 | 37 | b 7, nb 4 | 11 |
| | (all out 139.5 overs) | 352 | (5 wkts dec 50.5 overs) | 174 |

Bowling
Napier 16-6-41-0. Palladino 20-9-51-2. Danish Kaneria 49-14-112-5. Bopara 11-3-33-0.
Middlebrook 27-11-50-0. ten Doeschate 6-1-21-0. Phillips 10.5-3-28-3.
Napier 4-1-17-0. Palladino 6-1-16-0. Danish Kaneria 21.5-5-54-3.
Middlebrook 19-2-80-2.
Fall of Wickets: 1-24, 2-38, 3-155, 4-247, 5-270, 6-294, 7-315, 8-330, 9-340
1-28, 2-41, 3-73, 4-133, 5-136

| ESSEX | First Innings | | Second Innings | |
|---|---|---|---|---|
| V Chopra | lbw b Harris | 0 | c Maher b Cosker | 79 |
| ML Pettini (capt) | c Rees b Cosker | 27 | c Maher b Cosker | 79 |
| RS Bopara | c Wallace b Wharf | 4 | not out | 147 |
| GW Flower | b Waters | 44 | c Wallace b Wharf | 36 |
| TJ Phillips | c Maher b Waters | 1 | b Cosker | 7 |
| *JS Foster | c Harris b Wharf | 49 | run out | 36 |
| RN ten Doeschate | c Hemp b Croft | 36 | run out | 14 |
| JD Middlebrook | c Powell b Croft | 16 | not out | 20 |
| GR Napier | c & b Croft | 8 | | |
| Danish Kaneria | c Harris b Croft | 1 | | |
| AP Palladino | not out | 0 | | |
| Extras | b 2, lb 5, nb 4 | 11 | b 4, lb 9, w 2, nb 12 | 27 |
| | (all out 68.1 overs) | 204 | (6 wkts 77.2 overs) | 323 |

Bowling
Harris 14-4-27-1. Wharf 12-1-47-2. Cosker 17-2-53-1. Waters 8-3-18-2. Croft 17.1-3-52-4.
Harris 9-2-44-1. Wharf 17.2-2-85-1. Croft 25-2-74-0. Waters 4-1-19-0. Cosker 22-4-88-2.
Fall of Wickets: 1-0, 2-5, 3-85, 4-165, 5-167, 6-177, 7-195, 8-203, 9-203
1-6, 2-175, 3-202, 4-220, 5-281, 6-282

*Essex won by 4 wickets – Glamorgan (6pts), Essex (17pts)*

---

**MIDDLESEX v. SOMERSET – at Lord's**

| SOMERSET | First Innings | | Second Innings | |
|---|---|---|---|---|
| ME Trescothick | b Murtagh | 12 | b Silverwood | 0 |
| NJ Edwards | lbw b Silverwood | 0 | lbw b Richardson | 0 |
| JL Langer (capt) | c Silverwood | 0 | (5) lbw b Murtagh | 17 |
| JC Hildreth | c Nash b Wright | 5 | (7) b Silverwood | 127 |
| CL White | c Nash b Wright | 5 | (6) c Nash b Silverwood | 77 |
| ID Blackwell | c Shah b Richardson | 14 | (8) c Joyce b Silverwood | 0 |
| PD Trego | lbw b Silverwood | 1 | (4) c Nash b Silverwood | 16 |
| *C Kieswetter | c Nash b Murtagh | 6 | (3) c Joyce b Silverwood | 11 |
| PS Jones | not out | 0 | not out | 64 |
| AR Caddick | c Nash b Wright | 4 | b Murtagh | 4 |
| CM Willoughby | b Murtagh | 2 | | |
| Extras | lb 3, nb 2 | 5 | b 8, lb 11, w 1, nb 6 | 21 |
| | (8 wkts dec 26.3 overs) | 50 | (all out 87.5 overs) | 339 |

Bowling
Silverwood 10.3-6-13-3. Richardson 7-3-11-2. Murtagh 6-3-16-2. Wright 3-1-7-1.
Silverwood 21-7-49-6. Richardson 12-1-58-1. Murtagh 22.5-5-105-3.
Dalrymple 16-2-42-0. Wright 12-0-72-0. Shah 3.1-0-11-0.
Fall of Wickets: 1-9, 2-9, 3-19, 4-24, 5-36, 6-37, 7-43, 8-48
1-0, 2-0, 3-27, 4-36, 5-50, 6-189, 7-189, 8-332, 9-337

| MIDDLESEX | First Innings | | Second Innings | |
|---|---|---|---|---|
| BA Godleman | c Trescothick b Jones | 45 | lbw b Trego | 31 |
| NRD Compton | c sub b Willoughby | 47 | c Trescothick b Trego | 21 |
| OA Shah | lbw b Willoughby | 8 | c Trego b Jones | 28 |
| EC Joyce | c Edwards b Blackwell | 42 | not out | 45 |
| ET Smith (capt) | lbw b Willoughby | 8 | not out | 1 |
| *DC Nash | c Trego b Trego | 8 | | |
| JWM Dalrymple | c Jones b Trego | 7 | | |
| TJ Murtagh | not out | 36 | | |
| CJC Wright | c Trescothick b Blackwell | 12 | | |
| CEW Silverwood | b Trego | 15 | | |
| A Richardson | c Blackwell b Trego | 14 | lb 8, w 2, nb 2 | 12 |
| Extras | lb 6, w 2, nb 2 | 12 | | |
| | (all out 78.4 overs) | 252 | (3 wkts 37.3 overs) | 138 |

Bowling
Caddick 15-3-42-0. Willoughby 13-0-48-3. Jones 17-4-59-1. Trego 13.4-1-54-4. Blackwell 20-2-43-2.
Caddick 15-4-43-0. Willoughby 9-0-21-0. Trego 7-2-33-2. White 3.3-0-16-0. Jones 3-0-17-1.
Fall of Wickets: 1-97, 2-105, 3-117, 4-125, 5-161, 6-169, 7-171, 8-198, 9-236
1-48, 2-72, 3-136

*Middlesex won by 7 wickets – Middlesex (18pts), Somerset (3pts)*

painkillers – to send down six overs with the second new ball in a bid to break Kent's second-innings resolve. Typically, Gough took a wicket in his first over, but eventually the discomfort became too much even for him and James Tredwell's maiden first-class hundred saw Kent to safety.

Paul Wiseman was Durham's hero, batting 92 balls for his 7 not out against Lancashire and somehow surviving a nerve-tingling last over from Muttiah Muralitharan, while Mark Butcher dug deep to save his Surrey side at New Road. He battled through 142 balls, with a runner, after damaging an Achilles tendon and was joined in a ninth-wicket stand that lasted 21.4 overs by Matt Nicholson, who faced 67 balls for his unbeaten 20.

Gloucestershire's eight-day Championship marathon ended with a highly creditable draw at Derby, thanks in the main to the batting of Alex Gidman, Hamish Marshall and Mark Hardinges, but Derbyshire dismayed their supporters by amazingly opting not to chase a victory target of 200 from 31 overs.

Heroic batting from Robert Croft and James Harris at Swansea, plus a nine-wicket match haul from Dean Cosker, earned Glamorgan the prized scalp of Nottinghamshire at Swansea in what was their first win of the season in any competition, while a career-best 229 by Ravi Bopara, another double-hundred by Grant Flower and 14 wickets by spin pair Danish Kaneria and James Middlebrook meant Essex saw off Northamptonshire in a match which also contained the announcement of Ronnie Irani's enforced retirement

with chronic knee problems. Essex captain Irani has the proud record for the club he joined in 1994 of 12,994 runs at 43 and 316 wickets at 29.

At Taunton, meanwhile, Somerset's batting power was revealed in all its glory as Leicestershire were pulverised

## Round Eight: 5–9 June Division One

### SUSSEX v. HAMPSHIRE – at Arundel Castle

| SUSSEX | First Innings | | Second Innings | |
|---|---|---|---|---|
| CD Nash | c Adams b Warne | 61 | c Crawley b Mascarenhas | 28 |
| RR Montgomerie | c Carberry b Tremlett | 48 | c Warne b Udal | 82 |
| MH Yardy | c Adams b Warne | 15 | lbw b Mascarenhas | 3 |
| MW Goodwin | lbw b Tremlett | 2 | c Lumb b Udal | 99 |
| CJ Adams (capt) | c Warne b Udal | 52 | not out | 103 |
| *AJ Hodd | lbw b Tremlett | 28 | | |
| RSC Martin-Jenkins | c Adams b Warne | 12 | | |
| LJ Wright | c Pothas b Warne | 57 | (7) not out | 8 |
| Naved-ul-Hasan | c Tremlett b Warne | 21 | (6) c Carberry b Udal | 18 |
| Mushtaq Ahmed | b Clark | 54 | | |
| JD Lewry | not out | 1 | | |
| Extras | b 2, lb 2, w 1, nb 6 | 11 | b 6, lb 8, w 1, nb 4 | 19 |
| | (all out 111.2 overs) | 341 | (5 wkts dec 79 overs) | 360 |

Bowling
Clark 17-4-54-1. Tremlett 24-4-114-3. Mascarenhas 20-9-23-0. Adams 2-0-14-0. Udal 18-3-41-1. Warne 30.2-2-91-5.
Clark 14-3-49-0. Mascarenhas 16-2-53-2. Tremlett 11-0-42-0. Warne 13-0-70-0. Udal 19-1-83-3. Lumb 3-0-26-0. Adams 2-0-10-0. Crawley 1-0-13-0.
Fall of Wickets: 1-105, 2-127, 3-127, 4-130, 5-207, 6-223, 7-223, 8-233, 9-302
1-49, 2-59, 3-172, 4-292, 5-320

| HAMPSHIRE | First Innings | | Second Innings | |
|---|---|---|---|---|
| JHK Adams | lbw b Naved-ul-Hasan | 17 | c M'gomerie b Mushtaq Ahmed | 27 |
| MJ Brown | c M'gomerie b Martin-Jenkins | 4 | c Montgomerie b Lewry | 11 |
| JP Crawley | b Mushtaq Ahmed | 16 | lbw b Wright | 44 |
| MJ Lumb | c Adams b Mushtaq Ahmed | 51 | lbw b Naved-ul-Hasan | 62 |
| MA Carberry | b Goodwin | 9 | c Adams b Wright | 53 |
| *N Pothas | c Hodd b Mushtaq Ahmed | 13 | not out | 38 |
| AD Mascarenhas | c Naved-ul-Hasan b M'taq Ahmed | 22 | lbw b Martin-Jenkins | 41 |
| SK Warne (capt) | b Mushtaq Ahmed | 7 | lbw b Martin-Jenkins | 16 |
| SD Udal | not out | 17 | b Naved-ul-Hasan | 0 |
| CT Tremlett | c Adams b Mushtaq Ahmed | 21 | c Hodd b Martin-Jenkins | 3 |
| SR Clark | lbw b Mushtaq Ahmed | 0 | b Mushtaq Ahmed | 6 |
| Extras | b 4, nb 4 | 8 | b 5, lb 11, w 4, nb 12 | 32 |
| | (all out 58 overs) | 202 | (all out 103 overs) | 333 |

Bowling
Lewry 11-1-42-0. Naved-ul-Hasan 10-0-44-1. Martin-Jenkins 10-4-16-1. Wright 8-4-24-1. Mushtaq Ahmed 19-2-72-7.
Lewry 19-1-80-1. Naved-ul-Hasan 22-3-78-2. Mushtaq Ahmed 38-4-100-2. Martin-Jenkins 8-4-21-3. Wright 13-4-30-2. Yardy 3-0-8-0.
Fall of Wickets: 1-30, 2-53, 3-92, 4-109, 5-130, 6-131, 7-141, 8-166, 9-202
1-29, 2-49, 3-134, 4-216, 5-224, 6-288, 7-314, 8-317, 9-324

*Sussex won by 166 runs – Sussex (20pts), Hampshire (4pts)*

### KENT v. YORKSHIRE – at Tunbridge Wells

| YORKSHIRE | First Innings | |
|---|---|---|
| C White | c Hall b McLaren | 21 |
| JJ Sayers | c Key b Tredwell | 187 |
| A McGrath | lbw b Hall | 100 |
| Younus Khan | lbw b Cook | 7 |
| JA Rudolph | c Jones b McLaren | 43 |
| AU Rashid | c Key b Stevens | 54 |
| TT Bresnan | not out | 55 |
| *SM Guy | c Denly b Stevens | 25 |
| D Gough (capt) | c Cook b Stevens | 6 |
| JN Gillespie | not out | 13 |
| GJ Kruis | | |
| Extras | b 7, lb 20, w 11, nb 2 | 40 |
| | (8 wkts dec 166.2 overs) | 551 |

Bowling
Yasir Arafat 22-5-66-0. Hall 15-3-41-1. Cook 26-6-78-1. McLaren 21-2-76-2. Tredwell 47-8-149-1. Stevens 27.2-3-91-3. Denly 8-1-23-0.
Fall of Wickets: 1-52, 2-255, 3-281, 4-368, 5-415, 6-471, 7-511, 8-523

| KENT | First Innings | | Second Innings (following on) | |
|---|---|---|---|---|
| JL Denly | lbw b Gough | 10 | c Guy b Kruis | 9 |
| RWT Key (capt) | lbw b Gillespie | 62 | c Younus Khan b Kruis | 84 |
| M van Jaarsveld | c Rudolph b Gough | 10 | lbw b Gillespie | 56 |
| JC Tredwell | lbw b Kruis | 16 | not out | 116 |
| DI Stevens | c Guy b Kruis | 4 | c Sayers b Bresnan | 14 |
| NJ Dexter | c Younus Khan b Gough | 34 | c Guy b Bresnan | 0 |
| *GO Jones | c Guy b Bresnan | 61 | c Younus Khan b Gough | 15 |
| AJ Hall | lbw b Gough | 77 | not out | 63 |
| Yasir Arafat | b Gough | 4 | | |
| R McLaren | b Gough | 0 | | |
| SJ Cook | not out | 7 | | |
| Extras | lb 8, w 3, nb 6 | 17 | b 4, lb 13, w 3, nb 6 | 26 |
| | (all out 84.5 overs) | 292 | (6 wkts 129 overs) | 383 |

Bowling
Gough 16.2-6-47-6. Gillespie 17-5-58-1. Kruis 15-1-62-2. Bresnan 16.3-4-34-1. Rashid 11-1-55-0. Younus Khan 5-0-15-0. McGrath 4-0-13-0.
Kruis 24-2-89-2. Gillespie 21-3-51-1. Bresnan 22-3-82-2. McGrath 9-2-21-0. Rashid 35-4-77-0. White 5-0-9-0. Younus Khan 7-1-25-0. Gough 6-1-12-1.
Fall of Wickets: 1-12, 2-12, 3-55, 4-65, 5-141, 6-145, 7-271, 8-275, 9-279
1-14, 2-149, 3-173, 4-201, 5-201, 6-243

*Match drawn – Kent (7pts), Yorkshire (11pts)*

### DURHAM v. LANCASHIRE – at the Riverside

| LANCASHIRE | First Innings | | Second Innings | |
|---|---|---|---|---|
| MJ Chilton (capt) | st Mustard b Wiseman | 115 | (2) lbw b Davies | 29 |
| PJ Horton | c Di Venuto b Gibson | 15 | (1) lbw b Styris | 56 |
| MB Loye | c Mustard b Davies | 12 | lbw b Benkenstein | 41 |
| BJ Hodge | c Di Venuto b Styris | 1 | c Davies b Styris | 6 |
| SG Law | c Coetzer b Gibson | 60 | c Wiseman b Davies | 61 |
| *LD Sutton | lbw b Wiseman | 33 | c Di Venuto b Smith | 41 |
| G Chapple | c Onions b Davies | 57 | c Di Venuto b Davies | 7 |
| DG Cork | c Smith b Gibson | 9 | not out | 48 |
| TC Smith | c Mustard b Davies | 18 | not out | 4 |
| OJ Newby | c Wiseman b Davies | 10 | | |
| M Muralitharan | not out | 12 | | |
| JM Anderson† | | | | |
| Extras | b 4, lb 7, nb 14 | 25 | b 12, lb 2, nb 8 | 22 |
| | (all out 116.4 overs) | 367 | (7 wkts dec 73 overs) | 310 |

Bowling
Onions 25-5-79-0. Gibson 26-5-89-3. Davies 27.4-7-62-4. Styris 11-1-59-1. Benkenstein 2-0-8-0. Wiseman 21-2-59-2.
Onions 11-1-55-0. Gibson 11-1-64-0. Davies 14-5-34-3. Styris 13-3-56-2. Wiseman 10-0-38-0. Benkenstein 13-1-44-1. Smith 1-0-5-1.
Fall of Wickets: 1-37, 2-62, 3-63, 4-203, 5-237, 6-264, 7-294, 8-330, 9-350
1-92, 2-94, 3-110, 4-202, 5-204, 6-215, 7-305
† Replaced by OJ Newby

| DURHAM | First Innings | | Second Innings | |
|---|---|---|---|---|
| WR Smith | lbw b Smith | 16 | (2) b Chapple | 28 |
| MJ Di Venuto | c Hodge b Smith | 32 | (1) lbw b Cork | 15 |
| GJ Muchall | c Law b Muralitharan | 65 | c Sutton b Cork | 15 |
| KJ Coetzer | c Sutton b Anderson | 5 | c Law b Anderson | 16 |
| DM B'kenstein (capt) | c Sutton b Chapple | 35 | lbw b Muralitharan | 21 |
| SB Styris | st Sutton b Muralitharan | 48 | c Sutton b Smith | 39 |
| *P Mustard | lbw b Muralitharan | 54 | c Cork b Muralitharan | 18 |
| OD Gibson | c Law b Cork | 13 | lbw b Muralitharan | 54 |
| PJ Wiseman | lbw b Muralitharan | 10 | not out | 7 |
| M Davies | c Horton b Muralitharan | 0 | c Sutton b Anderson | 4 |
| G Onions | not out | 23 | not out | 6 |
| Extras | b 2, lb 4, w 1, nb 4 | 11 | b 20, lb 6, nb 6 | 32 |
| | (all out 76.3 overs) | 312 | (9 wkts 101 overs) | 229 |

Bowling
Cork 15-2-47-1. Newby 2-0-12-0. Anderson 16-3-80-1. Smith 12-3-47-2. Muralitharan 26.3-5-95-5. Chapple 5-0-25-1.
Anderson 26-11-46-2. Cork 14-4-35-2. Chapple 16-6-33-1. Smith 13-4-44-1. Muralitharan 32-14-45-3.
Fall of Wickets: 1-49, 2-53, 3-58, 4-125, 5-207, 6-226, 7-279, 8-279, 9-279
1-15, 2-35, 3-76, 4-95, 5-122, 6-136, 7-171, 8-224, 9-229

*Match drawn – Durham (10pts), Lancashire (11pts)*

### WORCESTERSHIRE v. SURREY – at Worcester

| WORCS | First Innings | |
|---|---|---|
| PA Jaques | c Batty b Nicholson | 124 |
| SC Moore | st Batty b Salisbury | 143 |
| VS Solanki (capt) | c Ramprakash b Clarke | 232 |
| BF Smith | b Clarke | 65 |
| GA Hick | lbw b Salisbury | 15 |
| *SM Davies | st Batty b Schofield | 81 |
| GJ Batty | not out | 9 |
| KW Hogg | not out | 2 |
| Kabir Ali | | |
| DE Bollinger | | |
| MN Malik | | |
| Extras | b 10, lb 12, w 8 | 30 |
| | (6 wkts dec 156 overs) | 701 |

Bowling
Azhar Mahmood 26.5-92-0. Nicholson 27-3-115-1. Saker 14-2-71-0. Clarke 16-1-84-2. Schofield 33-3-144-1. Salisbury 36-2-139-2. Brown 3-0-16-0. Ramprakash 1-0-18-0.
Fall of Wickets: 1-234, 2-329, 3-484, 4-517, 5-670, 6-697

| SURREY | First Innings | | Second Innings (following on) | |
|---|---|---|---|---|
| SA Newman | c Kabir Ali | 46 | c Davies b Kabir Ali | 34 |
| *JN Batty | c Davies b Batty | 114 | c Davies b Malik | 13 |
| MR Ramprakash | c Davies b Malik | 84 | (4) c Hick b Malik | 33 |
| AD Brown | c Jaques b Malik | 17 | (5) c Moore b Malik | 11 |
| R Clarke | c Davies b Batty | 4 | (6) lbw b Batty | 41 |
| Azhar Mahmood | c Davies b Batty | 18 | (7) c Davies b Kabir Ali | 44 |
| MA Butcher (capt) | c Malik b Hogg | 22 | (8) not out | 29 |
| CP Schofield | c Davies b Hogg | 20 | (9) b Malik | 17 |
| IDK Salisbury | b Hogg | 12 | (10) c Hick b Batty | 3 |
| MN Nicholson | c Smith b Batty | 7 | (11) not out | 20 |
| NC Saker | not out | 4 | (3) c Smith b Batty | 19 |
| Extras | b 4, w 1, nb 14 | 19 | b 1, lb 8, w 6, nb 2 | 17 |
| | (all out 113.2 overs) | 370 | (9 wkts 128 overs) | 281 |

Bowling
Bollinger 24-8-68-0. Kabir Ali 23-1-84-2. Malik 17-2-70-2. Hogg 15-4-44-3. Batty 34.2-6-100-3.
Kabir Ali 22-7-74-2. Bollinger 15-5-35-0. Malik 20-6-55-2. Hogg 16-10-16-0. Batty 50-20-84-5. Solanki 5-3-8-0.
Fall of Wickets: 1-80, 2-245, 3-271, 4-282, 5-284, 6-307, 7-336, 8-359, 9-362
1-48, 2-75, 3-75, 4-90, 5-126, 6-179, 7-220, 8-249, 9-255

*Match drawn – Worcestershire (12pts), Surrey (9pts)*

A rare moment of calm during a torrid season for Glamorgan as Will Bragg (left), Richard Grant (centre) and Dean Cosker enjoy a chat out in the middle.

## Round Eight: 5–9 June Division Two

### DERBYSHIRE v. GLOUCESTERSHIRE – at Derby

| DERBYSHIRE | First Innings | | Second Innings | |
|---|---|---|---|---|
| DJ Birch | c Taylor b Gidman | 95 | c Gidman b Hardinges | 2 |
| SD Stubbings | c Greenidge b Banerjee | 128 | not out | 11 |
| Hassan Adnan | c Marshall b Banerjee | 29 | not out | 23 |
| SM Katich (capt) | b Greenidge | 13 | | |
| TR Birt | c Marshall b Hardinges | 8 | | |
| GM Smith | c Marshall b Banerjee | 40 | | |
| AG Botha | run out | 98 | | |
| *DJ Pipe | not out | 53 | | |
| GG Wagg | c Banerjee b Fisher | 0 | | |
| T Lungley | c Taylor b Banerjee | 12 | | |
| ID Hunter | not out | 1 | | |
| Extras | b 5, lb 14, w 2, nb 2 | 23 | lb 1, w 3 | 4 |
| | (9 wkts dec 157 overs) | 500 | (1 wkt 15 overs) | 40 |

**Bowling**
Greenidge 28-5-91-1. Hardinges 29-5-126-1. Gidman 19-4-41-1. Brown 14-3-46-0. Fisher 28-7-68-1. Banerjee 37-6-103-4. Taylor 2-0-6-0.
Greenidge 7-3-11-0. Hardinges 5-0-22-1. Banerjee 2-1-4-0. Fisher 1-0-2-0.
**Fall of Wickets:** 1-181, 2-255, 3-280, 4-284, 5-288, 6-381, 7-466, 8-471, 9-499
1-7

| GLOS | First Innings | | Second Innings (following on) | |
|---|---|---|---|---|
| Kadeer Ali | lbw b Lungley | 27 | (2) b Lungley | 4 |
| ID Fisher | lbw b Wagg | 5 | (1) lbw b Lungley | 8 |
| HJH Marshall | c Pipe b Lungley | 47 | lbw b Smith | 120 |
| CG Taylor | b Lungley | 0 | c Pipe b Hunter | 6 |
| APR Gidman (capt) | lbw b Botha | 91 | c Lungley b Botha | 94 |
| SJ Adshead | c Pipe b Hunter | 13 | st Pipe b Botha | 3 |
| DO Brown | c Pipe b Lungley | 13 | c Pipe b Hunter | 43 |
| MA Hardinges | c Pipe b Wagg | 1 | c Botha b Wagg | 104 |
| *SD Snell | c Lungley b Botha | 11 | b Botha | 5 |
| CG Greenidge | not out | 13 | lbw b Katich | 27 |
| V Banerjee | c Pipe b Lungley | 0 | not out | 2 |
| Extras | b 18, lb 7, w 4, nb 8 | 37 | b 9, lb 11, w 5 | 25 |
| | (all out 81.1 overs) | 258 | (all out 130.4 overs) | 441 |

**Bowling**
Wagg 20-4-67-2. Hunter 21-2-67-1. Lungley 19.1-4-49-5. Botha 19-7-40-2. Smith 2-1-10-0.
Wagg 20.4-4-74-1. Lungley 21-5-84-2. Hunter 25-7-63-2. Smith 18-4-49-1. Botha 40-9-134-3. Katich 6-0-17-1.
**Fall of Wickets:** 1-9, 2-83, 3-83, 4-98, 5-120, 6-179, 7-190, 8-222, 9-247
1-4, 2-15, 3-34, 4-221, 5-230, 6-259, 7-323, 8-344, 9-439

*Match drawn – Derbyshire (12pts), Gloucestershire (8pts)*

### GLAMORGAN v. NOTTINGHAMSHIRE – at Swansea

| GLAMORGAN | First Innings | | Second Innings | |
|---|---|---|---|---|
| GP Rees | c Franks b Shreck | 0 | b Swann | 24 |
| N Peng | c Ealham b Shreck | 9 | c Ealham b Franks | 65 |
| *MA Wallace | c Read b Ealham | 24 | st Read b Swann | 22 |
| BJ Wright | c Shafayat b Swann | 28 | (7) not out | 18 |
| DL Hemp (capt) | c Ealham b Swann | 55 | c Shreck b Swann | 3 |
| RN Grant | c Franks b Swann | 41 | (4) c sub b Swann | 27 |
| AG Wharf | lbw b Ealham | 6 | (6) c Fleming b Shreck | 9 |
| MPO'Shea | c Hussey b Franks | 10 | (11) b Swann | 0 |
| RDB Croft | c Read b Ealham | 115 | (8) c Fleming b Shreck | 3 |
| JAR Harris | not out | 87 | (9) c Fleming b Swann | 11 |
| DA Cosker | c Ealham b Swann | 30 | (10) lbw b Swann | 6 |
| Extras | b 5, lb 6, w 1, nb 12 | 24 | b 4, w 1, nb 4 | 9 |
| | (all out 146.5 overs) | 429 | (all out 75.4 overs) | 197 |

**Bowling**
Shreck 32-9-83-2. Harris 24-3-72-0. Ealham 24-11-45-3. Franks 19-5-71-2. Swann 46.5-8-143-3. Hussey 1-0-4-0.
Shreck 24-9-43-2. Harris 9-2-34-0. Swann 31.4-2-100-7. Franks 10-2-16-1. Wagh 1-1-0-0.
**Fall of Wickets:** 1-0, 2-13, 3-45, 4-75, 5-144, 6-153, 7-178, 8-193, 9-378
1-78, 2-100, 3-120, 4-130, 5-157, 6-157, 7-164, 8-191, 9-197

| NOTTS | First Innings | | Second Innings | |
|---|---|---|---|---|
| JER Gallian | c Wharf b Cosker | 78 | c Wright b Cosker | 18 |
| BM Shafayat | c Croft b Wharf | 16 | lbw b Harris | 6 |
| MA Wagh | lbw b Harris | 57 | c Hemp b Cosker | 50 |
| SP Fleming (capt) | c Croft b Cosker | 8 | st Wallace b Cosker | 12 |
| DJ Hussey | c Rees b Cosker | 98 | b Croft | 63 |
| *CMW Read | c Peng b Harris | 4 | lbw b Croft | 5 |
| MA Ealham | run out | 74 | lbw b Cosker | 2 |
| PJ Franks | run out | 2 | c Hemp b Cosker | 1 |
| GP Swann | c Et b Cosker | 3 | b Wharf | 37 |
| AJ Harris | c Et b Croft | 5 | c Croft b Wharf | 0 |
| CE Shreck | not out | 0 | not out | 0 |
| Extras | b 11, lb 3, w 1, nb 4 | 19 | b 1, lb 8, nb 4 | 13 |
| | (all out 115.5 overs) | 364 | (all out 62.5 overs) | 207 |

**Bowling**
Harris 14-2-37-2. Wharf 14-1-62-1. Cosker 44-7-7-137-4. Croft 40.5-2-114-2. Croft 28-1-94-2. Harris 11-3-24-1. Cosker 18-4-69-5. Wharf 5.5-3-11-2.
**Fall of Wickets:** 1-24, 2-143, 3-153, 4-185, 5-199, 6-311, 7-320, 8-325, 9-364
1-14, 2-49, 3-69, 4-106, 5-115, 6-118, 7-136, 8-183, 9-190

*Glamorgan won by 55 runs –*
*Glamorgan (21pts), Nottinghamshire (7pts)*

### ESSEX v. NORTHAMPTONSHIRE – at Chelmsford

| ESSEX | First Innings | |
|---|---|---|
| V Chopra | c Peters b Brown | 50 |
| ML Pettini (capt) | c Sales b Crook | 8 |
| RS Bopara | lbw b White | 229 |
| GW Flower | c Klusener b Brown | 203 |
| *JS Foster | c O'Brien b Dawson | 69 |
| RN ten Doeschate | not out | 62 |
| JD Middlebrook | not out | 0 |
| GR Napier | | |
| Danish Kaneria | | |
| MJ Saggers | | |
| A Nel | | |
| Extras | b 10, lb 15, w 3 | 28 |
| | (5 wkts dec 173 overs) | 649 |

**Bowling**
Klusener 23-9-41-0. Lucas 29-2-121-0. Crook 37-6-140-1. Brown 42-9-148-2. Dawson 32-1-129-1. White 10-0-45-1.
**Fall of Wickets:** 1-11, 2-127, 3-447, 4-568, 5-632

| NORTHANTS | First Innings | | Second Innings (following on) | |
|---|---|---|---|---|
| SD Peters | lbw b Saggers | 10 | lbw b Middlebrook | 93 |
| DJ Jacobs | lbw b Saggers | 4 | b Nel | 16 |
| U Afzaal | c Flower b Danish Kaneria | 73 | c Flower b Danish Kaneria | 32 |
| DJG Sales (capt) | c Chopra b Middlebrook | 23 | b Danish Kaneria | 67 |
| DS Lucas | c Flower b Middlebrook | 12 | (10) not out | 9 |
| RA White | c Foster b Saggers | 6 | (5) c Foster b Danish Kaneria | 14 |
| L Klusener | not out | 70 | (6) c Bopara b Middlebrook | 25 |
| *NJO'Brien | c Pettini b Middlebrook | 0 | (7) lbw b Foster | 3 |
| SP Crook | c Chopra b Danish Kaneria | 6 | (8) c Flower b Middlebrook | 49 |
| RKJ Dawson | b ten Doeschate | 26 | (9) c Chopra b Nel | 7 |
| JF Brown | c Flower b Middlebrook | 0 | c ten Doeschate b D Kaneria | 21 |
| Extras | b 4, lb 10, w 1, nb 2 | 17 | b 14, lb 10, nb 4 | 28 |
| | (all out 82 overs) | 241 | (all out 112.2 overs) | 367 |

**Bowling**
Nel 11-3-39-0. Saggers 16-3-69-3. Bopara 5-1-17-0. Danish Kaneria 26-8-36-2. Middlebrook 20-4-53-4. ten Doeschate 4-2-13-1.
Nel 24-3-92-2. Saggers 16-4-48-0. Napier 7-2-16-0. Danish Kaneria 38.2-11-101-5. Middlebrook 25-0-77-3. Bopara 2-0-9-0.
**Fall of Wickets:** 1-6, 2-51, 3-121, 4-121, 5-127, 6-176, 7-176, 8-177, 9-236
1-39, 2-89, 3-223, 4-223, 5-263, 6-273, 7-290, 8-312, 9-354

*Essex won by an innings and 41 runs –*
*Essex (22pts), Northamptonshire (1pt)*

### SOMERSET v. LEICESTERSHIRE – at Taunton

| LEICESTERSHIRE | First Innings | | Second Innings | |
|---|---|---|---|---|
| TJ New | lbw b Caddick | 33 | c Trescothick b Caddick | 7 |
| DDJ Robinson (capt) | c Trego b Willoughby | 2 | c Kieswetter b Willoughby | 12 |
| JK Maunders | lbw b Caddick | 0 | c Kieswetter b Willoughby | 3 |
| HD Ackerman | c Kieswetter b Jones | 23 | c Kieswetter b Willoughby | 4 |
| A Jacobs | c Kieswetter b Jones | 22 | b Trego | 23 |
| J Allenby | c Trescothick b Jones | 20 | c Kieswetter b White | 43 |
| *PA Nixon | lbw b Jones | 21 | b Caddick | 18 |
| Mansoor Amjad | not out | 7 | c Trescothick b Caddick | 46 |
| SCJ Broad | lbw b Caddick | 5 | b Willoughby | 35 |
| DD Masters | lbw b Jones | 2 | not out | 31 |
| NGE Walker | c Edwards b Jones | 28 | c White b Willoughby | 8 |
| Extras | lb 2, nb 8 | 10 | b 4, lb 3, w 1, nb 10 | 18 |
| | (all out 41.2 overs) | 168 | (all out 61.1 overs) | 248 |

**Bowling**
Caddick 15-3-64-3. Willoughby 7-1-20-1. Jones 13.2-0-61-6. Trego 4-1-16-0. Blackwell 2-1-5-0.
Caddick 20-6-38-3. Willoughby 16.1-0-82-5. Trego 8-1-38-1. Jones 8-0-49-0. White 9-0-34-1.
**Fall of Wickets:** 1-6, 2-15, 3-60, 4-66, 5-88, 6-123, 7-124, 8-129, 9-132
1-12, 2-19, 3-23, 4-54, 5-56, 6-85, 7-157, 8-186, 9-234

| SOMERSET | First Innings | |
|---|---|---|
| ME Trescothick | c Maunders b Masters | 182 |
| NJ Edwards | c Robinson b Masters | 133 |
| JC Hildreth | c Nixon b Broad | 163 |
| CL White | c Nixon b Broad | 114 |
| *C Kieswetter | c Amjad b Masters | 36 |
| PD Trego | not out | 18 |
| JL Langer (capt) | | |
| ID Blackwell | | |
| PS Jones | | |
| AR Caddick | | |
| CM Willoughby | | |
| Extras | lb 14, w 5, nb 10 | 29 |
| | (5 wkts dec 122.4 overs) | 675 |

**Bowling**
Broad 24-1-142-2. Masters 28.4-4-130-3. Walker 14-0-131-0. Allenby 19-0-60-0. Amjad 23-0-120-0. Maunders 11-0-65-0. Jacobs 2-0-13-0. New 1-1-0-0.
**Fall of Wickets:** 1-233, 2-408, 3-610, 4-625, 5-675

*Somerset won by an innings and 259 runs –*
*Somerset (22pts), Leicestershire (1pt)*

by an innings and plenty. Justin Langer, the captain, did not even have to bat as the top four – Marcus Trescothick, Neil Edwards, James Hildreth and Cameron White – all reached three figures: a club record. Trescothick's 182 took only 185 balls, but young Cornishman Edwards reached his own hundred first, off 114 balls, as the pair put on 233 for the opening wicket. Steffan Jones, Andrew Caddick and Charl Willoughby also gave Stuart Broad, in particular, a lesson on how to bowl on a good pitch as Leicestershire's batting was blown away.

the first day and then sharing all ten second innings wickets with his new ball partner, Charl Willoughby. In between, after Marcus Trescothick had departed to the first ball of the innings, Neil Edwards hit 85 from 119 balls and there was even more aggressive batting from

## Round Nine: 15–18 June

Durham were 210 for 1 in their first innings and then 83 for no wicket second time around, chasing 254 for victory, before Shane Warne twice hauled his Hampshire team back into the match. Indeed, Warne was so successful – in company with Chris Tremlett on the final day – that Hampshire ended up winning by 50 runs a game that Durham several times seemed to have in the bag.

Brad Hodge's unbeaten 156, and eight wickets for Muttiah Muralitharan, enabled Lancashire to beat Kent comfortably at Old Trafford, while elsewhere in the first division there were rain-affected draws at Edgbaston and Headingley.

Andrew Caddick, 38, was at his brilliant best at Bristol as Somerset trounced Gloucestershire, taking 7 for 30 on

## Round Nine: 15–18 June Division One

### HAMPSHIRE v. DURHAM – at the Rose Bowl

| HAMPSHIRE | First Innings | | Second Innings | |
|---|---|---|---|---|
| MA Carberry | b Wiseman | 30 | b Onions | 6 |
| MJ Brown | lbw b Onions | 0 | c Muchall b Wiseman | 59 |
| JP Crawley | b Onions | 0 | b Davies | 23 |
| MJ Lumb | lbw b Wiseman | 70 | c Mustard b Davies | 7 |
| CC Benham | c Di Venuto b Gibson | 22 | b Davies | 15 |
| *N Pothas | c Mustard b Davies | 29 | c Mustard b Davies | 0 |
| CT Tremlett | lbw b Onions | 3 | (9) not out | 62 |
| AD Mascarenhas | b Plunkett | 34 | (7) c Mustard b Plunkett | 60 |
| SK Warne (capt) | c Plunkett b Davies | 4 | (8) c Smith b Onions | 33 |
| SR Clark | c Gibson b Plunkett | 17 | b Plunkett | 16 |
| JTA Bruce | not out | 0 | not out | 11 |
| Extras | b 1, lb 10, w 2, nb 10 | 23 | b 4, lb 5, w 6, nb 2 | 17 |
| | (all out 82.1 overs) | 232 | (9 wkts dec 79 overs) | 309 |

Bowling
Onions 21-6-61-3. Plunkett 20.1-7-57-2. Gibson 19-5-48-1. Wiseman 10-2-23-2.
Onions 13-0-55-2. Plunkett 20-4-79-2. Davies 15-5-48-4. Gibson 17-3-50-0. Wiseman 9-0-67-1. Styris 1-0-1-0.
Fall of Wickets: 1-1, 2-1, 3-83, 4-137, 5-145, 6-166, 7-187, 8-191, 9-230
1-8, 2-52, 3-68, 4-98, 5-98, 6-134, 7-179, 8-251, 9-273

| DURHAM | First Innings | | Second Innings | |
|---|---|---|---|---|
| MJ Di Venuto | c Brown b Clark | 124 | (2) c Crawley b Tremlett | 50 |
| WR Smith | lbw b Warne | 28 | (1) lbw b Warne | 41 |
| GJ Muchall | lbw b Warne | 59 | lbw b Warne | 4 |
| SB Styris | c Pothas b Warne | 6 | lbw b Warne | 41 |
| DM B'kenstein | lbw b Tremlett | 9 | c Benham b Warne | 0 |
| *P Mustard | c Warne b Tremlett | 1 | c Warne b Clark | 21 |
| OD Gibson | not out | 33 | lbw b Warne | 0 |
| LE Plunkett | lbw b Warne | 15 | c Warne b Tremlett | 15 |
| PJ Wiseman | lbw b Tremlett | 3 | not out | 2 |
| M Davies | c Benham b Warne | 1 | c Benham b Tremlett | 0 |
| G Onions | st Mustard b Warne | 1 | c Benham b Tremlett | 1 |
| Extras | b 5, lb 1, w 1, nb 8, p 5 | 20 | b 6, lb 3, w 2, nb 12 | 23 |
| | (all out 77.1 overs) | 288 | (all out 55 overs) | 203 |

Bowling
Clark 13-3-48-1. Bruce 9-0-52-0. Mascarenhas 7-1-22-0. Tremlett 21-4-63-3. Warne 26.1-3-83-6. Carberry 1-0-9-0.
Clark 16-4-56-1. Bruce 4-0-28-0. Mascarenhas 3-1-13-0. Tremlett 12-2-47-4. Warne 20-5-50-5.
Fall of Wickets: 1-116, 2-210, 3-226, 4-227, 5-230, 6-237, 7-247, 8-250, 9-277
1-83, 2-94, 3-115, 4-123, 5-173, 6-174, 7-189, 8-201, 9-201

*Hampshire won by 50 runs – Hampshire (18pts), Durham (5pts)*

### LANCASHIRE v. KENT – at Old Trafford

| LANCASHIRE | First Innings | | Second Innings | |
|---|---|---|---|---|
| PJ Horton | lbw b Cook | 29 | (2) c Yasir Arafat b Cook | 3 |
| IJ Sutcliffe | c Jones b McLaren | 57 | (1) c Jones b Cook | 0 |
| MB Loye | c Jones b Hall | 75 | not out | 8 |
| BJ Hodge | not out | 156 | not out | 0 |
| SG Law (capt) | c & b Denly | 58 | | |
| TC Smith | st Jones b Tredwell | 8 | | |
| DG Cork | run out | 40 | | |
| *LD Sutton† | | | | |
| JM Anderson | | | | |
| G Keedy | | | | |
| M Muralitharan | | | | |
| OJ Newby | | | | |
| Extras | lb 10, nb 18 | 28 | w 1 | 1 |
| | (5 wkts dec 112 overs) | 451 | (2 wkts 2.5 overs) | 12 |

Bowling
Yasir Arafat 18-3-65-0. Hall 18-0-100-1. Cook 16-1-46-1. McLaren 15-1-61-1. Tredwell 31-4-103-1. Stevens 6-0-32-0. Denly 8-0-34-1.
Cook 1.5-0-9-2. Hall 1-0-3-0.
Fall of Wickets: 1-71, 2-165, 3-217, 4-354, 5-377
1-1, 2-8
† Replaced by OJ Newby

| KENT | First Innings | | Second Innings (following on) | |
|---|---|---|---|---|
| JL Denly | b Cork | 77 | c & b Smith | 9 |
| RWT Key (capt) | lbw b Anderson | 28 | c Horton b Anderson | 17 |
| M van Jaarsveld | b Anderson | 7 | c Horton b Muralitharan | 85 |
| MJ Walker | c Sutton b Cork | 1 | lbw b Muralitharan | 7 |
| DI Stevens | c Horton b Muralitharan | 14 | run out | 55 |
| *GO Jones | c Sutcliffe b Keedy | 70 | b Anderson | 2 |
| JC Tredwell | c Law b Muralitharan | 10 | c Law b Muralitharan | 1 |
| AJ Hall | c Sutton b Muralitharan | 4 | c Law b Keedy | 6 |
| Yasir Arafat | c Smith b Muralitharan | 8 | c Anderson b Keedy | 0 |
| R McLaren | not out | 14 | b Muralitharan | 0 |
| SJ Cook | lbw b Anderson | 13 | not out | 1 |
| Extras | b 16, lb 8, nb 2 | 26 | lb 6, nb 2 | 7 |
| | (all out 88.4 overs) | 272 | (all out 63 overs) | 190 |

Bowling
Anderson 22.4-7-64-3. Cork 11.1-4-30-2. Muralitharan 34-7-73-4. Smith 6.5-0-37-0. Keedy 14-2-44-1.
Anderson 22-6-48-2. Smith 10-0-44-1. Muralitharan 25-1-72-4. Keedy 5-1-17-2. Hodge 1-0-4-0.
Fall of Wickets: 1-83, 2-105, 3-117, 4-120, 5-160, 6-182, 7-194, 8-210, 9-189
1-17, 2-39, 3-54, 4-158, 5-165, 6-172, 7-189, 8-189, 9-189

*Lancashire won by 8 wickets – Lancashire (22pts), Kent (3pts)*

### WARWICKSHIRE v. WORCESTERSHIRE – at Edgbaston

| WARWICKSHIRE | First Innings | | Second Innings | |
|---|---|---|---|---|
| IJ Westwood | c Hick b Kabir Ali | 18 | not out | 14 |
| DL Maddy | b Bollinger | 5 | | |
| KC Sangakkara | c Jaques b Kabir Ali | 20 | (2) not out | 34 |
| IJL Trott | c Smith b Kabir Ali | 27 | | |
| JO Troughton | c Smith b Kabir Ali | 109 | | |
| AGR Loudon | c Davies b Hogg | 36 | | |
| *TR Ambrose | c Davies b Hogg | 42 | | |
| TD Groenewald | not out | 41 | | |
| N Tahir | c Davies b Bollinger | 11 | | |
| DW Steyn | c Smith b Bollinger | 2 | | |
| JE Anyon | b Bollinger | 0 | | |
| Extras | b 8, lb 19, w 1, nb 4 | 32 | | 0 |
| | (all out 74 overs) | 343 | (0 wkts 18 overs) | 48 |

Bowling
Kabir Ali 24-4-85-3. Bollinger 24-6-102-4. Malik 5-0-32-0. Hogg 15-0-76-3. Batty 6-1-21-0.
Batty 9-2-25-0. Solanki 7-0-18-0. Malik 2-0-5-0.
Fall of Wickets: 1-32, 2-36, 3-79, 4-86, 5-162, 6-262, 7-297, 8-315, 9-327

| WORCS | First Innings | |
|---|---|---|
| PA Jaques | c Anyon b Groenewald | 34 |
| SC Moore | c Ambrose b Anyon | 112 |
| VS Solanki (capt) | c Trott b Groenewald | 41 |
| BF Smith | c Maddy b Troughton | 34 |
| GA Hick | c Ambrose b Steyn | 49 |
| *SM Davies | lbw b Steyn | 26 |
| GJ Batty | c Ambrose b Anyon | 25 |
| KW Hogg | c Groenewald b Loudon | 13 |
| Kabir Ali | b Steyn | 39 |
| DE Bollinger | b Anyon | 3 |
| MN Malik | not out | 1 |
| Extras | b 4, lb 10, nb 8 | 22 |
| | (all out 123.2 overs) | 399 |

Bowling
Steyn 28-9-59-3. Anyon 24.2-2-79-3. Tahir 18-4-74-0. Groenewald 16-4-61-2. Loudon 19-1-51-1. Trott 8-0-23-0. Troughton 10-2-38-1.
Fall of Wickets: 1-63, 2-144, 3-200, 4-268, 5-305, 6-338, 7-342, 8-388, 9-395

*Match drawn – Warwickshire (10pts), Worcestershire (11pts)*

### YORKSHIRE v. SUSSEX – at Headingley

| YORKSHIRE | First Innings | | Second Innings | |
|---|---|---|---|---|
| C White | c Montgomerie b Lewry | 0 | c Hodd b Lewry | 49 |
| JJ Sayers | b Lewry | 3 | lbw b Lewry | 3 |
| A McGrath (capt) | c Lewry b Naved-ul-Hasan | 9 | run out | 58 |
| Younus Khan | lbw b Lewry | 1 | b Martin-Jenkins | 31 |
| JA Rudolph | c Hodd b Naved-ul-Hasan | 46 | c Nash b Naved-ul-Hasan | 46 |
| *GL Brophy | c Martin-Jenkins b M'taq A | 0 | c Nash b Mushtaq Ahmed | 0 |
| AU Rashid | lbw b Martin-Jenkins | 22 | not out | 49 |
| TT Bresnan | c Hodd b Martin-Jenkins | 4 | not out | 27 |
| JN Gillespie | c Nash b Mushtaq Ahmed | 4 | | |
| A Shahzad | not out | 32 | | |
| GJ Kruis | c Naved-ul-Hasan b M'taq A | 17 | | |
| Extras | b 1, lb 2, w 1, nb 12 | 16 | b 2, lb 7, nb 12 | 21 |
| | (all out 48.2 overs) | 139 | (6 wkts dec 108 overs) | 284 |

Bowling
Lewry 15-8-30-2. Martin-Jenkins 8-2-20-2. Mushtaq Ahmed 11.2-2-40-3.
Lewry 24-10-37-2. Naved-ul-Hasan 22-1-85-1. Martin-Jenkins 17-7-28-1. Mushtaq Ahmed 29-7-72-1. Wright 10-2-30-0. Yardy 5-1-19-0. Nash 1-0-4-0.
Fall of Wickets: 1-0, 2-15, 3-16, 4-17, 5-26, 6-77, 7-81, 8-95, 9-95
1-9, 2-112, 3-121, 4-167, 5-174, 6-220

| SUSSEX | First Innings | | Second Innings | |
|---|---|---|---|---|
| CD Nash | c White b Gillespie | 28 | lbw b Kruis | 15 |
| RR Montgomerie | b Gillespie | 17 | b Gillespie | 0 |
| MH Yardy | c White b Bresnan | 20 | not out | 21 |
| MW Goodwin | c Sayers b Shahzad | 7 | not out | 21 |
| CJ Adams (capt) | c Brophy b Bresnan | 29 | | |
| *AJ Hodd | c Rudolph b Kruis | 7 | | |
| RSC Martin-Jenkins | c Bresnan b Kruis | 16 | | |
| LJ Wright | c Brophy b Shahzad | 2 | | |
| Naved-ul-Hasan | c Rudolph b Shahzad | 4 | | |
| Mushtaq Ahmed | not out | 2 | | |
| JD Lewry | b Shahzad | 0 | | |
| Extras | lb 3, w 6 | 9 | | 0 |
| | (all out 56.4 overs) | 141 | (2 wkts 22 overs) | 57 |

Bowling
Gillespie 16-3-54-2. Kruis 18-7-39-2. Rashid 2-0-6-0. Shahzad 8.4-1-22-4. Bresnan 9-2-14-2. McGrath 3-1-... 
Gillespie 6-0-25-1. Kruis 5-0-15-1. Bresnan 2-1-2-0. Shahzad 1-0-1-0. Younus Khan 4-2-9-0. Rashid 2-1-5-0. Rudolph 2-2-0-0.
Fall of Wickets: 1-43, 2-52, 3-77, 4-81, 5-99, 6-121, 7-132, 8-139, 9-141
1-15, 2-15

*Match drawn – Yorkshire (7pts), Sussex (7pts)*

Muttiah Muralitharan continued his remarkable level of wicket-taking success for Lancashire – but still a first Championship title since their shared triumph with Surrey in 1950 eluded them.

## Round Nine: 15–18 June Division Two

### NORTHAMPTONSHIRE v. LEICESTERSHIRE – at Northampton

| NORTHANTS | First Innings | | Second Innings | |
|---|---|---|---|---|
| SD Peters | c Allenby b Masters | 1 | (2) c Maunders b Walker | 26 |
| CJL Rogers | c Nixon b Broad | 4 | (1) lbw b Broad | 7 |
| U Afzaal | lbw b Masters | 0 | c & b Masters | 1 |
| DJG Sales (capt) | c Nixon b Broad | 92 | c Maunders b Allenby | 22 |
| *MH Wessels | c Allenby b Broad | 40 | c New b Walker | 20 |
| L Klusener | lbw b Walker | 7 | c Ackerman b Masters | 50 |
| JJ van der Wath | c Jacobs b Masters | 8 | c Allenby b Walker | 5 |
| SP Crook | c Nixon b Masters | 49 | not out | 23 |
| RKJ Dawson | c Nixon b Walker | 4 | not out | 8 |
| DS Lucas | not out | 31 | | |
| JF Brown | c Allenby b Masters | 6 | | |
| Extras | b 1, lb 7, w 1 | 9 | lb 5, w 2, nb 2 | 9 |
| | (all out 76.1 overs) | 251 | (7 wkts 47 overs) | 171 |

**Bowling**
Broad 27-3-102-3. Masters 29.1-13-59-5. Walker 12-1-57-2. Allenby 2-1-4-0.
Henderson 6-1-21-0.
Broad 7-2-9-1. Masters 14-2-62-2. Allenby 8-2-38-1. Walker 13-1-47-3.
Henderson 5-1-10-0.
**Fall of Wickets:** 1-5, 2-5, 3-9, 4-57, 5-72, 6-105, 7-209, 8-209, 9-228
1-18, 2-21, 3-45, 4-67, 5-114, 6-137, 7-145

| LEICESTERSHIRE | First Innings | |
|---|---|---|
| TJ New | c Wessels b Klusener | 29 |
| JK Maunders | lbw b Lucas | 14 |
| HD Ackerman | c Sales b Crook | 17 |
| A Jacobs | b Crook | 2 |
| J Allenby | not out | 30 |
| *PA Nixon | not out | 25 |
| DDJ Robinson (capt) | | |
| CW Henderson | | |
| SCJ Broad | | |
| DD Masters | | |
| NGE Walker | | |
| Extras | b 2, lb 4, w 4, nb 4 | 14 |
| | (4 wkts dec 42 overs) | 131 |

**Bowling**
van der Wath 11-1-38-0. Lucas 10-2-22-1. Crook 8-0-23-2. Klusener 8-2-25-1.
Brown 5-0-17-0.
**Fall of Wickets:** 1-40, 2-53, 3-62, 4-73

*Match drawn – Northamptonshire (7pts),
Leicestershire (7pts)*

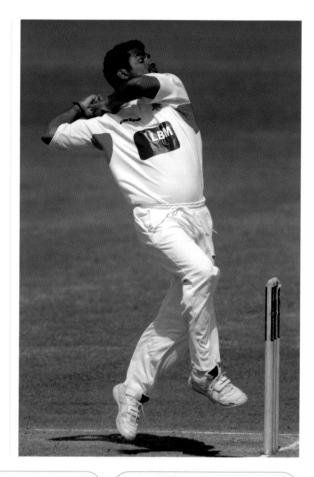

### GLOUCESTERSHIRE v. SOMERSET – at Bristol

| GLOS | First Innings | | Second Innings | |
|---|---|---|---|---|
| Kadeer Ali | c Trescothick b Caddick | 3 | (2) lbw b Willoughby | 14 |
| GP Hodnett | c Trescothick b Caddick | 52 | (1) c White b Willoughby | 21 |
| HJH Marshall | c Trescothick b Caddick | 4 | lbw b Willoughby | 31 |
| CG Taylor | c Trescothick b Caddick | 4 | c Kieswetter b Willoughby | 34 |
| APR Gidman (capt) | b Trego | 16 | c Hildreth b Caddick | 0 |
| DO Brown | c Hildreth b Willoughby | 9 | lbw b Willoughby | 12 |
| MA Hardinges | c Trescothick b Willoughby | 4 | c Langer b Caddick | 14 |
| *SD Snell | c Hildreth b Caddick | 12 | c Hildreth b Caddick | 1 |
| CG Greenidge | c Kieswetter b Caddick | 11 | b Caddick | 3 |
| V Banerjee | not out | 1 | not out | 1 |
| BM Edmondson | lbw b Caddick | 0 | lbw b Caddick | 1 |
| Extras | lb 5 | 5 | lb 2, lb 3, w 1 | 6 |
| | (all out 40.5 overs) | 121 | (all out 42.3 overs) | 138 |

**Bowling**
Caddick 18.5-7-30-7. Willoughby 16-1-65-2. Trego 4-0-12-1. Jones 2-0-9-0.
Caddick 16.3-4-41-5. Willoughby 14-4-56-5. Trego 4-1-15-0. Jones 4-0-21-0.
Blackwell 1-1-0-0.
**Fall of Wickets:** 1-14, 2-28, 3-32, 4-59, 5-87, 6-96, 7-97, 8-112, 9-121
1-29, 2-52, 3-102, 4-105, 5-113, 6-131, 7-131, 8-133, 9-136

| SOMERSET | First Innings | |
|---|---|---|
| ME Trescothick | lbw b Greenidge | 0 |
| NJ Edwards | c Snell b Edmondson | 85 |
| JL Langer (capt) | b Hardinges | 32 |
| JC Hildreth | c Snell b Banerjee | 68 |
| CL White | c Taylor b Greenidge | 65 |
| *C Kieswetter | c Hodnett b Greenidge | 23 |
| PD Trego | not out | 73 |
| ID Blackwell | c Greenidge b Marshall | 72 |
| PS Jones | | |
| AR Caddick | | |
| CM Willoughby | | |
| Extras | b 4, lb 5, w 1, nb 2 | 12 |
| | (7 wkts dec 78 overs) | 410 |

**Bowling**
Greenidge 15-3-73-3. Edmondson 19-2-82-1. Hardinges 13-1-66-1.
Gidman 8-0-32-0. Brown 7-0-48-0. Banerjee 13-1-76-1. Marshall 10-0-24-1.
**Fall of Wickets:** 1-0, 2-68, 3-148, 4-192, 5-260, 6-261, 7-410

*Somerset won by an innings and 151 runs –
Gloucestershire (2pts), Somerset (22pts)*

### MIDDLESEX v. ESSEX – at Lord's

| ESSEX | First Innings | |
|---|---|---|
| V Chopra | lbw b Silverwood | 9 |
| ML Pettini (capt) | lbw b Silverwood | 4 |
| RS Bopara | c Godleman b Vaas | 25 |
| GW Flower | lbw b Vaas | 4 |
| *JS Foster | c Smith b Kartik | 7 |
| RN ten Doeschate | lbw b Vaas | 20 |
| JD Middlebrook | c Kartik b Vaas | 127 |
| AJ Bichel | c Flower b Saggers | 102 |
| AJ Tudor | c Shah b Silverwood | 35 |
| Danish Kaneria | c Smith b Kartik | 9 |
| MJ Saggers | not out | 2 |
| Extras | lb 14, nb 18 | 32 |
| | (all out 114.4 overs) | 376 |

**Bowling**
Silverwood 24-5-81-3. Vaas 24.4-7-79-4. Murtagh 3.2-1-18-0. Kartik 41.4-12-93-3.
Joyce 8-1-30-0. Dalrymple 12-1-54-0. Shah 1-0-7-0.
**Fall of Wickets:** 1-9, 2-16, 3-46, 4-49, 5-55, 6-97, 7-258, 8-351, 9-372

| MIDDLESEX | First Innings | | Second Innings (following on) | |
|---|---|---|---|---|
| BA Godleman | c Foster b Tudor | 28 | lbw b Danish Kaneria | 68 |
| NRD Compton | c Flower b Saggers | 5 | lbw b Saggers | 11 |
| OA Shah | c sub b Tudor | 22 | c Foster b Danish Kaneria | 131 |
| M Kartik | lbw b Saggers | 7 | | |
| EC Joyce | c Middlebrook b Tudor | 0 | (4) c Foster b Bichel | 23 |
| ET Smith (capt) | c Foster b ten Doeschate | 49 | (5) c Chopra b Danish Kaneria | 30 |
| JWM Dalrymple | c Bopara b Saggers | 1 | (6) b Saggers | 48 |
| *BJM Scott | not out | 30 | (7) not out | 11 |
| WPUJC Vaas | c Tudor b Saggers | 5 | (8) not out | 18 |
| TJ Murtagh | c Foster b Saggers | 5 | | |
| CEW Silverwood | c ten Doeschate b Bichel | 0 | | |
| Extras | b 4, lb 10, w 1, nb 10 | 25 | b 13, lb 4, w 1, nb 2 | 20 |
| | (all out 72.3 overs) | 177 | (6 wkts dec 113 overs) | 360 |

**Bowling**
Bichel 19.3-4-52-1. Saggers 24-8-39-5. Bopara 5-2-10-0. Danish Kaneria 11-6-16-0.
Tudor 8-0-29-3. ten Doeschate 4-0-16-1. Middlebrook 1-0-1-0.
Bichel 21-3-83-1. Saggers 25-5-88-2. Tudor 10-2-23-0. Danish Kaneria 36-6-97-3.
ten Doeschate 8-0-25-0. Middlebrook 11-3-23-0. Flower 2-1-4-0.
**Fall of Wickets:** 1-21, 2-55, 3-74, 4-76, 5-80, 6-84, 7-155, 8-164, 9-173
1-32, 2-155, 3-203, 4-248, 5-317, 6-337

*Match drawn – Middlesex (7pts),
Essex (11pts)*

### NOTTINGHAMSHIRE v. DERBYSHIRE – at Trent Bridge

| DERBYSHIRE | First Innings | | Second Innings | |
|---|---|---|---|---|
| DJ Birch | c Francis b Shreck | 3 | lbw b Shreck | 5 |
| SD Stubbings | c Ealham b Francis | 13 | b Shreck | 10 |
| CR Taylor | c Fleming b Ealham | 12 | lbw b Ealham | 1 |
| SM Katich (capt) | c Patel b Shreck | 14 | not out | 50 |
| TR Birt | b Shreck | 18 | not out | 16 |
| GM Smith | c Read b Shreck | 1 | | |
| AG Botha | run out | 0 | | |
| *DJ Pipe | c Hussey b Shreck | 4 | | |
| GG Wagg | c & b Shreck | 11 | | |
| T Lungley | not out | 18 | | |
| R Hodgkinson | lbw b Shreck | 6 | | |
| Extras | lb 6, nb 2 | 8 | lb 10, w 3 | 13 |
| | (all out 35.3 overs) | 108 | (3 wkts 26 overs) | 95 |

**Bowling**
Shreck 13.3-3-35-7. Ealham 13-5-24-1. Francis 9-1-43-1.
Shreck 9-3-16-2. Ealham 8-1-16-1. Francis 3-0-31-0. Footitt 4-0-10-0.
Swann 2-0-12-0.
**Fall of Wickets:** 1-14, 2-27, 3-29, 4-52, 5-54, 6-60, 7-68, 8-75, 9-88
1-10, 2-19, 3-25

| NOTTS | First Innings | |
|---|---|---|
| JER Gallian | c Botha b Smith | 62 |
| SP Fleming (capt) | c Pipe b Wagg | 13 |
| MA Wagh | not out | 123 |
| SR Patel | not out | 89 |
| DJ Hussey | | |
| *CMW Read | | |
| MA Ealham | | |
| SRG Francis | | |
| GP Swann | | |
| CE Shreck | | |
| MHA Footitt | | |
| Extras | lb 6, w 7, nb 2 | 15 |
| | (2 wkts dec 54 overs) | 302 |

**Bowling**
Wagg 17-5-59-1. Smith 11-2-65-1. Lungley 13-1-75-0. Hodgkinson 10-0-75-0.
Birt 3-0-22-0.
**Fall of Wickets:** 1-23, 2-116

*Match drawn – Nottinghamshire (10pts),
Derbyshire (4pts)*

Cameron White, Peter Trego and Ian Blackwell, who featured four sixes and six fours in his 68-ball 72.

The three other second-division games all finished in draws, as the weather again disrupted proceedings, although Owais Shah's 131 saved Middlesex against Essex at Lord's and Nottinghamshire were particularly unlucky to be denied against Derbyshire following Charlie Shreck's seven-wicket opening salvo and flowing strokeplay from both Mark Wagh and Samit Patel.

## Round Ten: 8–11 July

The fall-out from the abandonment of Worcestershire's match against Kent at Worcester was to be felt for the rest of the season, after umpires Martin Bodenham and Richard Kettleborough officially called it off at noon on the scheduled third day. It was the first four-day fixture in six seasons to be abandoned without a ball being bowled, and Kent felt cheated because they believed the game should have been switched to Kidderminster. They were even more upset when

Surrey's victory over Durham was confirmed, dragging them deeper into the relegation mire.

There is no doubt that Kent were the injured, innocent party as Worcestershire attempted to safeguard the playing of their upcoming televised NatWest Pro40 game against Hampshire at New Road. Yet there was clearly no hope of play at the flood-ravaged Worcester ground, and Kent coach Graham Ford countered claims by Worcestershire chief executive Mark Newton that his club had business interests to protect by saying: 'Cricket is the most important thing, and this affair plainly hasn't had cricket's interests at heart.' Later, Kent were cheered somewhat by an ECB decision to replay the match in late July, but this plan was ruled out when ten counties, led by Yorkshire, objected.

Surrey's win at The Oval was a hard-fought, low-scoring affair settled in the end by Rikki Clarke, who came in at 50 for 4 in Surrey's second innings and struck 68 not out from 78 balls, with 12 fours and a six, while Mark Butcher held firm at the other end. Phil Mustard, with 70 from 82 balls, was the only Durham batsman to get on top of a Surrey attack in which Matt Nicholson was outstanding.

## Round Ten: 8–11 July Division One

### SURREY v. DURHAM – at The Oval

| DURHAM | First Innings | | Second Innings | |
|---|---|---|---|---|
| WR Smith | b Nicholson | 10 | (7) b Nicholson | 41 |
| GR Breese | c Walters b Saker | 23 | (1) c Batty b Dernbach | 8 |
| GJ Muchall | lbw b Nicholson | 1 | (6) b Nicholson | 0 |
| SB Styris | b Nicholson | 1 | c Schofield b Clarke | 23 |
| DM B'kenstein (capt) | c Schofield b Clarke | 26 | c Newman b Saker | 48 |
| *P Mustard | c Newman b Harbhajan Singh | 70 | c Newman b Schofield | 2 |
| OD Gibson | c Clarke b Dernbach | 10 | (8) lbw b Saker | 0 |
| LE Plunkett | c Clarke b Harbhajan Singh | 5 | (9) c Walters b Nicholson | 33 |
| PJ Wiseman | c Newman b Harbhajan Singh | 6 | (2) lbw b Schofield | 44 |
| M Davies | not out | 20 | c Batty b Nicholson | 0 |
| SJ Harmison | c Nicholson b Schofield | 8 | not out | 0 |
| Extras | b 9, lb 2 | 11 | lb 4, w 1 | 5 |
| | (all out 44.3 overs) | 191 | (all out 57.1 overs) | 204 |

**Bowling**
Nicholson 14-3-37-3. Dernbach 6-1-30-1. Saker 7-0-40-1. Clarke 5-0-27-1. Harbhajan Singh 11-2-44-3. Schofield 1.3-1-2-1.
Nicholson 14.1-2-44-4. Dernbach 4-1-29-1. Clarke 5-2-9-1. Harbhajan Singh 15-1-66-0. Schofield 12-4-29-2. Saker 7-1-23-2.
**Fall of Wickets:** 1-22, 2-34, 3-34, 4-40, 5-74, 6-96, 7-117, 8-123, 9-168
1-10, 2-11, 3-56, 4-126, 5-130, 6-132, 7-132, 8-197, 9-203

| SURREY | First Innings | | Second Innings | |
|---|---|---|---|---|
| SA Newman | c sub b Harmison | 0 | c Mustard b Harmison | 7 |
| *JN Batty | run out | 17 | c Gibson b Harmison | 4 |
| MR Ramprakash | b Gibson | 18 | c Mustard b Harmison | 1 |
| MA Butcher | lbw b Plunkett | 25 | not out | 40 |
| SJ Walters | lbw b Gibson | 70 | c Muchall b Harmison | 8 |
| R Clarke | b Wiseman | 30 | not out | 68 |
| CP Schofield | c Mustard b Gibson | 28 | | |
| MJ Nicholson | c Breese b Harmison | 19 | | |
| Harbhajan Singh | lbw b Gibson | 0 | | |
| NC Saker | not out | 16 | | |
| JW Dernbach | b Harmison | 0 | | |
| Extras | lb 10, w 2, nb 8 | 20 | b 4, lb 15, w 5, nb 2 | 26 |
| | (all out 67.4 overs) | 243 | (4 wkts 36.3 overs) | 154 |

**Bowling**
Plunkett 13-4-44-1. Harmison 18.4-5-75-3. Gibson 16-5-61-4. Davies 9-3-18-0. Wiseman 11-2-35-1.
Plunkett 8.3-3-32-0. Harmison 14-5-1-4. Gibson 5-1-18-0. Davies 5-0-17-0. Wiseman 4-1-17-0.
**Fall of Wickets:** 1-2, 2-49, 3-53, 4-115, 5-168, 6-198, 7-217, 8-217, 9-231
1-13, 2-18, 3-23, 4-50

*Surrey won by 6 wickets –*
*Surrey (18pts), Durham (3pts)*

### LANCASHIRE v. YORKSHIRE – at Old Trafford

| YORKSHIRE | First Innings | |
|---|---|---|
| JJ Sayers | lbw b Nicholson | 0 |
| MP Vaughan | b Jayasuriya | 74 |
| A McGrath | lbw b Anderson | 56 |
| Younus Khan | b Keedy | 6 |
| JA Rudolph | c Law b Cork | 25 |
| *GL Brophy | c Sutton b Anderson | 73 |
| AU Rashid | c Sutton b Anderson | 28 |
| TT Bresnan | not out | 28 |
| JN Gillespie | b Keedy | 13 |
| D Gough (capt) | c Loye b Keedy | 0 |
| MJ Hoggard | c Sutton b Anderson | 7 |
| Extras | b 1, lb 9 | 10 |
| | (all out 110.3 overs) | 320 |

**Bowling**
Anderson 33.3-7-98-5. Cork 18-5-47-1. Smith 16-2-54-0. Croft 8-31-0.
Keedy 31-7-70-3. Jayasuriya 4-0-10-1.
**Fall of Wickets:** 1-0, 2-90, 3-111, 4-160, 5-172, 6-249, 7-280, 8-297, 9-299

| LANCASHIRE | First Innings | |
|---|---|---|
| MJ Chilton (capt) | c sub b Younus Khan | 47 |
| ST Jayasuriya | c Bresnan b Rashid | 38 |
| MB Loye | c Hoggard b Rashid | 47 |
| BJ Hodge | lbw b Rashid | 24 |
| SG Law | st sub b Rashid | 55 |
| SJ Croft | st Brophy b Rashid | 5 |
| *LD Sutton | not out | 20 |
| DG Cork | | |
| TC Smith | | |
| JM Anderson | | |
| G Keedy | | |
| Extras | b 4, lb 5, nb 2 | 11 |
| | (6 wkts 69 overs) | 247 |

**Bowling**
Hoggard 6-2-6-0. Gough 13-4-29-0. Rashid 28-2-114-5. Gillespie 5-2-17-0. Bresnan 4-1-22-0. Younus Khan 13-1-50-1.
**Fall of Wickets:** 1-61, 2-117, 3-149, 4-166, 5-180, 6-247

*Match drawn – Lancashire (8pts),*
*Yorkshire (9pts)*

### HAMPSHIRE v. WARWICKSHIRE – at the Rose Bowl

| WARWICKSHIRE | First Innings | | Second Innings – Forfeited |
|---|---|---|---|
| IJ Westwood | c Pothas b Mascarenhas | 23 | |
| DL Maddy (capt) | c sub b Tremlett | 123 | |
| IJL Trott | c Brown b Carberry | 50 | |
| JO Troughton | c sub b Tremlett | 44 | |
| AGR Loudon | not out | 41 | |
| *TR Ambrose | b Mascarenhas | 32 | |
| HH Streak | not out | 5 | |
| TD Groenewald | | | |
| N Tahir | | | |
| PL Harris | | | |
| JE Anyon | | | |
| Extras | b 11, lb 8, w 2, nb 14 | 35 | |
| | (5 wkts dec 119.4 overs) | 353 | |

**Bowling**
Tremlett 29-9-82-2. Bruce 21-4-74-0. Tomlinson 18.4-4-49-0. Mascarenhas 19-7-30-2. Warne 22-1-60-0. Carberry 9-1-35-1. Lumb 1-0-4-0.
**Fall of Wickets:** 1-47, 2-166, 3-252, 4-283, 5-343

| HAMPSHIRE | First Innings | | Second Innings | |
|---|---|---|---|---|
| MA Carberry | c Anyon b Westwood | 7 | not out | 192 |
| MJ Brown | not out | 16 | b Anyon | 10 |
| JP Crawley | not out | 0 | c Trott b Maddy | 10 |
| MJ Lumb | | | c Westwood b Harris | 15 |
| CC Benham | | | run out | 40 |
| *N Pothas | | | run out | 12 |
| AD Mascarenhas (capt) | | | not out | 38 |
| SK Warne (capt) | | | | |
| CT Tremlett | | | | |
| JTA Bruce | | | | |
| JA Tomlinson | | | | |
| Extras | | | b 1, lb 8, w 1, nb 4 | 14 |
| | (1 wkt dec 1.5 overs) | 23 | (5 wkts 91.3 overs) | 331 |

**Bowling**
Troughton 1-0-14-0. Westwood 0.5-0-9-1.
Anyon 17-4-69-1. Streak 25-7-63-0. Maddy 7-1-25-1. Tahir 4-0-13-0. Harris 29-3-96-1. Loudon 1-0-6-0. Groenewald 8.3-1-50-0.
**Fall of Wickets:** 1-15
1-27, 2-47, 3-111, 4-228, 5-245

*Hampshire won by 5 wickets –*
*Hampshire (15pts), Warwickshire (4pts)*

### WORCESTERSHIRE v. KENT – at New Road

*Match abandoned – Worcestershire (4pts), Kent (4pts)*

The Roses match at Old Trafford was a rain-hit draw, although some quality performances from Michael Vaughan, Jimmy Anderson and Adil Rashid followed the washed-out first two days, while at the Rose Bowl there was a first Championship defeat of the season for Warwickshire. Darren Maddy's 123 gave the visitors an early advantage but there was no play on day three and Shane Warne's persuasive powers set up a seemingly tough Hampshire run chase that merely proved to be the showcase for Michael Carberry to bat quite brilliantly as he hit a six and 24 fours in a career-best unbeaten 192 from 281 balls.

Captained for the first time by Paul Nixon, Leicestershire beat Glamorgan by ten wickets, despite a century from the highly promising Ben Wright. From 88 for 5, in reply to the Welsh county's 268, Hylton Ackerman and Nixon himself transformed the second-division match by adding 213 for Leicestershire's sixth wicket. Chris Taylor's first-innings 112 not out, meanwhile, could not save Gloucestershire from defeat against Northamptonshire, for whom Monty Panesar took a match-winning 6 for 65.

Tom Lungley added to his growing reputation by taking 5 for 33 in Derbyshire's gusty 15-run win over Middlesex, who collapsed from 208 for 4 to 266 all out in their second innings – a slide which included a desperate 32-run last-wicket stand between Jamie Dalrymple and Alan Richardson. At Chelmsford, meanwhile, Nottinghamshire replied to Essex's massive 700 for 9 declared by building a mammoth 791 themselves. It was their highest first-class score and featured an innings of 240 from 328 balls by Chris Read, including 23 fours and eight sixes. James Foster also made 204 in the match, from 302 balls with 23 fours and three sixes, and it is believed this is the first

## Round Ten: 8–11 July Division Two

### LEICESTERSHIRE v. GLAMORGAN – at Leicester

**GLAMORGAN**

| | First Innings | | Second Innings | |
|---|---|---|---|---|
| GP Rees | b Masters | 2 | c Nixon b Masters | 0 |
| N Peng | b Kruger | 0 | b Kruger | 4 |
| JP Maher | c Nixon b Rowe | 19 | lbw b Kruger | 55 |
| BJ Wright | c sub b Masters | 108 | b Masters | 6 |
| DL Hemp (capt) | c Nixon b Masters | 23 | c Nixon b Kruger | 43 |
| *MA Wallace | run out | 42 | c Nixon b Allenby | 9 |
| AG Wharf | c Allenby b Maunders | 19 | c Nixon b Kruger | 5 |
| RDB Croft | c Nixon b Kruger | 29 | c Allenby b Masters | 71 |
| JAR Harris | c Ackerman b Kruger | 0 | c Nixon b Kruger | 2 |
| DA Cosker | not out | 2 | lbw b Amjad | 6 |
| HT Waters | b Masters | 0 | not out | 13 |
| Extras | b 1, lb 5, w 4, nb 16 | 26 | b 4, lb 2, w 2, nb 14 | 22 |
| | (all out 90.2 overs) | 268 | (all out 76.1 overs) | 236 |

**Bowling**
Masters 22.3-5-44-4. Kruger 21-3-66-3. Rowe 8-0-50-1. Amjad 18-3-65-0. Allenby 15-4-29-0. Maunders 5.5-1-8-1.
Masters 16.1-5-34-3. Kruger 21-6-62-5. Amjad 20-5-74-1. Rowe 8-2-38-0. Allenby 11-3-22-1.
Fall of Wickets: 1-2, 2-2, 3-47, 4-89, 5-161, 6-205, 7-251, 8-264, 9-267
1-4, 2-4, 3-35, 4-99, 5-122, 6-131, 7-136, 8-140, 9-174

**LEICESTERSHIRE**

| | First Innings | | Second Innings | |
|---|---|---|---|---|
| TJ New | c Wallace b Harris | 15 | not out | 11 |
| DD Masters | lbw b Wharf | 11 | | |
| HD Ackerman | c Maher b Wharf | 153 | | |
| A Jacobs | c Wallace b Harris | 2 | (2) not out | 13 |
| J Allenby | c Maher b Harris | 0 | | |
| MC Rosenberg | c Wallace b Waters | 11 | | |
| *PA Nixon (capt) | lbw b Croft | 126 | | |
| Mansoor Amjad | not out | 105 | | |
| DT Rowe | b Harris | 0 | | |
| JK Maunders | c Peng b Croft | 30 | | |
| GJP Kruger | c Maher b Wharf | 9 | | |
| Extras | b 4, lb 4, w 1, nb 10 | 19 | w 1, nb 2 | 3 |
| | (all out 135 overs) | 481 | (0 wkts 7.1 overs) | 27 |

**Bowling**
Harris 31-8-95-4. Wharf 26-3-81-3. Waters 6-0-99-1. Cosker 16-2-80-0. Croft 22-6-108-2. Wright 2-0-10-0.
Harris 4-1-10-0. Wharf 3.1-0-17-0.
Fall of Wickets: 1-24, 2-31, 3-37, 4-37, 5-88, 6-301, 7-337, 8-348, 9-446

*Leicestershire won by 10 wickets –*
*Leicestershire (22pts), Glamorgan (5pts)*

### NORTHAMPTONSHIRE v. GLOUCESTERSHIRE – at Northampton

**NORTHANTS**

| | First Innings | | Second Innings | |
|---|---|---|---|---|
| SD Peters | c Spearman b Banerjee | 55 | (2) b Gidman | 92 |
| CJL Rogers | c Banerjee b Greenidge | 4 | (1) c Adshead b Edmondson | 15 |
| U Afzaal | b Kirby | 66 | c Spearman b Taylor | 72 |
| DJG Sales (capt) | b Edmondson | 10 | st Adshead b Banerjee | 22 |
| *MH Wessels | c Marshall b Kirby | 57 | lbw b Banerjee | 22 |
| L Klusener | c Adshead b Kirby | 40 | lbw b Taylor | 9 |
| SP Crook | c & b Taylor | 4 | c Hodnett b Taylor | 6 |
| JJ van der Wath | c Adshead b Kirby | 4 | lbw b Greenidge | 15 |
| MS Panesar | c Taylor b Kirby | 0 | c Marshall b Banerjee | 0 |
| DS Lucas | not out | 32 | c Marshall b Banerjee | 0 |
| JF Brown | b Greenidge | 25 | not out | 5 |
| Extras | b 6, lb 4, w 3 | 13 | lb 11, w 1 | 12 |
| | (all out 81.3 overs) | 310 | (all out 91.4 overs) | 270 |

**Bowling**
Greenidge 17.2-4-56-2. Edmondson 19-2-90-1. Kirby 21-8-60-5. Gidman 6-3-13-0. Banerjee 20-6-57-1. Taylor 8-1-24-1.
Greenidge 6.4-1-12-1. Edmondson 15-2-48-1. Kirby 15-6-30-0. Banerjee 27-1-103-3. Taylor 22-4-52-4. Gidman 6-1-14-1.
Fall of Wickets: 1-5, 2-127, 3-143, 4-151, 5-240, 6-249, 7-249, 8-251, 9-254
1-31, 2-184, 3-184, 4-230, 5-241, 6-241, 7-255, 8-255, 9-260

**GLOS**

| | First Innings | | Second Innings | |
|---|---|---|---|---|
| CM Spearman | run out | 0 | (2) c Rogers b Lucas | 3 |
| Kadeer Ali | lbw b van der Wath | 25 | (1) lbw b Lucas | 3 |
| GP Hodnett | c van der Wath b Lucas | 0 | c Wessels b Lucas | 1 |
| SP Kirby | c Wessels b van der Wath | 37 | (6) c Wessels b Panesar | 5 |
| HJH Marshall | c Klusener b van der Wath | 2 | (4) b Panesar | 58 |
| APR Gidman | (3) c van der Wath | 112 | (5) lbw b Panesar | 36 |
| CG Taylor | not out | 112 | b Panesar | 0 |
| *SJ Adshead | c Lucas b Brown | 46 | c Peters b Panesar | 13 |
| CG Greenidge | c Sales b Panesar | 3 | b Panesar | 10 |
| V Banerjee | c Crook b Panesar | 4 | not out | 11 |
| BM Edmondson | c Sales b Crook | 0 | c Sales b Crook | 5 |
| Extras | b 8, lb 5, w 4, nb 4 | 21 | b 1, lb 18, nb 4 | 23 |
| | (all out 113.1 overs) | 250 | (all out 74.4 overs) | 192 |

**Bowling**
van der Wath 17-1-54-4. Lucas 10-2-35-1. Crook 10-3-39-0. Klusener 9-4-24-0. Panesar 19.3-3-47-3. Brown 12-2-38-1.
van der Wath 7-1-20-0. Lucas 9-4-26-3. Brown 19-6-30-0. Panesar 28-7-65-6. Crook 1.4-1-2-1.
Fall of Wickets: 1-6, 2-8, 3-50, 4-50, 5-52, 6-125, 7-227, 8-238, 9-248
1-8, 2-14, 3-33, 4-113, 5-119, 6-119, 7-139, 8-150, 9-153

*Northamptonshire won by 138 runs –*
*Northamptonshire (20pts), Gloucestershire (5pts)*

### MIDDLESEX v. DERBYSHIRE – at Southgate

**DERBYSHIRE**

| | First Innings | | Second Innings | |
|---|---|---|---|---|
| SD Stubbings | b Richardson | 15 | (2) c Scott b Silverwood | 8 |
| WPC Weston | lbw b Silverwood | 0 | (1) c Godleman b Richardson | 16 |
| MG Dighton | b Dalrymple | 68 | b Richardson | 9 |
| SM Katich (capt) | b Murtagh | 80 | b Murtagh | 68 |
| TR Birt | lbw b Dalrymple | 32 | lbw b Kartik | 1 |
| GM Smith | b Dalrymple | 5 | b Murtagh | 4 |
| AG Botha | b Richardson | 32 | b Murtagh | 4 |
| *TJ Poynton | run out | 2 | c Strauss b Kartik | 0 |
| GG Wagg | c Richardson b Kartik | 27 | lbw b Kartik | 28 |
| T Lungley | not out | 22 | c Scott b Kartik | 2 |
| KJ Dean | c Strauss b Kartik | 16 | c Godleman b Kartik | 16 |
| Extras | b 6, lb 22, nb 20 | 48 | lb 1, nb 8 | 9 |
| | (all out 93.5 overs) | 340 | (all out 70.2 overs) | 199 |

**Bowling**
Silverwood 14-2-47-1. Murtagh 12-7-22-1. Richardson 17-4-44-2. Kartik 26.5-2-108-2. Dalrymple 24-3-91-3.
Silverwood 8-2-35-1. Richardson 21-4-56-2. Murtagh 12-2-41-2. Kartik 25.2-8-38-5. Dalrymple 4-1-18-0.
Fall of Wickets: 1-2, 2-35, 3-201, 4-205, 5-208, 6-247, 7-247, 8-285, 9-292
1-11, 2-20, 3-69, 4-84, 5-114, 6-118, 7-121, 8-191, 9-199

**MIDDLESEX**

| | First Innings | | Second Innings | |
|---|---|---|---|---|
| AJ Strauss | c Wagg b Dean | 38 | lbw b Lungley | 53 |
| BA Godleman | lbw b Lungley | 11 | lbw b Lungley | 11 |
| OA Shah | b Smith | 24 | c Katich b Wagg | 26 |
| EC Joyce | lbw b Lungley | 81 | c & b Botha | 32 |
| ET Smith (capt) | c Dighton b Wagg | 26 | lbw b Smith | 65 |
| JWM Dalrymple | lbw b Wagg | 9 | not out | 48 |
| *BJM Scott | c Weston b Botha | 4 | lbw b Smith | 0 |
| TJ Murtagh | lbw b Lungley | 35 | c Poynton b Botha | 4 |
| M Kartik | lbw b Lungley | 0 | c Smith b Botha | 2 |
| CEW Silverwood | c Poynton b Lungley | 2 | c Lungley b Smith | 4 |
| A Richardson | not out | 6 | b Wagg | 19 |
| Extras | b 14, lb 1, w 3, nb 4 | 22 | b 2, lb 8, w 2 | 12 |
| | (all out 90.3 overs) | 258 | (all out 89.1 overs) | 266 |

**Bowling**
Wagg 23-7-59-2. Dean 14-4-42-1. Lungley 14.3-3-33-5. Botha 21-7-51-1. Smith 13-0-45-1. Dighton 3-0-10-0. Katich 2-0-3-0.
Lungley 16-3-50-2. Wagg 19.1-3-76-2. Botha 22-4-69-3. Dean 17-8-30-0. Smith 15-5-31-3.
Fall of Wickets: 1-44, 2-52, 3-105, 4-166, 5-185, 6-198, 7-229, 8-229, 9-231
1-7, 2-77, 3-87, 4-155, 5-208, 6-214, 7-222, 8-234, 9-234

*Derbyshire won by 15 runs – Middlesex (5pts), Derbyshire (20pts)*

### ESSEX v. NOTTINGHAMSHIRE – at Chelmsford

**ESSEX**

| | First Innings | | Second Innings | |
|---|---|---|---|---|
| V Chopra | lbw b Swann | 35 | not out | 29 |
| ML Pettini (capt) | c Read b Franks | 4 | c Swann b Patel | 1 |
| RS Bopara | c Sidebottom b Swann | 59 | not out | 33 |
| GW Flower | c Read b Ealham | 34 | | |
| *JS Foster | c Shafayat b Swann | 204 | | |
| RN ten Doeschate | c Patel b Swann | 17 | | |
| JD Middlebrook | c Ealham b Franks | 13 | | |
| AJ Bichel | lbw b Ferley | 148 | | |
| GR Napier | c Ealham b Shafayat | 125 | | |
| AJ Tudor | not out | 19 | | |
| Danish Kaneria | not out | 0 | | |
| Extras | lb 20, w 1, nb 14 | 35 | | 0 |
| | (9 wkts dec 151.5 overs) | 700 | (1 wkt 26 overs) | 63 |

**Bowling**
Sidebottom 30-7-101-0. Ealham 30-8-110-1. Franks 19-1-91-2. Swann 38-5-166-4. Ferley 27-3-151-1. Patel 3-0-30-0. Shafayat 3.5-0-24-1. Wagh 1-0-7-0.
Swann 1-0-1-0. Patel 10.1-1-29-1. Ferley 12-2-25-0. Hussey 0.5-0-2-0. Read 2-0-6-0.
Fall of Wickets: 1-42, 2-60, 3-129, 4-163, 5-199, 6-224, 7-478, 8-673, 9-696
1-4

**NOTTS**

| | First Innings | |
|---|---|---|
| JER Gallian | b Bichel | 21 |
| BM Shafayat | c Chopra b Danish Kaneria | 24 |
| MA Wagh | b Danish Kaneria | 107 |
| SR Patel | c Foster b Bopara | 117 |
| DJ Hussey (capt) | c Foster b Bichel | 36 |
| *CMW Read | c Middlebrook b ten Doeschate | 240 |
| MA Ealham | lbw b Middlebrook | 54 |
| PJ Franks | c Foster b Danish Kaneria | 1 |
| GP Swann | c Middlebrook b Flower | 97 |
| RS Ferley | not out | 43 |
| RJ Sidebottom | c Napier b Tudor | 10 |
| Extras | b 16, lb 9, w 2, nb 14 | 41 |
| | (all out 212.5 overs) | 791 |

**Bowling**
Bichel 32-5-127-2. Tudor 16.5-1-89-1. ten Doeschate 20-6-65-1. Napier 23-3-72-0. Middlebrook 45-11-140-1. Danish Kaneria 42-5-153-3. Bopara 17-4-61-1. Flower 14-4-50-1. Chopra 3-0-9-0.
Fall of Wickets: 1-29, 2-70, 3-262, 4-296, 5-343, 6-498, 7-501, 8-717, 9-735

*Match drawn – Essex (10pts), Nottinghamshire (11pts)*

Paul Nixon notched up another landmark honour in the year he finally made his England debut at the age of 36 – he captained Leicestershire for the first time.

instance of two wicketkeepers passing 200 in the same game. Of the four other century-makers in the predictably drawn match, Graham Napier's 101-ball 125 with 11 fours and eight sixes was by far the most explosive, while Graeme Swann reached 97 despite batting down at No. 9.

## Round Eleven: 13–16 July Division One

### SUSSEX v. DURHAM – at Horsham

| DURHAM | First Innings | | Second Innings | |
|---|---|---|---|---|
| WR Smith | c & b Mushtaq Ahmed | 21 | c sub b Naved-ul-Hasan | 8 |
| MD Stoneman | lbw b Lewry | 2 | b Naved-ul-Hasan | 15 |
| KJ Coetzer | c M-Jenkins b Mushtaq Ahmed | 31 | lbw b Mushtaq Ahmed | 36 |
| SB Styris | c M'gomerie b Naved-ul-Hasan | 47 | c Yardy b Wright | 6 |
| DM B'kenstein (capt) | b Naved-ul-Hasan | 32 | c Montgomerie b M-Jenkins | 50 |
| *P Mustard | c M-Jenkins b Mushtaq Ahmed | 35 | c Adams b Mushtaq Ahmed | 0 |
| BW Harmison | c Adams b Mushtaq Ahmed | 4 | c Adams b Mushtaq Ahmed | 0 |
| OD Gibson | c Martin-Jenkins b Lewry | 25 | b Mushtaq Ahmed | 68 |
| LE Plunkett | c M'gomerie b Mushtaq Ahmed | 0 | c Yardy b Martin-Jenkins | 4 |
| PJ Wiseman | lbw b Lewry | 0 | not out | 8 |
| SJ Harmison | not out | 0 | absent hurt | |
| Extras | b 7, lb 2, w 1, nb 2 | 12 | lb 4, nb 7 | 11 |
| | (60.1 overs) | 209 | (all out 56 overs) | 206 |

**Bowling**
Lewry 12-4-33-3. Naved-ul-Hasan 14-2-52-2. Mushtaq Ahmed 26.1-3-91-5. Martin-Jenkins 5-1-10-0. Wright 2-0-11-0. Yardy 1-0-3-0.
Naved-ul-Hasan 17-3-60-2. Martin-Jenkins 11-3-35-2. Wright 5-0-23-1. Mushtaq Ahmed 21-6-77-4. Yardy 2-0-7-0.
**Fall of Wickets:** 1-3, 2-46, 3-63, 4-131, 5-146, 6-167, 7-200, 8-209, 9-209
1-23, 2-26, 3-48, 4-92, 5-98, 6-100, 7-164, 8-176, 9-206

| SUSSEX | First Innings | |
|---|---|---|
| CD Nash | c Mustard b Wiseman | 63 |
| RR Montgomerie | lbw b Styris | 21 |
| MH Yardy | c Mustard b Wiseman | 14 |
| MW Goodwin | c Benkenstein b Wiseman | 44 |
| CJ Adams (capt) | st Mustard b Wiseman | 193 |
| *AJ Hodd | lbw b Plunkett | 72 |
| RSC Martin-Jenkins | c Coetzer b Plunkett | 43 |
| LJ Wright | b Wiseman b Plunkett | 15 |
| Naved-ul-Hasan | c Mustard b Plunkett | 0 |
| Mushtaq Ahmed | not out | 9 |
| JD Lewry | absent hurt | |
| Extras | b 13, lb 8, w 4, nb 18 | 43 |
| | (all out 110 overs) | 517 |

**Bowling**
Gibson 23-3-87-0. Harmison SJ 5-0-14-0. Plunkett 26.5-5-123-4. Styris 15-2-77-1. Wiseman 27-3-124-4. Harmison BW 9-0-48-0. Benkenstein 4-0-15-0. Smith 1-0-8-0.
**Fall of Wickets:** 1-47, 2-107, 3-124, 4-197, 5-355, 6-477, 7-503, 8-504, 9-517

*Sussex won by an innings and 102 runs –*
*Sussex (22pts), Durham (4pts)*

### WARWICKSHIRE v. YORKSHIRE – at Edgbaston

| YORKSHIRE | First Innings | |
|---|---|---|
| JJ Sayers | c Barnes b Streak | 16 |
| MP Vaughan | c Powell b Tahir | 6 |
| A McGrath | not out | 188 |
| Younus Khan | b Tahir | 49 |
| JA Rudolph | c Bell b Anyon | 82 |
| C White | run out | 7 |
| *SM Guy | c Barnes b Streak | 0 |
| JN Gillespie | c Barnes b Tahir | 1 |
| D Gough (capt) | c Barnes b Tahir | 10 |
| MJ Hoggard | c Barnes b Streak | 30 |
| GJ Kruis | not out | 0 |
| Extras | lb 4, w 3, nb 4 | 11 |
| | (9 wkts dec 128.4 overs) | 400 |

**Bowling**
Anyon 25-6-102-1. Tahir 29-7-93-4. Streak 30.4-4-105-3. Maddy 7-2-30-0. Harris 27-6-44-0. Westwood 6-1-17-0. Troughton 4-1-5-0.
**Fall of Wickets:** 1-12, 2-24, 3-111, 4-286, 5-309, 6-310, 7-313, 8-325, 9-396

| WARWICKSHIRE | First Innings | |
|---|---|---|
| IJ Westwood | c Rudolph b Hoggard | 51 |
| DL Maddy (capt) | not out | 135 |
| IR Bell | c Kruis b Gillespie | 65 |
| JO Troughton | not out | 1 |
| MJ Powell | | |
| HH Streak | | |
| LC Parker | | |
| *MW Barnes | | |
| PL Harris | | |
| N Tahir | | |
| JE Anyon | | |
| Extras | lb 2 | 2 |
| | (2 wkts 57 overs) | 254 |

**Bowling**
Hoggard 10-2-43-1. Gough 6-4-12-0. Kruis 13-3-59-0. Gillespie 11-2-48-1. Younus Khan 7-0-36-0. Rudolph 5-0-18-0. McGrath 4-0-26-0. Vaughan 1-0-10-0.
**Fall of Wickets:** 1-103, 2-237

*Match drawn – Warwickshire (9pts),*
*Yorkshire (9pts)*

# RAIN STOPS PLAY

Time lost in County Championship cricket in 2007
by Andrew Hignell

I t was with a certain amount of irony that 2007, the wettest summer since records began, should see Lancashire – so often the victims of bad weather in Manchester – come so close to being crowned winners of Division One and a first outright title since 1934.

After a bold and record-breaking run chase on the final day of the first-class season, Lancashire ended a couple of dozen runs short of their mammoth target, as the title went to the South Coast where Sussex once again were the county to lose the least amount of time when playing at home.

But before the supporters of the Red Rose county bemoan the weather gods once more, the statistics below show that Sussex were also hit by the weather, especially when playing away from Hove – losing, in all during 2007, 44 per cent more playing time than average as record-breaking amounts of rain fell over the UK, particularly in midsummer.

To explain these above average amounts of precipitation, scientists have pointed to disturbances with the jet stream so that the high-pressure system, which is normally so dominant over the Bay of Biscay and Azores in midsummer, was unable to develop in its usual location. Instead, a series of rain-bearing, low-pressure systems – usually blocked out by the high pressure – were able to sweep in from the Atlantic, cutting a swathe across England and Wales.

Summer flooding hit the headlines for several weeks with the residents of the Severn Valley, as well as those living in the Thames and Don Valleys, severely affected. As far as county cricket was concerned, Worcestershire and Gloucestershire were among the hardest hit, with Worcestershire losing 13 entire days' play, home matches at New Road against Kent and Lancashire completely washed out, and fixtures transferred to Kidderminster, Himley and several 'neutral' venues loaned by other counties.

Gloucestershire lost the entire Cheltenham Festival – the oldest of the county circuit – and although they were able to transfer matches to their headquarters in Bristol, it was a huge blow to lose this festive occasion which is such a lucrative event for both the Cotswold town and the county alike.

As Table 1 below shows, Gloucestershire suffered a 40 per cent increase in 2007 in the amount of time lost in Championship cricket – a figure, though, that pales into insignificance when compared with the 78 per cent increase in lost time which afflicted Worcestershire.

## Table 1 – Time lost (in hours) in County Championship cricket 2007, relative to trends during the past ten years

| | Time lost in 2007 | Average 1998–2006 | +/- Average (%) |
|---|---|---|---|
| Derbyshire | 66.50 | 69.86 | - 5 |
| Durham | 53.50 | 65.33 | - 18 |
| Essex | 77.75 | 54.05 | +44 |
| Glamorgan | 84.75 | 70.77 | + 20 |
| Gloucestershire | 92.00 | 65.08 | + 41 |
| Hampshire | 105.75 | 67.58 | + 56 |
| Kent | 91.50 | 62.25 | + 47 |
| Lancashire | 88.25 | 75.58 | + 17 |
| Leicestershire | 104.25 | 77.64 | + 36 |
| Middlesex | 78.75 | 60.74 | + 29 |
| Northamptonshire | 61.25 | 62.67 | - 2 |
| Nottinghamshire | 70.50 | 70.88 | - 0.5 |
| Somerset | 70.25 | 66.78 | + 5 |
| Surrey | 82.00 | 64.47 | + 27 |
| Sussex | 71.75 | 49.94 | + 44 |
| Warwickshire | 94.50 | 65.94 | + 43 |
| Worcestershire | 124.25 | 69.64 | + 78 |
| Yorkshire | 97.25 | 65.81 | + 48 |

Several other counties had a significant increase in lost time, including Yorkshire, Warwickshire, Hampshire, Essex and Kent. But it wasn`t all doom and gloom as four others reported a below average amount of time lost in Championship matches. Three were in the East Midlands – Nottinghamshire, Derbyshire and Northamptonshire, while the fourth were Durham, who enjoyed their most successful season since their elevation to first-class status.

Table 1 also shows that Durham were the county to lose least time in Championship cricket during 2007. Supporters of the north-eastern county will no doubt be hoping that 2008 sees a repetition of these weather patterns, allowing Dale Benkenstein and his team to improve on their second place in Division One and to lift the Championship crown for the first time in the club's history.

For people living in the rain-soaked Severn Valley it will come as no surprise to discover that Worcestershire were the 'raining champions of 2007', losing 124.25 hours' play in Championship matches. They fared much better in one-day games, and after a sequence of wins in the NatWest Pro40 League, the New Road club were able to add this title to the rather more dubious one in the rainfall league.

## Table 2 – Total time lost (in hours) both home and away in County Championship matches in 2007

| | Home | Away | Total | Entire days lost |
|---|---|---|---|---|
| Derbyshire | 46.50 | 20.00 | 66.50 | 4 |
| Durham | 22.25 | 31.25 | 53.50 | 3 |
| Essex | 17.75 | 60.00 | 77.75 | 7 |
| Glamorgan | 67.75 | 17.00 | 84.75 | 10 |
| Gloucestershire | 37.75 | 54.25 | 92.00 | 9 |
| Hampshire | 58.25 | 47.50 | 105.75 | 9 |
| Kent | 28.50 | 63.00 | 91.50 | 9 |
| Lancashire | 37.00 | 51.25 | 88.25 | 10 |
| Leicestershire | 45.00 | 59.25 | 104.25 | 10 |
| Middlesex | 27.50 | 51.25 | 78.75 | 4 |
| Northamptonshire | 40.50 | 20.75 | 61.25 | 3 |
| Nottinghamshire | 46.50 | 24.00 | 70.50 | 6 |
| Somerset | 16.50 | 53.75 | 70.25 | 5 |
| Surrey | 58.00 | 24.00 | 82.00 | 4 |
| Sussex | 15.00 | 56.75 | 71.75 | 6 |
| Warwickshire | 61.50 | 33.00 | 94.50 | 7 |
| Worcestershire | 65.25 | 59.00 | 124.25 | 13 |
| Yorkshire | 58.25 | 39.00 | 97.25 | 8 |

**Above** There was a lot of sloshing about on waterlogged outfields during the wettest summer since records began.

**Below** Another familiar sight in the so-called summer of 2007 – a sea of umbrellas as crowds wait patiently for the rain to go away.

Fingers will no doubt be crossed in the Worcester area that Spring 2008 is kinder to the New Road ground, allowing the recently sown and partly re-laid square to recover after the deluges of 2007. Many other counties will also be hoping that the weather gods look more kindly on them next year.

As shown in Table 2, there were three counties lost ten entire days: Lancashire, Leicestershire and Glamorgan. The latter two had their Championship match at Abergavenny in July washed out – the first time that an entire four-day game in Wales has been lost to the weather.

Three other counties saw nine of their Championship days washed out, and they too will be hoping for drier conditions in 2008. But we have to end on a note of caution, as several climate scientists believe that the events of 2007 are a taste of what to expect more often in the future, as the overall British climate as well as the local microclimates become more variable and volatile as a result of global warming. Only time will tell whether the summer of 2007 was a damp blip in the rainfall records, or instead, was the start of warmer and wetter summers.

## Round Eleven: 13–16 July Division Two

```
NOTTINGHAMSHIRE v. GLOUCESTERSHIRE – at Trent Bridge

NOTTS          First Innings
JER Gallian    c Gidman b Kirby              45
SP Fleming (capt) c Hodnett b Edmondson      1
MA Wagh        c sub b Banerjee             74
SR Patel       run out                       2
DJ Hussey      c Marshall b Taylor         180
*CMW Read      c Kadeer Ali b Lewis         52
MA Ealham      c Adshead b Edmondson        23
GP Swann       c Edmondson b Taylor          0
KW Hogg        not out                      10
RS Ferley      not out                       2
SRG Francis
Extras         b 3, lb 3, w 1, nb 4         11
               (8 wkts dec 85.1 overs)     400

Bowling
Lewis 18.1-2-55-1. Edmondson 16-1-93-2. Kirby 17-5-63-1. Marshall 3-0-18-0.
Gidman 10-0-81-0. Banerjee 16-0-53-1. Taylor 5-0-31-2.
Fall of Wickets: 1-12, 2-84, 3-101, 4-170, 5-363, 6-364, 7-365, 8-398

GLOS           First Innings
V Banerjee     not out                       0
Kadeer Ali     not out                       0
CM Spearman
GP Hodnett
HJH Marshall
APR Gidman
CG Taylor
*SJ Adshead
J Lewis (capt)
SP Kirby
BM Edmondson
Extras                                       0
               (0 wkts 0.1 overs)            0

Bowling
Ealham 0.1-0-0-0.
```

*Match drawn – Nottinghamshire (9pts),*
*Gloucestershire (6pts)*

```
SOMERSET v. NORTHAMPTONSHIRE – at Taunton

NORTHANTS      First Innings                    Second Innings
SD Peters      c Trescothick b Willoughby  25   (2) lbw b Willoughby      1
CJL Rogers     lbw b Caddick                9   (1) lbw b Caddick         0
U Afzaal       lbw b Caddick                1   c White b Caddick        46
DJG Sales (capt) c Trescothick b Caddick   17   lbw b Willoughby         12
*MH Wessels    lbw b Jones                 37   (6) c Kieswetter b Jones 28
AG Wakely      b Trego                     38   (7) lbw b White          66
L Klusener     c Kieswetter b Jones         0   (8)c White b Caddick    122
SP Crook       c Kieswetter b White        60   (10) lbw b Willoughby     6
JJ van der Wath c Kieswetter b Trego        5   c Edwards b White        37
DS Lucas       not out                     10   (5) c White b Caddick     4
JF Brown       b White                      8   not out                   0
Extras         b 7, nb 4                   11   b 3, lb 17, w 2, nb 14   36
               (all out 61.3 overs)       221   (all out 97.1 overs)    358

Bowling
Caddick 19-3-70-3. Willoughby 14-6-53-1. Trego 14-1-58-2. Jones 11-4-24-2.
White 3.3-2-9-2.
Caddick 20-4-113-4. Willoughby 19-6-83-3. Jones 13-2-36-1. Blackwell 12-4-12-0.
White 16.1-2-55-2. Trego 8-1-39-0.
Fall of Wickets: 1-27, 2-33, 3-39, 4-66, 5-116, 6-116, 7-153, 8-183, 9-211
1-0, 2-10, 3-72, 4-80, 5-84, 6-120, 7-293, 8-343, 9-358

SOMERSET       First Innings                    Second Innings
ME Trescothick c Wessels b Wakely          146  not out                  69
NJ Edwards     b Brown                      96  c Peters b van der Wath  46
JL Langer (capt) c Wessels b Lucas          83
JC Hildreth    c Rogers b Wakely            51
CL White       c Lucas b van der Wath       37  (3) not out               6
ID Blackwell   c Wessels b Lucas             9
PD Trego       c Afzaal b van der Wath       2
*C Kieswetter  c Wessels b van der Wath      7
PS Jones       lbw b Lucas                   0
AR Caddick     b van der Wath                9
CM Willoughby  not out                       0
Extras         lb 5, w 4, nb 10             19  lb 3                      3
               (all out 100 overs)         459  (1 wkt 13.5 overs)      124

Bowling
van der Wath 24-2-91-4. Lucas 15-0-88-3. Crook 6-0-35-0. Brown 25-3-101-1.
Klusener 17-1-77-0. Wakely 13-1-62-2.
van der Wath 7-0-60-1. Lucas 2-0-23-0. Brown 4.5-0-38-0.
Fall of Wickets: 1-217, 2-303, 3-379, 4-407, 5-425, 6-430, 7-438, 8-443, 9-455
1-95
```

*Somerset won by 9 wickets –*
*Somerset (22pts), Northamptonshire (4pts)*

## Round Eleven: 13–16 July

Sizeable crowds gloried both in the sylvan Horsham setting and an emphatic Sussex win as Chris Adams's brutal 202-ball 193, with 23 fours and five sixes, and Mushtaq Ahmed's nine wickets in the match put paid to Durham, who were not helped when Steve Harmison broke down after just five overs with a hernia problem. Yorkshire's draw at Edgbaston, however, where there was no play on the first and third days, kept them above Sussex by a single point at the top of Division One. Yorkshire fielded eight Test players – one of whom, Anthony McGrath, scored a superb 188 – but Darren Maddy was replying in kind when time ran out.

Powerful batting kept up Somerset's promotion push as Northamptonshire could not prevent the second-division leaders from completing a nine-wicket win that also defied the unpredictable weather. Marcus Trescothick and Neil Edwards's first innings opening stand of 217 was a big deciding factor in the match, but the two burly left-handers also needed to produce a scintillating 95-run alliance in the second innings to whisk Somerset on the way to reaching a target of 121 in just 16 overs. Trescothick added 69 not out to his earlier 146 from 173 balls, while the equally impressive Edwards scored 96 from 131 balls and then a 42-ball 46 as victory was clinched with 13 balls to spare.

Alex Wakely, with 66 on debut, helped Lance Klusener to lead some brave Northants resistance after their second innings had slipped to 120 for 6, but ultimately it was their first innings batting display – allied to Somerset's top-order dominance – which made all the difference. At Trent Bridge, in a rain-ruined contest, there were celebrations for another powerful batsman, Nottinghamshire's Australian David Hussey, who became the first to reach 1,000 first-class runs for the season while savaging a 164-ball 180, with 17 fours and six sixes, off Gloucestershire's bowlers.

**Opposite** One that got away: Mushtaq Ahmed, who for the fifth summer in succession took more first-class wickets than any other bowler, appeals unsuccessfully for lbw against Durham's Ottis Gibson.

### Round Twelve: 20–23 July

A remarkable game at the Riverside ended with Hampshire holding out for a draw through the last 5.3 overs with just one second-innings wicket standing. That, though, was only a small part of the drama in a match which saw Ottis Gibson, the 38-year old Barbadian, become the 78th bowler to take all ten wickets in a first-class innings and Michael Brown, Hampshire's batting hero, almost become only the seventh man in cricket history to carry his bat throughout both innings.

Brown was unbeaten on 56 when Hampshire's first innings ended on 115, with Gibson taking two wickets in three balls following a rain break to earn himself

figures of 10 for 47 from 17.3 overs. 'I feel like I'm 16 again,' said the veteran fast bowler, who then took the first two Hampshire second-innings wickets to fall after Durham had batted again to set their visitors a win target of 359. Off-spinner Paul Wiseman picked up 5 for 65 but the 27-year-old Brown held firm again as partners came and went, eventually finishing up on 126 not out and, fittingly, even seeing off Gibson's final over of the match.

Rain, arriving at lunchtime on the last day, prevented a frustrated Kent from finishing off Warwickshire at Canterbury, although Darren Maddy's superb run of form continued as he fought for 404 minutes and 334 balls to score an unbeaten 148 and hold his team's

## Round Twelve: 20–23 July Division One

### YORKSHIRE v. SURREY – at Headingley

| YORKSHIRE | First Innings | | Second Innings | |
|---|---|---|---|---|
| C White | lbw b Nicholson | 6 | c Clarke b Nicholson | 2 |
| JJ Sayers | b Nicholson | 5 | not out | 0 |
| A McGrath | c Walters b Harbhajan Singh | 72 | not out | 0 |
| Younus Khan | c Newman b Clarke | 29 | | |
| JA Rudolph | lbw b Clarke | 4 | | |
| *GL Brophy | lbw b Nicholson | 22 | | |
| AU Rashid | not out | 91 | | |
| TT Bresnan | c Walters b Harbhajan Singh | 3 | | |
| JN Gillespie | c Walters b Harbhajan Singh | 3 | | |
| D Gough (capt) | b Saker | 28 | | |
| GJ Kruis | b Saker | 20 | | |
| Extras | b 7, lb 8, w 5, nb 4 | 24 | | 0 |
| | (all out 91.5 overs) | 307 | (1 wkt 1.1 overs) | 2 |

Bowling
Nicholson 24.5-5-85-4. Dernbach 10-3-28-0. Saker 10-3-42-1. Clarke 19-0-81-2. Harbhajan Singh 28-10-56-3.
Nicholson 1-0-2-1. Dernbach 0.1-0-0-0.
Fall of Wickets: 1-9, 2-24, 3-67, 4-75, 5-124, 6-191, 7-199, 8-203, 9-252 1-2

| SURREY | First Innings | |
|---|---|---|
| SA Newman | c Rudolph b Gough | 9 |
| *JN Batty | lbw b Gough | 5 |
| MR Ramprakash | c Brophy b McGrath | 59 |
| MA Butcher (capt) | c Brophy b Gough | 11 |
| SJ Walters | c Bresnan b Gillespie | 27 |
| R Clarke | c Rashid b Gough | 65 |
| RS Clinton | c Brophy b McGrath | 0 |
| MJ Nicholson | c Brophy b Gough | 1 |
| Harbhajan Singh | c Gillespie b Gough | 10 |
| NC Saker | not out | 6 |
| JW Dernbach | c Sayers b Rashid | 0 |
| Extras | b 2, lb 16, nb 18 | 36 |
| | (all out 77.1 overs) | 229 |

Bowling
Gillespie 16.4-4-52-1. Gough 21-6-50-6. Kruis 1.2-0-5-0. Bresnan 11-3-18-0. Rashid 20.1-2-64-1. McGrath 7-0-22-2.
Fall of Wickets: 1-11, 2-16, 3-40, 4-107, 5-161, 6-161, 7-173, 8-183, 9-220

*Match drawn – Yorkshire (10pts), Surrey (8pts)*

### KENT v. WARWICKSHIRE – at Canterbury

| KENT | First Innings | |
|---|---|---|
| JL Denly | c Ambrose b Tahir | 36 |
| RWT Key (capt) | c Loudon b Groenewald | 25 |
| M van Jaarsveld | c Maddy b Trott | 117 |
| JC Tredwell | lbw b Carter | 11 |
| DI Stevens | c Ambrose b Tahir | 6 |
| NJ Dexter | c Groenewald b Trott | 86 |
| *GO Jones | c sub b Harris | 105 |
| AJ Hall | run out | 2 |
| Yasir Arafat | not out | 101 |
| R McLaren | b Carter | 21 |
| SJ Cook | not out | 0 |
| Extras | b 3, lb 18, w 5, nb 14 | 40 |
| | (9 wkts dec 156 overs) | 550 |

Bowling
Carter 30-3-110-2. Daggett 20-6-62-0. Tahir 26-5-78-2. Groenewald 21-4-81-1. Harris 29-5-95-1. Maddy 10-5-13-0. Trott 12-4-33-2. Loudon 8-0-57-0.
Fall of Wickets: 1-49, 2-88, 3-106, 4-120, 5-292, 6-307, 7-317, 8-494, 9-543

| WARWICKSHIRE | First Innings | | Second Innings (following on) | |
|---|---|---|---|---|
| IJ Westwood | c Jones b Tredwell | 15 | c Jones b McLaren | 47 |
| DL Maddy | c Tredwell b McLaren | 23 | not out | 148 |
| PL Harris | c Jones b McLaren | 4 | | |
| IJL Trott | lbw b Cook | 0 | (3) c Jones b McLaren | 0 |
| JO Troughton | b McLaren | 0 | (7) c Jones b Hall | 31 |
| AGR Loudon | c Jones b McLaren | 4 | (4) c Hall b McLaren | 0 |
| *TR Ambrose | c Hall b Stevens | 13 | (5) c Dexter b Tredwell | 8 |
| TD Groenewald | b McLaren | 0 | (6) b Tredwell | 3 |
| N Tahir | c Yasir Arafat b Stevens | 2 | (8) lbw b Tredwell | 6 |
| NM Carter | c Yasir Arafat b Stevens | 2 | | |
| LM Daggett | not out | 6 | | |
| Extras | b 4, lb 5, nb 14 | 23 | b 4, lb 8, w 3, nb 10 | 25 |
| | (all out 36.3 overs) | 107 | (7 wkts 109.2 overs) | 268 |

Bowling
Yasir Arafat 4-1-13-0. Hall 8-1-37-1. Cook 9-2-19-1. McLaren 11-4-24-5. Tredwell 1-1-0-1. Stevens 3.3-2-5-2.
McLaren 23-6-46-3. Hall 27-3-49, 4-51, 5-61, 6-70, 7-82, 8-91, 9-95 Stevens 7-3-8-0. van Jaarsveld 4-2-5-0. Denly 2-2-0-0.
Fall of Wickets: 1-41, 2-43, 3-49, 4-51, 5-61, 6-70, 7-82, 8-91, 9-95 1-122, 2-124, 3-124, 4-141, 5-145, 6-235, 7-268

*Match drawn – Kent (12pts), Warwickshire (6pts)*

### DURHAM v. HAMPSHIRE – at the Riverside

| DURHAM | First Innings | | Second Innings | |
|---|---|---|---|---|
| WR Smith | c Pothas b Mascarenhas | 3 | c Pothas b Warne | 48 |
| MD Stoneman | lbw b Mascarenhas | 2 | lbw b Udal | 50 |
| KJ Coetzer | c Pothas b Mascarenhas | 9 | b Griffiths | 26 |
| SB Styris | c Brown b Mascarenhas | 2 | (5) b Griffiths | 17 |
| DM Benkenstein (capt) | b Griffiths | 114 | (6) not out | 29 |
| *P Mustard | c Warne b Griffiths | 5 | (7) not out | 35 |
| BW Harmison | lbw b Carberry | 66 | | |
| OD Gibson | lbw b Bruce | 28 | | |
| LE Plunkett | c Lumb b Griffiths | 6 | (4) st Pothas b Warne | 12 |
| PJ Wiseman | c Pothas b Griffiths | 2 | | |
| G Onions | not out | 0 | | |
| Extras | b 5, lb 1, w 1, p 5 | 12 | b 1, w 1, nb 2 | 4 |
| | (all out 93.4 overs) | 252 | (5 wkts dec 51 overs) | 221 |

Bowling
Bruce 22-5-55-1. Mascarenhas 23-8-33-4. Griffiths 19.4-4-46-4. Udal 9-1-21-0. Warne 17-2-73-0. Carberry 3-0-13-1.
Mascarenhas 8-3-25-0. Bruce 11-1-52-0. Griffiths 16-2-78-2. Warne 14-1-56-2. Udal 2-0-9-1.
Fall of Wickets: 1-2, 2-5, 3-29, 4-5, 5-29, 6-185, 7-237, 8-245, 9-247 1-95, 2-107, 3-136, 4-140, 5-175

| HAMPSHIRE | First Innings | | Second Innings | |
|---|---|---|---|---|
| MA Carberry | c Harmison b Gibson | 4 | c Plunkett b Gibson | 4 |
| MJ Brown | not out | 56 | not out | 126 |
| JP Crawley | c Mustard b Gibson | 6 | lbw b Gibson | 12 |
| MJ Lumb | lbw b Gibson | 16 | lbw b Onions | 28 |
| CC Benham | b Gibson | 0 | b Wiseman | 3 |
| *N Pothas | b Gibson | 2 | run out | 0 |
| AD Mascarenhas | c Mustard b Gibson | 8 | c Coetzer b Wiseman | 8 |
| SK Warne (capt) | c Mustard b Gibson | 1 | c Stoneman b Wiseman | 50 |
| SD Udal | c Mustard b Gibson | 4 | c Coetzer b Wiseman | 4 |
| DA Griffiths | b Gibson | 3 | (11) not out | 0 |
| JTA Bruce | b Gibson | 0 | (10) c Smith b Wiseman | 0 |
| Extras | lb 4, nb 12 | 16 | b 4, lb 10, nb 12 | 26 |
| | (all out 35.3 overs) | 115 | (9 wkts 75 overs) | 262 |

Bowling
Onions 5-1-14-0. Gibson 17.3-1-47-10. Styris 7-1-24-0. Benkenstein 6-1-26-0.
Onions 15-3-71-1. Gibson 20-3-53-2. Plunkett 18-2-59-0. Wiseman 22-4-65-5. Udal 2-0-9-1.
Fall of Wickets: 1-13, 2-29, 3-65, 4-67, 5-67, 6-81, 7-85, 8-89, 9-115 1-21, 2-39, 3-100, 4-121, 5-121, 6-157, 7-241, 8-252, 9-252

*Match drawn – Durham (9pts), Hampshire (7pts)*

### WORCESTERSHIRE v. LANCASHIRE – at New Road

*Match abandoned – Worcestershire (4pts), Lancashire (4pts)*

## Round Twelve: 20–23 July Division Two

### SOMERSET v. ESSEX – at Taunton

| ESSEX | First Innings | | Second Innings | |
|---|---|---|---|---|
| V Chopra | lbw b Willoughby | 44 | c Kieswetter b Caddick | 0 |
| ML Pettini (capt) | b White | 73 | lbw b Jones | 14 |
| RS Bopara | c Trego b Caddick | 69 | c Willoughby b Blackwell | 126 |
| GW Flower | b Caddick | 0 | lbw b Willoughby | 7 |
| *JS Foster | lbw b Trego | 1 | c Langer b Blackwell | 71 |
| RN ten Doeschate | c Kieswetter b Jones | 24 | c Bresnan b Blackwell | 45 |
| JD Middlebrook | c Caddick b White | 24 | not out | 29 |
| AJ Bichel | c Kieswetter b Jones | 19 | not out | 5 |
| GR Napier | not out | 8 | | |
| AJ Tudor | lbw b White | 1 | | |
| AP Palladino | lbw b White | 0 | | |
| Extras | b 1, lb 7, w 1, nb 10 | 19 | lb 7 | 7 |
| | (all out 84.5 overs) | 282 | (6 wkts 76 overs) | 294 |

Bowling
Caddick 22-3-51-2. Willoughby 17-1-59-1. Blackwell 4-0-16-0. Trego 15-5-39-1. Jones 17-0-81-2. White 9.5-2-28-4.
Caddick 10-1-33-1. Jones 9-2-36-1. Willoughby 10-3-55-1. Trego 2-0-9-0. White 22-2-76-0. Blackwell 23-0-78-3.
Fall of Wickets: 1-59, 2-152, 3-185, 4-188, 5-221, 6-235, 7-269, 8-275, 9-282 1-2, 2-30, 3-61, 4-202, 5-237, 6-271

| SOMERSET | First Innings | |
|---|---|---|
| MJ Wood | lbw b Bichel | 20 |
| NJ Edwards | lbw b Palladino | 5 |
| JL Langer (capt) | lbw b Bichel | 24 |
| JC Hildreth | c Foster b Bichel | 38 |
| CL White | c Foster b Bichel | 1 |
| ID Blackwell | c Bopara b Tudor | 15 |
| PD Trego | b Napier | 20 |
| *C Kieswetter | c Flower b Bichel | 0 |
| PS Jones | c Foster b Bichel | 4 |
| AR Caddick | c Middlebrook b Napier | 8 |
| CM Willoughby | not out | 0 |
| Extras | lb 14, nb 4 | 18 |
| | (all out 35.1 overs) | 153 |

Bowling
Bichel 18-5-63-6. Palladino 8-1-38-1. Tudor 7-1-27-1. Napier 2.1-0-11-2.
Fall of Wickets: 1-12, 2-45, 3-76, 4-90, 5-115, 6-123, 7-125, 8-133, 9-134

*Match drawn – Somerset (7pts), Essex (9pts)*

### LEICESTERSHIRE v. MIDDLESEX – at Leicester

| LEICESTERSHIRE | First Innings | |
|---|---|---|
| TJ New | lbw b Murtagh | 56 |
| JK Maunders | st Scott b Dalrymple | 97 |
| HD Ackerman | lbw b Richardson | 118 |
| A Jacobs | c Scott b Vaas | 55 |
| J Allenby | not out | 38 |
| MC Rosenberg | st Scott b Murtagh | 17 |
| *PA Nixon (capt) | c Scott b Murtagh | 4 |
| Mansoor Amjad | | |
| DD Masters | | |
| SCJ Broad | | |
| GJP Kruger | | |
| Extras | lb 2, nb 16 | 18 |
| | (5 wkts dec 91 overs) | 403 |

Bowling
Vaas 15-2-87-1. Silverwood 20-3-95-0. Richardson 21-2-82-1. Murtagh 12-3-66-2. Dalrymple 14-1-43-1. Shah 9-3-28-0.
Fall of Wickets: 1-104, 2-207, 3-336, 4-368, 5-399

| MIDDLESEX | First Innings | |
|---|---|---|
| BA Godleman | not out | 7 |
| NRD Compton | b Broad | 1 |
| OA Shah | not out | 23 |
| EC Joyce | | |
| ET Smith (capt) | | |
| JWM Dalrymple | | |
| *BJM Scott | | |
| WPUJC Vaas | | |
| TJ Murtagh | | |
| A Richardson | | |
| CEW Silverwood | | |
| Extras | lb 1, nb 2 | 3 |
| | (1 wkt 9.4 overs) | 34 |

Bowling
Broad 5-1-23-1. Masters 4.4-1-10-0.
Fall of Wickets: 1-7

*Match drawn – Leicestershire (9pts), Middlesex (5pts)*

### DERBYSHIRE v. GLAMORGAN – at Derby

| GLAMORGAN | First Innings | | Second Innings | |
|---|---|---|---|---|
| JP Maher | lbw b Wagg | 16 | lbw b Lungley | 3 |
| GP Rees | lbw b Botha | 51 | lbw b Lungley | 19 |
| RE Watkins | c Redfern b Smith | 2 | (4) c Katich b Smith | 12 |
| BJ Wright | c Birt b Lungley | 2 | (8) lbw b Dean | 4 |
| DL Hemp (capt) | c Dighton b Lungley | 97 | lbw b Dean | 1 |
| RN Grant | lbw b Botha | 17 | lbw b Dean | 5 |
| *MA Wallace | c Birt b Lungley | 20 | c Poynton b Dean | 1 |
| AG Wharf | b Wagg | 14 | (9) c Dighton b Lungley | 5 |
| RDB Croft | c Et b Botha | 24 | (10) b Smith | 17 |
| JAR Harris | c Birt b Smith | 21 | (11) not out | 18 |
| AP Davies | not out | 1 | (3) c Dighton b Dean | 10 |
| Extras | lb 10, w 3, nb 20 | 33 | b 9, lb 3, w 8, nb 12 | 32 |
| | (all out 99 overs) | 298 | (all out 49.1 overs) | 127 |

Bowling
Lungley 21-4-67-3. Wagg 20-5-67-2. Smith 20-7-51-2. Dean 6-3-6-0. Botha 23-6-64-3. Redfern 9-1-33-0.
Lungley 13-5-40-3. Wagg 8-2-19-0. Smith 10-1-6-16-2. Botha 5-1-16-0. Dean 13-2-24-5.
Fall of Wickets: 1-29, 2-34, 3-46, 4-107, 5-161, 6-202, 7-239, 8-247, 9-296 1-19, 2-29, 3-62, 4-64, 5-70, 6-72, 7-76, 8-77, 9-85

| DERBYSHIRE | First Innings | | Second Innings | |
|---|---|---|---|---|
| SD Stubbings | b Croft | 41 | (2) c Grant b Croft | 25 |
| TR Birt | c Wallace b Davies | 11 | (1) c Et b Croft | 70 |
| MG Dighton | c Wallace b Wharf | 43 | c Wright b Croft | 0 |
| SM Katich (capt) | not out | 42 | c Wright b Croft | 3 |
| GM Smith | not out | 1 | c Watkins b Croft | 1 |
| DJ Redfern | | | b Harris | 15 |
| AG Botha | | | c Maher b Davies | 12 |
| GG Wagg | | | not out | 48 |
| *TJ Poynton | | | b Davies | 2 |
| T Lungley | | | c Wright b Croft | 0 |
| KJ Dean | | | not out | 0 |
| Extras | b 4, lb 1, w 1, nb 6 | 12 | b 1, lb 6, w 1, nb 8 | 16 |
| | (3 wkts dec 30.3 overs) | 150 | (9 wkts 46 overs) | 195 |

Bowling
Harris 11-3-24-0. Davies 6-1-41-1. Croft 3-0-12-1. Wharf 2-0-4-0. Watkins 6.3-0-41-0.
Harris 11-1-49-1. Davies 9-3-43-2. Wharf 7-0-52-0. Croft 19-5-44-6.
Fall of Wickets: 1-12, 2-78, 3-146 1-84, 2-84, 3-95, 4-115, 5-129, 6-131, 7-170, 8-178, 9-195

*Match drawn – Derbyshire (7pts), Glamorgan (7pts)*

second innings together. Only two overs were possible on day two as Yorkshire and Surrey drew at Headingley, with Darren Gough producing his best figures on the ground and Mark Ramprakash becoming the first Englishman to reach 1,000 first-class runs for the season. Worcestershire's match against Lancashire at New Road became the second four-day fixture there to be abandoned without a ball bowled, with the area around Worcester also now under an official flood warning from the Environment Agency.

In Division Two, Derbyshire just managed to deny Robert Croft and hang on for a draw, after initially having a dart at a target of 276, but there was no sign of any attempts to reach a positive result at either Grace Road or Taunton where bad weather also caused major disruptions.

### Round Thirteen: 25–29 July

Rain again badly affected this round of matches, with all three first-division fixtures ending in draws and Somerset's crushing 278-run victory at Derbyshire being the only result in Division Two. Glamorgan's match against Leicestershire at lovely Abergavenny was completely washed out.

Mark Ramprakash's 233-ball 142 against Worcestershire at Guildford, featuring 14 fours and three sixes, was his 93rd first-class hundred, and there were quality centuries in the other Division One games for John Crawley, Phil Jaques, Anthony McGrath and Joe Denly, whose 114 at Scarborough was his fourth at first-class level in just his 24th innings. Younus Khan, meanwhile, turned his hundred in the same game into a majestic unbeaten 217, with 18 fours and six sixes.

Charl Willoughby's 4 for 12 was chiefly responsible for undermining Derbyshire at Derby, where the home side disintegrated to 52 all out in a sad second innings, while there was no play for the first three days at Bristol. After a washed-out opening day at Trent Bridge, the bat dominated the ball with Stephen Fleming scoring 100 out of 162 for Nottinghamshire and Mark Wagh reaching 152.

Ottis Gibson became the 78th bowler in cricket history to take all ten wickets in an innings when he single-handedly ran through Hampshire at the Riverside. It was the undoubted highlight of a magnificent season for the 38-year-old all-rounder.

## Round Thirteen: 25–29 July Division One

### YORKSHIRE v. KENT – at Scarborough

| KENT | First Innings | | Second Innings | |
|---|---|---|---|---|
| JL Denly | b Rashid | 114 | not out | 11 |
| RWT Key (capt) | c Brophy b Bresnan | 21 | not out | 6 |
| M van Jaarsveld | c Brophy b Bresnan | 5 | | |
| JC Tredwell | lbw b Gough | 44 | | |
| DI Stevens | lbw b Rashid | 87 | | |
| NJ Dexter | c Brophy b Bresnan | 55 | | |
| *GO Jones | c Brophy b Rashid | 43 | | |
| AJ Hall | c Rudolph b Bresnan | 18 | | |
| R McLaren | c Brophy b Rashid | 17 | | |
| SJ Cook | not out | 50 | | |
| MJ Saggers | c Bresnan b Rashid | 11 | | |
| Extras | b 1, lb 12, nb 8 | 21 | | 0 |
| | (all out 124.3 overs) | 486 | (0 wkts 10 overs) | 17 |

**Bowling**
Gough 28-7-81-1. Gillespie 20-5-55-0. Rashid 23.3-1-112-5. Bresnan 35-7-140-4. McGrath 7-3-10-0. Lawson 7-0-54-0. Younus Khan 4-0-21-0.
Gough 3-2-1-0. Rashid 5-3-5-0. Lawson 2-0-11-0.
**Fall of Wickets:** 1-56, 2-66, 3-149, 4-263, 5-294, 6-352, 7-386, 8-419, 9-426

| YORKSHIRE | First Innings | |
|---|---|---|
| C White | c Jones b Cook | 49 |
| JJ Sayers | c Jones b Hall | 4 |
| A McGrath | c Jones b McLaren | 120 |
| Younus Khan | not out | 217 |
| JA Rudolph | c Tredwell b McLaren | 0 |
| *GL Brophy | c van Jaarsveld b McLaren | 43 |
| AU Rashid | c van Jaarsveld b McLaren | 0 |
| TT Bresnan | c Stevens b Dexter | 58 |
| D Gough (capt) | c Dexter b van Jaarsveld | 17 |
| MAK Lawson | c Key b van Jaarsveld | 5 |
| JN Gillespie | not out | 5 |
| Extras | b 4, lb 10, w 2, nb 16 | 32 |
| | (9 wkts dec 144.5 overs) | 550 |

**Bowling**
McLaren 28-7-89-4. Saggers 29-7-83-0. Hall 7-3-9-1. Cook 18-2-76-1. Stevens 16-4-72-0. Tredwell 17-5-96-0. Dexter 4-0-35-1. Denly 6-0-35-0. Key 6-0-27-0. van Jaarsveld 5.5-0-37-2.
**Fall of Wickets:** 1-17, 2-150, 3-262, 4-262, 5-354, 6-356, 7-479, 8-499, 9-513

*Match drawn – Yorkshire (12pts),
Kent (11pts)*

### SURREY v. WORCESTERSHIRE – at Guildford

| SURREY | First Innings | |
|---|---|---|
| SA Newman | b Batty | 32 |
| *JN Batty | c Sillence b Batty | 45 |
| MR Ramprakash | c Davies b Batty | 142 |
| MA Butcher (capt) | c Davies b Kabir Ali | 46 |
| SJ Walters | b Nel | 30 |
| R Clarke | c Solanki b Kabir Ali | 14 |
| RS Clinton | lbw b Kabir Ali | 0 |
| CP Schofield | c Hick b Sillence | 10 |
| MJ Nicholson | not out | 12 |
| Harbhajan Singh | c Batty b Batty | 14 |
| NC Saker | c Batty b Kabir Ali | 1 |
| Extras | lb 8, nb 15 | 23 |
| | (all out 106.4 overs) | 369 |

**Bowling**
Bollinger 22.7-57-0. Kabir Ali 29.4-3-104-4. Nel 12-1-57-1. Batty 33-6-101-4. Sillence 9-1-37-1. Solanki 1-0-5-0.
**Fall of Wickets:** 1-81, 2-104, 3-202, 4-260, 5-290, 6-304, 7-342, 8-342, 9-366

| WORCS | First Innings | | Second Innings (following on) | |
|---|---|---|---|---|
| PA Jaques | c Batty b Nicholson | 3 | c Batty b Harbhajan Singh | 103 |
| SC Moore | c Walters b Harbhajan Singh | 31 | c Clinton b Harbhajan Singh | 55 |
| VS Solanki (capt) | c Clarke b Nicholson | 13 | c Clarke b Harbhajan Singh | 11 |
| BF Smith | c Clarke b Harbhajan Singh | 15 | c Clarke b Harbhajan Singh | 66 |
| GA Hick | c Batty b Nicholson | 30 | c Clarke b Harbhajan Singh | 4 |
| *SM Davies | c Clarke b Harbhajan Singh | 58 | not out | 38 |
| GJ Batty | c Butcher b Harbhajan Singh | 18 | not out | 15 |
| RJ Sillence | b Saker | 6 | | |
| Kabir Ali | lbw b Schofield | 21 | | |
| DE Bollinger | b Schofield | 8 | | |
| JD Nel | not out | 2 | | |
| Extras | b 7, lb 3, nb 2 | 12 | b 8, lb 7 | 15 |
| | (all out 71.3 overs) | 217 | (5 wkts 98 overs) | 307 |

**Bowling**
Nicholson 14-4-43-3. Clarke 4-0-23-0. Saker 10-3-33-1. Harbhajan Singh 29-7-64-4. Schofield 14.3-1-44-2.
Nicholson 18-2-60-0. Clarke 9-0-31-0. Harbhajan Singh 34-12-64-5. Saker 13-3-50-0. Schofield 24-1-87-0.
**Fall of Wickets:** 1-12, 2-30, 3-49, 4-90, 5-98, 6-141, 7-148, 8-187, 9-211
1-94, 2-118, 3-230, 4-238, 5-261

*Match drawn – Surrey (11pts),
Worcestershire (8pts)*

### HAMPSHIRE v. SUSSEX – at the Rose Bowl

| SUSSEX | First Innings | | Second Innings | |
|---|---|---|---|---|
| CD Nash | c Lumb b Bruce | 0 | lbw b Bruce | 7 |
| RR Montgomerie | c Benham b Powell | 46 | c Warne b Powell | 2 |
| MH Yardy | c Pothas b Bruce | 1 | c Pothas b Mascarenhas | 1 |
| MW Goodwin | lbw b Bruce | 19 | not out | 68 |
| CJ Adams (capt) | c Warne b Powell | 1 | lbw b Powell | 38 |
| *AJ Hodd | b Warne | 9 | not out | 8 |
| RSC Martin-Jenkins | c Lumb b Griffiths | 6 | | |
| LJ Wright | c Bruce b Powell | 43 | | |
| Naved-ul-Hasan | run out | 4 | | |
| Mushtaq Ahmed | c Griffiths b Bruce | 5 | | |
| JD Lewry | not out | 5 | | |
| Extras | lb 2, nb 4 | 6 | b 1, lb 1 | 2 |
| | (all out 40.3 overs) | 145 | (4 wkts 37 overs) | 124 |

**Bowling**
Powell 13.3-4-46-3. Bruce 18-3-64-5. Griffiths 7-0-31-1. Mascarenhas 2-1-2-0.
Powell 11-1-32-2. Bruce 9-4-14-1. Mascarenhas 7-0-25-1. Griffiths 3-0-15-0. Warne 7-0-36-0.
**Fall of Wickets:** 1-1, 2-7, 3-29, 4-30, 5-43, 6-64, 7-111, 8-115, 9-125
1-3, 2-8, 3-21, 4-110

| HAMPSHIRE | First Innings | |
|---|---|---|
| MA Carberry | lbw b Naved-ul-Hasan | 20 |
| MJ Brown | b Lewry | 0 |
| JP Crawley | not out | 113 |
| MJ Lumb | c Hodd b Martin-Jenkins | 22 |
| CC Benham | lbw b Mushtaq Ahmed | 31 |
| *N Pothas | c Adams b Naved-ul-Hasan | 9 |
| AD Mascarenhas | b Naved-ul-Hasan | 0 |
| SK Warne (capt) | st Hodd b Mushtaq Ahmed | 15 |
| DB Powell | c Goodwin b Naved-ul-Hasan | 11 |
| DA Griffiths | lbw b Naved-ul-Hasan | 4 |
| JTA Bruce | not out | 0 |
| Extras | lb 15, nb 10 | 25 |
| | (9 wkts dec 58.4 overs) | 250 |

**Bowling**
Lewry 8-2-37-1. Naved-ul-Hasan 19.4-7-106-5. Martin-Jenkins 11-4-27-1. Wright 6.2-1-11-0. Mushtaq Ahmed 13.4-1-54-2.
**Fall of Wickets:** 1-3, 2-39, 3-82, 4-150, 5-165, 6-165, 7-198, 8-235, 9-249

*Match drawn – Hampshire (9pts),
Sussex (7pts)*

## Round Thirteen: 25–29 July Division Two

### DERBYSHIRE v. SOMERSET – at Derby

| SOMERSET | First Innings | | Second Innings | |
|---|---|---|---|---|
| ME Trescothick | c Pipe b Lungley | 18 | not out | 32 |
| NJ Edwards | c Pipe b Botha | 94 | c Dighton b Dean | 5 |
| JL Langer (capt) | c Wagg b Botha | 22 | lbw b Botha | 17 |
| JC Hildreth | c sub b Redfern | 13 | lbw b Redfern | 16 |
| CL White | c Pipe b Botha | 7 | not out | 4 |
| ID Blackwell | lbw b Botha | 30 | | |
| PD Trego | c Katich b Smith | 56 | | |
| *C Kieswetter | not out | 52 | | |
| AR Caddick | c Wagg b Botha | 5 | | |
| MK Munday | c Key b Botha | 0 | | |
| CM Willoughby | c Pipe b Botha | 9 | | |
| Extras | b 1, lb 11, w 2, nb 20 | 34 | b 6, nb 4 | 10 |
| | (all out 77.2 overs) | 340 | (3 wkts dec 20 overs) | 84 |

**Bowling**
Lungley 10-1-57-1. Wagg 12-3-65-1. Dean 14-4-32-0. Smith 14-1-66-1. Botha 22.2-2-101-6. Redfern 5-2-7-1.
Dean 5-0-22-1. Wagg 4-0-26-0. Smith 5-2-11-0. Botha 5-0-11-1. Redfern 1-0-8-1.
**Fall of Wickets:** 1-78, 2-140, 3-155, 4-169, 5-180, 6-268, 7-268, 8-296, 9-298
1-29, 2-57, 3-80

| DERBYSHIRE | First Innings | | Second Innings | |
|---|---|---|---|---|
| TR Birt | lbw b Willoughby | 8 | (3) b Willoughby | 4 |
| SD Stubbings | c Edwards b Blackwell | 14 | (1) lbw b Willoughby | 1 |
| MG Dighton | c not out | 36 | (4) c Trescothick b Caddick | 0 |
| SM Katich (capt) | not out | 29 | (5) b Willoughby | 1 |
| KJ Dean | | | (2) c Munday b Willoughby | 2 |
| GM Smith | | | c Langer b Blackwell | 6 |
| DJ Redfern | | | c Kieswetter b Caddick | 6 |
| AG Botha | | | c Hildreth b Blackwell | 21 |
| *DJ Pipe | | | c Kieswetter b White | 1 |
| GG Wagg | | | lbw b Blackwell | 0 |
| T Lungley | lbw 7 | | not out | 2 |
| Extras | | 7 | lb 4, w 2, nb 2 | 8 |
| | (2 wkts dec 31 overs) | 94 | (all out 27.5 overs) | 52 |

**Bowling**
Caddick 9-2-19-0. Blackwell 10-2-27-1. Willoughby 5-3-8-1. Munday 4-0-32-0. Trego 3-2-1-0.
Caddick 11-3-25-2. Blackwell 3.5-1-8-3. Willoughby 9-5-12-4. White 4-2-3-1.
**Fall of Wickets:** 1-15, 2-38
1-4, 2-11, 3-11, 4-13, 5-13, 6-24, 7-43, 8-50, 9-50

*Somerset won by 278 runs – Derbyshire (3pts),
Somerset (17pts)*

### GLOUCESTERSHIRE v. ESSEX – at Bristol

| GLOS | First Innings | |
|---|---|---|
| CM Spearman | b Palladino | 5 |
| Kadeer Ali | c Foster b Bichel | 0 |
| GP Hodnett | c Flower b Bopara | 24 |
| HJH Marshall | c Foster b Bichel | 1 |
| APR Gidman | c Middlebrook b Bichel | 10 |
| CG Taylor | c Foster b Bopara | 101 |
| MA Hardinges | c Foster b Bichel | 5 |
| *SJ Adshead | c Bopara b Bichel | 11 |
| J Lewis (capt) | c Middlebrook b Bichel | 1 |
| SP Kirby | c Bichel b Middlebrook | 4 |
| BM Edmondson | not out | 6 |
| Extras | lb 6, w 4, nb 6 | 16 |
| | (all out 55.3 overs) | 184 |

**Bowling**
Bichel 19-6-55-5. Palladino 7-2-21-1. Bopara 16.3-4-60-3. Napier 7-0-27-0. Middlebrook 6-0-15-1.
**Fall of Wickets:** 1-5, 2-5, 3-7, 4-23, 5-81, 6-88, 7-115, 8-122, 9-149

| ESSEX | First Innings | |
|---|---|---|
| ML Pettini (capt) | c Adshead b Kirby | 7 |
| JD Middlebrook | c Kadeer Ali b Kirby | 13 |
| V Chopra | c Edmondson b Lewis | 33 |
| RS Bopara | c Adshead b Kirby | 6 |
| GW Flower | b Kirby | 8 |
| *JS Foster | c Spearman b Hardinges | 3 |
| RN ten Doeschate | c Hodnett b Hardinges | 1 |
| T Westley | not out | 16 |
| AJ Bichel | not out | 22 |
| GR Napier | | |
| AP Palladino | | |
| Extras | lb 2, nb 2 | 4 |
| | (7 wkts 37.3 overs) | 129 |

**Bowling**
Lewis 8-1-23-1. Kirby 12-3-33-4. Edmondson 8-1-40-0. Hardinges 4-0-12-2. Taylor 3-0-9-0. Hodnett 2.3-0-10-0.
**Fall of Wickets:** 1-7, 2-22, 3-32, 4-44, 5-88, 6-89, 7-89

*Match drawn – Gloucestershire (4pts),
Essex (4pts)*

### NORTHAMPTONSHIRE v. NOTTINGHAMSHIRE – at Northampton

| NORTHANTS | First Innings | | Second Innings | |
|---|---|---|---|---|
| SD Peters | st Read b Swann | 54 | c Read b Harris | 8 |
| CJL Rogers | c Kadeer b Ealham | 7 | not out | 58 |
| DJG Sales (capt) | b Ealham | 59 | c Fleming b Harris | 1 |
| AG Wakely | b Ealham | 55 | c Fleming b Swann | 4 |
| RA White | c Read b Harris | 46 | not out | 74 |
| *MH Wessels | b Ealham | 32 | | |
| L Klusener | c Ealham b Swann | 0 | | |
| JJ van der Wath | not out | 59 | | |
| DS Lucas | c Wagh b Swann | 33 | | |
| RJ Logan | c Fleming b Harris | 4 | | |
| JF Brown | c Patel b Swann | 3 | | |
| Extras | b 7, lb 4, w 1, nb 2 | 14 | lb 2, nb 4, p 5 | 11 |
| | (all out 132 overs) | 366 | (3 wkts 42 overs) | 152 |

**Bowling**
Harris 34-10-106-2. Ealham 31-13-43-4. Hogg 16-5-49-0. Swann 36-6-90-4. Ferley 15-1-68-0.
Harris 11-2-39-3. Hogg 10-2-30-0. Swann 11-2-36-0. Ferley 9-2-40-0.
**Fall of Wickets:** 1-14, 2-111, 3-134, 4-205, 5-259, 6-260, 7-262, 8-331, 9-347
1-12, 2-16, 3-18

| NOTTS | First Innings | |
|---|---|---|
| JER Gallian | b van der Wath | 18 |
| SP Fleming (capt) | st Wessels b Brown | 100 |
| MA Wagh | c Wessels b van der Wath | 152 |
| SR Patel | c Peters b Brown | 54 |
| DJ Hussey | st Wessels b Wakely | 37 |
| RS Ferley | b van der Wath | 40 |
| *CMW Read | c Klusener b Logan | 38 |
| MA Ealham | retired hurt | 25 |
| KW Hogg | c Sales b Brown | 26 |
| GP Swann | c White b Logan | 2 |
| AJ Harris | not out | 2 |
| Extras | b 2, lb 11, w 8, nb 10 | 31 |
| | (all out 113.3 overs) | 526 |

**Bowling**
Lucas 11-0-55-0. van der Wath 21-4-90-3. Brown 36-3-122-3. Klusener 13-3-65-0. Logan 12.3-0-91-2. Wakely 16-0-65-1. White 4-0-25-0.
**Fall of Wickets:** 1-50, 2-162, 3-273, 4-327, 5-420, 6-433, 7-511, 8-522, 9-526

*Match drawn – Northamptonshire (11pts),
Nottinghamshire (12pts)*

### GLAMORGAN v. LEICESTERSHIRE – at Abergavenny

*Match abandoned – Glamorgan (4pts), Leicestershire (4pts)*

## Round Fourteen: 31 July–3 August

As the weather improved for a while, Kyle Coetzer's dedicated seven-and-a-half-hour 142 helped Durham to put themselves into a winning position against Warwickshire at the Riverside. Ben Harmison also more than did his bit, with a 242-ball 101, but Warwickshire battled hard for survival in their second innings – with Ian Westwood and Kumar Sangakkara both reaching three figures – before the home side made short work of a last-day target. Phil Mustard's 58-ball 76 made sure they would not be short of time, and Michael Di Venuto's 91 not out rounded off an excellent team performance in which the bowling of Liam Plunkett, Ottis Gibson and Paul Wiseman were other important factors.

In the other first division match Sussex won themselves a vital 108-run triumph against title rivals Lancashire at Liverpool, where fine crowds turned out

In Murali Kartik, the Indian slow left-arm spinner, Middlesex had one of the best overseas signings of the season.

## Round Fourteen: 31 July–3 August Division One

### LANCASHIRE v. SUSSEX – at Liverpool

| SUSSEX | First Innings | | Second Innings | |
|---|---|---|---|---|
| CD Nash | lbw b Chapple | 75 | c Sutton b Cork | 0 |
| RR Montgomerie | c Croft b Chapple | 12 | c Flintoff b Chapple | 1 |
| MH Yardy | c Law b Cork | 47 | c Sutton b Cork | 52 |
| MW Goodwin | not out | 74 | c Flintoff b Chapple | 68 |
| CJ Adams (capt) | c & b Muralitharan | 2 | c Mahmood b Muralitharan | 42 |
| CD Hopkinson | c Law b Muralitharan | 8 | lbw b Muralitharan | 32 |
| *AJ Hodd | b Chapple | 4 | c Chapple b Mahmood | 10 |
| RSC Martin-Jenkins | c Croft b Muralitharan | 8 | c Croft b Mahmood | 17 |
| Naved-ul-Hasan | b Muralitharan | 1 | not out | 21 |
| Mushtaq Ahmed | b Muralitharan | 8 | c Loye b Muralitharan | 0 |
| JD Lewry | c Sutton b Cork | 4 | run out | 5 |
| Extras | b 7, lb 4, w 8, nb 20 | 39 | b 4, lb 6, w 2, nb 8 | 20 |
| | (all out 88.3 overs) | 274 | (all out 92.2 overs) | 268 |

**Bowling**
Cork 22.3-3-66-2. Chapple 19-2-60-3. Mahmood 13-3-47-0. Muralitharan 25-8-53-5. Croft 9-0-37-0. Cork 17-5-23-2. Chapple 17-5-38-2. Muralitharan 31.2-3-120-3. Mahmood 17-3-43-2. Flintoff 8-5-26-0. Croft 2-0-8-0.
**Fall of Wickets:** 1-34, 2-131, 3-154, 4-176, 5-221, 6-228, 7-239, 8-241, 9-269
1-0, 2-2, 3-127, 4-129, 5-205, 6-209, 7-225, 8-247, 9-248

| LANCASHIRE | First Innings | | Second Innings | |
|---|---|---|---|---|
| MJ Chilton (capt) | b Lewry | 18 | (2) c Hodd b Lewry | 9 |
| MB Loye | c Yardy b Naved-ul-Hasan | 6 | (1) b Martin-Jenkins | 40 |
| BJ Hodge | c Adams b Lewry | 7 | c Hodd b Martin-Jenkins | 15 |
| SG Law | c Adams b Naved-ul-Hasan | 95 | c Adams b Naved-ul-Hasan | 16 |
| A Flintoff | lbw b Naved-ul-Hasan | 34 | c Hopkinson b Mushtaq A | 9 |
| SJ Croft | c Montgomerie b M-Jenkins | 25 | c M-Jenkins b Mushtaq Ahmed | 19 |
| *LD Sutton | c Adams b Mushtaq Ahmed | 18 | c M'gomerie b Mushtaq Ahmed | 2 |
| DG Cork | c Hodd b Mushtaq Ahmed | 9 | b Naved-ul-Hasan | 6 |
| G Chapple | not out | 30 | c Adams b Naved-ul-Hasan | 0 |
| SI Mahmood | b Lewry | 0 | not out | 6 |
| M Muralitharan | b Naved-ul-Hasan | 28 | c Goodwin b Mushtaq Ahmed | 6 |
| Extras | b 3, w 12, nb 16 | 31 | lb 3, nb 6 | 9 |
| | (all out 70.4 overs) | 301 | (all out 44 overs) | 133 |

**Bowling**
Lewry 19-3-81-4. Naved-ul-Hasan 18.4-1-99-3. Mushtaq Ahmed 19-2-81-2. Martin-Jenkins 14-4-37-1. Lewry 5-0-27-1. Naved-ul-Hasan 9-4-10-3. Mushtaq Ahmed 21-5-71-4. Martin-Jenkins 9-3-22-2.
**Fall of Wickets:** 1-14, 2-25, 3-70, 4-127, 5-183, 6-229, 7-243, 8-251, 9-251
1-23, 2-65, 3-66, 4-85, 5-97, 6-108, 7-119, 8-119, 9-126

*Sussex won by 108 runs – Lancashire (6pts),*
*Sussex (19pts)*

### DURHAM v. WARWICKSHIRE – at the Riverside

| WARWICKSHIRE | First Innings | | Second Innings | |
|---|---|---|---|---|
| IJ Westwood | lbw b Gibson | 0 | c Di Venuto b Wiseman | 116 |
| DL Maddy (capt) | c Davies b Plunkett | 7 | b Gibson | 16 |
| KC Sangakkara | c Coetzer b Plunkett | 59 | b Gibson | 119 |
| IJL Trott | c Mustard b Harmison | 20 | c Wiseman b Davies | 4 |
| AGR Loudon | c Plunkett b Gibson | 32 | c Plunkett b Wiseman | 45 |
| *TR Ambrose | c Plunkett b Gibson | 11 | c Coetzer b Wiseman | 24 |
| HH Streak | lbw b Plunkett | 0 | lbw b Gibson | 0 |
| N Tahir | c Gibson b Plunkett | 32 | c Mustard b Gibson | 0 |
| JE Anyon | c Di Venuto b Gibson | 7 | not out | 37 |
| PL Harris | c Plunkett b Harmison | 55 | st Mustard b Wiseman | 0 |
| LM Daggett | not out | 0 | b Plunkett | 33 |
| Extras | lb 5, w 1, nb 10 | 16 | b 5, lb 16, w 1, nb 10 | 32 |
| | (all out 65.2 overs) | 239 | (all out 135.1 overs) | 426 |

**Bowling**
Plunkett 22-5-74-4. Gibson 19-5-56-4. Davies 16-4-68-0. Harmison 6.2-1-29-2. Wiseman 2-0-7-0.
Plunkett 29.1-7-84-1. Gibson 30-8-99-4. Benkenstein 5-0-15-0. Davies 23-9-46-1. Wiseman 41-8-131-4. Harmison 5-1-17-0. Chanderpaul 2-0-13-0.
**Fall of Wickets:** 1-6, 2-27, 3-81, 4-128, 5-128, 6-128, 7-150, 8-168, 9-239
1-38, 2-257, 3-262, 4-296, 5-342, 6-353, 7-353, 8-354, 9-355

| DURHAM | First Innings | | Second Innings | |
|---|---|---|---|---|
| MJ Di Venuto | c Maddy b Tahir | 24 | not out | 91 |
| MD Stoneman | b Maddy | 32 | | |
| KJ Coetzer | c Trott b Maddy | 142 | | |
| S Chanderpaul | c Trott b Streak | 12 | (3) not out | 16 |
| DM B'kenstein (capt) | c Sangakkara b Maddy | 45 | | |
| *P Mustard | b Daggett | 1 | (2) b Anyon | 76 |
| BW Harmison | c Ambrose b Maddy | 101 | | |
| OD Gibson | c Ambrose b Maddy | 22 | | |
| LE Plunkett | c Westwood b Harris | 20 | | |
| PJ Wiseman | not out | 33 | | |
| M Davies | lbw b Harris | 0 | | |
| Extras | lb 10, b 17, w 1, nb 14 | 42 | b 4, lb 1, nb 6 | 11 |
| | (all out 159.5 overs) | 474 | (1 wkt 30.1 overs) | 194 |

**Bowling**
Daggett 17-3-61-1. Streak 23-7-59-1. Anyon 30-6-108-0. Tahir 23-7-63-1. Maddy 27-5-63-5. Harris 22.5-6-50-2. Trott 12-3-20-0. Loudon 5-0-23-0. Streak 5-0-38-0. Tahir 1-0-17-0. Loudon 5-0-32-0. Harris 13-0-56-0. Maddy 2-0-12-0. Anyon 4.1-0-34-1.
**Fall of Wickets:** 1-48, 2-86, 3-105, 4-189, 5-196, 6-378, 7-408, 8-423, 9-462
1-157

*Durham won by 9 wickets – Durham (21pts),*
*Warwickshire (2pts)*

## Round Fourteen: 31 July–3 August Division Two

**MIDDLESEX v. GLAMORGAN – at Lord's**

| MIDDLESEX | First Innings | |
|---|---|---|
| BA Godleman | c Wallace b Wharf | 38 |
| NRD Compton | c Hemp b Wharf | 67 |
| OA Shah | lbw b Wharf | 24 |
| EC Joyce | c Wallace b Cosker | 51 |
| ET Smith (capt) | c Rees b Cosker | 16 |
| *BJM Scott | c Watkins b Cosker | 65 |
| WPUJC Vaas | c Watkins b Waters | 79 |
| TJ Murtagh | run out | 2 |
| M Kartik | c Wallace b Wharf | 1 |
| CEW Silverwood | c Wharf b Waters | 5 |
| A Richardson | not out | 0 |
| Extras | lb 4, w 7, nb 2 | 13 |
| | (all out 112.5 overs) | 361 |

Bowling
Waters 27.5-8-73-2. Jones 19-2-61-0. Wharf 21-1-77-4. Watkins 7-0-34-0. Croft 20-3-50-0. Cosker 18-1-62-3.
Fall of Wickets: 1-87, 2-135, 3-136, 4-168, 5-220, 6-320, 7-337, 8-341, 9-355

| GLAMORGAN | First Innings | | Second Innings (following on) | |
|---|---|---|---|---|
| JP Maher | lbw b Silverwood | 4 | lbw b Silverwood | 0 |
| GP Rees | c Scott b Vaas | 0 | lbw b Vaas | 8 |
| DD Cherry | lbw b Kartik | 32 | c Godleman b Richardson | 10 |
| DL Hemp (capt) | c Scott b Silverwood | 9 | c Compton b Kartik | 36 |
| RE Watkins | c Godleman b Kartik | 30 | c Scott b Murtagh | 20 |
| *MA Wallace | lbw b Kartik | 11 | c Godleman b Kartik | 9 |
| AG Wharf | c Scott b Kartik | 10 | lbw b Richardson | 55 |
| RDB Croft | c Scott b Murtagh | 0 | lbw b Silverwood | 20 |
| DA Cosker | c Godleman b Kartik | 0 | b Kartik | 2 |
| HT Waters | not out | 0 | c Compton b Murtagh | 8 |
| SP Jones | c Silverwood b Kartik | 0 | not out | 2 |
| Extras | lb 3, nb 4 | 7 | b 3, lb 8, w 1, nb 2 | 14 |
| | (all out 53.5 overs) | 106 | (all out 64.1 overs) | 184 |

Bowling
Silverwood 11-2-42-2. Vaas 9-2-15-1. Richardson 12-5-15-0. Murtagh 8-4-10-1. Kartik 13.5-5-21-6.
Silverwood 12-2-34-2. Vaas 9-3-17-1. Richardson 14.1-4-45-2. Murtagh 10-3-24-2. Kartik 18-5-52-3. Shah 1-0-1-0.
Fall of Wickets: 1-4, 2-10, 3-27, 4-78, 5-85, 6-100, 7-103, 8-103, 9-103
1-0, 2-12, 3-34, 4-74, 5-90, 6-96, 7-132, 8-149, 9-182

*Middlesex won by an innings and 71 runs –
Middlesex (21pts), Glamorgan (3pts)*

**GLOUCESTERSHIRE v. DERBYSHIRE – at Bristol**

| DERBYSHIRE | First Innings | | Second Innings | |
|---|---|---|---|---|
| SD Stubbings | lbw b Lewis | 1 | (2) lbw b Lewis | 0 |
| TR Birt | lbw b Lewis | 140 | (1) st Adshead b Banerjee | 162 |
| MG Dighton | b Kirby | 40 | c Marshall b Kirby | 42 |
| SM Katich (capt) | c Adshead b Edmondson | 41 | not out | 124 |
| GM Smith | c Lewis b Taylor | 12 | | |
| DJ Redfern | c Adshead b Edmondson | 12 | (5) not out | 7 |
| AG Botha | c Adshead b Edmondson | 0 | | |
| *DJ Pipe | c Gidman b Kirby | 23 | | |
| GG Wagg | c Spearman b Kirby | 23 | | |
| WA White | lbw b Edmondson | 9 | | |
| KJ Dean | not out | 0 | | |
| Extras | lb 7, nb 2 | 11 | b 10, lb 3, w 2, nb 6 | 21 |
| | (all out 93.3 overs) | 312 | (3 wkts dec 88 overs) | 356 |

Bowling
Lewis 20-5-66-2. Kirby 19.3-3-66-3. Edmondson 15-0-50-4. Banerjee 24-4-69-0. Taylor 15-1-54-1.
Lewis 13-3-33-1. Kirby 13-1-44-1. Edmondson 11-4-43-0. Banerjee 30-6-126-1. Taylor 15-1-76-0. Gidman 6-1-21-0.
Fall of Wickets: 1-7, 2-86, 3-171, 4-212, 5-237, 6-237, 7-274, 8-278, 9-308
1-3, 2-71, 3-336

| GLOS | First Innings | | Second Innings | |
|---|---|---|---|---|
| CM Spearman | c Dighton b Wagg | 52 | (2) c Birt b Wagg | 35 |
| Kadeer Ali | lbw b Smith | 28 | (1) lbw b White | 13 |
| GP Hodnett | c Redfern b Wagg | 168 | (6) not out | 30 |
| HJH Marshall | c Dighton b Wagg | 38 | (3) b White | 0 |
| APR Gidman | lbw b Wagg | 111 | b Smith | 17 |
| CG Taylor | c White b Dean | 19 | (4) c Dighton b Botha | 28 |
| *SJ Adshead | c Pipe b Smith | 1 | not out | 36 |
| J Lewis (capt) | c Katich b Botha | 3 | | |
| SP Kirby | c Redfern b Smith | 6 | | |
| V Banerjee | c Et b Wagg | 3 | | |
| BM Edmondson | not out | 3 | | |
| Extras | b 7, lb 5, w 4, nb 4 | 20 | b 3, lb 3, w 3, nb 2 | 11 |
| | (all out 137.3 overs) | 454 | (5 wkts 37 overs) | 170 |

Bowling
Wagg 30.3-6-119-5. Dean 19-5-41-1. Botha 31-6-73-1. White 20-2-97-0. Smith 30-2-73-3. Dighton 2-0-14-0. Redfern 2-0-11-0. Katich 3-0-14-0.
Wagg 12-0-55-1. White 5-0-32-2. Botha 7-3-22-1. Smith 6-2-18-1. Katich 5-0-26-0. Redfern 2-0-11-0.
Fall of Wickets: 1-79, 2-91, 3-148, 4-347, 5-380, 6-390, 7-397, 8-430, 9-437
1-26, 2-26, 3-73, 4-85, 5-105

*Match drawn – Gloucestershire (12pts),
Derbyshire (9pts)*

to see a high-quality contest decided in the end by Sussex's ruthless bowling display after the home side, chasing 242, moved encouragingly to 65 for 1. The combined power of Mushtaq Ahmed, who whirled away for 21 successive overs, Rana Naved-ul-Hasan, Robin Martin-Jenkins and Jason Lewry, however, then carried the day.

The left-arm spin of Indian Murali Kartik, who took nine wickets in all, enabled Middlesex to dispose highly efficiently of Glamorgan at Lord's, while an enterprising declaration by Simon Katich breathed new life into a hard-fought game between Derbyshire and Gloucestershire at Bristol. The home side won the opening exchanges, with Grant Hodnett hitting a career-best 168 in front of his visiting parents from South Africa, but Travis Birt's second hundred of the match, and an unbeaten 124 from Katich himself, blunted Gloucestershire's victory bid with the ball. Katich's move left a target of 215 in 37 overs, on a turning pitch, and Gloucestershire chased hard until Alex Gidman was fifth out with 110 more needed from 16 overs.

## Round Fifteen: 8–12 August

Having walked out on Surrey, Nayan Doshi was prevented by his old club from playing immediately for new club Warwickshire, and it was his last-minute replacement, Adam Shantry, who initially put the skids under Sussex at Hove with four wickets in 11 balls. Set a mountainous 504, however, Sussex built their 150-over escape act around Richard Montgomerie's nine-and-a-half-hour 195, in which he faced 440 balls.

Hampshire thrashed Worcestershire at the Rose Bowl, with Daren Powell's extra pace and bounce and James Bruce's underrated seamers dismissing them for the ground's lowest ever total, 86, after the home team had cruised past 450 themselves. Harbhajan Singh's 11 wickets at Canterbury enabled Surrey to heap more relegation pressure on Kent, and also underline what an inspired overseas signing he had been, although Kent's homegrown off-spinner James Tredwell also showed up well in this fixture. Lancashire took the Roses honours at Headingley, overpowering Yorkshire with penetrative bowling from Muttiah Muralitharan,

**Overleaf** Leicestershire's John Maunders is in flamboyant mood against Derbyshire's left-arm swing bowler Kevin Dean at Grace Road.

## Round Fifteen: 8–12 August Division One

### KENT v. SURREY – at Canterbury

| KENT | First Innings | | Second Innings | |
|---|---|---|---|---|
| JL Denly | b Ormond | 12 | b Ormond | 14 |
| RWT Key (capt) | not out | 75 | c Batty b Harbhajan Singh | 18 |
| M van Jaarsveld | c Batty b Jordan | 22 | c Harbhajan Singh b Nicholson | 3 |
| MJ Walker | c Ramprakash b Jordan | 0 | b Harbhajan Singh | 12 |
| DI Stevens | c Batty b Harbhajan Singh | 2 | c Benning b Jordan | 30 |
| *GO Jones | b Harbhajan Singh | 10 | (7) c Brown b Harbhajan Singh | 12 |
| JC Tredwell | c Batty b Nicholson | 13 | (8) c Butcher b Harbhajan Singh | 50 |
| Yasir Arafat | c Butcher b Harbhajan Singh | 4 | (6) c Brown b Jordan | 8 |
| R McLaren | lbw b Harbhajan Singh | 0 | c Ormond b Harbhajan Singh | 0 |
| SL Malinga | b Nicholson | 0 | c Walters b Harbhajan Singh | 12 |
| MJ Saggers | b Harbhajan Singh | 0 | not out | 5 |
| Extras | b 4, lb 4, nb 4 | 12 | b 2, lb 1, w 2, nb 2 | 7 |
| | (all out 60.4 overs) | 150 | (all out 58.3 overs) | 171 |

**Bowling**
Nicholson 15-4-48-2. Ormond 13-6-19-1. Jordan 13-3-41-2.
Harbhajan Singh 19.4-5-34-5.
Nicholson 12-4-43-1. Ormond 12-6-21-1. Harbhajan Singh 23.3-6-57-6.
Jordan 11-1-47-2.
**Fall of Wickets:** 1-17, 2-61, 3-63, 4-66, 5-102, 6-133, 7-138, 8-138, 9-139
1-19, 2-32, 3-38, 4-55, 5-78, 6-89, 7-111, 8-111, 9-163

| SURREY | First Innings | | Second Innings | |
|---|---|---|---|---|
| SA Newman | lbw b McLaren | 57 | b McLaren | 10 |
| *JN Batty | lbw b Malinga | 7 | c Denly b Tredwell | 12 |
| MR Ramprakash | b Tredwell | 61 | st Jones b Denly | 28 |
| MA Butcher (capt) | c Jones b Tredwell | 19 | b Saggers | 6 |
| SJ Walters | c Denly b Tredwell | 2 | (6) c van Jaarsveld b Denly | 4 |
| J Ormond | b McLaren | 15 | | |
| AD Brown | c Key b Tredwell | 7 | not out | 2 |
| JGE Benning | b Saggers | 26 | not out | 10 |
| MJ Nicholson | st Jones b Tredwell | 1 | | |
| Harbhajan Singh | not out | 5 | (5) c Jones b Tredwell | 29 |
| CJ Jordan | c Jones b Tredwell | 0 | | |
| Extras | b 8, lb 2, w 3, nb 2 | 15 | b 5, w 2 | 7 |
| | (all out 62 overs) | 215 | (6 wkts 24 overs) | 108 |

**Bowling**
Yasir Arafat 8-1-42-0. Malinga 7-0-40-1. McLaren 17-6-37-2. Saggers 11-1-38-1.
Tredwell 16-3-47-6. Stevens 3-2-1-0.
Saggers 6-0-25-1. McLaren 6-0-17-1. Tredwell 10-0-48-2. Denly 2-0-13-2.
**Fall of Wickets:** 1-14, 2-93, 3-138, 4-146, 5-160, 6-174, 7-196, 8-209, 9-215
1-15, 2-30, 3-47, 4-92, 5-92, 6-98

*Surrey won by 4 wickets –
Kent (3pts), Surrey (18pts)*

### HAMPSHIRE v. WORCESTERSHIRE – at the Rose Bowl

| HAMPSHIRE | First Innings | | Second Innings | |
|---|---|---|---|---|
| MA Carberry | c Moore b Batty | 116 | c Batty b Bollinger | 0 |
| MJ Brown | b Brown | 73 | lbw b Bollinger | 5 |
| JP Crawley | c Solanki b Mason | 96 | c Davies b Bollinger | 4 |
| MJ Lumb | lbw b Kabir Ali | 11 | c Jaques b Kabir Ali | 57 |
| CC Benham | c Moore b Kabir Ali | 0 | c & b Batty | 17 |
| *N Pothas | not out | 71 | lbw b Kabir Ali | 2 |
| AD Mascarenhas | c Moore b Batty | 30 | st Davies b Batty | 5 |
| SK Warne (capt) | c Jaques b Batty | 23 | | |
| DB Powell | c Hick b Batty | 5 | (8) b Batty | 8 |
| DA Griffiths | lbw b Batty | 4 | not out | 1 |
| JTA Bruce | not out | 1 | (9) not out | 1 |
| Extras | b 5, lb 22 | 27 | lb 3 | 3 |
| | (9 wkts dec 126 overs) | 455 | (8 wkts dec 35 overs) | 103 |

**Bowling**
Kabir Ali 29-3-101-2. Bollinger 20-0-83-0. Sillence 18-4-50-0. Mason 21-7-51-1.
Batty 36-8-125-6. Solanki 2-0-18-0.
Bollinger 7-2-21-3. Kabir Ali 8-3-26-2. Mason 3-1-11-0. Sillence 10-0-22-0.
Batty 10-3-20-3.
**Fall of Wickets:** 1-133, 2-246, 3-274, 4-292, 5-350, 6-395, 7-431, 8-432, 9-444
1-0, 2-7, 3-20, 4-73, 5-80, 6-91, 7-101, 8-101

| WORCS | First Innings | | Second Innings | |
|---|---|---|---|---|
| PA Jaques | c Crawley b Powell | 0 | (2) c Lumb b Bruce | 10 |
| SC Moore | c Pothas b Powell | 0 | c Pothas b Bruce | 19 |
| VS Solanki (capt) | c Warne b Griffiths | 22 | lbw b Bruce | 0 |
| BF Smith | c Pothas b Bruce | 5 | c Pothas b Powell | 1 |
| GA Hick | c Benham b Griffiths | 0 | c Benham b Warne | 69 |
| *SM Davies | c Pothas b Powell | 17 | b Warne | 28 |
| GJ Batty | lbw b Bruce | 0 | b Warne | 10 |
| RJ Sillence | c Bruce b Powell | 6 | c Brown b Warne | 28 |
| Kabir Ali | b Bruce | 5 | run out | 1 |
| MS Mason | b Bruce | 0 | c Brown b Bruce | 15 |
| DE Bollinger | not out | 0 | not out | 0 |
| Extras | b 4, lb 2 | 6 | b 6 | 6 |
| | (all out 34.2 overs) | 86 | (all out 42.3 overs) | 187 |

**Bowling**
Powell 10-5-8-4. Bruce 12.2-5-31-4. Griffiths 8-1-33-2. Warne 4-1-8-0.
Powell 9-1-39-1. Bruce 10.3-1-41-4. Mascarenhas 5-1-25-0. Warne 13-4-28-4.
Griffiths 3-0-26-0. Carberry 2-0-22-0.
**Fall of Wickets:** 1-0, 2-5, 3-28, 4-28, 5-49, 6-49, 7-62, 8-73, 9-73
1-25, 2-25, 3-34, 4-38, 5-85, 6-95, 7-165, 8-166, 9-183

*Hampshire won by 285 runs –
Hampshire (22pts), Worcestershire (3pts)*

### YORKSHIRE v. LANCASHIRE – at Headingley

| YORKSHIRE | First Innings | | Second Innings | |
|---|---|---|---|---|
| C White | c Sutton b Chapple | 0 | b Flintoff | 16 |
| JJ Sayers | c Sutton b Mahmood | 3 | c Sutton b Flintoff | 19 |
| A McGrath | lbw b Chapple | 0 | (4) run out | 40 |
| Younus Khan | b Mahmood | 0 | (5) c Flintoff b Muralitharan | 31 |
| AW Gale | c Keedy b Chapple | 15 | (6) lbw b Mahmood | 16 |
| *GL Brophy | c Croft b Muralitharan | 18 | (7) c Flintoff b Muralitharan | 0 |
| AU Rashid | c Horton b Chapple | 34 | (8) lbw b Muralitharan | 6 |
| TT Bresnan | c Hodge b Flintoff | 39 | (9) not out | 20 |
| JN Gillespie | not out | 18 | (3) c Croft b Muralitharan | 44 |
| D Gough (capt) | b Flintoff | 7 | b Mahmood | 10 |
| A Shahzad | lbw b Flintoff | 0 | c Hodge b Muralitharan | 15 |
| Extras | lb 1, w 1, nb 8 | 10 | b 16, lb 2, nb 12 | 30 |
| | (all out 55.5 overs) | 144 | (all out 67.4 overs) | 247 |

**Bowling**
Chapple 14-4-35-4. Mahmood 7-0-24-2. Muralitharan 20-6-35-1.
Flintoff 11.5-3-38-3. Keedy 3-0-11-0.
Chapple 9-2-31-0. Mahmood 18-0-75-2. Muralitharan 24.4-2-66-5.
Flintoff 6-1-31-2. Keedy 10-2-26-0.
**Fall of Wickets:** 1-0, 2-0, 3-1, 4-20, 5-22, 6-55, 7-96, 8-130, 9-144
1-33, 2-44, 3-123, 4-133, 5-180, 6-181, 7-186, 8-195, 9-230

| LANCASHIRE | First Innings | |
|---|---|---|
| MJ Chilton (capt) | run out | 24 |
| PJ Horton | c Younus Khan b Bresnan | 149 |
| BJ Hodge | lbw b Bresnan | 29 |
| SG Law | run out | 206 |
| A Flintoff | lbw b Younus Khan | 24 |
| SJ Croft | b Gough | 15 |
| *LD Sutton | c Younus Khan b Rashid | 7 |
| G Chapple | st Brophy b Rashid | 21 |
| SI Mahmood | lbw b Rashid | 1 |
| G Keedy | c Gale b Younus Khan | 6 |
| M Muralitharan | not out | 2 |
| Extras | b 14, lb 5, nb 14 | 33 |
| | (all out 135.5 overs) | 517 |

**Bowling**
Gough 21-4-74-1. Gillespie 15-5-54-0. Bresnan 26-7-98-2. Rashid 32-2-109-3.
Shahzad 19-3-68-0. Younus Khan 11.5-0-53-2. McGrath 9-1-40-0. White 1-0-2-0.
**Fall of Wickets:** 1-66, 2-125, 3-383, 4-436, 5-470, 6-476, 7-496, 8-504, 9-505

*Lancashire won by an innings and 126 runs –
Yorkshire (2pts), Lancashire (22pts)*

### SUSSEX v. WARWICKSHIRE – at Hove

| WARWICKSHIRE | First Innings | | Second Innings | |
|---|---|---|---|---|
| IJ Westwood | c Hodd b Saqlain Mushtaq | 110 | b Naved-ul-Hasan | 14 |
| DL Maddy (capt) | st Hodd b Mushtaq Ahmed | 53 | c Adams b Mushtaq Ahmed | 30 |
| KC Sangakkara | c & b Saqlain Mushtaq | 59 | c Lewry b Mushtaq Ahmed | 21 |
| IJL Trott | c Adams b Saqlain Mushtaq | 35 | (5) c M'gomerie b Saqlain M | 35 |
| JO Troughton | c Adams b Saqlain Mushtaq | 35 | c Hodd b Lewry | 26 |
| AGR Loudon | lbw b Mushtaq Ahmed | 0 | (7) c Adams b Mushtaq Ahmed | 0 |
| *TR Ambrose | lbw b Saqlain Mushtaq | 99 | (8) c Goodwin b Mushtaq A | 39 |
| HH Streak | lbw b Naved-ul-Hasan | 24 | (9) c Montgomerie b Mushtaq A | 7 |
| AJ Shantry | c Adams b Mushtaq Ahmed | 5 | (10) c Hodd b Mushtaq Ahmed | 5 |
| N Tahir | c Nash b Mushtaq Ahmed | 0 | (11) not out | 2 |
| JE Anyon | not out | 4 | (4) c Naved-ul-Hasan b Mushtaq A | 1 |
| Extras | b 11, lb 12, w 1, nb 12 | 37 | b 11, lb 11, nb 6 | 28 |
| | (all out 129.3 overs) | 433 | (all out 66.4 overs) | 238 |

**Bowling**
Lewry 20-4-45-0. Naved-ul-Hasan 22-1-71-1. Mushtaq Ahmed 47-6-170-4.
Wright 10-2-18-0. Saqlain Mushtaq 27.3-6-96-5. Yardy 3-0-9-0.
Lewry 12-6-22-1. Naved-ul-Hasan 10-3-30-1. Mushtaq Ahmed 29.4-3-111-7.
Saqlain Mushtaq 10-1-37-1. Wright 5-0-16-0.
**Fall of Wickets:** 1-125, 2-239, 3-240, 4-249, 5-250, 6-349, 7-393, 8-408, 9-431
1-27, 2-63, 3-82, 4-83, 5-136, 6-137, 7-175, 8-222, 9-233

| SUSSEX | First Innings | | Second Innings | |
|---|---|---|---|---|
| CD Nash | c Sangakkara b Shantry | 3 | c Westwood b Maddy | 50 |
| RR Montgomerie | c Westwood b Shantry | 2 | c Shantry b Loudon | 195 |
| MH Yardy | c Ambrose b Shantry | 0 | c Maddy b Loudon | 54 |
| MW Goodwin | c Ambrose b Shantry | 5 | c Maddy b Loudon | 28 |
| CJ Adams (capt) | c Westwood b Anyon | 7 | b Loudon | 1 |
| *AJ Hodd | lbw b Tahir | 18 | not out | 46 |
| LJ Wright | b Anyon | 61 | not out | 9 |
| Naved-ul-Hasan | b Tahir | 5 | | |
| Saqlain Mushtaq | c Ambrose b Anyon | 19 | | |
| Mushtaq Ahmed | not out | 13 | | |
| JD Lewry | b Anyon | 12 | | |
| Extras | b 5, lb 6, nb 10 | 21 | b 18, lb 9, w 5, nb 12 | 44 |
| | (all out 52.3 overs) | 168 | (5 wkts 150 overs) | 405 |

**Bowling**
Anyon 17.3-3-62-4. Shantry 16-8-31-4. Tahir 9-0-42-2. Streak 6-1-12-0.
Loudon 4-1-10-0.
Anyon 19-4-37-0. Shantry 13-3-49-0. Tahir 6-1-20-0. Troughton 22-5-61-0.
Loudon 49-8-123-4. Maddy 19-4-48-1. Trott 7-4-11-0. Streak 15-3-29-0.
**Fall of Wickets:** 1-4, 2-4, 3-7, 4-16, 5-34, 6-73, 7-85, 8-133, 9-168
1-121, 2-244, 3-262, 4-272, 5-385

*Match drawn – Sussex (7pts),
Warwickshire (12pts)*

## Round Fifteen: 8–12 August Division Two

### ESSEX v. GLOUCESTERSHIRE – at Southend

| GLOS | First Innings | | Second Innings | |
|---|---|---|---|---|
| Kadeer Ali | c Middlebrook b Bopara | 65 | (2) lbw b Bichel | 2 |
| CM Spearman | c ten Doeschate b Middlebrook | 75 | (1) c ten Doeschate b Tudor | 31 |
| GP Hodnett | c Bichel b Danish Kaneria | 0 | c Chopra b Bichel | 0 |
| HJH Marshall | lbw b Danish Kaneria | 22 | c Bopara b Bichel | 11 |
| APR Gidman | c Foster b Bopara | 4 | b Bichel | 12 |
| CG Taylor | c Foster b Bopara | 12 | c ten Doeschate b D Kaneria | 16 |
| *SJ Adshead | c Middlebrook b Tudor | 18 | c Bichel b Danish Kaneria | 50 |
| ID Fisher | c Danish Kaneria b Bichel | 41 | c Flower b Danish Kaneria | 7 |
| J Lewis (capt) | c Middlebrook b Tudor | 1 | c Tudor b Middlebrook | 2 |
| SP Kirby | c Pettini b Danish Kaneria | 8 | c Bichel b Danish Kaneria | 4 |
| V Banerjee | not out | 11 | not out | 3 |
| Extras | b 3, lb 3, nb 8 | 14 | lb 1 | 1 |
| | (all out 90.4 overs) | 278 | (all out 38.3 overs) | 139 |

Bowling
Bichel 19.4-6-48-1. Palladino 10-5-29-0. Tudor 13-4-48-2. Middlebrook 16-3-46-1. Bopara 11-0-63-3. Danish Kaneria 21-10-38-3.
Bichel 10-3-34-4. Palladino 2-0-13-0. Tudor 8-3-25-1. Bopara 4-0-18-0. Danish Kaneria 9.3-0-30-4. Middlebrook 5-0-18-1.
Fall of Wickets: 1-114, 2-133, 3-169, 4-173, 5-185, 6-197, 7-219, 8-221, 9-231
1-3, 2-3, 3-27, 4-47, 5-57, 6-88, 7-108, 8-121, 9-136

| ESSEX | First Innings | | Second Innings | |
|---|---|---|---|---|
| V Chopra | lbw b Kirby | 7 | c Spearman b Gidman | 36 |
| ML Pettini (capt) | lbw b Lewis | 0 | c Adshead b Lewis | 7 |
| RS Bopara | b Lewis | 14 | b Banerjee | 46 |
| GW Flower | c Adshead b Kirby | 15 | c Spearman b Kirby | 15 |
| AP Palladino | c Hodnett b Lewis | 17 | (11) lbw b Kirby | 8 |
| *JS Foster | c Kadeer Ali b Kirby | 0 | (5) b Kirby | 29 |
| RN ten Doeschate | lbw b Lewis | 6 | (6) c Spearman b Banerjee | 58 |
| JD Middlebrook | c Adshead b Kirby | 7 | (7) c Spearman b Kirby | 2 |
| AJ Bichel | not out | 14 | (8) b Kirby | 3 |
| AJ Tudor | b Kirby | 0 | (9) not out | 29 |
| Danish Kaneria | c Spearman b Lewis | 0 | (10) c Lewis b Banerjee | 4 |
| Extras | lb 6, nb 2 | 8 | lb 6, nb 16 | 22 |
| | (all out 31 overs) | 88 | (all out 70.5 overs) | 259 |

Bowling
Lewis 16-3-41-5. Kirby 15-2-41-5.
Lewis 16-3-56-1. Kirby 21.5-5-75-5. Banerjee 23-5-67-3. Gidman 4-0-30-1. Fisher 6-2-25-0.
Fall of Wickets: 1-3, 2-15, 3-33, 4-57, 5-59, 6-64, 7-65, 8-85, 9-85
1-21, 2-90, 3-102, 4-120, 5-171, 6-181, 7-195, 8-241, 9-245

*Gloucestershire won by 70 runs –*
*Essex (3pts), Gloucestershire (19pts)*

### NOTTINGHAMSHIRE v. SOMERSET – at Trent Bridge

| NOTTS | First Innings | | Second Innings | |
|---|---|---|---|---|
| WI Jefferson | run out | 44 | c Hildreth b Blackwell | 37 |
| JER Gallian | c Trescothick b Caddick | 22 | lbw b Blackwell | 15 |
| MA Wagh | c Trescothick b Caddick | 51 | b Jones | 8 |
| SP Fleming (capt) | lbw b Caddick | 145 | c Kieswetter b Caddick | 32 |
| DJ Hussey | c Langer b Caddick | 0 | not out | 108 |
| SR Patel | c Langer b Willoughby | 8 | lbw b Caddick | 19 |
| *CMW Read | lbw b Willoughby | 7 | c Trescothick b White | 37 |
| GP Swann | c Trescothick b White | 39 | b White | 1 |
| GD Clough | lbw b White | 2 | c Kieswetter b White | 7 |
| AJ Harris | c Edwards b Blackwell | 0 | lbw b Blackwell | 1 |
| MN Malik | not out | 12 | lbw b White | 1 |
| Extras | b 2, lb 10, w 1, nb 8, p 5 | 26 | b 5, lb 5, w 1, nb 2 | 13 |
| | (all out 81.3 overs) | 350 | (all out 80 overs) | 279 |

Bowling
Caddick 18.3-1-69-4. Willoughby 20-1-74-2. Jones 7-0-54-0. Trego 11-0-50-0. Blackwell 13-3-49-1. White 12-3-37-2.
Caddick 20-5-48-2. Willoughby 19-2-66-0. Jones 13-3-53-1. Blackwell 19-4-65-3. White 9-4-37-4.
Fall of Wickets: 1-55, 2-115, 3-151, 4-151, 5-160, 6-168, 7-254, 8-266, 9-267
1-43, 2-56, 3-68, 4-134, 5-166, 6-233, 7-237, 8-265, 9-272

| SOMERSET | First Innings | | Second Innings | |
|---|---|---|---|---|
| ME Trescothick | lbw b Harris | 49 | run out | 16 |
| NJ Edwards | c Patel b Swann | 31 | c Fleming b Swann | 23 |
| *C Kieswetter | b Malik | 14 | | |
| JL Langer (capt) | lbw b Clough | 36 | (3) st Read b Clough | 16 |
| JC Hildreth | c Gallian b Swann | 27 | (4) b Malik | 43 |
| CL White | b Clough | 124 | (5) not out | 47 |
| ID Blackwell | c Patel b Harris | 58 | (6) not out | 28 |
| PD Trego | lbw b Clough | 67 | | |
| PS Jones | b Swann | 9 | | |
| AR Caddick | not out | 5 | | |
| CM Willoughby | c Jefferson b Swann | 4 | | |
| Extras | b 10, lb 12, nb 6 | 28 | b 1, lb 6, w 1 | 8 |
| | (all out 116.2 overs) | 452 | (4 wkts 38.5 overs) | 181 |

Bowling
Harris 28-1-109-2. Malik 24-3-97-1. Clough 22-5-72-3. Swann 39.2-8-125-4. Patel 3-0-27-0.
Harris 9-0-45-0. Malik 11-2-43-1. Swann 12-1-49-1. Clough 4-0-10-1. Patel 1.5-0-18-0. Hussey 1-0-9-0.
Fall of Wickets: 1-66, 2-96, 3-102, 4-161, 5-211, 6-317, 7-433, 8-436, 9-444
1-40, 2-40, 3-82, 4-108

*Somerset won by 6 wickets –*
*Nottinghamshire (7pts), Somerset (22pts)*

### GLAMORGAN v. NORTHAMPTONSHIRE – at Colwyn Bay

| GLAMORGAN | First Innings | | Second Innings | |
|---|---|---|---|---|
| DD Cherry | b Logan | 28 | c Rogers b Brown | 18 |
| GP Rees | b Lucas | 11 | b Klusener | 0 |
| *MA Wallace | c & b Klusener | 19 | c sub b Logan | 15 |
| RN Grant | lbw b Lucas | 79 | c Wessels b Logan | 26 |
| DL Hemp (capt) | lbw b Logan | 82 | c Wessels b Brown | 0 |
| RE Watkins | run out | 4 | lbw b Logan | 4 |
| AG Wharf | not out | 111 | c Rogers b Brown | 37 |
| RDB Croft | lbw b Klusener | 14 | c Brown b GG White | 29 |
| DA Cosker | lbw b Brown | 10 | c Rogers b Brown | 26 |
| AP Davies | run out | 0 | (11) not out | 0 |
| SP Jones | c White G.G. b Brown | 39 | (10) c Rogers b Brown | 14 |
| Extras | b 12, lb 19, w 7 | 38 | b 11, lb 3, nb 14 | 28 |
| | (all out 170.4 overs) | 465 | (all out 93.2 overs) | 197 |

Bowling
Klusener 36-10-117-2. Lucas 36-6-104-2. Logan 31-7-90-2. Brown 47.4-17-81-2. White G.G. 20-7-42-0.
Klusener 17-4-57-1. Lucas 9-3-23-0. Brown 35.2-15-47-5. Logan 16-2-38-3. White G.G. 16-8-18-1.
Fall of Wickets: 1-22, 2-58, 3-58, 4-213, 5-218, 6-256, 7-287, 8-309, 9-386
1-7, 2-39, 3-43, 4-49, 5-70, 6-71, 7-133, 8-153, 9-192

| NORTHANTS | First Innings | | Second Innings | |
|---|---|---|---|---|
| SD Peters | c Wallace b Watkins | 25 | b Wharf | 2 |
| CJL Rogers | lbw b Davies | 8 | c Wallace b Wharf | 69 |
| IJ Sutcliffe | c Wallace b Watkins | 9 | | |
| DJG Sales (capt) | c Wallace b Croft | 219 | not out | 1 |
| RA White | c Wallace b Watkins | 6 | (3) not out | 45 |
| L Klusener | b Watkins | 6 | | |
| *MH Wessels | c Hemp b Croft | 1 | | |
| DS Lucas | b Davies | 18 | | |
| GG White | b Cosker | 65 | | |
| RJ Logan | c Wallace b Davies | 1 | | |
| JF Brown | not out | 8 | | |
| Extras | b 1, lb 6, w 6, nb 8 | 21 | b 5, lb 9 | 14 |
| | (all out 102.2 overs) | 387 | (2 wkts 32 overs) | 131 |

Bowling
Davies 25-5-70-3. Jones 11-2-30-0. Croft 19.2-3-76-2. Watkins 18-1-89-4. Wharf 14-2-60-0. Cosker 15-5-55-1.
Wharf 7-1-27-2. Croft 12-0-52-0. Cosker 13-2-38-0.
Fall of Wickets: 1-20, 2-37, 3-70, 4-77, 5-83, 6-107, 7-144, 8-289, 9-316
1-4, 2-129

*Match drawn – Glamorgan (10pts), Northamptonshire (10pts)*

### LEICESTERSHIRE v. DERBYSHIRE – at Leicester

| LEICESTERSHIRE | First Innings | | Second Innings | |
|---|---|---|---|---|
| TJ New | lbw b Lungley | 1 | lbw b Dean | 78 |
| JK Maunders | lbw b Lungley | 45 | c Hassan Adnan b Wagg | 9 |
| HD Ackerman | c Pipe b Lungley | 0 | b Wagg | 11 |
| MC Rosenberg | c Pipe b Dean | 19 | b Wagg | 0 |
| J Allenby | c Pipe b Wagg | 83 | c Birt b Lungley | 14 |
| *PA Nixon (capt) | lbw b Lungley | 7 | c Birt b Botha | 10 |
| Mansoor Amjad | c Birt b Botha | 4 | c Pipe b Botha | 4 |
| SCJ Broad | not out | 40 | not out | 91 |
| DD Masters | c Birt b Botha | 14 | c Dean b Botha | 46 |
| JE Taylor | c Pipe b Wagg | 40 | c Birch b Botha | 4 |
| GJP Kruger | b Wagg | 0 | st Pipe b Botha | 5 |
| Extras | lb 6, w 1, nb 14 | 21 | b 13, lb 15, w 16, nb 18 | 62 |
| | (all out 81 overs) | 274 | (all out 94.2 overs) | 344 |

Bowling
Lungley 24-5-110-4. Wagg 19-4-62-3. Dean 17-7-21-1. Smith 7-0-25-0. Botha 14-2-50-2.
Lungley 20-5-76-1. Wagg 26-7-98-3. Dean 23-6-73-1. Botha 24.2-5-69-5. Katich 1-1-0-0.
Fall of Wickets: 1-1, 2-4, 3-36, 4-136, 5-148, 6-174, 7-180, 8-211, 9-274
1-45, 2-60, 3-60, 4-96, 5-142, 6-155, 7-155, 8-247, 9-253

| DERBYSHIRE | First Innings | | Second Innings | |
|---|---|---|---|---|
| TR Birt | lbw b Masters | 0 | (2) b Amjad | 74 |
| SD Stubbings | b Broad | 0 | (1) c Nixon b Kruger | 21 |
| DJ Birch | c Maunders b Masters | 6 | (6) c Maunders b Broad | 1 |
| SM Katich (capt) | b Broad | 6 | c Allenby b Broad | 167 |
| GM Smith | lbw b Masters | 15 | c Maunders b Broad | 74 |
| Hassan Adnan | c Amjad b Masters | 5 | (3) b Taylor | 0 |
| AG Botha | lbw b Kruger | 10 | lbw b Masters | 1 |
| *DJ Pipe | lbw b Kruger | 32 | b Broad | 11 |
| GG Wagg | c Ackerman b Broad | 22 | c Nixon b Broad | 0 |
| T Lungley | c Wallace b Davies | 1 | c Nixon b Masters | 4 |
| KJ Dean | not out | 10 | not out | 2 |
| Extras | b 8, lb 9, w 3, nb 18 | 31 | b 8, lb 14, w 1, nb 18 | 41 |
| | (all out 54 overs) | 194 | (all out 93.2 overs) | 396 |

Bowling
Masters 19-7-42-5. Broad 11-4-49-3. Kruger 11-1-53-2. Taylor 10-2-40-0.
Masters 22.2-5-73-2. Broad 24-4-67-5. Kruger 12-3-73-1. Taylor 13-1-59-1. Amjad 15-2-84-1. Allenby 7-1-18-0.
Fall of Wickets: 1-0, 2-1, 3-8, 4-8, 5-27, 6-42, 7-96, 8-163, 9-170
1-57, 2-64, 3-132, 4-324, 5-330, 6-347, 7-373, 8-373, 9-384

*Leicestershire won by 28 runs –*
*Leicestershire (19pts), Derbyshire (3pts)*

Glen Chapple and Andrew Flintoff and magnificent batting from double-centurion Stuart Law and Paul Horton, who made 149.

Somerset took control of Division Two by dispatching Nottinghamshire, their nearest challengers, by six wickets at Trent Bridge. Stephen Fleming and David Hussey scored excellent hundreds for the home side, but an eye-catching all-round performance from Cameron White highlighted an irresistible Somerset display.

In the other second division games, there were narrow wins for Gloucestershire at Southend and for Leicestershire against local rivals Derbyshire, while at Colwyn Bay an innings of 219 from 247 balls by David Sales, featuring 28 fours and six sixes, enabled Northamptonshire to fight back and gain a draw after initially limping to 144 for 7 in reply to a Glamorgan first-innings total boosted by the addition of 156 runs for the last two wickets.

Derbyshire gallantly reached 324 for 3 at Grace Road, chasing 425, with Travis Birt and Greg Smith supporting well as Simon Katich's 232-ball 167 with 25 fours and four sixes led the charge. But then Stuart Broad, who had earlier hit a career-best 91 not out to push Derbyshire's win target beyond 400, followed up with a career-best 5 for 67 with the ball to clinch for Leicestershire an eventual 28-run win that came with a record four-point penalty for a slow over-rate. Steve

Kirby's match haul of 10 for 116, meanwhile, proved too hot for Essex to handle at Garon's Park.

## Round Sixteen: 13–17 August

Worcestershire's first Championship win of the season was also a blow to Yorkshire's title ambitions, with the home side chasing down a sizeable fourth-innings target at Kidderminster – to where the match had been switched due to the ongoing post-flooding problems at Worcester. The opening day, ironically, fell foul of yet more bad weather in the area, but two declarations following a maiden first-class hundred for Adil Rashid set up the last day run chase. Rashid's bowling, however, was not as influential as his batting as Worcestershire's top order made consistent progress, eventually reaching their 336-run target with eight overs unused and with Ben Smith's 98 not out from 102 balls guiding them home.

The first two days of play were lost at Edgbaston, where Kent had much the better of things against Warwickshire, and there was also a draw at the Riverside in a game which had started a day earlier than scheduled in order to give Durham time to travel down to Lord's at the end of the week for the Friends Provident Trophy final. Durham enjoyed the upper

### Round Sixteen: 13–17 August Division One

#### DURHAM v. SURREY – at the Riverside

| DURHAM | First Innings | | Second Innings | |
|---|---|---|---|---|
| MJ Di Venuto | lbw b Harbhajan Singh | 56 | (2) c Newman b Jordan | 77 |
| MD Stoneman | c Jordan b Nicholson | 6 | (1) c Walters b Nicholson | 28 |
| KJ Coetzer | b Jordan | 9 | c Batty b Nicholson | 19 |
| S Chanderpaul | c Batty b Ormond | 81 | c Newman b Jordan | 23 |
| DM B'kenstein (capt) | lbw b Walters | 30 | c & b Harbhajan Singh | 23 |
| *P Mustard | c Newman b Jordan | 2 | b Harbhajan Singh | 44 |
| BW Harmison | c Batty b Jordan | 1 | not out | 40 |
| OD Gibson | c Batty b Ormond | 8 | c Batty b Nicholson | 55 |
| LE Plunkett | not out | 9 | not out | 59 |
| PJ Wiseman | c & b Harbhajan Singh | 2 | | |
| SJ Harmison | c Butcher b Harbhajan Singh | 0 | | |
| Extras | lb 14, w 8, nb 6 | 28 | b 6, lb 8, w 1, nb 8 | 23 |
| | (all out 65.4 overs) | 232 | (7 wkts dec 103 overs) | 397 |

**Bowling**
Nicholson 15-2-51-1. Ormond 15-2-68-2. Jordan 13-2-42-3.
Harbhajan Singh 19.4-8-49-3. Brown 1-0-4-0. Walters 2-0-4-1.
Nicholson 25-4-86-3. Ormond 17-4-76-0. Jordan 18-2-69-2. Walters 3-0-22-0.
Harbhajan Singh 40-9-130-2.
**Fall of Wickets:** 1-21, 2-51, 3-129, 4-181, 5-184, 6-188, 7-212, 8-223, 9-232
1-80, 2-106, 3-161, 4-168, 5-226, 6-241, 7-324

| SURREY | First Innings | | Second Innings | |
|---|---|---|---|---|
| SA Newman | run out | 9 | c Gibson b Plunkett | 34 |
| *JN Batty | c Mustard b Harmison SJ | 18 | not out | 102 |
| MR Ramprakash | c Di Venuto b Plunkett | 62 | b Gibson | 15 |
| MA Butcher (capt) | c Chanderpaul b Gibson | 4 | c Mustard b Wiseman | 18 |
| SJ Walters | lbw b Gibson | 0 | not out | 14 |
| AD Brown | lbw b Gibson | 7 | | |
| JGE Benning | c Di Venuto b Wiseman | 36 | | |
| MJ Nicholson | c Chanderpaul b Plunkett | 32 | | |
| CJ Jordan | not out | 8 | | |
| J Ormond | b Plunkett | 0 | | |
| Harbhajan Singh | c Mustard b Gibson | 6 | | |
| Extras | lb 4, w 2, nb 2 | 8 | lb 6, w 1, nb 8 | 15 |
| | (all out 44.2 overs) | 183 | (3 wkts 78 overs) | 198 |

**Bowling**
Harmison SJ 9-2-39-1. Gibson 15.2-7-50-4. Plunkett 9-1-46-3. Harmison BW 5-1-16-0.
Wiseman 6-0-28-1.
Gibson 17-5-45-1. Plunkett 19-7-41-1. Wiseman 27-6-65-1. Harmison BW 6-2-27-0.
Benkenstein 3-2-4-0. Chanderpaul 6-3-10-0.
**Fall of Wickets:** 1-29, 2-30, 3-34, 4-38, 5-42, 6-109, 7-161, 8-176, 9-176
1-57, 2-81, 3-145

*Match drawn – Durham (8pts),
Surrey (7pts)*

#### WARWICKSHIRE v. KENT – at Edgbaston

| WARWICKSHIRE | First Innings | |
|---|---|---|
| DL Maddy (capt) | c Jones b Saggers | 8 |
| KC Sangakkara | c van Jaarsveld b Saggers | 26 |
| IJL Trott | c van Jaarsveld b Yasir Arafat | 10 |
| JO Troughton | lbw b McLaren | 36 |
| AGR Loudon | c van Jaarsveld b McLaren | 14 |
| *TR Ambrose | c van Jaarsveld b Malinga | 2 |
| LC Parker | c van Jaarsveld b McLaren | 49 |
| HH Streak | c Tredwell b Saggers | 15 |
| AC Thomas | not out | 21 |
| AJ Shantry | lbw b McLaren | 0 |
| LM Daggett | c Jones b van Jaarsveld | 3 |
| Extras | lb 1, w 4, nb 24 | 29 |
| | (all out 59.5 overs) | 213 |

**Bowling**
Yasir Arafat 15-2-50-1. Saggers 16-2-53-3. McLaren 13-0-42-4. Malinga 8-0-45-1.
Tredwell 7-1-21-0. van Jaarsveld 0.5-0-1-1.
**Fall of Wickets:** 1-31, 2-40, 3-48, 4-91, 5-94, 6-132, 7-166, 8-209, 9-209

| KENT | First Innings | |
|---|---|---|
| JL Denly | c Loudon b Streak | 31 |
| RWT Key (capt) | c Parker b Thomas | 153 |
| M van Jaarsveld | c & b Thomas | 85 |
| MJ Walker | c Parker b Thomas | 44 |
| NJ Dexter | not out | 59 |
| *GO Jones | not out | 6 |
| JC Tredwell | | |
| Yasir Arafat | | |
| R McLaren | | |
| SL Malinga | | |
| MJ Saggers | | |
| Extras | b 1, lb 13, w 2, nb 6 | 22 |
| | (4 wkts 121.3 overs) | 400 |

**Bowling**
Thomas 30-10-74-3. Shantry 4-0-31-0. Daggett 8-0-31-0. Streak 21-5-53-1.
Maddy 25-9-44-0. Trott 12-1-48-0. Loudon 15.3-0-65-0. Troughton 4-0-24-0.
Parker 2-0-16-0.
**Fall of Wickets:** 1-82, 2-283, 3-286, 4-371

*Match drawn – Warwickshire (6pts),
Kent (12pts)*

#### WORCESTERSHIRE v. YORKSHIRE – at Kidderminster

| YORKSHIRE | First Innings | | Second Innings | |
|---|---|---|---|---|
| C White | b Kabir Ali | 0 | c Davies b Kabir Ali | 0 |
| JJ Sayers | c Smith b Bollinger | 4 | lbw b Kabir Ali | 0 |
| A McGrath | c Jaques b Malik | 55 | c Davies b Kabir Ali | 6 |
| Younus Khan | c Jaques b Kabir Ali | 15 | b Kabir Ali | |
| JA Rudolph | b Kabir Ali | 29 | not out | 92 |
| *GL Brophy | c Smith b Sillence | 41 | b Bollinger | 13 |
| AU Rashid | c Davies b Bollinger | 108 | not out | 73 |
| TT Bresnan | c Davies b Malik | 13 | | |
| JN Gillespie | b Bollinger | 4 | | |
| D Gough (capt) | c Davies b Bollinger | 0 | | |
| MJ Hoggard | not out | 2 | | |
| Extras | b 10, lb 17, w 13, nb 8 | 48 | b 4 | 4 |
| | (all out 73.5 overs) | 319 | (5 wkts dec 41.4 overs) | 188 |

**Bowling**
Kabir Ali 24-7-69-3. Bollinger 16.5-1-82-4. Malik 18.5-2-85-2. Batty 9-2-28-0.
Sillence 5.1-0-28-1.
Kabir Ali 10-2-30-4. Bollinger 8.1-0-33-1. Malik 5.5-1-26-0. Batty 11-1-57-0.
Sillence 6.4-0-38-0.
**Fall of Wickets:** 1-4, 2-22, 3-51, 4-120, 5-125, 6-236, 7-276, 8-296, 9-302
1-0, 2-0, 3-5, 4-10, 5-35

| WORCS | First Innings | | Second Innings | |
|---|---|---|---|---|
| PA Jaques | lbw b Bresnan | 20 | c Rashid b Gillespie | 44 |
| SC Moore | b Hoggard | 10 | c & b Bresnan | 65 |
| VS Solanki (capt) | lbw b Hoggard | 0 | c Younus Khan b Hoggard | 44 |
| BF Smith | c McGrath b Gough | 36 | not out | 98 |
| GA Hick | c Brophy b Gough | 69 | c Brophy b Gillespie | 31 |
| *SM Davies | c Rashid b Bresnan | 22 | not out | 26 |
| GJ Batty | not out | 7 | | |
| RJ Sillence | | | | |
| Kabir Ali | | | | |
| MN Malik | | | | |
| DE Bollinger | | | | |
| Extras | lb 4, nb 4 | 8 | b 6, lb 8, w 5, nb 10 | 29 |
| | (5 wkts dec 42 overs) | 172 | (4 wkts 57 overs) | 337 |

**Bowling**
Gillespie 7-3-19-0. Hoggard 11-2-55-2. Bresnan 12-2-46-2. Gough 8-4-16-1.
Rashid 4-0-32-0.
Hoggard 9-1-49-1. Gough 9-2-55-0. Gillespie 11-2-74-2. Bresnan 12-1-45-1.
Rashid 13-0-75-0. Younus Khan 3-0-25-0.
**Fall of Wickets:** 1-28, 2-28, 3-48, 4-90, 5-141
1-62, 2-126, 3-205, 4-300

*Worcestershire won by 6 wickets –
Worcestershire (17pts), Yorkshire (4pts)*

## Round Sixteen: 13–17 August Division Two

Owais Shah, of Middlesex, forced his way back into England colours during another fine season for one of the English game's most talented strokemakers.

### NORTHAMPTONSHIRE v. MIDDLESEX – at Northampton

| MIDDLESEX | First Innings | |
|---|---|---|
| ET Smith (capt) | c Sales b Wigley | 15 |
| NRD Compton | b Logan | 9 |
| OA Shah | not out | 189 |
| EC Joyce | c Nelson b Wigley | 106 |
| EJG Morgan | c Rogers b Klusener | 0 |
| JWM Dalrymple | c Rogers b Nelson | 13 |
| *BJM Scott | c Rogers b Nelson | 1 |
| WPUJC Vaas | run out | 28 |
| M Kartik | not out | 17 |
| A Richardson | | |
| CEW Silverwood | | |
| Extras | b 5, lb 7, w 4, nb 6 | 22 |
| | (7 wkts dec 99.3 overs) | **400** |

**Bowling**
Logan 30-6-102-1. Wigley 23-2-83-2. Nelson 8-1-62-2. Klusener 14.3-2-51-1. Brown 12-1-43-0. White G.G. 12-0-47-0.
**Fall of Wickets:** 1-21, 2-36, 3-232, 4-232, 5-258, 6-266, 7-351

| NORTHANTS | First Innings | |
|---|---|---|
| SD Peters | c Morgan b Vaas | 4 |
| CJL Rogers | c Kartik b Dalrymple | 51 |
| MAG Nelson | c Morgan b Richardson | 13 |
| DJG Sales (capt) | c Richardson b Kartik | 8 |
| RA White | c Kartik b Vaas | 43 |
| L Klusener | c Compton b Dalrymple | 89 |
| *MH Wessels | b Kartik | 27 |
| GG White | c Compton b Dalrymple | 6 |
| DH Wigley | lbw b Richardson | 70 |
| RJ Logan | not out | 0 |
| JF Brown | | |
| Extras | b 4, lb 8, nb 12 | 24 |
| | (9 wkts 91.4 overs) | **335** |

**Bowling**
Silverwood 13-1-60-0. Vaas 11-2-45-2. Richardson 14.4-2-56-2. Kartik 31-8-76-2. Dalrymple 22-3-86-3.
**Fall of Wickets:** 1-9, 2-46, 3-69, 4-123, 5-123, 6-173, 7-190, 8-329, 9-335

*Match drawn – Northamptonshire (9pts), Middlesex (12pts)*

### GLAMORGAN v. SOMERSET – at Cardiff

| GLAMORGAN | First Innings | |
|---|---|---|
| JP Maher | lbw b Caddick | 4 |
| RE Watkins | c Kieswetter b Caddick | 0 |
| RN Grant | c Kieswetter b Willoughby | 5 |
| DL Hemp (capt) | c Langer b Trego | 28 |
| TL Maynard | c Kieswetter b Jones | 15 |
| *MA Wallace | c Langer b Caddick | 16 |
| AG Wharf | b Willoughby | 45 |
| RDB Croft | c Hildreth b Willoughby | 43 |
| DA Cosker | c Kieswetter b Jones | 4 |
| AP Davies | not out | 26 |
| HT Waters | c Kieswetter b Caddick | 0 |
| Extras | lb 4, w 2, nb 6 | 12 |
| | (all out 72.4 overs) | **198** |

**Bowling**
Caddick 25.4-10-48-4. Willoughby 21-5-65-3. Trego 15-4-44-1. Jones 11-2-37-2.
**Fall of Wickets:** 1-1, 2-8, 3-18, 4-56, 5-56, 6-92, 7-165, 8-172, 9-191

| SOMERSET | First Innings | |
|---|---|---|
| ME Trescothick | c Wallace b Croft | 28 |
| NJ Edwards | st Wallace b Cosker | 92 |
| JL Langer (capt) | c Wallace b Grant | 113 |
| ND McKenzie | c Hemp b Croft | 50 |
| JC Hildreth | run out | 26 |
| WJ Durston | st Wallace b Cosker | 58 |
| PD Trego | not out | 19 |
| *C Kieswetter | not out | 7 |
| PS Jones | | |
| AR Caddick | | |
| CM Willoughby | | |
| Extras | b 5, lb 1, w 1 | 7 |
| | (6 wkts 74.5 overs) | **400** |

**Bowling**
Davies 10-2-36-0. Waters 9-1-44-0. Croft 29-4-138-2. Wharf 7.5-0-55-0. Cosker 11-0-61-2. Grant 6-0-42-1. Maynard 2-0-18-0.
**Fall of Wickets:** 1-36, 2-153, 3-275, 4-307, 5-333, 6-387

*Match drawn – Glamorgan (6pts), Somerset (12pts)*

hand, despite an early torn back muscle injury to Steve Harmison, who had only recently returned to action following a hernia operation in a bid to win selection for the FPT final. In the end, though, Jon Batty's unbeaten 102 saw Surrey comfortably to safety.

Both second division matches were also badly rain-affected, with no play possible on the first two days at Cardiff and a first day washout, too, at Northampton, where the bat held sway thereafter with Owais Shah reaching his 1,000 runs for the season in an unbeaten 189 that featured 18 fours and three sixes.

## Round Seventeen: 21–25 August

Continuing unseasonal bad weather caused an historic first abandonment of an entire Championship match at The Oval in the month of August, with Champions Sussex the unlucky county to be caught up in Surrey's frustrations, while at Canterbury, too, there was the unprecedented sight of three successive Championship days being called off. As the St Lawrence Ground has a 160-year history, it was hardly surprising then that

neither Kent nor Worcestershire (it just had to be them, didn't it?) really knew how to approach the resulting 96-over one-innings game that, rather inevitably, quickly became a damp squib after hundreds from Rob Key and Martin van Jaarsveld.

No play on day one, and further interruptions, condemned Lancashire's meeting with Hampshire at Old Trafford to another draw, but despite initially bitter cold conditions there was a positive result up in Scarborough as Yorkshire trounced Warwickshire by an innings and 210 runs.

Half the Yorkshire team wore woolly hats in the field on the opening day, as biting winds blew in off the North Sea and Matthew Hoggard whistled through the Warwickshire batting. But temperatures did improve and a crowd of 5,000 turned up at North Marine Road on day two to see the home side take command as Jacques Rudolph scored 220 from 328 balls and Tim Bresnan propelled the total well past 500 with 15 fours and a six in his 124-ball unbeaten 101. Only Tim Ambrose then resisted as Darren Gough, with 5 for 52, and Hoggard clinched the win that took Yorkshire 14 points clear at the top of the Division One table.

## Round Seventeen: 21–25 August Division One

### LANCASHIRE v. HAMPSHIRE – Old Trafford

| HAMPSHIRE | First Innings | | Second Innings | |
|---|---|---|---|---|
| MA Carberry | c Sutton b Cork | 16 | not out | 66 |
| MJ Brown | lbw b Muralitharan | 29 | c Sutton b Chapple | 5 |
| JHK Adams | run out | 63 | c Cork b Muralitharan | 19 |
| JP Crawley | lbw b Muralitharan | 47 | not out | 15 |
| MJ Lumb | c Laxman b Cork | 64 | | |
| *N Pothas | c Sutton b Mahmood | 27 | | |
| SM Ervine | not out | 103 | | |
| SK Warne (capt) | c Laxman b Cork | 2 | | |
| DB Powell | run out | 15 | | |
| JTA Bruce | b Muralitharan | 1 | | |
| DA Griffiths | c Sutton b Chapple | 0 | | |
| Extras | b 9, lb 8, w 1, nb 8 | 26 | b 1, lb 1, nb 4 | 6 |
| | (all out 113.5 overs) | 393 | (2 wkts 47 overs) | 111 |

Bowling
Chapple 17.5-3-41-1. Mahmood 21-2-92-1. Cork 24-6-74-3. Muralitharan 38-6-107-3. Keedy 13-0-62-0.
Chapple 8-2-13-1. Mahmood 4-2-11-0. Muralitharan 16-3-35-1. Keedy 15-4-39-0. Croft 4-0-11-0.
Fall of Wickets: 1-30, 2-79, 3-153, 4-187, 5-245, 6-292, 7-296, 8-312, 9-341
1-19, 2-76

| LANCASHIRE | First Innings | |
|---|---|---|
| MJ Chilton (capt) | c Pothas b Powell | 4 |
| PJ Horton | b Griffiths | 152 |
| SJ Croft | c Brown b Powell | 0 |
| SG Law | b Bruce | 53 |
| VVS Laxman | c Pothas b Bruce | 12 |
| *LD Sutton | not out | 100 |
| G Chapple | c Lumb b Griffiths | 10 |
| DG Cork | b Ervine | 21 |
| SI Mahmood | b Griffiths | 17 |
| G Keedy | not out | 4 |
| M Muralitharan | | |
| Extras | b 9, lb 8, w 5, nb 8 | 30 |
| | (8 wkts dec 118.5 overs) | 403 |

Bowling
Powell 27-4-101-2. Bruce 27-6-86-2. Ervine 18-1-54-1. Griffiths 21.5-1-82-3.
Warne 16.3-3-37-0. Carberry 8.3-1-26-0.
Fall of Wickets: 1-7, 2-7, 3-138, 4-154, 5-319, 6-337, 7-362, 8-395

*Match drawn – Lancashire (12pts),
Hampshire (10pts)*

### YORKSHIRE v. WARWICKSHIRE – at Scarborough

| WARWICKSHIRE | First Innings | | Second Innings | |
|---|---|---|---|---|
| MJ Powell | lbw b Bresnan | 14 | c Brophy b Hoggard | 6 |
| DL Maddy (capt) | c Inzamam-ul-Haq b Hoggard | 0 | c Inzamam-ul-Haq b Hoggard | 2 |
| KC Sangakkara | c Brophy b Hoggard | 0 | lbw b Hoggard | 4 |
| JO Troughton | c Brophy b Shahzad | 9 | c Rashid b Gough | 0 |
| AGR Loudon | lbw b Shahzad | 33 | c Brophy b Gough | 2 |
| *TR Ambrose | c McGrath b Bresnan | 4 | not out | 89 |
| LC Parker | lbw b McGrath | 1 | c Brophy b Gough | 1 |
| HH Streak | lbw b McGrath | 24 | c McGrath b Gough | 0 |
| AC Thomas | c Brophy b Hoggard | 24 | c McGrath b Rashid | 42 |
| JE Anyon | c Brophy b Hoggard | 13 | c Gough b Rashid | 27 |
| SM Hole | not out | 0 | c Inzamam-ul-Haq b Gough | 24 |
| Extras | lb 5, nb 2 | 7 | b 4, w 1, nb 20 | 25 |
| | (all out 58.3 overs) | 129 | (all out 55.3 overs) | 222 |

Bowling
Gough 12-5-20-0. Hoggard 12.3-3-33-4. Bresnan 14-5-28-2. Shahzad 10-4-31-2. McGrath 10-5-12-2.
Gough 14.3-3-52-5. Hoggard 12-2-28-3. Shahzad 6-0-33-0. Bresnan 9-0-39-0. Rashid 14-2-66-2.
Fall of Wickets: 1-4, 2-4, 3-25, 4-29, 5-37, 6-47, 7-81, 8-107, 9-122
1-10, 2-14, 3-15, 4-21, 5-25, 6-31, 7-31, 8-126, 9-176

| YORKSHIRE | First Innings | |
|---|---|---|
| AW Gale | lbw b Thomas | 21 |
| MP Vaughan | c Ambrose b Anyon | 5 |
| A McGrath | lbw b Thomas | 58 |
| Inzamam-ul-Haq | c Ambrose b Anyon | 8 |
| JA Rudolph | c Ambrose b Thomas | 220 |
| *GL Brophy | lbw b Thomas | 38 |
| AU Rashid | c Sangakkara b Anyon | 52 |
| TT Bresnan | not out | 101 |
| A Shahzad | not out | 5 |
| D Gough (capt) | | |
| MJ Hoggard | | |
| Extras | b 8, lb 2, nb 43 | 53 |
| | (7 wkts dec 126.1 overs) | 561 |

Bowling
Hole 15-4-65-0. Thomas 32.1-5-109-4. Anyon 30-5-148-3. Streak 20-1-95-0.
Maddy 13-4-48-0. Loudon 10-1-52-0. Troughton 6-0-34-0.
Fall of Wickets: 1-25, 2-29, 3-50, 4-133, 5-231, 6-371, 7-554

*Yorkshire won by an innings and 210 runs.
Yorkshire (22pts), Warwickshire (2pts)*

### KENT v. WORCESTERSHIRE – at Canterbury

| KENT | First Innings – Forfeited | Second Innings | |
|---|---|---|---|
| JL Denly | | c Mitchell b Malik | 28 |
| RWT Key (capt) | | c & b Sillence | 125 |
| M van Jaarsveld | | not out | 122 |
| MJ Walker | | c Davies b Mitchell | 9 |
| NJ Dexter | | | |
| *GO Jones | | | |
| R McLaren | | | |
| JC Tredwell | | | |
| SJ Cook | | | |
| MJ Saggers | | | |
| SL Malinga | | | |
| Extras | | lb 1, w 2, nb 6 | 9 |
| | | (3 wkts dec 65 overs) | 293 |

Bowling
Kabir Ali 10-1-41-0. Malik 12-3-62-1. Abdul Razzaq 10-2-37-0. Sillence 10-0-44-1.
Batty 6-1-24-0. Smith 7-1-49-0. Moore 4-1-18-0. Solanki 3-0-14-0. Mitchell 3-2-3-1.
Fall of Wickets: 1-60, 2-250, 3-293

| WORCS | First Innings – Forfeited | Second Innings | |
|---|---|---|---|
| VS Solanki (capt) | | (2) b Saggers | 42 |
| BF Smith | | (5) not out | 17 |
| *SM Davies | | (1) c Dexter b Saggers | 21 |
| Abdul Razzaq | | (3) not out | 22 |
| Kabir Ali | | (4) c Jones b Saggers | 0 |
| SC Moore | | | |
| DKH Mitchell | | | |
| GA Hick | | | |
| GJ Batty | | | |
| RJ Sillence | | | |
| MN Malik | | | |
| Extras | | lb 2, nb 6 | 8 |
| | | (3 wkts 21 overs) | 110 |

Bowling
Saggers 7-2-37-3. Cook 7-0-42-0. Malinga 4-1-11-0. Tredwell 3-0-18-0.
Fall of Wickets: 1-66, 2-66, 3-66

*Match drawn – Kent (4pts),
Worcestershire (4pts)*

### SURREY v. SUSSEX – at The Oval

*Match abandoned – Surrey (4pts), Sussex (4pts)*

A number of Yorkshire's players follow their captain Darren Gough's lead and sport woolly hats instead of caps to combat the biting wind at Scarborough in August in a game they eventually won convincingly against Warwickshire.

Only at Lord's, however, where there was no play on the first day and just 8.2 overs bowled on the second, did the weather seriously affect matters in Division Two. Although a washed-out second day at Colchester took the sting out of Jerome Taylor's five-wicket haul, Leicestershire could not then take advantage of Essex's offer of a final day 291-run target and lost by 114 runs. At Trent Bridge and Cardiff, meanwhile, there were exciting finishes and narrow wins for Nottinghamshire and Derbyshire respectively.

Nottinghamshire's victory over Northamptonshire was particularly well earned in a contest closely fought throughout, with fifties from Samit Patel and Stephen Fleming proving critical in a tense fourth-innings run-chase, yet the home side were also exceedingly grateful for the presence of Mark Davies, on loan from Durham because of the extended injury list among their own faster bowlers. Davies took a career-best 7 for 59 in the Northants first innings, and also made other important contributions.

At Sophia Gardens there were 11 wickets in the match for Robert Croft and a fine batting performance from Gareth Rees, the 22-year-old opener from Swansea, but still Glamorgan found a way of losing after reaching 185 for 2 in pursuit of 269. Ant Botha took 5 for 67 to earn Derbyshire a remarkable 42-run win themselves as the Welsh county imploded.

## Round Seventeen: 21–25 August Division Two

### GLAMORGAN v. DERBYSHIRE – at Cardiff

| DERBYSHIRE | First Innings | | Second Innings | |
|---|---|---|---|---|
| WPC Weston | c Maher b Wharf | 6 | (2) c Wallace b Wharf | 32 |
| TR Birt | lbw b Harris | 0 | (1) lbw b Harris | 84 |
| MG Dighton | c Wharf b Jones | 29 | st Wallace b Croft | 60 |
| SM Katich (capt) | c Wallace b Wharf | 4 | c Wallace b Harris | 0 |
| GM Smith | c Wharf b Harris | 9 | c Wharf b Croft | 35 |
| Hassan Adnan | lbw b Croft | 18 | c Rees b Cosker | 18 |
| AG Botha | c Rees b Croft | 22 | c Hemp b Croft | 25 |
| *DJ Pipe | c Wharf b Croft | 33 | not out | 13 |
| GG Wagg | not out | 61 | c Rees b Croft | 5 |
| T Lungley | lbw b Croft | 15 | lbw b Croft | 1 |
| WB Rankin | c & b Croft | 0 | lbw b Croft | 2 |
| Extras | b 4, lb 2, w 1, nb 2 | 9 | b 1, lb 7, w 2, nb 2 | 12 |
| | (all out 65.5 overs) | 206 | (all out 105.3 overs) | 287 |

**Bowling**
Wharf 11-3-37-2. Harris 14-3-51-2. Croft 25.5-7-62-5. Jones 14-1-39-1.
Cosker 1-0-11-0.
Harris 15-3-34-2. Wharf 8-0-42-1. Croft 40.3-11-88-6. Jones 14-1-48-0.
Cosker 33-8-61-1. Grant 1-0-6-0.
**Fall of Wickets:** 1-6, 2-6, 3-21, 4-34, 5-60, 6-67, 7-111, 8-144, 9-206
1-90, 2-145, 3-145, 4-210, 5-231, 6-260, 7-271, 8-277, 9-283

| GLAMORGAN | First Innings | | Second Innings | |
|---|---|---|---|---|
| JP Maher | b Wagg | 31 | c Lungley b Botha | 29 |
| GP Rees | c Pipe b Lungley | 61 | c Birt b Katich | 109 |
| RN Grant | run out | 2 | c Pipe b Botha | 28 |
| DL Hemp (capt) | c Rankin b Botha | 6 | b Lungley | 12 |
| TL Maynard | c Birt b Botha | 18 | c Birt b Botha | 2 |
| *MA Wallace | lbw b Lungley | 21 | c Smith b Botha | 15 |
| AG Wharf | c Smith b Wagg | 21 | c Wagg b Botha | 0 |
| RDB Croft | not out | 11 | c Birt b Lungley | 8 |
| JAR Harris | c Pipe b Wagg | 0 | run out | 3 |
| DA Cosker | lbw b Wagg | 0 | not out | 1 |
| SP Jones | c Hassan Adnan b Botha | 23 | c Birt b Lungley | 0 |
| Extras | b 6, lb 2, w 4, nb 19 | 31 | b 4, w 3, nb 12 | 19 |
| | (all out 46 overs) | 225 | (all out 67 overs) | 226 |

**Bowling**
Lungley 14-2-64-2. Wagg 13-3-63-4. Rankin 7-0-43-0. Botha 12-2-47-3.
Lungley 16-6-52-3. Wagg 8-0-53-0. Botha 28-10-67-5. Rankin 5-0-24-0.
Smith 2-0-7-0. Katich 8-3-19-1.
**Fall of Wickets:** 1-71, 2-77, 3-114, 4-115, 5-151, 6-179, 7-191, 8-191, 9-191
1-54, 2-185, 3-185, 4-188, 5-214, 6-214, 7-214, 8-224, 9-226

*Derbyshire won by 42 runs – Glamorgan (4pts),*
*Derbyshire (18pts)*

### ESSEX v. LEICESTERSHIRE – at Colchester

| ESSEX | First Innings | | Second Innings | |
|---|---|---|---|---|
| V Chopra | c Allenby b Masters | 2 | not out | 62 |
| ML Pettini (capt) | b Taylor | 14 | not out | 86 |
| GW Flower | b Taylor | 7 | | |
| TJ Phillips | c Nixon b Masters | 5 | | |
| *JS Foster | c New b Allenby | 16 | | |
| RN ten Doeschate | c Ackerman b Taylor | 56 | | |
| JD Middlebrook | not out | 55 | | |
| AJ Bichel | c Ackerman b Taylor | 0 | | |
| AJ Tudor | c Nixon b Taylor | 3 | | |
| Danish Kaneria | c Maunders b Masters | 19 | | |
| AP Palladino | c Nixon b Masters | 2 | | |
| Extras | lb 4, nb 8 | 12 | b 1, w 2 | 3 |
| | (all out 54.3 overs) | 191 | (0 wkts dec 14 overs) | 151 |

**Bowling**
Masters 14.3-2-40-4. Taylor 16-3-77-5. Walker 7-3-18-0. Allenby 5-0-21-1.
Henderson 12-1-31-0.
New 5-0-64-0. Sadler 7-0-77-0. Nixon 2-0-9-0.
**Fall of Wickets:** 1-4, 2-11, 3-28, 4-28, 5-75, 6-122, 7-122, 8-132, 9-184

| LEICESTERSHIRE | First Innings | | Second Innings | |
|---|---|---|---|---|
| TJ New | not out | 35 | b Bichel | 0 |
| JK Maunders | c ten Doeschate b Bichel | 13 | c Pettini b Palladino | 8 |
| HD Ackerman | c Flower b Bichel | 1 | b Bichel | 15 |
| J Allenby | not out | 1 | c Flower b Middlebrook | 59 |
| JL Sadler | | | lbw b Danish Kaneria | 5 |
| *PA Nixon (capt) | | | lbw b Danish Kaneria | 0 |
| DD Masters | | | c Middlebrook b Bichel | 8 |
| CW Henderson | | | c Flower b Middlebrook | 27 |
| JE Taylor | | | not out | 20 |
| NGE Walker | | | st Foster b Danish Kaneria | 25 |
| MC Rosenberg | | | absent hurt | |
| Extras | lb 6 | 6 | lb 6 | 6 |
| | (2 wkts dec 11.3 overs) | 52 | (all out 47 overs) | 176 |

**Bowling**
Bichel 6-1-20-2. Palladino 3-0-18-0. Tudor 2.3-0-14-0.
Bichel 12-2-63-3. Palladino 6-0-22-1. Danish Kaneria 16-5-52-3.
Middlebrook 6-0-19-2. Tudor 7-4-14-0.
**Fall of Wickets:** 1-43, 2-47
1-0, 2-16, 3-42, 4-62, 5-74, 6-83, 7-126, 8-141, 9-176

*Essex won by 114 runs – Essex (14pts),*
*Leicestershire (3pts)*

### MIDDLESEX v. GLOUCESTERSHIRE – at Lord's

| MIDDLESEX | First Innings | | Second Innings | |
|---|---|---|---|---|
| AJ Strauss | c Hodnett b Stayt | 75 | b Hardinges | 36 |
| NRD Compton | b Kirby | 11 | c Hardinges b Kirby | 1 |
| ET Smith (capt) | c Spearman b Stayt | 69 | not out | 56 |
| EC Joyce | c Marshall b Kirby | 33 | | |
| JWM Dalrymple | b Kirby | 0 | (4) not out | 27 |
| *BJM Scott | c Adshead b Stayt | 0 | | |
| WPUJC Vaas | not out | 44 | | |
| TJ Murtagh | c Hardinges b Gidman | 16 | | |
| M Kartik | not out | 35 | | |
| A Richardson | | | | |
| D Evans | | | | |
| Extras | b 4, lb 13, w 1, nb 4 | 22 | lb 1 | 1 |
| | (7 wkts dec 81 overs) | 305 | (2 wkts dec 20 overs) | 121 |

**Bowling**
Lewis 25-8-80-0. Kirby 18-5-46-3. Hardinges 16-1-78-0. Stayt 16.4-4-51-3.
Gidman 4-0-22-1. Taylor 2-0-11-0.
Lewis 10-1-41-0. Kirby 7-0-50-1. Hardinges 3-0-29-1.
**Fall of Wickets:** 1-18, 2-135, 3-197, 4-197, 5-197, 6-198, 7-241
1-2, 2-77

| GLOS | First Innings | | Second Innings | |
|---|---|---|---|---|
| CM Spearman | c Joyce b Evans | 18 | (2) b Richardson | 32 |
| Kadeer Ali | st Scott b Kartik | 42 | (1) b Richardson | 24 |
| GP Hodnett | st Scott b Kartik | 1 | b Kartik | 22 |
| HJH Marshall | c Scott b Murtagh | 2 | not out | 59 |
| APR Gidman | c Scott b Richardson | 6 | not out | 9 |
| CG Taylor | not out | 62 | | |
| MA Hardinges | lbw b Vaas | 13 | | |
| *SJ Adshead | b Vaas | 0 | | |
| J Lewis (capt) | c Evans b Kartik | 11 | | |
| SP Kirby | c Scott b Kartik | 0 | | |
| TP Stayt | run out | 0 | | |
| Extras | b 1, lb 5, nb 2 | 8 | b 4, lb 2, nb 6 | 12 |
| | (all out 46.5 overs) | 163 | (3 wkts 50.3 overs) | 158 |

**Bowling**
Vaas 12-0-48-2. Richardson 11.5-2-42-1. Murtagh 6-2-16-1. Evans 2-1-5-1.
Kartik 13-4-41-4. Dalrymple 2-0-5-0.
Vaas 5-0-10-0. Richardson 13-5-34-2. Murtagh 10-3-20-0. Kartik 19-6-60-1.
Evans 3-1-6-0. Dalrymple 7.3-1-16-0.
**Fall of Wickets:** 1-50, 2-57, 3-64, 4-66, 5-82, 6-115, 7-125, 8-148, 9-155
1-59, 2-62, 3-118

*Match drawn – Middlesex (10pts),*
*Gloucestershire (6pts)*

### NOTTINGHAMSHIRE v. NORTHAMPTONSHIRE – at Trent Bridge

| NORTHANTS | First Innings | | Second Innings | |
|---|---|---|---|---|
| SD Peters | c Fleming b Davies | 0 | c Ealham b Swann | 43 |
| AR Crook | b Harris | 70 | c Fleming b Davies | 0 |
| RA White | c Read b Davies | 71 | c Fleming b Adams | 13 |
| DJG Sales (capt) | c Fleming b Patel | 57 | run out | 22 |
| L Klusener | c Swann b Davies | 0 | c Fleming b Ealham | 34 |
| N Boje | c Harris b Davies | 7 | c Read b Harris | 21 |
| *MH Wessels | lbw b Swann | 27 | c Fleming b Harris | 19 |
| DS Lucas | c Read b Davies | 51 | c Read b Swann | 13 |
| DH Wigley | c Harris b Davies | 25 | not out | 29 |
| RJ Logan | c Swann b Davies | 10 | b Adams | 6 |
| JF Brown | not out | 0 | c Gallian b Harris | 10 |
| Extras | lb 3, nb 4 | 7 | b 4, lb 5, nb 10 | 19 |
| | (all out 91.3 overs) | 285 | (all out 88.3 overs) | 229 |

**Bowling**
Harris 21-7-67-1. Davies 19.3-4-59-7. Adams 18-5-55-0. Ealham 13-3-55-0.
Swann 14-5-28-1. Patel 6-2-18-1.
Harris 15.3-1-66-3. Davies 13.3-4-31-1. Adams 17-3-48-2. Ealham 16-4-38-1.
Swann 20.3-5-32-2. Patel 6-2-5-0.
**Fall of Wickets:** 1-17, 2-147, 3-149, 4-150, 5-160, 6-216, 7-248, 8-256, 9-280
1-16, 2-55, 3-74, 4-119, 5-123, 6-151, 7-166, 8-196, 9-216

| NOTTS | First Innings | | Second Innings | |
|---|---|---|---|---|
| WI Jefferson | b Klusener | 18 | c & b Wigley | 25 |
| JER Gallian | lbw b Lucas | 10 | b Klusener | 6 |
| MA Wagh | c Wessels b Logan | 22 | lbw b Klusener | 16 |
| SP Fleming (capt) | c sub b Logan | 28 | c Wigley b Boje | 50 |
| SR Patel | c Sales b Wigley | 9 | c Crook b Boje | 50 |
| *CMW Read | c Boje b Lucas | 16 | (7) c Wessels b Brown | 24 |
| MA Ealham | b Boje | 21 | (8) b Boje | 4 |
| GP Swann | c Klusener b Wigley | 51 | (9) not out | 17 |
| AR Adams | c Wessels b Logan | 32 | (10) not out | 20 |
| M Davies | not out | 35 | | |
| AJ Harris | c Wessels b Wigley | 10 | (6) c Logan b Wigley | 6 |
| Extras | b 4, lb 5, w 10, nb 12 | 31 | b 4, lb 9, w 2 | 15 |
| | (all out 84.2 overs) | 283 | (8 wkts 70.1 overs) | 233 |

**Bowling**
Klusener 19-7-37-1. Logan 20-4-67-3. Lucas 16-2-86-2. Wigley 15.2-5-41-3.
Boje 12-3-32-1. Crook 2-0-11-0.
Klusener 11-1-43-2. Logan 13-3-32-0. Brown 17-1-59-1. Wigley 11-2-35-2.
Boje 18.1-2-51-3.
**Fall of Wickets:** 1-36, 2-38, 3-77, 4-102, 5-106, 6-127, 7-197, 8-203, 9-236
1-7, 2-33, 3-73, 4-124, 5-141, 6-179, 7-185, 8-197

*Nottinghamshire won by 2 wickets –*
*Nottinghamshire (19pts), Northamptonshire (5pts)*

Ryan ten Doeschate began the year playing World Cup cricket for Holland, but his development as a punishing middle-order batsman and useful seamer then continued apace at Essex.

## Round Eighteen: 28 August–2 September

Ottis Gibson's 7 for 46, his latest memorable display of bowling in what was to be a glorious final season, set up Durham for a five-wicket win against Worcestershire at the Riverside. But they were made to scrap far harder for the spoils than they expected when Liam Plunkett was thumping an unbeaten 50 from 62 balls to take their first-innings lead beyond 100. Worcestershire's fighting second innings, centred around an excellent 87 off 112 balls from Steven Davies, left Durham with a far from straightforward last-innings target which was reached in relative comfort only thanks to judicious half-centuries from Dale Benkenstein, their dependable captain, and Gordon Muchall.

A third-wicket partnership of 288 between Kent's Rob Key and Matthew Walker batted Lancashire right out of the match at Canterbury, where the visitors were also much hampered by the bicep muscle injury suffered by Muttiah Muralitharan late on the opening day. By then, though, Walker had already scored his first hundred of the game and not even Glen Chapple's five sixes could haul Lancashire past Kent's first-innings total as Martin Saggers celebrated his comeback to Kent colours, after long absences through injury and a loan spell at Essex, by taking 5 for 43. Key's second-innings 182 sent him past 1,000 runs for

the season and Walker added 157, with 16 fours and two sixes, to his earlier 142.

Nic Pothas did his best to deny Surrey a deserved innings victory at the Rose Bowl, batting four hours and 40 minutes for 92 and being joined in a stubborn ninth-wicket stand of 99 by young Isle of Wight seamer David Griffiths that went deep into the final session. But Surrey's spinners Harbhajan Singh and Chris Schofield, who claimed eight wickets in the match, eventually won the day to do justice to yet more magnificent batting from Mark Ramprakash, who completed 30,000 first-class career runs during his 188 and added 225 for Surrey's third wicket with fellow centurion Mark Butcher.

Essex kept their slender promotion hopes alive in Division Two by thrashing Derbyshire by 227 runs at Derby. Andy Bichel was an all-round inspiration throughout, while Ryan ten Doeschate's second-innings 132 ended all home interest in the contest and Danish Kaneria's irresistible 6 for 45 then helped Bichel to administer the last rites.

There were equally overwhelming victories for Somerset against Glamorgan at Taunton, where 19-year-old wicketkeeper Craig Kieswetter hit a career-best 93 from 103 balls, and for high-scoring Gloucestershire at Leicester. The run-getting, however, came from both sides at Lord's where Middlesex and Nottinghamshire settled on a draw.

## Round Eighteen: 28 August–2 September Division One

### DURHAM v. WORCESTERSHIRE – at the Riverside

| WORCS | First Innings | | Second Innings | |
|---|---|---|---|---|
| DKH Mitchell | c Muchall b Gibson | 5 | lbw b Gibson | 22 |
| SC Moore | c sub b Gibson | 27 | c Coetzer b Wiseman | 9 |
| VS Solanki (capt) | c Coetzer b Gibson | 6 | lbw b Wiseman | 0 |
| BF Smith | c Mustard b Gibson | 0 | c Et b Harmison | 60 |
| GA Hick | c Mustard b Gibson | 64 | b Gibson | 66 |
| *SM Davies | c Mustard b Wiseman | 26 | c Muchall b Wiseman | 87 |
| Abdul Razzaq | c Coetzer b Gibson | 23 | b Onions | 35 |
| GJ Batty | lbw b Gibson | 0 | c Benkenstein b Onions | 72 |
| Kabir Ali | c Mustard b Wiseman | 8 | c Di Venuto b Gibson | 4 |
| MN Malik | lbw b Plunkett | 4 | c Mustard b Gibson | 4 |
| JD Nel | not out | 0 | not out | 7 |
| Extras | lb 6, w 1, nb 12 | 19 | lb 9, lb 8, w 1, nb 6 | 24 |
| | (all out 48.2 overs) | 182 | (all out 84 overs) | 390 |

**Bowling**
Gibson 18-5-46-7. Plunkett 8.2-1-31-1. Onions 13-1-65-0. Harmison 4-0-29-0. Wiseman 5-3-5-2.
Gibson 23-4-104-4. Onions 17-5-54-2. Wiseman 28-4-110-3. Plunkett 10-0-59-0. Harmison 5-1-34-1. Benkenstein 1-0-12-0.
**Fall of Wickets:** 1-31, 2-43, 3-45, 4-50, 5-110, 6-159, 7-163, 8-176, 9-176
1-17, 2-17, 3-41, 4-138, 5-187, 6-273, 7-317, 8-330, 9-338

| DURHAM | First Innings | | Second Innings | |
|---|---|---|---|---|
| MJ Di Venuto | c Hick b Batty | 50 | lbw b Kabir Ali | 5 |
| *P Mustard | c Solanki b Malik | 6 | c Davies b Malik | 30 |
| KJ Coetzer | c Mitchell b Malik | 0 | c Smith b Abdul Razzaq | 44 |
| S Chanderpaul | b Batty | 54 | c Batty b Abdul Razzaq | 28 |
| DM B'kenstein (capt) | b Batty | 0 | c Malik b Nel | 68 |
| GJ Muchall | b Batty | 66 | not out | 64 |
| BW Harmison | lbw b Batty | 0 | not out | 24 |
| OD Gibson | b Batty | 14 | | |
| LE Plunkett | not out | 50 | | |
| PJ Wiseman | c Davies b Abdul Razzaq | 34 | | |
| G Onions | b Abdul Razzaq | 7 | | |
| Extras | lb 4, nb 12 | 16 | lb 1, lb 3, nb 12 | 16 |
| | (all out 69.3 overs) | 297 | (5 wkts 69.1 overs) | 279 |

**Bowling**
Kabir Ali 12-0-52-0. Malik 18-2-88-2. Abdul Razzaq 9.3-0-35-2. Batty 28-4-106-6. Mitchell 2-0-12-0.
Kabir Ali 8-0-46-1. Abdul Razzaq 16-4-54-2. Malik 11-2-58-1. Batty 17-6-37-0. Nel 14.1-3-61-1. Solanki 2-0-11-0. Mitchell 1-0-8-0.
**Fall of Wickets:** 1-14, 2-14, 3-86, 4-86, 5-171, 6-171, 7-195, 8-206, 9-281
1-10, 2-51, 3-120, 4-125, 5-228

*Durham won by 5 wickets – Durham (19pts), Worcestershire (3pts)*

### KENT v. LANCASHIRE – at Canterbury

| KENT | First Innings | | Second Innings | |
|---|---|---|---|---|
| JL Denly | c Laxman b Chapple | 19 | (5) b Croft | 5 |
| RWT Key (capt) | c Laxman b Newby | 17 | c Sutton b Cork | 182 |
| M van Jaarsveld | lbw b Chapple | 0 | c Horton b Cork | 28 |
| MJ Walker | c Law b Chapple | 142 | b Newby | 157 |
| NJ Dexter | b Cork | 42 | (6) not out | 29 |
| *GO Jones | lbw b Muralitharan | 7 | | |
| JC Tredwell | lbw b Muralitharan | 19 | (1) lbw b Chapple | 3 |
| R McLaren | run out | 2 | | |
| SJ Cook | lbw b Newby | 38 | (7) lbw b Newby | 0 |
| MJ Saggers | b Newby | 0 | | |
| SL Malinga | not out | 1 | | |
| Extras | b 8, lb 18, w 2, nb 12 | 40 | b 1, lb 10, w 2, nb 2 | 15 |
| | (all out 110 overs) | 327 | (6 wkts dec 112.4 overs) | 419 |

**Bowling**
Chapple 22-5-63-3. Cork 20-8-36-1. Muralitharan 33.3-5-81-2. Newby 21-4-65-3. Mahmood 13.3-2-56-0.
Chapple 19-1-50-1. Cork 32-4-107-2. Newby 15.4-1-74-2. Mahmood 17-1-69-0. Law 4-0-21-0. Croft 18-2-64-1. Laxman 5-1-15-0. Chilton 2-0-8-0.
**Fall of Wickets:** 1-30, 2-30, 3-50, 4-173, 5-186, 6-231, 7-236, 8-324, 9-324
1-15, 2-65, 3-353, 4-358, 5-419, 6-419

| LANCASHIRE | First Innings | | Second Innings | |
|---|---|---|---|---|
| MJ Chilton (capt) | c Dexter b Tredwell | 53 | (2) c van Jaarsveld b Saggers | 15 |
| PJ Horton | c sub b Saggers | 37 | (1) c van Jaarsveld b Tredwell | 69 |
| SJ Croft | lbw b Cook | 29 | not out | 54 |
| SG Law | b Tredwell | 66 | not out | 29 |
| VVS Laxman | c Tredwell b Saggers | 10 | run out | 22 |
| *LD Sutton | c Jones b Saggers | 12 | | |
| G Chapple | b Saggers | 88 | | |
| DG Cork | st Jones b Tredwell | 5 | | |
| OJ Newby | not out | 1 | | |
| SI Mahmood | c Tredwell b Saggers | 1 | | |
| M Muralitharan | absent hurt | | | |
| Extras | b 5, lb 10 | 15 | lb 3, w 5, nb 6 | 14 |
| | (all out 96.4 overs) | 317 | (3 wkts 67 overs) | 208 |

**Bowling**
Saggers 25.4-12-43-5. Malinga 9-1-41-0. Tredwell 36-6-146-3. Cook 19-9-43-1. Dexter 7-0-29-0.
Saggers 14-7-22-1. Malinga 12-0-60-0. Tredwell 24-5-71-1. Cook 6-1-27-0. Denly 7-1-17-0. van Jaarsveld 4-1-8-0.
**Fall of Wickets:** 1-85, 2-127, 3-135, 4-161, 5-179, 6-297, 7-315, 8-316, 9-317
1-46, 2-102, 3-163

*Match drawn – Kent (10pts), Lancashire (10pts)*

### HAMPSHIRE v. SURREY – at the Rose Bowl

| SURREY | First Innings | | |
|---|---|---|---|
| SA Newman | c Brown b Powell | 24 | |
| *JN Batty | c Bruce b Udal | 55 | |
| MR Ramprakash | b Powell | 188 | |
| MA Butcher (capt) | c Bruce b Bruce | 100 | |
| SJ Walters | b Bruce | 10 | |
| JGE Benning | c Ervine b Udal | 42 | |
| CP Schofield | b Powell | 0 | |
| CJ Jordan | c Ervine b Udal | 19 | |
| MJ Nicholson | not out | 34 | |
| Harbhajan Singh | c Powell b Ervine | 18 | |
| J Ormond | c Adams b Ervine | 18 | |
| Extras | b 10, lb 11, w 17, nb 10 | 48 | |
| | (all out 160.4 overs) | 556 | |

**Bowling**
Powell 32-7-117-3. Bruce 31-7-86-2. Griffiths 22-1-100-0. Ervine 31.4-2-116-2. Udal 41-12-106-3. Adams 3-0-10-0.

| HAMPSHIRE | First Innings | | Second Innings (following on) | |
|---|---|---|---|---|
| MA Carberry | lbw b Nicholson | 0 | c Butcher b Harbhajan Singh | 40 |
| MJ Brown | c Nicholson b Jordan | 30 | | |
| JHK Adams | c Nicholson b Harbhajan Singh | 110 | b Nicholson | 31 |
| JP Crawley | c Butcher b Nicholson | 0 | b Harbhajan Singh | 20 |
| MJ Lumb | lbw b Schofield | 17 | lbw b Harbhajan Singh | 20 |
| *N Pothas (capt) | c Nicholson b Schofield | 39 | lbw b Nicholson | 92 |
| SM Ervine | b Harbhajan Singh | 12 | lbw b Schofield | 10 |
| SD Udal | lbw b Schofield | 6 | c Butcher b Schofield | 0 |
| DB Powell | b Schofield | 4 | c Newman b Harbhajan Singh | 25 |
| DA Griffiths | not out | 0 | not out | 31 |
| JTA Bruce | not out | 0 | c Butcher b Schofield | 0 |
| Extras | b 7, lb 3, w 1 | 11 | b 2, lb 14, w 1, nb 2 | 19 |
| | (all out 90.2 overs) | 221 | (all out 115.5 overs) | 298 |

**Bowling**
Nicholson 16-6-38-2. Ormond 13-3-30-0. Jordan 13-3-43-0.
Harbhajan Singh 26.2-9-51-2. Schofield 22-6-52-5.
Nicholson 19-7-40-2. Ormond 6-2-28-0. Jordan 17-6-50-1. Harbhajan Singh 38-14-71-4. Schofield 33.5-9-87-3. Benning 2-0-6-0.
**Fall of Wickets:** 1-63, 2-86, 3-88, 4-121, 5-141, 6-167, 7-169, 8-198, 9-297
1-63, 2-86, 3-88, 4-121, 5-141, 6-167, 7-169, 8-198, 9-297

*Surrey won by an innings and 37 runs – Hampshire (3pts), Surrey (22pts)*

## Round Eighteen: 28 August–2 September Division Two

### DERBYSHIRE v. ESSEX – at Derby

| ESSEX | First Innings | | Second Innings | |
|---|---|---|---|---|
| GW Flower | c Dean b Wagg | 9 | b Dighton | 26 |
| ML Pettini (capt) | c Botha b Dean | 17 | lbw b Lungley | 2 |
| T Westley | b Wagg | 4 | c sub b Lungley | 0 |
| TJ Phillips | b Dean | 30 | c Weston b Stubbings | 0 |
| *JS Foster | lbw b Dean | 11 | c Stubbings b Dighton | 0 |
| RN ten Doeschate | c Needham b Botha | 38 | c Dighton b Botha | 132 |
| JD Middlebrook | not out | 81 | lbw b Needham | 15 |
| AJ Bichel | lbw b Botha | 23 | c Weston b Needham | 74 |
| AJ Tudor | c Pipe b Wagg | 1 | lbw b Botha | 0 |
| Danish Kaneria | c Birt b Needham | 16 | c Botha b Needham | 1 |
| AP Palladino | st Pipe b Needham | 18 | not out | 0 |
| Extras | lb 7, w 1, nb 16 | 24 | b 2, lb 2, w 4, nb 10 | 18 |
| | (all out 66.2 overs) | 272 | (all out 77.2 overs) | 268 |

Bowling
Lungley 11-0-61-0. Wagg 20-2-83-3. Dean 10-3-38-3. Botha 20-3-72-2. Needham 4.2-0-10-2. Dighton 1-0-1-0.
Lungley 17-7-58-3. Dighton 20-3-47-2. Botha 16.2-2-55-2. Needham 22-1-92-3. Weston 2-1-12-0.
Fall of Wickets: 1-25, 2-29, 3-39, 4-79, 5-80, 6-141, 7-175, 8-190, 9-264
1-9, 2-15, 3-19, 4-28, 5-57, 6-116, 7-238, 8-240, 9-243

| DERBYSHIRE | First Innings | | Second Innings | |
|---|---|---|---|---|
| TR Birt | b Bichel | 0 | (2) c Bichel b Danish Kaneria | 63 |
| WPC Weston | lbw b Palladino | 2 | (1) c Foster b Bichel | 15 |
| MG Dighton (capt) | c Foster b Bichel | 32 | b Bichel | 19 |
| Hassan Adnan | c Flower b Bichel | 5 | (5) lbw b Danish Kaneria | 15 |
| SD Stubbings | c Tudor b Bichel | 21 | (6) b Danish Kaneria | 3 |
| GG Wagg | c Bichel b ten Doeschate | 11 | (9) c Phillips b Bichel | 22 |
| AG Botha | run out | 9 | (8) c Palladino b Danish Kaneria | 1 |
| *DJ Pipe | c ten Doeschate b Bichel | 40 | (7) lbw b Bichel | 1 |
| J Needham | not out | 3 | (4) b Danish Kaneria | 4 |
| T Lungley | c Westley b Bichel | 0 | b Danish Kaneria | 22 |
| KJ Dean | c Middlebrook b Bichel | 2 | not out | 2 |
| Extras | nb 10 | 10 | lb 6, w 1 | 7 |
| | (all out 28.3 overs) | 139 | (all out 43.3 overs) | 174 |

Bowling
Bichel 10.3-2-36-7. Palladino 6-0-28-1. ten Doeschate 6-1-46-1. Tudor 4-1-28-0. Danish Kaneria 2-1-1-0.
Bichel 22-3-96-4. Palladino 4-1-17-0. Tudor 1-0-10-0. Danish Kaneria 16.3-5-45-6.
Fall of Wickets: 1-0, 2-4, 3-9, 4-48, 5-81, 6-81, 7-114, 8-135, 9-135
1-53, 2-83, 3-96, 4-121, 5-125, 6-126, 7-127, 8-130, 9-160

*Essex won by 227 runs –
Derbyshire (3pts), Essex (19pts)*

### LEICESTERSHIRE v. GLOUCESTERSHIRE – at Leicester

| LEICESTERSHIRE | First Innings | | Second Innings | |
|---|---|---|---|---|
| TJ New | b Greenidge | 4 | c Adshead b Kirby | 50 |
| JK Maunders | lbw b Greenidge | 6 | c Kadeer Ali b Greenidge | 1 |
| MAG Boyce | b Greenidge | 5 | absent hurt | |
| HD Ackerman | c Kadeer Ali b Greenidge | 4 | (3) b Kirby | 9 |
| J Allenby | c Spearman b Kirby | 25 | (4) c Adshead b Greenidge | 8 |
| JL Sadler | c & b Stayt | 18 | (5) b Banerjee | 42 |
| *PA Nixon (capt) | c Adshead b Marshall | 57 | (6) b Taylor | 77 |
| CW Henderson | c Gidman b Greenidge | 81 | (7) c Gidman b Banerjee | 5 |
| DD Masters | b Banerjee | 8 | (8) c Taylor b Banerjee | 46 |
| DT Rowe | not out | 6 | (9) run out | 0 |
| RAG Cummins | run out | 0 | (10) not out | 26 |
| Extras | b 2, lb 5, w 1, nb 4 | 12 | b 1, lb 4, w 1 | 6 |
| | (all out 60.1 overs) | 229 | (all out 58.2 overs) | 270 |

Bowling
Kirby 14-2-51-1. Greenidge 14-1-54-5. Stayt 12-0-44-1. Banerjee 13.1-2-50-1. Gidman 4-0-14-0. Marshall 3-1-9-1.
Kirby 17-1-51-2. Greenidge 13-0-70-2. Stayt 10-2-43-0. Banerjee 15.2-3-74-3. Taylor 3-0-27-1.
Fall of Wickets: 1-5, 2-15, 3-19, 4-20, 5-57, 6-77, 7-197, 8-210, 9-224
1-12, 2-21, 3-32, 4-110, 5-122, 6-129, 7-228, 8-228, 9-270

| GLOUCS | First Innings | |
|---|---|---|
| Kadeer Ali | c Ackerman b Masters | 140 |
| CM Spearman | c Nixon b Masters | 110 |
| GP Hodnett | c New b Cummins | 16 |
| HJH Marshall | run out | 123 |
| APR Gidman (capt) | lbw b Allenby | 59 |
| CG Taylor | c Henderson b New | 61 |
| *SJ Adshead | b New | 99 |
| CG Greenidge | c Nixon b Cummins | 1 |
| SP Kirby | not out | 18 |
| TP Stayt | | |
| V Banerjee | | |
| Extras | b 9, lb 7, w 1, nb 6 | 23 |
| | (8 wkts dec 161.1 overs) | 650 |

Bowling
Masters 36-7-102-2. Rowe 17-1-113-0. Allenby 22-4-64-1. Cummins 33-4-144-2. Henderson 48-5-193-0. New 5.1-1-18-2.
Fall of Wickets: 1-201, 2-243, 3-326, 4-412, 5-529, 6-542, 7-557, 8-650

*Gloucestershire won by an innings and 151 runs –
Leicestershire (2pts), Gloucestershire (22pts)*

### SOMERSET v. GLAMORGAN – at Taunton

| SOMERSET | First Innings | | Second Innings | |
|---|---|---|---|---|
| ME Trescothick | lbw b Wharf | 52 | c Wallace b Harris | 13 |
| NJ Edwards | c & b Wharf | 52 | b Harris | 3 |
| JL Langer (capt) | c Croft b Wharf | 31 | c Rees b Croft | 47 |
| JC Hildreth | c Wright b Waters | 4 | (5) run out | 69 |
| ND McKenzie | c Wright b Waters | 55 | (4) c Davies b Croft | 84 |
| ID Blackwell | c Wright b Croft | 54 | c Maher b Croft | 42 |
| PD Trego | c Wallace b Waters | 0 | c Maher b Croft | 41 |
| *C Kieswetter | c Davies b Waters | 93 | c Waters b Croft | 20 |
| PS Jones | lbw b Croft | 0 | not out | 2 |
| AR Caddick | c Wright b Harris | 43 | b Grant | 0 |
| CM Willoughby | not out | 0 | | |
| Extras | b 9, lb 5 | 14 | lb 3, w 1, nb 4 | 8 |
| | (all out 85.5 overs) | 402 | (9 wkts dec 73.4 overs) | 329 |

Bowling
Davies 12-0-67-0. Harris 17.5-2-94-1. Waters 21.3-3-76-4. Wharf 15-1-82-3. Croft 20-4-69-2.
Waters 21-0-107-0. Harris 16-0-55-2. Wharf 14-0-25-0. Croft 24-2-102-5. Davies 7-0-34-0. Grant 1.4-0-7-1.
Fall of Wickets: 1-101, 2-106, 3-111, 4-171, 5-250, 6-250, 7-260, 8-268, 9-398
1-6, 2-29, 3-83, 4-191, 5-227, 6-278, 7-320, 8-324, 9-329

| GLAMORGAN | First Innings | | Second Innings | |
|---|---|---|---|---|
| JP Maher | lbw b Trego | 25 | c Kieswetter b Caddick | 39 |
| GP Rees | c Kieswetter b Willoughby | 7 | c Kieswetter b Caddick | 12 |
| WD Bragg | c McKenzie b Willoughby | 24 | c Kieswetter b Willoughby | 9 |
| RN Grant | lbw b Jones | 64 | c Trescothick b Blackwell | 13 |
| BJ Wright | c Trescothick b Caddick | 4 | c Kieswetter b Blackwell | 39 |
| *MA Wallace (capt) | lbw b Caddick | 0 | lbw b Jones | 12 |
| AG Wharf | c Kieswetter b Caddick | 3 | absent hurt | |
| RDB Croft | lbw b Willoughby | 5 | (7) c Hildreth b Caddick | 38 |
| JAR Harris | lbw b Jones | 5 | (8) c Kieswetter b Blackwell | 9 |
| AP Davies | c Trescothick b Jones | 54 | (9) c Langer b Caddick | 9 |
| HT Waters | not out | 1 | (10) not out | 0 |
| Extras | b 8, lb 11, nb 4 | 23 | b 8, lb 7, nb 4 | 19 |
| | (all out 65.1 overs) | 233 | (all out 57.5 overs) | 199 |

Bowling
Willoughby 21-6-65-3. Caddick 19-3-64-3. Blackwell 10-0-2-0. Trego 11-3-38-1. Jones 13.1-1-45-3.
Caddick 22-6-48-4. Trego 7-0-36-0. Willoughby 10-5-17-1. Blackwell 13.5-1-60-3. Jones 5-1-23-1.
Fall of Wickets: 1-13, 2-55, 3-84, 4-89, 5-89, 6-101, 7-158, 8-163, 9-208
1-48, 2-69, 3-69, 4-97, 5-118, 6-159, 7-181, 8-199, 9-199

*Somerset won by 299 runs –
Somerset (22pts), Glamorgan (4pts)*

### MIDDLESEX v. NOTTINGHAMSHIRE – at Lord's

| NOTTS | First Innings | | Second Innings | |
|---|---|---|---|---|
| WI Jefferson | b Vaas | 11 | b Richardson | 73 |
| JER Gallian | c Scott b Vaas | 26 | b Vaas | 0 |
| MA Wagh | c Godleman b Murtagh | 92 | c Scott b Kartik | 94 |
| SP Fleming (capt) | c Vaas | 110 | (6) c Morgan b Strauss | 81 |
| SR Patel | lbw b Richardson | 41 | (4) c Godleman b Morgan | 112 |
| BM Shafayat | c Godleman b Vaas | 21 | (5) lbw b Kartik | 36 |
| *CMW Read | b Kartik | 61 | (8) not out | 14 |
| GP Swann | c Dalrymple b Murtagh | 17 | (9) not out | 11 |
| AR Adams | lbw b Vaas | 33 | | |
| PJ Franks | c Kartik b Murtagh | 46 | | |
| CE Shreck | not out | 0 | (7) c Smith b Morgan | 3 |
| Extras | b 2, lb 18, nb 18 | 38 | b 2, lb 8, w 4, nb 18 | 32 |
| | (all out 122.1 overs) | 473 | (7 wkts 111 overs) | 456 |

Bowling
Vaas 29-3-126-5. Murtagh 29.1-3-134-3. Kartik 30-5-104-1. Richardson 19-7-45-1. Dalrymple 15-1-44-0.
Vaas 19-3-62-1. Murtagh 14-3-77-0. Kartik 30-6-82-2. Richardson 13-1-57-1. Dalrymple 10-1-64-0. Joyce 5-0-29-0. Godleman 5-1-35-0. Strauss 6-0-16-1. Morgan 8-2-24-2. Smith 1-1-0-0.
Fall of Wickets: 1-26, 2-57, 3-245, 4-277, 5-295, 6-321, 7-346, 8-417, 9-455
1-11, 2-175, 3-177, 4-263, 5-424, 6-426, 7-434

| MIDDLESEX | First Innings | |
|---|---|---|
| AJ Strauss | c Read b Adams | 16 |
| BA Godleman | c Read b Franks | 30 |
| ET Smith (capt) | c Swann b Patel | 122 |
| EC Joyce | c Read b Adams | 19 |
| EJG Morgan | c Fleming b Adams | 72 |
| JWM Dalrymple | c Swann b Adams | 43 |
| *BJM Scott | run out | 20 |
| WPUJC Vaas | c Gallian b Shreck | 37 |
| TJ Murtagh | c Swann b Shreck | 20 |
| M Kartik | st Read b Patel | 35 |
| A Richardson | not out | 24 |
| Extras | b 2, lb 8, w 8, nb 16 | 34 |
| | (all out 144.2 overs) | 472 |

Bowling
Shreck 37-11-87-2. Adams 43-13-127-4. Franks 23-2-115-1. Swann 34-5-108-0. Shafayat 2-1-7-0. Patel 5.2-1-18-2.
Fall of Wickets: 1-19, 2-93, 3-125, 4-274, 5-296, 6-351, 7-351, 8-397, 9-416

*Match drawn – Middlesex (12pts),
Nottinghamshire (11pts)*

## Round Nineteen: 5–9 September
### Division One

---

### WORCESTERSHIRE v. HAMPSHIRE – at Kidderminster

| HAMPSHIRE | First Innings | | Second Innings | |
|---|---|---|---|---|
| MA Carberry | c Davies b Sillence | 127 | c Hick b Price | 120 |
| MJ Brown | run out | 47 | c Davies b Price | 88 |
| JHK Adams | c Abdul Razzaq b Sillence | 80 | not out | 82 |
| JP Crawley | run out | 8 | not out | 75 |
| MJ Lumb | c Hick b Abdul Razzaq | 63 | | |
| *N Pothas | c Batty b Mitchell | 8 | | |
| SM Ervine | c Mitchell b Malik | 26 | | |
| SK Warne (capt) | st Davies b Price | 46 | | |
| SD Udal | c Mitchell b Abdul Razzaq | 0 | | |
| JTA Bruce | st Davies b Price | 5 | | |
| JA Tomlinson | not out | 1 | | |
| Extras | b 5, lb 7, w 19, nb 2 | 33 | b 6, lb 5 | 11 |
| | (all out 123.5 overs) | 444 | (2 wkts dec 67 overs) | 376 |

Bowling
Abdul Razzaq 23-6-70-2. Malik 27-2-109-1. Sillence 23-3-79-2. Batty 16-5-54-0. Price 22.5-1-89-2. Ali 1-0-4-0. Mitchell 14-4-27-1.
Malik 11-1-57-0. Abdul Razzaq 9-3-23-0. Sillence 9-1-108-0. Batty 12-0-64-0. Price 19-1-104-2. Mitchell 1-0-9-0.
Fall of Wickets: 1-111, 2-253, 3-272, 4-278, 5-300, 6-369, 7-428, 8-438, 9-438
1-199, 2-214

| WORCS | First Innings | | Second Innings | |
|---|---|---|---|---|
| DKH Mitchell | c Pothas b Tomlinson | 0 | c Pothas b Udal | 8 |
| SC Moore | c Pothas b Tomlinson | 24 | c sub b Udal | 37 |
| MM Ali | c Pothas b Bruce | 5 | c Brown b Warne | 77 |
| BF Smith | lbw b Bruce | 10 | (11) absent hurt | |
| GA Hick | lbw b Tomlinson | 29 | (4) c Lumb b Tomlinson | 19 |
| *SM Davies | c Brown b Warne | 84 | (5) lbw b Warne | 2 |
| Abdul Razzaq | c Pothas b Ervine | 78 | (6) b Warne | 14 |
| GJ Batty (capt) | lbw b Tomlinson | 5 | (7) c Warne b Bruce | 8 |
| RJ Sillence | c Adams b Warne | 11 | (8) c Adams b Warne | 36 |
| RW Price | lbw b Tomlinson | 3 | (9) b Warne | 6 |
| MN Malik | not out | 1 | (10) not out | 24 |
| Extras | b 5, lb 9, nb 6 | 20 | b 5, lb 1 | 6 |
| | (all out 73.1 overs) | 289 | (all out 67.2 overs) | 237 |

Bowling
Bruce 14-5-36-2. Tomlinson 22-3-78-5. Ervine 9.1-2-47-1. Adams 4-3-9-0. Udal 8-1-19-0. Warne 16-0-86-2.
Bruce 17-2-76-1. Tomlinson 18-4-45-1. Warne 22.2-5-68-5. Udal 10-1-42-2.
Fall of Wickets: 1-1, 2-10, 3-28, 4-71, 5-88, 6-210, 7-217, 8-232, 9-241
1-34, 2-62, 3-97, 4-112, 5-158, 6-167, 7-173, 8-194, 9-237

*Hampshire won by 294 runs –*
*Worcestershire (5pts), Hampshire (22pts)*

---

### SUSSEX v. YORKSHIRE – at Hove

| SUSSEX | First Innings | |
|---|---|---|
| CD Nash | lbw b Shahzad | 1 |
| RR Montgomerie | b Bresnan | 73 |
| MH Yardy | c Gale b Rashid | 119 |
| MW Goodwin | c Rudolph b Rashid | 47 |
| CJ Adams (capt) | lbw b Hoggard | 46 |
| *AJ Hodd | c Hoggard b Rashid | 123 |
| RSC Martin-Jenkins | c Rudolph b Hoggard | 49 |
| Naved-ul-Hasan | c Inzaman-ul-Haq b Bresnan | 46 |
| Saqlain Mushtaq | not out | 57 |
| Mushtaq Ahmed | | |
| JD Lewry | | |
| Extras | b 4, lb 13, w 3, nb 16 | 36 |
| | (8 wkts dec 157.1 overs) | 597 |

Bowling
Hoggard 27-7-75-2. Shahzad 19-1-92-1. Bresnan 26-3-104-2. McGrath 6-0-13-0. Rashid 35.1-3-136-3. Imran Tahir 37-2-141-0. Vaughan 7-0-19-0.
Fall of Wickets: 1-9, 2-187, 3-266, 4-283, 5-331, 6-410, 7-500, 8-597

| YORKSHIRE | First Innings | | Second Innings (following on) | |
|---|---|---|---|---|
| AW Gale | c Adams b Mushtaq Ahmed | 51 | c Adams b Saqlain Mushtaq | 16 |
| MP Vaughan | c Yardy b Lewry | 8 | b Naved-ul-Hasan | 5 |
| A McGrath (capt) | c Montgomerie b Mushtaq | 31 | lbw b Lewry | 20 |
| Inzamam-ul-Haq | c Adams b Mushtaq Ahmed | 8 | c Montgomerie b Lewry | 22 |
| JA Rudolph | c Montgomerie b M-Jenkins | 23 | b Lewry | 1 |
| *GL Brophy | c Nash b Martin-Jenkins | 4 | c Montgomerie b Saqlain M | 3 |
| AU Rashid | not out | 54 | c M'gomerie b Naved-ul-Hasan | 10 |
| TT Bresnan | c Naved-ul-Hasan b Mushtaq A | 9 | lbw b Naved-ul-Hasan | 1 |
| A Shahzad | c Nash b Saqlain Mushtaq | 11 | not out | 1 |
| MJ Hoggard | c Lewry b Mushtaq Ahmed | 9 | b Naved-ul-Hasan | 0 |
| Imran Tahir | run out | 0 | b Naved-ul-Hasan | 5 |
| Extras | b 6, lb 16, nb 22 | 44 | b 4, lb 2 | 6 |
| | (all out 69.1 overs) | 247 | (all out 44.1 overs) | 89 |

Bowling
Lewry 11-4-38-1. Naved-ul-Hasan 16.1-2-74-0. Mushtaq Ahmed 30.5-5-89-5. Martin-Jenkins 6-2-17-2. Saqlain Mushtaq 4-0-7-1.
Lewry 13-4-23-3. Naved-ul-Hasan 6.1-3-15-4. Saqlain Mushtaq 17-6-28-3. Mushtaq Ahmed 1-0-1-0. Martin-Jenkins 7-3-16-0.
Fall of Wickets: 1-31, 2-79, 3-87, 4-118, 5-122, 6-164, 7-180, 8-225, 9-246
1-18, 2-33, 3-51, 4-53, 5-66, 6-70, 7-75, 8-83, 9-83

*Sussex won by an innings and 261 runs –*
*Sussex (22pts), Yorkshire (3pts)*

---

### LANCASHIRE v. DURHAM – at Blackpool

| DURHAM | First Innings | | Second Innings | |
|---|---|---|---|---|
| MJ Di Venuto | b Chapple | 78 | (2) lbw b Chapple | 8 |
| MD Stoneman | b Mahmood | 24 | (1) lbw b Mahmood | 1 |
| KJ Coetzer | c Law b Mahmood | 11 | lbw b Croft | 24 |
| BW Harmison | b Chapple | 3 | b Chapple | 0 |
| DM B'kenstein (capt) | c Laxman b Chapple | 15 | c Sutton b Mahmood | 77 |
| GJ Muchall | b Chapple | 0 | lbw b Croft | 0 |
| *P Mustard | c Sutton b Chapple | 15 | b Chapple | 36 |
| OD Gibson | c Sutton b Chapple | 8 | c Chapple b Mahmood | 33 |
| LE Plunkett | c Chilton b Chapple | 5 | b Mahmood | 0 |
| PJ Wiseman | c Law b Cork | 4 | c Sutton b Croft | 5 |
| M Davies | not out | 0 | not out | 0 |
| Extras | lb 3 | 3 | w 1 | 1 |
| | (all out 58.3 overs) | 166 | (all out 48 overs) | 185 |

Bowling
Chapple 27-5-53-7. Cork 14.3-2-45-1. Newby 7-2-20-0. Mahmood 14-2-45-2. Chapple 13-4-33-3. Mahmood 11-2-51-4. Cork 13-2-31-0. Newby 3-0-30-0. Croft 8-3-40-3.
Fall of Wickets: 1-57, 2-91, 3-106, 4-121, 5-121, 6-136, 7-153, 8-159, 9-162
1-3, 2-17, 3-17, 4-47, 5-47, 6-114, 7-170, 8-180, 9-181

| LANCASHIRE | First Innings | | Second Innings | |
|---|---|---|---|---|
| MJ Chilton (capt) | lbw b Gibson | 0 | (2) c Mustard b Plunkett | 14 |
| PJ Horton | c Harmison b Gibson | 2 | (1) c Mustard b Gibson | 1 |
| SJ Croft | c Mustard b Davies | 7 | c Harmison b Plunkett | 1 |
| SG Law | c Davies b Gibson | 2 | not out | 82 |
| VVS Laxman | lbw b Plunkett | 25 | not out | 55 |
| *LD Sutton | not out | 66 | | |
| G Chapple | c Di Venuto b Gibson | 16 | | |
| DG Cork | c Muchall b Gibson | 19 | | |
| OJ Newby | b Gibson | 0 | | |
| SI Mahmood | lbw b Gibson | 41 | | |
| G Keedy | b Gibson | 0 | | |
| Extras | lb 2, w 3 | 5 | b 4, lb 1, w 1, nb 10 | 16 |
| | (all out 55 overs) | 183 | (3 wkts 37.2 overs) | 169 |

Bowling
Gibson 20-4-68-8. Davies 14-5-43-1. Harmison 5-0-28-0. Plunkett 15-2-52-1. Gibson 10-0-59-1. Plunkett 12-3-51-2. Davies 8-3-20-0. Harmison 2-0-18-0. Wiseman 5.2-1-16-0.
Fall of Wickets: 1-0, 2-9, 3-11, 4-13, 5-56, 6-82, 7-114, 8-114, 9-183
1-2, 2-7, 3-44

*Lancashire won by 7 wickets –*
*Lancashire (17pts), Durham (3pts)*

---

### WARWICKSHIRE v. SURREY – at Edgbaston

| WARWICKSHIRE | First Innings | | Second Innings | |
|---|---|---|---|---|
| IJ Westwood | c Walters b Ormond | 4 | c Benning b Dernbach | 79 |
| MJ Powell | c Nicholson b Dernbach | 82 | c Dernbach b Nicholson | 33 |
| UL Trott | c Batty b Nicholson | 19 | c Batty b Ormond | 33 |
| JO Troughton | c Batty b Nicholson | 76 | (7) c Ramprakash b Dernbach | 43 |
| AGR Loudon | c Ramprakash b Ormond | 13 | (4) c Newman b Ormond | 20 |
| *TR Ambrose (capt) | c Hussain b Jordan | 33 | (5) c Newman b Hussain | 11 |
| AG Botha | lbw b Hussain | 1 | (6) c Batty b Hussain | 9 |
| AC Thomas | c Benning b Jordan | 9 | lbw b Hussain | 7 |
| CR Woakes | c Newman b Jordan | 9 | (10) not out | 14 |
| NM Carter | not out | 14 | (9) c Batty b Jordan | 27 |
| JE Anyon | b Hussain | 13 | c Ramprakash b Jordan | 8 |
| Extras | b 3, lb 1, w 2, nb 6 | 12 | lb 6, nb 2 | 8 |
| | (all out 78 overs) | 285 | (all out 79.5 overs) | 264 |

Bowling
Nicholson 16-6-41-2. Ormond 16-2-70-2. Jordan 15-2-46-3. Dernbach 11-1-45-1. Benning 2-0-22-0. Hussain 18-2-57-2.
Nicholson 15-2-60-1. Ormond 14-2-42-2. Jordan 8.5-2-27-2. Hussain 21-5-50-3. Dernbach 18-4-77-2. Walters 3-1-2-0.
Fall of Wickets: 1-7, 2-44, 3-193, 4-193, 5-221, 6-222, 7-249, 8-258, 9-259
1-21, 2-122, 3-142, 4-157, 5-157, 6-194, 7-213, 8-223, 9-256

| SURREY | First Innings | | Second Innings | |
|---|---|---|---|---|
| SA Newman | c Ambrose b Carter | 0 | c Ambrose b Woakes | 87 |
| *JN Batty | c Ambrose b Thomas | 21 | not out | 68 |
| MR Ramprakash | c Trott b Botha | 175 | not out | 15 |
| MA Butcher (capt) | c Carter | 14 | | |
| SJ Walters | b Anyon | 13 | | |
| JGE Benning | c Ambrose b Thomas | 44 | | |
| CJ Jordan | c Ambrose b Anyon | 17 | | |
| MJ Nicholson | lbw b Botha | 41 | | |
| Murtaza Hussain | c Woakes b Anyon | 6 | | |
| J Ormond | not out | 25 | | |
| JW Dernbach | c Carter b Thomas | 10 | | |
| Extras | lb 7 | 7 | b 2, lb 1, nb 6 | 9 |
| | (all out 139.1 overs) | 373 | (1 wkt 45.4 overs) | 179 |

Bowling
Carter 27-6-75-2. Thomas 27.1-10-57-3. Anyon 36-7-107-3. Woakes 12-3-48-0. Botha 34-11-73-2. Trott 3-1-6-0.
Carter 6-0-26-0. Thomas 10-3-37-0. Woakes 7.4-0-42-1. Botha 15-2-44-0. Anyon 7-0-27-0.
Fall of Wickets: 1-0, 2-70, 3-141, 4-169, 5-244, 6-267, 7-303, 8-334, 9-344
1-149

*Surrey won by 9 wickets –*
*Warwickshire (5pts), Surrey (21pts)*

---

## Round Nineteen: 5–9 September

The clash of the top two at Hove finished with Sussex emerging as comprehensive winners and Yorkshire's title aspirations looking in ruins after they had been skittled for a sad 89 on the third afternoon. There were 13 internationals in the game, but Yorkshire's big names did not fire and it was two of the lesser names, Mike Yardy and Andrew Hodd, who provided Sussex with much of their initial impetus. Yardy's 119 was his first Championship hundred of the season and Hodd, deputising behind the wicket for England's Matt Prior, scored his maiden Championship century.

Mushtaq Ahmed, brought on as early as the ninth over when Yorkshire began their reply to Sussex's intimidating 597 for 8 declared, took 5 for 89 to force the follow-on – but, second time around, Yorkshire's brittleness was such that Mushtaq only bowled one over. The margin of defeat, indeed, was the second heaviest in the white rose county's proud history. 'People will now say we are favourites, and it's good that things are in our own hands after this win,' said Chris Adams, the Sussex captain, 'but I'm taking nothing for granted over the last two rounds of games because this season has been the tightest and most hard-fought Championship I have known.'

Lancashire kept up their challenge, meanwhile, by beating Durham by seven wickets at Blackpool and avoiding the threat of an eight-point penalty for a sub-

Sussex wicketkeeper Andrew Hodd took his chance magnificently when Matt Prior was called up into regular England action during the 2007 season. He scored his maiden Championship hundred against Yorkshire at Hove to help to set up a crushing win for the Champions against one of their closest challengers for the title.

standard pitch at Stanley Park in the process. Glen Chapple and Ottis Gibson held sway in the first half of the game, but Stuart Law and VVS Laxman defied the unpredictable surface to hurry Lancashire to victory inside two days.

Hampshire, with Shane Warne back at the helm after injury and picking up five second-innings wickets himself, were too strong for Worcestershire at Kidderminster in a game that will be fondly remembered in particular by Michael Carberry, who scored 127 and 120 as the home bowlers struggled to contain Hampshire's batsmen. The division's other match was won by Surrey, who put Warwickshire director of cricket Mark Greatbatch under even more pressure with a nine-wicket success that, once again, owed much to Mark Ramprakash. Dropped on 104 when offering a dolly to Alfonso Thomas at mid on, off the unfortunate Neil

Carter, Ramprakash went on to score 175 – his 95th first-class hundred, three days after his 38th birthday.

Somerset clinched the second division title by beating Essex by six wickets in a solid all-round team performance at Chelmsford. Charl Willoughby made the early inroads, with only 18-year-old Tom Westley showing any kind of fight or technique in Essex's first innings slide to 144 all out. Justin Langer, Somerset's captain, singled out Andrew Caddick when praising his entire side on their achievement. 'He's been the catalyst, and I can't believe he hasn't played every Test for England in the past ten years,' said Langer of his 38-year-old strike bowler.

Nottinghamshire, sure to go up with Somerset in second place, demolished Derbyshire by an innings and six runs at the Racecourse Ground, where Stephen Fleming made hay with 243 from 264 balls, including 40 fours and two sixes.

## Round Nineteen: 5–9 September Division Two

### ESSEX v. SOMERSET – at Chelmsford

| ESSEX | First Innings | | Second Innings | |
|---|---|---|---|---|
| V Chopra | lbw b Willoughby | 5 | c Trescothick b Willoughby | 8 |
| ML Pettini (capt) | c Langer b Willoughby | 0 | lbw b Willoughby | 4 |
| T Westley | c Kieswetter b Willoughby | 72 | c McKenzie b Willoughby | 10 |
| TJ Phillips | c Trescothick b Willoughby | 2 | lbw b Blackwell | 68 |
| *JS Foster | lbw b Trego | 15 | lbw b Munday | 96 |
| RN ten Doeschate | c Trescothick b Trego | 5 | lbw b Caddick | 34 |
| JD Middlebrook | lbw b Munday | 8 | b Caddick | 0 |
| AJ Bichel | c Kieswetter b Willoughby | 12 | not out | 60 |
| GR Napier | c Trescothick b Blackwell | 0 | c Kieswetter b Munday | 10 |
| Danish Kaneria | c Hildreth b Blackwell | 8 | c Blackwell b Munday | 27 |
| JS Ahmed | not out | 7 | c Trescothick b Willoughby | 7 |
| Extras | b 4, lb 4, nb 2 | 10 | b 12, lb 11, nb 2 | 25 |
| | (all out 46.1 overs) | 144 | (all out 83.3 overs) | 349 |

**Bowling**
Caddick 8-2-22-0. Willoughby 18-8-36-5. Blackwell 15.1-3-47-2. Trego 4-0-22-2. Munday 1-0-9-1.
Caddick 25-4-95-2. Willoughby 13.3-1-53-4. Trego 8-2-46-0. Blackwell 18-5-46-1. Munday 19-0-86-3.
**Fall of Wickets:** 1-0, 2-5, 3-13, 4-53, 5-59, 6-91, 7-103, 8-104, 9-126
1-6, 2-13, 3-26, 4-161, 5-235, 6-235, 7-239, 8-253, 9-313

| SOMERSET | First Innings | | Second Innings | |
|---|---|---|---|---|
| ME Trescothick | c Ahmed b Danish Kaneria | 59 | c Phillips b Bichel | 6 |
| NJ Edwards | c Foster b Danish Kaneria | 55 | c Phillips b Bichel | 35 |
| JL Langer (capt) | c Ahmed b Danish Kaneria | 43 | (4) st Foster b Danish Kaneria | 28 |
| JC Hildreth | c Napier b Danish Kaneria | 61 | (5) not out | 32 |
| ND McKenzie | run out | 49 | (6) not out | 33 |
| ID Blackwell | c ten Doeschate b D Kaneria | 9 | | |
| PD Trego | st Foster b Danish Kaneria | 44 | (3) lbw b Bichel | 44 |
| *C Kieswetter | b Bichel | 14 | | |
| AR Caddick | b Bichel | 0 | | |
| MK Munday | not out | 4 | | |
| CM Willoughby | b Danish Kaneria | 7 | | |
| Extras | | 0 | lb 5, w 1 | 6 |
| | (all out 60.4 overs) | 312 | (4 wkts 31.5 overs) | 184 |

**Bowling**
Bichel 19-2-100-2. Ahmed 8-0-58-0. Napier 2-0-19-0. Danish Kaneria 24.4-5-95-7.
Middlebrook 7-0-40-0.
Bichel 9-1-65-3. Napier 7.5-0-36-0. Danish Kaneria 12-2-56-1. Middlebrook 3-1-22-0.
**Fall of Wickets:** 1-114, 2-114, 3-197, 4-236, 5-246, 6-260, 7-293, 8-293, 9-301
1-14, 2-90, 3-93, 4-130

*Somerset won by 6 wickets –*
*Essex (3pts), Somerset (20pts)*

### GLOUCESTERSHIRE v. MIDDLESEX – at Bristol

| MIDDLESEX | First Innings | |
|---|---|---|
| AJ Strauss | b Kirby | 32 |
| BA Godleman | lbw b Greenidge | 5 |
| ET Smith (capt) | c Kirby b Banerjee | 111 |
| EC Joyce | c Kadeer Ali b Greenidge | 8 |
| EJG Morgan | c Stayt b Gidman | 76 |
| *BJM Scott | b Greenidge | 112 |
| TJ Murtagh | lbw b Kirby | 32 |
| M Kartik | c Adshead b Greenidge | 10 |
| A Richardson | c Spearman b Kirby | 15 |
| D Evans | c sub b Kirby | 0 |
| ST Finn | not out | 1 |
| Extras | b 9, lb 8, w 13, nb 8 | 38 |
| | (all out 116.1 overs) | 440 |

**Bowling**
Kirby 29-5-99-4. Greenidge 20.1-5-99-4. Stayt 21-3-80-0. Gidman 13-0-35-1.
Banerjee 28-4-90-1. Marshall 5-0-20-0.
**Fall of Wickets:** 1-14, 2-59, 3-81, 4-255, 5-265, 6-364, 7-385, 8-424, 9-428

| GLOS | First Innings | | Second Innings (following on) | |
|---|---|---|---|---|
| Kadeer Ali | b Richardson | 7 | (2) c Godleman b Murtagh | 2 |
| CM Spearman | c Kartik b Murtagh | 18 | (1) b Kartik | 46 |
| GP Hodnett | c Scott b Finn | 35 | lbw b Murtagh | 55 |
| HJH Marshall | b Evans | 6 | (5) lbw b Kartik | 0 |
| APR Gidman | c Strauss b Evans | 27 | (6) c Smith b Kartik | 1 |
| JG Thompson | lbw b Evans | 11 | (7) b Finn | 21 |
| *SJ Adshead | b Kartik | 9 | (8) c Morgan b Finn | 32 |
| CG Greenidge† | c Kartik b Murtagh | 19 | | |
| SP Kirby | c Scott b Kartik | 4 | (4) b Kartik | 0 |
| V Banerjee | not out | 2 | c Kartik b Finn | 0 |
| TP Stayt | lbw b Murtagh | 6 | not out | 3 |
| J Lewis | | | (9) c Joyce b Finn | 31 |
| Extras | b 2, lb 7, w 1, nb 6 | 16 | b 1, lb 3, nb 4 | 8 |
| | (all out 55.4 overs) | 152 | (all out 67.5 overs) | 199 |

**Bowling**
Richardson 11-4-29-1. Murtagh 11.4-3-36-4. Evans 10-3-31-3. Finn 8-1-21-1.
Kartik 15-4-26-1.
Richardson 6-0-20-0. Murtagh 12-3-39-2. Finn 12.5-2-51-4. Evans 10-2-24-0.
Kartik 26-9-57-4. Morgan 1-0-4-0.
**Fall of Wickets:** 1-24, 2-26, 3-37, 4-86, 5-107, 6-108, 7-116, 8-143, 9-144
1-6, 2-84, 3-94, 4-94, 5-106, 6-116, 7-145, 8-184, 9-184
† Replaced by J Lewis

*Middlesex won by an innings and 89 runs –*
*Gloucestershire (3pts), Middlesex (22pts)*

### DERBYSHIRE v. NOTTINGHAMSHIRE – at Chesterfield

| NOTTS | First Innings | |
|---|---|---|
| WI Jefferson | b Clare | 36 |
| JER Gallian | lbw b Lungley | 43 |
| MA Wagh | c Birt b White | 13 |
| SP Fleming (capt) | c Dighton b Clare | 243 |
| SR Patel | c Stubbings b Dighton | 24 |
| BM Shafayat | lbw b Dighton | 0 |
| *CMW Read | c Lungley b Clare | 90 |
| GP Swann | c Hassan Adnan b Clare | 56 |
| AR Adams | c White b Clare | 2 |
| PJ Franks | not out | 1 |
| CE Shreck | | |
| Extras | b 6, lb 13, w 1, nb 20 | 40 |
| | (9 wkts dec 113.2 overs) | 548 |

**Bowling**
Lungley 27-4-132-1. White 17-3-117-1. Clare 23.2-4-90-5. Needham 22-5-80-0.
Dighton 15-1-61-2. Smith 9-0-49-0.
**Fall of Wickets:** 1-82, 2-95, 3-132, 4-193, 5-195, 6-381, 7-535, 8-543, 9-548

| DERBYSHIRE | First Innings | | Second Innings (following on) | |
|---|---|---|---|---|
| SD Stubbings | c Jefferson b Adams | 1 | (2) b Patel | 48 |
| WPC Weston | b Shreck | 38 | (1) run out | 16 |
| MG Dighton (capt) | c Adams b Swann | 32 | lbw b Franks | 8 |
| TR Birt | c Jefferson b Adams | 12 | lbw b Patel | 85 |
| GM Smith | b Adams | 0 | (6) lbw b Swann | 51 |
| Hassan Adnan | lbw b Franks | 50 | (7) c Read b Patel | 4 |
| *DJ Pipe | b Shreck | 4 | (8) not out | 26 |
| JL Clare | b Franks | 20 | (9) lbw b Swann | 0 |
| J Needham | c Fleming b Adams | 13 | (5) c Swann b Franks | 48 |
| WA White | c Read b Franks | 17 | c Fleming b Adams | 19 |
| T Lungley | not out | 9 | lbw b Adams | 0 |
| Extras | lb 5, nb 4 | 9 | b 7, lb 8, w 11, nb 6 | 32 |
| | (all out 52.5 overs) | 205 | (all out 100.2 overs) | 337 |

**Bowling**
Shreck 17-3-60-2. Adams 14.5-0-74-4. Franks 10-2-28-3. Swann 10-3-34-1.
Shafayat 1-0-4-0.
Shreck 20-3-76-0. Adams 19.2-4-78-2. Franks 13-1-57-2. Swann 27-7-72-2.
Patel 21-3-39-3.
**Fall of Wickets:** 1-1, 2-64, 3-86, 4-86, 5-86, 6-110, 7-163, 8-166, 9-184
1-46, 2-58, 3-138, 4-227, 5-257, 6-271, 7-301, 8-301, 9-337

*Nottinghamshire won by an innings and 6 runs –*
*Derbyshire (4pts), Nottinghamshire (22pts)*

### LEICESTERSHIRE v. NORTHAMPTONSHIRE – at Leicester

| NORTHANTS | First Innings | | Second Innings | |
|---|---|---|---|---|
| SD Peters | c Nixon b Allenby | 36 | lbw b Cummins | 0 |
| AR Crook | b Cummins | 0 | b New | 72 |
| RA White | c Henderson b Allenby | 23 | c Nixon b Cummins | 14 |
| DJG Sales (capt) | c Maunders b Cummins | 43 | not out | 187 |
| N Boje | c Et b Cummins | 125 | c Nixon b Cummins | 4 |
| AG Wakely | c Ackerman b New | 2 | c Nixon b Henderson | 0 |
| L Klusener | run out | 45 | (8) not out | 37 |
| *NJO'Brien | c Allenby b Gurney | 1 | (7) c Maunders b Gurney | 109 |
| DS Lucas | b Cummins | 5 | | |
| DH Wigley | lbw b Cummins | 0 | | |
| RJ Logan | not out | 1 | | |
| Extras | b 4, lb 12, w 6, nb 8 | 30 | b 10, lb 5, w 5, nb 16 | 36 |
| | (all out 88.2 overs) | 310 | (6 wkts dec 108 overs) | 459 |

**Bowling**
Cummins 21.2-7-60-5. Gurney 22-4-89-1. Allenby 12-4-37-2. Henderson 15-5-24-0.
New 7-1-27-1. Cobb 3-0-17-0. Cliff 5-0-33-0. Sadler 3-2-7-0.
Cummins 22-7-94-3. Gurney 14-1-84-1. Cliff 13-0-65-0. Allenby 7-2-19-0.
Henderson 36-11-96-1. New 10-1-59-1. Cobb 6-0-27-0.
**Fall of Wickets:** 1-7, 2-66, 3-67, 4-146, 5-158, 6-293, 7-294, 8-301, 9-301
1-0, 2-44, 3-143, 4-159, 5-160, 6-345

| LEICESTERSHIRE | First Innings | | Second Innings | |
|---|---|---|---|---|
| TJ New | c White b Boje | 45 | c White b Boje | 40 |
| JK Maunders | lbw b Lucas | 51 | lbw b Klusener | 30 |
| HD Ackerman | c O'Brien b Lucas | 18 | b Boje | 4 |
| JL Sadler | c O'Brien b Wigley | 26 | (8) c O'Brien b Boje | 5 |
| J Allenby | c Peters b Lucas | 9 | (4) c Sales b Logan | 58 |
| *PA Nixon (capt) | c O'Brien b Logan | 30 | (5) b Boje | 110 |
| JJ Cobb | c Wigley b Klusener | 3 | (6) c Sales b Wigley | 21 |
| CW Henderson | c O'Brien b Lucas | 22 | (7) lbw b Boje | 38 |
| RAG Cummins | lbw b Boje | 1 | c Wakely b Boje | 11 |
| SJ Cliff | not out | 1 | c Sales b Klusener | 11 |
| HF Gurney | c Sales b Logan | 1 | not out | 0 |
| Extras | b 4, lb 13, w 11, nb 2 | 30 | b 9, lb 9, w 4, nb 6 | 28 |
| | (all out 63.3 overs) | 236 | (all out 114.2 overs) | 356 |

**Bowling**
Wigley 13-0-71-1. Logan 12.3-4-39-2. Lucas 17-2-49-5. Klusener 13-1-30-1.
Boje 8-1-30-1.
Klusener 22.2-3-71-2. Lucas 5-1-25-0. Boje 44-8-110-6. Crook 15-5-49-0.
Logan 18-2-49-1. Wigley 10-2-34-1.
**Fall of Wickets:** 1-101, 2-105, 3-135, 4-157, 5-173, 6-192, 7-221, 8-222, 9-235
1-54, 2-59, 3-90, 4-207, 5-260, 6-315, 7-330, 8-335, 9-346

*Northamptonshire won by 177 runs –*
*Leicestershire (4pts), Northamptonshire (20pts)*

Michael Carberry, Hampshire's opener, is pictured pulling to the boundary during the second of his two centuries in the match against Worcestershire at Kidderminster.

Amid the carnage, though, there were creditable figures of 5 for 90 for 21-year-old debutant Jonathan Clare, the first Derbyshire bowler to take five wickets or more on his first-class debut for 25 years.

More second-division wins were recorded by Middlesex and Northamptonshire. Another highly promising young fast bowler, the 18-year-old Steven Finn, impressed with a four-wicket second-innings return as Middlesex thumped Gloucestershire at Bristol, while Nicky Boje's all-round dominance and aggressive hundreds from David Sales and Niall O'Brien enabled Northants to overcome a Leicestershire side so full of inexperience that one of their number, 19-year-old seamer Sam Cliff, had to abandon a painting and decorating job in Preston to head back to Grace Road at the last minute.

# ROBERT CROFT

Mark Baldwin talks to Robert Croft about Glamorgan cricket and his own
1,000-wicket landmark in 2007 that set the seal on a legendary Welsh sporting career.

On Thursday 19 September the rain fell unforgivingly from grey Cardiff skies, ruling out any play for the day in Glamorgan's final County Championship fixture of a depressing season and also washing out a planned public lunchtime presentation to Robert Croft, to commemorate the taking of his 1,000th first-class wicket the week before.

That the damp day was also the 10th anniversary of Glamorgan's proud 1997 Championship victory, clinched amid memorable scenes against Somerset at Taunton by a side in which Croft played a leading role, made the gloomy scene of a deserted stadium even more poignant.

By mid-afternoon, however, even though the saturated outfield had meant no cricket, the sun was shining again and the sky above a Sophia Gardens transformed by recent building work was an azure blue. As Croft spoke about his career and the club's future, perhaps there was hope after all of more glory days for a county that has fallen fast, and far, in the past decade.

Glamorgan had gone into their final match, against Gloucestershire, knowing that nothing they could do over those four days could prevent them from finishing last. Moreover, the Championship's wooden spoon followed a one-from-bottom finish in 2006 while a chronic lack of funds on the playing side – mainly due to the massive redevelopment of Sophia Gardens – had condemned David Hemp's side to battling on in 2007 without any official overseas players and no new recruits bar what has emerged from the club's successful youth systems.

It is a fall from grace that has angered county loyalists but Croft, their senior player and former captain, insists that the club can recover the lost ground and be champions again.

The optimism Croft offers, however, is guarded – accompanied as it is by the rider that success can only be achieved again if the club manages its clutch of promising young players correctly, and realises that it will take a careful leavening of senior cricketers to help to fulfil the potential of the likes of James Harris, Ben Wright, Huw Waters, Michael O'Shea and Gareth Rees.

Croft himself, 38 in May 2008, is contracted for one more year but still has to thrash out a rolling contract deal with the club if he is to extend a Glamorgan career that began in 1989.

'The role of the senior player is first and foremost to perform,' said Croft, 'and I feel I have done quite well this summer with more than 50 wickets and more than 500 runs.

'But players like myself are also vital for the development of the youngsters, because it is our experience and guidance which can head them off from the pitfalls which are all too easily found if you come on to the county circuit and have no guidance.

'Take James Harris, for instance. The key to his immediate future is how he is managed. If you uncover a gem, as James unquestionably is despite being only 17, then you have to manage him exceptionally well through the rest of his teenage years and into his early 20s.

Welsh hero: Robert Croft's distinguished career has brought him 21 England Test caps and also domestic titles, including the 1997 County Championship, with Glamorgan.

'I don't want to see players being treated as stars at 18 and then being broken by 21. Look at another young player here at Glamorgan, Adam Harrison. He first played senior cricket at 18 and was a very promising young fast bowler indeed. But he's now just turned 22 and has played only three first-class games. He has huge ankle problems and is struggling.

'Overall, however, I think Glamorgan can be competitive again, but it will take our current group of younger players another six to ten years to get there – if they are managed properly. Don't forget, our team which won in 1997 had been growing together for eight or nine years.'

Bob Willis, the former England captain and Sky pundit, made something of a splash during the last weeks of the summer by calling for ex-England players like Croft, who played 21 Tests and 50 one-day internationals, to 'stop clogging up the county game' and retire.

Croft, however, sees it differently. 'After we had won the Championship in 1997 we lost a clutch of senior players at the same time, and they were not replaced. If too many young lads are asked to swim before they are ready, it is a recipe for seeing them fail to fulfil their potential.

'You need a spine of senior players so that you can blood your youngsters around them and drip-feed them, in effect, into the team. In my early years at Glamorgan there were others around me who were far more experienced and consistent in their performances.

'That's what allows you to develop correctly, and in my case if players like Hugh Morris, Steve Watkin, Viv Richards, Alan Butcher and Colin Metson had not been around to offer me real guidance and wisdom then I don't think I would have achieved what I've done in the game.'

Glamorgan, meanwhile, are more determined than most counties to produce their own talent – irrespective of their

Croft has always regarded playing for England as similar to representing the British Lions at rugby – the highest accolade for a proud Welshman.

inability to buy in star names from overseas. Croft broadly agrees with this approach, but says the club will also need to bring in experienced hands from outside. 'I would like to see a Glamorgan team featuring around seven or eight homegrown players, with the rest made up of overseas

Croft (far right) congratulates a Glamorgan team-mate and has always been a loyal member of the county side. A former captain, he is now back in the ranks but still good enough to do the modern 'double' of 500 runs and 50 wickets during the 2007 season.

players – whether official or Kolpak – and guys brought in from other counties.

'Your first port of call has to be your own backyard, which in Glamorgan's case means Wales, because otherwise what's the point of having youth and academy structures. But if you can't fill a particular position in the team with your own talent then there's no point in cutting off your nose to spite your face. You then have to recruit carefully those extra players you need from outside.'

Croft said he felt very emotional when Niall O'Brien, the Northamptonshire wicketkeeper, became his 1,000th first-class victim during a Championship fixture in mid-September. Another left-hander, Graham Thorpe, had been his maiden first-class scalp, caught by Alan Butcher – Croft's first captain at Glamorgan.

'It means a hell of a lot to me for many reasons, but chiefly because it means I have stayed fit and performed for a long time – and, at around 10 to 12 overs per wicket, it means I have bowled a lot of overs. Also, to do it for one club means I have shown real loyalty.

'But it felt like my head would explode when I took that wicket because my emotions were running so strongly. You never know what will happen during another winter, so I wanted to reach the milestone before the season was over. Of course, it has also been a very frustrating summer both on the field and off it with all the bad weather.

'I was also very proud to become the first Welshman to complete 1,000 wickets and 10,000 runs and I have dedicated my 1,000th wicket to my mother Susan, who has not been in the best of health during the past few years but – like the rest of my family – has been an enormous support to me throughout my career. And that, for me, has been incredibly important.'

## Round Twenty: 11–14 September

A twist in the tale here, as Sussex collapsed to a nine-wicket defeat at Durham, for whom Mark Stoneman, 20, made an impressive five-and-a-half-hour maiden first-class hundred, and Lancashire moved six points clear at the top of the first division table by brushing aside relegated Warwickshire at Old Trafford. Kent, meanwhile, confirmed their first-division status – and their record as the only county never to play second-division Championship cricket – by completing a superb ten-wicket win over Hampshire at the Rose Bowl, in which James Tredwell showed up strongly with both bat and ball in a sturdy overall team performance.

Nine wickets for Murali Kartik and a century for the third successive Championship match by Ed Smith, their captain, proved just enough for Middlesex to overturn a battling Leicestershire at Southgate, while in the other second-division match there was a notable landmark for Robert Croft. Though Glamorgan slid to their ninth defeat in 15 games, Monty Panesar helping Northamptonshire to clean up, Croft had earlier

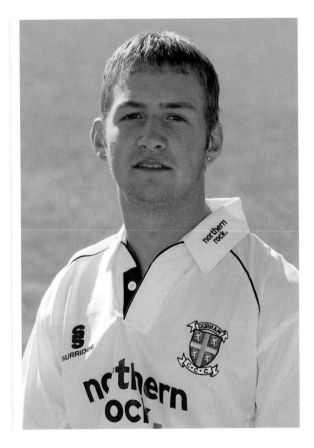

Mark Stoneman, the 20-year-old Durham opener, will long remember a maiden first-class hundred scored against Mushtaq Ahmed, Saqlain Mushtaq and the rest of Sussex's formidable attack.

### Round Twenty: 11–14 September Division One

#### DURHAM v. SUSSEX – at the Riverside

| SUSSEX | First Innings | | Second Innings | |
|---|---|---|---|---|
| CD Nash | lbw b Onions | 49 | lbw b Gibson | 4 |
| RR Montgomerie | lbw b Gibson | 20 | c Coetzer b Gibson | 8 |
| MH Yardy | c Plunkett b Gibson | 0 | c Mustard b Gibson | 9 |
| MW Goodwin | c Muchall b Onions | 66 | c Di Venuto b Davies | 23 |
| CJ Adams (capt) | c Muchall b Onions | 6 | lbw b Plunkett | 44 |
| *AJ Hodd | not out | 2 | b Davies | 0 |
| RSC Martin-Jenkins | not out | 77 | c Mustard b Plunkett | 23 |
| Naved-ul-Hasan | c Mustard b Plunkett | 27 | absent hurt | |
| Saqlain Mushtaq | c Davies b Gibson | 5 | (8) c Wiseman b Davies | 0 |
| Mushtaq Ahmed | run out | 8 | (9) c Di Venuto b Plunkett | 0 |
| JD Lewry | | | (10) not out | 4 |
| Extras | b 2, lb 8, nb 14 | 24 | nb 16 | 16 |
| | (all out 67.2 overs) | 291 | (all out 35.1 overs) | 131 |

Bowling
Gibson 18-3-78-4. Onions 14-5-56-3. Davies 13-3-51-1. Plunkett 16.2-2-60-1. Wiseman 6-0-36-0.
Gibson 14-3-60-3. Onions 5-0-34-0. Davies 12.1-7-28-3. Plunkett 4-2-9-3.
Fall of Wickets: 1-41, 2-41, 3-115, 4-125, 5-149, 6-187, 7-256, 8-273, 9-281
1-4, 2-20, 3-27, 4-85, 5-89, 6-122, 7-127, 8-127, 9-131

| DURHAM | First Innings | | Second Innings | |
|---|---|---|---|---|
| MJ Di Venuto | c Hodd b Martin-Jenkins | 28 | (2) not out | 35 |
| MD Stoneman | b Saqlain Mushtaq | 101 | (1) c Goodwin b Nash | 46 |
| KJ Coetzer | c Davies b Mushtaq Ahmed | 30 | not out | 21 |
| DM B'enstein (capt) | b Mushtaq Ahmed | 67 | | |
| GJ Muchall | c Yardy b Saqlain Mushtaq | 17 | | |
| *P Mustard | c Goodwin b Saqlain Mushtaq | 0 | | |
| OD Gibson | c Goodwin b Saqlain Mushtaq | 0 | | |
| LE Plunkett | lbw b Mushtaq Ahmed | 14 | | |
| PJ Wiseman | c Adams b Martin-Jenkins | 17 | | |
| M Davies | c Montgomerie b M-Jenkins | 19 | | |
| G Onions | not out | 1 | | |
| Extras | b 2, lb 15, w 1, nb 4 | 22 | lb 5 | 5 |
| | (all out 104.3 overs) | 316 | (all out 24.3 overs) | 107 |

Bowling
Lewry 14-3-36-0. Naved-ul-Hasan 15-4-46-0. Martin-Jenkins 16.3-6-33-3. Mushtaq Ahmed 36-3-125-3. Saqlain Mushtaq 23-3-59-4.
Lewry 4-0-10-0. Martin-Jenkins 6-0-27-0. Saqlain Mushtaq 3-0-8-0. Mushtaq Ahmed 1-0-8-0. Nash 5-0-23-1. Yardy 4.3-1-20-0. Goodwin 1-0-6-0.
Fall of Wickets: 1-36, 2-118, 3-233, 4-247, 5-252, 6-256, 7-270, 8-283, 9-315
1-81

*Durham won by 9 wickets – Durham (20pts), Sussex (5pts)*

#### LANCASHIRE v. WARWICKSHIRE – at Old Trafford

| WARWICKSHIRE | First Innings | | Second Innings | |
|---|---|---|---|---|
| IJ Westwood | c Keedy b Mahmood | 2 | c Horton b Keedy | 50 |
| MJ Powell | b Cork | 27 | c Laxman b Keedy | 23 |
| UL Trott | c Sutton b Chapple | 1 | lbw b Chapple | 42 |
| AGR Loudon | c Sutton b Mahmood | 0 | b Mahmood | 80 |
| LC Parker | c Sutton b Cork | 16 | b Newby | 14 |
| *TR Ambrose (capt) | b Mahmood | 2 | c Mahmood b Cork | 16 |
| AG Botha | c Croft b Mahmood | 27 | c Sutton b Cork | 0 |
| HH Streak | c Sutton b Chapple | 7 | c Sutton b Chapple | 4 |
| AC Thomas | c Laxman b Chapple | 12 | lbw b Chapple | 15 |
| NM Carter | c Horton b Chapple | 1 | not out | 12 |
| JE Anyon | not out | 9 | b Mahmood | 0 |
| Extras | nb 2 | 2 | b 6, lb 7, w 1, nb 2 | 16 |
| | (all out 45.2 overs) | 106 | (all out 86 overs) | 272 |

Bowling
Chapple 13.2-3-42-4. Mahmood 15-6-21-4. Cork 9-2-21-2. Newby 6-2-20-0. Keedy 2-0-2-0.
Chapple 20-3-71-3. Mahmood 20-3-72-2. Keedy 24-2-66-2. Cork 13-4-19-2. Newby 9-1-31-1.
Fall of Wickets: 1-13, 2-14, 3-25, 4-41, 5-46, 6-75, 7-84, 8-84, 9-85
1-60, 2-119, 3-133, 4-164, 5-199, 6-201, 7-212, 8-246, 9-272

| LANCASHIRE | First Innings | | Second Innings | |
|---|---|---|---|---|
| MJ Chilton (capt) | c Thomas b Anyon | 18 | (2) not out | 20 |
| PJ Horton | c Ambrose b Botha | 71 | (1) c Ambrose b Carter | 13 |
| SJ Croft | c Ambrose b Carter | 1 | not out | 24 |
| SG Law | c Powell b Carter | 43 | | |
| VVS Laxman | c Ambrose b Carter | 103 | | |
| *LD Sutton | c Ambrose b Streak | 7 | | |
| G Chapple | c Parker b Streak | 16 | | |
| DG Cork | c Anyon b Carter | 0 | | |
| SI Mahmood | c Ambrose b Carter | 10 | | |
| OJ Newby | b Botha | 26 | | |
| G Keedy | not out | 4 | | |
| Extras | lb 3, w 3, nb 6 | 12 | b 6, lb 2, w 1, nb 8 | 17 |
| | (all out 98.4 overs) | 311 | (1 wkt 22.3 overs) | 71 |

Bowling
Anyon 17-1-62-1. Thomas 25-9-75-0. Carter 17.4-2-62-5. Streak 14-2-67-2. Botha 23-9-37-2. Trott 2-1-5-0.
Thomas 5-0-15-0. Streak 11-3-37-0. Carter 5-3-10-1. Botha 1.3-0-1-0.
Fall of Wickets: 1-44, 2-54, 3-128, 4-156, 5-181, 6-212, 7-213, 8-245, 9-305
1-29

*Lancashire won by 9 wickets – Lancashire (20pts), Warwickshire (3pts)*

#### HAMPSHIRE v. KENT – at the Rose Bowl

| KENT | First Innings | | Second Innings | |
|---|---|---|---|---|
| JL Denly | st Pothas b Warne | 54 | not out | 6 |
| RWT Key (capt) | lbw b Ervine | 84 | not out | 0 |
| M van Jaarsveld | b Balcombe | 112 | | |
| MJ Walker | c Brown b Warne | 38 | | |
| DI Stevens | c Pothas b Bruce | 8 | | |
| NJ Dexter | c Pothas b Balcombe | 6 | | |
| *GO Jones | b Tomlinson | 63 | | |
| JC Tredwell | lbw b Adams | 62 | | |
| R McLaren | not out | 35 | | |
| SJ Cook | lbw b Warne | 9 | | |
| MJ Saggers | lbw b Warne | 1 | | |
| Extras | b 3, lb 5, w 1, nb 4 | 13 | | 0 |
| | (all out 146.3 overs) | 495 | (0 wkts 0.3 overs) | 6 |

Bowling
Bruce 30-4-101-1. Tomlinson 21-6-81-1. Balcombe 28-5-106-2. Warne 44.3-6-134-4. Ervine 16-4-47-1. Carberry 4-1-8-0. Adams 3-0-10-1.
Carberry 0.3-0-6-0.
Fall of Wickets: 1-122, 2-169, 3-249, 4-296, 5-310, 6-342, 7-425, 8-462, 9-481

| HAMPSHIRE | First Innings | | Second Innings (following on) | |
|---|---|---|---|---|
| MA Carberry | lbw b Tredwell | 46 | b Tredwell | 31 |
| MJ Brown | c Stevens b Tredwell | 42 | c Jones b Cook | 53 |
| JHK Adams | c Dexter b Tredwell | 3 | lbw b Cook | 16 |
| MJ Lumb | b Cook | 5 | c Jones b van Jaarsveld | 89 |
| CC Benham | c Stevens b McLaren | 17 | lbw b Denly | 32 |
| *N Pothas | c Jones b Cook | 0 | c Walker b Tredwell | 1 |
| SM Ervine | c Jones b Tredwell | 20 | c van Jaarsveld b Tredwell | 1 |
| SK Warne (capt) | c van Jaarsveld b Saggers | 37 | c Stevens b Denly | 4 |
| DJ Balcombe | c Cook b McLaren | 29 | c McLaren b Tredwell | 25 |
| JTA Bruce | not out | 4 | not out | 9 |
| JA Tomlinson | not out | 4 | c Stevens b van Jaarsveld | 3 |
| Extras | lb 5, w 1, nb 8 | 14 | b 5, lb 5, w 1, nb 2 | 18 |
| | (all out 63.4 overs) | 216 | (all out 100.4 overs) | 282 |

Bowling
Saggers 11-1-47-1. McLaren 19.4-3-96-3. Tredwell 23-8-46-4. Cook 10-3-22-2.
Saggers 9-2-26-0. McLaren 12-1-39-0. Tredwell 44.8-114-4. Cook 12-3-37-2. Denly 18-3-34-2. van Jaarsveld 5.4-1-17-2.
Fall of Wickets: 1-79, 2-98, 3-99, 4-99, 5-104, 6-133, 7-139, 8-196, 9-201
1-77, 2-104, 3-117, 4-198, 5-201, 6-207, 7-216, 8-270, 9-270

*Kent won by 10 wickets – Hampshire (3pts), Kent (22pts)*

Kent celebrate another wicket for James Tredwell, their much-underrated 25-year-old off spinner, during the county's vital victory against Hampshire at the Rose Bowl.

celebrated becoming only the third Welshman to reach 1,000 first-class wickets after the great Don Shepherd and fellow slow bowler Johnnie Clay.

It was a memorable achievement for former England off spinner Croft, who played the last of his 21 Tests in 2001. What pleased him more than anything was that it completed a notable all-round double of 10,000 first-class runs and 1,000 wickets, and that it meant that he had bowled consistently well for a long period of time.

Croft, in fact, finished as one of only two cricketers (Derbyshire's seam bowling all-rounder Graham Wagg was the other) to take more than 50 wickets and score 500 runs in the 2007 season – another illustration, if it was needed, that the chirpy Welshman remains a potent force in the domestic game.

## Round Twenty: 11-14 September
## Division Two

### NORTHAMPTONSHIRE v. GLAMORGAN - at Northampton

| GLAMORGAN | First Innings | | Second Innings | |
|---|---|---|---|---|
| GP Rees | lbw b Klusener | 0 | c & b Wigley | 4 |
| WD Bragg | lbw b Logan | 13 | lbw b Panesar | 5 |
| RN Grant | c O'Brien b Klusener | 34 | c & b Wigley | 9 |
| DL Hemp (capt) | b Wigley | 9 | c Peters b Panesar | 31 |
| BJ Wright | lbw b Wigley | 0 | c Sales b Wigley | 0 |
| *MA Wallace | c Sales b Klusener | 120 | b Panesar | 6 |
| AG Wharf | lbw b Klusener | 12 | c Peters b Boje | 18 |
| RDB Croft | c O'Brien b Klusener | 20 | c White b Brown | 1 |
| DA Cosker | lbw b Brown | 14 | c Brown b Panesar | 18 |
| AP Davies | not out | 49 | c Sales b Boje | 4 |
| HT Waters | run out | 0 | not out | 0 |
| Extras | lb 9 | 9 | b 1, lb 5 | 6 |
| | (all out 85.1 overs) | 280 | (all out 39.2 overs) | 102 |

Bowling
Klusener 17.1-6-40-5. Wigley 16-4-75-2. Logan 16-4-68-1. Panesar 12-3-35-0.
Boje 9-2-25-0. Brown 15-4-28-1.
Klusener 6-0-18-0. Wigley 7-3-13-3. Brown 13-3-32-1. Panesar 12.2-1-29-4.
Boje 1-0-4-2.
Fall of Wickets: 1-0, 2-29, 3-48, 4-50, 5-67, 6-87, 7-141, 8-198, 9-272
1-5, 2-23, 3-25, 4-31, 5-62, 6-63, 7-68, 8-94, 9-98

| NORTHANTS | First Innings | | Second Innings | |
|---|---|---|---|---|
| SD Peters | b Cosker | 104 | not out | 5 |
| AR Crook | c Rees b Davies | 41 | not out | 0 |
| RA White | lbw b Croft | 75 | | |
| DJG Sales (capt) | c Waters b Croft | 78 | | |
| N Boje | c Wallace b Cosker | 4 | | |
| L Klusener | lbw b Croft | 23 | | |
| *NJO'Brien | lbw b Croft | 0 | | |
| MS Panesar | lbw b Croft | 30 | | |
| DH Wigley | c Wallace b Cosker | 3 | | |
| RJ Logan | not out | 3 | | |
| JF Brown | c Wallace b Croft | 0 | | |
| Extras | b 2, lb 6, w 6, nb 6 | 20 | | 0 |
| | (all out 131.3 overs) | 381 | (0 wkts 1.3 overs) | 5 |

Bowling
Davies 11-2-48-1. Waters 11-0-34-0. Cosker 51-12-126-3. Croft 53.3-10-138-6.
Wharf 5-0-27-0.
Croft 1-0-1-0. Cosker 0.3-0-4-0.
Fall of Wickets: 1-89, 2-213, 3-250, 4-264, 5-318, 6-320, 7-350, 8-367, 9-381

*Northamptonshire won by 10 wickets –*
*Northamptonshire (21pts), Glamorgan (4pts)*

### MIDDLESEX v. LEICESTERSHIRE - at Southgate

| MIDDLESEX | First Innings | | Second Innings | |
|---|---|---|---|---|
| AJ Strauss | lbw b Taylor | 11 | lbw b Henderson | 23 |
| BA Godleman | b Taylor | 3 | c Nixon b Sadler | 37 |
| ET Smith (capt) | lbw b Masters | 5 | c Nixon b Sadler | 134 |
| EJG Morgan | b Taylor | 1 | (5) c Nixon b Cummins | 1 |
| EC Joyce | c Nixon b Taylor | 74 | (4) c Sadler b Naik | 19 |
| JWM Dalrymple | c Naik b Henderson | 17 | b Henderson | 57 |
| *BJM Scott | c Ackerman b Henderson | 35 | c New b Henderson | 4 |
| TJ Murtagh | c New b Henderson | 0 | c Naik b Henderson | 9 |
| M Kartik | b Taylor | 14 | c & b Cummins | 17 |
| ST Finn | not out | 0 | c Nixon b Cummins | 0 |
| D Evans | b Taylor | 0 | not out | 0 |
| Extras | b 8, nb 4, p 5 | 17 | b 8, lb 7, w 7, nb 8 | 30 |
| | (all out 64 overs) | 176 | (all out 114.3 overs) | 331 |

Bowling
Masters 16-7-30-1. Taylor 17-5-35-6. Allenby 7-1-15-2. Cummins 8-2-21-0.
Henderson 16-3-52-3.
Masters 20-9-43-0. Taylor 16-3-76-0. Henderson 43.3-15-80-5. Naik 19-3-58-1.
Cummins 14-2-54-3. Sadler 2-0-5-1.
Fall of Wickets: 1-8, 2-23, 3-23, 4-27, 5-79, 6-141, 7-141, 8-173, 9-176
1-35, 2-94, 3-165, 4-172, 5-292, 6-300, 7-309, 8-331, 9-331

| LEICESTERSHIRE | First Innings | | Second Innings | |
|---|---|---|---|---|
| TJ New | lbw b Kartik | 47 | b Murtagh | 4 |
| JK Maunders | lbw b Kartik | 58 | c Kartik b Finn | 10 |
| HD Ackerman | c Scott b Murtagh | 22 | c Scott b Murtagh | 7 |
| JL Sadler | c Scott b Kartik | 3 | c Scott b Evans | 25 |
| J Allenby | c & b Murtagh | 1 | c Godleman b Kartik | 46 |
| *PA Nixon (capt) | st Scott b Kartik | 4 | b Kartik | 57 |
| CW Henderson | c Scott b Murtagh | 0 | c Murtagh b Dalrymple | 34 |
| DD Masters | c Strauss b Kartik | 6 | c Kartik b Dalrymple | 39 |
| JE Taylor | c Scott b Finn | 2 | b Kartik | 20 |
| RAG Cummins | not out | 13 | c Scott b Murtagh | 11 |
| JHK Naik | lbw b Kartik | 15 | not out | 0 |
| Extras | b 1, lb 6, w 2, nb 10 | 19 | b 4, lb 4, w 1, nb 12 | 21 |
| | (all out 69.5 overs) | 190 | (all out 90.3 overs) | 279 |

Bowling
Murtagh 19-7-36-3. Evans 4-0-20-0. Finn 13-2-37-1. Kartik 28.5-6-85-6.
Dalrymple 5-1-5-0.
Murtagh 18.3-4-54-3. Finn 11-3-50-1. Kartik 39-10-83-3. Evans 6-2-23-1.
Dalrymple 16-2-61-2.
Fall of Wickets: 1-67, 2-144, 3-144, 4-147, 5-152, 6-153, 7-155, 8-161, 9-161
1-6, 2-14, 3-32, 4-61, 5-153, 6-164, 7-226, 8-253, 9-263

*Middlesex won by 38 runs – Middlesex (17pts),*
*Leicestershire (3pts)*

## Round Twenty-One: 19-22 September

After a title race which many believed to be the closest, and finest, of modern times, it was Sussex who duly retained the crown. It was their third triumph in five seasons – after none at all in their previous long history – and fittingly it was Mushtaq Ahmed, the leg spin sorcerer from Pakistan, who led them off at Hove at the end of an innings and 14-run thrashing of bottom team Worcestershire.

'Little Mushy' had just taken 7 for 132, to go with his first innings 6 for 93, to take his season's wicket tally to 90. For the fifth successive season it was the country's leading haul, and it was a remarkable 39th time that he had taken five wickets or more in an innings in five summers as a cherished Sussex player. In the absence through England calls or injury in this game of Matt Prior, Luke Wright, James Kirtley, Naved-ul-Hasan and Murray Goodwin, the contribution of the tireless Mushtaq was even more valuable, although it was the batting of Chris Nash, Richard Montgomerie and Robin Martin-Jenkins which had given him the runs to play with.

Sussex's celebrations, however, could only start in earnest once news filtered through from The Oval that a magnificent, courageous last day chase of 489 by Lancashire had only narrowly failed. Surrey – or more precisely, Mark Ramprakash – had totally dominated the previous three days, and few would have forecast such a Lancashire fightback when they began the final day at 27 without loss following a Surrey declaration. But a run-a-ball 100 by VVS Laxman, a typically combative 79 from Stuart Law and a series of determined innings right down the order culminated in Dominic Cork heroically leading a last-ditch charge for the line.

In the end, only 4.1 overs remained when Cork, on 47, inside-edged off spinner Murtaza Hussain on to his stumps to leave Surrey breathless winners by 24 runs and Sussex players and fans to crack open the champagne at Hove. 'I have never seen a changing room like it in my life,' said Lancashire captain Mark Chilton. 'The lads are just broken.' Ramprakash, meanwhile, had batted for 730 minutes in the match, and his majestic 196 and 130 not out had made him the first batsman to average more than 100 in successive first-class seasons in England. He also ended the season with 2,026 runs and 97 first-class centuries – 44 of which have come in exactly 100 matches for Surrey.

Elsewhere in the first division a fine captain's innings of 117 by Dale Benkenstein highlighted Durham's eight-wicket win at Kent, but rain put

## Round Twenty-One: 19-22 September Division One

### KENT v. DURHAM – at Canterbury

| KENT | First Innings | | Second Innings | |
|---|---|---|---|---|
| JL Denly | b Onions | 4 | lbw b Wiseman | 30 |
| RWT Key (capt) | c Di Venuto b Gibson | 3 | c Mustard b Wiseman | 33 |
| M van Jaarsveld | c Di Venuto b Davies | 15 | lbw b Plunkett | 25 |
| MJ Walker | c Di Venuto b Davies | 7 | c Di Venuto b Wiseman | 10 |
| NJ Dexter | c Di Venuto b Gibson | 28 | c Mustard b Plunkett | 11 |
| SA Northeast | c Benkenstein b Gibson | 5 | c Stoneman b Plunkett | 0 |
| *GO Jones | b Onions | 32 | not out | 25 |
| JC Tredwell | lbw b Plunkett | 18 | c Chanderpaul b Onions | 5 |
| R McLaren | not out | 54 | c Chanderpaul b Gibson | 8 |
| SJ Cook | c Mustard b Onions | 3 | b Gibson | 0 |
| MJ Saggers | b Davies | 16 | b Wiseman | 14 |
| Extras | b 4, lb 4, w 1, nb 8 | 17 | lb 2, nb 7 | 9 |
| | (all out 50.5 overs) | 212 | (all out 44.1 overs) | 160 |

**Bowling**
Gibson 13-1-60-3. Onions 15-2-49-3. Davies 11.5-4-43-3. Plunkett 11-2-52-1.
Onions 8-2-32-1. Gibson 12-2-42-2. Davies 2-0-12-0. Plunkett 10-1-27-3.
Wiseman 12.1-2-45-4.
**Fall of Wickets:** 1-7, 2-9, 3-27, 4-46, 5-57, 6-84, 7-122, 8-136, 9-147
1-67, 2-68, 3-80, 4-100, 5-104, 6-113, 7-118, 8-137, 9-137

| DURHAM | First Innings | | Second Innings | |
|---|---|---|---|---|
| MJ Di Venuto | c Jones b McLaren | 32 | (2) not out | 23 |
| MD Stoneman | lbw b Saggers | 0 | (1) c Denly b Walker | 6 |
| KJ Coetzer | c Dexter b Tredwell | 4 | c Walker b Denly | 1 |
| S Chanderpaul | c van Jaarsveld b Tredwell | 4 | | |
| DM B'kenstein (capt) | c Tredwell b Saggers | 117 | | |
| *P Mustard | c Jones b McLaren | 22 | | |
| OD Gibson | b Tredwell | 40 | | |
| LE Plunkett | lbw b Saggers | 6 | | |
| PJ Wiseman | lbw b Saggers | 36 | (4) not out | 17 |
| M Davies | not out | 0 | | |
| G Onions | c Walker b McLaren | 3 | | |
| Extras | b 1, lb 8, nb 8 | 17 | lb 2, w 1, nb 2 | 5 |
| | (all out 88 overs) | 321 | (2 wkts 10.1 overs) | 52 |

**Bowling**
Saggers 28-2-89-4. McLaren 19-2-86-3. Cook 13-4-39-0. Tredwell 26-4-96-3.
Denly 2-1-2-0.
Dexter 2-0-8-0. Walker 2-0-10-1. Denly 3.1-2-12-1. Jones 2-0-14-0. Key 1-0-6-0.
**Fall of Wickets:** 1-3, 2-86, 3-86, 4-92, 5-156, 6-242, 7-251, 8-317, 9-318
1-14, 2-32

*Durham won by 8 wickets –*
*Kent (4pts), Durham (20pts)*

---

### SUSSEX v. WORCESTERSHIRE – at Hove

| SUSSEX | First Innings | |
|---|---|---|
| CD Nash | c Davies b Kabir Ali | 89 |
| RR Montgomerie | c Davies b Malik | 82 |
| MH Yardy | c Jones b Mitchell | 52 |
| CJ Adams (capt) | c Davies b Kabir Ali | 74 |
| CD Hopkinson | b Batty b Jones | 7 |
| *AJ Hodd | c Malik b Jones | 8 |
| RSC Martin-Jenkins | c Moore b Mitchell | 99 |
| OP Rayner | c Mitchell b Kabir Ali | 4 |
| Mushtaq Ahmed | c Davies b Malik | 19 |
| CJ Liddle | c sub b Mitchell | 53 |
| JD Lewry | not out | 8 |
| Extras | b 6, lb 13, w 2, nb 16 | 37 |
| | (all out 130.3 overs) | 532 |

**Bowling**
Kabir Ali 17-4-79-3. Malik 23-1-103-2. Jones 24-5-125-2. Batty 26-6-83-0.
Ali 4-1-10-0. Price 17-4-63-0. Mitchell 19.3-3-50-3.
**Fall of Wickets:** 1-155, 2-217, 3-250, 4-262, 5-304, 6-332, 7-340, 8-382, 9-502

| WORCS | First Innings | | Second Innings (following on) | |
|---|---|---|---|---|
| DKH Mitchell | not out | 70 | b Rayner | 31 |
| SC Moore | c Montgomerie b Mushtaq A | 48 | b Martin-Jenkins | 5 |
| MM Ali | c Nash b Rayner | 1 | b Mushtaq Ahmed | 85 |
| GA Hick | lbw b Mushtaq Ahmed | 16 | lbw b Mushtaq Ahmed | 22 |
| *SM Davies | c Nash b Rayner | 31 | c Hopkinson b Mushtaq A | 0 |
| JP Knappett | c Montgomerie b Mushtaq A | 7 | st Hodd b Mushtaq Ahmed | 4 |
| GJ Batty | c Hopkinson b Mushtaq A | 23 | st Hodd b Mushtaq Ahmed | 84 |
| Kabir Ali | lbw b Mushtaq Ahmed | 4 | b Martin-Jenkins | 23 |
| RW Price | b Mushtaq Ahmed | 0 | not out | 15 |
| RA Jones | b Lewry | 0 | c Adams b Mushtaq Ahmed | 2 |
| MN Malik | b Lewry | 0 | c Hopkinson b Mushtaq A | 3 |
| Extras | b 4, lb 2, w 3, nb 4 | 13 | b 10, lb 17, w 2, nb 2 | 31 |
| | (all out 88 overs) | 213 | (all out 72.5 overs) | 305 |

**Bowling**
Lewry 23-3-44-3. Liddle 12-5-34-0. Martin-Jenkins 5-1-22-0.
Mushtaq Ahmed 39-8-93-6. Rayner 9-3-14-1.
Lewry 13-2-39-0. Martin-Jenkins 14-1-41-2. Liddle 5-0-16-0.
Mushtaq Ahmed 27.5-2-132-7. Rayner 12-1-47-1. Nash 1-0-3-0.
**Fall of Wickets:** 1-79, 2-84, 3-107, 4-162, 5-171, 6-197, 7-205, 8-205, 9-208
1-7, 2-67, 3-111, 4-111, 5-117, 6-234, 7-277, 8-287, 9-301

*Sussex won by an innings and 14 runs –*
*Sussex (22pts), Worcestershire (4pts)*

---

### YORKSHIRE v. HAMPSHIRE – at Headingley

| YORKSHIRE | First Innings | |
|---|---|---|
| AW Gale | c Pothas b Bruce | 0 |
| JJ Sayers | c Warne b Ervine | 6 |
| MP Vaughan | b Balcombe | 26 |
| Inzamam-ul-Haq | lbw b Bruce | 51 |
| JA Rudolph | c Warne b Ervine | 0 |
| *GL Brophy | c Lumb b Balcombe | 41 |
| AU Rashid | b Bruce | 14 |
| TT Bresnan | c Ervine b Bruce | 11 |
| D Gough (capt) | c Pothas b Balcombe | 25 |
| MJ Hoggard | c Warne b Bruce | 7 |
| GJ Kruis | not out | 0 |
| Extras | b 4, lb 5, w 1, nb 4 | 14 |
| | (all out 61.1 overs) | 195 |

**Bowling**
Bruce 25-6-73-5. Balcombe 20.1-4-58-3. Ervine 14-2-48-2. Warne 2-0-7-0.
**Fall of Wickets:** 1-0, 2-17, 3-45, 4-46, 5-122, 6-150, 7-156, 8-173, 9-193

| HAMPSHIRE | First Innings | |
|---|---|---|
| MA Carberry | not out | 113 |
| MJ Brown | b Hoggard | 9 |
| JHK Adams | lbw b Hoggard | 18 |
| JP Crawley | c Inzamam-ul-Haq b Bresnan | 57 |
| MJ Lumb | run out | 0 |
| *N Pothas | not out | 34 |
| SM Ervine | | |
| SK Warne (capt) | | |
| DJ Balcombe | | |
| JTA Bruce | | |
| LA Dawson | | |
| Extras | lb 5, w 2, nb 6 | 13 |
| | (4 wkts 60.3 overs) | 244 |

**Bowling**
Hoggard 15-2-76-2. Gough 12-2-56-0. Kruis 10-4-21-0. Bresnan 14.3-4-36-1.
Rashid 9-1-50-0.
**Fall of Wickets:** 1-13, 2-42, 3-179, 4-179

*Match drawn – Yorkshire (5pts),*
*Hampshire (8pts)*

---

### SURREY v. LANCASHIRE – at The Oval

| SURREY | First Innings | | Second Innings | |
|---|---|---|---|---|
| SA Newman | c Sutton b Cork | 39 | c Chilton b Cork | 8 |
| *JN Batty | c Law b Mahmood | 0 | c Mahmood b Newby | 45 |
| MR Ramprakash | c Newby b Chapple | 196 | not out | 130 |
| MA Butcher (capt) | c Croft b Mahmood | 21 | c Sutton b Chapple | 47 |
| SJ Walters | c Croft b Keedy | 36 | c Sutton b Chapple | 14 |
| JGE Benning | c Law b Keedy | 51 | c Croft b Mahmood | 12 |
| CJ Jordan | c Sutton b Mahmood | 34 | not out | 19 |
| MJ Nicholson | c Sutton b Mahmood | 10 | | |
| IDK Salisbury | lbw b Chapple | 12 | | |
| Murtaza Hussain | not out | 9 | | |
| JW Dernbach | not out | 6 | | |
| Extras | lb 11, nb 2 | 13 | lb 11, w 1, nb 8 | 20 |
| | (9 wkts dec 106 overs) | 427 | (5 wkts dec 93 overs) | 295 |

**Bowling**
Chapple 26-10-82-2. Mahmood 26-6-93-4. Newby 14-2-83-0. Cork 15-2-50-1.
Keedy 23-5-97-2. Croft 2-0-11-0.
Chapple 15-3-34-1. Mahmood 17-2-65-1. Cork 15-2-52-1. Keedy 31-10-68-0.
Newby 15-0-65-2.
**Fall of Wickets:** 1-2, 2-74, 3-117, 4-213, 5-301, 6-361, 7-391, 8-407, 9-412
1-23, 2-112, 3-189, 4-217, 5-243

| LANCASHIRE | First Innings | | Second Innings | |
|---|---|---|---|---|
| MJ Chilton (capt) | lbw b Nicholson | 4 | (2) st Batty b Hussain | 30 |
| PJ Horton | c Batty b Dernbach | 48 | (1) c Batty b Jordan | 39 |
| SJ Croft | c Batty b Nicholson | 0 | (5) c Batty b Dernbach | 45 |
| SG Law | b Nicholson | 45 | c Batty b Dernbach | 79 |
| VVS Laxman | c Nicholson b Jordan | 53 | (3) c Ramprakash b Salisbury | 100 |
| *LD Sutton | lbw b Hussain | 17 | c Benning b Jordan | 32 |
| G Chapple | c Benning b Salisbury | 1 | c sub b Hussain | 29 |
| DG Cork | not out | 46 | b Hussain | 47 |
| SI Mahmood | c Newman b Hussain | 3 | c Batty b Hussain | 26 |
| OJ Newby | c Batty b Jordan | 0 | c Ramprakash b Dernbach | 4 |
| G Keedy | c Batty b Jordan | 2 | not out | 4 |
| Extras | b 3, lb 1, w 1, nb 10 | 15 | b 8, lb 14, w 1, nb 6 | 29 |
| | (all out 67.2 overs) | 234 | (all out 101.5 overs) | 464 |

**Bowling**
Nicholson 8-3-30-3. Dernbach 11-2-41-1. Hussain 21-4-49-2. Jordan 12.2-1-50-3.
Salisbury 15-1-60-1.
Nicholson 20-1-102-0. Dernbach 18-2-85-3. Hussain 34.4-14-126-4.
Jordan 18-0-78-2. Salisbury 11.1-0-51-1.
**Fall of Wickets:** 1-4, 2-8, 3-86, 4-120, 5-158, 6-161, 7-198, 8-205, 9-206
1-56, 2-114, 3-229, 4-306, 5-307, 6-358, 7-379, 8-431, 9-452

*Surrey won by 24 runs – Surrey (22pts),*
*Lancashire (4pts)*

The peerless Mark Ramprakash, England's best batsman of his generation – whatever the evidence provided seemingly to the contrary by the national selectors – flips another ball away for runs during the second successive season he reached both 2,000 first-class runs and topped 100 in the batting averages.

## Round Twenty-One: 19-22 September Division Two

### SOMERSET v. NOTTINGHAMSHIRE – at Taunton

| NOTTS | First Innings | | Second Innings | |
|---|---|---|---|---|
| WI Jefferson | c Edwards b Jones | 28 | c Jones b Munday | 44 |
| JER Gallian | c Trescothick b Willoughby | 18 | (10) c Hildreth b Munday | 14 |
| MA Wagh | b Trego | 41 | c Kieswetter b Munday | 3 |
| SP Fleming (capt) | lbw b Munday | 16 | lbw b Munday | 10 |
| SR Patel | c Kieswetter b Munday | 2 | lbw b Blackwell | 4 |
| BM Shafayat | b Trego | 10 | (2) c & b Munday | 57 |
| *CMW Read | b Willoughby | 9 | (6) c Trescothick b Munday | 8 |
| AR Adams | c Willoughby b Munday | 1 | (7) c Jones b Munday | 16 |
| PJ Franks | c Trescothick b Willoughby | 28 | (8) b Blackwell | 30 |
| RJ Sidebottom | c Langer b Willoughby | 4 | (9) b Munday | 0 |
| CE Shreck | not out | 0 | not out | 0 |
| Extras | lb 1 | 1 | lb 4 | 4 |
| | (all out 39 overs) | 158 | (all out 49.4 overs) | 190 |

**Bowling**
Willoughby 14-4-39-4. Jones 12-1-53-1. Trego 7-0-50-3. Blackwell 2-1-5-0.
Munday 4-1-10-2.
Willoughby 9-1-43-0. Jones 5-1-23-0. Blackwell 19.4-4-65-2. Munday 16-1-55-8.
**Fall of Wickets:** 1-37, 2-59, 3-102, 4-105, 5-105, 6-124, 7-125, 8-133, 9-145
1-98, 2-104, 3-109, 4-118, 5-122, 6-130, 7-143, 8-152, 9-182

| SOMERSET | First Innings | |
|---|---|---|
| ME Trescothick | c Shafayat b Franks | 112 |
| NJ Edwards | lbw b Shreck | 4 |
| JL Langer (capt) | lbw b Adams | 16 |
| JC Hildreth | c Read b Adams | 0 |
| WJ Durston | c Fleming b Shreck | 17 |
| ID Blackwell | c sub b Shreck | 141 |
| PD Trego | not out | 113 |
| *C Kieswetter | b Patel | 1 |
| PS Jones | c Shreck b Patel | 37 |
| MK Munday | b Wagh | 9 |
| CM Willoughby | c Shafayat b Wagh | 0 |
| Extras | b 1, lb 12, nb 6 | 19 |
| | (all out 104 overs) | 469 |

**Bowling**
Sidebottom 22-5-63-0. Shreck 22-1-110-3. Adams 25-4-119-2. Franks 16-0-90-1.
Patel 17-4-68-2. Wagh 2-0-6-2.
**Fall of Wickets:** 1-8, 2-54, 3-54, 4-98, 5-302, 6-310, 7-318, 8-401, 9-469

*Somerset won by an innings and 121 runs –*
*Somerset (22pts), Nottinghamshire (3pts)*

---

### ESSEX v. MIDDLESEX – at Chelmsford

| ESSEX | First Innings | | Second Innings | |
|---|---|---|---|---|
| V Chopra | c Joyce b Finn | 4 | not out | 24 |
| GW Flower | c Strauss b Williams | 157 | not out | 20 |
| T Westley | c Kartik b Williams | 29 | | |
| TJ Phillips | b Williams | 7 | | |
| ML Pettini (capt) | c Smith b Williams | 6 | | |
| *JS Foster | run out | 96 | | |
| JD Middlebrook | b Finn | 21 | | |
| GR Napier | lbw b Williams | 6 | | |
| AJ Tudor | c Scott b Finn | 11 | | |
| AP Palladino | c Kartik b Finn | 5 | | |
| JS Ahmed | not out | 0 | | |
| Extras | b 6, lb 5, w 4, nb 8 | 23 | lb 7, w 2 | 9 |
| | (all out 95.4 overs) | 365 | (0 wkts 17.1 overs) | 53 |

**Bowling**
Finn 22-5-61-4. Williams 28.4-4-112-5. Evans 16-4-51-0. Kartik 20-2-79-0.
Dalrymple 5-0-25-0. Joyce 4-0-26-0.
Finn 6-0-19-0. Williams 6-3-14-0. Evans 3-1-9-0. Morgan 2-1-0-4-0.
**Fall of Wickets:** 1-7, 2-54, 3-72, 4-86, 5-267, 6-310, 7-326, 8-349, 9-361

| MIDDLESEX | First Innings | | Second Innings (following on) | |
|---|---|---|---|---|
| AJ Strauss | c Chopra b Palladino | 11 | c Chopra b Palladino | 7 |
| BA Godleman | c Flower b Ahmed | 0 | lbw b Ahmed | 17 |
| ET Smith (capt) | c Chopra b Napier | 24 | b Ahmed | 13 |
| EJG Morgan | b Palladino | 7 | (5) c Foster b Middlebrook | 71 |
| EC Joyce | lbw b Ahmed | 9 | (4) lbw b Palladino | 38 |
| JWM Dalrymple | c Pettini b Napier | 0 | b Napier | 21 |
| *BJM Scott | not out | 61 | c Westley b Middlebrook | 31 |
| M Kartik | c Chopra b Tudor | 30 | not out | 11 |
| REM Williams | c Middlebrook b Tudor | 15 | c Flower b Tudor | 6 |
| ST Finn | lbw b Palladino | 0 | c Chopra b Tudor | 3 |
| D Evans | c Westley b Palladino | 0 | st Foster b Middlebrook | 0 |
| Extras | b 4, lb 1, nb 2 | 7 | b 4, lb 8, w 2, nb 14 | 28 |
| | (all out 45.5 overs) | 171 | (all out 69.5 overs) | 246 |

**Bowling**
Tudor 13-3-48-3. Palladino 15.5-5-44-4. Napier 10-4-44-2. Ahmed 7-2-30-1.
Tudor 18-5-56-2. Palladino 19-6-53-2. Napier 16-3-71-1. Ahmed 10-2-41-2.
Middlebrook 6.5-1-13-3.
**Fall of Wickets:** 1-5, 2-11, 3-27, 4-47, 5-51, 6-64, 7-128, 8-148, 9-155
1-9, 2-45, 3-52, 4-117, 5-170, 6-225, 7-230, 8-239, 9-245

*Essex won by 10 wickets –*
*Essex (21pts), Middlesex (3pts)*

---

### GLAMORGAN v. GLOUCESTERSHIRE – at Cardiff

| GLOS | First Innings | |
|---|---|---|
| CM Spearman | c Harris b Waters | 14 |
| Kadeer Ali | c & b Croft | 79 |
| GP Hodnett | c Wallace b Harris | 4 |
| HJH Marshall | c Cosker b Harris | 121 |
| APR Gidman | not out | 17 |
| CG Taylor | not out | 20 |
| *SJ Adshead | | |
| J Lewis (capt) | | |
| CG Greenidge | | |
| SP Kirby | | |
| V Banerjee | | |
| Extras | lb 3, nb 4 | 7 |
| | (4 wkts 63 overs) | 262 |

**Bowling**
Harris 14-2-63-2. Waters 13-1-59-1. Owen 8-0-37-0. Croft 21-2-65-1.
Grant 3-0-23-0. Cosker 4-1-12-0.
**Fall of Wickets:** 1-15, 2-22, 3-214, 4-226

**GLAMORGAN**
MP O'Shea
GP Rees
RN Grant
DL Hemp (capt)
BJ Wright
*MA Wallace
RDB Croft
JAR Harris
DA Cosker
WT Owen
HT Waters

*Match drawn – Glamorgan (5pts),*
*Gloucestershire (6pts)*

---

### DERBYSHIRE v. NORTHAMPTONSHIRE – at Derby

| DERBYSHIRE | First Innings | | Second Innings | |
|---|---|---|---|---|
| SD Stubbings (capt) | lbw b Lucas | 18 | (2) run out | 46 |
| PM Borrington | c O'Brien b Klusener | 50 | (1) c O'Brien b Lucas | 14 |
| Hassan Adnan | c Sales b Wigley | 0 | lbw b Boje | 4 |
| GM Smith | b Klusener | 21 | b Boje | 8 |
| DJ Redfern | c White b Brown | 43 | c O'Brien b Wigley | 51 |
| FA Klokker | c O'Brien b Klusener | 23 | c O'Brien b Wigley | 48 |
| *DJ Pipe | b Klusener | 35 | b Wigley | 1 |
| GG Wagg | st O'Brien b Boje | 82 | not out | 17 |
| JL Clare | run out | 22 | | |
| J Needham | not out | 36 | | |
| T Lungley | lbw b Klusener | 24 | | |
| Extras | lb 21, w 1, nb 6 | 28 | b 9, lb 3, w 1, nb 6 | 19 |
| | (all out 112.3 overs) | 382 | (7 wkts dec 64.2 overs) | 208 |

**Bowling**
Klusener 29.3-6-98-5. Lucas 23-5-55-1. Wigley 14-4-64-1. Logan 16-4-63-0.
Boje 21-9-53-1. Brown 9-3-28-1.
Klusener 14-2-31-0. Lucas 10-0-39-1. Logan 4-0-17-0. Boje 23-4-77-2.
Brown 9-3-22-0. Wigley 4.2-0-10-3.
**Fall of Wickets:** 1-43, 2-54, 3-54, 4-98, 5-135, 6-194, 7-257, 8-297, 9-343
1-49, 2-62, 3-74, 4-76, 5-167, 6-187, 7-208

| NORTHANTS | First Innings | | Second Innings | |
|---|---|---|---|---|
| AG Wakely | b Clare | 7 | c Redfern b Wagg | 1 |
| AR Crook | b Lungley | 40 | c Pipe b Smith | 46 |
| RA White | c Smith b Wagg | 17 | lbw b Lungley | 0 |
| DJG Sales (capt) | c Pipe b Clare | 0 | | |
| N Boje | c Stubbings b Lungley | 37 | not out | 53 |
| L Klusener | c Pipe b Clare | 6 | not out | 86 |
| *NJO'Brien | c Redfern b Lungley | 0 | (4) c Pipe b Clare | 30 |
| DS Lucas | lbw b Lungley | 37 | | |
| DH Wigley | c Borrington b Clare | 10 | | |
| RJ Logan | c Borrington b Needham | 8 | | |
| JF Brown | not out | 23 | | |
| Extras | b 12, lb 14, w 4, nb 20 | 50 | w 1, nb 12 | 13 |
| | (all out 60.1 overs) | 235 | (4 wkts 48 overs) | 229 |

**Bowling**
Lungley 18.1-3-61-4. Wagg 16-2-75-1. Clare 18-5-59-4. Needham 7-3-14-1.
Smith 1-1-0-0.
Lungley 11-0-63-1. Wagg 12-2-56-1. Smith 9-2-43-1. Clare 8-1-54-1.
Needham 8-3-13-0.
**Fall of Wickets:** 1-58, 2-62, 3-66, 4-97, 5-138, 6-140, 7-142, 8-160, 9-185
1-5, 2-10, 3-76, 4-80

*Match drawn – Derbyshire (11pts),*
*Northamptonshire (8pts)*

Mike Munday, Somerset's 22-year-old leg-spin prodigy, finished off the county's superb season in some style by demolishing Nottinghamshire's second innings at Taunton with an eight-wicket haul that promises much for the future.

paid to any play on the final two days at Headingley, where Hampshire had moved into a strong position against Yorkshire.

A final round tussle between the two promoted second division sides, at Taunton, ended in an eye-catching innings and 121-run victory for Somerset, for whom Marcus Trescothick, Ian Blackwell and Pete Trego hit rollicking hundreds and Michael Munday, a 22-year-old leg spinner, picked up a magnificent 8 for 55 as Nottinghamshire tumbled from 98 for 0 to 190 all out.

Grant Flower's 157, and 96 from James Foster, anchored Essex's ten-wicket win against Middlesex at Chelmsford, Lance Klusener enlivened proceedings with bat and ball as Northamptonshire drew with Derbyshire at Derby and Hamish Marshall's attractive 123-ball 121 proved to be the last notable action of the season at Cardiff, where the final three days of Glamorgan's match against Gloucestershire all disappeared under the weight of a series of torrential storms in South Wales that left the Sophia Gardens outfield completely sodden.

### Final Division One Table

|  | P | W | L | D | T | Ab | Bat | Bowl | Pens | Pts |
|---|---|---|---|---|---|---|---|---|---|---|
| Sussex | 16 | 7 | 3 | 5 | 0 | 1 | 37 | 43 | 0.00 | 202.00 |
| Durham | 16 | 7 | 5 | 4 | 0 | 0 | 38 | 47 | 1.50 | 197.50 |
| Lancashire | 16 | 5 | 2 | 8 | 0 | 1 | 40 | 44 | 0.00 | 190.00 |
| Surrey | 16 | 5 | 4 | 6 | 0 | 1 | 41 | 40 | 1.00 | 178.00 |
| Hampshire | 16 | 5 | 3 | 8 | 0 | 0 | 32 | 43 | 0.00 | 177.00 |
| Yorkshire | 16 | 4 | 4 | 8 | 0 | 0 | 49 | 38 | 0.00 | 175.00 |
| Kent | 16 | 3 | 5 | 7 | 0 | 1 | 43 | 36 | 0.00 | 153.00 |
| Warwickshire | 16 | 2 | 5 | 9 | 0 | 0 | 40 | 35 | 0.00 | 139.00 |
| Worcestershire | 16 | 1 | 8 | 5 | 0 | 2 | 18 | 35 | 0.00 | 95.00 |

### Final Division Two Table

|  | P | W | L | D | T | Ab | Bat | Bowl | Pens | Pts |
|---|---|---|---|---|---|---|---|---|---|---|
| Somerset | 16 | 10 | 1 | 5 | 0 | 0 | 65 | 41 | 0.00 | 266.00 |
| Nottinghamshire | 16 | 6 | 3 | 7 | 0 | 0 | 60 | 43 | 0.50 | 214.50 |
| Middlesex | 16 | 6 | 2 | 8 | 0 | 0 | 35 | 43 | 1.50 | 192.50 |
| Essex | 16 | 6 | 4 | 6 | 0 | 0 | 40 | 36 | 2.00 | 182.00 |
| Northamptonshire | 16 | 5 | 5 | 6 | 0 | 0 | 44 | 38 | 0.00 | 176.00 |
| Derbyshire | 16 | 3 | 5 | 8 | 0 | 0 | 30 | 44 | 1.00 | 147.00 |
| Gloucestershire | 16 | 3 | 5 | 8 | 0 | 0 | 32 | 37 | 3.50 | 139.50 |
| Leicestershire | 16 | 2 | 8 | 5 | 0 | 1 | 32 | 35 | 4.00 | 115.00 |
| Glamorgan | 16 | 1 | 9 | 5 | 0 | 1 | 26 | 37 | 8.50 | 92.50 |

Glamorgan had eight points deducted for a poor pitch.

# SUSSEX

Bruce Talbot, who has covered Sussex cricket for the *Brighton Evening Argus* for more than a decade, offers a personal view of the county's latest Championship triumph.

Y ou never forget your first time. For Sussex supporters the wonderful images of the county's Championship win in 2003 are ingrained in the memory. Hardly surprising really – they had waited since the days when players wore top hats and bowled underarm to celebrate one.

But 2007 ran it close, especially the nerve-shredding final afternoon when Lancashire threatened to pickpocket the title. In their own way, the scenes that greeted Sussex's third title were as memorable as that moment in 2003 when Murray Goodwin's boundary off Phil DeFreitas secured the first Championship after more than a hundred summers of trying. Sussex had done their bit much earlier in the day when they eased to victory over Worcestershire before being led off the

field by Richard Montgomerie, who had announced his retirement, and the brilliant leg spinner Mushtaq Ahmed. All they could do was wait for events at The Oval to unfold. Hundreds stayed behind to enjoy the late-summer sunshine and watch as the players' children staged an impromptu game out in the middle.

With no live TV coverage in the bars, they were forced to rely on text messages from friends viewing at home. Several dozen sat transfixed in front of the pavilion TV, watching the score change on Ceefax. The numbers in the crowd swelled as hundreds of Brighton supporters arrived from Withdean. And, up in the press box, I discovered that every time I went to the toilet another Lancashire wicket fell. As Dominic Cork defiantly inched Lancashire towards their target, colleagues urged me to make yet another visit to the loo. I hadn't even

got halfway down the steps when a huge roar erupted. And I knew it wasn't because Mark Robinson's daughter had just hit a boundary.

It was a surreal afternoon but the celebrations which followed were pure Sussex. A couple of hours after he had held the trophy aloft, Chris Adams and his players emerged from the dressing room and marched like some triumphant band of brothers returning from the battlefield to the place that is the heartbeat of the club – the Sussex Cricketer pub at the ground entrance. As they arrived, an ear-shattering rendition of the county's hoary old anthem 'Sussex by the Sea' pierced the air. As one, players, backroom staff and supporters – many of them in tears – savoured a special moment. Within minutes the trophy was being passed around the garden and countless pictures were taken of fans with the trophy and their favourite player (or both). It was a scene hard to imagine being repeated at Old Trafford or The Oval.

It has been my good fortune to be writing about Sussex during the county's golden age – an unprecedented era of success that has brought them six trophies since Adams took over as captain in 1998. The 2003 victory is still my favourite memory, but 2007 comes a very close second because it was not really until that last Lancashire wicket fell that I felt Sussex were going to win. A week earlier I had made the long journey back down the A1 convinced Lancashire would be champions. Sussex had just been beaten by Durham, which meant they no longer controlled their own destiny and injuries were decimating the squad, just as they had done at the start of the season. But somehow Sussex always found a way to win. And I'm not just thinking about the final game against Worcestershire, which they controlled from the moment Adams won the toss and Mushtaq was thrown the ball.

For the first time in the Adams era, the squad was weakened by England call-ups with Matt Prior missing nearly all summer and Mike Yardy, James Kirtley and Luke Wright all part of the England one-day squads. Sussex have had an enviable record of keeping their players fit but in 2007 they had to cope with a

**Above** Skipper Chris Adams (front left) leads the celebrations as Sussex's players hear that they are Champions again.

**Opposite** Another wicket for the maestro: Mushtaq Ahmed dismisses Worcestershire's Richard Jones as Sussex close in on the title at Hove.

series of injuries. Yardy, the bedrock of their top order, missed two months with a broken finger while at some stage key players like Jason Lewry, Rana Naved and Murray Goodwin were all missing. After they lost successive games by an innings to Warwickshire and Kent in early season most people were predicting relegation. And they weren't all from outside the county.

But new talent blossomed. Chris Nash and Andrew Hodd emerged from second-team cricket to play key roles, Wright realised his potential while the senior players quietly glued the whole thing together, and none more so than 'Mushy'. He barely had the strength to acknowledge the cheers when he led the team off against Worcestershire as the physical effort of bowling 667 overs – more than anyone else in the country – took its toll on the 36-year-old's creaking knees. But 459 Championship wickets in five years are testament to the massive part he has played and will continue to do so, at least for two more years.

'The team, the supporters – everyone at Sussex is united as one,' he said, during a moment of quiet reflection. 'That's what brings us success and makes this club so special'. Long may it continue.

## COUNTY CHAMPIONSHIP FEATURES 2007

### INDIVIDUAL SCORES OVER 200

| | | | |
|---|---|---|---|
| JL Langer | 315 | Somerset v. Middlesex | at Taunton |
| ME Trescothick | 284 | Somerset v. Northamptonshire | at Northampton |
| DJ Hussey | 275 | Nottinghamshire v. Essex | at Trent Bridge |
| MR Ramprakash | 266* | Surrey v. Sussex | at Hove |
| TR Ambrose | 251* | Warwickshire v. Worcestershire | at Worcester |
| SP Fleming | 243 | Nottinghamshire v. Derbyshire | at Chesterfield |
| CL White | 241 | Somerset v. Gloucestershire | at Taunton |
| CMW Read | 240 | Nottinghamshire v. Essex | at Chelmsford |
| VS Solanki | 232 | Worcestershire v. Surrey | at Worcester |
| RS Bopara | 221 | Derbyshire v. Somerset | at Taunton |
| JA Rudolph | 220 | Yorkshire v. Warwickshire | at Scarborough |
| DJG Sales | 219 | Northamptonshire v. Glamorgan | at Colwyn Bay |
| RC Irani | 218 | Essex v. Glamorgan | at Chelmsford |
| Younus Khan | 217* | Yorkshire v. Kent | at Scarborough |
| SG Law | 206 | Lancashire v. Yorkshire | at Headingley |
| MW Goodwin | 205* | Sussex v. Surrey | at Hove |
| MJ Di Venuto | 204* | Durham v. Kent | at the Riverside |
| JS Foster | 204 | Essex v. Nottinghamshire | at Chelmsford |
| GW Flower | 203 | Essex v. Northamptonshire | at Chelmsford |
| Younus Khan | 202* | Yorkshire v. Hampshire | at the Rose Bowl |

### BEST INNINGS BOWLING (6 WICKETS OR MORE)

| | | | |
|---|---|---|---|
| OD Gibson | 10/47 | Durham v. Hampshire | at the Riverside |
| Kabir Ali | 8/50 | Worcestershire v. Lancashire | at Old Trafford |
| MK Munday | 8/55 | Somerset v. Nottinghamshire | at Taunton |
| OD Gibson | 8/68 | Durham v. Lancashire | at Blackpool |
| G Onions | 8/101 | Durham v. Warwickshire | at Edgbaston |
| AR Caddick | 7/30 | Somerset v. Gloucestershire | at Bristol |
| CE Shreck | 7/35 | Nottinghamshire v. Derbyshire | at Trent Bridge |
| AJ Bichel | 7/36 | Essex v. Derbyshire | at Derby |
| OD Gibson | 7/46 | Durham v. Worcestershire | at the Riverside |
| G Chapple | 7/53 | Lancashire v. Durham | at Blackpool |
| M Davies | 7/59 | Nottinghamshire v. Northamptonshire | at Trent Bridge |
| JAR Harris | 7/66 | Glamorgan v. Gloucestershire | at Bristol |
| Mushtaq Ahmed | 7/72 | Sussex v. Hampshire | at Arundel |
| OD Gibson | 7/81 | Durham v. Yorkshire | at the Riverside |
| SR Clark | 7/82 | Hampshire v. Lancashire | at the Rose Bowl |
| Danish Kaneria | 7/95 | Essex v. Somerset | at Chelmsford |
| GP Swann | 7/100 | Nottinghamshire v. Glamorgan | at Swansea |
| Danish Kaneria | 7/105 | Essex v. Glamorgan | at Chelmsford |
| Mushtaq Ahmed | 7/111 | Sussex v. Warwickshire | at Hove |
| Mushtaq Ahmed | 7/132 | Sussex v. Worcestershire | at Hove |

### BEST MATCH BOWLING

| | | | |
|---|---|---|---|
| Danish Kaneria | 13/181 | Essex v. Glamorgan | at Chelmsford |
| Mushtaq Ahmed | 13/225 | Sussex v. Worcestershire | at Hove |
| AR Caddick | 12/71 | Somerset v. Gloucestershire | at Bristol |
| OD Gibson | 12/100 | Durham v. Hampshire | at the Riverside |
| JAR Harris | 12/118 | Glamorgan v. Gloucestershire | at Bristol |
| Harbhajan Singh | 11/91 | Surrey v. Kent | at Canterbury |
| AJ Bichel | 11/132 | Essex v. Derbyshire | at Derby |
| SK Warne | 11/133 | Hampshire v. Durham | at the Rose Bowl |
| RDB Croft | 11/150 | Glamorgan v. Derbyshire | at Cardiff |
| OD Gibson | 11/150 | Durham v. Worcestershire | at the Riverside |
| Mushtaq Ahmed | 11/281 | Sussex v. Warwickshire | at Hove |
| MK Munday | 10/65 | Somerset v. Nottinghamshire | at Taunton |
| G Chapple | 10/86 | Lancashire v. Durham | at Blackpool |
| Kabir Ali | 10/102 | Worcestershire v. Lancashire | at Old Trafford |
| SP Kirby | 10/116 | Gloucestershire v. Essex | at Southend |
| OD Gibson | 10/144 | Durham v. Yorkshire | at the Riverside |
| Mushtaq Ahmed | 10/219 | Sussex v. Kent | at Hove |
| GP Swann | 10/243 | Nottinghamshire v. Glamorgan | at Swansea |
| CE Shreck | 9/51 | Nottinghamshire v. Derbyshire | at Trent Bridge |
| CEW Silverwood | 9/62 | Middlesex v. Somerset | at Lord's |

## HIGHEST TEAM TOTALS

| | | |
|---|---|---|
| 850 for 7d | Somerset v. Middlesex | at Taunton |
| 801 for 8d | Derbyshire v. Somerset | at Taunton |
| 791 | Nottinghamshire v. Essex | at Chelmsford |
| 701 for 6d | Worcestershire v. Surrey | at Worcester |
| 700 for 9d | Essex v. Nottinghamshire | at Chelmsford |
| 675 for 5d | Somerset v. Leicestershire | at Taunton |
| 664 for 7d | Nottinghamshire v. Essex | at Trent Bridge |
| 650 for 8d | Gloucestershire v. Leicestershire | at Leicester |
| 649 for 5d | Essex v. Northamptonshire | at Chelmsford |
| 641 for 6d | Somerset v. Northamptonshire | at Northampton |
| 626 for 3d | Surrey v. Sussex | at Hove |
| 610 for 6d | Warwickshire v. Worcestershire | at Worcester |
| 600 for 4d | Middlesex v. Somerset | at Taunton |
| 597 for 8d | Sussex v. Yorkshire | at Hove |
| 594 for 9d | Yorkshire v. Surrey | at The Oval |
| 584 for 7d | Essex v. Glamorgan | at Chelmsford |
| 564 for 5d | Kent v. Surrey | at Whitgift School |
| 561 for 7d | Yorkshire v. Warwickshire | at Scarborough |
| 556 | Surrey v. Hampshire | at the Rose Bowl |
| 551 for 8d | Yorkshire v. Kent | at Tunbridge Wells |
| 551 | Derbyshire v. Essex | at Chelmsford |

## LOWEST TEAM TOTALS

| | | |
|---|---|---|
| 52 | Derbyshire v. Somerset | at Derby |
| 60 | Glamorgan v. Middlesex | at Swansea |
| 86 | Worcestershire v. Hampshire | at the Rose Bowl |
| 88 | Essex v. Gloucestershire | at Southend |
| 89 | Yorkshire v. Sussex | at Hove |
| 100 | Worcestershire v. Sussex | at Worcester |
| 102 | Sussex v. Kent | at Canterbury |
| 102 | Glamorgan v. Northamptonshire | at Northampton |
| 106 | Glamorgan v. Middlesex | at Lord's |
| 106 | Warwickshire v. Lancashire | at Old Trafford |
| 107 | Warwickshire v. Kent | at Canterbury |
| 108 | Derbyshire v. Nottinghamshire | at Trent Bridge |
| 115 | Hampshire v. Durham | at the Riverside |
| 120 | Surrey v. Lancashire | at Old Trafford |
| 121 | Gloucestershire v. Somerset | at Bristol |
| 127 | Glamorgan v. Derbyshire | at Derby |
| 129 | Worcestershire v. Yorkshire | at Headingley |
| 129 | Warwickshire v. Yorkshire | at Scarborough |
| 131 | Sussex v. Durham | at the Riverside |
| 132 | Worcestershire v. Yorkshire | at Headingley |

## LEADING RUN SCORERS

| Player | Runs | Matches |
|---|---|---|
| MR Ramprakash (Surrey) | 2026 | 15 |
| DJG Sales (Northamptonshire) | 1384 | 16 |
| MJ Di Venuto (Durham) | 1329 | 13 |
| ME Trescothick (Somerset) | 1315 | 15 |
| SM Katich (Derbyshire) | 1284 | 13 |
| DM Benkenstein (Durham) | 1278 | 16 |
| SG Law (Lancashire) | 1277 | 14 |
| MA Wagh (Nottinghamshire) | 1253 | 16 |
| RWT Key (Kent) | 1250 | 15 |
| JL Langer (Somerset) | 1231 | 16 |
| DJ Hussey (Nottinghamshire) | 1219 | 12 |
| JC Hildreth (Somerset) | 1147 | 16 |
| CL White (Somerset) | 1083 | 12 |
| MW Goodwin (Sussex) | 1078 | 14 |
| JA Rudolph (Yorkshire) | 1078 | 15 |
| MJ Brown (Hampshire) | 1078 | 16 |
| ET Smith (Middlesex) | 1070 | 16 |
| MA Carberry (Hampshire) | 1067 | 13 |
| NJ Edwards (Somerset) | 1039 | 16 |
| PJ Horton (Lancashire) | 1034 | 13 |

## MOST SIXES

| Player | Sixes | Matches |
|---|---|---|
| DJ Hussey (Nottinghamshire) | 32 | 12 |
| DJG Sales (Northamptonshire) | 24 | 16 |
| MR Ramprakash (Surrey) | 19 | 15 |
| GR Napier (Essex) | 18 | 9 |
| ID Blackwell (Somerset) | 16 | 14 |
| CMW Read (Nottinghamshire) | 16 | 16 |
| CL White (Somerset) | 14 | 12 |
| SM Katich (Derbyshire) | 14 | 13 |
| CJ Adams (Sussex) | 14 | 15 |
| OD Gibson (Durham) | 13 | 15 |
| M van Jaarsveld (Kent) | 13 | 15 |
| PD Trego (Somerset) | 13 | 16 |
| SR Patel (Nottinghamshire) | 11 | 13 |
| DJ Pipe (Derbyshire) | 11 | 14 |
| SP Fleming (Nottinghamshire) | 10 | 11 |
| DI Stevens (Kent) | 10 | 11 |
| ME Trescothick (Somerset) | 10 | 15 |
| JA Rudolph (Yorkshire) | 10 | 15 |
| MA Wagh (Nottinghamshire) | 10 | 16 |
| C White (Yorkshire) | 9 | 11 |
| LE Plunkett (Durham) | 9 | 11 |

## COUNTY CHAMPIONSHIP FEATURES 2007

### MOST FOURS

| Player | Fours | Matches |
|---|---|---|
| MR Ramprakash (Surrey) | 258 | 15 |
| MJ Di Venuto (Durham) | 197 | 13 |
| ME Trescothick (Somerset) | 197 | 15 |
| SG Law (Lancashire) | 169 | 14 |
| NJ Edwards (Somerset) | 166 | 16 |
| JC Hildreth (Somerset) | 164 | 16 |
| SM Katich (Derbyshire) | 163 | 13 |
| DJG Sales (Northamptonshire) | 161 | 16 |
| RWT Key (Kent) | 157 | 15 |
| MA Wagh (Nottinghamshire) | 153 | 16 |
| DM Benkenstein (Durham) | 150 | 16 |
| PJ Horton (Lancashire) | 149 | 13 |
| MA Carberry (Hampshire) | 145 | 13 |
| JL Langer (Somerset) | 145 | 16 |
| JA Rudolph (Yorkshire) | 143 | 15 |
| DJ Hussey (Nottinghamshire) | 138 | 12 |
| GA Hick (Worcestershire) | 138 | 14 |
| JN Batty (Surrey) | 138 | 15 |
| MW Goodwin (Sussex) | 137 | 14 |
| ET Smith (Middlesex) | 134 | 16 |
| MJ Brown (Hampshire) | 134 | 16 |

### LEADING WICKET-TAKERS

| Player | Wickets | Matches |
|---|---|---|
| Mushtaq Ahmed (Sussex) | 90 | 15 |
| OD Gibson (Durham) | 80 | 15 |
| Danish Kaneria (Essex) | 74 | 13 |
| AR Caddick (Somerset) | 70 | 15 |
| CM Willoughby (Somerset) | 62 | 16 |
| T Lungley (Derbyshire) | 59 | 15 |
| AG Botha (Derbyshire) | 55 | 16 |
| RDB Croft (Glamorgan) | 53 | 15 |
| GG Wagg (Derbyshire) | 53 | 15 |
| M Muralitharan (Lancashire) | 51 | 8 |
| M Kartik (Middlesex) | 51 | 12 |
| Naved-ul-Hasan (Sussex) | 50 | 14 |
| SK Warne (Hampshire) | 50 | 15 |
| G Chapple (Lancashire) | 47 | 12 |
| Kabir Ali (Worcestershire) | 45 | 13 |
| MJ Nicholson (Surrey) | 44 | 12 |
| R McLaren (Kent) | 44 | 15 |
| CE Shreck (Nottinghamshire) | 43 | 10 |
| GP Swann (Nottinghamshire) | 43 | 15 |
| AJ Bichel (Essex) | 41 | 8 |

### LEADING CATCHES (EXCLUDING WICKETKEEPERS)

| Player | Catches | Matches |
|---|---|---|
| ME Trescothick (Somerset) | 33 | 15 |
| CJ Adams (Sussex) | 27 | 15 |
| RR Montgomerie (Sussex) | 27 | 15 |
| DJG Sales (Northamptonshire) | 23 | 16 |
| TR Birt (Derbyshire) | 22 | 13 |
| SP Fleming (Nottinghamshire) | 21 | 11 |
| MJ Di Venuto (Durham) | 21 | 13 |
| BA Godleman (Middlesex) | 20 | 14 |
| JA Rudolph (Yorkshire) | 19 | 15 |
| GW Flower (Essex) | 17 | 10 |
| SG Law (Lancashire) | 17 | 14 |
| SK Warne (Hampshire) | 17 | 15 |
| SA Newman (Surrey) | 17 | 15 |
| M van Jaarsveld (Kent) | 17 | 15 |
| DJ Hussey (Nottinghamshire) | 16 | 12 |
| PJ Horton (Lancashire) | 16 | 13 |
| IJL Trott (Warwickshire) | 16 | 14 |
| CM Spearman (Gloucestershire) | 15 | 11 |
| GA Hick (Worcestershire) | 15 | 14 |
| HD Ackerman (Leicestershire) | 15 | 15 |

### LEADING DISMISSALS (WICKETKEEPERS)

| Player | Dismissals | Matches |
|---|---|---|
| P Mustard (Durham) | 65 | 16 |
| SM Davies (Worcestershire) | 47 | 14 |
| JN Batty (Surrey) | 47 | 15 |
| DJ Pipe (Derbyshire) | 46 | 14 |
| C Kieswetter (Somerset) | 46 | 14 |
| GO Jones (Kent) | 46 | 15 |
| CMW Read (Nottinghamshire) | 45 | 16 |
| N Pothas (Hampshire) | 44 | 15 |
| LD Sutton (Lancashire) | 44 | 15 |
| MA Wallace (Glamorgan) | 43 | 15 |
| GL Brophy (Yorkshire) | 38 | 13 |
| PA Nixon (Leicestershire) | 37 | 13 |
| JS Foster (Essex) | 36 | 15 |
| TR Ambrose (Warwickshire) | 36 | 15 |
| SJ Adshead (Gloucestershire) | 30 | 12 |
| BJM Scott (Middlesex) | 28 | 10 |
| NJ O'Brien (Northamptonshire) | 25 | 8 |
| MH Wessels (Northamptonshire) | 25 | 8 |
| AJ Hodd (Sussex) | 24 | 12 |
| DC Nash (Middlesex) | 19 | 6 |

## MOST HUNDREDS

| Player | Hundreds | Matches |
|---|---|---|
| MR Ramprakash (Surrey) | 10 | 15 |
| CL White (Somerset) | 5 | 12 |
| MA Carberry (Hampshire) | 5 | 13 |
| RWT Key (Kent) | 5 | 15 |
| M van Jaarsveld (Kent) | 5 | 15 |
| SP Fleming (Nottinghamshire) | 4 | 11 |
| DJ Hussey (Nottinghamshire) | 4 | 12 |
| SR Patel (Nottinghamshire) | 4 | 13 |
| DL Maddy (Warwickshire) | 4 | 14 |
| JN Batty (Surrey) | 4 | 15 |
| ME Trescothick (Somerset) | 4 | 15 |
| JA Rudolph (Yorkshire) | 4 | 15 |
| ET Smith (Middlesex) | 4 | 16 |
| JC Hildreth (Somerset) | 4 | 16 |
| MJ North (Gloucestershire) | 3 | 5 |
| OA Shah (Middlesex) | 3 | 10 |
| RS Bopara (Essex) | 3 | 10 |
| MJ Walker (Kent) | 3 | 12 |
| MJ Di Venuto (Durham) | 3 | 13 |
| SM Katich (Derbyshire) | 3 | 13 |
| Younus.Khan (Yorkshire) | 3 | 13 |
| PJ Horton (Lancashire) | 3 | 13 |
| HJH Marshall (Gloucestershire) | 3 | 13 |

## MOST FIFTIES (INCLUDING HUNDREDS)

| Player | Fifties | Matches |
|---|---|---|
| MR Ramprakash (Surrey) | 14 | 15 |
| MA Wagh (Nottinghamshire) | 13 | 16 |
| MJ Di Venuto (Durham) | 12 | 13 |
| SG Law (Lancashire) | 12 | 14 |
| SM Katich (Derbyshire) | 11 | 13 |
| DM Benkenstein (Durham) | 11 | 16 |
| DJG Sales (Northamptonshire) | 10 | 16 |
| DJ Hussey (Nottinghamshire) | 9 | 12 |
| A McGrath (Yorkshire) | 9 | 14 |
| ME Trescothick (Somerset) | 9 | 15 |
| RWT Key (Kent) | 9 | 15 |
| NJ Edwards (Somerset) | 9 | 16 |
| JC Hildreth (Somerset) | 9 | 16 |
| CL White (Somerset) | 8 | 12 |
| MA Carberry (Hampshire) | 8 | 13 |
| SR Patel (Nottinghamshire) | 8 | 13 |
| GA Hick (Worcestershire) | 8 | 14 |
| MW Goodwin (Sussex) | 8 | 14 |
| TJ New (Leicestershire) | 8 | 15 |
| M van Jaarsveld (Kent) | 8 | 15 |

## LEADING DUCK-MAKERS

| Player | Ducks | Matches |
|---|---|---|
| T Lungley (Derbyshire) | 6 | 15 |
| BW Harmison (Durham) | 5 | 8 |
| GP Rees (Glamorgan) | 5 | 10 |
| C White (Yorkshire) | 5 | 11 |
| BF Smith (Worcestershire) | 5 | 13 |
| N Pothas (Hampshire) | 5 | 15 |
| AGR Loudon (Warwickshire) | 5 | 15 |
| J Ormond (Surrey) | 4 | 7 |
| AJ Tudor (Essex) | 4 | 10 |
| M Davies (Durham) | 4 | 10 |
| HT Waters (Glamorgan) | 4 | 10 |
| SP Kirby (Gloucestershire) | 4 | 11 |
| JTA Bruce (Hampshire) | 4 | 14 |
| Naved-ul-Hasan (Sussex) | 4 | 14 |
| IJL Trott (Warwickshire) | 4 | 14 |
| SC Moore (Worcestershire) | 4 | 14 |
| RR Montgomerie (Sussex) | 4 | 15 |
| Mushtaq Ahmed (Sussex) | 4 | 15 |
| OD Gibson (Durham) | 4 | 15 |
| SA Newman (Surrey) | 4 | 15 |
| M van Jaarsveld (Kent) | 4 | 15 |
| R McLaren (Kent) | 4 | 15 |

## HUNDREDS IN EACH INNINGS

| Name | For | Against | Venue | Date | 1st | 2nd |
|---|---|---|---|---|---|---|
| Younus Khan | Yorks | Hants | the Rose Bowl | 2 May | 106 | 202* |
| MW Goodwin | Sussex | Surrey | Hove | 16 May | 119 | 205* |
| APR Gidman | Glos | Northants | Gloucester | 1 June | 130 | 105* |
| TR Birt | Derbys | Glos | Bristol | 31 July | 140 | 162 |
| MJ Walker | Kent | Lancs | Canterbury | 28 August | 142 | 157 |
| MA Carberry | Hants | Worcs | Kidderminster | 4 Sept | 127 | 120 |
| MR Ramprakash | Surrey | Lancs | The Oval | 19 Sept | 196 | 130* |

## FASTEST COUNTY CHAMPIONSHIP HUNDREDS

| Name | No. of balls | Match | Venue | Date |
|---|---|---|---|---|
| MJ North | 73 balls | Glos v. Leicestershire | at Taunton | 5 May |
| GR Napier | 78 balls | Essex v. Notts | at Chelmsford | 9 July |
| ID Blackwell | 91 balls | Somerset v. Notts | at Taunton | 20 September |
| CJ Adams | 93 balls | Sussex v. Hampshire | at Arundel | 8 June |
| GO Jones | 94 balls | Kent v. Surrey | at Whitgift School | 1 June |
| VVS Laxman | 97 balls | Lancashire v. Surrey | at The Oval | 22 September |
| CM Spearman | 98 balls | Glos v. Notts | at Bristol | 26 April |

# DERBYSHIRE CCC

## FIRST-CLASS MATCHES
### BATTING

| | SD Stubbings | GG Wagg | T Lungley | DJ Pipe | AG Botha | SM Katich | TR Birt | GM Smith | Hassan Adnan | KJ Dean | WPC Weston | MG Dighton | DJ Redfern | DJ Birch | J Needham | CR Taylor | WA White | WB Rankin | LJ Harvey | FA Klokker | JL Clare | T Poynton | A Patel | PM Borrington | SMJ Cusden | R Hodgkinson | ID Hunter | OHJ Saffell | Extras | Total | Wickets | Result |
|---|---|---|---|---|---|---|---|---|---|---|---|---|---|---|---|---|---|---|---|---|---|---|---|---|---|---|---|---|---|---|---|---|
| v. Essex (Chelmsford) 18-21 April | 33 | 51 | 3 | 133* | 8 | 50 | | 33 | 10 | 21 | | | | | | 55 | | | 136 | | | | | | | | | | 18 | 551 | 10 | |
| | 9 | | | | | 88* | | 33 | | | | | | | | 96 | | | 0* | | | | | | | | | | 5 | 231 | 3 | D 12 |
| v. Cambridge UCCE (Fenner's) 25-27 April | 43 | | | | | | | 30 | 17 | | | 46 | | 130 | 21 | 2 | | | | 100* | | | 31 | 14 | | | | 35* | 35 | 504 | 9 | |
| | 45* | | | | | | | 21 | 3 | | | | | | | | | | | | | | 12* | | | | | | 14 | 95 | 2 | D |
| v. Somerset (Taunton) 2-5 May | 58 | 55* | 30* | 106 | 101 | 221 | | 21 | 0 | | | | | | | 0 | | | 153 | | | | | | | | | | 56 | 801 | 8 | |
| | | | | | | | | | | | | | | | | | | | | | | | | | | | | | | | | D 12 |
| v. Leicestershire (Derby) 9-12 May | 63 | 4 | 0 | 36 | 0 | 94 | 25 | 0 | | 5 | | | | | | 4 | 0* | | | | | | | | | | | | 28 | 259 | 10 | |
| | 16 | | 10* | | | | 45* | 1 | | 8 | | | | | | | | | | | | | | | | | | | 8 | 88 | 3 | W 19 |
| v. Middlesex (Derby) 16-19 May | 23 | 40 | 0 | 11 | 9 | 59 | 28 | 29 | 2* | 14 | | | | | | 3 | | | | | | | | | | | | | 7 | 225 | 10 | |
| | 21* | | | | | | | 12* | 12 | | | | | | | | | | | | | | | | | | | | 8 | 53 | 1 | D 8 |
| v. Northamptonshire (Northampton) 23-26 May | 36 | 11 | 0 | 4 | 53* | 0 | 5 | 8 | 15 | | 13 | | | | | | 10 | | | | | | | | | | | | 5 | 160 | 10 | |
| | 104 | 8 | 0* | 0 | 4 | 85 | 37 | 17 | 7 | | | | | | | | 4 | | | | | | | | | | | | 17 | 283 | 10 | L 3 |
| v. Gloucestershire (Derby) 5-8 June | 128 | 0 | 12 | 53* | 98 | 13 | 8 | 40 | 29 | | | | | 95 | | | | | | | | | | | | | 1* | | 23 | 500 | 9 | |
| | 11* | | | | | | | | 23* | | | | | 2 | | | | | | | | | | | | | | | 4 | 40 | 1 | D 12 |
| v. Nottinghamshire (Trent Bridge) 15-18 June | 13 | 11 | 18* | 4 | 0 | 14 | 18 | 1 | 3 | | | 12 | | | | | | | | | | | | | | 6 | | | 8 | 108 | 10 | |
| | 10 | | | | | | 50* | 16* | | | | 5 | 1 | | | | | | | | | | | | | | | | 13 | 95 | 3 | D 4 |
| v. Middlesex (Southgate) 8-11 July | 15 | 27 | 22* | | 32 | 80 | 32 | 0 | 16 | 0 | | 68 | | | 0 | | | | | | | | | | | | | | 48 | 340 | 10 | |
| | 8 | 28 | 2 | | 4 | 68 | 1 | 54* | 0 | | | 16 | | | 9 | 0 | | | | | | | | | | | | | 9 | 199 | 10 | W 20 |
| v. Glamorgan (Derby) 20-23 July | 41 | | | 42* | 11 | 1* | | | | | | 43 | | | | | | | | | | | | | | | | | 12 | 150 | 3 | |
| | 25 | 48* | 0 | 12 | 3 | 70 | 4 | 0* | 0 | | | | | | | 15 | | | | | | 2 | | | | | | | 16 | 195 | 9 | D 7 |
| v. Somerset (Derby) 25-28 July | 14 | | | | | 29* | 8 | | 36* | | | | | | | | | | | | | | | | | | | | 7 | 94 | 2 | |
| | 1 | 0 | 2* | 1 | 21 | | 4 | 6 | 2 | | | 0 | 6 | | | | | | | | | | | | | | | | 8 | 52 | 10 | L 3 |
| v. Gloucestershire (Bristol) 31 July-3 August | 1 | 23 | | 23 | 0 | 41 | 140 | 12 | 0* | | | 40 | 12 | | 9 | | | | | | | | | | | | | | 11 | 312 | 10 | |
| | 0 | | | | | 124* | 162 | 0* | | | | 42 | 7* | | | | | | | | | | | | | | | | 21 | 356 | 3 | D 9 |
| v. Leicestershire (Leicester) 9-12 August | 0 | 22 | 5 | 32 | 10 | 6 | 0 | 15 | 63 | 10* | 0 | | | | | | | | | | | | | | | | | | 31 | 194 | 10 | |
| | 21 | 0 | 4 | 11 | 1 | 167 | 74 | 74 | 0 | 2* | | | | | | | 1 | | | | | | | | | | | | 41 | 396 | 10 | L 3 |
| v. Glamorgan (Cardiff) 22-24 August | | 61* | 15 | 33 | 22 | 4 | 0 | 9 | 18 | | 6 | 29 | | | | 0 | | | | | | | | | | | | | 9 | 206 | 10 | |
| | | 5 | 1 | 13* | 25 | 0 | 84 | 35 | 18 | | 32 | 60 | | | | 0 | | | | | | | | | | | | | 12 | 287 | 10 | W 18 |
| v. Essex (Derby) 30 August-1 September | 21 | 15 | 0 | 40 | 9 | | 0 | | 5 | 2 | 32 | | | | | | 3* | | | | | | | | | | | | 10 | 139 | 10 | |
| | 3 | 22 | 22 | 1 | 1 | | | 63 | 15 | 2* | 15 | 19 | | | | | 4 | | | | | | | | | | | | 7 | 174 | 10 | L 3 |
| v. Nottinghamshire (Chesterfield) 6-8 September 2007 | 1 | | 9* | 4 | | 12 | 0 | 50 | 38 | | 32 | | 13 | | | | 17 | | | | 20 | | | | | | | | 9 | 205 | 10 | |
| | 48 | | 0 | 26* | | 85 | 51 | 4 | 16 | | 8 | | 48 | | | | 19 | | | | 0 | | | | | | | | 32 | 337 | 10 | L 4 |
| v. Northamptonshire (Derby) 19-22 September | 18 | 82 | 24 | 35 | | | 21 | 0 | 43 | | | 36* | | | 23 | | | | | | 22 | | | 50 | | | | | 28 | 382 | 10 | |
| | 46 | 17* | | 1 | | | 8 | 4 | | | | | 51 | | 48 | | | | | | | | | | 14 | | | | 19 | 208 | 7 | D 11 |
| **Matches** | 16 | 15 | 15 | 14 | 14 | 13 | 13 | 12 | 11 | 10 | 9 | 7 | 5 | 4 | 4 | 4 | 4 | 3 | 2 | 2 | 2 | 2 | 1 | 1 | 1 | 1 | 1 | 1 | | | | |
| **Innings** | 31 | 21 | 21 | 21 | 19 | 23 | 24 | 20 | 21 | 12 | 15 | 14 | 7 | 7 | 6 | 6 | 6 | 4 | 3 | 3 | 3 | 3 | 2 | 2 | 1 | 1 | 1 | 1 | | | | |
| **Not Out** | 3 | 4 | 6 | 5 | 1 | 6 | 1 | 2 | 2 | 6 | 0 | 1 | 1 | 0 | 2 | 0 | 0 | 1 | 1 | 1 | 0 | 0 | 1 | 0 | 0 | 0 | 1 | 1 | | | | |
| **Highest Score** | 128 | 82 | 30* | 133* | 101 | 221 | 162 | 74 | 63 | 16 | 38 | 68 | 51 | 130 | 48 | 96 | 19 | 3 | 153 | 100* | 22 | 2 | 31 | 50 | 14 | 6 | 1* | 35* | | | | |
| **Runs** | 876 | 530 | 169 | 577 | 410 | 1284 | 884 | 407 | 399 | 46 | 198 | 418 | 180 | 236 | 125 | 168 | 61 | 5 | 289 | 171 | 42 | 2 | 43 | 64 | 14 | 6 | 1 | 35 | | | | |
| **Average** | 31.28 | 31.17 | 11.26 | 36.06 | 22.77 | 75.52 | 38.43 | 22.61 | 21.00 | 7.66 | 13.20 | 32.15 | 30.00 | 33.71 | 31.25 | 28.00 | 10.16 | 1.66 | 144.50 | 85.50 | 14.00 | 0.66 | 43.00 | 32.00 | 14.00 | 6.00 | – | – | | | | |
| **100s** | 2 | 0 | 0 | 2 | 1 | 3 | 2 | 0 | 0 | 0 | 0 | 0 | 0 | 1 | 0 | 0 | 0 | 0 | 2 | 1 | 0 | 0 | 0 | 0 | 0 | 0 | 0 | 0 | | | | |
| **50s** | 2 | 4 | 0 | 1 | 2 | 8 | 5 | 3 | 2 | 0 | 0 | 2 | 1 | 1 | 0 | 2 | 0 | 0 | 0 | 0 | 0 | 0 | 0 | 1 | 0 | 0 | 0 | 0 | | | | |
| **Catches/Stumpings** | 7/0 | 7/0 | 5/0 | 42/4 | 11/0 | 9/0 | 22/0 | 4/0 | 5/0 | 2/0 | 5/0 | 10/0 | 5/0 | 1/0 | 2/0 | 4/0 | 3/0 | 3/0 | 4/0 | 3/0 | 0/0 | 3/0 | 0/0 | 2/0 | 0/0 | 0/0 | 0/0 | 0/0 | | | | |

---

**Home Ground:** Derby
**Address:** County Ground, Nottingham Road, Derby, DE21 6DA
**Tel:** 01332 383211
**Fax:** 01332 290251
**Email:** sue.evans@debyshireccc.com
**Directions:** *By road:* From the South & East, exit M1 junction 25, follow the A52 into Derby, take the fourth exit off the Pentagon Island. From the North, exit M1 junction 28, join the A38 into Derby, follow directional signs, the cricket ground is seen on the left approaching the city. From the West, on A50 follow signs for A52 Nottingham and on leaving the city centre inner ring road take the second exit off the Pentagon Island into the ground.

**Capacity:** 9,500
**Other grounds used:** Chesterfield
**Year Formed:** 1870

**Chief Executive:** Tom Sears
**Head of Cricket:** John Morris
**Academy Director & 2nd XI Coach:** Karl Krikken
**Captain:** Simon Katich
**County colours:** Blue, brown and gold

### Honours
County Championship
1936
Sunday League/NCL/Pro40
1990
Benson & Hedges Cup
1993
Gillette Cup/NatWest/C&G Trophy
1981

### Website:
www.derbyshireccc.com

# FIRST-CLASS MATCHES
## BOWLING

| | T Lungley | GG Wagg | AG Botha | KJ Dean | GM Smith | WA White | JL Clare | WB Rankin | J Needham | OHJ Saffell | MG Dighton | ID Hunter | DJ Redfern | SMJ Cusden | IJ Harvey | SM Katich | WPC Weston | R Hodgkinson | A Patel | TR Birt | Overs | Total | Byes/Leg-byes | Wickets | Run outs |
|---|---|---|---|---|---|---|---|---|---|---|---|---|---|---|---|---|---|---|---|---|---|---|---|---|---|
| **v. Essex** (Chelmsford) 18-21 April | 22.3-7-69-3 | 26-6-70-1 | 35-13-108-3 | 24-7-65-3 | | | | | | | | | | 12-0-47-0 | 5-0-29-0 | | | | | | 124.3 | 407 | 19 | 10 | |
| | 13-4-37-0 | 6-1-16-0 | 18-5-30-1 | 11-7-13-1 | | | | | | | | | | 6-1-14-1 | 4-0-19-0 | | | | | | 58 | 131 | 2 | 3 | |
| **v. Cambridge UCCE** (Fenner's) 25-27 April | | | | | 6-1-16-1 | 31-6-79-2 | | 16-2-44-1 | | 9.1-2-37-3 | | | | 16-1-67-2 | | | | | 7-2-23-0 | | 85.1 | 279 | 13 | 10 | 1 |
| | | | | | 5-1-17-1 | 6-2-17-1 | | 4-1-3-0 | | 7-0-22-2 | | | | 8-1-31-0 | | | | | 2-0-7-0 | | 32 | 107 | 10 | 4 | |
| **v. Somerset** (Taunton) 2-5 May | 28-7-99-0 | 34.4-1-148-5 | 37-6-178-1 | 29-9-64-3 | | | | | | | | | | | | 8-4-25-1 | | | | | 136.4 | 530 | 16 | 10 | |
| | 14-1-85-2 | 16-3-45-2 | 16-2-66-0 | 14-1-59-0 | | | | | | | | | | | 4-0-30-0 | 4-0-17-0 | | | | | 68 | 309 | 7 | 4 | |
| **v. Leicestershire** (Derby) 9-12 May | 20-3-54-4 | 10-3-28-1 | 1.4-0-8-1 | 22-6-54-2 | | | | | | | | | 13-1-58-0 | | | | | | | | 66.4 | 209 | 7 | 10 | |
| | 15.3-9-20-5 | 15-3-39-3 | 5-3-7-0 | 9-2-16-0 | | | | | | | | | 13-0-46-2 | | | | | | | | 57.3 | 137 | 9 | 10 | |
| **v. Middlesex** (Derby) 16-19 May | 15-7-20-3 | 25-6-71-2 | 8-3-10-0 | 20-6-59-1 | | | | | 22.3-7-80-4 | | | | | | | | | | | | 91.3 | 248 | 8 | 10 | |
| | 17-7-30-2 | 23-8-46-2 | | | | | | | 17-5-54-2 | | | | | | | | | | | | 72 | 180 | 9 | 10 | |
| | | | | | | | | | 15-3-41-4 | | | | | | | | | | | | | | | | |
| **v. Northamptonshire** (Northampton) 23-26 May | 5-3-9-0 | | 28-3-120-0 | 30.5-11-59-3 | 30-14-84-2 | 27-8-87-5 | | | | | | | | | | | | | | | 120.5 | 365 | 6 | 10 | |
| | | 8-1-26-3 | | 1-0-3-0 | 1-0-13-0 | 7-0-34-1 | | | | | | | | | | | | | 0.3-0-4-0 | | 17.3 | 80 | 0 | 4 | |
| **v. Gloucestershire** (Derby) 5-8 June | 19.1-4-49-5 | 20-4-67-2 | 19-7-40-2 | | 2-1-10-0 | | | | | | 21-2-67-1 | | | | | | | | | | 81.1 | 258 | 25 | 10 | |
| | 21-5-84-2 | 20.4-4-74-1 | 40-9-134-3 | | | 18-4-49-1 | | | | | 25-7-63-2 | | | | | 6-0-17-1 | | | | | 130.4 | 441 | 20 | 10 | |
| **v. Nottinghamshire** (Trent Bridge) 15-18 June | 13-1-75-0 | 17-5-59-1 | | | 11-2-65-1 | | | | | | | | | | | | | 10-0-75-0 | | 3-0-22-0 | 54 | 302 | 6 | 2 | |
| **v. Middlesex** (Southgate) 8-11 July | 14.3-3-33-5 | 23-7-59-2 | 21-7-51-1 | 14-4-42-1 | 13-0-45-1 | | | | | | | 3-0-10-0 | | | | 2-0-3-0 | | | | | 90.3 | 258 | 15 | 10 | |
| | 16-3-50-2 | 19.1-3-76-2 | 22-4-69-3 | 17-8-30-0 | 15-5-31-3 | | | | | | | | | | | | | | | | 89.1 | 266 | 10 | 10 | |
| **v. Glamorgan** (Derby) 20-23 July | 21-4-67-3 | 20-5-67-2 | 23-6-64-3 | 6-3-6-0 | 20-7-51-2 | | | | | | | | | | 9-1-33-0 | | | | | | 99 | 298 | 10 | 10 | |
| | 13-5-40-3 | 8-2-19-0 | 5-1-16-0 | 13-2-24-5 | 10.1-6-16-2 | | | | | | | | | | | | | | | | 49.1 | 127 | 12 | 10 | |
| **v. Somerset** (Derby) 25-28 July | 10-1-57-1 | 12-3-65-1 | 22.2-2-101-6 | 14-4-32-0 | 14-1-66-1 | | | | | | | | | | | 5-2-7-1 | | | | | 77.2 | 340 | 12 | 10 | |
| | | 4-0-26-0 | 5-0-11-1 | 5-0-22-1 | 5-2-11-0 | | | | | | | | | | | 1-0-8-1 | | | | | 20 | 84 | 6 | 3 | |
| **v. Gloucestershire** (Bristol) 31 July-3 August | | 30.3-6-119-5 | 31-6-73-1 | 19-5-41-1 | 30-2-73-3 | | | | | | | | | | 2-0-14-0 | 2-0-11-0 | 3-0-14-0 | | | | 137.3 | 454 | 12 | 10 | |
| | | 12-0-55-1 | 7-3-22-1 | | 6-2-18-1 | 5-0-32-2 | | | | | | | | | | 2-0-11-0 | 5-0-26-0 | | | | 37 | 170 | 6 | 5 | |
| **v. Leicestershire** (Leicester) 9-12 August | 24-5-110-4 | 19-4-62-3 | 14-2-50-2 | 17-7-21-1 | 7-0-25-0 | | | | | | | | | | | | | | | | 81 | 274 | 6 | 10 | |
| | 20-5-76-1 | 26-7-98-3 | 24.2-5-69-5 | 23-6-73-1 | | | | | | | | | | | | 1-1-0-0 | | | | | 94.2 | 344 | 28 | 10 | |
| **v. Glamorgan** (Cardiff) 22-24 August | 14-2-64-2 | 13-3-63-4 | 12-2-47-3 | | | | 7-0-43-0 | | | | | | | | | | | | | | 46 | 225 | 8 | 10 | 1 |
| | 16-6-52-3 | 8-0-53-0 | | 28-10-67-5 | 2-0-7-0 | | 5-0-24-0 | | | | | | | | | 8-3-19-1 | | | | | 67 | 226 | 4 | 10 | 1 |
| **v. Essex** (Derby) 30 August-1 September | 11-0-61-0 | 20-2-83-3 | 20-3-72-2 | 10-3-38-3 | | | | 4.2-0-10-2 | 1-0-1-0 | | | | | | | | | 2-1-12-0 | | | 66.2 | 272 | 7 | 10 | |
| | 17-7-58-3 | 16.2-2-55-2 | | | | | | 22-1-92-3 | 20-3-47-2 | | | | | | | | | | | | 77.2 | 268 | 4 | 10 | |
| **v. Nottinghamshire** (Chesterfield) 6-8 September | 27-4-132-1 | | | | 9-0-49-0 | 17-3-117-1 | 23.2-4-90-5 | 22-5-80-0 | | | | 15-1-61-2 | | | | | | | | | 113.2 | 548 | 19 | 9 | |
| **v. Northamptonshire** (Derby) 19-22 September | 18.1-3-61-4 | 16-2-75-1 | | | 1-1-0-0 | | | 18-5-59-4 | 7-3-14-1 | | | | | | | | | | | | 60.1 | 235 | 26 | 10 | |
| | 11-0-63-1 | 12-2-56-1 | | | 9-2-43-1 | | | 8-1-54-1 | 8-3-13-0 | | | | | | | | | | | | 48 | 229 | 0 | 4 | |
| **Overs** | 435.5 | 492 | 479.3 | 267 | 214.1 | 113 | 49.2 | 76.3 | 83.2 | 16.1 | 41 | 46 | 19 | 24 | 30 | 38 | 2 | 10 | 9 | 3.3 | | | | | |
| **Maidens** | 106 | 94 | 117 | 80 | 51 | 21 | 10 | 11 | 15 | 2 | 4 | 9 | 3 | 2 | 5 | 4 | 1 | 0 | 2 | 0 | | | | | |
| **Runs** | 1555 | 1785 | 1464 | 659 | 689 | 463 | 203 | 292 | 256 | 59 | 133 | 130 | 70 | 98 | 116 | 144 | 12 | 75 | 30 | 26 | | | | | |
| **Wickets** | 59 | 53 | 51 | 23 | 20 | 12 | 10 | 10 | 7 | 5 | 4 | 3 | 2 | 2 | 2 | 2 | 0 | 0 | 0 | 0 | | | | | |
| **Average** | 26.35 | 33.67 | 28.70 | 28.65 | 34.45 | 38.58 | 20.30 | 29.20 | 36.57 | 11.80 | 33.25 | 43.33 | 35.00 | 49.00 | 58.00 | 72.00 | - | - | - | - | | | | | |

## FIELDING

| | |
|---|---|
| 46 | DJ Pipe (42 ct, 4 st) |
| 22 | TR Birt |
| 11 | AG Botha |
| 10 | MG Dighton |
| 9 | SM Katich |
| 7 | SD Stubbings |
| 7 | GG Wagg |
| 5 | WPC Weston |
| 5 | T Lungley |
| 5 | Hassan Adnan |
| 5 | DJ Redfern |
| 4 | IJ Harvey |
| 4 | CR Taylor |
| 4 | GM Smith |
| 3 | FA Klokker |
| 3 | WB Rankin |
| 3 | WA White |
| 3 | T Poynton |
| 2 | KJ Dean |
| 2 | PM Borrington |
| 2 | J Needham |
| 1 | DJ Birch |
| 0 | ID Hunter |
| 0 | R Hodgkinson |
| 0 | A Patel |
| 0 | SMJ Cusden |
| 0 | OHJ Saffell |
| 0 | JL Clare |

### Final Division Two Table

| | P | W | L | D | T | Ab | Bat | Bowl | Pens | Pts |
|---|---|---|---|---|---|---|---|---|---|---|
| Somerset | 16 | 10 | 1 | 5 | 0 | 0 | 65 | 41 | 0.00 | 266.00 |
| Nottinghamshire | 16 | 6 | 3 | 7 | 0 | 0 | 60 | 43 | 0.50 | 214.50 |
| Middlesex | 16 | 6 | 2 | 8 | 0 | 0 | 35 | 43 | 1.50 | 192.50 |
| Essex | 16 | 6 | 4 | 6 | 0 | 0 | 40 | 36 | 2.00 | 182.00 |
| Northamptonshire | 16 | 5 | 5 | 6 | 0 | 0 | 44 | 38 | 0.00 | 176.00 |
| **Derbyshire** | **16** | **3** | **5** | **8** | **0** | **0** | **30** | **44** | **1.00** | **147.00** |
| Gloucestershire | 16 | 3 | 5 | 8 | 0 | 0 | 32 | 37 | 3.50 | 139.50 |
| Leicestershire | 16 | 2 | 8 | 5 | 0 | 1 | 32 | 35 | 4.00 | 115.00 |
| Glamorgan | 16 | 1 | 9 | 5 | 0 | 1 | 26 | 37 | 8.50 | 92.50 |

Glamorgan had eight points deducted for a poor pitch.

Limited overs nickname:
DERBYSHIRE PHANTOMS

# DURHAM CCC

## FIRST-CLASS MATCHES
### BATTING

| | P Mustard | DM Benkenstein | OD Gibson | KJ Coetzer | MJ Di Venuto | PJ Wiseman | GJ Muchall | WR Smith | LE Plunkett | G Onions | M Davies | BW Harmison | MD Stoneman | SJ Harmison | SB Styris | GR Breese | S Chanderpaul | GT Park | CD Thorp | N Killeen | ME Claydon | LJ Goddard | PD Collingwood | WRS Gidman | L Evans | Extras | Total | Wickets | Result | Points |
|---|---|---|---|---|---|---|---|---|---|---|---|---|---|---|---|---|---|---|---|---|---|---|---|---|---|---|---|---|---|---|
| v. Worcestershire (Worcester) 18-21 April | 23 | 10 | 25 | | 155* | | 6 | 5 | | 16 | | 6 | | 30 | | 3 | | 1 | | | | | | | | 33 | 313 | 10 | | |
| | 38 | 103* | 19 | | 83 | | 29 | 22 | | 19 | | 0 | | 6 | | 53 | | 9 | | | | | | | | 35 | 416 | 10 | W | 20 |
| v. Yorkshire (Headingley) 25-27 April | 10 | 83 | 38 | | 27 | | 17 | 34 | | 24 | | 6 | | 2* | | 19 | | 0 | | | | | | | | 14 | 274 | 10 | | |
| | 32 | 3 | 0 | | | | 1 | 1 | | 41 | | | | 23 | | 21 | | 30* | | | | | | | | 6 | 169 | 10 | L | 4 |
| v. Durham UCCE (Durham) 2-4 May | 7 | | | 153* | | | 4 | 105 | 31* | | | 82 | | | | | | 3 | | | | | | | | 12 | 397 | 5 | | |
| | 35 | | | 19* | | 32 | 14 | 3 | 4 | | | 25 | | | | | | 2 | | | | | | | | 7 | 141 | 7 | W | |
| v. Kent (Riverside) 9-12 May | 23 | 2 | | 74 | 204* | | 13 | 35 | 4 | | | | | 5 | | 5 | | 0 | | | | | 0 | | | 42 | 407 | 10 | | |
| | 5 | 77* | | 3 | 58 | | 21 | | | | | | | | | 0* | | 61 | | | | | 58 | | | 36 | 319 | 6 | W | 22 |
| v. Warwickshire (Edgbaston) 16-19 May | 16 | 93* | 14* | 46 | 9 | | 30 | 38 | | | | | | | | | 15 | | | | | | | | | 13 | 274 | 6 | | |
| | | | | | | | | | | | | | | | | | | | | | | | | | | | | | D | 9 |
| v. Yorkshire (Riverside) 23-26 May | 59 | 68 | 71 | 91 | 11 | 27 | 48 | 6 | | 21 | 21 | | | | | | | | | | 14* | | | | | 44 | 481 | 10 | | |
| | 22* | 32* | 6 | 53 | 6 | 3 | | | | | | | | | | | | | | | | | | | | 9 | 131 | 4 | W | 22 |
| v. Lancashire (Riverside) 6-9 June | 54 | 35 | 13 | 5 | 32 | 10 | 65 | 16 | 23* | 0 | | | | | 48 | | | | | | | | | | | 11 | 312 | 10 | | |
| | 18 | 21 | 54 | 16 | 15 | 7* | 15 | 28 | 0* | 4 | | | | | 19 | | | | | | | | | | | 32 | 229 | 9 | D | 10 |
| v. Hampshire (Rose Bowl) 15-18 June | 1 | 9 | 33* | | 124 | 2 | 59 | 28 | 2 | 1 | 3 | | | | 6 | | | | | | | | | | | 20 | 288 | 10 | | |
| | 21 | 1 | 0 | | 50 | 2* | 9 | 41 | 15 | 0 | 0 | | | | 41 | | | | | | | | | | | 23 | 203 | 10 | L | 5 |
| v. Surrey (The Oval) 8-10 July | 70 | 26 | 10 | 6 | 1 | | 10 | 5 | 20* | | | | | 8 | | 1 | 23 | | | | | | | | | 11 | 191 | 10 | | |
| | 2 | 48 | 0 | 44 | 0 | | 41 | 33 | 0 | | | | | 0* | | 23 | 8 | | | | | | | | | 5 | 204 | 10 | L | 3 |
| v. Sussex (Horsham) 13-15 July | 35 | 32 | 25 | 31 | 0 | | 21 | 0 | | | | 4 | | 2 | | 0* | 47 | | | | | | | | | 12 | 209 | 10 | | |
| | 0 | 50 | 68 | 36 | | | 8* | 8 | | | | 4 | | 0 | | | 15 | | | | | | | | | 11 | 206 | 10 | L | |
| v. Hampshire (Riverside) 20-23 July | 5 | 114 | 28 | 9 | 2 | | 3 | 6 | 3* | | | 66 | | 2 | 2 | | | | | | | | | | | 12 | 252 | 10 | | |
| | 35* | 29* | | 26 | | | | 48 | 12 | | | 50 | | | 17 | | | | | | | | | | | 4 | 221 | 5 | D | 9 |
| v. Warwickshire (Riverside) 31 July-3 August | 1 | 45 | 22 | 142 | 24 | 33* | | 20 | | 0 | | 101 | 32 | | | 12 | | | | | | | | | | 42 | 474 | 10 | | |
| | 76 | | | | 91* | | | | | | | | | | | 16* | | | | | | | | | | 11 | 194 | 1 | W | 21 |
| v. Sri Lanka A (Riverside) 8-10 August | | | 17 | | | 25 | 7 | 2 | | | | 35 | | 17 | 9 | 45 | | | | | | 52 | | 0 | 0* | 11 | 220 | 10 | | |
| | | | 3 | | | 44 | 39 | 26* | | | | 21 | | 0 | 4 | 51 | | | | | | 7 | | 8 | 1 | 13 | 217 | 10 | | |
| v. Surrey (Riverside) 13-16 August | 2 | 30 | 8 | 9 | 56 | 2 | | | 9* | | | 1 | | 6 | 0 | | 81 | | | | | | | | | 28 | 232 | 10 | | |
| | 44 | 23 | 55 | 19 | 77 | | | | 59* | | | 40* | | 28 | | | 29 | | | | | | | | | 23 | 397 | 7 | D | |
| v. Worcestershire (Riverside) 29-31 August | 6 | 0 | 14 | 0 | 50 | 34 | 66 | 50* | 7 | | | 0 | | | | | 54 | | | | | | | | | 16 | 297 | 10 | | |
| | 30 | 68 | | 44 | 5 | | 64* | | | | | 24* | | | | | 28 | | | | | | | | | 16 | 279 | 5 | W | 19 |
| v. Lancashire (Blackpool) 6-7 September | 15 | 15 | 8 | 11 | 78 | 4 | 0 | 5 | 0* | 3 | | 24 | | | | | | | | | | | | | | 3 | 166 | 10 | | |
| | 36 | 77 | 33 | 24 | 8 | 5 | 0 | 0 | 0* | 0 | | 1 | | | | | | | | | | | | | | 1 | 185 | 10 | L | 3 |
| v. Sussex (Riverside) 11-13 September | 0 | 67 | 0 | 30 | 28 | 17 | 17 | 14 | | 1* | 19 | | 101 | | | | | | | | | | | | | 22 | 316 | 10 | | |
| | 21* | | | 35* | | | | | | | | | 46 | | | | | | | | | | | | | 5 | 107 | 1 | W | 20 |
| v. Kent (Canterbury) 19-21 September | 22 | 117 | 40 | 44 | 32 | 36 | | 6 | 3 | 0* | | 0 | | | | | | | 4 | | | | | | | 17 | 321 | 10 | | |
| | | | | 1 | 23* | 17* | | | | | | 6 | | | | | | | | | | | | | | 5 | 52 | 2 | W | 20 |

| | P Mustard | DM Benkenstein | OD Gibson | KJ Coetzer | MJ Di Venuto | PJ Wiseman | GJ Muchall | WR Smith | LE Plunkett | G Onions | M Davies | BW Harmison | MD Stoneman | SJ Harmison | SB Styris | GR Breese | S Chanderpaul | GT Park | CD Thorp | N Killeen | ME Claydon | LJ Goddard | PD Collingwood | WRS Gidman | L Evans |
|---|---|---|---|---|---|---|---|---|---|---|---|---|---|---|---|---|---|---|---|---|---|---|---|---|---|
| Matches | 17 | 16 | 15 | 14 | 13 | 13 | 12 | 12 | 12 | 12 | 10 | 9 | 8 | 7 | 5 | 5 | 4 | 4 | 2 | 2 | 2 | 1 | 1 | 1 | 1 |
| Innings | 31 | 28 | 23 | 26 | 25 | 19 | 22 | 23 | 19 | 16 | 12 | 16 | 15 | 11 | 10 | 10 | 7 | 7 | 4 | 0 | 1 | 2 | 2 | 2 | 2 |
| Not Out | 2 | 5 | 2 | 3 | 5 | 5 | 1 | 0 | 4 | 5 | 4 | 3 | 0 | 1 | 1 | 0 | 1 | 0 | 1 | 0 | 0 | 0 | 0 | 0 | 1 |
| Highest Score | 76 | 117 | 71 | 153* | 204* | 44 | 66 | 105 | 59* | 41 | 21 | 101 | 101 | 30 | 48 | 53 | 81 | 61 | 30* | 0 | 14* | 52 | 58 | 8 | 1 |
| Runs | 743 | 1278 | 578 | 880 | 1329 | 288 | 520 | 551 | 310 | 191 | 67 | 358 | 369 | 91 | 210 | 145 | 224 | 177 | 40 | 0 | 14 | 59 | 58 | 8 | 1 |
| Average | 25.62 | 55.56 | 27.52 | 38.26 | 66.45 | 20.57 | 24.76 | 23.95 | 20.66 | 17.36 | 8.37 | 25.57 | 24.60 | 11.37 | 21.00 | 16.11 | 37.33 | 25.28 | 13.33 | - | - | 29.50 | 29.00 | 4.00 | 1.00 |
| 100s | 0 | 3 | 0 | 2 | 3 | 0 | 0 | 1 | 0 | 0 | 0 | 1 | 1 | 0 | 0 | 0 | 0 | 0 | 0 | 0 | 0 | 0 | 0 | 0 | 0 |
| 50s | 4 | 8 | 4 | 2 | 9 | 0 | 4 | 0 | 2 | 0 | 0 | 2 | 1 | 0 | 0 | 1 | 2 | 2 | 0 | 0 | 0 | 1 | 1 | 0 | 0 |
| Catches/Stumpings | 70/3 | 5/0 | 6/0 | 14/0 | 21/0 | 6/0 | 9/0 | 7/0 | 9/0 | 3/0 | 5/0 | 7/0 | 5/0 | 1/0 | 0/0 | 6/0 | 4/0 | 1/0 | 0/0 | 0/0 | 0/0 | 5/0 | 1/0 | 0/0 | 0/0 |

**Home Ground:** Chester-le-Street
**Address:** County Ground, The Riverside, Chester-le-Street, County Durham, DH3 3QR
**Tel:** 0191 3871717
**Fax:** 0191 3871616
**Email:** reception@durhamccc.co.uk
**Directions:** *By rail:* Chester-le-Street Station (approx 5 minutes by taxi or a 10-minute walk). *By road:* Easily accessible from junction 63 of the A1(M).

**Capacity:** 10,000
**Other grounds used:** Darlington CC, Hartlepool CC, Stockton CC
**Year formed:** 1882

**Chief Executive:** David Harker
**Head Coach:** Geoff Cook
**Captain:** Dale Benkenstein
**County colours:** Yellow, blue and burgundy

**Honours**
Friends Provident Trophy 2007

Website:
www.durhamccc.co.uk

## FIRST-CLASS MATCHES
## BOWLING

| | OD Gibson | LE Plunkett | G Onions | SJ Harmison | PJ Wiseman | M Davies | N Killeen | CD Thorp | ME Claydon | GR Breese | WRS Gidman | L Evans | SB Styris | BW Harmison | WR Smith | DM Benkenstein | S Chanderpaul | PD Collingwood | GT Park | Overs | Total | Byes/Leg-byes | Wickets | Run outs |
|---|---|---|---|---|---|---|---|---|---|---|---|---|---|---|---|---|---|---|---|---|---|---|---|---|
| v. Worcestershire (Worcester) 18-21 April | 13-3-37-3 | | 15-5-47-3 | 19-6-52-3 | | | | 10-2-43-1 | | | | | | | | | | | | 57 | 191 | 12 | 10 | |
| | 12-4-29-0 | 13-1-46-1 | | 24-5-63-5 | | | | 12.4-1-51-3 | | 14-1-82-0 | | | | | 3-0-15-0 | | | | | 78.4 | 297 | 11 | 10 | 1 |
| v. Yorkshire (Headingley) 25-27 April | 27-7-88-1 | | 27-9-58-1 | 37.3-9-87-6 | | | 25-7-69-2 | | | 19-3-59-0 | | | | 3-0-22-0 | 4-2-6-0 | | | | | 142.3 | 414 | 25 | 10 | |
| | | | 3.3-0-22-0 | 3-1-7-1 | | | | | | | | | | | | | | | | 6.3 | 30 | 1 | 1 | |
| v. Durham UCCE (Durham) 2-4 May | | 21-8-36-2 | | 19-9-40-1 | 16-5-53-2 | 13.3-5-26-2 | | | 16-5-54-2 | | | | | | 5-2-8-1 | | | | | 90.3 | 238 | 21 | 10 | |
| | | 10.2-2-40-3 | | | 5-0-31-0 | 11-2-22-4 | | | 9-4-26-3 | | | | | | | | 3-0-18-0 | | | 38.2 | 137 | 0 | 10 | |
| v. Kent (Riverside) 9-12 May | | 32-5-105-5 | 23-1-92-1 | 24.3-3-75-4 | | | | | | 14-0-55-0 | | | | | 6-1-22-0 | | | 14-3-27-0 | | 113.3 | 400 | 24 | 10 | |
| | | 20-7-54-3 | 8-0-38-1 | 19.3-3-61-5 | | | | | | | | | | | | | | 3-1-12-0 | | 50.3 | 169 | 4 | 10 | |
| v. Warwickshire (Edgbaston) 16-19 May | 21-6-78-1 | | 26.2-8-101-8 | | | 19-6-45-0 | 18-2-69-0 | | | | | | | | 2-0-10-0 | 8-4-24-1 | | | | 94.2 | 335 | 8 | 10 | |
| | | | | | | | | | | | | | | | | | | | | - | - | - | - | - |
| v. Yorkshire (Riverside) 23-26 May | 28-8-81-7 | | 26-6-99-1 | | 19-6-43-0 | 18-5-44-2 | | | 17-0-94-0 | | | | | | 7-0-26-0 | | | | | 115 | 393 | 6 | 10 | |
| | 15-1-63-3 | | 15.2-3-53-5 | | 4-3-1-1 | 14-3-49-0 | | | 11-0-45-1 | | | | | | | | | | | 59.2 | 218 | 7 | 10 | |
| v. Lancashire (Riverside) 6-9 June | 26-5-89-3 | | 25-5-79-0 | | 21-2-59-2 | 27.4-7-62-4 | | | | | | | 15-1-59-1 | 13-3-56-2 | | | | | | 116.4 | 367 | 14 | 7 | |
| | 11-1-64-0 | | 11-1-55-0 | | 10-0-38-0 | 14-5-34-3 | | | | | | | | 1-0-5-1 | 13-1-44-1 | | | | | 73 | 310 | 14 | 7 | |
| v. Hampshire (Rose Bowl) 15-18 June | 19-5-48-1 | 20.1-7-57-2 | 21-6-61-3 | | 10-2-23-2 | 12-0-32-2 | | | | | | | 1-0-1-0 | | | | | | | 82.1 | 232 | 11 | 10 | |
| | 17-3-50-0 | 20-4-79-2 | 13-0-55-2 | | 9-0-67-1 | 19-5-48-4 | | | | | | | | | | | | | | 79 | 309 | 9 | 9 | |
| v. Surrey (The Oval) 8-10 July | 16-5-61-4 | 13-4-44-1 | | 18.4-5-75-3 | 11-2-35-1 | 9-3-18-0 | | | | | | | | | | | | | | 67.4 | 243 | 10 | 10 | 1 |
| | 5-1-18-0 | 8.3-3-32-0 | | 14-5-51-4 | 4-1-17-0 | 5-0-17-0 | | | | | | | | | | | | | | 36.3 | 154 | 19 | 4 | |
| v. Sussex (Horsham) 13-15 July | 23-3-87-0 | 26-5-123-4 | | 5-0-14-0 | 27-3-124-4 | | | | | | | | 15-2-77-1 | 9-0-48-0 | 1-0-8-0 | 4-0-15-0 | | | | 110 | 517 | 21 | 10 | |
| v. Hampshire (Riverside) 20-23 July | 17.3-1-47-10 | | 5-1-14-0 | | | | | | | | | | 7-1-24-0 | | 6-1-26-0 | | | | | 35.3 | 115 | 4 | 10 | |
| | 20-3-53-2 | 18-2-59-0 | 15-3-71-1 | | 22-4-65-5 | | | | | | | | | | | | | | | 75 | 262 | 14 | 9 | 1 |
| v. Warwickshire (Riverside) 31 July-3 August | 19-5-56-4 | 22-5-74-4 | | | 2-0-7-0 | 16-4-68-0 | | | | | | | | 6.2-1-29-2 | | | | | | 65.2 | 239 | 5 | 10 | |
| | 30-8-99-4 | 29.1-7-84-1 | | | 41-8-131-4 | 23-9-46-1 | | | | | | | | 5-1-17-0 | | 5-0-15-0 | 2-0-13-0 | | | 135.1 | 426 | 21 | 10 | |
| v. Sri Lanka A (Riverside) 8-10 August | | 19-2-79-3 | | 4-1-21-1 | | | | | | 25-3-102-3 | 13-3-49-1 | 13.1-1-76-2 | | | | | | | 7-1-39-0 | 81.1 | 379 | 13 | 10 | |
| | | 7-2-26-0 | | 6-0-33-1 | | | | | | 12-1-70-2 | 10-1-37-3 | 7-0-39-2 | | | | | | | | 42 | 212 | 7 | 8 | |
| v. Surrey (Riverside) 13-16 August | 15.2-7-50-4 | 9-1-46-3 | | 9-2-39-1 | | | | | | | | | | 5-1-16-0 | | | | | | 44.2 | 183 | 4 | 10 | |
| | 17-5-45-1 | 19-7-41-1 | | | 27-6-65-1 | | | | | | | | | 6-2-27-0 | 3-2-4-0 | 6-3-10-0 | | | | 78 | 198 | 6 | 3 | |
| v. Worcestershire (Riverside) 29-31 August | 18-5-46-7 | 8.2-1-31-1 | 13-1-65-0 | | 5-3-5-2 | | | | | | | | | 4-0-29-0 | | | | | | 48.2 | 182 | 6 | 10 | |
| | 23-4-104-4 | 10-0-59-0 | 17-5-54-2 | | 28-4-110-3 | | | | | | | | | 5-1-34-1 | | | 1-0-12-0 | | | 84 | 390 | 17 | 10 | |
| v. Lancashire (Blackpool) 6-7 September | 20-4-68-8 | 15-2-52-1 | | | | 15-4-33-1 | | | | | | | | 5-0-28-0 | | | | | | 55 | 183 | 2 | 10 | |
| | 10-0-59-1 | 12-3-51-2 | | | 5.2-1-16-0 | 8-3-20-0 | | | | | | | | 2-0-16-0 | | | | | | 37.2 | 169 | 5 | 3 | |
| v. Sussex (Riverside) 11-13 September | 18-3-78-4 | 16.2-2-60-1 | 14-5-56-3 | | 6-0-36-0 | | | | | | | | 13-3-51-1 | | | | | | | 67.2 | 291 | 10 | 10 | 1 |
| | 14-3-60-3 | 4-2-9-3 | 5-0-34-0 | | 12.1-7-28-3 | | | | | | | | | | | | | | | 35.1 | 131 | 0 | 10 | |
| v. Kent (Canterbury) 19-21 September | 13-1-60-3 | 11-2-52-1 | 15-2-49-3 | | | 11.5-4-43-3 | | | | | | | | | | | | | | 50.5 | 212 | 8 | 10 | |
| | 12-1-42-2 | 10-1-27-3 | 8-2-32-1 | | 12.1-2-45-4 | 2-0-12-0 | | | | | | | | | | | | | | 44.1 | 160 | 2 | 10 | |

| | OD Gibson | LE Plunkett | G Onions | SJ Harmison | PJ Wiseman | M Davies | N Killeen | CD Thorp | ME Claydon | GR Breese | WRS Gidman | L Evans | SB Styris | BW Harmison | WR Smith | DM Benkenstein | S Chanderpaul | PD Collingwood | GT Park |
|---|---|---|---|---|---|---|---|---|---|---|---|---|---|---|---|---|---|---|---|
| Overs | 479.5 | 354.5 | 345.1 | 184.1 | 288.3 | 259.4 | 42.3 | 47.4 | 53 | 84 | 23 | 20.1 | 51 | 53.2 | 12 | 59 | 8 | 17 | 7 |
| Maidens | 103 | 80 | 68 | 40 | 56 | 73 | 9 | 10 | 9 | 8 | 4 | 1 | 7 | 6 | 2 | 11 | 3 | 4 | 1 |
| Runs | 1660 | 1215 | 1286 | 578 | 955 | 734 | 117 | 163 | 219 | 368 | 86 | 115 | 217 | 286 | 46 | 202 | 23 | 39 | 39 |
| Wickets | 80 | 43 | 39 | 34 | 32 | 26 | 6 | 6 | 6 | 5 | 4 | 4 | 4 | 3 | 2 | 2 | 0 | 0 | 0 |
| Average | 20.75 | 28.25 | 32.97 | 17.00 | 29.84 | 28.23 | 19.50 | 27.16 | 36.50 | 73.60 | 21.50 | 28.75 | 54.25 | 95.33 | 23.00 | 101.00 | - | - | - |

## FIELDING

| | |
|---|---|
| 73 | P Mustard (70 ct, 3 st) |
| 21 | MJ Di Venuto |
| 14 | KJ Coetzer |
| 9 | GJ Muchall |
| 9 | LE Plunkett |
| 7 | WR Smith |
| 7 | BW Harmison |
| 6 | OD Gibson |
| 6 | GR Breese |
| 6 | PJ Wiseman |
| 5 | M Davies |
| 5 | DM Benkenstein |
| 5 | LJ Goddard |
| 5 | MD Stoneman |
| 4 | S Chanderpaul |
| 3 | G Onions |
| 1 | PD Collingwood |
| 1 | SJ Harmison |
| 1 | GT Park |
| 0 | N Killeen |
| 0 | SB Styris |
| 0 | WRS Gidman |
| 0 | CD Thorp |
| 0 | ME Claydon |
| 0 | L Evans |

### Final Division One Table

| | P | W | L | D | T | Ab | Bat | Bowl | Pens | Pts |
|---|---|---|---|---|---|---|---|---|---|---|
| Sussex | 16 | 7 | 3 | 5 | 0 | 1 | 37 | 43 | 0.00 | 202.00 |
| Durham | 16 | 7 | 5 | 4 | 0 | 0 | 38 | 47 | 1.50 | 197.50 |
| Lancashire | 16 | 5 | 2 | 8 | 0 | 1 | 40 | 44 | 0.00 | 190.00 |
| Surrey | 16 | 5 | 4 | 6 | 0 | 1 | 41 | 40 | 1.00 | 178.00 |
| Hampshire | 16 | 5 | 3 | 8 | 0 | 0 | 32 | 43 | 0.00 | 177.00 |
| Yorkshire | 16 | 4 | 4 | 8 | 0 | 0 | 49 | 38 | 0.00 | 175.00 |
| Kent | 16 | 3 | 5 | 7 | 0 | 1 | 43 | 36 | 0.00 | 153.00 |
| Warwickshire | 16 | 2 | 5 | 9 | 0 | 0 | 40 | 35 | 0.00 | 139.00 |
| Worcestershire | 16 | 1 | 8 | 5 | 0 | 2 | 18 | 35 | 0.00 | 95.00 |

DURHAM DYNAMOS

Limited overs nickname:
DURHAM DYNAMOS

# ESSEX CCC

## FIRST-CLASS MATCHES
### BATTING

| | JD Middlebrook | ML Pettini | RN ten Doeschate | V Chopra | JS Foster | Danish Kaneria | RS Bopara | GW Flower | GR Napier | TJ Phillips | AJ Tudor | AJ Bichel | AP Palladino | T Westley | RC Irani | AC McGarry | A Nel | AN Cook | JS Ahmed | MJ Saggers | MS Westfield | Extras | Total | Wickets | Result | Points |
|---|---|---|---|---|---|---|---|---|---|---|---|---|---|---|---|---|---|---|---|---|---|---|---|---|---|---|
| v. Derbyshire (Chelmsford) 18-21 April | 19 | 0 | 2 | 10 | 61 | 5 | | | | 20 | 3 | | | | 144 | | | 100 | | | 4* | 39 | 407 | 10 | | 11 |
| | | 2 | | 69 | 4* | | | | | | | | | | 28* | | | 21 | | | | 7 | 131 | 3 | D | |
| v. Glamorgan (Chelmsford) 25-28 April | 13* | 86 | 148 | 86 | 7 | | | | 0 | 10* | | | | | 218 | | | 0 | | | | 16 | 584 | 7 | W | 22 |
| v. Northamptonshire (Northampton) 2-5 May | 0 | 67 | 0 | 38 | 0 | 21 | 26 | | | | 0 | | | | 34* | 0 | | 136 | | | | 12 | 334 | 10 | | |
| | 0 | 50 | 33* | 9 | 17 | 12 | 12 | | | | 0 | | | | 1 | | 1 | 37 | | | | 18 | 190 | 10 | L | 5 |
| v. Cambridge UCCE (Fenner's) 9-11 May | 23 | 37 | 4 | 52 | | | 82 | 54 | 11* | 49 | | | 46* | | | | | | | | | 43 | 401 | 7 | D | |
| v. Leicestershire (Leicester) 16-19 May | 12 | 1 | 3 | 4 | | 18 | 2 | | 72* | 4 | | | | | 40 | 10 | 10 | | | | | 25 | 201 | 10 | D | 8 |
| v. Nottinghamshire (Trent Bridge) 23-25 May | 81 | 0 | 33 | 32 | 7 | 65 | 1 | | 40 | 1 | | | | | | | 5* | 8 | | | | 44 | 317 | 10 | | |
| | 4 | 1 | 102 | 1 | 12 | 4 | 50 | | 37 | 0 | | | | | | | | 0* | | | | 24 | 235 | 9 | L | 5 |
| v. Glamorgan (Swansea) 30 May-2 June | 16 | 27 | 36 | 0 | 49 | 7 | 4 | 44 | 8 | 1 | | 1* | | | | | | | | | | 11 | 204 | 10 | | |
| | 20* | 79 | 0 | 0 | 36 | | 147* | 8 | | 6 | | | | | | | | | | | | 27 | 323 | 6 | W | 17 |
| v. Northamptonshire (Chelmsford) 6-9 June | 0* | 8 | 62* | 50 | 69 | | 229 | 203 | | | | | | | | | | | | | | 28 | 649 | 5 | W | 22 |
| v. Middlesex (Lord's) 15-18 June | 127 | 4 | 20 | 9 | 7 | 9 | 25 | 4 | | | 35 | 102 | | | | | | | | 2* | | 32 | 376 | 10 | | 11 |
| v. Nottinghamshire (Chelmsford) 8-11 July | 13 | 11 | 17 | 35 | 204 | 0* | 59 | 34 | 125 | | 19* | 148 | | | | | | | | | | 35 | 700 | 9 | | |
| | | 1 | | 29* | | | 33* | | | | | | | | | | | | | | | 0 | 63 | 1 | | 10 |
| v. Somerset (Taunton) 20-23 July | 24 | 73 | 24 | 44 | 1 | | 69 | 0 | 8* | | 1 | 19 | 0 | | | | | | | | | 19 | 282 | 10 | | |
| | 29* | 14 | 35 | 0 | 71 | | 126 | | | | | 5* | | | | | | | | | | 7 | 294 | 6 | W | 17 |
| v. Gloucestershire (Bristol) 25-28 July | 13 | 7 | 1 | 33 | 19 | | 6 | 8 | | | | 22* | | 16* | | | | | | | | 4 | 129 | 7 | D | 4 |
| v. Gloucestershire (Southend) 8-10 August | 7 | 0 | 6 | 7 | 0 | 0 | 14 | 15 | | | 0 | 14* | 17 | | | | | | | | | 8 | 88 | 10 | | |
| | 2 | 7 | 58 | 36 | 29 | 4 | 46 | 15 | | | 29* | 3 | 8 | | | | | | | | | 22 | 259 | 10 | L | 3 |
| v. Leicestershire (Colchester) 22-25 August | 55* | 14 | 56 | 2 | 16 | 19 | | 7 | | 5 | 3 | 0 | 2 | | | | | | | | | 12 | 191 | 10 | | |
| | | 86* | | 62* | | | | | | | | | | | | | | | | | | 3 | 151 | 0 | W | 14 |
| v. Derbyshire (Derby) 30 August-1 September | 81* | 17 | 38 | | 11 | 16 | 9 | | 30 | 1 | 23 | 18 | 4 | | | | | | | | | 24 | 272 | 10 | | |
| | 15 | 2 | 132 | 0 | 1 | | 26 | | 0 | 0 | 74 | 0* | 0 | | | | | | | | | 18 | 268 | 10 | W | 19 |
| v. Somerset (Chelmsford) 5-7 September | 8 | 0 | 5 | 5 | 15 | 8 | | 0 | | | 2 | 12 | | | 72 | | | | | 7* | | 10 | 144 | 10 | | |
| | 0 | 4 | 34 | 8 | 96 | 27 | | 10 | 68 | | | 60* | | | 10 | | | | | 7 | | 25 | 349 | 10 | L | 3 |
| v. Middlesex (Chelmsford) 19-21 September | 21 | 6 | | 4 | | | 157 | 6 | 7 | 11 | | | | 5 | 29 | | | | | 0* | | 23 | 365 | 10 | | |
| | | | | 24* | | | 20* | | | | | | | | | | | | | | | 9 | 53 | 0 | W | 21 |
| | | | | | | | | | | | | | | | | | | | | | | | | | | |
| Matches | 17 | 17 | 16 | 16 | 15 | 13 | 11 | 11 | 10 | 10 | 10 | 8 | 7 | 5 | 4 | 4 | 4 | 3 | 3 | 2 | 1 | | | | | |
| Innings | 24 | 27 | 23 | 26 | 23 | 16 | 17 | 16 | 10 | 14 | 13 | 12 | 8 | 7 | 6 | 2 | 5 | 5 | 3 | 1 | 1 | | | | | |
| Not Out | 6 | 1 | 2 | 3 | 1 | 1 | 2 | 1 | 3 | 0 | 3 | 4 | 2 | 2 | 2 | 1 | 1 | 0 | 2 | 1 | 1 | | | | | |
| Highest Score | 127 | 86* | 148 | 86 | 204 | 65 | 229 | 203 | 125 | 68 | 35 | 148 | 18 | 72 | 218 | 10 | 10 | 136 | 7* | 2* | 4* | | | | | |
| Runs | 583 | 604 | 849 | 649 | 827 | 216 | 931 | 611 | 317 | 193 | 112 | 482 | 51 | 177 | 465 | 15 | 19 | 294 | 14 | 2 | 4 | | | | | |
| Average | 32.38 | 23.23 | 40.42 | 28.21 | 37.59 | 14.40 | 62.06 | 40.73 | 45.28 | 13.78 | 11.20 | 60.25 | 8.50 | 35.40 | 116.25 | 15.00 | 4.75 | 58.80 | 14.00 | - | - | | | | | |
| 100s | 1 | 0 | 3 | 0 | 1 | 0 | 3 | 2 | 1 | 0 | 0 | 2 | 0 | 0 | 2 | 0 | 0 | 2 | 0 | 0 | 0 | | | | | |
| 50s | 3 | 6 | 3 | 5 | 5 | 1 | 4 | 1 | 1 | 1 | 0 | 2 | 0 | 1 | 0 | 0 | 0 | 0 | 0 | 0 | 0 | | | | | |
| Catches/Stumpings | 15/0 | 17/0 | 10/0 | 15/0 | 31/5 | 1/0 | 4/0 | 17/0 | 4/0 | 4/0 | 3/0 | 7/0 | 1/0 | 3/0 | 4/0 | 1/0 | 0/0 | 2/0 | 2/0 | 0/0 | 0/0 | | | | | |

**Home Ground:** Chelmsford
**Address:** Ford County Ground, New Writtle Street, Chelmsford, Essex, CM2 0PG
**Tel:** 01245 252420
**Fax:** 01245 254030
**Email:** administration.essex@ecb.co.uk
**Directions:** *By rail:* Chelmsford Station (8 minutes' walk away). *By road:* M25 then A12 to Chelmsford. Exit Chelmsford and follow AA signs to Essex Cricket Club.

**Capacity:** 6,000
**Other grounds used:** Colchester, Southend-on-Sea
**Year formed:** 1876

**Chief Executive:** David East
**Cricket Operations Manager:** Alan Lilley
**First Team Coach:** Paul Grayson
**Captain:** Mark Pettini
**County colours:** Blue, gold and red

**Honours**
County Championship
1979, 1983, 1984, 1986, 1991, 1992
Sunday League/NCL/Pro40
1981, 1984, 1985, 2005, 2006
Refuge Assurance Cup
1989
Benson & Hedges Cup
1979, 1998
Gillette Cup/NatWest/C&G Trophy
1985, 1997

Website:
www.essexcricket.org.uk

FIRST-CLASS MATCHES

# BOWLING

| | Danish Kaneria | AJ Bichel | JD Middlebrook | AJ Tudor | AP Palladino | RS Bopara | MJ Saggers | A Nel | GR Napier | RN ten Doeschate | TJ Phillips | JS Ahmed | AC McGarry | GW Flower | AN Cook | MS Westfield | V Chopra | Overs | Total | Byes/Leg-byes | Wickets | Run outs |
|---|---|---|---|---|---|---|---|---|---|---|---|---|---|---|---|---|---|---|---|---|---|---|
| v. Derbyshire (Chelmsford) 18-21 April | 52.3-8-152-5<br>21-0-76-1 | 22-3-77-2<br>19-0-84-0 | 19-5-66-1<br>8-2-22-0 | | | | | | | 19-2-98-1<br>6-1-24-1 | 17-2-79-1<br>7-0-20-0 | | | | 1-0-6-0 | 13-1-64-0 | | 143.3<br>61 | 551<br>231 | 9<br>5 | 10<br>3 | <br>1 |
| v. Glamorgan (Chelmsford) 25-28 April | 47.4-16-105-7<br>25.5-4-76-6 | 32-9-61-0<br>34-8-76-3 | 21-6-48-1 | | | | | | 9-1-47-0 | 20-3-58-1<br>3-2-5-1 | | | 15-3-52-0<br>7-3-20-0 | | | | 1-0-5-0 | 145.4<br>69.5 | 394<br>183 | 18<br>6 | 10<br>10 | 1 |
| v. Northamptonshire (Northampton) 2-5 May | 41-9-108-4<br>12-1-61-2 | | 24-5-62-1<br>18-5-55-2 | | | | | 19-1-73-0<br>3-0-15-1 | 26.2-5-62-3<br>12-7-20-1 | 8-1-35-0<br>23-2-12-0 | | | | | | | | 136.2<br>29.3 | 416<br>110 | 21<br>2 | 10<br>4 | |
| v. Cambridge UCCE (Fenner's) 9-11 May | | | | | | | | | 10-4-29-2 | 6-0-24-0 | 1-0-2-0 | 3.3-1-14-0 | 6-1-18-0 | | | | | 26.3 | 89 | 2 | 2 | |
| v. Leicestershire (Leicester) 16-19 May | 6-1-48-1 | | 6-1-9-0 | | | | | 14-3-39-1 | 15-4-58-2<br>3-1-17-0 | 19.1-6-55-3<br>3-0-23-0 | 10-0-63-1 | 5.1-1-6-0 | 15-3-62-2 | | | | | 79.1<br>17.1 | 335<br>56 | 10<br>1 | 10<br>0 | |
| v. Nottinghamshire (Trent Bridge) 23-25 May | 29-2-131-3 | | 7-0-54-0 | | | | | 22.5-5-98-2 | 31-8-103-2 | 23-3-128-0 | 11-1-63-0 | 7-0-48-0 | 2.1-0-8-0 | | | | 1-0-11-0 | 134 | 664 | 20 | 7 | |
| v. Glamorgan (Swansea) 30 May-2 June | 49-14-112-5<br>21.5-5-54-3 | | 27-11-50-0<br>19-2-80-2 | | 20-9-51-2<br>6-1-16-0 | 11-3-33-0 | | | 16-6-41-0<br>4-1-17-0 | 6-1-21-0<br>10.5-3-28-3 | | | | | | | | 139.5<br>50.5 | 352<br>174 | 16<br>7 | 10<br>5 | |
| v. Northamptonshire (Chelmsford) 6-9 June | 26-8-36-2<br>38.2-11-101-5 | | 20-4-53-4<br>25-0-77-3 | | | | 5-1-17-0<br>2-0-9-0 | 16-3-69-3<br>16-4-48-0 | 11-3-39-0<br>24-3-92-2 | 4-2-13-1<br>7-2-16-0 | | | | | | | | 82<br>112.2 | 241<br>367 | 14<br>24 | 10<br>10 | |
| v. Middlesex (Lord's) 15-18 June | 11-6-16-0<br>36-6-97-3 | 19.3-4-52-1<br>21-3-83-1 | 1-0-1-0<br>11-3-23-0 | 8-0-29-3<br>10-2-23-0 | | | 24-8-39-5<br>25-5-88-2 | 5-2-10-0 | | 4-0-16-1<br>8-0-25-0 | | | | 2-1-4-0 | | | | 72.3<br>113 | 177<br>360 | 14<br>17 | 10<br>6 | |
| v. Nottinghamshire (Chelmsford) 8-11 July | 42-5-153-3 | 32-5-127-2 | 45-11-140-1 | 16.5-1-89-1 | | | | 17-4-61-0 | 23-3-72-0 | 20-6-65-1 | | | | 14-4-50-1 | | | 3-0-9-0 | 212.5 | 791 | 25 | 10 | |
| v. Somerset (Taunton) 20-23 July | | 18-5-63-6 | | 7-1-27-1 | | | | 8-1-38-1 | 2.1-0-11-2 | | | | | | | | | 35.1 | 153 | 14 | 10 | |
| v. Gloucestershire (Bristol) 25-28 July | | 19-6-55-5 | 6-0-15-1 | | | | | 7-2-21-1 | 16.3-4-60-3 | 7-0-27-0 | | | | | | | | 55.3 | 184 | 6 | 10 | |
| v. Gloucestershire (Southend) 8-10 August | 21-10-38-3<br>9.3-0-30-4 | 19.4-6-48-1<br>10-3-34-4 | 16-3-46-1<br>5-0-18-1 | 13-4-48-2<br>8-3-25-1 | 10-5-29-0<br>2-0-13-0 | 11-0-63-3<br>4-0-18-0 | | | | | | | | | | | | 90.4<br>38.3 | 278<br>139 | 6<br>1 | 10<br>10 | |
| v. Leicestershire (Colchester) 22-25 August | 16-5-52-3 | | 6-1-20-2<br>12-2-63-3 | 2.3-0-14-0<br>7-4-14-0 | 3-0-18-0<br>6-0-22-1 | | | | | | | | | | | | | 11.3<br>47 | 52<br>176 | 0<br>6 | 2<br>10 | |
| v. Derbyshire (Derby) 30 August-1 September | 2-1-1-0<br>16.3-5-45-6 | 10.3-2-36-7<br>22-3-96-4 | | 4-1-28-0<br>1-0-10-0 | 6-0-28-1<br>4-1-17-0 | | | | | 6-1-46-1 | | | | | | | | 28.3<br>43.3 | 139<br>174 | 0<br>6 | 10<br>10 | 1 |
| v. Somerset (Chelmsford) 5-7 September | 24.4-5-95-7<br>12-2-56-1 | 19-2-100-2<br>9-1-65-3 | 7-0-40-0<br>3-1-22-0 | | | | | | 2-0-19-0<br>7.5-0-36-0 | | | | 8-0-58-0 | | | | | 60.4<br>31.5 | 312<br>184 | 0<br>5 | 10<br>4 | 1 |
| v. Middlesex (Chelmsford) 19-21 September | | | 6.5-1-13-3<br>18-5-56-2 | 13-3-48-3<br>19-6-53-2 | | 15.5-5-44-4 | | | 10-4-44-2<br>16-3-71-1 | | 7-2-30-1<br>10-2-41-2 | | | | | | | 45.5<br>69.5 | 171<br>246 | 5<br>12 | 10<br>10 | |
| **Overs** | 560.5 | 217.4 | 341.5 | 174.2 | 106.5 | 130.2 | 81 | 122.2 | 150.1 | 119.3 | 71 | 28.3 | 45.1 | 16 | 1 | 13 | 5 | | | | | |
| **Maidens** | 124 | 43 | 62 | 42 | 30 | 23 | 20 | 31 | 32 | 18 | 11 | 5 | 10 | 5 | 0 | 1 | 0 | | | | | |
| **Runs** | 1643 | 842 | 1020 | 602 | 350 | 496 | 244 | 391 | 589 | 552 | 246 | 143 | 160 | 54 | 6 | 64 | 25 | | | | | |
| **Wickets** | 74 | 41 | 24 | 17 | 12 | 11 | 10 | 10 | 10 | 7 | 6 | 3 | 2 | 1 | 0 | 0 | 0 | | | | | |
| **Average** | 22.20 | 20.53 | 42.50 | 35.41 | 29.16 | 45.09 | 24.40 | 39.10 | 58.90 | 78.85 | 41.00 | 47.66 | 80.00 | 54.00 | - | - | - | | | | | |

# FIELDING

| | |
|---|---|
| 36 | JS Foster (31 ct, 5 st) |
| 17 | GW Flower |
| 17 | ML Pettini |
| 15 | JD Middlebrook |
| 15 | V Chopra |
| 10 | RN ten Doeschate |
| 7 | AJ Bichel |
| 4 | RC Irani |
| 4 | GR Napier |
| 4 | TJ Phillips |
| 4 | RS Bopara |
| 3 | AJ Tudor |
| 3 | T Westley |
| 2 | AN Cook |
| 2 | JS Ahmed |
| 1 | AC McGarry |
| 1 | AP Palladino |
| 1 | Danish Kaneria |
| 0 | MJ Saggers |
| 0 | A Nel |
| 0 | MS Westfield |

## Final Division Two Table

| | P | W | L | D | T | Ab | Bat | Bowl | Pens | Pts |
|---|---|---|---|---|---|---|---|---|---|---|
| Somerset | 16 | 10 | 1 | 5 | 0 | 0 | 65 | 41 | 0.00 | 266.00 |
| Nottinghamshire | 16 | 6 | 3 | 7 | 0 | 0 | 60 | 43 | 0.50 | 214.50 |
| Middlesex | 16 | 6 | 2 | 8 | 0 | 0 | 35 | 43 | 1.50 | 192.50 |
| Essex | 16 | 6 | 4 | 6 | 0 | 0 | 40 | 36 | 2.00 | 182.00 |
| Northamptonshire | 16 | 5 | 5 | 6 | 0 | 0 | 44 | 38 | 0.00 | 176.00 |
| Derbyshire | 16 | 3 | 5 | 8 | 0 | 0 | 30 | 44 | 1.00 | 147.00 |
| Gloucestershire | 16 | 3 | 5 | 8 | 0 | 0 | 32 | 37 | 3.50 | 139.50 |
| Leicestershire | 16 | 2 | 8 | 5 | 0 | 1 | 32 | 35 | 4.00 | 115.00 |
| Glamorgan | 16 | 1 | 9 | 5 | 0 | 1 | 26 | 37 | 8.50 | 92.50 |

Glamorgan had eight points deducted for a poor pitch.

Limited overs nickname:
ESSEX EAGLES

# GLAMORGAN CCC

## FIRST-CLASS MATCHES

### BATTING

| Match | RDB Croft | MA Wallace | DL Hemp | AG Wharf | BJ Wright | DA Cosker | GP Rees | HT Waters | JAR Harris | RN Grant | JP Maher | RE Watkins | AP Davies | DD Cherry | MJ Powell | MTG Elliott | SP Jones | N Peng | WD Bragg | TL Maynard | MP O'Shea | DG Wright | WT Owen | Extras | Total | Wickets | Result | Poi |
|---|---|---|---|---|---|---|---|---|---|---|---|---|---|---|---|---|---|---|---|---|---|---|---|---|---|---|---|---|
| v. Oxford UCCE | 26 | 97 | 152* | 100* | 2 | | | | | | 28 | 1* | 19 | | 114 | 0 | | | | | | | | 27 | 566 | 7 | | |
| (The Parks) 18-20 Apil | | | | | | | | | | | | | | | | | | | | | | | | | | | W | |
| v. Essex | 0 | 13 | 13 | 38 | 11 | | 33 | | | | 29 | 24* | | 48 | 64 | 95 | | | | | | | | 26 | 394 | 10 | | |
| (Chelmsford) 25-28 April | 42* | 10 | 2 | 2 | 4 | | 0 | | | | 2 | 12 | | 18 | 8 | 75 | | | | | | | | 8 | 183 | 10 | L | 4 |
| v. Nottinghamshire | 17 | 7 | 54 | 19 | 10 | | 6* | 21 | | | 4 | 0 | 53 | 47 | | | | | | | | | | 24 | 262 | 10 | | |
| (Trent Bridge) 2-4 May | 9 | 6 | 47 | 0 | 66* | | 2 | 11 | | | 20 | 0 | 0 | 30 | | | | | | | | | | 14 | 205 | 10 | L | 5 |
| v. Gloucestershire | 11 | 128 | 15 | 128* | 19 | | 7 | | | 17 | | | 0 | 16 | 4 | 5 | | | | | | | | 42 | 392 | 10 | | |
| (Bristol) 16-19 May | | | | | | | | | | | | | | | | | | | | | | | | | | | D | 10 |
| v. Middlesex | 11 | 4 | 7 | 14 | 5 | 0 | | 0* | | 1 | | | 10 | 0 | | | | | | | | 0 | | 8 | 60 | 10 | | |
| (Swansea) 23-24 May | 5 | 7 | 13 | 15 | 3 | 10 | | 19 | | 3 | | | 15 | 39* | | | | | | | | 1 | | 29 | 159 | 10 | L | 3 |
| v. Essex | 8 | 34 | 53 | 18 | 10 | | 107 | 5* | 1 | 4 | | | | | 62 | 13 | | | | | | | | 37 | 352 | 10 | | |
| (Swansea) 30 May-2 June | | 1 | 36 | 22* | 14 | | 19 | | | | | | | | 51* | 20 | | | | | | | | 11 | 174 | 5 | L | 6 |
| v. Nottinghamshire | 115 | 24 | 55 | 6 | 28 | 30 | 0 | | 87* | 41 | | | | | | | | 9 | | | 10 | | | 24 | 429 | 10 | | |
| (Swansea) 5-8 June | 3 | 22 | 3 | 9 | 18* | 6 | 24 | | 11 | 27 | | | | | | | | 65 | | | 0 | | | 9 | 197 | 10 | W | 21 |
| v. Leicestershire | 29 | 42 | 23 | 19 | 108 | 0* | 2 | 0 | 0 | | 19 | | | | | | 0 | | | | | | | 26 | 268 | 10 | | |
| (Leicester) 8-11 July | 71 | 9 | 43 | 5 | 6 | 6 | 0 | 13* | 2 | | 55 | | | | | | 4 | | | | | | | 22 | 236 | 10 | L | |
| v. Derbyshire | 24 | 20 | 97 | 14 | 2 | | 51 | | 21 | 17 | 16 | 2 | 1* | | | | | | | | | | | 33 | 298 | 10 | | |
| (Derby) 20-23 July | 17 | 1 | 1 | 5 | 4 | | 19 | | 18* | 5 | 3 | 12 | 10 | | | | | | | | | | | 32 | 127 | 10 | D | 7 |
| v. Middlesex | 0 | 11 | 9 | 10 | 0 | 0 | 0* | | 4 | 30 | | | 32 | | | | 3 | | | | | | | 7 | 106 | 10 | | |
| (Lord's) 31 July-2 August | 20 | 9 | 36 | 55 | 2 | 8 | 8 | | 0 | 20 | | | 10 | | | | 2* | | | | | | | 14 | 184 | 10 | L | 3 |
| v. Northamptonshire | 14 | 19 | 82 | 111* | 10 | 11 | | | | 79 | 4 | 30 | 28 | | | | 39 | | | | | | | 38 | 465 | 10 | | |
| (Colwyn Bay) 8-11 August | 29 | 15 | 0 | 37 | 26 | 0 | | | | 26 | 4 | 0* | 18 | | | | 14 | | | | | | | 28 | 197 | 10 | L | 10 |
| v. Somerset | 43 | 16 | 28 | 45 | 4 | | 0 | | 5 | 4 | 0 | 26* | | | | | | | | 15 | | | | 12 | 198 | 10 | | |
| (Cardiff) 14-17 August | | | | | | | | | | | | | | | | | | | | | | | | | | | D | 6 |
| v. Derbyshire | 11* | 21 | 6 | 21 | 0 | | 61 | | 0 | 2 | 31 | | | | | 23 | | | | 18 | | | | 31 | 225 | 10 | | |
| (Cardiff) 22-24 August | 8 | 15 | 12 | 0 | 1* | | 109 | | 3 | 28 | 29 | | | | | 0 | | | | 2 | | | | 19 | 226 | 10 | L | 4 |
| v. Somerset | 23 | 0 | 3 | 4 | 7 | 1* | 5 | | 64 | 25 | | | 54 | | | | | | 24 | | | | | 23 | 233 | 10 | | |
| (Taunton) 30 August-1 September | 38 | 12 | 39 | | 12 | 0* | 9 | | 13 | 39 | | | 9 | | | | | | 9 | | | | | 19 | 199 | 10 | L | 4 |
| v. Northamptonshire | 20 | 120 | 9 | 12 | 0 | 14 | 0 | | | 34 | | | 49* | | | | | | 13 | | | | | 9 | 280 | 10 | | |
| (Northampton) 11-13 September | 1 | 6 | 31 | 18 | 0 | 18 | 4 | | 0* | 9 | | | 4 | | | | | | 5 | | | | | 6 | 102 | 10 | L | 4 |
| v. Gloucestershire | | | | | | | | | | | | | | | | | | | | | | | | | | | | |
| (Cardiff) 19-22 September | | | | | | | | | | | | | | | | | | | | | | | | | | | D | 5 |
| | | | | | | | | | | | | | | | | | | | | | | | | | | | | |
| Matches | 16 | 16 | 15 | 15 | 11 | 11 | 10 | 10 | 9 | 8 | 8 | 8 | 7 | 7 | 6 | 4 | 4 | 3 | 2 | 2 | 2 | 1 | 1 | | | | | |
| Innings | 26 | 27 | 25 | 26 | 18 | 16 | 18 | 16 | 14 | 13 | 15 | 13 | 12 | 12 | 10 | 6 | 7 | 6 | 4 | 3 | 2 | 2 | 0 | | | | | |
| Not Out | 2 | 0 | 1 | 4 | 2 | 2 | 0 | 8 | 2 | 0 | 0 | 0 | 6 | 0 | 2 | 0 | 1 | 0 | 0 | 0 | 0 | 0 | 0 | | | | | |
| Highest Score | 115 | 128 | 152* | 128* | 108 | 30 | 109 | 33 | 87* | 79 | 55 | 30 | 54 | 48 | 114 | 95 | 39 | 65 | 24 | 18 | 10 | 1 | 0 | | | | | |
| Runs | 595 | 669 | 827 | 726 | 329 | 137 | 429 | 87 | 196 | 350 | 252 | 172 | 220 | 198 | 407 | 251 | 86 | 111 | 51 | 35 | 10 | 1 | 0 | | | | | |
| Average | 24.79 | 24.77 | 34.45 | 33.00 | 20.56 | 9.78 | 23.83 | 10.87 | 16.33 | 26.92 | 16.80 | 13.23 | 36.66 | 16.50 | 50.87 | 41.83 | 14.33 | 18.50 | 12.75 | 11.66 | 5.00 | 0.50 | - | | | | | |
| 100s | 1 | 2 | 1 | 3 | 1 | 0 | 2 | 0 | 0 | 0 | 0 | 0 | 0 | 0 | 1 | 1 | 0 | 0 | 0 | 0 | 0 | 0 | 0 | | | | | |
| 50s | 1 | 1 | 5 | 1 | 1 | 0 | 2 | 0 | 1 | 2 | 1 | 0 | 1 | 0 | 4 | 2 | 0 | 1 | 0 | 0 | 0 | 0 | 0 | | | | | |
| Catches/Stumpings | 10/0 | 40/6 | 8/0 | 7/0 | 13/0 | 2/0 | 8/0 | 4/0 | 4/0 | 1/0 | 9/0 | 3/0 | 3/0 | 3/0 | 4/0 | 6/0 | 0/0 | 2/0 | 0/0 | 0/0 | 0/0 | 1/0 | 0/0 | | | | | |

**Home Ground:** Cardiff
**Address:** Sophia Gardens, Cardiff, CF11 9XR
**Tel:** 0871 2823401
**Fax:** 0871 2823405
**Email:** info@glamorgancricket.co.uk
**Directions:** By rail: Cardiff Central train station.
By road: From North, A470 and follow signs to Cardiff until junction with Cardiff bypass then A48 Port Talbot and City Centre. Cathedral Road is situated off A48 for Sophia Gardens.

**Capacity:** 4,000
**Other grounds used:** Swansea, Colwyn Bay, Abergavenny
**Year formed:** 1888

**Chief Executive:** Mike Fatkin
**First XI Coach:** Adrian Shaw
**Captain:** David Hemp
**County colours:** Navy blue and yellow/gold

**Honours**
County Championship
1948, 1969, 1997
Sunday League/NCL/Pro40
1993, 2002, 2004

Website:
www.glamorgancricket.com

FIRST-CLASS MATCHES

# BOWLING

| | RDB Croft | AG Wharf | JAR Harris | DA Cosker | HT Waters | AP Davies | RE Watkins | DG Wright | RN Grant | BJ Wright | SP Jones | DL Hemp | DD Cherry | TL Maynard | WT Owen | Overs | Total | Byes/Leg-byes | Wickets | Run outs |
|---|---|---|---|---|---|---|---|---|---|---|---|---|---|---|---|---|---|---|---|---|
| **Oxford UCCE** The Parks 18-20 April | 19-4-68-0 | 13.5-2-54-1 | | 12-3-19-2 | | 18-6-46-4 | 15-2-54-3 | | | | | 4-1-8-0 | | | | 81.5 | 251 | 2 | 10 | |
| | 19-3-61-3 | 11.4-5-16-4 | | 16-5-42-1 | | 5-0-19-0 | 8-2-26-1 | | | | | | | | | 59.4 | 170 | 6 | 10 | |
| **Essex** (Chelmsford) 25-28 April | 54-6-142-3 | 31-2-110-1 | | | 30-5-117-2 | 31-3-138-0 | 17-5-52-0 | | | 4-0-14-1 | | | | | | 167 | 584 | 11 | 7 | |
| **Nottinghamshire** (Trent Bridge) 2-4 May | 24-1-101-0 | 26-1-97-4 | 25-7-86-2 | | | 20.4-2-73-2 | 16-2-78-1 | | | 11-0-37-1 | | | | | | 122.4 | 475 | 3 | 10 | |
| **Gloucestershire** Bristol 16-19 May | 15-4-42-1 | 9.4-2-18-1 | 22-6-66-7 | | | | 7-2-22-1 | | | | | 18-4-61-0 | | | | 71.4 | 219 | 10 | 10 | |
| | 28-3-94-3 | 19-0-75-1 | 19-6-52-5 | | | | 5-1-15-0 | | | 3-0-24-0 | | 19-4-51-0 | 2-0-5-0 | | | 95 | 328 | 12 | 9 | |
| **Middlesex** Swansea 23-24 May | 10-1-30-0 | 16-1-82-2 | | 10.3-0-21-4 | 8-1-22-1 | | | 16-4-60-3 | | 2-0-4-0 | | | | | | 62.3 | 221 | 2 | 10 | |
| **Essex** Swansea 30 May-2 June | 17.1-3-52-4 | 12-1-47-2 | 14-4-27-1 | 17-2-53-1 | 8-3-18-2 | | | | | | | | | | | 68.1 | 204 | 7 | 10 | |
| | 25-2-74-0 | 17.2-2-85-1 | 9-2-44-1 | 22-4-88-2 | 4-1-19-0 | | | | | | | | | | | 77.2 | 323 | 13 | 6 | 2 |
| **Nottinghamshire** Swansea 5-8 June | 40.5-2-114-2 | 14-1-62-1 | 14-2-37-2 | 47-7-137-4 | | | | | | | | | | | | 115.5 | 364 | 14 | 10 | 1 |
| | 28-1-94-2 | 5.5-3-11-2 | 11-3-24-1 | 18-4-69-5 | | | | | | | | | | | | 62.5 | 207 | 9 | 10 | |
| **Leicestershire** (Leicester) 8-11 July | 32-6-108-2 | 26-3-81-3 | 31-8-95-4 | 16-2-80-0 | 28-6-99-1 | | | | | 2-0-10-0 | | | | | | 135 | 481 | 8 | 10 | |
| | | 3.1-0-17-0 | 4-1-10-0 | | | | | | | | | | | | | 7.1 | 27 | | | |
| **Derbyshire** Derby 20-23 July | 3-0-12-1 | 4-0-27-1 | 11-3-24-0 | | | | 6-1-41-1 | 6.3-0-41-0 | | | | | | | | 30.3 | 150 | 5 | 3 | |
| | 19-5-44-6 | 7-0-52-0 | 11-1-49-1 | | | | 9-3-43-2 | | | | | | | | | 46 | 195 | 7 | 9 | |
| **Middlesex** (Lord's) 31 July-2 August | 20-3-50-0 | 21-1-77-4 | | 18-1-62-3 | | 27.5-8-73-2 | 7-0-34-0 | | | | 19-2-61-0 | | | | | 112.5 | 361 | 4 | 10 | 1 |
| **Northamptonshire** (Colwyn Bay) 8-11 August | 19.2-3-76-2 | 14-2-60-0 | | 15-5-55-1 | | 25-5-70-3 | 18-1-89-4 | | | | 11-2-30-0 | | | | | 102.2 | 387 | 7 | 10 | |
| | 12-0-52-0 | 7-1-27-2 | | 13-2-38-0 | | | | | | | | | | | | 32 | 131 | 14 | 2 | |
| **Somerset** (Cardiff) 14-17 August | 29-4-138-2 | 7.5-0-55-0 | | 11-0-61-2 | | 9-1-44-0 | 10-2-36-0 | | 6-0-42-1 | | | | 2-0-18-0 | | | 74.5 | 400 | 6 | 6 | |
| **Derbyshire** (Cardiff) 22-24 August | 25.5-7-62-5 | 11-3-37-2 | 14-3-51-2 | 1-0-11-0 | | | | | | | | | 14-1-39-1 | | | 65.5 | 206 | 6 | 10 | |
| | 40.3-11-88-6 | 8-0-42-1 | 15-3-34-2 | 33-8-61-1 | | | | | 1-0-6-0 | | | | 8-0-48-0 | | | 105.3 | 287 | 8 | 10 | |
| **Somerset** Taunton 30 August-1 September | 20-4-69-2 | 15-1-82-3 | 17.5-2-94-1 | | | 21-3-76-4 | 12-0-67-0 | | | | | | | | | 85.5 | 402 | 14 | 10 | |
| | 24-2-102-5 | 4-0-21-0 | 16-0-55-2 | | | 21-0-107-0 | 7-0-34-0 | | | 1.4-0-7-1 | | | | | | 73.4 | 329 | 3 | 9 | 1 |
| **Northamptonshire** (Northampton) 11-13 September | 53.3-10-138-6 | 5-0-27-0 | | 51-12-126-3 | 11-0-34-0 | 11-2-48-1 | | | | | | | | | | 131.3 | 381 | 8 | 10 | |
| | 1-0-1-0 | | | 0.3-0-4-0 | | | | | | | | | | | | 1.3 | 5 | 0 | 0 | |
| **Gloucestershire** (Cardiff) 19-22 September | 21-2-65-1 | | 14-2-63-2 | 4-1-12-0 | 13-1-58-1 | | | | 3-0-23-0 | | | | | | 8-0-37-0 | 63 | 262 | 3 | 4 | |
| **Overs** | 600.1 | 309.2 | 247.5 | 305 | 201.3 | 134 | 99.3 | 16 | 11.4 | 22 | 89 | 4 | 2 | 2 | 8 | | | | | |
| **Maidens** | 87 | 31 | 53 | 56 | 31 | 22 | 15 | 4 | 0 | 0 | 13 | 1 | 0 | 0 | 0 | | | | | |
| **Runs** | 1877 | 1262 | 811 | 939 | 741 | 542 | 411 | 60 | 78 | 89 | 290 | 8 | 5 | 18 | 37 | | | | | |
| **Wickets** | 56 | 36 | 33 | 29 | 15 | 11 | 10 | 3 | 2 | 2 | 1 | 0 | 0 | 0 | 0 | | | | | |
| **Average** | 33.51 | 35.05 | 24.57 | 32.37 | 49.40 | 49.27 | 41.10 | 20.00 | 39.00 | 44.50 | 290.00 | - | - | - | - | | | | | |

# FIELDING

- 46 MA Wallace (40 ct, 6 st)
- 13 BJ Wright
- 10 RDB Croft
- 9 JP Maher
- 8 DL Hemp
- 8 GP Rees
- 7 AG Wharf
- 6 MTG Elliott
- 4 MJ Powell
- 4 HT Waters
- 4 JAR Harris
- 3 AP Davies
- 3 DD Cherry
- 3 RE Watkins
- 2 DA Cosker
- 2 N Peng
- 2 DG Wright
- 1 RN Grant
- 1 SP Jones
- 0 WD Bragg
- 0 MP O'Shea
- 0 TL Maynard
- 0 WT Owen

## Final Division Two Table

| | P | W | L | D | T | Ab | Bat | Bowl | Pens | Pts |
|---|---|---|---|---|---|---|---|---|---|---|
| **Somerset** | 16 | 10 | 1 | 5 | 0 | 0 | 65 | 41 | 0.00 | 266.00 |
| **Nottinghamshire** | 16 | 6 | 3 | 7 | 0 | 0 | 60 | 43 | 0.50 | 214.50 |
| **Middlesex** | 16 | 6 | 2 | 8 | 0 | 0 | 35 | 43 | 1.50 | 192.50 |
| **Essex** | 16 | 6 | 4 | 6 | 0 | 0 | 40 | 36 | 2.00 | 182.00 |
| **Northamptonshire** | 16 | 5 | 5 | 6 | 0 | 0 | 44 | 38 | 0.00 | 176.00 |
| **Derbyshire** | 16 | 3 | 5 | 8 | 0 | 0 | 30 | 44 | 1.00 | 147.00 |
| **Gloucestershire** | 16 | 3 | 5 | 8 | 0 | 0 | 32 | 37 | 3.50 | 139.50 |
| **Leicestershire** | 16 | 2 | 8 | 5 | 0 | 1 | 32 | 35 | 4.00 | 115.00 |
| **Glamorgan** | 16 | 1 | 9 | 5 | 0 | 1 | 26 | 37 | 8.50 | 92.50 |

Glamorgan had eight points deducted for a poor pitch.

DRAGONS CRICKET

Limited overs nickname: GLAMORGAN DRAGONS

# GLOUCESTERSHIRE CCC

## FIRST-CLASS MATCHES

### BATTING

| Match | APR Gidman | Kadeer Ali | CG Taylor | GP Hodnett | HJH Marshall | SJ Adshead | CM Spearman | SP Kirby | V Banerjee | MA Hardinges | J Lewis | CG Greenidge | MJ North | BM Edmondson | SD Snell | AA Noffke | DO Brown | ID Fisher | AJ Ireland | TP Stayt | JG Thompson | WD Rudge | Extras | Total | Wickets | Result | Points |
|---|---|---|---|---|---|---|---|---|---|---|---|---|---|---|---|---|---|---|---|---|---|---|---|---|---|---|---|
| v. Nottinghamshire (Bristol) 25-28 April | 17 | 48 | 0 | 25 | 0 | 100 | 16 | | | 31 | 42* | | 24 | 16 | | | | | | | | | 9 | 328 | 10 | | |
| | 88 | 9 | 5 | 61 | 21 | 85 | 0 | | | 18* | 0 | | 22 | 15 | | | | | | | | | 29 | 353 | 10 | L | 6 |
| v. Leicestershire (Bristol) 2-5 May | 17 | 92 | 8 | 67 | 81 | 38 | 22 | | | 36 | | | 86 | | 2 | | | 4* | | | | | 54 | 507 | 10 | | |
| | 0* | 43 | | 55 | | 26 | | | | | | | 106 | | | | | | | | | | 19 | 249 | 4 | D | 12 |
| v. Glamorgan (Bristol) 16-19 May | 8 | 13 | 10 | 8 | | 19 | | | | 19 | | | 94 | | | 15 | 6 | | 10* | | | 0 | 17 | 219 | 10 | | |
| | 0 | 102 | 31 | 55 | | 3 | | | | 68 | | | 13 | | | 61 | 0 | | 4* | | | 3* | 22 | 328 | 9 | D | 7 |
| v. Somerset (Taunton) 23-26 May | 22 | 7 | 21 | 32 | 86 | | | 4* | 0 | | | 6 | 6 | | | | 3 | | | | | | 11 | 202 | 10 | | |
| | 13 | 95 | 101* | 108 | 20 | | | 1 | 0 | | | 0 | 106 | 6 | | | 0 | | | | | | 15 | 465 | 10 | L | 4 |
| v. Northamptonshire (Gloucester) 1-4 June | 130 | 0 | 36 | 60 | 30 | | | 1* | 2 | | | 2 | 109 | 10 | 5 | | | | | | | | 9 | 394 | 10 | | |
| | 105* | 2 | 46 | 11 | 38 | | | | 20 | | | | 1 | 6 | 10 | | | | | | | | 5 | 244 | 8 | W | 21 |
| v. Derbyshire (Derby) 5-8 June | 91 | 27 | 0 | 47 | 13 | | | 0 | 1 | 13* | | 11 | 13 | | | | 5 | | | | | | 37 | 258 | 10 | | |
| | 94 | 4 | 6 | 120 | 3 | | | 2* | | 104 | | 27 | 5 | | | | 43 | 8 | | | | | 25 | 441 | 10 | D | 8 |
| v. Somerset (Bristol) 15-17 June | 16 | 3 | 4 | 52 | 4 | | | 1* | 4 | 11 | | 0 | 12 | | 9 | | | | | | | | 5 | 121 | 10 | | |
| | 0 | 14 | 34 | 21 | 31 | | | 1* | 14 | 3 | | 1 | 1 | | 12 | | | | | | | | 6 | 138 | 10 | L | 5 |
| v. Northamptonshire (Northampton) 8-11 July | 2 | 25 | 112* | 0 | 0 | 46 | 0 | 37 | 4 | | | 3 | 0 | | | | | | | | | | 21 | 250 | 10 | | |
| | 36 | 17 | 0 | 3 | 58 | 13 | 3 | 0 | 11* | | | | 10 | 18 | | | | | | | | | 23 | 192 | 10 | L | 5 |
| v. Nottinghamshire (Trent Bridge) 13-16 July | | | 0* | | | | | | 0* | | | | | | | | | | | | | | 0 | 0 | 0 | D | 6 |
| v. Essex (Bristol) 25-28 July | 10 | 0 | 101 | 24 | 1 | 11 | 5 | 4 | | | 5 | 1 | 6* | | | | | | | | | | 16 | 184 | 10 | D | 4 |
| v. Derbyshire (Bristol) 31 July-3 August | 111 | 28 | 19 | 168 | 38 | 1 | 52 | 6 | 5 | | | 3 | 3* | | | | | | | | | | 20 | 454 | 10 | | |
| | 17 | 13 | 28 | 30* | 0 | 36* | 35 | | | | | | 11 | | | | | | | | | | 11 | 170 | 5 | D | 12 |
| v. Essex (Southend) 8-10 August | 4 | 65 | 12 | 7 | 22 | 18 | 75 | 8 | 11* | | | 1 | | | | | | 41 | | | | | 14 | 278 | 10 | W | 19 |
| | 12 | 2 | 16 | 0 | 11 | 50 | 31 | 4 | 3* | | | 2 | | | | | | 7 | | | | | 1 | 139 | 10 | | |
| v. Middlesex (Lord's) 22-25 August | 6 | 42 | 62* | 1 | 2 | 0 | 18 | 0 | 13 | 11 | | | | | | | | | 0 | | | | 8 | 163 | 10 | | |
| | 9* | 24 | | 22 | 59* | | 32 | | | | | | | | | | | | | | | | 12 | 158 | 3 | D | 6 |
| v. Leicestershire (Leicester) 30 August-1 September | 59 | 140 | 61 | 16 | 123 | 99 | 110 | 18* | | | 1 | | | | | | | | | | | | 23 | 650 | 8 | W | 22 |
| v. Middlesex (Bristol) 5-7 September | 27 | 7 | | 35 | 6 | 1 | 18 | 4 | 2* | | | | 19 | | | | | | | 6 | 11 | | 16 | 152 | 10 | | |
| | 1 | 2 | | 55 | 0 | 32 | 46 | 0 | 0 | | | | 31 | | | | | | | 3* | 21 | | 8 | 199 | 10 | L | 3 |
| v. Glamorgan (Cardiff) 19-22 September | 17* | 79 | 20* | 4 | 121 | 14 | | | | | | | | | | | | | | | | | 7 | 262 | 4 | D | 6 |
| **Matches** | 16 | 16 | 15 | 15 | 13 | 13 | 11 | 11 | 11 | 9 | 8 | 8 | 8 | 5 | 5 | 4 | 3 | 3 | 3 | 3 | 1 | 1 | | | | | |
| **Innings** | 27 | 28 | 23 | 25 | 21 | 18 | 17 | 13 | 15 | 15 | 8 | 11 | 10 | 6 | 8 | 5 | 6 | 6 | 5 | 3 | 2 | 2 | | | | | |
| **Not Out** | 4 | 1 | 4 | 1 | 1 | 1 | 0 | 1 | 10 | 1 | 1 | 1 | 0 | 2 | 0 | 0 | 0 | 0 | 3 | 1 | 0 | 1 | | | | | |
| **Highest Score** | 130 | 140 | 112* | 168 | 123 | 99 | 110 | 37 | 11* | 104 | 42* | 27 | 109 | 18 | 12 | 61 | 43 | 41 | 10* | 6 | 21 | 3* | | | | | |
| **Runs** | 912 | 903 | 733 | 886 | 817 | 447 | 688 | 119 | 46 | 335 | 91 | 95 | 565 | 28 | 57 | 109 | 92 | 67 | 21 | 9 | 32 | 3 | | | | | |
| **Average** | 39.65 | 33.44 | 38.57 | 36.91 | 40.85 | 26.29 | 40.47 | 9.91 | 9.20 | 23.92 | 13.00 | 9.50 | 56.50 | 7.00 | 7.12 | 21.80 | 15.33 | 11.16 | 10.50 | 4.50 | 16.00 | 3.00 | | | | | |
| **100s** | 3 | 2 | 3 | 2 | 3 | 0 | 2 | 0 | 0 | 3 | 0 | 0 | 3 | 0 | 0 | 0 | 0 | 0 | 0 | 0 | 0 | 0 | | | | | |
| **50s** | 4 | 4 | 2 | 6 | 3 | 3 | 3 | 0 | 0 | 1 | 0 | 0 | 2 | 0 | 0 | 1 | 0 | 0 | 0 | 0 | 0 | 0 | | | | | |
| **Catches/Stumpings** | 9/0 | 8/0 | 13/0 | 8/0 | 9/0 | 28/2 | 15/0 | 1/0 | 3/0 | 6/0 | 2/0 | 3/0 | 4/0 | 2/0 | 8/0 | 1/0 | 0/0 | 1/0 | 2/0 | 2/0 | 0/0 | 1/0 | | | | | |

**Home Ground:** Bristol
**Address:** County Ground, Nevil Road, Bristol, BS7 9EJ
**Tel:** 0117 9108000
**Fax:** 0117 9241193
**Email:** reception@glosccc.co.uk
**Directions:** *By road:* M5, M4, M32 into Bristol, exit at second exit (Fishponds/Horfield), then third exit - Muller Road. Almost at end of Muller Road (bus station on right), turn left at Ralph Road. Go to the top, turn left and then right almost immediately into Kennington Avenue. Follow the signs for County Cricket.

**Capacity:** 8,000
**Other grounds used:** Gloucester, Cheltenham College
**Year formed:** 1870

**Chief Executive:** Tom Richardson
**Cricket Development Manager:** Andy Stovold
**Head Coach:** Mark Alleyne
**Captain:** Jon Lewis
**County colours:** Blue, brown, gold, green and red

**Honours**
Sunday League/NCL/Pro40
2000
Benson & Hedges Cup
1977, 1999, 2000
Gillette Cup/NatWest/C&G Trophy
1973, 1999, 2000, 2003, 2004

Website:
www.glosccc.co.uk

# FIRST-CLASS MATCHES
## BOWLING

| | SP Kirby | CG Greenidge | V Banerjee | MA Hardinges | AA Noffke | J Lewis | CG Taylor | MJ North | BM Edmondson | APR Gidman | AJ Ireland | TP Stayt | HJH Marshall | DO Brown | ID Fisher | WD Rudge | GP Hodnett | Overs | Total | Byes/Leg-byes | Wickets | Run outs |
|---|---|---|---|---|---|---|---|---|---|---|---|---|---|---|---|---|---|---|---|---|---|---|
| **v. Nottinghamshire** (Bristol) 25-28 April | 27-8-75-2 | | | 20-4-93-1 | 24.1-6-68-6 | 18-4-65-1 | | 14-2-37-0 | | 8-0-34-0 | | | | | | | | 111.1 | 399 | 27 | 10 | |
| | 17-5-46-0 | | | 15-1-80-1 | 18-5-45-3 | 6-3-12-0 | 5-0-28-0 | 11-1-46-1 | | 8-0-67-0 | | | | | | | | 80 | 333 | 9 | 5 | |
| **v. Leicestershire** (Bristol) 2-5 May | 28.3-9-75-3 | | | 16-5-54-0 | 32-10-94-2 | | | 26-2-53-3 | | 6-2-4-1 | 19-1-71-0 | | | | | | | 127.3 | 376 | 25 | 10 | |
| | 20.5-5-56-1 | | | 7-1-21-1 | 21-5-66-1 | 11-6-13-1 | | 6-1-15-0 | | | 14-4-39-3 | | | | | | | 79.5 | 218 | 8 | 7 | |
| **v. Glamorgan** (Bristol) 16-19 May | | | | 27-11-59-3 | 29.3-8-62-3 | | | 16-4-30-1 | | 12-4-31-0 | 18-8-32-2 | | | | 20-4-58-1 | 12-2-40-0 | | 147.3 | 392 | 20 | 10 | |
| | | | | | | | | | | | | | | | - | - | | - | - | - | - | |
| **v. Somerset** (Taunton) 23-26 May | | 29-2-143-4 | 27.3-6-74-1 | 26-5-101-3 | | | | 5-0-17-0 | | 8-3-25-0 | 23-2-112-2 | 5-0-10-0 | | | | | | 123.3 | 496 | 14 | 10 | |
| | | 8-0-57-2 | 13-1-54-0 | | | | | 8-0-29-0 | | | 3-0-18-0 | | | | | | | 32 | 172 | 14 | 2 | |
| **v. Northamptonshire** (Gloucester) 1-4 June | | 14-2-54-0 | 24.5-6-38-4 | 19-7-49-1 | | | | 18-3-23-2 | | 14-3-27-1 | | | | 10-3-25-2 | | | | 99.5 | 223 | 7 | 10 | |
| | | 10.5-2-32-4 | 35-5-140-2 | | | | | 26-3-109-2 | | 16-4-57-1 | | | | 7-2-21-0 | | | | 109.5 | 411 | 15 | 10 | 1 |
| **v. Derbyshire** (Derby) 5-8 June | | 28-5-91-1 | | 37-6-103-4 | 29-5-126-1 | | 2-0-6-0 | | | 19-4-41-1 | | | | 14-3-46-0 | 28-7-68-1 | | | 157 | 500 | 19 | 9 | |
| | | 7-3-11-0 | 2-1-4-0 | | 5-0-22-1 | | | | | | | | | | 1-0-2-0 | | | 15 | 40 | 1 | 1 | |
| **v. Somerset** (Bristol) 15-17 June | | 15-3-73-3 | 13-1-76-1 | 13-1-66-1 | | | | | 19-2-82-1 | 8-0-32-0 | | | | 3-0-24-1 | 7-0-48-0 | | | 78 | 410 | 9 | 7 | |
| | | | | | | | | | | | | | | | - | - | | - | - | - | - | |
| **v. Northamptonshire** (Northampton) 8-11 July | 21-8-60-5 | | 17.2-4-56-2 | 20-6-57-1 | | | 8-1-24-1 | | 19-2-90-1 | 6-3-13-0 | | | | | | | | 91.2 | 310 | 10 | 10 | |
| | 15-6-30-0 | | 6.4-1-12-1 | 27-1-103-3 | | | 22-4-52-4 | | 15-2-48-1 | 6-1-14-1 | | | | | | | | 91.4 | 270 | 11 | 10 | |
| **v. Nottinghamshire** (Trent Bridge) 13-16 July | 17-5-63-1 | | | 16-0-53-1 | | 18.1-2-55-1 | 5-0-31-2 | 16-1-93-2 | | 10-0-81-0 | | | | 3-0-18-0 | | | | 85.1 | 400 | 6 | 8 | 1 |
| | | | | | | | | | | | | | | | - | - | | - | - | - | - | |
| **v. Essex** (Bristol) 25-28 July | 12-3-33-4 | | | 4-0-12-2 | | 8-1-23-1 | 3-0-9-0 | | 8-1-40-0 | | | | | | | | 2.3-0-10-0 | 37.3 | 129 | 2 | 7 | |
| | | | | | | | | | | | | | | | - | - | | - | - | - | - | |
| **v. Derbyshire** (Bristol) 31 July-3 August | 19.3-3-66-3 | | 24-4-69-0 | | | | | 20-5-66-2 | 15-1-54-1 | 15-0-50-4 | | | | | | | | 93.3 | 312 | 7 | 10 | |
| | 13-1-44-1 | | 30-6-126-1 | | | | | 13-3-33-1 | 15-1-76-0 | 11-4-43-0 | 6-1-21-0 | | | | | | | 88 | 356 | 13 | 3 | |
| **v. Essex** (Southend) 8-10 August | 15-2-41-5 | | | | | | | 16-3-41-5 | | | | | | | | | | 31 | 88 | 6 | 10 | |
| | 21.5-5-75-5 | | 23-6-57-3 | | | | | 16-3-56-1 | | 4-0-30-1 | | | | | 6-2-25-0 | | | 70.5 | 259 | 6 | 10 | |
| **v. Middlesex** (Lord's) 22-25 August | 18-5-46-3 | | | 16-1-78-0 | | | 2-0-11-0 | 25-8-80-0 | | 4-0-22-1 | | 16-4-51-3 | | | | | | 81 | 305 | 17 | 7 | |
| | 7-0-50-1 | | | 3-0-29-1 | | | 10-1-41-0 | | | | | | | | | | | 20 | 121 | 1 | 2 | |
| **v. Leicestershire** (Leicester) 30 August-1 September | 14-2-51-1 | | | | 14-1-54-5 | 13.1-2-50-1 | | | | 4-0-14-0 | | 12-0-44-1 | 3-1-9-1 | | | | | 60.1 | 229 | 7 | 10 | |
| | 17-1-51-2 | | | | 13-0-70-2 | 15.2-3-74-3 | 3-0-27-1 | | | | | 10-2-43-0 | | | | | | 58.2 | 270 | 5 | 10 | 1 |
| **v. Middlesex** (Bristol) 5-7 September | 29-5-99-4 | 20.1-5-99-4 | | 28-4-90-1 | | | | | 13-0-35-1 | | | 21-3-80-0 | 5-0-20-0 | | | | | 116.1 | 440 | 17 | 10 | |
| | | | | | | | | | | | | | | | - | - | | - | - | - | - | |
| **v. Glamorgan** (Cardiff) 19-22 September | | | | | | | | | | | | | | | - | - | | - | - | - | - | |
| | | | | | | | | | | | | | | | - | - | | - | - | - | - | |
| **Overs** | 312.4 | 183 | 348.5 | 215 | 124.4 | 150.1 | 91 | 130 | 103 | 152 | 90 | 59 | 19 | 38 | 55 | 12 | 2.3 | | | | | |
| **Maidens** | 73 | 28 | 57 | 45 | 34 | 33 | 13 | 16 | 12 | 25 | 15 | 9 | 1 | 8 | 13 | 2 | 0 | | | | | |
| **Runs** | 961 | 752 | 1178 | 822 | 335 | 472 | 331 | 359 | 446 | 548 | 332 | 218 | 81 | 140 | 153 | 40 | 10 | | | | | |
| **Wickets** | 41 | 28 | 26 | 16 | 15 | 12 | 10 | 9 | 9 | 8 | 7 | 4 | 2 | 2 | 2 | 0 | 0 | | | | | |
| **Average** | 23.43 | 26.85 | 45.30 | 51.37 | 22.33 | 39.33 | 33.10 | 39.88 | 49.55 | 68.50 | 47.42 | 54.50 | 40.50 | 70.00 | 76.50 | - | - | | | | | |

## FIELDING

| | |
|---|---|
| 30 | SJ Adshead (28 ct, 2 st) |
| 15 | CM Spearman |
| 13 | CG Taylor |
| 9 | APR Gidman |
| 9 | HJH Marshall |
| 8 | Kadeer Ali |
| 8 | SD Snell |
| 8 | GP Hodnett |
| 6 | MA Hardinges |
| 4 | MJ North |
| 3 | CG Greenidge |
| 3 | V Banerjee |
| 2 | J Lewis |
| 2 | BM Edmondson |
| 2 | TP Stayt |
| 2 | AJ Ireland |
| 1 | ID Fisher |
| 1 | SP Kirby |
| 1 | AA Noffke |
| 1 | WD Rudge |
| 1 | JG Thompson |
| 0 | DO Brown |

### Final Division Two Table

| | P | W | L | D | T | Ab | Bat | Bowl | Pens | Pts |
|---|---|---|---|---|---|---|---|---|---|---|
| Somerset | 16 | 10 | 1 | 5 | 0 | 0 | 65 | 41 | 0.00 | 266.00 |
| Nottinghamshire | 16 | 6 | 3 | 7 | 0 | 0 | 60 | 43 | 0.50 | 214.50 |
| Middlesex | 16 | 6 | 2 | 8 | 0 | 0 | 35 | 43 | 1.50 | 192.50 |
| Essex | 16 | 6 | 4 | 6 | 0 | 0 | 40 | 36 | 2.00 | 182.00 |
| Northamptonshire | 16 | 5 | 5 | 6 | 0 | 0 | 44 | 38 | 0.00 | 176.00 |
| Derbyshire | 16 | 3 | 5 | 8 | 0 | 0 | 30 | 44 | 1.00 | 147.00 |
| Gloucestershire | 16 | 3 | 5 | 8 | 0 | 0 | 32 | 37 | 3.50 | 139.50 |
| Leicestershire | 16 | 2 | 8 | 5 | 0 | 1 | 32 | 35 | 4.00 | 115.00 |
| Glamorgan | 16 | 1 | 9 | 5 | 0 | 1 | 26 | 37 | 8.50 | 92.50 |

Glamorgan had eight points deducted for a poor pitch.

Limited overs nickname:
**GLOUCESTERSHIRE GLADIATORS**

# HAMPSHIRE CCC

**FIRST-CLASS MATCHES**

## BATTING

| Match | MJ Brown | MJ Lumb | N Pothas | JP Crawley | SK Warne | JTA Bruce | MA Carberry | JHK Adams | AD Mascarenhas | CC Benham | SM Ervine | CT Tremlett | SR Clark | JA Tomlinson | DA Griffiths | SD Udal | DB Powell | DJ Balcombe | TG Burrows | LA Dawson | Extras | Total | Wickets | Result | Points |
|---|---|---|---|---|---|---|---|---|---|---|---|---|---|---|---|---|---|---|---|---|---|---|---|---|---|
| v. Surrey (The Oval) 25-28 April | 42 | 49 | 85* | 7 | 48 | 32 | | 86 | 18 | 76 | | | | 2 | | | | | | | 36 | 481 | 9 | | |
| | 115* | | | 66* | | | 29 | | | | | | | | | | | | | | 14 | 224 | 1 | W | 22 |
| v. Yorkshire (Rose Bowl) 2-5 May | 105 | 5 | 70* | 32 | 10 | 7 | | 22 | | 2 | 12 | | 3 | 5 | | | | | | | 23 | 296 | 10 | | |
| | 8 | 57 | 76* | 50 | 33 | 4 | | 90 | | 5 | 14 | | 3* | | | | | | | | 26 | 366 | 8 | D | 9 |
| v. Lancashire (Rose Bowl) 9-12 May | 18 | 3 | 0 | 40 | 12 | 16 | | 16 | 74 | 46 | | 14* | 12 | | | | | | | | 21 | 272 | 10 | | |
| | | | | | | | | | | | | | | | | | | | | | | | | D | 9 |
| v. Kent (Canterbury) 23-26 May | 0 | 0 | | 16 | 19 | | 7 | 21 | 90 | | 22 | 11* | 14 | | | | 35 | | | | 37 | 272 | 10 | | |
| | 24 | 48 | | 38 | | | 6 | 31 | 33* | | 56* | | | | | | | | | | 39 | 275 | 5 | D | 9 |
| v. Warwickshire (Edgbaston) 30 May-2 June | 39 | 5 | 22 | 18 | 4 | 0 | 52 | 1 | 8 | | 6 | 0* | | | | | | | | | 14 | 169 | 10 | | |
| | 21 | 16 | 126* | 73 | 0 | | 2 | 11 | 20 | | 30* | | | | | | | | | | 13 | 312 | 7 | D | 7 |
| v. Sussex (Arundel Castle) 6-9 June | 25 | 51 | 9 | 16 | 7 | | 9 | 17 | 22 | | 21 | 0 | | | | 17* | | | | | 8 | 202 | 10 | | |
| | 11 | 62 | 38* | 44 | | | 53 | 27 | 41 | | 3 | 6 | | | | 0 | | | | | 32 | 333 | 10 | L | 4 |
| v. Durham (Rose Bowl) 15-18 June | 0 | 70 | 29 | 0 | 4 | 0* | 30 | | 34 | 22 | 3 | 17 | | | | | | | | | 23 | 232 | 10 | | |
| | 59 | 7 | 0 | 23 | 33 | 11* | 6 | | 60 | 15 | | 62* | 16 | | | | | | | | 17 | 309 | 9 | W | 18 |
| v. Warwickshire (Rose Bowl) 8-11 July | 16* | | | 0* | | | 7 | | | | | | | | | | | | | | 0 | 23 | 1 | | |
| | 10 | 15 | 12 | 10 | | | 192* | | 38* | 40 | | | | | | | | | | | 14 | 331 | 5 | W | 22 |
| v. Durham (Riverside) 20-23 July | 56* | 16 | 0 | 6 | 1 | 0 | 4 | | 8 | 2 | | | | 2 | 4 | | | | | | 16 | 115 | 10 | | |
| | 126* | 28 | 0 | 12 | 50 | 0 | 4 | | 8 | 3 | | | | 0* | 5 | | | | | | 26 | 262 | 9 | D | 7 |
| v. Sussex (Rose Bowl) 25-28 July | 0 | 22 | 9 | 113* | 15 | 0* | 20 | | 0 | 31 | | | | 4 | | 11 | | | | | 25 | 250 | 9 | | |
| | | | | | | | | | | | | | | | | | | | | | | | | D | 9 |
| v. Worcestershire (Rose Bowl) 8-10 August | 73 | 11 | 71* | 96 | 23 | 0* | 116 | | 30 | 4 | | | | 4 | | 0 | | | | | 27 | 455 | 9 | | |
| | 5 | 57 | 2 | 4 | | 1* | | | 5 | 17 | | | | 1* | | 8 | | | | | 3 | 103 | 8 | W | 22 |
| v. Lancashire (Old Trafford) 21-24 August | 29 | 64 | 27 | 47 | 2 | 1 | 16 | 63 | | | 103* | | | 0 | | 15 | | | | | 26 | 393 | 10 | | |
| | 5 | | | 15* | | | 66* | 19 | | | | | | | | | | | | | 6 | 111 | 2 | D | 10 |
| v. Surrey (Rose Bowl) 30 August-2 September | 22 | 17 | 39 | 0 | 0* | | 110 | | | | 12 | | | 0 | 6 | 4 | | | | | 11 | 221 | 10 | | |
| | 30 | 20 | 92 | 0 | | 0 | 40 | 31 | | | 10 | | | 31* | 0 | 25 | | | | | 19 | 298 | 10 | L | 3 |
| v. Worcestershire (Kidderminster) 4-7 September | 47 | 63 | 8 | 8 | 46 | 5 | 127 | 80 | | | 26 | | | 1* | | 0 | | | | | 33 | 444 | 10 | | |
| | 88 | | | 75* | | | 120 | 82* | | | | | | | | | | | | | 11 | 376 | 2 | W | 22 |
| v. Kent (Rose Bowl) 11-13 September | 42 | 0 | 0 | | 37 | 4 | 46 | 3 | | | 17 | 20 | | 4* | | | | 29 | | | 14 | 216 | 10 | | |
| | 53 | 89 | 1 | | 4 | 3* | 31 | 16 | | | 32 | 1 | | 9 | | | | 25 | | | 18 | 282 | 10 | L | 3 |
| v. Yorkshire (Headingley) 19-22 September | 9 | 0 | 34* | 57 | | | 113* | 18 | | | | | | | | | | | | | 13 | 244 | 4 | | |
| | | | | | | | | | | | | | | | | | | | | | | | | D | 8 |
| Matches | 16 | 16 | 15 | 15 | 15 | 14 | 13 | 11 | 10 | 9 | 7 | 6 | 6 | 5 | 5 | 5 | 4 | 2 | 1 | 1 | | | | | |
| Innings | 29 | 25 | 23 | 27 | 19 | 18 | 24 | 20 | 16 | 14 | 10 | 8 | 9 | 4 | 8 | 8 | 6 | 2 | 1 | 0 | | | | | |
| Not Out | 4 | 0 | 7 | 5 | 0 | 7 | 3 | 1 | 2 | 0 | 2 | 4 | 2 | 2 | 3 | 1 | 0 | 0 | 0 | 0 | | | | | |
| Highest Score | 126* | 89 | 126* | 113* | 50 | 32 | 192* | 110 | 90 | 76 | 103* | 62* | 17 | 9 | 31* | 17* | 25 | 29 | 35 | 0 | | | | | |
| Runs | 1078 | 775 | 750 | 866 | 364 | 84 | 1067 | 773 | 489 | 312 | 276 | 150 | 71 | 19 | 42 | 34 | 63 | 54 | 35 | 0 | | | | | |
| Average | 43.12 | 31.00 | 46.87 | 39.36 | 19.15 | 7.63 | 50.80 | 40.68 | 34.92 | 22.28 | 34.50 | 37.50 | 10.14 | 9.50 | 8.40 | 4.85 | 10.50 | 27.00 | 35.00 | - | | | | | |
| 100s | 3 | 0 | 1 | 1 | 0 | 0 | 5 | 0 | 0 | 0 | 1 | 0 | 0 | 0 | 0 | 0 | 0 | 0 | 0 | 0 | | | | | |
| 50s | 5 | 8 | 5 | 6 | 1 | 0 | 3 | 5 | 3 | 1 | 1 | 1 | 0 | 0 | 0 | 0 | 0 | 0 | 0 | 0 | | | | | |
| Catches/Stumpings | 14/0 | 13/0 | 38/6 | 4/0 | 17/0 | 4/0 | 2/0 | 10/0 | 2/0 | 10/0 | 5/0 | 1/0 | 3/0 | 1/0 | 1/0 | 0/0 | 1/0 | 0/0 | 4/0 | 0/0 | | | | | |

**Home Ground:** Southampton
**Address:** The Rose Bowl, Botley Road, West End, Southampton, SO30 3XH
**Tel:** 02380 472002
**Fax:** 02380 472122
**Email:** enquiries@rosebowlplc.com
**Directions:** From the North: M3 Southbound to junction 14, follow signs for M27 Eastbound (Fareham and Portsmouth). At junction 7 of M27, filter left onto Charles Watts Way (A334) and from there follow the brown road signs to the Rose Bowl. From the South: M27 to junction 7 and follow the brown road signs to the Rose Bowl.

**Capacity:** 9,950
**Year formed:** 1863

**Chief Executive:** Rod Bransgrove
**Director of Cricket:** Tim Tremlett
**Captain:** Shane Warne
**County colours:** Navy blue, old gold

**Honours**
County Championship
1961, 1973
Sunday League/NCL/Pro40
1975, 1978, 1986
Benson & Hedges Cup
1988, 1992
Gillette Cup/NatWest/C&G Trophy
1991, 2005

Website:
www.hampshirecricket.com

# FIRST-CLASS MATCHES
## BOWLING

| | SK Warne | JTA Bruce | SR Clark | DB Powell | AD Mascarenhas | CT Tremlett | SD Udal | JA Tomlinson | DA Griffiths | SM Ervine | DJ Balcombe | JHK Adams | MA Carberry | JP Crawley | MJ Lumb | Overs | Total | Byes/Leg-byes | Wickets | Run outs |
|---|---|---|---|---|---|---|---|---|---|---|---|---|---|---|---|---|---|---|---|---|
| **v. Surrey** (The Oval) 25-28 April | 15-2-45-5 | 9-0-48-2 | | | 13-4-39-1 | | 3-0-10-0 | 20-7-53-2 | | | | | | | | 60 | 203 | 8 | 10 | |
| | 44-13-128-3 | 17-2-81-1 | | | 9-4-25-0 | | 40.1-6-138-4 | 19.2-4-76-2 | | | | 4-2-6-0 | | | | 133.3 | 467 | 13 | 10 | |
| **v. Yorkshire** (Rose Bowl) 2-5 May | 18-1-63-1 | 20-2-56-4 | 12-3-37-1 | | | | | | | 20.4-2-68-2 | 14-3-42-1 | 9-2-25-0 | | | | 93.4 | 299 | 8 | 10 | 1 |
| | 29-2-114-1 | 17-7-44-0 | 22.5-0-83-3 | | | | | | | 15-1-78-0 | 21-3-86-0 | 2-0-16-0 | | | | 106.5 | 439 | 18 | 4 | |
| **v. Lancashire** (Rose Bowl) 9-12 May | 3-0-11-1 | 18-4-63-2 | 23.3-6-82-7 | | 10-3-21-0 | 8-3-10-0 | | | | | | | | | | 62.3 | 207 | 20 | 10 | |
| **v. Kent** (Canterbury) 23-26 May | 14-2-42-3 | | 14-1-48-4 | | 15-6-29-2 | 9.4-0-54-1 | | | | 6-3-14-0 | | | | | | 58.4 | 199 | 12 | 10 | |
| | 37-2-142-1 | | 28-5-80-3 | | 20-3-76-1 | 30-4-76-1 | | | | 20-3-95-0 | | 11-1-37-2 | 2-0-6-0 | 1-0-9-0 | | 149 | 533 | 12 | 8 | |
| **v. Warwickshire** (Edgbaston) 30 May-2 June | 10.2-1-47-2 | 11-3-38-2 | 15-3-65-3 | | 13-3-40-2 | 17-3-71-1 | | | | | | | | | | 66.2 | 262 | 1 | 10 | |
| **v. Sussex** (Arundel Castle) 6-9 June | 30.2-2-91-5 | | 17-4-54-1 | | 20-9-23-0 | 24-4-114-3 | 18-3-41-1 | | | | | 2-0-14-0 | | | | 111.2 | 341 | 4 | 10 | |
| | 13-0-70-0 | | 14-3-49-0 | | 16-2-53-2 | 11-0-42-0 | 19-1-83-3 | | | | | 2-0-10-0 | | 1-0-13-0 | 3-0-26-0 | 79 | 360 | 14 | 5 | |
| **v. Durham** (Rose Bowl) 15-18 June | 26.1-3-83-6 | 9-0-52-0 | 13-3-48-1 | | 7-1-22-0 | | | | 21-4-63-3 | | | 1-0-9-0 | | | | 77.1 | 288 | 6 | 10 | |
| | 20-5-50-5 | 4-0-28-0 | 16-4-56-1 | | 3-1-13-0 | | | | 12-2-47-4 | | | | | | | 55 | 203 | 9 | 10 | |
| **v. Warwickshire** (Rose Bowl) 8-11 July | 22-1-60-0 | 21-4-74-0 | | | 19-7-30-2 | 29-9-82-2 | | | | 18.4-4-49-0 | | 9-1-35-1 | | 1-0-4-0 | | 119.4 | 353 | 19 | 5 | |
| **v. Durham** (Riverside) 20-23 July | 17-2-73-0 | 22-5-55-1 | | | 23-8-33-4 | | 9-1-21-0 | | | 19.4-4-46-4 | | 3-0-13-1 | | | | 93.4 | 252 | 6 | 10 | |
| | 14-1-56-2 | 11-1-52-0 | | | 8-3-25-0 | | 2-0-9-1 | | | 16-2-78-2 | | | | | | 51 | 221 | 1 | 5 | |
| **v. Sussex** (Rose Bowl) 25-28 July | | 18-3-64-5 | | 13.3-4-46-3 | 2-1-2-0 | | | | | 7-0-31-1 | | | | | | 40.3 | 145 | 2 | 10 | 1 |
| | 7-0-36-0 | 9-4-14-1 | | 11-1-32-2 | 7-0-25-1 | | | | | 3-0-15-0 | | | | | | 37 | 124 | 2 | 4 | |
| **v. Worcestershire** (Rose Bowl) 8-10 August | 4-1-8-0 | | 12.2-5-31-4 | 10-5-8-4 | | | | | | 8-1-33-2 | | | | | | 34.2 | 86 | 6 | 10 | |
| | 13-4-28-4 | | 10.3-1-41-4 | 9-1-39-1 | 5-1-25-0 | | | | | 3-0-26-0 | | 2-0-22-0 | | | | 42.3 | 187 | 6 | 10 | 1 |
| **v. Lancashire** (Old Trafford) 21-24 August | 16.3-3-37-0 | 27-6-86-2 | | 27-4-101-2 | | | | 21.5-1-82-3 | | 18-1-54-1 | | | 8.3-1-26-0 | | | 118.5 | 403 | 17 | 8 | |
| **v. Surrey** (Rose Bowl) 30 August-2 September | | 31-7-86-2 | | 32-7-117-3 | | | 41-12-106-3 | 22-1-100-0 | | 31.4-2-116-2 | | 3-0-10-0 | | | | 160.4 | 556 | 21 | 10 | |
| **v. Worcestershire** (Kidderminster) 4-7 September | 16-0-86-2 | 14-5-36-2 | | | | | 8-1-19-0 | 22-3-78-5 | | 9.1-2-47-1 | | 4-3-9-0 | | | | 73.1 | 289 | 14 | 10 | |
| | 22.2-5-68-5 | 17-2-76-1 | | | | | 10-1-42-2 | 18-4-45-1 | | | | | | | | 67.2 | 237 | 6 | 9 | |
| **v. Kent** (Rose Bowl) 11-13 September | 44.3-6-134-4 | 30-4-101-1 | | | | | | 21-6-81-1 | | 16.4-4-47-1 | 28-5-106-2 | 3-0-10-1 | 4-1-8-0 | | | 146.3 | 495 | 8 | 10 | |
| | | | | | | | | | | | | | 0.3-0-6-0 | | | 0.3 | 6 | | 0 | |
| **v. Yorkshire** (Headingley) 19-22 September | 2-0-7-0 | 25-6-73-5 | | | | | | | | 14-2-48-2 | 20.1-4-58-3 | | | | | 61.1 | 195 | 9 | 10 | |
| **Overs** | 438.1 | 352.5 | 175.2 | 102.3 | 190 | 161.4 | 150.1 | 154.4 | 100.3 | 149.5 | 48.1 | 40 | 30 | 2 | 4 | | | | | |
| **Maidens** | 56 | 71 | 32 | 22 | 56 | 29 | 25 | 31 | 9 | 23 | 9 | 8 | 3 | 0 | 0 | | | | | |
| **Runs** | 1479 | 1199 | 602 | 343 | 481 | 559 | 469 | 528 | 411 | 549 | 164 | 137 | 125 | 22 | 30 | | | | | |
| **Wickets** | 50 | 39 | 24 | 15 | 15 | 15 | 14 | 13 | 12 | 8 | 5 | 3 | 2 | 0 | 0 | | | | | |
| **Average** | 29.58 | 30.74 | 25.08 | 22.86 | 32.06 | 37.26 | 33.50 | 40.61 | 34.25 | 68.62 | 32.80 | 45.66 | 62.50 | – | – | | | | | |

## FIELDING

| | |
|---|---|
| 44 | N Pothas (38 ct, 6 st) |
| 17 | SK Warne |
| 14 | MJ Brown |
| 13 | MJ Lumb |
| 10 | JHK Adams |
| 10 | CC Benham |
| 5 | SM Ervine |
| 4 | JP Crawley |
| 4 | JTA Bruce |
| 4 | TG Burrows |
| 3 | SR Clark |
| 2 | AD Mascarenhas |
| 2 | MA Carberry |
| 1 | CT Tremlett |
| 1 | JA Tomlinson |
| 1 | DB Powell |
| 1 | DA Griffiths |
| 0 | SD Udal |
| 0 | DJ Balcombe |
| 0 | LA Dawson |

### Final Division One Table

| | P | W | L | D | T | Ab | Bat | Bowl | Pens | Pts |
|---|---|---|---|---|---|---|---|---|---|---|
| **Sussex** | 16 | 7 | 3 | 5 | 0 | 1 | 37 | 43 | 0.00 | 202.00 |
| **Durham** | 16 | 7 | 5 | 4 | 0 | 0 | 38 | 47 | 1.50 | 197.50 |
| **Lancashire** | 16 | 5 | 2 | 8 | 0 | 1 | 40 | 44 | 0.00 | 190.00 |
| **Surrey** | 16 | 5 | 4 | 6 | 0 | 1 | 41 | 40 | 1.00 | 178.00 |
| **Hampshire** | 16 | 5 | 3 | 8 | 0 | 0 | 32 | 43 | 0.00 | 177.00 |
| **Yorkshire** | 16 | 4 | 4 | 8 | 0 | 0 | 49 | 38 | 0.00 | 175.00 |
| **Kent** | 16 | 3 | 5 | 7 | 0 | 1 | 43 | 36 | 0.00 | 153.00 |
| **Warwickshire** | 16 | 2 | 5 | 9 | 0 | 0 | 40 | 35 | 0.00 | 139.00 |
| **Worcestershire** | 16 | 1 | 8 | 5 | 0 | 2 | 18 | 35 | 0.00 | 95.00 |

HAMPSHIRE HAWKS

Limited overs nickname:
HAMPSHIRE HAWKS

## KENT CCC

### FIRST-CLASS MATCHES
### BATTING

| | RWT Key | M van Jaarsveld | JL Denly | GO Jones | R McLaren | JC Tredwell | MJ Walker | SJ Cook | DI Stevens | Yasir Arafat | NJ Dexter | AJ Hall | MJ Saggers | SL Malinga | RH Joseph | MM Patel | SA Northeast | Extras | Total | Wickets | Result | Points |
|---|---|---|---|---|---|---|---|---|---|---|---|---|---|---|---|---|---|---|---|---|---|---|
| v. Sussex | 6 | 0 | 37 | 2 | 44 | | 21 | 3 | 35 | 33 | | | | | 11* | 15 | | 9 | 216 | 10 | | |
| (Hove) 18-21 April | 0 | 26 | 63 | 9 | 29 | | 59 | 5 | 19 | 40 | | | | | 36* | 52 | | 11 | 349 | 10 | L | 3 |
| v. Sussex | 5 | 6 | 24 | 49 | 12 | 0 | 103 | 14* | 9 | 122 | | | | | 4 | | | 20 | 368 | 10 | | |
| (Canterbury) 2-3 May | | | | | | | | | | | | | | | | | | | | | W | 21 |
| v. Durham | 169 | 10 | 17 | 1 | 1 | 25 | 72 | | 10 | 17 | | 42 | | | 7* | | | 29 | 400 | 10 | | |
| (Riverside) 9-12 May | 11 | 0 | 92 | 1 | 6* | 0 | 1 | | 35 | 6 | | 3 | | | 2* | | | 12 | 169 | 10 | L | 8 |
| v. Hampshire | 0 | 12 | 115* | 0 | 4 | 17 | 4 | 8 | 11 | 7 | 1 | | | | | | | 20 | 199 | 10 | | |
| (Canterbury) 23-26 May | 120 | 109 | 0 | 4 | 25* | 27* | 46 | | 105 | 19 | | 48 | | | | | | 30 | 533 | 8 | D | 7 |
| v. Surrey | 6 | 166 | 85 | 106* | | 17 | | | 174 | | | | | | | | | 10 | 564 | 5 | | |
| (Whitgift School) 30 May-2 June | | | | | | | | | | | | | | | | | | | | | W | 22 |
| v. Yorkshire | 62 | 0 | 10 | 61 | 0 | 16 | | 7* | 4 | 4 | 34 | 77 | | | | | | 17 | 292 | 10 | | |
| (Tunbridge Wells) 6-9 June | 84 | 56 | 9 | 15 | | 116* | | | 14 | | 0 | 63* | | | | | | 26 | 383 | 6 | D | 7 |
| v. Lancashire | 28 | 7 | 77 | 70 | 14* | 10 | 1 | 13 | 14 | 8 | | 4 | | | | | | 26 | 272 | 10 | | |
| (Old Trafford) 15-18 June | 17 | 85 | 9 | 2 | 0 | 1 | 7 | 1* | 55 | 0 | | 6 | | | | | | 7 | 190 | 10 | L | 3 |
| v. Warwickshire | 25 | 117 | 36 | 105 | 21 | 11 | | 0* | 6 | 101* | 86 | 2 | | | | | | 40 | 550 | 9 | | |
| (Canterbury) 20-23 July | | | | | | | | | | | | | | | | | | | | | D | 12 |
| v. Yorkshire | 21 | 5 | 114 | 43 | 17 | 44 | | 50* | 87 | | 55 | 18 | 11 | | | | | 21 | 486 | 10 | | |
| (Scarborough) 25-28 July | 6* | | 11* | | | | | | | | | | | | | | | 0 | 17 | 0 | | 11 |
| v. Surrey | 75* | 22 | 12 | 10 | 0 | 13 | 0 | | 2 | 4 | | | 0 | 0 | | | | 12 | 150 | 10 | | |
| (Canterbury) 8-9 August | 18 | 3 | 14 | 12 | 0 | 50 | 12 | | 30 | 8 | | | 5* | 12 | | | | 7 | 171 | 10 | L | 3 |
| v. Warwickshire | 153 | 85 | 31 | 6* | | | 44 | | | | 59* | | | | | | | 22 | 400 | 4 | | |
| (Edgbaston) 14-17 August | | | | | | | | | | | | | | | | | | | | | D | 12 |
| v. Worcestershire | 125 | 122* | 28 | | | | | 9 | | | | | | | | | | 9 | 293 | 3 | D | 4 |
| (Canterbury) 21-24 August | | | | | | | | | | | | | | | | | | | | | | |
| v. Lancashire | 17 | 0 | 19 | 7 | 2 | 19 | 142 | 38 | | | 42 | | 0 | 1* | | | | 40 | 327 | 10 | | |
| (Canterbury) 28-31 August | 182 | 28 | 5 | | | 3 | 157 | 0 | | | 29* | | | | | | | 15 | 419 | 6 | D | 10 |
| v. Hampshire | 84 | 112 | 54 | 63 | 35* | 62 | 38 | 9 | 18 | | | 6 | | | | | | 13 | 495 | 10 | | |
| (Rose Bowl) 11-13 September | 0* | | 6* | | | | | | | | | 1 | | | | | | 0 | 6 | 0 | W | 22 |
| v. Durham | 3 | 25 | 4 | 32 | 54* | 18 | 7 | 3 | | | 28 | | 16 | | | | 5 | 17 | 212 | 10 | | |
| (Canterbury) 19-21 September | 33 | 15 | 30 | 25* | 8 | 5 | 10 | 0 | | | 11 | | 14 | | | | 0 | 9 | 160 | 10 | L | 4 |
| Matches | 15 | 15 | 15 | 15 | 15 | 14 | 12 | 12 | 11 | 10 | 8 | 7 | 7 | 4 | 3 | 1 | 1 | | | | | |
| Innings | 25 | 23 | 25 | 21 | 18 | 19 | 18 | 14 | 17 | 13 | 10 | 10 | 7 | 3 | 5 | 2 | 2 | | | | | |
| Not Out | 3 | 1 | 3 | 3 | 5 | 2 | 0 | 5 | 0 | 1 | 2 | 1 | 1 | 1 | 4 | 0 | 0 | | | | | |
| Highest Score | 182 | 166 | 115* | 106* | 54* | 116* | 157 | 50* | 174 | 122 | 86 | 77 | 16 | 12 | 36* | 52 | 5 | | | | | |
| Runs | 1250 | 1011 | 902 | 623 | 272 | 454 | 733 | 151 | 628 | 369 | 350 | 264 | 47 | 13 | 60 | 67 | 5 | | | | | |
| Average | 56.81 | 45.95 | 41.00 | 34.61 | 20.92 | 26.70 | 40.72 | 16.77 | 36.94 | 30.75 | 43.75 | 29.33 | 7.83 | 6.50 | 60.00 | 33.50 | 2.50 | | | | | |
| 100s | 5 | 5 | 2 | 2 | 0 | 1 | 3 | 0 | 2 | 2 | 0 | 0 | 0 | 0 | 0 | 0 | 0 | | | | | |
| 50s | 4 | 3 | 5 | 3 | 1 | 2 | 2 | 1 | 2 | 0 | 3 | 2 | 0 | 0 | 0 | 1 | 0 | | | | | |
| Catches/Stumpings | 4/0 | 17/0 | 9/0 | 42/4 | 7/0 | 11/0 | 6/0 | 4/0 | 7/0 | 2/0 | 6/0 | 6/0 | 0/0 | 0/0 | 2/0 | 1/0 | 0/0 | | | | | |

**Home Ground:** Canterbury
**Address:** St Lawrence Ground, Old Dover Road, Canterbury, CT1 3NZ
**Tel:** 01227 456886
**Fax:** 01227 762168
**Email:** jon.fordham.kent@ecb.co.uk
**Directions:** From the North, from M20 junction 7 turn left onto A249. At M2 junction 5 (Sittingbourne) bear right onto M2. At junction 7 (Boughton Street) turn right on to A2. Follow this to junction with A2050, turn left. Follow yellow signs to cricket ground. From the South, from M20 junction 13 bear right onto A20. Follow this road to junction with A260. Bear left and continue to junction with A2 (north). Continue to junction with A2050 and then proceed as north.

**Capacity:** 10,000
**Other grounds used:** Beckenham, Maidstone, Tunbridge Wells
**Year formed:** 1870

**Chief Executive:** Paul Millman
**Director of Cricket:** Graham Ford
**Coaching Coordinator:** Simon Willis
**Captain:** Robert Key
**County colours:** Maroon

**Honours**
County Championship
1906, 1909, 1910, 1913, 1970, 1978
Joint Champions 1977
Sunday League/NCL/Pro40
1972, 1973, 1976, 1995, 2001
Benson & Hedges Cup
1973, 1978
Gillette Cup/NatWest/C&G Trophy
1967, 1974
Twenty20 Cup
2007

**Website:**
**www.kentccc.com**

## FIRST-CLASS MATCHES
# BOWLING

| | R McLaren | JC Tredwell | Yasir Arafat | SJ Cook | MJ Saggers | AJ Hall | DI Stevens | JL Denly | M van Jaarsveld | RH Joseph | SL Malinga | MJ Walker | NJ Dexter | MM Patel | RWT Key | GO Jones | Overs | Total | Byes/Leg-byes | Wickets | Run outs |
|---|---|---|---|---|---|---|---|---|---|---|---|---|---|---|---|---|---|---|---|---|---|
| v. Sussex (Hove) 18-21 April | 28-6-95-1 | 28.2-5-104-2 | 23-5-61-2 | | | | 24-5-42-2 | 6-3-17-0 | | 22-2-78-3 | | | | 25-4-90-0 | | | 156.2 | 510 | 23 | 10 | |
| | 1-0-2-0 | 3.1-1-10-1 | 2-0-12-0 | | | | | | | 6-1-16-0 | | | | 6-0-17-1 | | | 18.1 | 57 | 0 | 2 | |
| v. Sussex (Canterbury) 2-3 May | 7.3-2-12-4 | | 10-3-36-4 | 5-0-31-0 | | | 3-2-5-2 | | | 8-6-13-0 | | | | | | | 33.3 | 102 | 5 | 10 | |
| | 5-1-19-1 | | 8-0-62-1 | 13.5-5-35-6 | | | 9-0-27-2 | | | 7-2-13-0 | | | | | | | 42.5 | 160 | 4 | 10 | |
| v. Durham (Riverside) 9-12 May | 19.5-2-91-4 | 27-2-88-4 | | 17-2-85-2 | | 10-0-48-0 | 5-1-15-0 | | | 8-0-62-0 | | | | | | | 86.5 | 407 | 18 | 10 | |
| | 10-2-33-0 | 13-1-47-0 | | 19.5-3-85-2 | | 17-3-68-4 | 7-3-19-0 | | | 6-0-51-0 | | | | | | | 72.5 | 319 | 16 | 6 | |
| v. Hampshire (Canterbury) 23-26 May | 18-4-61-2 | 11-1-25-0 | | 21.3-4-63-5 | 19-4-56-2 | | 15-3-49-0 | | | | | | | | | | 84.3 | 272 | 18 | 10 | 1 |
| | 13-5-41-0 | 19-3-53-0 | | 23-4-90-4 | 13-7-13-0 | | 16-4-47-1 | | 5-2-16-0 | | | | | | | | 89 | 275 | 15 | 5 | |
| v. Surrey (Whitgift School) 30 May-2 June | 6-0-26-1 | | 15.5-4-49-3 | 3-0-19-0 | | | 17-4-59-5 | 2-1-5-1 | | | | | | | | | 43.5 | 166 | 8 | 10 | |
| | 23-4-86-3 | | 25-6-62-2 | 7-2-15-1 | | | 19-4-76-0 | 2-0-6-0 | | | | | | | | | 92.1 | 319 | 21 | 10 | 1 |
| v. Yorkshire (Tunbridge Wells) 6-9 June | 21-2-76-2 | 47-8-149-1 | | 22-5-66-0 | | 15-3-41-1 | 27.2-3-91-3 | 8-1-23-0 | | | | | | | | | 166.2 | 551 | 27 | 8 | |
| | - | - | | - | | - | - | - | | | | | | | | | - | - | - | - | |
| v. Lancashire (Old Trafford) 15-18 June | 15-1-61-1 | 31-4-103-1 | | 18-3-65-0 | 16-1-46-1 | | 18-0-100-1 | 6-0-32-0 | 8-0-34-1 | | | | | | | | 112 | 451 | 10 | 5 | |
| | 2.5 | | | | 1.5-0-9-2 | | 1-0-3-0 | | | | | | | | | | 2.5 | 12 | 0 | 2 | |
| v. Warwickshire (Canterbury) 20-23 July | 11-4-24-5 | 1-1-0-1 | 4-1-13-0 | 9-2-19-1 | | | 8-1-37-1 | 3.3-2-5-2 | | 4-2-5-0 | | | | | | | 36.3 | 107 | 9 | 10 | |
| | 23-6-46-3 | 34.2-13-64-3 | | 19-4-60-0 | | | 7-3-8-0 | | 2-2-0-0 | | | | | | | | 109.2 | 342 | 12 | 7 | |
| v. Yorkshire (Scarborough) 25-28 July | 28-7-89-4 | 27-5-96-0 | | 18-2-76-1 | 29-7-83-0 | 7-3-9-1 | 14-2-48-0 | 6-0-35-0 | 5.5-0-37-2 | | | | | 4-0-35-1 | 6-0-27-0 | | 144.5 | 550 | 14 | 9 | |
| v. Surrey (Canterbury) 8-9 August | 17-6-37-2 | 16-3-47-6 | 8-1-42-0 | | 11-1-38-1 | | 3-2-1-0 | | | 7-0-40-1 | | | | | | | 62 | 215 | 10 | 10 | |
| | 6-0-17-1 | 10-0-48-2 | | | 6-0-25-1 | | | 2-0-13-2 | | | | | | | | | 24 | 108 | 5 | 6 | |
| v. Warwickshire (Edgbaston) 14-17 August | 13-0-42-4 | 7-1-21-0 | 15-2-50-1 | | 16-2-53-3 | | | | 0.5-0-1-1 | 8-0-45-1 | | | | | | | 59.5 | 213 | 1 | 10 | |
| | - | | | | | | | | | | | | | | | | - | - | - | - | |
| v. Worcestershire (Canterbury) 21-24 August | | 3-0-18-0 | | 7-0-42-0 | 7-2-37-3 | | | | | 4-1-11-0 | | | | | | | 21 | 110 | 2 | 3 | |
| v. Lancashire (Canterbury) 28-31 August | | 36-6-146-3 | | 19-9-43-1 | 25.4-12-43-5 | | | | | 9-1-41-0 | | 7-0-29-0 | | | | | 96.4 | 317 | 15 | 10 | |
| | | 24-5-71-1 | | 6-1-27-0 | 14-7-22-1 | | | 7-1-17-0 | 4-1-8-0 | 12-0-60-0 | | | | | | | 67 | 208 | 3 | 3 | 1 |
| v. Hampshire (Rose Bowl) 11-13 September | 19.4-3-96-3 | 23-8-46-4 | | 10-3-22-2 | 11-1-47-1 | | | | | | | | | | | | 63.4 | 216 | 5 | 10 | |
| | 12-1-39-0 | 44-8-114-4 | | 12-3-37-2 | 9-2-26-0 | | | | 18-3-34-2 | 5.4-1-17-2 | | | | | | | 100.4 | 282 | 15 | 10 | |
| v. Durham (Canterbury) 19-21 September | 19-2-86-3 | 26-4-96-3 | | 13-4-39-0 | 28-2-89-4 | | 2-1-2-0 | | | | | | 2-0-10-1 | 2-0-8-0 | 1-0-6-0 | 2-0-14-0 | 88 | 321 | 9 | 10 | |
| | | | | | | | 3.1-2-12-1 | | | | | | | | | | 10.1 | 52 | 2 | 2 | |

| | R McLaren | JC Tredwell | Yasir Arafat | SJ Cook | MJ Saggers | AJ Hall | DI Stevens | JL Denly | M van Jaarsveld | RH Joseph | SL Malinga | MJ Walker | NJ Dexter | MM Patel | RWT Key | GO Jones |
|---|---|---|---|---|---|---|---|---|---|---|---|---|---|---|---|---|
| Overs | 316 | 415.3 | 238.4 | 242.4 | 156.4 | 163 | 112.5 | 67.1 | 20.2 | 57 | 40 | 2 | 13 | 31 | 7 | 2 |
| Maidens | 58 | 76 | 44 | 58 | 36 | 27 | 24 | 15 | 4 | 11 | 2 | 0 | 0 | 4 | 0 | 0 |
| Runs | 1079 | 1285 | 882 | 740 | 463 | 610 | 305 | 203 | 68 | 233 | 197 | 10 | 72 | 107 | 33 | 14 |
| Wickets | 44 | 36 | 27 | 22 | 19 | 15 | 12 | 6 | 5 | 3 | 2 | 1 | 1 | 1 | 0 | 0 |
| Average | 24.52 | 35.69 | 32.66 | 33.63 | 24.36 | 40.66 | 25.41 | 33.83 | 13.60 | 77.66 | 98.50 | 10.00 | 72.00 | 107.00 | - | - |

# FIELDING

| | |
|---|---|
| 46 | GO Jones (42 ct, 4 st) |
| 17 | M van Jaarsveld |
| 11 | JC Tredwell |
| 9 | JL Denly |
| 7 | DI Stevens |
| 7 | R McLaren |
| 6 | MJ Walker |
| 6 | AJ Hall |
| 6 | NJ Dexter |
| 4 | SJ Cook |
| 4 | RWT Key |
| 2 | Yasir Arafat |
| 2 | RH Joseph |
| 1 | MM Patel |
| 0 | MJ Saggers |
| 0 | SL Malinga |
| 0 | SA Northeast |

## Final Division One Table

| | P | W | L | D | T | Ab | Bat | Bowl | Pens | Pts |
|---|---|---|---|---|---|---|---|---|---|---|
| Sussex | 16 | 7 | 3 | 5 | 0 | 1 | 37 | 43 | 0.00 | 202.00 |
| Durham | 16 | 7 | 5 | 4 | 0 | 0 | 38 | 47 | 1.50 | 197.50 |
| Lancashire | 16 | 5 | 2 | 8 | 0 | 1 | 40 | 44 | 0.00 | 190.00 |
| Surrey | 16 | 5 | 4 | 6 | 0 | 1 | 41 | 40 | 1.00 | 178.00 |
| Hampshire | 16 | 5 | 3 | 8 | 0 | 0 | 32 | 43 | 0.00 | 177.00 |
| Yorkshire | 16 | 4 | 4 | 8 | 0 | 0 | 49 | 38 | 0.00 | 175.00 |
| Kent | 16 | 3 | 5 | 7 | 0 | 1 | 43 | 36 | 0.00 | 153.00 |
| Warwickshire | 16 | 2 | 5 | 9 | 0 | 0 | 40 | 35 | 0.00 | 139.00 |
| Worcestershire | 16 | 1 | 8 | 5 | 0 | 2 | 18 | 35 | 0.00 | 95.00 |

Limited overs nickname:
KENT SPITFIRES

# LANCASHIRE CCC

## FIRST-CLASS MATCHES
## BATTING

| Match | LD Sutton | SG Law | PJ Horton | MJ Chilton | DG Cork | G Chapple | SJ Croft | SI Mahmood | G Keedy | OJ Newby | MB Loye | BJ Hodge | M Muralitharan | TC Smith | JM Anderson | VVS Laxman | IJ Sutcliffe | A Flintoff | KW Hogg | GD Cross | ST Jayasuriya | KR Brown | SJ Marshall | SJ Mullaney | SP Cheetham | SD Parry | Extras | Total | Wickets | Result | Points |
|---|---|---|---|---|---|---|---|---|---|---|---|---|---|---|---|---|---|---|---|---|---|---|---|---|---|---|---|---|---|---|---|
| v. Warwickshire | 111 | 21 | 76 | 14 | 12 | 30 | | 1* | 0 | 4 | | | | | | | 4 | 29 | | | | | | | | | 31 | 333 | 10 | | |
| (Edgbaston) 18-21 April | | 38 | 8* | 14 | | | | | | | 105* | | | | | | 9 | | | | | | | | | | 15 | 189 | 3 | D | 9 |
| v. Durham UCCE | | | 59 | | 0 | | | | | | | | | | | | 104* | | | 61* | | 27 | | | | | 3 | 254 | 3 | | |
| (Durham) 25-27 April | | | 23 | | 5 | | | | | | | | | | | | 15* | | 30 | 10 | | 0 | 7 | 165* | | | 7 | 262 | 6 | W | |
| v. Surrey | 0 | 120 | 36 | 31 | 17 | 9 | | 9 | 7 | | 35 | | 26* | | | | 2 | | | | | | | | | | 23 | 315 | 10 | | |
| (Old Trafford) 2-4 May | | 1 | 49* | 34* | | | | | | | 1 | | | | | | 3 | | | | | | | | | | 2 | 90 | 3 | W | 20 |
| v. Hampshire | 37 | 20 | 9 | | | 17 | 13 | 4* | | | 13 | 4 | 0 | | | | | 61 | | | | | | | | | 26 | 207 | 10 | D | 8 |
| (Rose Bowl) 9-12 May | | | | | | | | | | | | | | | | | | | | | | | | | | | | | | | |
| v. Worcestershire | 25 | | 10 | 6 | 14 | 5 | 21 | 13 | | | 5 | 49 | 1* | | 0 | | | | | | | | | | | | 12 | 161 | 10 | | |
| (Old Trafford) 15-18 May | 14 | | 139 | 59 | 11* | 2 | 1 | 4* | | | 35 | 10 | | | | | | | | | | | | | | | 21 | 296 | 7 | D | 7 |
| v. Sussex | 40 | 119 | 20 | 26 | 17 | | 9 | 8 | | | 43 | 1* | 19 | 1 | | | | | | | | | | | | | 27 | 330 | 10 | | |
| (Hove) 30 May-2 June | 5 | 8 | 9 | 23 | 8 | | 65 | 5* | | | 15 | 8* | 44 | | | | | | | | | | | | | | 16 | 206 | 8 | D | 10 |
| v. Durham | 33 | 60 | 15 | 115 | 9 | 57 | | | | 10 | 12 | 1 | 12* | 18 | | | | | | | | | | | | | 25 | 367 | 10 | | |
| (Riverside) 6-9 June | 41 | 61 | 56 | 29 | 48* | 7 | | | | | 41 | 1 | | 4* | | | | | | | | | | | | | 22 | 310 | 7 | D | 11 |
| v. Kent | | 58 | 29 | | | 40* | | | | | 75 | 156* | 8 | | | | 57 | | | | | | | | | | 28 | 451 | 5 | | |
| (Old Trafford) 15-18 June | | | 3 | | | | | | | | 8* | 0* | | | | | 0 | | | | | | | | | | 1 | 12 | 2 | W | |
| v. Yorkshire | 20* | 55 | 47 | | | 5 | | | | | 47 | 24 | | | | | | | | | 38 | | | | | | 11 | 247 | 6 | D | 8 |
| (Old Trafford) 8-11 July | | | | | | | | | | | | | | | | | | | | | | | | | | | | | | | |
| v. Sussex | 18 | 95 | 18 | 9 | 30* | 25 | 0 | | | | 6 | 7 | 28 | | | | | 34 | | | | | | | | | 31 | 301 | 10 | | |
| (Liverpool) 31 July-2 August | 2 | 16 | 9 | 6 | 0 | 19 | 6* | | | | 40 | 15 | 6 | | | | | 9 | | | | | | | | | 5 | 133 | 10 | L | 6 |
| v. Yorkshire | 7 | 206 | 149 | 24 | | 21 | 15 | 1 | 6 | | 29 | 2* | | | | | | 24 | | | | | | | | | 33 | 517 | 10 | W | 22 |
| (Headingley) 9-11 August | | | | | | | | | | | | | | | | | | | | | | | | | | | | | | | |
| v. Hampshire | 100* | 53 | 152 | 4 | 21 | 10 | 0 | 17 | 4* | | | | | | | 12 | | | | | | | | | | | 30 | 403 | 8 | D | 12 |
| (Old Trafford) 21-24 August | | | | | | | | | | | | | | | | | | | | | | | | | | | | | | | |
| v. Kent | 12 | 66 | 37 | 53 | 5 | 88 | 29 | 1 | 1* | | | | | | | 10 | | | | | | | | | | | 15 | 317 | 10 | | |
| (Canterbury) 28-31 August | | 29* | 69 | 15 | | 59* | | | | | | | | | | 22 | | | | | | | | | | | 14 | 208 | 3 | D | 10 |
| v. Durham | 66* | 2 | 2 | 0 | 19 | 16 | 7 | 41 | 0 | 0 | | | | | | 25 | | | | | | | | | | | 5 | 183 | 10 | | |
| (Blackpool) 6-7 September | | 82* | 2 | 14 | | 1 | | | | | | | | | | 55* | | | | | | | | | | | 16 | 169 | 3 | W | 17 |
| v. Warwickshire | 7 | 43 | 71 | 18 | 0 | 16 | 1 | 10 | 4* | 26 | | | | | | 103 | | | | | | | | | | | 12 | 311 | 10 | | |
| (Old Trafford) 11-13 September | | 13 | 20* | | | | | 21* | | | | | | | | | | | | | | | | | | | 17 | 71 | 1 | W | 20 |
| v. Surrey | 17 | 45 | 48 | 4 | 46* | 1 | 0 | 3 | 2 | 0 | | | | | | 53 | | | | | | | | | | | 15 | 234 | 10 | | |
| (The Oval) 19-22 September | 32 | 79 | 39 | 30 | 47 | 29 | 45 | 26 | 4* | 4 | | | | | | 100 | | | | | | | | | | | 29 | 464 | 10 | L | 4 |

| | LD Sutton | SG Law | PJ Horton | MJ Chilton | DG Cork | G Chapple | SJ Croft | SI Mahmood | G Keedy | OJ Newby | MB Loye | BJ Hodge | M Muralitharan | TC Smith | JM Anderson | VVS Laxman | IJ Sutcliffe | A Flintoff | KW Hogg | GD Cross | ST Jayasuriya | KR Brown | SJ Marshall | SJ Mullaney | SP Cheetham | SD Parry |
|---|---|---|---|---|---|---|---|---|---|---|---|---|---|---|---|---|---|---|---|---|---|---|---|---|---|---|
| Matches | 15 | 14 | 14 | 14 | 13 | 12 | 11 | 10 | 10 | 9 | 8 | 8 | 8 | 6 | 6 | 5 | 4 | 3 | 2 | 1 | 1 | 1 | 1 | 1 | 1 | 1 |
| Innings | 19 | 22 | 25 | 24 | 17 | 16 | 19 | 14 | 9 | 8 | 14 | 13 | 7 | 6 | 3 | 8 | 8 | 4 | 2 | 2 | 1 | 2 | 1 | 1 | 0 | 0 |
| Not Out | 3 | 2 | 2 | 2 | 4 | 1 | 2 | 3 | 5 | 1 | 2 | 2 | 5 | 2 | 0 | 1 | 2 | 0 | 0 | 1 | 0 | 0 | 0 | 1 | 0 | 0 |
| Highest Score | 111 | 206 | 152 | 115 | 48* | 88 | 65 | 41 | 9 | 26 | 105* | 156* | 28 | 44 | 1 | 103 | 104* | 61 | 30 | 61* | 38 | 27 | 7 | 165* | 0 | 0 |
| Runs | 587 | 1277 | 1116 | 616 | 329 | 338 | 328 | 148 | 34 | 48 | 427 | 354 | 58 | 119 | 1 | 380 | 194 | 128 | 59 | 71 | 38 | 27 | 7 | 165 | 0 | 0 |
| Average | 36.68 | 63.85 | 48.52 | 28.00 | 25.30 | 22.53 | 19.29 | 13.45 | 8.50 | 6.85 | 35.58 | 32.18 | 29.00 | 29.75 | 0.33 | 54.28 | 32.33 | 32.00 | 29.50 | 71.00 | 38.00 | 13.50 | 7.00 | - | - | - |
| 100s | 2 | 3 | 3 | 1 | 0 | 0 | 0 | 0 | 0 | 0 | 1 | 1 | 0 | 0 | 0 | 2 | 1 | 0 | 0 | 0 | 0 | 0 | 0 | 1 | 0 | 0 |
| 50s | 1 | 9 | 5 | 2 | 0 | 2 | 2 | 0 | 0 | 0 | 1 | 0 | 0 | 0 | 0 | 2 | 1 | 1 | 0 | 1 | 0 | 0 | 0 | 0 | 0 | 0 |
| Catches/Stumpings | 42/2 | 17/0 | 17/0 | 7/0 | 4/0 | 4/0 | 12/0 | 3/0 | 3/0 | 2/0 | 5/0 | 4/0 | 1/0 | 4/0 | 1/0 | 7/0 | 5/0 | 4/0 | 0/0 | 4/2 | 0/0 | 1/0 | 1/0 | 2/0 | 1/0 | 0/0 |

**Home Ground:** Old Trafford
**Address:** Old Trafford Cricket Ground, Talbot Road, Manchester, M16 0PX
**Tel:** 0161 282 4000
**Fax:** 0161 873 8353 (Ticket office)
**Email:** enquiries@lccc.co.uk
**Directions:** By rail: Manchester Piccadilly or Victoria then Metro link to Old Trafford. By road: M63, Stretford slip-road (junction 7) on to A56; follow signs.
**Capacity:** 21,500
**Other grounds used:** Blackpool, Liverpool

**Year formed:** 1864
**Chairman:** Jack Simmons
**Chief Executive:** Jim Cumbes
**Cricket Manager:** Mike Watkinson
**Captain:** Mark Chilton
**County colours:** Red and white

Website:
**www.lccc.co.uk**

**Honours**
County Championship
1881, 1897, 1904, 1926, 1927, 1928, 1930, 1934. Joint champions 1879, 1882, 1889, 1950
Sunday League/NCL/Pro40
1970, 1989, 1998, 1999
Benson & Hedges Cup
1984, 1990, 1995, 1996
Gillette Cup/NatWest/C&GTrophy
1970, 1971, 1972, 1975, 1990, 1996, 1998

## FIRST-CLASS MATCHES
## BOWLING

| FIRST-CLASS MATCHES | M Muralitharan | G Chapple | SI Mahmood | DG Cork | G Keedy | OJ Newby | JM Anderson | TC Smith | SJ Croft | SD Parry | A Flintoff | SJ Marshall | ST Jayasuriya | SP Cheetham | KW Hogg | SG Law | MJ Chilton | VVS Laxman | BJ Hodge | KR Brown | SJ Mullaney | Overs | Total | Byes/Leg-byes | Wickets | Run outs |
|---|---|---|---|---|---|---|---|---|---|---|---|---|---|---|---|---|---|---|---|---|---|---|---|---|---|---|
| v. Warwickshire (Edgbaston) 18-21 April | 29-6-88-2 | | | 32-5-93-0 | 52.3-12-159-5 | 24-5-85-3 | | | | | | | | | 22-7-58-0 | | | | | | | 159.3 | 490 | 7 | 10 | |
| | 12-4-22-0 | | | 9-3-24-0 | 22-2-73-4 | 11-1-52-3 | | | | | | | | | 2-0-7-0 | | | | | | | 56 | 189 | 11 | 7 | |
| v. Durham UCCE (Durham) 25-27 April | | | | | | | | 19-7-40-2 | 20-5-54-2 | 10-2-23-0 | 13-2-32-1 | | | 14-1-83-0 | 18-8-35-0 | | | | | 3-0-7-0 | 7-2-13-0 | 104 | 298 | 11 | 6 | 1 |
| | | | | | | | | 10-1-36-2 | 6-0-25-0 | 9.1-2-23-5 | 15-4-52-1 | | | 10-0-44-1 | 11-2-31-1 | | | | | | | 61.1 | 217 | 6 | 10 | |
| v. Surrey (Old Trafford) 2-4 May | | 16-1-51-0 | 15-3-59-1 | 22.3-6-57-4 | 18-1-44-3 | | | | 20-5-56-2 | | | | | | | | 2-0-5-0 | | | | | 93.3 | 284 | 12 | 10 | |
| | | 15-4-40-4 | 14-3-39-3 | | 3-1-13-1 | | | | 3-0-17-1 | | | | | | | | | | | | | 35 | 120 | 11 | 10 | 1 |
| v. Hampshire (Rose Bowl) 9-12 May | | 20-2-65-3 | 14-0-69-3 | | 4.3-2-2-1 | | 16-0-83-3 | | | | 9-1-25-0 | | | | | | | | | | | 63.3 | 272 | 8 | 10 | |
| | | | | | | | | | | | | | | | | | | | | | | - | - | - | - | |
| v. Worcestershire (Old Trafford) 15-18 May | 33.3-9-72-6 | 16-2-57-1 | 16-3-52-1 | | 19-1-61-1 | | | 12-0-62-1 | 1-0-4-0 | | | | | | | | | | | | | 97.3 | 327 | 19 | 10 | |
| | | | | | | | | | | | | | | | | | | | | | | - | - | - | - | |
| v. Sussex (Hove) 30 May-2 June | 27-8-73-5 | | 15-5-32-2 | 11.4-2-37-2 | | | | 11-5-46-0 | 11-4-44-1 | 2-0-5-0 | | | | | | | | | | | | 75.4 | 235 | 3 | 10 | |
| | 26-13-25-4 | | 12-1-38-0 | 7-2-15-0 | | | | 12-1-42-1 | 3-2-4-0 | | | | | | | | | 1-0-1-0 | | | | 63 | 145 | 15 | 5 | |
| v. Durham (Riverside) 6-9 June | 26.3-5-95-5 | | 5-0-25-1 | 15-2-47-1 | | 2-0-12-0 | | 16-3-80-1 | 12-3-47-2 | | | | | | | | | | | | | 76.3 | 312 | 6 | 10 | |
| | 32-14-45-3 | | 16-6-33-1 | 14-4-35-2 | | | | 26-11-46-2 | 13-4-44-1 | | | | | | | | | | | | | 101 | 229 | 26 | 9 | |
| v. Kent (Old Trafford) 15-18 June | 34-7-73-4 | | | 11.1-4-30-2 | 14-2-44-1 | | | 22.4-7-64-3 | 6.5-0-37-0 | | | | | | | | | | | | | 88.4 | 272 | 24 | 10 | |
| | 25-1-72-4 | | | | 5-1-17-2 | | | 22-6-48-2 | | | | | | | | | | 1-0-4-0 | | | | 63 | 190 | 5 | 10 | 1 |
| v. Yorkshire (Old Trafford) 8-11 July | | | | 18-5-47-1 | 31-7-70-3 | | | 33.3-7-98-5 | 16-2-54-0 | 8-1-31-0 | | | | 4-0-10-1 | | | | | | | | 110.3 | 320 | 10 | 10 | |
| | | | | | | | | | | | | | | | | | | | | | | - | - | - | - | |
| v. Sussex (Liverpool) 31 July- 2 August | 25-8-53-5 | 19-2-60-3 | 13-3-47-0 | 22.3-3-66-2 | | | | | 9-0-37-0 | | | | | | | | | | | | | 88.3 | 274 | 11 | 10 | |
| | 31.2-3-120-3 | 17-5-38-2 | 17-3-43-2 | 17-5-23-2 | | | | | 2-0-8-0 | 8-5-26-0 | | | | | | | | | | | | 92.2 | 268 | 10 | 10 | 1 |
| v. Yorkshire (Headingley) 9-11 August | 20-6-35-1 | 14-4-35-4 | 7-0-24-2 | | 3-0-11-0 | | | | | | 11.5-3-38-3 | | | | | | | | | | | 55.5 | 144 | 1 | 10 | |
| | 24.4-2-66-5 | 9-2-31-0 | 18-0-75-2 | | 10-2-26-0 | | | | | | 6-1-31-2 | | | | | | | | | | | 67.4 | 247 | 18 | 10 | |
| v. Hampshire (Old Trafford) 21-24 August | 38-6-107-3 | 17.5-3-41-1 | 21-2-92-1 | 24-6-74-3 | 13-0-62-0 | | | | | | | | | | | | | | | | | 113.5 | 393 | 17 | 10 | 2 |
| | 16-3-35-1 | 8-2-13-1 | 4-2-11-0 | | 15-4-39-0 | | | | 4-0-11-0 | | | | | | | | | | | | | 47 | 111 | 2 | 2 | |
| v. Kent (Canterbury) 28-31 August | 33.3-5-81-2 | 22-5-63-3 | 13.3-2-56-0 | 20-8-36-1 | 21-4-65-3 | | | | 18-2-64-1 | | | | | | | | | | | | | 110 | 327 | 26 | 10 | |
| | 19-1-50-1 | 17-1-80-2 | 11-2-51-1 | 32-4-107-2 | 15.4-1-74-2 | | | | | | | | | | | 4-0-21-0 | 2-0-8-0 | 5-1-15-0 | | | | 112.4 | 419 | 11 | 6 | |
| v. Durham (Blackpool) 6-7 September | | 23-7-53-7 | 14-2-45-2 | 14.3-2-45-1 | | | | | 7-2-20-0 | | | | | | | | | | | | | 58.3 | 166 | 3 | 10 | |
| | | 13-4-33-1 | 11-2-51-4 | 13-2-31-0 | | | | | 3-0-30-0 | 8-3-40-3 | | | | | | | | | | | | 48 | 185 | 0 | 10 | |
| v. Warwickshire (Old Trafford) 11-13 September | | 13.2-3-42-4 | 15-6-21-4 | 9-2-21-2 | | 2-0-2-0 | | | 6-2-20-0 | | | | | | | | | | | | | 45.2 | 106 | 0 | 10 | |
| | | 20-3-71-3 | 20-3-72-2 | 13-4-19-2 | | 24-6-62-2 | | | 9-1-31-1 | | | | | | | | | | | | | 86 | 272 | 13 | 10 | |
| v. Surrey (The Oval) 19-22 September | | 26-10-82-2 | 26-6-93-4 | 15-2-50-1 | 23-5-97-2 | | | | 14-2-83-0 | | | | | | | | | | | | | 106 | 427 | 11 | 9 | |
| | | 15-3-34-1 | 17-2-65-1 | 15-2-65-2 | 31-10-68-0 | | | | 15-0-65-2 | | 2-0-11-0 | | | | | | | | | | | 93 | 295 | 11 | 5 | |

| | M Muralitharan | G Chapple | SI Mahmood | DG Cork | G Keedy | OJ Newby | JM Anderson | TC Smith | SJ Croft | SD Parry | A Flintoff | SJ Marshall | ST Jayasuriya | SP Cheetham | KW Hogg | SG Law | MJ Chilton | VVS Laxman | BJ Hodge | KR Brown | SJ Mullaney |
|---|---|---|---|---|---|---|---|---|---|---|---|---|---|---|---|---|---|---|---|---|---|
| Overs | 392.3 | 365.1 | 270.3 | 360.5 | 272.3 | 177.4 | 171.1 | 95.5 | 79 | 19.1 | 34.5 | 28 | 4 | 24 | 53 | 4 | 4 | 5 | 2 | 3 | 7 |
| Maidens | 90 | 79 | 43 | 74 | 55 | 28 | 40 | 20 | 11 | 4 | 10 | 6 | 0 | 1 | 17 | 0 | 0 | 1 | 0 | 0 | 2 |
| Runs | 952 | 1027 | 955 | 1011 | 813 | 670 | 569 | 351 | 286 | 46 | 120 | 84 | 10 | 127 | 131 | 21 | 13 | 15 | 5 | 7 | 13 |
| Wickets | 51 | 47 | 30 | 30 | 24 | 22 | 18 | 8 | 6 | 5 | 5 | 2 | 1 | 1 | 1 | 0 | 0 | 0 | 0 | 0 | 0 |
| Average | 18.66 | 21.85 | 31.83 | 33.70 | 33.87 | 30.45 | 31.61 | 43.87 | 47.66 | 9.20 | 24.00 | 42.00 | 10.00 | 127.00 | 131.00 | - | - | - | - | - | - |

## FIELDING

| | |
|---|---|
| 44 | LD Sutton (42 ct, 2 st) |
| 17 | SG Law |
| 17 | PJ Horton |
| 12 | SJ Croft |
| 7 | MJ Chilton |
| 7 | VVS Laxman |
| 6 | GD Cross (4 ct, 2 st) |
| 5 | MB Loye |
| 5 | IJ Sutcliffe |
| 4 | DG Cork |
| 4 | G Chapple |
| 4 | A Flintoff |
| 4 | BJ Hodge |
| 4 | TC Smith |
| 3 | G Keedy |
| 3 | SI Mahmood |
| 2 | OJ Newby |
| 2 | SJ Mullaney |
| 1 | M Muralitharan |
| 1 | JM Anderson |
| 1 | SJ Marshall |
| 1 | KR Brown |
| 1 | SP Cheetham |
| 0 | ST Jayasuriya |
| 0 | KW Hogg |
| 0 | SD Parry |

### Final Division One Table

| | P | W | L | D | T | Ab | Bat | Bowl | Pens | Pts |
|---|---|---|---|---|---|---|---|---|---|---|
| Sussex | 16 | 7 | 3 | 5 | 0 | 1 | 37 | 43 | 0.00 | 202.00 |
| Durham | 16 | 7 | 5 | 4 | 0 | 0 | 38 | 47 | 1.50 | 197.50 |
| Lancashire | 16 | 5 | 2 | 8 | 0 | 1 | 40 | 44 | 0.00 | 190.00 |
| Surrey | 16 | 5 | 4 | 6 | 0 | 1 | 41 | 40 | 1.00 | 178.00 |
| Hampshire | 16 | 5 | 3 | 8 | 0 | 0 | 32 | 43 | 0.00 | 177.00 |
| Yorkshire | 16 | 4 | 4 | 8 | 0 | 0 | 49 | 38 | 0.00 | 175.00 |
| Kent | 16 | 3 | 5 | 7 | 0 | 1 | 43 | 36 | 0.00 | 153.00 |
| Warwickshire | 16 | 2 | 5 | 9 | 0 | 1 | 40 | 35 | 0.00 | 139.00 |
| Worcestershire | 16 | 1 | 8 | 5 | 0 | 2 | 18 | 35 | 0.00 | 95.00 |

Limited overs nickname:
LANCASHIRE LIGHTNING

# LEICESTERSHIRE CCC

## FIRST-CLASS MATCHES
### BATTING

| Match | TJ New | J Allenby | HD Ackerman | PA Nixon | JK Maunders | DD Masters | CW Henderson | JL Sadler | Mansoor Amjad | DDJ Robinson | NGE Walker | MC Rosenberg | A Jacobs | SCJ Broad | DT Rowe | RAG Cummins | GJP Kruger | CK Langeveldt | JE Taylor | SJ Cliff | RP Singh | JHK Naik | JJ Cobb | MAG Boyce | PW Harrison | HF Gurney | Extras | Total | Wickets | Result | Points |
|---|---|---|---|---|---|---|---|---|---|---|---|---|---|---|---|---|---|---|---|---|---|---|---|---|---|---|---|---|---|---|---|
| v. Nottinghamshire (Trent Bridge) 18-21 April | 16 | 14 | 18 | | 82 | 1 | 47 | 18 | 5 | 50 | 0* | | | | | | | | | | 25 | | | | | | 23 | 299 | 10 | | |
| | 57 | 3 | 112 | | 31 | 9 | 10 | 0 | 20 | 37 | 0* | | | | | | | | | | 0 | | | | | | 32 | 311 | 10 | L | 5 |
| v. Somerset (Leicester) 25-28 April | 53 | 77 | 1 | | 26 | 9 | 4 | 3 | 67 | 122 | 2* | | | | | | | | | 1 | | | | | | | 20 | 385 | 10 | | |
| | 54 | 2 | 17 | | 10 | 7 | 1 | 22 | 1 | 10 | 9* | | | | | | | | | 2 | | | | | | | 15 | 150 | 10 | L | 7 |
| v. Gloucestershire (Bristol) 2-5 May | 98 | 0 | 59 | 30 | | 0 | | 45 | | 14 | | 64* | 22 | | | | 9 | | | | | | | | | | 35 | 376 | 10 | | |
| | 16 | 47* | 28 | 15 | | 5* | | 32 | | 36 | | 17 | 9 | | | | | | | | | | | | | | 13 | 218 | 7 | D | 10 |
| v. Derbyshire (Derby) 9-12 May | 0 | 36 | 1 | 40 | 15 | | | 1 | 41 | 19 | 24 | | 5 | | | | | 3* | | | | | | | | | 24 | 209 | 10 | | |
| | 4 | 0 | 27 | 42 | 5 | | | 5 | 6 | 14 | 16 | | 1 | | | | | 3* | | | | | | | | | 14 | 137 | 10 | L | 4 |
| v. Essex (Leicester) 16-19 May | 0 | 21 | 20 | 85 | | | 15 | 9 | 43 | 31 | 0 | | 85 | | | | | 10* | | | | | | | | | 16 | 335 | 10 | | |
| | 14* | | | | | | | | | 41* | | | | | | | | | | | | | | | | | 1 | 56 | 0 | D | 10 |
| v. Oxford UCCE (The Parks) 23-25 May | 125 | 24 | | | 31 | | 25 | 39 | | | 2 | 28 | 34 | 34* | | | | 9* | | | | | | | 1 | | 32 | 384 | 9 | W | |
| v. Nottinghamshire (Oakham School) 30 May-2 June | 51 | 93 | 14 | 98 | | 32 | | 4 | 0 | 0* | | 0 | 12 | 4 | | | | | | | | | | | | | 56 | 364 | 10 | | |
| | 14 | | 20 | 20* | | | | | 7 | | 39* | | | | | | | | | | | | | | | | 14 | 114 | 3 | D | 9 |
| v. Somerset (Taunton) 6-9 June | 33 | 20 | 23 | 21 | 0 | 2 | | 7* | 2 | 28 | | 22 | 0 | | | | | | | | | | | | | | 10 | 168 | 10 | | |
| | 7 | 43 | 4 | 18 | 3 | 31* | | 46 | 12 | 8 | | 23 | 35 | | | | | | | | | | | | | | 18 | 248 | 10 | L | 1 |
| v. Northamptonshire (Northampton) 15-18 June | 29 | 30* | 17 | 25* | 14 | | | | | | | | 2 | | | | | | | | | | | | | | 14 | 131 | 4 | D | 7 |
| v. Glamorgan (Leicester) 8-11 July | 15 | 0 | 153 | 126 | 30 | 11 | | 105* | | | 11 | 2 | | | | | 9 | | | | | | | | | | 19 | 481 | 10 | | |
| | 11* | | | | | | | | | | | 13* | | | | | | | | | | | | | | | 3 | 27 | 0 | W | 22 |
| v. Middlesex (Leicester) 20-23 July | 56 | 38* | 118 | 4* | 97 | | | | | 17 | 55 | | | | | | | | | | | | | | | | 18 | 403 | 5 | D | 9 |
| v. Derbyshire (Leicester) 9-12 August | 1 | 83 | 0 | 7 | 45 | 14 | | 4 | | | 19 | | | 40* | | | 0 | | 40 | | | | | | | | 21 | 274 | 10 | | |
| | 78 | 14 | 11 | 10 | 9 | 46 | | 4 | | | 0 | | | 91* | | | 15 | | 4 | | | | | | | | 62 | 344 | 10 | W | 19 |
| v. Essex (Colchester) 22-25 August | 35* | 3* | 1 | | 13 | | | | | | 25 | | | | | | | | | | | | | | | | 0 | 52 | 2 | | |
| | 0 | 59 | 15 | 3 | 8 | 8 | 27 | 5 | | | | | | | | 20* | | | | | | | | | | | 6 | 176 | 10 | L | 3 |
| v. Gloucestershire (Leicester) 30 August-1 September | 4 | 25 | 4 | 57 | 6 | 8 | 81 | 18 | | | | | | 6* | 3 | | | | | | | | | 5 | | | 12 | 229 | 10 | | |
| | 50 | 8 | 9 | 77 | 1 | 46 | 5 | 42 | | | | | | 0 | 26* | | | | | | | | | | | | 6 | 270 | 10 | L | 2 |
| v. Northamptonshire (Leicester) 5-8 September | 45 | 10 | 18 | 30 | 51 | | 22 | 26 | | 0 | | | | | | | | | 1* | | | | 2 | | | 1 | 30 | 236 | 10 | | |
| | 40 | 58 | 4 | 110 | 30 | | 38 | 5 | | 11 | | | | | | | | | 11 | | | | 21 | | | 0* | 28 | 356 | 10 | L | 4 |
| v. Middlesex (Southgate) 11-14 September | 47 | 1 | 22 | 4 | 58 | 6 | 0 | 3 | | 13* | | | | | | | | | 2 | | | 15 | | | | | 19 | 190 | 10 | | |
| | 4 | 46 | 7 | 57 | 10 | 39 | 34 | 25 | | 11 | | | | | | | | | 20 | | | 5* | | | | | 21 | 279 | 10 | L | 3 |
| Matches | 16 | 16 | 15 | 13 | 13 | 11 | 10 | 10 | 9 | 8 | 8 | 7 | 6 | 5 | 5 | 5 | 4 | 3 | 3 | 2 | 2 | 1 | 1 | 1 | 1 | 1 | | | | | |
| Innings | 29 | 26 | 26 | 21 | 22 | 16 | 13 | 17 | 13 | 14 | 11 | 8 | 9 | 6 | 6 | 9 | 4 | 4 | 5 | 3 | 4 | 2 | 2 | 1 | 1 | 2 | | | | | |
| Not Out | 3 | 4 | 0 | 3 | 0 | 2 | 0 | 0 | 2 | 1 | 5 | 1 | 2 | 2 | 1 | 3 | 0 | 3 | 1 | 2 | 0 | 1 | 0 | 0 | 0 | 1 | | | | | |
| Highest Score | 125 | 93 | 153 | 126 | 97 | 46 | 81 | 45 | 105* | 122 | 31 | 64* | 55 | 91* | 85 | 34* | 15 | 10* | 40 | 11 | 25 | 15 | 21 | 5 | 1 | 1 | | | | | |
| Runs | 957 | 755 | 723 | 879 | 575 | 242 | 326 | 304 | 319 | 407 | 143 | 130 | 184 | 197 | 137 | 104 | 28 | 25 | 86 | 21 | 28 | 20 | 23 | 5 | 1 | 1 | | | | | |
| Average | 36.80 | 34.31 | 27.80 | 48.83 | 26.13 | 17.28 | 25.07 | 17.88 | 29.00 | 31.30 | 23.83 | 18.57 | 26.28 | 49.25 | 27.40 | 17.33 | 7.00 | 25.00 | 21.50 | 21.00 | 7.00 | 20.00 | 11.50 | 5.00 | 1.00 | 1.00 | | | | | |
| 100s | 1 | 0 | 3 | 2 | 0 | 0 | 0 | 0 | 1 | 1 | 0 | 0 | 0 | 0 | 0 | 0 | 0 | 0 | 0 | 0 | 0 | 0 | 0 | 0 | 0 | 0 | | | | | |
| 50s | 8 | 5 | 1 | 5 | 4 | 0 | 1 | 0 | 1 | 1 | 0 | 1 | 1 | 1 | 1 | 1 | 0 | 0 | 0 | 0 | 0 | 0 | 0 | 0 | 0 | 0 | | | | | |
| Catches/Stumpings | 19/1 | 15/0 | 15/0 | 36/1 | 12/0 | 1/0 | 3/0 | 7/0 | 6/0 | 5/0 | 4/0 | 2/0 | 5/0 | 0/0 | 0/0 | 2/0 | 1/0 | 0/0 | 0/0 | 0/0 | 2/0 | 0/0 | 0/0 | 0/0 | 1/0 | 0/0 | | | | | |

**Home Ground:** Grace Road, Leicester
**Address:** County Ground, Grace Road, Leicester, LE2 8AD
**Tel:** 0871 2821879
**Fax:** 0871 2821873
**Email:** enquiries@leicestershireccc.co.uk
**Directions:** *By road:* Follow signs from city centre, or from southern ring road from M1 or A6.
**Capacity:** 5,500
**Other grounds used:** Oakham School
**Year formed:** 1879

**Chief Executive:** Paul Maylard-Mason
**Senior Coach:** Tim Boon
**Club Captain:** Jeremy Snape
**County colours:** Dark green and scarlet

Website:
www.leicestershireccc.co.uk

**Honours**
County Championship
1975, 1996, 1998
Sunday League/NCL/Pro40
1974, 1977
Benson & Hedges Cup
1972, 1975, 1985
Twenty20 Cup
2004, 2006

# FIRST-CLASS MATCHES
## BOWLING

| | DD Masters | CW Henderson | SCJ Broad | NGE Walker | J Allenby | GJP Kruger | DT Rowe | RAG Cummins | JE Taylor | Mansoor Amjad | RP Singh | CK Langeveldt | TJ New | HF Gurney | JK Maunders | DDJ Robinson | JHK Naik | JL Sadler | SJ Cliff | PA Nixon | MC Rosenberg | A Jacobs | JJ Cobb | Overs | Total | Byes/Leg-byes | Wickets | Run outs |
|---|---|---|---|---|---|---|---|---|---|---|---|---|---|---|---|---|---|---|---|---|---|---|---|---|---|---|---|---|
| **v. Nottinghamshire** (Trent Bridge) 18-21 April | 34-8-101-2 | 21-5-64-1 | | 28-4-106-3 | 6-0-26-0 | | | | | | 15-0-76-0 | 25.4-6-106-3 | | | | | | | | | | | | 129.4 | 500 | 21 | 10 | 1 |
| | 4-1-11-0 | 9-0-50-1 | | 2-0-10-0 | | | | | | | 7.3-1-28-0 | 4-1-12-0 | | | | | | | | | | | | 26.3 | 112 | 1 | 1 | |
| **v. Somerset** (Leicester) 25-28 April | 20-4-60-6 | 15-1-61-2 | | 19-2-99-0 | | | | | | 17-4-70-2 | | | 13-2-51-0 | | | | | | | | | | | 84.4 | 357 | 16 | 10 | |
| | 9-4-21-1 | 30-5-111-3 | | 9-0-89-0 | | | | | | 17.4-1-52-3 | 14-3-62-3 | | 7-0-28-0 | | | | | | | | | | | 86.4 | 376 | 33 | 10 | |
| **v. Gloucestershire** (Bristol) 2-5 May | 17-3-62-1 | 23-4-69-0 | | 33-6-111-3 | 34.2-6-125-5 | | | | | | 35-8-97-0 | | | | | 1-0-2-0 | | | | 9.2-1-45-0 | | | | 143.2 | 507 | 41 | 10 | 1 |
| | | 7-1-23-1 | | | | | | | | | 14-3-71-1 | | | | | 7-0-48-1 | | | | | | | | 51.2 | 249 | 9 | 4 | 1 |
| **v. Derbyshire** (Derby) 9-12 May | | | | 19-3-67-3 | 14-6-23-1 | | 15-3-45-0 | | | 7.4-1-16-3 | 23-9-64-3 | | 5-0-32-0 | | | | | | | | | | | 83.4 | 259 | 12 | 10 | |
| | | | | 5-1-24-0 | | | | | | 5.3-1-22-2 | 7-1-40-1 | | | | | | | | | | | | | 17.3 | 88 | 2 | 3 | |
| **v. Essex** (Leicester) 16-19 May | | | | 19-7-55-3 | 5-0-30-1 | | | 5-1-27-2 | | 8-2-32-0 | 22.4-8-41-4 | | | | | | | | | | | | | 59.4 | 201 | 16 | 10 | |
| | | | | | | | | | | | | | | | | | | | | | | | | – | – | – | – | |
| **v. Oxford UCCE** (The Parks) 23-25 May | | 28.5-9-56-5 | | | | | 16-6-50-3 | 20-5-49-0 | | | | | 7-1-14-1 | | | | 10-0-28-1 | | | | | | | 81.5 | 205 | 8 | 10 | |
| | | 28.1-10-44-4 | | 3-2-2-1 | | | 15-4-45-0 | | | | | | 1-0-5-0 | | | | 2-0-6-0 | | | | | | | 69.1 | 165 | 2 | 10 | |
| **v. Nottinghamshire** (Oakham School) 30 May-2 June | | 7-2-18-0 | 6-1-24-0 | | 9-1-32-2 | 5-1-26-1 | | | | | | | | | | | | | | | | | | 27 | 102 | 2 | 3 | |
| | | 9-1-55-1 | 18-4-70-4 | 18.4-4-48-0 | 11-2-38-0 | 10-1-62-1 | | | | | 24-1-76-2 | | | | | | | | | | | | | 91 | 363 | 14 | 8 | |
| **v. Somerset** (Taunton) 6-9 June | 28-4-100-3 | | | 24-1-142-2 | 14-0-131-0 | 19-0-60-0 | | | | 23-0-120-0 | | 1-1-0-0 | | 11-0-65-0 | | | | | | | | 2-0-13-0 | | 122.4 | 675 | 14 | 5 | |
| | | | | | | | | | | | | | | | | | | | | | | | | – | – | – | – | |
| **v. Northamptonshire** (Northampton) 15-18 June | 28.1-13-59-5 | 6-1-21-0 | | 27-3-102-3 | 12-1-57-2 | 2-1-4-0 | | | | | | | | | | | | | | | | | | 76.1 | 251 | 8 | 10 | |
| | 14-2-62-2 | 5-1-10-0 | | 7-2-9-1 | 13-1-47-3 | 8-2-38-1 | | | | | | | | | | | | | | | | | | 47 | 171 | 5 | 7 | |
| **v. Glamorgan** (Leicester) 8-11 July | 22.3-5-44-4 | | | | 15-4-29-0 | 21-3-66-3 | 8-0-50-1 | | | 18-3-65-0 | | | 5.5-1-8-1 | | | | | | | | | | | 90.2 | 268 | 6 | 10 | 1 |
| | 16.1-5-34-3 | | | | 11-3-22-1 | 21-6-62-5 | 8-2-38-0 | | | 20-5-74-1 | | | | | | | | | | | | | | 76.1 | 236 | 6 | 10 | |
| **v. Middlesex** (Leicester) 20-23 July | 4.4-1-10-0 | | | 5-1-23-1 | | | | | | | | | | | | | | | | | | | | 9.4 | 34 | 1 | 1 | |
| | | | | | | | | | | | | | | | | | | | | | | | | – | – | – | – | |
| **v. Derbyshire** (Leicester) 9-12 August | 19-7-42-5 | | | 14-1-49-3 | | | | 11-1-53-2 | 10-2-40-0 | | | | | | | | | | | | | | | 54 | 194 | 10 | 10 | |
| | 22.2-5-73-2 | | | 24-4-67-5 | 7-1-18-0 | | | 12-3-73-1 | 13-1-59-1 | 15-2-84-1 | | | | | | | | | | | | | | 93.2 | 396 | 22 | 10 | |
| **v. Essex** (Colchester) 22-25 August | 14.3-2-40-4 | 12-1-31-0 | | 7-3-18-0 | 5-0-21-1 | | | | 16-3-77-5 | | | | | | | | | | | | | | | 54.3 | 191 | 4 | 10 | |
| | | | | | | | | | | | | | 5-0-64-0 | | | | | 7-0-77-0 | | 2-0-9-0 | | | | 14 | 151 | 1 | 0 | |
| **v. Gloucestershire** (Leicester) 30 August-1 September | 36-7-102-2 | 48-5-193-0 | | | 22-4-64-1 | | | 17-1-113-0 | 33-4-144-2 | | | | 5.1-1-18-2 | | | | | | | | | | | 161.1 | 650 | 16 | 8 | 1 |
| | | | | | | | | | | | | | | | | | | | | | | | | – | – | – | – | |
| **v. Northamptonshire** (Leicester) 5-8 September | | 15-5-24-0 | | | | | 12-4-37-2 | | | 21.2-7-60-5 | | | 7-1-27-1 | | 22-4-89-1 | | | 3-2-7-0 | 5-0-33-0 | | | | 3-0-17-0 | 88.2 | 310 | 16 | 10 | 1 |
| | | 36-11-96-1 | | | | | 7-2-19-0 | | | 22-7-94-3 | | | 10-1-59-1 | | 14-1-84-1 | | | | 13-0-65-0 | | | | 6-0-27-0 | 108 | 459 | 15 | 6 | |
| **v. Middlesex** (Southgate) 11-14 September | 16-7-30-1 | 16-3-52-1 | | | 7-1-25-0 | | | | | 8-2-21-0 | 17-5-35-6 | | | | | | | 19-3-58-1 | 2-0-5-1 | | | | | 64 | 176 | 8 | 10 | |
| | 20-9-43-0 | 43.3-15-80-5 | | | | | | | | 14-2-54-3 | 16-3-76-0 | | | | | | | | | | | | | 114.3 | 331 | 15 | 10 | |

| | DD Masters | CW Henderson | SCJ Broad | NGE Walker | J Allenby | GJP Kruger | DT Rowe | RAG Cummins | JE Taylor | Mansoor Amjad | RP Singh | CK Langeveldt | TJ New | HF Gurney | JK Maunders | DDJ Robinson | JHK Naik | JL Sadler | SJ Cliff | PA Nixon | MC Rosenberg | A Jacobs | JJ Cobb |
|---|---|---|---|---|---|---|---|---|---|---|---|---|---|---|---|---|---|---|---|---|---|---|---|
| Overs | 327.4 | 352.3 | 141 | 171 | 210.2 | 85 | 89 | 148.2 | 72 | 161.2 | 60.4 | 101.4 | 28.1 | 36 | 49.5 | 8 | 19 | 14 | 28 | 2 | 9.2 | 2 | 9 |
| Maidens | 89 | 79 | 19 | 27 | 43 | 16 | 16 | 34 | 14 | 17 | 14 | 27 | 4 | 5 | 4 | 0 | 3 | 2 | 0 | 0 | 1 | 0 | 0 |
| Runs | 924 | 1035 | 526 | 777 | 662 | 324 | 427 | 512 | 287 | 645 | 250 | 295 | 168 | 173 | 203 | 50 | 58 | 95 | 16 | 9 | 45 | 13 | 44 |
| Wickets | 41 | 26 | 19 | 18 | 15 | 13 | 13 | 12 | 12 | 8 | 8 | 8 | 4 | 2 | 2 | 1 | 1 | 1 | 0 | 0 | 0 | 0 | 0 |
| Average | 22.53 | 39.80 | 27.68 | 43.16 | 44.13 | 24.92 | 32.84 | 39.38 | 23.91 | 53.75 | 31.25 | 36.87 | 42.00 | 86.50 | 101.5 | 50.00 | 50.00 | 58.00 | 95.00 | 126.0 | – | – | – |

## FIELDING

| | |
|---|---|
| 37 | PA Nixon (36 ct, 1 st) |
| 20 | TJ New (19 ct, 1 st) |
| 15 | HD Ackerman |
| 15 | J Allenby |
| 12 | JK Maunders |
| 7 | JL Sadler |
| 6 | Mansoor Amjad |
| 5 | DDJ Robinson |
| 5 | A Jacobs |
| 4 | NGE Walker |
| 3 | CW Henderson |
| 2 | JHK Naik |
| 2 | RAG Cummins |
| 2 | MC Rosenberg |
| 2 | RP Singh |
| 1 | DD Masters |
| 1 | GJP Kruger |
| 1 | PW Harrison |
| 0 | CK Langeveldt |
| 0 | MAG Boyce |
| 0 | SCJ Broad |
| 0 | DT Rowe |
| 0 | JE Taylor |
| 0 | SJ Cliff |
| 0 | JJ Cobb |
| 0 | HF Gurney |

Limited overs nickname:
**LEICESTERSHIRE FOXES**

### Final Division Two Table

| | P | W | L | D | T | Ab | Bat | Bowl | Pens | Pts |
|---|---|---|---|---|---|---|---|---|---|---|
| **Somerset** | 16 | 10 | 1 | 5 | 0 | 0 | 65 | 41 | 0.00 | 266.00 |
| **Nottinghamshire** | 16 | 6 | 3 | 7 | 0 | 0 | 60 | 43 | 0.50 | 214.50 |
| **Middlesex** | 16 | 6 | 2 | 8 | 0 | 0 | 35 | 43 | 1.50 | 192.50 |
| **Essex** | 16 | 6 | 4 | 6 | 0 | 0 | 40 | 36 | 2.00 | 182.00 |
| **Northamptonshire** | 16 | 5 | 5 | 6 | 0 | 0 | 44 | 38 | 0.00 | 176.00 |
| **Derbyshire** | 16 | 3 | 5 | 8 | 0 | 0 | 30 | 44 | 1.00 | 147.00 |
| **Gloucestershire** | 16 | 3 | 5 | 8 | 0 | 0 | 32 | 37 | 3.50 | 139.50 |
| **Leicestershire** | 16 | 2 | 8 | 5 | 0 | 1 | 32 | 35 | 4.00 | 115.00 |
| **Glamorgan** | 16 | 1 | 9 | 5 | 0 | 1 | 26 | 37 | 8.50 | 92.50 |

Glamorgan had eight points deducted for a poor pitch.

# MIDDLESEX CCC

## FIRST-CLASS MATCHES
### BATTING

| Match | ET Smith | BA Godleman | EC Joyce | TJ Murtagh | A Richardson | JWM Dalrymple | M Kartik | BJM Scott | CEW Silverwood | OA Shah | NRD Compton | DC Nash | WPUJC Vaas | AJ Strauss | EJG Morgan | BL Hutton | RL Johnson | D Evans | ST Finn | CT Peploe | CJC Wright | REM Williams | CD Whelan | Extras | Total | Wickets | Result | Points |
|---|---|---|---|---|---|---|---|---|---|---|---|---|---|---|---|---|---|---|---|---|---|---|---|---|---|---|---|---|
| v. Oxford UCCE (The Parks) 14–16 April | 149* | 55 | | | | | | | | | 45* | | | | | 118 | | | | | | | | 12 | 379 | 2 | | |
| | | 55 | 26 | 5* | | 15 | | | | | | 102 | | | | 39 | | | | 7 | | | 0 | 15 | 264 | 7 | D | |
| v. Somerset (Taunton) 18–21 April | 68 | 113* | | | | | | | | 193 | 67 | 100* | | 17 | | | | | | | | | | 42 | 600 | 4 | | |
| | 103* | | | | | | | | | 72* | 15 | | | 10 | | | | | | | | | | 9 | 209 | 2 | D | 10 |
| v. Northamptonshire (Lord's) 25–28 April | 25 | 77 | 40 | 0* | | 25 | | 4 | | 41 | 12 | 10 | | | | 6 | 0 | | | | | | | 18 | 258 | 10 | | |
| | 38 | 40 | 34 | 0 | | 5 | | 30 | | 24 | 8 | 103* | | | | 37 | 9 | | | | | | | 34 | 362 | 10 | W | 19 |
| v. Nottinghamshire (Trent Bridge) 9–12 May | 38 | 6 | 36 | 5 | 0 | 8 | | 0* | 29 | | | | 4 | | | | | | | | | | | 29 | 176 | 10 | | |
| | | 80 | 1* | | | | | | 21* | | | | | 120 | | | | | | | | | | 21 | 243 | 2 | D | 7 |
| v. Derbyshire (Derby) 16–19 May | 28 | 23 | 21 | 1 | 9 | 2 | | 10 | | 51 | 21 | 56* | | | 10 | | | | | | | | | 16 | 248 | 10 | | |
| | 1 | 57 | 8 | 2 | 2 | 4 | | 14 | | 30 | 6 | 10 | | | 32* | | | | | | | | | 14 | 180 | 10 | D | 8 |
| v. Glamorgan (Swansea) 23–24 May | 29 | 15 | 58 | 9 | 0 | | | | 25* | 15 | 29 | 10 | | | | | | | | 13 | 3 | | | 15 | 221 | 10 | | |
| | | | | | | | | | | | | | | | | | | | | | | | | | | | W | 18 |
| v. Somerset (Lord's) 30 May–2 June | 4 | 45 | 42 | 36* | 15 | 7 | | 16 | 8 | 47 | 8 | | | | | | | | | | 12 | | | 12 | 252 | 10 | | |
| | 1* | 31 | 45* | | | | | | 28 | 21 | | | | | | | | | | | | | | 12 | 138 | 3 | W | 18 |
| v. Essex (Lord's) 15–18 June | 49 | 28 | 0 | 5 | | 1 | 7 | 30* | 0 | 22 | 5 | | 5 | | | | | | | | | | | 25 | 177 | 10 | | |
| | 30 | 68 | 23 | | 48 | | | 11* | | 131 | 11 | | 18* | | | | | | | | | | | 20 | 360 | 10 | D | 7 |
| v. Derbyshire (Southgate) 8–11 July | 26 | 11 | 81 | 35 | 6* | 9 | 0 | 4 | 2 | | 24 | | | | 38 | | | | | | | | | 22 | 258 | 10 | | |
| | 65 | 1 | 32 | 4 | 19 | 48* | 2 | 0 | 4 | | 26 | | | | 53 | | | | | | | | | 12 | 266 | 10 | L | 5 |
| v. Leicestershire (Leicester) 20–23 July | | 7* | | | | | | | 23* | | 1 | | | | | | | | | | | | | 3 | 34 | 1 | | |
| | | | | | | | | | | | | | | | | | | | | | | | | | | | D | 5 |
| v. Glamorgan (Lord's) 31 July–2 August | 16 | 38 | 51 | 2 | 0* | 1 | | 65 | 5 | 24 | 67 | | 79 | | | | | | | | | | | 13 | 361 | 10 | | |
| | | | | | | | | | | | | | | | | | | | | | | | | | | | W | 21 |
| v. Northamptonshire (Northampton) 14–17 August | 15 | 106 | | | | 13 | 17* | 1 | | 189* | 9 | | 28 | 0 | | | | | | | | | | 22 | 400 | 7 | | |
| | | | | | | | | | | | | | | | | | | | | | | | | | | | D | 12 |
| v. Gloucestershire (Lord's) 22–25 August | 69 | | 33 | 16 | 0 | | 35* | 0 | | | 11 | | 44* | 75 | | | | | | | | | | 22 | 305 | 7 | | |
| | 56* | | | | 27* | | | | | | 1 | | | 36 | | | | | | | | | | 1 | 121 | 2 | D | 10 |
| v. Nottinghamshire (Lord's) 29 August–1 September | 122 | 30 | 19 | 20 | 24* | 43 | 35 | 20 | | | | 37 | 16 | 72 | | | | | | | | | | 34 | 472 | 10 | | |
| | | | | | | | | | | | | | | | | | | | | | | | | | | | D | 12 |
| v. Gloucestershire (Bristol) 5–7 September | 111 | 5 | 8 | 32 | 15 | | 10 | 112 | | | | | 32 | | 76 | | 0 | 1* | | | | | | 38 | 440 | 10 | | |
| | | | | | | | | | | | | | | | | | | | | | | | | | | | W | 22 |
| v. Leicestershire (Southgate) 11–14 September | 5 | 3 | 74 | 0 | | 17 | 14 | 35 | | | | | 11 | 0 | | | 0 | 0* | | | | | | 17 | 176 | 10 | | |
| | 134 | 37 | 19 | 9 | | 57 | 17 | 4 | | | | | 23 | 1 | | | 0* | 0 | | | | | | 30 | 331 | 10 | W | 17 |
| v. Essex (Chelmsford) 19–21 September | 24 | 0 | 9 | | 0 | | 30 | 61* | | | | | 11 | 7 | | | | 7 | 0 | | | 15 | | 7 | 171 | 10 | | |
| | 13 | 17 | 38 | | 21 | | 11* | 31 | | | | | 7 | 71 | | | | 0 | 3 | | | 6 | | 28 | 246 | 10 | L | 3 |

| | ET Smith | BA Godleman | EC Joyce | TJ Murtagh | A Richardson | JWM Dalrymple | M Kartik | BJM Scott | CEW Silverwood | OA Shah | NRD Compton | DC Nash | WPUJC Vaas | AJ Strauss | EJG Morgan | BL Hutton | RL Johnson | D Evans | ST Finn | CT Peploe | CJC Wright | REM Williams | CD Whelan |
|---|---|---|---|---|---|---|---|---|---|---|---|---|---|---|---|---|---|---|---|---|---|---|---|
| Matches | 17 | 15 | 14 | 14 | 14 | 12 | 12 | 11 | 11 | 10 | 10 | 7 | 7 | 7 | 5 | 4 | 4 | 4 | 3 | 2 | 2 | 1 | 1 |
| Innings | 25 | 24 | 20 | 16 | 13 | 17 | 15 | 14 | 10 | 16 | 16 | 10 | 8 | 12 | 7 | 7 | 4 | 5 | 5 | 2 | 2 | 2 | 1 |
| Not Out | 4 | 2 | 2 | 1 | 5 | 2 | 4 | 3 | 1 | 4 | 0 | 3 | 3 | 0 | 0 | 1 | 0 | 1 | 2 | 0 | 0 | 0 | 0 |
| Highest Score | 149* | 113* | 106 | 40 | 24* | 57 | 35* | 112 | 30 | 193 | 67 | 103* | 79 | 120 | 76 | 118 | 39 | 7 | 3 | 13 | 12 | 15 | 0 |
| Runs | 1219 | 842 | 704 | 267 | 104 | 305 | 209 | 389 | 110 | 870 | 385 | 426 | 277 | 426 | 227 | 230 | 48 | 7 | 4 | 20 | 15 | 21 | 0 |
| Average | 58.04 | 38.27 | 39.11 | 17.80 | 13.00 | 20.33 | 19.00 | 35.36 | 12.22 | 72.50 | 24.06 | 60.85 | 55.40 | 35.50 | 32.42 | 38.33 | 12.00 | 1.75 | 1.33 | 10.00 | 7.50 | 10.50 | 0.00 |
| 100s | 5 | 1 | 1 | 0 | 0 | 0 | 0 | 1 | 0 | 3 | 0 | 1 | 0 | 1 | 0 | 1 | 0 | 0 | 0 | 0 | 0 | 0 | 0 |
| 50s | 4 | 6 | 4 | 0 | 0 | 1 | 0 | 2 | 0 | 1 | 3 | 0 | 2 | 3 | 0 | 0 | 0 | 0 | 0 | 0 | 0 | 0 | 0 |
| Catches/Stumpings | 9/0 | 22/0 | 5/0 | 2/0 | 5/0 | 3/0 | 12/0 | 23/5 | 2/0 | 6/0 | 6/0 | 20/2 | 2/0 | 7/0 | 4/0 | 4/0 | 1/0 | 1/0 | 2/0 | 0/0 | 0/0 | 0/0 | 0/0 |

**Home Ground:** Lord's
**Address:** Lord's Cricket Ground, London, NW8 8QN
**Tel:** 0207 289 1300
**Fax:** 0207 289 5831
**Email:** enquiries@middlesexccc.com
**Directions:** *By underground:* St John's Wood on Jubilee Line. *By bus:* 13, 82, 113 stop along east side of ground; 139 at south-west corner; 274 at top of Regent's Park.
**Capacity:** 28,000

**Other grounds used:** Southgate, Uxbridge, Richmond
**Year formed:** 1864

**Chief Executive:** Vinny Codrington
**Head Coach:** John Emburey
**Captain:** Ed Smith
**County colours:** Navy blue

Website:
www.middlesexccc.com

**Honours**
County Championship
1903, 1920, 1921, 1947, 1976, 1980, 1982, 1985, 1990, 1993. Joint champions 1949, 1977
Sunday League/NCL/Pro40 1992
Benson & Hedges Cup 1983, 1986
Gillette Cup/NatWest/C&G Trophy 1977, 1980, 1984, 1988, 1989

## FIRST-CLASS MATCHES
# BOWLING

| Match | M Kartik | A Richardson | TJ Murtagh | CEW Silverwood | WPUJC Vaas | JWM Dalrymple | ST Finn | RL Johnson | CT Peploe | REM Williams | D Evans | CD Whelan | CJC Wright | EJG Morgan | AJ Strauss | OA Shah | ET Smith | BL Hutton | EC Joyce | NRD Compton | BA Godleman | Overs | Total | Byes/Leg-byes | Wickets | Run outs |
|---|---|---|---|---|---|---|---|---|---|---|---|---|---|---|---|---|---|---|---|---|---|---|---|---|---|---|
| v. Oxford UCCE (The Parks) 14–16 April | 12-2-26-1 | 12-3-34-4 | 14-1-48-2 | | | | | 15-4-27-1 | 4-2-10-0 | | | | 5.1-1-13-2 | | | | | | | | | 62.1 | 179 | 21 | 10 | |
| | 5-0-19-0 | 6-1-25-1 | 5-1-18-0 | | | | | 5-1-19-1 | 4-1-20-0 | | | | 4-0-18-2 | | | | | | | | | 29 | 122 | 3 | 4 | |
| v. Somerset (Taunton) 18–21 April | 50-8-168-4 | 26-0-127-0 | 25-1-147-1 | 30-4-125-2 | | | | 27.3-1-142-0 | | | | | | | | 16-0-90-0 | | | | 4-0-20-0 | | 178.3 | 850 | 31 | 7 | |
| v. Northamptonshire (Lord's) 25–28 April | 5-2-13-1 | 13-2-44-4 | 7-2-17-1 | 13-1-55-2 | | | | 13.4-2-49-2 | | | | | | | | | | | | | | 51.4 | 211 | 13 | 10 | |
| | 28-6-76-3 | 20-4-55-4 | 7-3-13-0 | 19-3-55-2 | | | | 13-1-45-1 | | | | | | | | | | | | | | 87 | 255 | 11 | 10 | |
| v. Nottinghamshire (Trent Bridge) 9–12 May | 4-1-11-0 | 32.5-9-80-2 | 38-16-87-6 | | | 14-2-47-1 | | 22-1-82-1 | | | | | | | | | | | | 3-0-18-0 | | 113.5 | 336 | 11 | 10 | |
| v. Derbyshire (Derby) 16–19 May | | 23-9-50-5 | 1.5-0-1-0 | 22.1-6-65-3 | 20.2-5-49-2 | | 9-1-34-0 | | | | | | | | 4-1-21-0 | | | | | | | 80.2 | 225 | 5 | 10 | |
| | | 7-4-4-0 | | 6-1-10-0 | 8-3-14-1 | | 4-0-10-0 | | | | | | | | 4-1-7-0 | | | | | | | 29 | 53 | 8 | 1 | |
| v. Glamorgan (Swansea) 23–24 May | | 11-7-7-4 | | 11-3-23-2 | | | | 4-0-7-2 | | | | 8-2-21-2 | | | | | | | | | | 34 | 60 | 2 | 10 | |
| | | 13.5-6-23-4 | | 7-2-10-0 | | 19-3-44-2 | | 21-5-58-3 | | | | 5-2-7-0 | | | | | | | | | | 65.5 | 159 | 17 | 10 | 1 |
| v. Somerset (Lord's) 30 May–2 June | | 7-3-11-2 | 6-3-16-2 | 10.3-6-13-3 | | | | | | | | 3-1-7-1 | | | | | | | | | | 26.3 | 50 | 3 | 8 | |
| | | 12.5-3-46-1 | 22.5-5-105-3 | 21-7-49-6 | | 16-2-42-0 | | | | | | 12-0-72-0 | | | | 3.1-0-11-0 | | | | | | 87.5 | 339 | 14 | 10 | |
| v. Essex (Lord's) 15–18 June | 41.4-12-93-3 | | 3.2-1-18-0 | 24-5-81-3 | 24.4-7-79-4 | | 12-1-54-0 | | | | | | | | | 1-0-7-0 | | 8-1-30-0 | | | | 114.4 | 376 | | 14 | |
| v. Derbyshire (Southgate) 8–11 July | 26.5-2-108-2 | 17-4-44-2 | 12-7-22-1 | 14-2-47-1 | | | | 24-3-91-3 | | | | | | | | | | | | | | 93.5 | 340 | 28 | 10 | 1 |
| | 25.2-4-38-5 | 21-4-56-2 | 12-2-41-2 | 8-2-45-1 | | | 4-1-18-0 | | | | | | | | | | | | | | | 70.2 | 199 | 1 | 10 | |
| v. Leicestershire (Leicester) 20–23 July | | 21-2-82-1 | 12-3-66-2 | 20-3-95-0 | 15-2-87-1 | | 14-1-43-1 | | | | | | | | 9-3-28-0 | | | | | | | 91 | 403 | 2 | 5 | |
| v. Glamorgan (Lord's) 31 July–2 August | 13.5-5-21-6 | 12-5-15-0 | 8-4-10-1 | 11-2-42-2 | 9-2-15-1 | | | | | | | | | | | | | | | | | 53.5 | 106 | 3 | 10 | |
| | 18-5-52-3 | 14.1-4-45-2 | 10-3-24-2 | 12-2-34-2 | 9-3-17-1 | | | | | | | | | | | 1-0-1-0 | | | | | | 64.1 | 184 | 11 | 10 | |
| v. Northamptonshire (Northampton) 14–17 August | 31-8-76-2 | 14.4-2-56-2 | | 13-1-60-0 | 11-2-45-2 | | 22-3-86-3 | | | | | | | | | | | | | | | 91.4 | 335 | 12 | 9 | |
| v. Gloucestershire (Lord's) 22–25 August | 13-4-41-4 | 11.5-2-42-1 | 6-2-16-1 | | 12-0-48-2 | 2-0-5-0 | | | | | 2-1-5-1 | | | | | | | | | | | 46.5 | 163 | 6 | 10 | 1 |
| | 19-6-60-1 | 13.5-3-34-2 | 3-0-26-0 | | 5-0-10-0 | 7.3-1-16-0 | | | | | 3-1-6-0 | | | | | | | | | | | 50.3 | 158 | 6 | 3 | |
| v. Nottinghamshire (Lord's) 29 August–1 September | 30-5-104-1 | 19-7-45-1 | 29.1-3-134-3 | | 29-3-126-5 | | 15-1-44-0 | | | | | | 8-2-24-2 | 6-0-16-1 | | 1-1-0-0 | | | | 5-0-29-0 | 5-1-35-0 | 122.1 | 473 | 20 | 10 | |
| | 30-6-82-2 | 13-1-57-1 | 14-3-77-0 | | 19-3-62-1 | | 10-1-54-0 | | | | | | | | | | | | | | | 111 | 456 | 10 | 7 | |
| v. Gloucestershire (Bristol) 5–7 September | 15-4-26-1 | 11-4-29-1 | 11.4-3-36-4 | | | | 8-1-21-1 | | | | 10-3-31-3 | | | | 1-0-4-0 | | | | | | | 55.4 | 152 | 9 | 10 | |
| | 26-9-57-4 | 6-0-20-0 | 12-3-39-2 | | | | 12.5-2-51-4 | | | | 10-2-24-0 | | | | | | | | | | | 67.5 | 199 | 4 | 10 | |
| v. Leicestershire (Southgate) 11–14 September | 28.5-6-85-6 | | 19-7-36-3 | | | | 5-1-5-0 | | | | 13-2-37-1 | 4-0-20-0 | | | | | | | | | | 69.5 | 190 | 7 | 10 | |
| | 39-10-83-3 | | 18.3-4-54-3 | | | | 16-2-61-2 | | | | 11-3-50-1 | 6-2-23-1 | | | | | | | | | | 90.3 | 279 | 8 | 10 | |
| v. Essex (Chelmsford) 19–21 September | 20-2-79-0 | | | | | | 5-0-25-0 | | | 22-5-61-4 | 16-4-51-0 | | | | | | | | | 4-0-26-0 | | 95.4 | 365 | 11 | 10 | |
| | | | | | | | 6-0-19-0 | | | 28.4-4-112-5 | 6-3-14-0 | 3-1-9-0 | | | 2.1-0-4-0 | | | | | | | 17.1 | 53 | 7 | 0 | |

| | M Kartik | A Richardson | TJ Murtagh | CEW Silverwood | WPUJC Vaas | JWM Dalrymple | ST Finn | RL Johnson | CT Peploe | REM Williams | D Evans | CD Whelan | CJC Wright | EJG Morgan | AJ Strauss | OA Shah | ET Smith | BL Hutton | EC Joyce | NRD Compton | BA Godleman |
|---|---|---|---|---|---|---|---|---|---|---|---|---|---|---|---|---|---|---|---|---|---|
| Overs | 464.3 | 357.1 | 296.2 | 260.4 | 162 | 198.3 | 72.5 | 96.1 | 33 | 34.4 | 54 | 9.1 | 28 | 11.1 | 6 | 30.1 | 1 | 8 | 20 | 4 | 5 |
| Maidens | 109 | 89 | 79 | 52 | 30 | 23 | 13 | 10 | 8 | 7 | 14 | 1 | 5 | 2 | 0 | 3 | 1 | 2 | 1 | 0 | 1 |
| Runs | 1273 | 1017 | 1044 | 875 | 552 | 689 | 239 | 384 | 95 | 126 | 169 | 31 | 107 | 32 | 16 | 137 | 0 | 28 | 103 | 20 | 35 |
| Wickets | 51 | 42 | 42 | 31 | 20 | 12 | 11 | 6 | 5 | 5 | 5 | 4 | 3 | 2 | 1 | 0 | 0 | 0 | 0 | 0 | 0 |
| Average | 24.96 | 24.21 | 24.85 | 28.22 | 27.60 | 57.41 | 21.72 | 64.00 | 19.00 | 25.20 | 33.80 | 7.75 | 35.66 | 16.00 | 16.00 | – | – | – | – | – | – |

## FIELDING

| | |
|---|---|
| 28 | BJM Scott (23 ct, 5 st) |
| 22 | DC Nash (20 ct, 2 st) |
| 22 | BA Godleman |
| 12 | M Kartik |
| 9 | ET Smith |
| 7 | AJ Strauss |
| 6 | OA Shah |
| 6 | NRD Compton |
| 5 | A Richardson |
| 5 | EC Joyce |
| 4 | BL Hutton |
| 4 | EJG Morgan |
| 3 | JWM Dalrymple |
| 2 | CEW Silverwood |
| 2 | WPUJC Vaas |
| 2 | TJ Murtagh |
| 2 | CT Peploe |
| 1 | RL Johnson |
| 1 | D Evans |
| 0 | CD Whelan |
| 0 | CJC Wright |
| 0 | ST Finn |
| 0 | REM Williams |

### Final Division Two Table

| | P | W | L | D | T | Ab | Bat | Bowl | Pens | Pts |
|---|---|---|---|---|---|---|---|---|---|---|
| Somerset | 16 | 10 | 1 | 5 | 0 | 0 | 65 | 41 | 0.00 | 266.00 |
| Nottinghamshire | 16 | 6 | 3 | 7 | 0 | 0 | 60 | 43 | 0.50 | 214.50 |
| Middlesex | 16 | 6 | 2 | 8 | 0 | 0 | 35 | 43 | 1.50 | 192.50 |
| Essex | 16 | 6 | 4 | 6 | 0 | 0 | 40 | 36 | 2.00 | 182.00 |
| Northamptonshire | 16 | 5 | 5 | 6 | 0 | 0 | 44 | 38 | 0.00 | 176.00 |
| Derbyshire | 16 | 3 | 5 | 8 | 0 | 0 | 30 | 44 | 1.00 | 147.00 |
| Gloucestershire | 16 | 3 | 5 | 8 | 0 | 0 | 32 | 37 | 3.50 | 139.50 |
| Leicestershire | 16 | 2 | 8 | 5 | 0 | 1 | 32 | 35 | 4.00 | 115.00 |
| Glamorgan | 16 | 1 | 9 | 5 | 0 | 1 | 26 | 37 | 8.50 | 92.50 |

Glamorgan had eight points deducted for a poor pitch.

crusaders

Limited overs nickname:
MIDDLESEX CRUSADERS

# NORTHAMPTONSHIRE CCC

## FIRST-CLASS MATCHES
### BATTING

| | DJG Sales | L Klusener | SD Peters | JF Brown | RA White | MH Wessels | JJ van der Wath | SP Crook | DH Wigley | DS Lucas | U Afzaal | CJL Rogers | NJ O'Brien | RJ Logan | AR Crook | MS Panesar | N Boje | AG Wakely | DJ Jacobs | GG White | RKJ Dawson | MAG Nelson | PS Coverdale | IJ Sutcliffe | Extras | Total | Wickets | Result | Points |
|---|---|---|---|---|---|---|---|---|---|---|---|---|---|---|---|---|---|---|---|---|---|---|---|---|---|---|---|---|---|
| v. Cambridge UCCE (Fenner's) 14–15 April | | | 112 | 108 | 97 | 25* | 29* | | | | | 138 | | | 0 | | | | | | | | 11 | | 57 | 577 | 6 | W | |
| v. Middlesex (Lord's) 25–28 April | 14 | 44* | 8 | 8 | 16 | 16 | 0 | 11 | 23 | | 39 | 12 | | | | | | | | | | | | | 20 | 211 | 10 | | |
| | 81 | 25 | 0 | 4 | 8 | 58 | 5 | 8* | 4 | | 16 | 20 | | | | | | | | | | | | | 26 | 255 | 10 | L | 4 |
| v. Essex (Northampton) 2–5 May | 35 | 8 | 39 | 0* | | 0 | 94 | 53 | 53 | | 66 | 3 | | | 33 | | | | | | | | | | 32 | 416 | 10 | | |
| | 37 | 12* | 5 | | | 0 | | | | 39 | | 13* | | | | | | | | | | | | | 4 | 110 | 4 | W | 22 |
| v. Somerset (Northampton) 8–11 May | 150* | 36 | 2 | | 45 | 45 | 53* | 11 | | | | 4 | | | | | | | 32 | | | | | | 22 | 400 | 7 | | |
| | 18* | | 4 | | 7* | | | | | | | | | | | | | | 3 | | | | | | 0 | 32 | 2 | D | 9 |
| v. Derbyshire (Northampton) 23–26 May | 4 | 32 | 107 | 0 | 7 | 2 | 33 | | | 0 | 54 | 49* | | | | | | | 56 | | | | | | 21 | 365 | 10 | | |
| | 2 | 28* | | | 43* | | | | | 0 | 4 | | | | | | | | 1 | | | | | | 2 | 80 | 4 | W | 21 |
| v. Gloucestershire (Gloucester) 1–4 June | 4 | 96 | 31 | 0 | | 25 | 1 | 5* | | | 24 | 2 | | | 20 | | | | 4 | | | | | | 11 | 223 | 10 | | |
| | 99 | 111 | 46 | 35 | | 9 | 2 | 1* | | | 37 | 18 | | | 0 | | | | 27 | | | | | | 26 | 411 | 10 | L | 4 |
| v. Essex (Chelmsford) 6–9 June | 23 | 70* | 10 | 0 | 6 | | 0 | | | 12 | 73 | 0 | | | 20 | | | | 4 | | 26 | | | | 17 | 241 | 10 | | |
| | 67 | 25 | 93 | 7 | 14 | | 49 | | | 9* | 32 | 20 | | | | | | | 16 | | 7 | | | | 28 | 367 | 10 | L | 1 |
| v. Leicestershire (Northampton) 15–18 June | 92 | 7 | 1 | 6 | | 40 | 8 | 49 | | 31* | 0 | 4 | | | | | | | | | 4 | | | | 9 | 251 | 10 | | |
| | 22 | 50 | 26 | | | 20 | 5 | 23* | | | 1 | 7 | | | | | | | | | 8* | | | | 9 | 171 | 7 | D | 7 |
| v. Gloucestershire (Northampton) 8–11 July | 10 | 40 | 55 | 25 | | 57 | 4 | 5 | | 32* | 66 | 4 | | | 0 | | | | | | | | | | 13 | 310 | 10 | | |
| | 22 | 9 | 92 | 6* | | 22 | 15 | 5 | | 0 | 72 | 15 | | | 0 | | | | | | | | | | 12 | 270 | 10 | W | 20 |
| v. Somerset (Taunton) 13–16 July | 17 | 0 | 25 | 8 | | 37 | 5 | 60 | | 10* | 9 | | | | | | | 38 | | | | | | | 11 | 221 | 10 | | |
| | 12 | 122 | 1 | 0* | | 28 | 37 | 6 | | 4 | 46 | 0 | | | | | | 66 | | | | | | | 36 | 358 | 10 | L | 4 |
| v. Nottinghamshire (Northampton) 26–29 July | 59 | 0 | 54 | 3 | 46 | 32 | 59* | | | 33 | | 7 | | 4 | | | | 55 | | | | | | | 14 | 366 | 10 | | |
| | 1 | 8 | | | 74* | | | | | | | 58* | | | | | | 0 | | | | | | | 11 | 152 | 3 | D | 11 |
| v. Glamorgan (Colwyn Bay) 8–11 August | 219 | 6 | 25 | 8* | 6 | 1 | | | | 18 | 8 | 1 | | | | | | | | 65 | | | | 9 | 21 | 387 | 10 | | |
| | 1* | | 2 | | 45* | | | | | | 69 | | | | | | | | | | | | | | 14 | 131 | 2 | D | 10 |
| v. Middlesex (Northampton) 14–17 August | 8 | 89 | 4 | | 43 | 27 | | | 70 | | | 51 | | 0* | | | | | | 6 | | 13 | | | 24 | 335 | 9 | D | 9 |
| v. Nottinghamshire (Trent Bridge) 22–25 August | 57 | 0 | 43 | 0* | 71 | 27 | | 25 | 11 | | | | | | 10 | 70 | 7 | | | | | | | | 7 | 285 | 10 | | |
| | 22 | 34 | 43 | 10 | 19 | | | 29* | 13 | | | | | | 6 | 0 | 21 | | | | | | | | 19 | 229 | 10 | L | 5 |
| v. Leicestershire (Leicester) 5–8 September | 43 | 45 | 36 | | 23 | | | | | | 0 | 5 | 1 | | 0* | 0 | 125 | 2 | | | | | | | 30 | 310 | 10 | | |
| | 187* | 37* | 0 | | 14 | | | | | | | | 109 | | 72 | | 4 | 0 | | | | | | | 36 | 459 | 6 | W | 20 |
| v. Glamorgan (Northampton) 11–13 September | 78 | 23 | 104 | 0 | 75 | | 3 | | | | | 0 | 3* | 41 | 30 | 4 | | | | | | | | | 20 | 381 | 10 | | |
| | | | 5* | | | | | | | | | | | 0* | | | | | | | | | | | 0 | 5 | 0 | W | 21 |
| v. Derbyshire (Derby) 19–22 September | 0 | 6 | | 23* | 17 | | | | | 10 | 37 | | 0 | 8 | 40 | 37 | 7 | | | | | | | | 50 | 235 | 10 | | |
| | | 86* | | 0 | | | | | | | | | 30 | 46 | 53* | 1 | | | | | | | | | 13 | 229 | 4 | D | 8 |
| **Matches** | 16 | 16 | 16 | 14 | 13 | 11 | 10 | 10 | 10 | 9 | 8 | 8 | 8 | 7 | 5 | 5 | 4 | 4 | 4 | 3 | 3 | 1 | 1 | 1 | | | | | |
| **Innings** | 29 | 26 | 30 | 17 | 22 | 18 | 15 | 16 | 13 | 13 | 16 | 14 | 13 | 8 | 9 | 6 | 7 | 8 | 8 | 2 | 4 | 1 | 1 | 1 | | | | | |
| **Not Out** | 4 | 5 | 2 | 6 | 3 | 1 | 3 | 3 | 3 | 4 | 0 | 1 | 2 | 3 | 1 | 0 | 1 | 0 | 0 | 0 | 1 | 0 | 0 | 0 | | | | | |
| **Highest Score** | 219 | 122 | 112 | 25 | 108 | 97 | 94 | 60 | 70 | 37 | 73 | 138 | 109 | 10 | 72 | 33 | 125 | 66 | 56 | 65 | 26 | 13 | 11 | 9 | | | | | |
| **Runs** | 1384 | 1013 | 966 | 108 | 709 | 533 | 346 | 344 | 223 | 215 | 570 | 402 | 249 | 32 | 269 | 83 | 251 | 169 | 143 | 71 | 45 | 13 | 11 | 9 | | | | | |
| **Average** | 55.36 | 48.23 | 34.50 | 9.81 | 37.31 | 31.35 | 28.83 | 26.46 | 22.30 | 23.88 | 35.62 | 30.92 | 22.63 | 6.40 | 33.62 | 13.83 | 41.83 | 21.12 | 17.87 | 35.50 | 15.00 | 13.00 | 11.00 | 9.00 | | | | | |
| **100s** | 3 | 2 | 3 | 0 | 1 | 0 | 0 | 0 | 0 | 0 | 0 | 1 | 1 | 0 | 0 | 0 | 1 | 0 | 0 | 0 | 0 | 0 | 0 | 0 | | | | | |
| **50s** | 7 | 5 | 4 | 0 | 3 | 3 | 3 | 2 | 2 | 0 | 5 | 3 | 0 | 0 | 2 | 0 | 1 | 2 | 1 | 1 | 0 | 0 | 0 | 0 | | | | | |
| **Catches/Stumpings** | 23/0 | 6/0 | 14/0 | 3/0 | 9/0 | 28/2 | 3/0 | 3/0 | 6/0 | 2/0 | 3/0 | 13/0 | 23/2 | 1/0 | 4/0 | 2/0 | 1/0 | 1/0 | 2/0 | 1/0 | 2/0 | 1/0 | 0/0 | 0/0 | | | | | |

**Home Ground:** County Ground
**Address:** Abingdon Avenue, Northampton, NN1 4PR
**Tel:** 01604 514455/514444
**Fax:** 01604 514488
**Email:** commercial@nccc.co.uk
**Directions:** Junction 15 from M1 onto A508 (A45) towards Northampton. Follow the dual carriageway for approx. 3 miles. Keeping in left-hand lane, take next exit from dual carriageway marked A428 Bedford and Town Centre. Move into middle lane approaching the roundabout at bottom of slip road. Take second exit following signs for Abington/Kingsthorpe on to Rushmere Road. Follow Rushmere Road (A5095) across the junction with Billing Road and continue straight on through Abington Park to traffic lights at main junction with Wellingborough Road.
**Capacity:** 4,250
**Other grounds used:** Campbell Park, Milton Keynes, Stowe School
**Year formed:** 1878

**Chief Executive:** Mark Tagg
**First XI Manager:** David Capel
**Captain:** David Sales
**County colours:** Claret and gold

**Honours**
Benson & Hedges Cup 1980
Gillette Cup/NatWest/C&G Trophy 1976, 1992

Website: www.nccc.co.uk

# FIRST-CLASS MATCHES
## BOWLING

| Match | JJ van der Wath | DH Wigley | L Klusener | JF Brown | SP Crook | MS Panesar | DS Lucas | N Boje | RJ Logan | RKJ Dawson | AG Wakely | GG White | MAG Nelson | RA White | U Afzaal | PS Coverdale | DJG Sales | AR Crook | Overs | Total | Byes/Leg-byes | Wickets | Run outs |
|---|---|---|---|---|---|---|---|---|---|---|---|---|---|---|---|---|---|---|---|---|---|---|---|
| v. Cambridge UCCE (Fenner's) 14-15 April | 7.4-1-12-5 | | | 6-2-20-2 | | | | | 5-2-14-1 | | | | | | | 6-5-3-0 | | | 32.4 | 79 | 3 | 10 | 1 |
| | 5-1-8-0 | 7-0-30-3 | | 9-2-33-0 | | | | | 10-3-25-3 | | | 14-3-35-2 | | | | 7.1-1-36-1 | | | 52.1 | 169 | 2 | 10 | 1 |
| v. Middlesex (Lord's) 25-28 April | 18.3-6-49-6 | 16-3-52-0 | 16-2-59-2 | 16-6-29-1 | 15-2-58-1 | | | | | | | | | | | | | | 81.3 | 258 | 11 | 10 | |
| | 26-7-102-3 | 19-3-65-3 | 13-5-21-1 | 30-12-54-2 | 25-5-91-0 | | | | | | | | | | 2-0-5-0 | | | | 115 | 362 | 24 | 10 | 1 |
| v. Essex (Northampton) 2-5 May | 3-1-6-0 | 15.5-1-91-2 | 25-9-54-2 | 25-8-50-1 | 18-4-58-4 | 18-2-72-1 | | | | | | | | | | | | | 104.5 | 334 | 5 | 10 | |
| | 11-4-32-1 | 4-0-27-0 | 10-2-29-1 | 13-3-40-3 | 13-4-24-1 | | | | | | | | | | | | | | 64 | 190 | 12 | 8 | |
| v. Somerset (Northampton) 8-11 May | 22-3-71-0 | | 27-7-99-1 | 39-5-184-2 | 23-3-109-0 | 32.4-3-149-3 | | | | | | | | 3-0-17-0 | | | | | 146.4 | 641 | 12 | 6 | |
| | | | | | | | | | | | | | | | | | | | – | – | – | – | |
| v. Derbyshire (Northampton) 23-26 May | 17-5-41-2 | | 7-1-41-2 | 14-6-31-1 | 7-2-10-2 | 15-6-34-3 | | | | | | | | | | | | | 60 | 160 | 3 | 10 | |
| | 23-6-67-4 | | 10.3-1-33-3 | 19-5-55-0 | 22-7-48-0 | 14-3-40-1 | | | | | | | | 6-1-35-1 | | | | | 94.3 | 283 | 5 | 10 | |
| v. Gloucestershire (Gloucester) 1-4 June | 6-1-34-1 | | 18-1-77-1 | 31-7-85-3 | | 19-1-71-3 | 35-12-84-2 | | | | | | | 11-0-37-0 | | | | | 120 | 394 | 6 | 10 | |
| | | 10-0-67-1 | 8-3-22-1 | | | 12-3-40-2 | 19-3-75-2 | | | | | | | 5-0-29-0 | 1-0-5-1 | | 1-0-3-0 | | 56 | 244 | 3 | 8 | 1 |
| v. Essex (Chelmsford) 6-9 June | | | 23-9-41-0 | 42-9-148-2 | 37-6-140-1 | | | 29-2-121-0 | 32-1-129-0 | | | | | 10-0-45-1 | | | | | 173 | 649 | 25 | 5 | |
| v. Leicestershire (Northampton) 15-18 June | 11-1-38-0 | | 8-2-25-1 | 5-0-17-0 | 8-0-23-2 | | | 10-2-22-1 | | | | | | | | | | | 42 | 131 | 6 | 4 | |
| v. Gloucestershire (Northampton) 8-11 July | 21-7-54-4 | | 9-4-24-0 | | 12-2-38-1 | 10-3-39-0 | 19.3-3-47-3 | 10-2-35-1 | | | | | | | | | | | 81.3 | 250 | 13 | 10 | 1 |
| | 17-5-50-0 | | | | 19-6-30-0 | 1.4-1-2-1 | 28-7-65-6 | 9-4-26-3 | | | | | | | | | | | 74.4 | 192 | 19 | 10 | |
| v. Somerset (Taunton) 13-16 July | 24-2-91-4 | | | 17-1-77-0 | 25-3-101-1 | 6-0-35-0 | 15-0-88-3 | | | | 13-1-62-2 | | | | | | | | 100 | 459 | 5 | 10 | |
| | 7-0-60-1 | | | | 4.5-0-38-0 | | 2-0-23-0 | | | | | | | | | | | | 13.5 | 124 | 3 | 1 | |
| v. Nottinghamshire (Northampton) 26-29 July | 21-4-90-3 | | 13-3-65-0 | | 36-3-122-3 | | 11-0-55-0 | | 12.3-0-91-2 | | 16-0-65-1 | | | 4-0-25-0 | | | | | 113.3 | 526 | 13 | 9 | |
| | | | | | | | | | | | | | | | | | | | – | – | – | – | |
| v. Glamorgan (Colwyn Bay) 8-11 August | | | 36-10-117-2 | 47.4-17-81-2 | | | 36-6-104-2 | | 31-7-90-2 | | | 20-7-42-0 | | | | | | | 170.4 | 465 | 31 | 10 | 2 |
| | | | 17-4-57-1 | 35.2-15-47-5 | | | | 9-3-23-0 | 16-2-38-3 | | | 16-8-18-1 | | | | | | | 93.2 | 197 | 14 | 10 | |
| v. Middlesex (Northampton) 14-17 August | | 23-2-83-2 | 14.3-2-51-1 | 12-1-43-0 | | | | | 30-6-102-1 | | | 12-0-47-0 | 8-1-62-2 | | | | | | 99.3 | 400 | 12 | 7 | 1 |
| v. Nottinghamshire (Trent Bridge) 22-25 August | | | 15.2-5-41-3 | 19-7-37-1 | | | 16-2-86-2 | 12-3-32-1 | 20-4-67-3 | | | | | | | | | 2-0-11-0 | 84.2 | 283 | 9 | 10 | |
| | | | 11-2-35-2 | 11-1-43-2 | 17-1-59-1 | | | 18.1-2-51-3 | 13-3-32-0 | | | | | | | | | | 70.1 | 233 | 13 | 8 | |
| v. Leicestershire (Leicester) 5-8 September | | | 13-0-71-1 | 13-1-30-1 | | | | 17-2-49-5 | 8-1-30-1 | 12.3-4-39-2 | | | | | | | | | 63.3 | 236 | 17 | 10 | |
| | | | 10-2-34-1 | 22.2-3-71-2 | | | | 5-1-25-0 | 44-8-110-6 | 18-2-49-1 | | | | | | | | 15-5-49-0 | 114.2 | 356 | 18 | 10 | |
| v. Glamorgan (Northampton) 11-13 September | | | 16-4-75-2 | 17.1-6-40-5 | 15-4-28-1 | 12-3-35-0 | | | 9-2-25-0 | 16-4-68-1 | | | | | | | | | 85.1 | 280 | 9 | 10 | 1 |
| | | | 7-3-13-3 | 6-0-18-0 | 13-3-32-1 | 12.2-1-29-4 | | | | | | | | | | | | | 39.2 | 102 | 6 | 10 | |
| v. Derbyshire (Derby) 19-22 September | | | 14-4-64-1 | 29.3-6-98-5 | 9-3-28-1 | | | 23-5-55-1 | 21-9-53-1 | 16-4-63-0 | | | | | | | | | 112.3 | 382 | 21 | 10 | 1 |
| | | | 4.2-0-10-3 | 14-2-31-0 | 9-3-22-0 | | | 10-0-39-1 | 23-4-77-2 | 4-0-17-0 | | | | | | | | | 64.2 | 208 | 12 | 7 | 1 |
| **Overs** | 240.1 | 229 | 432.3 | 453.5 | 231.4 | 189.3 | 202 | 136.1 | 189 | 47 | 29 | 62 | 8 | 39 | 3 | 13.1 | 1 | 17 | | | | | |
| **Maidens** | 54 | 33 | 107 | 113 | 44 | 38 | 29 | 29 | 36 | 6 | 1 | 18 | 1 | 1 | 0 | 6 | 0 | 5 | | | | | |
| **Runs** | 805 | 936 | 1280 | 1235 | 831 | 580 | 751 | 382 | 656 | 168 | 127 | 142 | 62 | 188 | 10 | 39 | 3 | 60 | | | | | |
| **Wickets** | 34 | 34 | 33 | 30 | 23 | 22 | 19 | 16 | 15 | 5 | 3 | 3 | 2 | 2 | 1 | 1 | 0 | 0 | | | | | |
| **Average** | 23.67 | 27.52 | 38.78 | 41.16 | 36.13 | 26.36 | 39.52 | 23.87 | 43.73 | 33.60 | 42.33 | 47.33 | 31.00 | 94.00 | 10.00 | 39.00 | – | – | | | | | |

## FIELDING

| | |
|---|---|
| 30 | MH Wessels (28 ct, 2 st) |
| 25 | NJ O'Brien (23 ct, 2 st) |
| 23 | DJG Sales |
| 14 | SD Peters |
| 13 | CJL Rogers |
| 9 | RA White |
| 6 | L Klusener |
| 6 | DH Wigley |
| 4 | AR Crook |
| 3 | U Afzaal |
| 3 | JF Brown |
| 3 | SP Crook |
| 3 | JJ van der Wath |
| 2 | DS Lucas |
| 2 | RKJ Dawson |
| 2 | MS Panesar |
| 2 | DJ Jacobs |
| 1 | N Boje |
| 1 | RJ Logan |
| 1 | AG Wakely |
| 1 | GG White |
| 1 | MAG Nelson |
| 0 | IJ Sutcliffe |
| 0 | PS Coverdale |

### Final Division Two Table

| | P | W | L | D | T | Ab | Bat | Bowl | Pens | Pts |
|---|---|---|---|---|---|---|---|---|---|---|
| Somerset | 16 | 10 | 1 | 5 | 0 | 0 | 65 | 41 | 0.00 | 266.00 |
| Nottinghamshire | 16 | 6 | 3 | 7 | 0 | 0 | 60 | 43 | 0.50 | 214.50 |
| Middlesex | 16 | 6 | 2 | 8 | 0 | 0 | 35 | 43 | 1.50 | 192.50 |
| Essex | 16 | 6 | 4 | 6 | 0 | 0 | 40 | 36 | 2.00 | 182.00 |
| Northamptonshire | 16 | 5 | 5 | 6 | 0 | 0 | 44 | 38 | 0.00 | 176.00 |
| Derbyshire | 16 | 3 | 5 | 8 | 0 | 0 | 30 | 44 | 1.00 | 147.00 |
| Gloucestershire | 16 | 3 | 5 | 8 | 0 | 0 | 32 | 37 | 3.50 | 139.50 |
| Leicestershire | 16 | 2 | 8 | 5 | 0 | 1 | 32 | 35 | 4.00 | 115.00 |
| Glamorgan | 16 | 1 | 9 | 5 | 0 | 1 | 26 | 37 | 8.50 | 92.50 |

Glamorgan had eight points deducted for a poor pitch.

Limited overs nickname:
STEELBACKS

# NOTTINGHAMSHIRE CCC

## FIRST-CLASS MATCHES
### BATTING

| Match | MA Wagh | CMW Read | JER Gallian | GP Swann | SR Patel | DJ Hussey | MA Ealham | BM Shafayat | SP Fleming | PJ Franks | CE Shreck | RJ Sidebottom | AJ Harris | WI Jefferson | AR Adams | RS Ferley | MHA Footitt | KW Hogg | SRG Francis | MN Malik | GD Clough | M Davies | Extras | Total | Wickets | Result | Points |
|---|---|---|---|---|---|---|---|---|---|---|---|---|---|---|---|---|---|---|---|---|---|---|---|---|---|---|---|
| v. Durham UCCE (Durham) 14-16 April | 6 | 15 | 73 | 9 | 3 | 0 | 9 | 38 | | | 0 | 7 | 15* | | | | | | | | | | 8 | 183 | 10 | | |
| | 51 | 65 | | 40* | 73 | 40 | 30* | 34 | | | | | | | | | | | | | | | 8 | 341 | 5 | D | |
| v. Leicestershire (Trent Bridge) 18-21 April | 74 | 36 | 150 | 46 | 6 | 105 | 2 | 0 | | 32 | 1* | 0 | | | | | | | | | | | 48 | 500 | 10 | | |
| | 30* | | 37 | | | | | | 41* | | | | | | | | | | | | | | 4 | 112 | 1 | W | 22 |
| v. Gloucestershire (Bristol) 25-28 April | 71 | 7 | 10 | 0 | 89 | 21 | 27 | 79 | 26 | 8* | 0 | | | | | | | | | | | | 61 | 399 | 10 | | |
| | 12 | 43* | 0 | | 176 | 77 | 5* | 0 | | | | | | | | | | | | | | | 20 | 333 | 5 | W | 21 |
| v. Glamorgan (Trent Bridge) 2-4 May | 3 | 34 | 178 | 25 | 108 | 81 | 12 | 2 | | 4 | 0* | 18 | | | | | | | | | | | 10 | 475 | 10 | | |
| | | | | | | | | | | | | | | | | | | | | | | | | | | W | 22 |
| v. Middlesex (Trent Bridge) 9-12 May | 10 | 20 | 17 | 47 | 0 | 48 | 1 | 67 | | 92 | 0* | 15 | | | | | | | | | | | 19 | 336 | 10 | | |
| | | | | | | | | | | | | | | | | | | | | | | | | | | D | 10 |
| v. Essex (Trent Bridge) 23-25 May | 68 | 165* | 0 | 6* | | 275 | 2 | 67 | 32 | 1 | | | | | | | | | | | | | 48 | 664 | 7 | | |
| | | | | | | | | | | | | | | | | | | | | | | | | | | W | 22 |
| v. Leicestershire (Oakham School) 30 May-2 June | 4 | | 19 | | 11* | | 17 | 32* | | | | | | | | | | | | | | | 19 | 102 | 3 | | |
| | 78 | 17* | 60 | 11 | 79 | 9 | 45 | 17 | 11 | 0* | | | | | | | | | | | | | 36 | 363 | 8 | D | 7 |
| v. Glamorgan (Swansea) 5-8 June | 57 | 4 | 78 | 3 | 98 | 74* | 16 | 8 | 2 | 0 | | 5 | | | | | | | | | | | 19 | 364 | 10 | | |
| | 50 | 5 | 18 | 37 | 63 | 2 | 6 | 12 | 1 | 0* | | 0 | | | | | | | | | | | 13 | 207 | 10 | L | 7 |
| v. Derbyshire (Trent Bridge) 15-18 June | 123* | | 62 | 89* | | | | | 13 | | | | | | | | | | | | | | 15 | 302 | 2 | | |
| | | | | | | | | | | | | | | | | | | | | | | | | | | D | 10 |
| v. Essex (Chelmsford) 8-11 July | 107 | 240 | 21 | 97 | 117 | 36 | 54 | 24 | | 1 | | | 10 | | | 43* | | | | | | | 41 | 791 | 10 | | |
| | | | | | | | | | | | | | | | | | | | | | | | | | | D | 11 |
| v. Gloucestershire (Trent Bridge) 13-16 July | 74 | 52 | 45 | 0 | 2 | 180 | 23 | | 1 | | | | | | | 2* | | 10* | | | | | 11 | 400 | 8 | | |
| | | | | | | | | | | | | | | | | | | | | | | | | | | D | 9 |
| v. Northamptonshire (Northampton) 26-29 July | 152 | 38 | 18 | 3 | 54 | 37 | 25* | | 100 | | 2* | | | | | 40 | | 26 | | | | | 31 | 526 | 9 | | |
| | | | | | | | | | | | | | | | | | | | | | | | | | | D | 12 |
| v. Somerset (Trent Bridge) 8-11 August | 51 | 1 | 22 | 39 | 8 | 0 | | | 145 | | 0 | | | | 44 | | | | | 12* | 2 | | 26 | 350 | 10 | | |
| | 8 | 37 | 15 | 1 | 19 | 108* | | | 32 | | 1 | | | | 37 | | | | | 1 | 7 | | 13 | 279 | 10 | L | 7 |
| v. Northamptonshire (Trent Bridge) 22-25 August | 22 | 16 | 10 | 51 | 9 | | 21 | | 28 | | | | 10 | 18 | 32 | | | | | | | 35* | 31 | 283 | 10 | | |
| | 16 | 24 | 6 | 17* | 50 | | 4 | | 50 | | | | 6 | 25 | 20* | | | | | | | | 15 | 233 | 8 | W | 19 |
| v. Middlesex (Lord's) 29 August-1 September | 92 | 61 | 26 | 17 | 18 | | 21 | 110 | 46 | 0* | | | | 11 | 33 | | | | | | | | 38 | 473 | 10 | | |
| | 94 | 14* | | 11* | 112 | | 36 | 81 | 3 | | | | | 73 | | | | | | | | | 32 | 456 | 7 | D | 11 |
| v. Derbyshire (Chesterfield) 6-8 September | 13 | 90 | 43 | 56 | 24 | | | 0 | 243 | 1* | | | | 36 | 2 | | | | | | | | 40 | 548 | 9 | | |
| | | | | | | | | | | | | | | | | | | | | | | | | | | W | 22 |
| v. Somerset (Taunton) 19-21 September | 41 | 9 | 18 | 2 | | | 10 | 16 | 28 | 0* | 4 | | | | 28 | 1 | | | | | | | 1 | 158 | 10 | | |
| | 3 | 8 | 14 | 4 | | | 57 | 10 | 30 | 0* | 0 | | | | 44 | 16 | | | | | | | 4 | 190 | 10 | L | 3 |

| | MA Wagh | CMW Read | JER Gallian | GP Swann | SR Patel | DJ Hussey | MA Ealham | BM Shafayat | SP Fleming | PJ Franks | CE Shreck | RJ Sidebottom | AJ Harris | WI Jefferson | AR Adams | RS Ferley | MHA Footitt | KW Hogg | SRG Francis | MN Malik | GD Clough | M Davies |
|---|---|---|---|---|---|---|---|---|---|---|---|---|---|---|---|---|---|---|---|---|---|---|
| Matches | 17 | 17 | 17 | 16 | 14 | 13 | 13 | 12 | 11 | 11 | 11 | 7 | 6 | 5 | 4 | 3 | 3 | 2 | 2 | 1 | 1 | 1 |
| Innings | 26 | 23 | 25 | 20 | 20 | 17 | 16 | 19 | 17 | 13 | 11 | 8 | 9 | 9 | 6 | 3 | 0 | 2 | 0 | 2 | 2 | 1 |
| Not Out | 2 | 4 | 0 | 4 | 1 | 2 | 4 | 1 | 1 | 1 | 8 | 1 | 2 | 0 | 1 | 2 | 0 | 1 | 0 | 1 | 0 | 1 |
| Highest Score | 152 | 240 | 178 | 97 | 176 | 275 | 74* | 79 | 243 | 92 | 3 | 18 | 15* | 73 | 33 | 43* | 0 | 26 | 0 | 12* | 7 | 35* |
| Runs | 1310 | 1001 | 940 | 516 | 963 | 1259 | 300 | 560 | 930 | 275 | 4 | 62 | 39 | 316 | 104 | 85 | 0 | 36 | 0 | 13 | 9 | 35 |
| Average | 54.58 | 52.68 | 37.60 | 32.25 | 50.68 | 83.93 | 25.00 | 31.11 | 58.12 | 22.91 | 1.33 | 8.85 | 5.57 | 35.11 | 20.80 | 85.00 | - | 36.00 | - | 13.00 | 4.50 | - |
| 100s | 3 | 2 | 2 | 0 | 4 | 4 | 0 | 0 | 4 | 0 | 0 | 0 | 0 | 0 | 0 | 0 | 0 | 0 | 0 | 0 | 0 | 0 |
| 50s | 11 | 4 | 4 | 3 | 5 | 5 | 2 | 4 | 2 | 1 | 0 | 0 | 0 | 1 | 0 | 0 | 0 | 0 | 0 | 0 | 0 | 0 |
| Catches/Stumpings | 2/0 | 42/6 | 9/0 | 15/0 | 8/0 | 16/0 | 16/0 | 15/1 | 21/0 | 5/0 | 6/0 | 1/0 | 2/0 | 3/0 | 1/0 | 0/0 | 0/0 | 0/0 | 1/0 | 0/0 | 0/0 | 0/0 |

**Home Ground:** Trent Bridge
**Address:** Trent Bridge, Nottingham, NG2 6AG
**Tel:** 0115 9823000
**Fax:** 0115 9823037
**Email:** administration@nottsccc.co.uk
**Directions:** By road: Follow signs from ring road towards city centre.
**Capacity:** 14,500 (16,000 during international matches)
**Year formed:** 1841
**Chief Executive:** Derek Brewer

**Director of Cricket:** Mick Newell
**Captain:** Stephen Fleming
**County colours:** Green and gold

**Website:**
www.trentbridge.co.uk

**Honours**
County Championship
1883, 1884, 1885, 1886, 1907, 1929, 1981, 1987, 2005
Sunday League/NCL/Pro40
1991
Benson & Hedges Cup
1976, 1989
Gillette Cup/NatWest/C&G Trophy
1987

# FIRST–CLASS MATCHES
## BOWLING

| | CE Shreck | GP Swann | MA Ealham | PJ Franks | AJ Harris | RJ Sidebottom | SR Patel | AR Adams | M Davies | MHA Footitt | GD Clough | MA Wagh | MN Malik | JER Gallian | SRG Francis | BM Shafayat | RS Ferley | CMW Read | KW Hogg | DJ Hussey | Overs | Total | Byes/Leg-byes | Wickets | Run outs |
|---|---|---|---|---|---|---|---|---|---|---|---|---|---|---|---|---|---|---|---|---|---|---|---|---|---|
| v. Durham UCCE (Durham) 14-16 April | 15-5-24-0 | 7-6-1-2 | 7-0-24-1 | | 12.3-2-69-4 | 12-4-23-2 | | | | 8-3-20-0 | | | | 8-2-36-1 | | 15-2-45-0 | | 3-0-29-0 | | | 53.3 | 142 | 1 | 10 | 1 |
| | 13-5-37-4 | 17-5-30-0 | | | | 11-5-18-0 | 23-6-68-4 | | | | | | | | | | | | | | 98 | 294 | 11 | 9 | |
| v. Leicestershire (Trent Bridge) 18-21 April | 24-3-98-2 | 13-6-30-3 | 21-8-63-1 | 20.1-6-49-3 | 24-9-43-1 | | | | | | | | | | | | | | | | 102.1 | 299 | 16 | 10 | |
| | 20.5-2-84-1 | 20-6-71-1 | 17-7-43-4 | 12-1-41-0 | 20-3-49-3 | | | | | | | | | | | | | | | | 89.5 | 311 | 23 | 10 | 1 |
| v. Gloucestershire (Bristol) 25-28 April | | 11-2-31-1 | 13-3-47-0 | 14-3-53-3 | 23-2-120-3 | 24.4-4-72-3 | | | | | | | | | | | | | | | 85.4 | 328 | 5 | 10 | |
| | | 24-0-122-3 | 18.2-6-53-2 | 20.3-4-89-3 | 10-2-35-1 | 20-5-43-1 | 2-0-3-0 | | | | | | | | | | | | | | 94.5 | 353 | 8 | 10 | |
| v. Glamorgan (Trent Bridge) 2-4 May | 18-3-73-0 | 10-2-35-2 | 14-5-37-4 | 14-4-41-0 | 14-0-54-3 | 0.4-0-0-1 | | | | | | | | | | | | | | | 70.4 | 262 | 22 | 10 | |
| | 22-4-62-6 | 15-5-30-1 | 6-2-25-0 | 11-3-34-1 | 21-7-43-1 | 1-0-1-0 | | | | | | | | | | | | | | | 76 | 205 | 10 | 10 | 1 |
| v. Middlesex (Trent Bridge) 9-12 May | 27-8-79-6 | | 21.5-10-34-3 | 12-2-50-1 | | | | | | | | | | | | | | | | | 60.5 | 176 | 13 | 10 | |
| | 18-3-78-0 | | 17-2-44-1 | 11-3-44-0 | 14-4-39-1 | 4-1-5-0 | | | | | | | | | | | | | | | 71 | 243 | 1 | 2 | |
| v. Essex (Trent Bridge) 23-25 May | 24-8-84-1 | 5-1-20-1 | 18-4-66-1 | 11-0-75-2 | | | | | | 15.4-3-58-5 | | | | | | | | 2-0-8-0 | | | 73.4 | 317 | 13 | 10 | |
| | 18-6-48-2 | 7-1-28-0 | 18.2-5-47-4 | 7-0-42-3 | | | | | | 7-0-51-0 | | | | | | | | | | | 59.2 | 235 | 11 | 9 | |
| v. Leicestershire (Oakham School) 30 May-2 June | 28.3-5-97-5 | 17-1-65-1 | | 15-1-68-2 | | | | | | 11-3-32-1 | | | | | | | | | | | 98.3 | 364 | 18 | 10 | |
| | | | | 6-0-36-2 | | | | | | 8-0-39-1 | | | | 2-0-17-0 | | 4-0-20-0 | | | | | 20 | 114 | 2 | 3 | |
| v. Glamorgan (Swansea) 5-8 June | 32-9-83-2 | 46.5-8-143-3 | 24-11-45-3 | 19.5-7-71-2 | 24-3-72-0 | | | | | | | 1-1-0-0 | | | | | | | | 1-0-4-0 | 146.5 | 429 | 11 | 10 | |
| | 24-9-43-2 | 31.4-2-100-7 | | 10-2-16-1 | 9-2-34-0 | | | | | | | | | | | | | | | | 75.4 | 197 | 4 | 10 | |
| v. Derbyshire (Trent Bridge) 15-18 June | 13.3-3-35-7 | 2-0-12-0 | | | | | | | | | | 4-0-10-0 | | | 9-1-43-1 | | | | | | 35.3 | 108 | 6 | 10 | 3 |
| | 9-3-16-2 | 8-1-16-1 | | | | | | | | | | | | | 3-0-31-0 | | | | | | 26 | 95 | 10 | 3 | |
| v. Essex (Chelmsford) 8-11 July | | 38-5-166-4 | 30-8-110-1 | 19-1-91-2 | 30-7-101-0 | | 3-0-30-0 | | | | | 1-0-7-0 | | | | 3.5-0-24-1 | 27-3-151-1 | | | 0.5-0-2-0 | 151.5 | 700 | 20 | 9 | |
| | | 1-0-1-0 | | | | | 10.1-1-29-1 | | | | | | | | | 2-0-6-0 | 12-2-25-0 | | | | 26 | 63 | 0 | 0 | |
| v. Gloucestershire (Trent Bridge) 13-16 July | | | 0.1-0-0-0 | | | | | | | | | | | | | | | | | | 0.1 | 0 | 0 | 0 | |
| | | | | | | | | | | | | | | | | | | | | | – | – | – | – | |
| v. Northamptonshire (Northampton) 26-29 July | | 36-6-90-4 | 31-13-43-4 | 34-10-106-2 | | | | | | | | | | | | | 15-1-67-0 | | 16-5-49-0 | | 132 | 366 | 11 | 10 | |
| | | 12-1-36-0 | | 11-2-39-3 | | | | | | | | | | | | | 9-2-40-0 | | 10-2-30-0 | | 42 | 152 | 2 | 3 | |
| v. Somerset (Trent Bridge) 8-11 August | | 39.2-8-125-4 | | 28-1-109-2 | | | 3-0-27-0 | | | | 22-5-72-3 | | 24-3-97-1 | | | | | | | | 116.2 | 452 | 22 | 10 | |
| | | 12-1-49-1 | | 9-0-45-0 | | | 1.5-0-18-0 | | | | 4-0-10-1 | | 11-2-43-1 | | | | | | | 1-0-9-0 | 38.5 | 181 | 7 | 4 | |
| v. Northamptonshire (Trent Bridge) 22-25 August | | 14-5-28-1 | 13-3-55-0 | 21-7-67-1 | | 6-2-18-1 | | 18-5-55-0 | 19.3-4-59-7 | | | | | | | | | | | | 91.3 | 285 | 3 | 10 | |
| | | 20.3-5-32-2 | 16-4-38-1 | 15.3-1-66-3 | | 6-2-5-0 | | 17-3-48-2 | 13.3-4-31-1 | | | | | | | | | | | | 88.3 | 229 | 9 | 10 | |
| v. Middlesex (Lord's) 29 August-1 September | 37-11-87-2 | 34-5-108-0 | | 23-2-115-1 | | 5.2-1-18-2 | 43-13-127-4 | | | | | 2-1-7-0 | | | | | | | | | 144.2 | 472 | 10 | 10 | 1 |
| | | | | | | | | | | | | | | | | | | | | | – | – | – | – | |
| v. Derbyshire (Chesterfield) 6-8 September | 17-3-60-2 | 10-3-34-1 | | 10-2-28-1 | | | | 14.5-0-74-4 | | | | | | | | | | | | 1-0-4-0 | 52.5 | 205 | 5 | 10 | |
| | 20-3-76-0 | 27-7-72-2 | | 13-1-57-2 | | 21-3-39-3 | | 19.2-4-78-2 | | | | | | | | | | | | | 100.2 | 337 | 15 | 10 | 1 |
| v. Somerset (Taunton) 19-21 September | 22-1-110-3 | | | 16-0-90-1 | | 22-5-63-0 | 17-4-68-2 | 25-4-119-2 | | | | 2-0-6-2 | | | | | | | | | 104 | 469 | 13 | 10 | |
| | | | | | | | | | | | | | | | | | | | | | – | – | – | – | |

| | CE Shreck | GP Swann | MA Ealham | PJ Franks | AJ Harris | RJ Sidebottom | SR Patel | AR Adams | M Davies | MHA Footitt | GD Clough | MA Wagh | MN Malik | JER Gallian | SRG Francis | BM Shafayat | RS Ferley | CMW Read | KW Hogg | DJ Hussey |
|---|---|---|---|---|---|---|---|---|---|---|---|---|---|---|---|---|---|---|---|---|
| Overs | 400.5 | 487.2 | 325.4 | 263.4 | 197 | 212.4 | 104 | 137.1 | 33 | 45.4 | 26 | 12 | 35 | 10 | 12 | 25.5 | 63 | 5 | 26 | 4.5 |
| Maidens | 94 | 93 | 101 | 90 | 32 | 53 | 20 | 29 | 8 | 6 | 5 | 4 | 5 | 2 | 1 | 3 | 8 | 0 | 7 | 0 |
| Runs | 1274 | 1503 | 886 | 1090 | 762 | 548 | 329 | 501 | 90 | 191 | 82 | 33 | 140 | 53 | 74 | 100 | 283 | 35 | 79 | 23 |
| Wickets | 47 | 45 | 32 | 32 | 19 | 15 | 14 | 14 | 8 | 7 | 4 | 2 | 2 | 1 | 1 | 1 | 1 | 0 | 0 | 0 |
| Average | 27.10 | 33.40 | 27.68 | 34.06 | 40.10 | 36.53 | 23.50 | 35.78 | 11.25 | 27.28 | 20.50 | 16.50 | 70.00 | 53.00 | 74.00 | 100.00 | 283.00 | – | – | – |

## FIELDING

| | |
|---|---|
| 48 | CMW Read (42 ct, 6 st) |
| 21 | SP Fleming |
| 16 | MA Ealham |
| 16 | BM Shafayat (15 ct, 1 st) |
| 16 | DJ Hussey |
| 15 | GP Swann |
| 9 | JER Gallian |
| 8 | SR Patel |
| 6 | CE Shreck |
| 5 | PJ Franks |
| 3 | WI Jefferson |
| 2 | AJ Harris |
| 2 | MA Wagh |
| 1 | RJ Sidebottom |
| 1 | SRG Francis |
| 1 | AR Adams |
| 0 | GD Clough |
| 0 | M Davies |
| 0 | MN Malik |
| 0 | RS Ferley |
| 0 | KW Hogg |
| 0 | MHA Footitt |

### Final Division Two Table

| | P | W | L | D | T | Ab | Bat | Bowl | Pens | Pts |
|---|---|---|---|---|---|---|---|---|---|---|
| Somerset | 16 | 10 | 1 | 5 | 0 | 0 | 65 | 41 | 0.00 | 266.00 |
| Nottinghamshire | 16 | 6 | 3 | 7 | 0 | 0 | 60 | 43 | 0.50 | 214.50 |
| Middlesex | 16 | 6 | 2 | 8 | 0 | 0 | 35 | 43 | 1.50 | 192.50 |
| Essex | 16 | 6 | 4 | 6 | 0 | 0 | 40 | 36 | 2.00 | 182.00 |
| Northamptonshire | 16 | 5 | 5 | 6 | 0 | 0 | 44 | 38 | 0.00 | 176.00 |
| Derbyshire | 16 | 3 | 5 | 8 | 0 | 0 | 30 | 44 | 1.00 | 147.00 |
| Gloucestershire | 16 | 3 | 5 | 8 | 0 | 0 | 32 | 37 | 3.50 | 139.50 |
| Leicestershire | 16 | 2 | 8 | 5 | 0 | 1 | 32 | 35 | 4.00 | 115.00 |
| Glamorgan | 16 | 1 | 9 | 5 | 0 | 1 | 26 | 37 | 8.50 | 92.50 |

Glamorgan had eight points deducted for a poor pitch.

NOTTS OUTLAWS

Limited overs nickname:
NOTTS OUTLAWS

# SOMERSET CCC

## FIRST-CLASS MATCHES
### BATTING

| Match | JC Hildreth | PD Trego | NJ Edwards | ME Trescothick | JL Langer | AR Caddick | CM Willoughby | ID Blackwell | C Kieswetter | PS Jones | CL White | ND McKenzie | WJ Durston | ML Turner | SHP Spurway | MK Munday | AV Suppiah | JD Francis | MJ Wood | Extras | Total | Wickets | Result | Points |
|---|---|---|---|---|---|---|---|---|---|---|---|---|---|---|---|---|---|---|---|---|---|---|---|---|
| v. Loughborough UCCE | 44 | 18* | 212 | 28 | | | | 27* | | | | | | | | | 51 | 10 | | 27 | 417 | 5 | | |
| (Taunton) 14-16 April | 79 | 4 | | | | | | 50 | | 1 | | | | 1* | 1 | | 41* | 30 | | 7 | 214 | 6 | W | |
| v. Middlesex | 116 | 130 | 9 | 70 | 315 | | 6 | | | 1* | 114 | | | | 44* | | | | | 45 | 850 | 7 | D | 10 |
| (Taunton) 18-21 April | | | | | | | | | | | | | | | | | | | | | | | | |
| v. Leicestershire | 0 | 50 | 13 | 77 | 14 | 51 | 4* | 0 | | 114 | 11 | | | | 0 | | | | | 23 | 357 | 10 | | |
| (Leicester) 25-28 April | 9 | 6 | 79 | 17 | 92 | 1 | 1* | 29 | | 19 | 69 | | | | 1 | | | | | 53 | 376 | 10 | W | 21 |
| v. Derbyshire | 45 | 67 | 5 | 32 | 4 | 2 | 23* | | 63 | | 138 | 50 | | 57 | | | | | | 44 | 530 | 10 | | |
| (Taunton) 2-5 May | 32 | | 81 | 24 | 136* | | | | | | 6 | | 15* | | | | | | | 15 | 309 | 4 | D | 11 |
| v. Northamptonshire | 111 | 32* | 28 | 284 | 86 | | | 81 | 0* | | 1 | | | | | | | | | 18 | 641 | 6 | D | 11 |
| (Northampton) 8-11 May | | | | | | | | | | | | | | | | | | | | | | | | |
| v. Gloucestershire | 60 | 48 | 21 | 17 | 18 | 25 | 0* | 2 | 30 | | 241 | | | 5 | | | | | | 29 | 496 | 10 | | |
| (Taunton) 23-26 May | 51* | | 44 | | 41 | | | | | | 16* | | | | | | | | | 20 | 172 | 2 | W | 22 |
| v. Middlesex | 5 | 1 | 0 | 12 | 0 | 2* | | 14 | 6 | 0* | 5 | | | | | | | | | 5 | 50 | 8 | | |
| (Lord's) 30 May-2 June | 127 | 16 | 0 | 0 | 17 | 4 | 2 | 0 | 11 | 64* | 77 | | | | | | | | | 21 | 339 | 10 | L | 3 |
| v. Leicestershire | 163 | 18* | 133 | 182 | | | | | 36 | | 114 | | | | | | | | | 29 | 675 | 5 | W | 22 |
| (Taunton) 6-9 June | | | | | | | | | | | | | | | | | | | | | | | | |
| v. Gloucestershire | 48 | 73* | 85 | 0 | 32 | | | 72 | 23 | | 65 | | | | | | | | | 12 | 410 | 7 | W | 22 |
| (Bristol) 15-17 June | | | | | | | | | | | | | | | | | | | | | | | | |
| v. Northamptonshire | 51 | 2 | 96 | 146 | 83 | 9 | 0* | 9 | 7 | 0 | 37 | | | | | | | | | 19 | 459 | 10 | | |
| (Taunton) 13-16 July | | | 46 | 69* | | | | | | | 6* | | | | | | | | | 3 | 124 | 1 | W | 22 |
| v. Essex | 38 | 20 | 5 | 24 | 0 | 8* | | 15 | 0 | 4 | 1 | | | | | | | | 20 | 18 | 153 | 10 | D | 7 |
| (Taunton) 20-23 July | | | | | | | | | | | | | | | | | | | | | | | | |
| v. Derbyshire | 13 | 56 | 94 | 18 | 22 | 5 | 9 | 30 | 52* | | 7 | | | | | 0 | | | | 34 | 340 | 10 | | |
| (Derby) 25-28 July | 16 | | 5 | 32* | 17 | | | | | | 4* | | | | | | | | | 10 | 84 | 3 | W | 17 |
| v. Nottinghamshire | 27 | 67 | 31 | 49 | 36 | 5* | 4 | 58 | 14 | 9 | 124 | | | | | | | | | 28 | 452 | 10 | | |
| (Trent Bridge) 8-11 August | 43 | | 23 | 16 | 16 | | | 28* | | | 47* | | | | | | | | | 8 | 181 | 4 | W | 22 |
| v. Glamorgan | 26 | 19* | 92 | 28 | 113 | | | | 7* | | | 50 | 58 | | | | | | | 7 | 400 | 6 | D | 12 |
| (Cardiff) 14-17 August | | | | | | | | | | | | | | | | | | | | | | | | |
| v. Glamorgan | 4 | 0 | 52 | 52 | 31 | 43 | 0* | 54 | 93 | 4 | 55 | | | | | | | | | 14 | 402 | 10 | | |
| (Taunton) 30 August-1 September | 69 | 41 | 3 | 13 | 47 | 0 | | 42 | 20 | 2* | 84 | | | | | | | | | 8 | 329 | 9 | W | 22 |
| v. Essex | 61 | 11 | 55 | 59 | 43 | 0 | 7 | 9 | 14 | | 49 | | | | | 4* | | | | 0 | 312 | 10 | | |
| (Chelmsford) 5-7 September | 32* | 44 | 35 | 6 | 28 | | | | | | 33* | | | | | | | | | 6 | 184 | 4 | W | 20 |
| v. Nottinghamshire | 0 | 113* | 4 | 112 | 16 | | 0 | 141 | 1 | 37 | | 17 | | | | 9 | | | | 19 | 469 | 10 | W | 22 |
| (Taunton) 19-21 September | | | | | | | | | | | | | | | | | | | | | | | | |
| **Matches** | 17 | 17 | 17 | 16 | 16 | 16 | 16 | 15 | 14 | 13 | 12 | 3 | 3 | 3 | 3 | 3 | 1 | 1 | 1 | | | | | |
| **Innings** | 26 | 22 | 26 | 24 | 23 | 13 | 12 | 19 | 16 | 12 | 19 | 5 | 4 | 3 | 4 | 3 | 2 | 2 | 1 | | | | | |
| **Not Out** | 2 | 6 | 0 | 2 | 1 | 2 | 7 | 2 | 3 | 4 | 4 | 1 | 1 | 1 | 1 | 1 | 1 | 0 | 0 | | | | | |
| **Highest Score** | 163 | 130 | 212 | 284 | 315 | 51 | 23* | 141 | 93 | 114 | 241 | 84 | 58 | 57 | 44* | 9 | 51 | 30 | 20 | | | | | |
| **Runs** | 1270 | 836 | 1251 | 1343 | 1231 | 147 | 58 | 667 | 377 | 255 | 1083 | 271 | 140 | 63 | 46 | 13 | 92 | 40 | 20 | | | | | |
| **Average** | 52.91 | 52.25 | 48.11 | 61.04 | 55.95 | 13.36 | 11.60 | 39.23 | 29.00 | 31.87 | 72.20 | 67.75 | 46.66 | 31.50 | 15.33 | 6.50 | 92.00 | 20.00 | 20.00 | | | | | |
| **100s** | 4 | 2 | 2 | 4 | 3 | 0 | 0 | 1 | 0 | 1 | 5 | 0 | 0 | 0 | 0 | 0 | 0 | 0 | 0 | | | | | |
| **50s** | 6 | 5 | 8 | 5 | 3 | 1 | 0 | 5 | 3 | 1 | 3 | 3 | 2 | 1 | 0 | 0 | 1 | 0 | 0 | | | | | |
| **Catches/Stumpings** | 15/0 | 4/0 | 10/0 | 34/0 | 14/0 | 2/0 | 2/0 | 2/0 | 46/0 | 3/0 | 7/0 | 2/0 | 0/0 | 1/0 | 9/0 | 2/0 | 2/0 | 0/0 | 0/0 | | | | | |

**Home Ground:** Taunton
**Address:** County Ground, St James Street, Taunton, Somerset, TA1 1JT
**Tel:** 0845 337 1875
**Fax:** 01823 332395
**Email:** info@somersetcountycc.co.uk
**Directions:** By road: M5 junction 25, follow A358 to town centre. Signposted from there.
**Capacity:** 6,500

**Other grounds used:** Bath
**Year formed:** 1875

**Chief Executive:** Richard Gould
**Director of Cricket:** Brian Rose
**Head Coach:** Andy Hurry
**Captain:** Justin Langer
**County colours:** Black, white and maroon

**Honours**
Sunday League/NCL/Pro40
1979
Benson & Hedges Cup
1981, 1982
Gillette Cup/NatWest/C&G Trophy
1979, 1983, 2001
Twenty20 Cup
2005

**Website:**
www.somersetcountycc.co.uk

## FIRST-CLASS MATCHES
## BOWLING

| | AR Caddick | CM Willoughby | PD Trego | ID Blackwell | PS Jones | CL White | MK Munday | ML Turner | JC Hildreth | WJ Durston | AV Suppiah | Overs | Total | Byes/Leg-byes | Wickets | Run outs |
|---|---|---|---|---|---|---|---|---|---|---|---|---|---|---|---|---|
| v. Loughborough UCCE | 8-4-14-5 | | 2.1-1-2-1 | | 5-1-15-2 | | | 10-0-42-2 | 5-2-13-1 | | | 25.1 | 77 | 4 | 10 | |
| (Taunton) 14-16 April | 11-1-29-0 | | 17-8-49-1 | 26-9-52-3 | 11-4-29-1 | | | 11.2-2-30-4 | | | 3-1-5-0 | 84.2 | 224 | 17 | 10 | |
| v. Middlesex | 34-7-127-0 | 30-6-89-0 | 18-6-48-1 | 24-4-88-1 | 27-5-109-1 | 21-0-79-0 | | | 3-0-27-0 | | | 157 | 600 | 33 | 8 | 1 |
| (Taunton) 18-21 April | 10-1-54-1 | 10-2-38-0 | | 18-7-27-1 | 8-1-47-0 | 6-0-42-0 | | | | | | 52 | 209 | 1 | 2 | |
| v. Leicestershire | 22-4-83-0 | 28-9-97-5 | 20.4-3-72-4 | 23-6-43-1 | 17-3-79-0 | | | | | | | 110.4 | 385 | 11 | 10 | |
| (Leicester) 25-28 April | 10-3-29-2 | 3-0-15-0 | 9-2-49-4 | 4-3-2-1 | 3-1-5-0 | 9.1-0-42-3 | | | | | | 38.1 | 150 | 8 | 10 | |
| v. Derbyshire | 35-10-150-3 | 31-7-85-1 | 24-1-113-1 | | | 28.3-0-115-0 | | 26-1-126-1 | 13-2-62-1 | 24-1-117-0 | | 181.3 | 801 | 33 | 8 | 1 |
| (Taunton) 2-5 May | | | | | | | | | | | | - | - | - | - | |
| v. Northamptonshire | 23.1-3-105-4 | 21-4-77-0 | 18-1-71-3 | 16-5-41-0 | 20-2-90-0 | | | | | | | 98.1 | 400 | 11 | 7 | |
| (Northampton) 8-11 May | 4.2-0-18-2 | | 4-0-14-0 | | | | | | | | | 8.2 | 32 | 0 | 2 | |
| v. Gloucestershire | 9-0-50-3 | 14-6-33-5 | 9-2-40-0 | | | 15-0-46-1 | | 7.1-2-30-1 | | | | 54.1 | 202 | 3 | 10 | |
| (Taunton) 23-26 May | 36.5-7-111-6 | 28-8-76-2 | 19-1-73-0 | 36-11-79-1 | | 10-0-36-0 | | 23-2-84-0 | | | | 152.5 | 465 | 6 | 10 | 1 |
| v. Middlesex | 15-3-42-0 | 13-0-48-3 | 13.4-1-54-4 | 20-2-43-2 | 17-4-59-1 | | | | | | | 78.4 | 252 | 6 | 10 | |
| (Lord's) 30 May-2 June | 15-4-43-0 | 9-0-21-0 | 7-2-33-2 | | 3-0-17-1 | 3.3-0-16-0 | | | | | | 37.3 | 138 | 8 | 3 | |
| v. Leicestershire | 15-3-64-3 | 7-1-20-1 | 4-1-16-0 | 2-1-5-0 | 13.2-0-61-6 | | | | | | | 41.2 | 168 | 2 | 10 | |
| (Taunton) 6-9 June | 20-6-38-3 | 16.1-0-82-5 | 8-1-38-1 | | 8-0-49-0 | 9-0-34-1 | | | | | | 61.1 | 248 | 7 | 10 | |
| v. Gloucestershire | 18.5-7-30-7 | 16-1-65-2 | 4-0-12-1 | | 2-0-9-0 | | | | | | | 40.5 | 121 | 5 | 10 | |
| (Bristol) 15-17 June | 16.3-4-41-5 | 17-4-56-5 | 4-1-15-0 | 1-1-0-0 | 4-0-21-0 | | | | | | | 42.3 | 138 | 5 | 10 | |
| v. Northamptonshire | 19-3-70-3 | 14-6-53-1 | 14-1-58-2 | | 11-4-24-2 | 3.3-2-9-2 | | | | | | 61.3 | 221 | 7 | 10 | |
| (Taunton) 13-16 July | 29-4-113-4 | 19-6-83-3 | 8-1-39-0 | 12-4-12-0 | 13-2-36-1 | 16.1-2-55-2 | | | | | | 97.1 | 358 | 20 | 10 | |
| v. Essex | 22-3-51-2 | 17-1-59-1 | 15-5-39-1 | 4-0-16-0 | 17-0-81-2 | 9.5-2-28-4 | | | | | | 84.5 | 282 | 8 | 10 | |
| (Taunton) 20-23 July | 10-1-33-1 | 10-3-55-1 | 2-0-9-0 | 23-0-78-3 | 9-2-36-1 | 22-2-76-0 | | | | | | 76 | 294 | 7 | 6 | |
| v. Derbyshire | 9-2-19-0 | 5-3-8-1 | 3-2-1-0 | 10-2-27-1 | | | 4-0-32-0 | | | | | 31 | 94 | 7 | 2 | |
| (Derby) 25-28 July | 11-3-25-2 | 9-5-12-4 | | 3.5-1-8-3 | | 4-2-3-1 | | | | | | 27.5 | 52 | 4 | 10 | |
| v. Nottinghamshire | 18.3-1-69-4 | 20-1-74-2 | 11-0-50-0 | 13-3-49-1 | 7-0-54-0 | 12-3-37-2 | | | | | | 81.3 | 350 | 12 | 10 | 1 |
| (Trent Bridge) 8-11 August | 20-5-48-2 | 19-2-66-0 | | 19.4-6-65-3 | 13-3-53-1 | 9-4-37-4 | | | | | | 80 | 279 | 10 | 10 | |
| v. Glamorgan | 25.4-10-48-4 | 21-5-65-3 | 15-4-44-1 | | 11-2-37-2 | | | | | | | 72.4 | 198 | 4 | 10 | |
| (Cardiff) 14-17 August | | | | | | | | | | | | - | - | - | - | |
| v. Glamorgan | 19-3-64-3 | 21-6-65-3 | 11-3-38-1 | 1-0-2-0 | 13.1-1-45-3 | | | | | | | 65.1 | 233 | 19 | 10 | |
| (Taunton) 30 August-1 September | 22-6-48-4 | 10-5-17-1 | 7-0-36-0 | 13.5-1-60-3 | 5-1-23-1 | | | | | | | 57.5 | 199 | 15 | 10 | |
| v. Essex | 8-2-22-0 | 18-8-36-5 | 4-0-22-2 | 15.1-3-47-2 | | | 1-0-9-1 | | | | | 46.1 | 144 | 8 | 10 | |
| (Chelmsford) 5-7 September | 25-4-95-2 | 13.3-1-53-4 | 8-2-46-0 | 18-5-46-1 | | | 19-0-86-3 | | | | | 83.3 | 349 | 23 | 10 | |
| v. Nottinghamshire | | 14-4-39-4 | 7-0-50-3 | 2-1-5-0 | 12-1-53-1 | | 4-1-10-2 | | | | | 39 | 158 | 1 | 10 | |
| (Taunton) 19-21 September | | 9-1-43-0 | | 19.4-4-65-2 | 5-1-23-0 | | 16-1-55-8 | | | | | 49.4 | 190 | 4 | 10 | |

| | AR Caddick | CM Willoughby | PD Trego | ID Blackwell | PS Jones | CL White | MK Munday | ML Turner | JC Hildreth | WJ Durston | AV Suppiah |
|---|---|---|---|---|---|---|---|---|---|---|---|
| Overs | 541.5 | 462.4 | 286.3 | 324.3 | 254.3 | 178.4 | 44 | 77.3 | 21 | 24 | 3 |
| Maidens | 114 | 105 | 49 | 77 | 38 | 17 | 2 | 7 | 4 | 1 | 1 |
| Runs | 1733 | 1530 | 1131 | 860 | 1055 | 655 | 192 | 312 | 102 | 117 | 5 |
| Wickets | 75 | 62 | 33 | 29 | 26 | 20 | 14 | 8 | 2 | 0 | 0 |
| **Average** | 23.10 | 24.67 | 34.27 | 29.65 | 40.57 | 32.75 | 13.71 | 39.00 | 51.00 | – | – |

## FIELDING

| | |
|---|---|
| 46 | C Kieswetter (46 ct) |
| 34 | ME Trescothick |
| 15 | JC Hildreth |
| 14 | JL Langer |
| 10 | NJ Edwards |
| 9 | SHP Spurway (9 ct) |
| 7 | CL White |
| 4 | PD Trego |
| 3 | PS Jones |
| 2 | AR Caddick |
| 2 | ID Blackwell |
| 2 | AV Suppiah |
| 2 | MK Munday |
| 2 | ND McKenzie |
| 2 | CM Willoughby |
| 1 | ML Turner |
| 0 | WJ Durston |
| 0 | JD Francis |
| 0 | MJ Wood |

### Final Division Two Table

| | P | W | L | D | T | Ab | Bat | Bowl | Pens | Pts |
|---|---|---|---|---|---|---|---|---|---|---|
| Somerset | 16 | 10 | 1 | 5 | 0 | 0 | 65 | 41 | 0.00 | 266.00 |
| Nottinghamshire | 16 | 6 | 3 | 7 | 0 | 0 | 60 | 43 | 0.50 | 214.50 |
| Middlesex | 16 | 6 | 2 | 8 | 0 | 0 | 35 | 43 | 1.50 | 192.50 |
| Essex | 16 | 6 | 4 | 6 | 0 | 0 | 40 | 36 | 2.00 | 182.00 |
| Northamptonshire | 16 | 5 | 5 | 6 | 0 | 0 | 44 | 38 | 0.00 | 176.00 |
| Derbyshire | 16 | 3 | 5 | 8 | 0 | 0 | 30 | 44 | 1.00 | 147.00 |
| Gloucestershire | 16 | 3 | 5 | 8 | 0 | 0 | 32 | 37 | 3.50 | 139.50 |
| Leicestershire | 16 | 2 | 8 | 5 | 0 | 1 | 32 | 35 | 4.00 | 115.00 |
| Glamorgan | 16 | 1 | 9 | 5 | 0 | 1 | 26 | 37 | 8.50 | 92.50 |

Glamorgan had eight points deducted for a poor pitch.

Limited overs nickname:
SOMERSET SABRES

# SURREY CCC

## FIRST-CLASS MATCHES
### BATTING

| | MR Ramprakash | JN Batty | SA Newman | MA Butcher | MJ Nicholson | R Clarke | AD Brown | JGE Benning | SJ Walters | NC Saker | J Ormond | IDK Salisbury | CP Schofield | Harbhajan Singh | CJ Jordan | ND Doshi | JW Dernbach | Azhar Mahmood | Mohammad Akram | RS Clinton | Murtaza Hussain | SJ Magoffin | Extras | Total | Wickets | Result | Points |
|---|---|---|---|---|---|---|---|---|---|---|---|---|---|---|---|---|---|---|---|---|---|---|---|---|---|---|---|
| v. Yorkshire (The Oval) 18-21 April | 115 | 5 | 124 | | | 42 | 4 | 0 | | | 0 | | 0* | | 1 | | | 32 | | | | 6 | 15 | 344 | 10 | | |
| | 5 | 14 | 89 | | | 3 | 7 | 7 | | | 1 | | 11 | | 15 | | | 0 | | | | 9* | 9 | 170 | 10 | L | 5 |
| v. Hampshire (The Oval) 25-28 April | 107* | 2 | 0 | 50 | | 8 | 0 | | | | 0 | 18 | | | 0 | | | 5 | 0 | | | | 13 | 203 | 10 | | |
| | 43 | 121 | 3 | 72 | | 0 | 24 | | | | 0 | 103 | | | 2* | | | 69 | 4 | | | | 26 | 467 | 10 | L | |
| v. Lancashire (Old Trafford) 2-4 May | 13 | 70 | 60 | 9 | | 19 | 69 | 13 | 8 | | 4* | 4 | | | | | 1 | | | | | | 14 | 284 | 10 | | |
| | 7 | 0 | 0 | 32 | | 3 | 0 | 36 | 1 | | 20 | 2 | | | | | 8* | | | | | | 11 | 120 | 10 | L | 5 |
| v. Warwickshire (The Oval) 9-12 May | 120* | 154* | 73 | | | | | | | | | | | | | | | | | | | | 53 | 400 | 1 | D | 12 |
| v. Sussex (Hove) 16-19 May | 266* | 39 | 38 | 179 | | 50* | | | | | | | | | | | | | | | | | 54 | 626 | 3 | D | 12 |
| v. Kent (Whitgift School) 30 May-2 June | 35 | 9 | 9 | 4 | 48* | 1 | 18 | | | | 6 | 6 | | 13 | 4 | | | | | | | | 13 | 166 | 10 | | |
| | 108 | 25 | 20 | 4 | 13 | 0 | 68 | | | | 13 | 16 | | 11 | 0* | | | | | | | | 41 | 319 | 10 | L | 1 |
| v. Worcestershire (Worcester) 6-9 June | 84 | 114 | 46 | 22 | 7 | 7 | 17 | | 4* | | 12 | 20 | | | | | | 18 | | | | | 19 | 370 | 10 | | |
| | 33 | 13 | 34 | 29* | 20* | 41 | 11 | | 19 | | 3 | 17 | | | | | | 44 | | | | | 17 | 281 | 9 | D | 9 |
| v. Durham (The Oval) 8-10 July | 18 | 17 | 0 | 25 | 19 | 30 | | | 70 | 16* | | | 28 | 0 | | 0 | | | | | | | 20 | 243 | 10 | | |
| | 1 | 4 | 7 | 40* | | 68* | | | 8 | | | | | | | | | | | | | | 26 | 154 | 4 | W | 18 |
| v. Yorkshire (Headingley) 20-23 July | 59 | 5 | 9 | 11 | 1 | 65 | | | 27 | 6* | | | 10 | 0 | | 0 | | | | | 0 | | 36 | 229 | 10 | D | 8 |
| v. Worcestershire (Guildford) 25-28 July | 142 | 45 | 32 | 46 | 12* | 14 | | | 30 | 1 | | | 10 | 14 | | | | | | 0 | | | 23 | 369 | 10 | D | 11 |
| v. Kent (Canterbury) 8-9 August | 61 | 7 | 57 | 19 | 1 | | 7 | 26 | 2 | | 15 | | 5* | 0 | | | | | | | | | 15 | 215 | 10 | | |
| | 28 | 12 | 10 | 6 | | | 2* | 10* | 4 | | | | | 29 | | | | | | | | | 7 | 108 | 6 | W | 18 |
| v. Durham (Riverside) 13-16 August | 62 | 18 | 9 | 4 | 32 | 0 | | 36 | 0 | | 0 | | 6 | 8* | | | | | | | | | 8 | 183 | 10 | | |
| | 15 | 102* | 34 | 18 | | | | 14* | | | | | 19* | | | | | | | | | | 15 | 198 | 3 | D | 7 |
| v. Hampshire (Rose Bowl) 30 August-2 September | 188 | 55 | 24 | 100 | 34* | | 42 | 10 | 18 | | 0 | | 18 | 19 | | | | | | | | | 48 | 556 | 10 | W | 22 |
| v. Warwickshire (Edgbaston) 6-9 September | 175 | 21 | 0 | 14 | 41 | | 44 | 13 | | | 25* | | 17 | | 10 | | | | | | 6 | | 7 | 373 | 10 | | |
| | 15* | 68* | 87 | | | | | | | | | | | | | | | | | | 9 | | 9 | 179 | 1 | W | 21 |
| v. Lancashire (The Oval) 19-22 September | 196 | 0 | 39 | 21 | 12 | | 51 | 36 | | | 10 | | | 6* | 34 | | | | | | 9* | | 13 | 427 | 9 | | |
| | 130* | 45 | 8 | 47 | | | 12 | 14 | | | | | 19* | | | | | | | | | | 20 | 295 | 5 | W | 22 |
| **Matches** | 15 | 15 | 15 | 14 | 12 | 10 | 9 | 8 | 8 | 8 | 7 | 6 | 6 | 6 | 5 | 5 | 4 | 3 | 3 | 3 | 2 | 1 | | | | | |
| **Innings** | 25 | 25 | 25 | 21 | 12 | 14 | 14 | 11 | 12 | 9 | 10 | 7 | 7 | 6 | 6 | 4 | 6 | 6 | 2 | 2 | 2 | 2 | | | | | |
| **Not Out** | 5 | 3 | 0 | 2 | 4 | 1 | 2 | 1 | 1 | 3 | 2 | 0 | 1 | 1 | 2 | 1 | 1 | 0 | 2 | 0 | 1 | 1 | | | | | |
| **Highest Score** | 266* | 154* | 124 | 179 | 48* | 68* | 69 | 51 | 70 | 19 | 25* | 103 | 28 | 29 | 34 | 15 | 10 | 69 | 8* | 0 | 9* | 9* | | | | | |
| **Runs** | 2026 | 965 | 812 | 752 | 240 | 301 | 277 | 277 | 228 | 74 | 83 | 174 | 86 | 82 | 97 | 42 | 16 | 168 | 17 | 0 | 15 | 15 | | | | | |
| **Average** | 101.30 | 43.86 | 32.48 | 39.57 | 30.00 | 23.15 | 23.08 | 27.70 | 20.72 | 12.33 | 10.37 | 19.33 | 14.33 | 13.66 | 24.25 | 8.40 | 5.33 | 28.00 | 4.25 | 0.00 | 15.00 | 15.00 | | | | | |
| **100s** | 10 | 4 | 1 | 2 | 0 | 0 | 0 | 0 | 0 | 0 | 0 | 1 | 0 | 0 | 0 | 0 | 0 | 0 | 0 | 0 | 0 | 0 | | | | | |
| **50s** | 4 | 3 | 5 | 2 | 0 | 2 | 3 | 1 | 1 | 0 | 0 | 0 | 0 | 0 | 0 | 0 | 0 | 1 | 0 | 0 | 0 | 0 | | | | | |
| **Catches/Stumpings** | 13/0 | 42/5 | 17/0 | 14/0 | 6/0 | 10/0 | 7/0 | 5/0 | 9/0 | 1/0 | 1/0 | 4/0 | 3/0 | 3/0 | 1/0 | 1/0 | 1/0 | 2/0 | 0/0 | 1/0 | 1/0 | 0/0 | | | | | |

**Home Ground:** The Brit Oval
**Address:** The Brit Oval, Kennington, London, SE11 5SS
**Tel:** 0207 582 6660
**Fax:** 0207 735 7769
**Email:** enquiries@surreycricket.com
**Directions:** *By road:* The Brit Oval is located south of the Thames in Kennington on the A202, near the junction with the A3 and A24, just south of Vauxhall Bridge and 10 minutes from Victoria and Waterloo (Eurostar). *By rail:* Take South West Trains to Vauxhall which is a short walk from the ground. The station is well served by trains from throughout Surrey and Hampshire as well as from the Greater London area. Connections include Clapham Junction and Waterloo.

**Capacity:** 16,500
**Other grounds used:** Guildford, Whitgift School
**Year formed:** 1845

**Chief Executive:** Paul Sheldon
**Cricket Manager:** Alan Butcher
**Captain:** Mark Butcher
**County colours:** Blue, white and yellow

Website:
www.surreycricket.com

**Honours**
County Championship
1890, 1891, 1892, 1894, 1895, 1899, 1914,
1952, 1953, 1954, 1955, 1956, 1957, 1958,
1971, 1999, 2000, 2002
Joint Champions 1950
Sunday League/NCL/Pro40
1996, 2003
Benson & Hedges Cup
1974, 1997, 2001
Gillette Cup/NatWest/C&G Trophy
1982, 1992
Twenty20 Cup
2003

# FIRST-CLASS MATCHES
## BOWLING

| | MJ Nicholson | Harbhajan Singh | CJ Jordan | CP Schofield | R Clarke | NC Saker | ND Doshi | J Ormond | Murtaza Hussain | IDK Salisbury | JW Dernbach | Mohammad Akram | Azhar Mahmood | SJ Magoffin | SJ Walters | MR Ramprakash | AD Brown | MA Butcher | RS Clinton | JGE Benning | Overs | Total | Byes/Leg-byes | Wickets | Run outs |
|---|---|---|---|---|---|---|---|---|---|---|---|---|---|---|---|---|---|---|---|---|---|---|---|---|---|
| v. Yorkshire (The Oval) 18-21 April | | | 23-1-114-0 / 16-1-71-1 | 16-3-71-2 | | | 35-10-118-1 / 21.1-3-111-6 | 24-6-101-1 / 8-2-24-0 | | | | | 27-4-73-3 / 7-0-27-0 | 24-8-73-2 / 6-1-21-0 | | | | | | 5-0-25-0 | 154 / 58.1 | 594 / 266 | 19 / 12 | 9 / 7 | |
| v. Hampshire (The Oval) 25-28 April | | | | 15-1-57-1 | 18.4-2-61-1 / 18-0-80-0 | | 24-8-78-1 / 3-0-13-0 | | 31-3-121-4 / 15-0-76-1 | | | 16-2-71-2 / 6-0-25-0 | 22-7-66-0 / 5-0-20-0 | | | | | | | | 126.4 / 47 | 481 / 224 | 27 / 10 | 9 / 1 | |
| v. Lancashire (Old Trafford) 2-4 May | | | | 16-2-62-1 / 22-0-12-0 | 20-4-76-5 / 4-1-24-1 | | 20-5-52-2 / 4-0-18-0 | | 20.2-4-59-1 / 3-0-12-0 | | | 16-7-37-1 / 8-3-22-2 | | | | | | | | 4-0-18-0 | 96.2 / 21.2 | 315 / 90 | 11 / 2 | 10 / 3 | |
| v. Warwickshire (The Oval) 9-12 May | 26-5-68-3 | | 7-2-20-1 | 15-4-60-1 / 1-0-4-0 | 19-3-98-4 | | 16-3-56-1 | | | | | | | | | 1-0-1-0 | | | | 4-0-20-0 | 87 / 2 | 329 / 5 | 7 / 0 | 10 / 0 | |
| v. Sussex (Hove) 16-19 May | 29-7-89-5 / 19-3-73-2 | | | 16-4-57-3 / 10-0-39-0 | 23-7-71-0 / 15-5-50-0 | | 23.3-6-60-2 / 22-0-88-1 | | 12-0-44-0 / 24-3-81-0 | | | | | | | 3-0-17-0 | 1-1-0-0 | 14-3-38-0 / 3-0-17-0 | | | 118.3 / 96 | 365 / 372 | 6 / 7 | 10 / 3 | |
| v. Kent (Whitgift School) 30 May-2 June | 30-2-134-1 | | | | 5.3-2-16-1 | 14-1-71-0 | 20-2-123-1 | | 21.2-4-102-1 | | | | 27-8-81-1 | | | | 5.3-0-28-0 | | | | 123.3 | 564 | - | 9 | - |
| v. Worcestershire (Worcester) 6-9 June | 27-3-115-1 | | | 33-3-144-1 | 16-1-84-2 | 14-2-71-0 | | | | 36-2-139-2 | | | 26-5-92-0 | | | 1-0-18-0 | 3-0-16-0 | | | | 156 | 701 | - | 6 | - |
| v. Durham (The Oval) 8-10 July | 14-3-37-3 / 14.1-2-44-4 | | | 11-2-44-3 / 15-1-66-0 | 1.3-1-2-1 / 12-4-29-2 | 5-0-27-1 / 5-2-9-1 | 7-0-40-1 / 7-1-23-2 | | | | | 6-1-30-1 / 4-1-29-1 | | | | | | | | | 44.3 / 57.1 | 191 / 204 | 11 / 4 | 10 / 10 | |
| v. Yorkshire (Headingley) 20-23 July | 24.5-5-85-4 / 1-0-2-1 | 28-10-56-3 | | | | 19-0-81-2 | 10.3-2-42-1 | | | | | 10-3-28-0 / 0.1-0-0-0 | | | | | | | | | 91.5 / 1.1 | 307 / 2 | 15 / 0 | 10 / 1 | |
| v. Worcestershire (Guildford) 25-28 July | 14-4-43-3 / 18-2-60-0 | 29-7-64-4 / 34-12-64-5 | | | 14.3-1-44-2 / 24-1-87-0 | 4-0-23-0 / 9-0-31-0 | 10.3-3-31-1 / 13-3-50-0 | | | | | | | | | | | | | | 71.3 / 98 | 217 / 307 | 10 / 15 | 10 / 15 | |
| v. Kent (Canterbury) 8-9 August | 15-4-48-2 / 12-4-43-1 | 19.4-5-34-5 / 23.3-6-57-6 | 13-3-41-2 / 11-1-47-2 | | | | | 13-6-19-1 / 12-6-21-1 | | | | | | | | | | | | | 60.4 / 58.3 | 150 / 171 | 8 / 3 | 10 / 10 | |
| v. Durham (Riverside) 13-16 August | 15-2-51-1 / 25-4-86-3 | 19.4-8-49-3 / 40-9-130-2 | 13-2-42-3 / 18-2-69-2 | | | | | | 15-2-68-2 / 17-4-76-0 | | | | | | 2-0-4-1 / 3-0-22-0 | | 1-0-4-0 | | | | 65.4 / 103 | 232 / 397 | 14 / 7 | 14 / 7 | |
| v. Hampshire (Rose Bowl) 30 August-2 September | 16-6-38-2 / 19-7-40-2 | 26.2-9-51-2 / 38-14-71-4 | 13-3-40-0 / 17-6-50-1 | 22-6-52-5 / 33.5-9-87-3 | | | | | 13-3-30-0 / 6-2-28-0 | | | | | | | | | | 2-0-6-0 | | 90.2 / 115.5 | 221 / 298 | 10 / 16 | 10 / 10 | 1 |
| v. Warwickshire (Edgbaston) 6-9 September | 16-6-41-2 / 15-2-60-1 | | 15-2-46-3 / 8.5-2-27-2 | | | | | | 16-2-70-2 / 14-2-42-2 | 18-2-57-2 / 21-5-50-3 | 11-1-45-1 / 18-4-77-2 | | | | | 3-1-2-0 | | | 2-0-22-0 | | 78 / 79.5 | 285 / 264 | 4 / 6 | 10 / 10 | |
| v. Lancashire (The Oval) 19-22 September | 8-3-30-3 / 20-1-102-0 | | 12.2-1-50-3 / 18-0-78-2 | | | | | | 21-4-49-2 / 34.4-14-126-4 | 15-1-60-1 / 11.1-0-51-1 | 11-2-41-1 / 18-2-85-3 | | | | | | | | | | 67.2 / 101.5 | 234 / 464 | 4 / 22 | 10 / 10 | |

| | MJ Nicholson | Harbhajan Singh | CJ Jordan | CP Schofield | R Clarke | NC Saker | ND Doshi | J Ormond | Murtaza Hussain | IDK Salisbury | JW Dernbach | Mohammad Akram | Azhar Mahmood | SJ Magoffin | SJ Walters | MR Ramprakash | AD Brown | MA Butcher | RS Clinton | JGE Benning |
|---|---|---|---|---|---|---|---|---|---|---|---|---|---|---|---|---|---|---|---|---|
| Overs | 378 | 284.1 | 139.1 | 186.5 | 154.5 | 156 | 174.2 | 189 | 94.4 | 188.5 | 78.1 | 73 | 87 | 30 | 8 | 1 | 8 | 6.3 | 17 | 17 |
| Maidens | 75 | 83 | 22 | 29 | 19 | 33 | 26 | 48 | 25 | 15 | 14 | 20 | 16 | 9 | 1 | 0 | 0 | 1 | 3 | 0 |
| Runs | 1289 | 686 | 490 | 650 | 633 | 649 | 697 | 640 | 282 | 745 | 335 | 236 | 287 | 94 | 28 | 18 | 38 | 28 | 55 | 91 |
| Wickets | 44 | 37 | 20 | 16 | 15 | 15 | 13 | 12 | 11 | 11 | 9 | 6 | 3 | 2 | 1 | 0 | 0 | 0 | 0 | 0 |
| Average | 29.29 | 18.54 | 24.50 | 40.62 | 42.20 | 43.26 | 53.61 | 53.33 | 25.63 | 67.72 | 37.22 | 39.33 | 92.66 | 47.00 | 28.00 | - | - | - | - | - |

## FIELDING

| | |
|---|---|
| 47 | JN Batty (42 ct, 5 st) |
| 17 | SA Newman |
| 14 | MA Butcher |
| 13 | MR Ramprakash |
| 10 | R Clarke |
| 9 | SJ Walters |
| 7 | AD Brown |
| 6 | MJ Nicholson |
| 5 | JGE Benning |
| 4 | IDK Salisbury |
| 3 | CP Schofield |
| 3 | Harbhajan Singh |
| 2 | Azhar Mahmood |
| 1 | J Ormond |
| 1 | RS Clinton |
| 1 | ND Doshi |
| 1 | NC Saker |
| 1 | JW Dernbach |
| 1 | CJ Jordan |
| 1 | Murtaza Hussain |
| 0 | Mohammad Akram |
| 0 | SJ Magoffin |

## Final Division One Table

| | P | W | L | D | T | Ab | Bat | Bowl | Pens | Pts |
|---|---|---|---|---|---|---|---|---|---|---|
| Sussex | 16 | 7 | 3 | 5 | 0 | 1 | 37 | 43 | 0.00 | 202.00 |
| Durham | 16 | 7 | 5 | 4 | 0 | 0 | 38 | 47 | 1.50 | 197.50 |
| Lancashire | 16 | 5 | 2 | 8 | 0 | 1 | 40 | 44 | 0.00 | 190.00 |
| Surrey | 16 | 5 | 4 | 6 | 0 | 1 | 41 | 40 | 1.00 | 178.00 |
| Hampshire | 16 | 5 | 3 | 8 | 0 | 0 | 32 | 43 | 0.00 | 177.00 |
| Yorkshire | 16 | 4 | 4 | 8 | 0 | 0 | 49 | 38 | 0.00 | 175.00 |
| Kent | 16 | 3 | 5 | 7 | 0 | 1 | 43 | 36 | 0.00 | 153.00 |
| Warwickshire | 16 | 2 | 5 | 9 | 0 | 0 | 40 | 35 | 0.00 | 139.00 |
| Worcestershire | 16 | 1 | 8 | 5 | 0 | 2 | 18 | 35 | 0.00 | 95.00 |

SURREY CRICKET

Limited overs nickname:
**SURREY BROWN CAPS**

# SUSSEX CCC

## FIRST-CLASS MATCHES
### BATTING

| Match | RR Montgomerie | CD Nash | MW Goodwin | CJ Adams | RSC Martin-Jenkins | Mushtaq Ahmed | AJ Hodd | Naved-ul-Hasan | JD Lewry | MH Yardy | LJ Wright | CD Hopkinson | RJ Kirtley | CJ Liddle | MJ Prior | Saqlain Mushtaq | OP Rayner | MA Thornley | BC Brown | JAG Green | TMJ Smith | Extras | Total | Wickets | Result | Points |
|---|---|---|---|---|---|---|---|---|---|---|---|---|---|---|---|---|---|---|---|---|---|---|---|---|---|---|
| v. MCC (Lord's) 13–16 April | | 15 | 134 | 0 | 99* | 8* | 8 | | | | 8 | 20 | 26 | | 37 | 0 | | | | | | 30 | 385 | 10 | | |
| | | 7 | 2 | 6* | | | 35* | | | | | 11 | | | 47 | | | | | | | 13 | 121 | 4 | D | |
| v. Kent (Hove) 18–21 April | 175 | 50 | 23 | 0 | 27 | | 75 | 13* | | 7 | | 13 | 51 | | 14 | | | | | | | 62 | 510 | 10 | | |
| | 33* | 1 | 7* | | | | | | | 7 | | 11 | | | | | | | | | | 5 | 57 | 2 | W | 22 |
| v. Warwickshire (Edgbaston) 25–27 April | 0 | 0 | 8 | 41 | 20 | 4 | 4 | | | | | 47 | 13* | 4 | 3 | | | | | | | 7 | 151 | 10 | | |
| | 6 | 24 | 31 | 27 | 8 | 0 | 0 | | | | | 55 | 2* | 15 | 18 | | | | | | | 20 | 206 | 10 | L | 3 |
| v. Kent (Canterbury) 2–3 May | 0 | 22 | 0 | 42 | 2* | | 0 | 0 | | | | 6 | 0 | | 4 | | | | | | | 22 | 102 | 10 | | |
| | 11 | 16 | 1 | 16 | 24* | 0 | 4 | 6 | | | | 26 | 4 | | 35 | | | | | | | 17 | 160 | 10 | L | 3 |
| v. Surrey (Hove) 16–19 May | 78 | 53 | 119 | 32 | 4 | 14 | 43 | 0 | | 14* | | 0 | 0 | | | | | | | | | 8 | 365 | 10 | | |
| | 3 | 46 | 205* | 102* | | | | | | | | 8 | | | | | | | | | | 8 | 372 | 3 | D | 9 |
| v. Worcestershire (Worcester) 24–26 May | 9 | 16 | 112 | 91 | 17 | | 72 | 26 | | 55* | | 83 | | | | | | | | | | 31 | 512 | 8 | W | 22 |
| v. Lancashire (Hove) 30 May–2 June | 28 | 47 | 0 | 40 | 7 | 4 | 9 | 15 | 0 | 42 | 32* | | | | | | | | | | | 11 | 235 | 10 | | |
| | 50 | 35 | 23 | 1 | 4* | | 16* | | 0 | | | | | | | | | | | | | 16 | 145 | 5 | D | 8 |
| v. Hampshire (Arundel Castle) 6–9 June | 48 | 61 | 2 | 52 | 12 | 54 | 28 | 1 | 0* | 15 | 57 | | | | | | | | | | | 11 | 341 | 10 | | |
| | 82 | 28 | 99 | 103* | | | | 18 | | 3 | 8* | | | | | | | | | | | 19 | 360 | 5 | W | 20 |
| v. Yorkshire (Headingley) 15–18 June | 17 | 28 | 7 | 29 | 16 | 2* | 7 | 4 | 0 | 20 | 2 | | | | | | | | | | | 9 | 141 | 10 | | |
| | 0 | 15 | 21* | | | | | | | 21* | | | | | | | | | | | | 0 | 57 | 2 | D | 7 |
| v. India (Hove) 7–10 July | 18 | 28 | | 42 | | | 106* | | | 53 | | 5 | | | | | 19* | 2 | | | | 27 | 300 | 6 | | |
| | 59 | 0 | | 45* | | | 4 | 8* | | 5 | | 6 | 8 | | | 9 | 3 | 11 | | | | 32 | 190 | 9 | D | |
| v. Durham (Horsham) 13–15 July | 21 | 63 | 44 | 193 | 43 | 9* | 72 | 0 | | 14 | 15 | | | | | | | | | | | 43 | 517 | 10 | W | 22 |
| v. Sri Lanka A (Hove) 19–21 July | 52 | | | | | | | | | 125 | 36 | 21 | | | | 1* | 35 | 2 | 46 | 28 | 2 | 24 | 372 | 9 | D | |
| v. Hampshire (Rose Bowl) 25–28 July | 46 | 0 | 19 | 1 | 6 | 5 | 9 | 4 | 5* | 1 | 43 | | | | | | | | | | | 6 | 145 | 10 | | |
| | 0 | 7 | 68* | 38 | | | 8* | | | 1 | | | | | | | | | | | | 2 | 124 | 4 | D | 7 |
| v. Lancashire (Liverpool) 31 July–2nd August | 12 | 75 | 74* | 2 | 0 | 8 | 4 | 1 | 4 | 47 | 8 | | | | | | | | | | | 39 | 274 | 10 | | |
| | 1 | 0 | 68 | 42 | 17 | 0 | 10 | 21* | 5 | 52 | 32 | | | | | | | | | | | 20 | 268 | 10 | W | 19 |
| v. Warwickshire (Hove) 8–11 August | 2 | 5 | 5 | 7 | 13* | | 18 | 5 | 12 | 0 | 61 | | | | | 19 | | | | | | 21 | 168 | 10 | | |
| | 195 | 50 | 6 | 1 | | | 46* | | | 54 | 9* | | | | | | | | | | | 44 | 405 | 5 | D | 7 |
| v. Yorkshire (Hove) 5–7 September | 73 | 1 | 47 | 46 | 49 | | 123 | 46 | | 119 | | | | | | 57* | | | | | | 36 | 597 | 8 | W | 22 |
| v. Durham (Riverside) 11–13 September | 20 | 49 | 66 | 6 | 77* | 7 | 2 | 27 | 8 | 0 | | | | | | 5 | | | | | | 24 | 291 | 10 | | |
| | 8 | 4 | 23 | 44 | 23 | 0 | 0 | 4* | | 9 | | | | | | 0 | | | | | | 16 | 131 | 10 | L | 5 |
| v. Worcestershire (Hove) 19–22 September | 82 | 89 | | 74 | 99 | 19 | 8 | 8* | | 52 | | 7 | | 53 | | | 4 | | | | | 37 | 532 | 10 | W | 22 |
| **Matches** | 17 | 17 | 15 | 15 | 15 | 15 | 14 | 14 | 14 | 13 | 11 | 10 | 7 | 5 | 4 | 4 | 4 | 2 | 1 | 1 | 1 | | | | | |
| **Innings** | 29 | 30 | 27 | 24 | 22 | 17 | 21 | 18 | 14 | 21 | 13 | 17 | 8 | 5 | 7 | 5 | 5 | 3 | 1 | 1 | 1 | | | | | |
| **Not Out** | 1 | 0 | 5 | 2 | 6 | 3 | 5 | 1 | 6 | 2 | 6 | 0 | 2 | 1 | 0 | 1 | 1 | 0 | 0 | 0 | 0 | | | | | |
| **Highest Score** | 195 | 89 | 205* | 193 | 99 | 54 | 123 | 75 | 13* | 125 | 61 | 83 | 51 | 53 | 47 | 57* | 35 | 11 | 46 | 28 | 2 | | | | | |
| **Runs** | 1129 | 835 | 1214 | 1030 | 521 | 170 | 628 | 251 | 73 | 732 | 347 | 347 | 98 | 99 | 158 | 90 | 61 | 15 | 46 | 28 | 2 | | | | | |
| **Average** | 40.32 | 27.83 | 55.18 | 46.81 | 32.56 | 12.14 | 39.25 | 14.76 | 9.12 | 38.52 | 49.57 | 20.41 | 16.33 | 24.75 | 22.57 | 22.50 | 15.25 | 5.00 | 46.00 | 28.00 | 2.00 | | | | | |
| **100s** | 2 | 0 | 4 | 3 | 0 | 0 | 2 | 0 | 0 | 2 | 0 | 0 | 0 | 0 | 0 | 0 | 0 | 0 | 0 | 0 | 0 | | | | | |
| **50s** | 7 | 7 | 5 | 3 | 2 | 1 | 2 | 1 | 0 | 5 | 3 | 2 | 1 | 1 | 0 | 1 | 0 | 0 | 0 | 0 | 0 | | | | | |
| **Catches/Stumpings** | 31/0 | 10/0 | 10/0 | 27/0 | 8/0 | 3/0 | 21/7 | 5/0 | 4/0 | 11/0 | 3/0 | 10/0 | 6/0 | 3/0 | 11/2 | 1/0 | 3/0 | 4/0 | 0/0 | 0/0 | 0/0 | | | | | |

**Home Ground:** Hove
**Address:** County Ground, Eaton Road, Hove, BN3 3AN
**Tel:** 08712 461100
**Fax:** 01273 771549
**Email:** simon.dyke@sussexcricket.co.uk
**Directions:** *By rail:* Hove station is a 10-minute walk. *By road:* Follow AA signs. Street parking at no cost.
**Capacity:** 5,500

**Other grounds used:** Arundel Castle, Horsham
**Year formed:** 1839

**Chief Executive:** Gus MacKay
**Club Coach:** Mark Robinson
**Captain:** Chris Adams
**County colours:** Red, black and white

### Honours
County Championship
2003, 2006, 2007
Sunday League/NCL/Pro40
1982
Gillette Cup/NatWest/C&G Trophy
1963, 1964, 1978, 1986, 2006

Website:
www.sussexcricket.co.uk

# FIRST-CLASS MATCHES
## BOWLING

| v. | Mushtaq Ahmed | Naved-ul-Hasan | RSC Martin-Jenkins | JD Lewry | Saqlain Mushtaq | OP Rayner | LJ Wright | RJ Kirtley | CJ Liddle | MH Yardy | CD Nash | TMJ Smith | CJ Adams | MW Goodwin | CD Hopkinson | JAG Green | Overs | Total | Byes/Leg-byes | Wickets | Run outs |
|---|---|---|---|---|---|---|---|---|---|---|---|---|---|---|---|---|---|---|---|---|---|
| v. MCC (Lord's) 13-16 April | | | 25-11-50-2 | | 16-5-51-0 | 24-2-117-3 | 31-9-71-4 | 20.4-2-91-1 | 4-1-18-0 | | | | | | 3-0-19-0 | | 123.4 | 425 | 8 | 10 | |
| | | | 12-2-36-1 | | 39-3-136-2 | 12-2-38-0 | 11-3-30-0 | 22-3-67-2 | | 1-0-4-0 | | | | | 2-0-10-0 | | 99 | 327 | 6 | 5 | |
| v. Kent (Hove) 18-21 April | 21.3-2-74-6 | 15.5-1-64-1 | | 8-4-23-2 | | | | | | 14-2-46-1 | 10-2-39-0 | | | | | | 59.2 | 216 | 9 | 10 | |
| | 41.1-4-145-4 | 24-2-106-4 | | 9.1-2-35-1 | | | 3.5-2-13-1 | | | | | | | | | | 88.1 | 349 | 11 | 10 | |
| v. Warwickshire (Edgbaston) 25-27 April | 41.3-7-124-4 | | 37-7-123-5 | 12-3-26-0 | | | 21-8-51-0 | 17-5-43-0 | | | | | | | | | 128.3 | 391 | 24 | 10 | 1 |
| | | | | | | | | | | | | | | | | | - | - | - | - | |
| v. Kent (Canterbury) 2-3 May | 25-2-117-1 | 12-1-44-3 | 23.3-4-67-5 | 20-4-53-0 | | | | 16-2-78-0 | | | | | | | | | 96.3 | 368 | 9 | 10 | 1 |
| | | | | | | | | | | | | | | | | | - | - | - | - | |
| v. Surrey (Hove) 16-19 May | 35-2-178-1 | 26-4-103-1 | 28-6-97-0 | | | | 24-0-107-1 | 27-5-89-0 | | | 0.4-0-5-0 | | 4-0-3-0 | | 2-0-16-0 | | 146.4 | 626 | 22 | 3 | |
| | | | | | | | | | | | | | | | | | - | - | - | - | |
| v. Worcestershire (Worcester) 24-26 May | 8-3-22-5 | 5-2-17-1 | | 6-1-21-2 | | | 8.2-0-34-2 | | | | | | | | | | 27.2 | 100 | 6 | 10 | |
| | 31-2-117-3 | 12-0-63-3 | 7-5-17-3 | 13-3-47-0 | | | 8-0-43-1 | | | | | | | | | | 71 | 303 | 16 | 10 | |
| v. Lancashire (Hove) 30 May-2 June | 32-6-88-2 | 23-2-94-3 | | 12-4-36-1 | | | 15-0-53-1 | | | 13-1-1-2 | | | | | | | 103.3 | 330 | 9 | 10 | |
| | 23-4-58-2 | 9-2-36-1 | | 4-2-9-1 | 18-3-81-3 | | 2-0-10-1 | | | | | | | | | | 56 | 206 | 12 | 8 | |
| v. Hampshire (Arundel Castle) 6-9 June | 19-2-72-7 | 10-0-44-1 | 10-4-16-1 | 11-1-42-0 | | | 8-4-24-1 | | | | | | | | | | 58 | 202 | 4 | 10 | |
| | 38-4-100-2 | 22-3-78-2 | 8-4-21-3 | 19-1-80-1 | | | 13-4-30-2 | | | 3-0-8-0 | | | | | | | 103 | 333 | 16 | 10 | |
| v. Yorkshire (Headingley) 15-18 June | 11.2-2-40-3 | 12-4-34-3 | 8-2-20-2 | 15-8-30-2 | | | 2-0-12-0 | | | | | | | | | | 48.2 | 139 | 9 | 10 | |
| | 29-7-72-1 | 22-1-85-1 | 17-7-28-1 | 24-10-37-2 | | | 10-2-30-0 | | | | 5-1-19-0 | | 1-0-4-0 | | | | 108 | 284 | 9 | 6 | 1 |
| v. India (Hove) 7-10 July | | | 21-5-48-1 | 21-6-53-0 | 29.5-4-71-3 | 8-0-34-2 | | 24-7-69-0 | 15-1-48-0 | | 9-0-33-1 | | | | 3-0-14-0 | | 130.5 | 388 | 18 | 7 | |
| | | | 7-3-13-2 | 8-1-31-2 | 4-1-10-1 | 9-2-36-0 | | 12-4-31-1 | | | 7-0-32-0 | | | | 4-0-20-0 | | 51 | 184 | 11 | 8 | |
| v. Durham (Horsham) 13-15 July | 26.1-3-91-5 | 14-2-52-2 | 5-1-10-0 | 12-4-33-3 | | | 2-0-11-0 | | | | 1-0-3-0 | | | | | | 60.1 | 209 | 9 | 10 | |
| | 21-6-77-4 | 17-3-60-2 | 11-3-35-2 | | | | 5-0-23-1 | | | | 2-0-7-0 | | | | | | 56 | 206 | 4 | 10 | |
| v. Sri Lanka A (Hove) 19-21 July | | | | | | 7.4-0-28-3 | 6-1-14-0 | 14-1-44-4 | 12-2-40-2 | 13-4-32-1 | | | 4-0-27-0 | | | 8-1-32-0 | 64.4 | 225 | 5 | 10 | |
| | | | | | | 16.4-2-68-5 | 4-1-15-0 | 5-1-19-2 | 8-2-23-0 | | | | 9-1-52-1 | | | | 42.4 | 191 | 14 | 8 | |
| v. Hampshire (Rose Bowl) 25-28 July | 13.4-1-54-2 | 19.4-7-106-5 | 11-4-27-1 | 8-2-37-1 | | | 6.2-1-11-0 | | | | | | | | | | 58.4 | 250 | 15 | 9 | |
| | | | | | | | | | | | | | | | | | - | - | - | - | |
| v. Lancashire (Liverpool) 31 July-2 August | 19-2-81-2 | 18.4-1-99-3 | 14-4-37-1 | 19-3-81-4 | | | | | | | | | | | | | 70.4 | 301 | 3 | 10 | |
| | 21-5-71-4 | 9-4-10-3 | 9-3-22-2 | 5-0-27-1 | | | | | | | | | | | | | 44 | 133 | 3 | 10 | |
| v. Warwickshire (Hove) 8-11 August | 47-6-170-4 | 22-1-71-1 | | 20-4-45-0 | 27.3-6-96-5 | | 10-2-18-0 | | | 3-0-9-0 | | | | | | | 129.3 | 433 | 24 | 10 | |
| | 29.4-3-111-7 | 10-3-30-1 | | 12-6-22-1 | 10-1-37-1 | | 5-0-16-0 | | | | | | | | | | 66.4 | 238 | 22 | 10 | |
| v. Yorkshire (Hove) 5-7 September | 30-5-89-5 | 16.1-2-74-0 | 6-2-17-2 | 13-4-38-1 | 4-0-7-1 | | 17-6-28-3 | | | | | | | | | | 69.1 | 247 | 22 | 10 | 1 |
| | 1-0-1-0 | 6.1-3-15-4 | 7-3-16-0 | 13-4-23-3 | | | | | | | | | | | | | 44.1 | 89 | 6 | 10 | |
| v. Durham (Riverside) 11-13 September | 36.3-125-3 | 15.4-46-0 | 16.3-6-33-3 | 14-3-36-0 | 23-4-58-4 | | | | | | 4.3-1-20-0 | 5-0-23-1 | | | 1-0-6-0 | | 104.3 | 316 | 17 | 10 | |
| | 1-0-8-0 | | | 6-0-27-0 | 4-0-10-0 | 3-0-8-0 | | | | | | | | | | | 24.3 | 107 | 5 | 1 | |
| v. Worcestershire (Hove) 19-22 September | 39-8-93-6 | | 5-1-22-0 | 23-3-44-3 | | | 9-3-14-1 | | | | 12-5-34-0 | | | | | | 88 | 213 | 6 | 10 | |
| | 27.5-2-132-7 | | 14-1-41-2 | 13-2-39-0 | | | 12-1-47-1 | | | | 5-0-16-0 | 1-0-3-0 | | | | | 72.5 | 305 | 27 | 10 | |
| **Overs** | 667.5 | 377.3 | 299 | 348.1 | 118.2 | 117.2 | 168.3 | 185 | 111.4 | 51.3 | 10.1 | 13 | 4 | 1 | 14 | 8 | | | | | |
| **Maidens** | 91 | 59 | 90 | 85 | 21 | 16 | 21 | 44 | 20 | 7 | 1 | 1 | 0 | 0 | 0 | 1 | | | | | |
| **Runs** | 2310 | 1454 | 771 | 1017 | 316 | 414 | 619 | 567 | 365 | 181 | 40 | 79 | 9 | 6 | 79 | 32 | | | | | |
| **Wickets** | 90 | 50 | 36 | 33 | 18 | 14 | 14 | 12 | 5 | 4 | 3 | 1 | 0 | 0 | 0 | 0 | | | | | |
| **Average** | 25.66 | 29.08 | 21.41 | 30.81 | 17.55 | 29.57 | 44.21 | 47.25 | 73.00 | 45.25 | 13.33 | 79.00 | - | - | - | - | | | | | |

## FIELDING

| | |
|---|---|
| 31 | RR Montgomerie |
| 28 | AJ Hodd (21 ct, 7 st) |
| 27 | CJ Adams |
| 13 | MJ Prior (11 ct, 2 st) |
| 11 | MH Yardy |
| 10 | MW Goodwin |
| 10 | CD Hopkinson |
| 10 | CD Nash |
| 8 | RSC Martin-Jenkins |
| 6 | RJ Kirtley |
| 5 | Naved-ul-Hasan |
| 4 | JD Lewry |
| 4 | MA Thornley |
| 3 | Mushtaq Ahmed |
| 3 | LJ Wright |
| 3 | CJ Liddle |
| 3 | OP Rayner |
| 1 | Saqlain Mushtaq |
| 0 | JAG Green |
| 0 | TMJ Smith |
| 0 | BC Brown |

## Final Division One Table

| | P | W | L | D | T | Ab | Bat | Bowl | Pens | Pts |
|---|---|---|---|---|---|---|---|---|---|---|
| Sussex | 16 | 7 | 3 | 5 | 0 | 1 | 37 | 43 | 0.00 | 202.00 |
| Durham | 16 | 7 | 5 | 4 | 0 | 0 | 38 | 47 | 1.50 | 197.50 |
| Lancashire | 16 | 5 | 2 | 8 | 0 | 1 | 40 | 44 | 0.00 | 190.00 |
| Surrey | 16 | 5 | 4 | 6 | 0 | 1 | 41 | 40 | 1.00 | 178.00 |
| Hampshire | 16 | 5 | 3 | 8 | 0 | 0 | 32 | 43 | 0.00 | 177.00 |
| Yorkshire | 16 | 4 | 4 | 8 | 0 | 0 | 49 | 38 | 0.00 | 175.00 |
| Kent | 16 | 3 | 5 | 7 | 0 | 1 | 43 | 36 | 0.00 | 153.00 |
| Warwickshire | 16 | 2 | 5 | 9 | 0 | 0 | 40 | 35 | 0.00 | 139.00 |
| Worcestershire | 16 | 1 | 8 | 5 | 0 | 2 | 18 | 35 | 0.00 | 95.00 |

Limited overs nickname:
SUSSEX SHARKS

# WARWICKSHIRE CCC

## FIRST–CLASS MATCHES
### BATTING

| Match | TR Ambrose | AGR Loudon | DL Maddy | JO Troughton | IJ Westwood | UL Trott | JE Anyon | HH Streak | N Tahir | TD Groenewald | KC Sangakkara | DW Steyn | LC Parker | MJ Powell | AC Thomas | PL Harris | LM Daggett | NM Carter | IR Bell | AG Botha | AJ Shantry | SM Hole | CR Woakes | MW Barnes | Extras | Total | Wickets | Result | Points |
|---|---|---|---|---|---|---|---|---|---|---|---|---|---|---|---|---|---|---|---|---|---|---|---|---|---|---|---|---|---|
| v. Lancashire | 30 | 104 | 71 | 100 | 33 | 0 | 37 | 55* | 12 | 16 | 9 | | | | | | | | | | | | | | 23 | 490 | 10 | | |
| (Edgbaston) 18-21 April | 51* | 3 | 14 | 25 | 32 | 0 | | 4 | | 30 | 17* | | | | | | | | | | | | | | 13 | 189 | 7 | D | 12 |
| v. Sussex | 72 | 32 | 2 | 26 | 82 | 84 | 0 | | 7 | 20 | 31* | 0 | | | | | | | | | | | | | 35 | 391 | 10 | W | 21 |
| (Edgbaston) 25-27 April | | | | | | | | | | | | | | | | | | | | | | | | | | | | | |
| v. Worcestershire | 251* | 45 | 0 | 162 | 2 | 39 | | 66 | | 13* | | | | | | | | | | | | | | | 32 | 610 | 6 | W | 22 |
| (Worcester) 2-5 May | | | | | | | | | | | | | | | | | | | | | | | | | | | | | |
| v. Surrey | 14 | 0 | 134 | 24 | 24 | 20 | 5* | 21 | 6 | | 51 | | | | | | | | 9 | | | | | | 21 | 329 | 10 | | |
| (The Oval) 9-12 May | | | 1* | | 4* | | | | | | | | | | | | | | | | | | | | 0 | 5 | 0 | D | 7 |
| v. Durham | 15 | 105 | 0 | 1 | 0 | 3 | 34 | 16* | 0 | 149 | 0 | | | | | | | | | | | | | | 12 | 335 | 10 | D | 9 |
| (Edgbaston) 16-19 May | | | | | | | | | | | | | | | | | | | | | | | | | | | | | |
| v. Hampshire | 0 | 103 | 24 | 18 | 51 | 3 | 14* | 5 | 10 | 5 | 26 | | | | | | | | | | | | | | 3 | 262 | 10 | D | 9 |
| (Edgbaston) 30 May-2 June | | | | | | | | | | | | | | | | | | | | | | | | | | | | | |
| v. Worcestershire | 42 | 36 | 5 | 109 | 18 | 27 | 2 | | 0 | 41* | 20 | 11 | | | | | | | | | | | | | 32 | 343 | 10 | | |
| (Edgbaston) 15-18 June | | | | | 14* | | | | | 34* | | | | | | | | | | | | | | | 0 | 48 | 0 | D | 10 |
| v. Hampshire | 32 | 41* | 123 | 44 | 23 | 50 | 5* | | | | | | | | | | | | | | | | | | 35 | 353 | 5 | L | 1 |
| (Rose Bowl) 8-11 July | | | | | | | | | | | | | | | | | | | | | | | | | | | | | |
| v. Yorkshire | | 135* | 1* | 51 | | | | | | | | | | | | | | | 65 | | | | | | 2 | 254 | 2 | D | 9 |
| (Edgbaston) 13-16 July | | | | | | | | | | | | | | | | | | | | | | | | | | | | | |
| v. Kent | 13 | 4 | 23 | 5 | 15 | 0 | | 12 | 0 | | | | | 4 | 6* | 2 | | | | | | | | | 23 | 107 | 10 | | |
| (Canterbury) 20-23 July | 8 | 0 | 148* | 31 | 47 | 0 | | 6 | 3 | | | | | | | | | | | | | | | | 25 | 268 | 7 | D | 6 |
| v. Durham | 11 | 32 | 7 | | 0 | 20 | 7 | 0 | 32 | | 59 | | | | | 55 | 0* | | | | | | | | 16 | 239 | 10 | | |
| (Riverside) 31 July-3 August | 24 | 45 | 16 | | 116 | 4 | 37* | 0 | 0 | | 119 | | | | | 0 | 33 | | | | | | | | 32 | 426 | 10 | L | 2 |
| v. Sussex | 99 | 0 | 53 | 35 | 110 | 6 | 0* | 24 | 5 | | 59 | | | | | | | | | | 5 | | | | 37 | 433 | 10 | | |
| (Hove) 8-11 August | 39 | 0 | 30 | 26 | 14 | 35 | 1 | 37 | 2* | | 21 | | | | | | | | | | 5 | | | | 28 | 238 | 10 | D | 12 |
| v. Kent | 2 | 14 | 8 | 36 | | 10 | | 15 | | | 26 | | 49 | 21* | 3 | | | | | 0 | | | | | 29 | 213 | 10 | D | 6 |
| (Edgbaston) 14-17 August | | | | | | | | | | | | | | | | | | | | | | | | | | | | | |
| v. Yorkshire | 4 | 33 | 0 | 9 | | | 13 | 24 | | | 0 | | 1 | 14 | 24 | | | | | | | 0* | | | 7 | 129 | 10 | | |
| (Scarborough) 22-24 August | 89* | 2 | 2 | 0 | | | 27 | 0 | | | 4 | | 1 | 6 | 42 | | | | | | | 24 | | | 25 | 222 | 10 | L | |
| v. Surrey | 33 | 13 | | 76 | 4 | 19 | 13 | | | | | | | 82 | 9 | | 14* | 1 | | | | | 9 | | 12 | 285 | 10 | | |
| (Edgbaston) 6-9 September | 11 | 20 | | 43 | 79 | 33 | 0 | | | | | | | 13 | 7 | | 27 | 9 | | | | | 14* | | 8 | 264 | 10 | L | 5 |
| v. Lancashire | 2 | 0 | | 2 | 1 | 9* | 7 | | | | | | 16 | | 27 | 12 | 1 | | | 27 | | | | | 2 | 106 | 10 | | |
| (Old Trafford) 11-13 September | 16 | 80 | | 50 | 42 | 0 | 4 | | | | | | 14 | | 23 | 15 | 12* | | | 0 | | | | | 16 | 272 | 10 | L | |
| **Matches** | 15 | 15 | 14 | 14 | 14 | 14 | 14 | 11 | 11 | 8 | 7 | 7 | 5 | 4 | 4 | 4 | 3 | 3 | 2 | 2 | 2 | 1 | 1 | 1 | | | | | |
| **Innings** | 22 | 22 | 20 | 19 | 22 | 20 | 16 | 15 | 11 | 9 | 11 | 7 | 6 | 6 | 3 | 4 | 5 | 2 | 4 | 3 | 2 | 2 | 2 | 0 | | | | | |
| **Not Out** | 3 | 1 | 3 | 1 | 2 | 0 | 5 | 3 | 1 | 2 | 1 | 2 | 0 | 0 | 1 | 0 | 2 | 2 | 0 | 0 | 0 | 1 | 1 | 0 | | | | | |
| **Highest Score** | 251* | 105 | 148* | 162 | 116 | 84 | 37* | 66 | 32 | 41* | 149 | 51 | 49 | 82 | 42 | 55 | 33 | 27 | 65 | 27 | 5 | 24 | 14* | 0 | | | | | |
| **Runs** | 858 | 712 | 796 | 771 | 771 | 396 | 199 | 278 | 87 | 133 | 496 | 145 | 81 | 165 | 130 | 59 | 42 | 56 | 74 | 37 | 10 | 24 | 23 | 0 | | | | | |
| **Average** | 45.15 | 33.90 | 46.82 | 42.83 | 38.55 | 19.80 | 18.09 | 23.16 | 8.70 | 19.00 | 49.60 | 29.00 | 13.50 | 27.50 | 21.66 | 19.66 | 21.00 | 18.66 | 37.00 | 9.25 | 3.33 | 24.00 | 23.00 | - | | | | | |
| **100s** | 1 | 3 | 4 | 3 | 2 | 0 | 0 | 0 | 0 | 0 | 2 | 0 | 0 | 0 | 0 | 0 | 0 | 0 | 0 | 0 | 0 | 0 | 0 | 0 | | | | | |
| **50s** | 4 | 2 | 1 | 1 | 5 | 2 | 0 | 2 | 0 | 0 | 1 | 1 | 0 | 1 | 0 | 1 | 0 | 0 | 1 | 0 | 0 | 0 | 0 | 0 | | | | | |
| **Catches/Stumpings** | 36/0 | 8/0 | 14/0 | 1/0 | 8/0 | 16/0 | 3/0 | 0/0 | 0/0 | 4/0 | 0/0 | 3/0 | 2/0 | 2/0 | 0/0 | 0/0 | 1/0 | 1/0 | 1/0 | 1/0 | 0/0 | 1/0 | 0/0 | 5/0 | | | | | |

**Home Ground:** Edgbaston
**Address:** County Ground, Edgbaston, Birmingham, B5 7QU
**Tel:** 0870 0621902
**Fax:** 0121 4464544
**Email:** info@edgbaston.com
**Directions:** By rail: New Street station, Birmingham.
By road: M6 to A38(M) to city centre, then follow signs to county ground.
**Capacity:** 20,000

**Other grounds used:** Stratford upon Avon
**Year formed:** 1882

**Chief Executive:** Colin Povey
**Director of Coaching:** Ashley Giles
**Captain:** Tim Ambrose
**County colours:** Blue and white

**Honours**
County Championship
1911, 1951, 1972, 1994, 1995, 2004
Sunday League/NCL/Pro40
1980, 1994, 1997
Benson & Hedges Cup
1994, 2002
Gillette Cup/NatWest/C&G Trophy
1989, 1993, 1995

Website:
www.thebears.co.uk

## FIRST-CLASS MATCHES
## BOWLING

| | JE Anyon | N Tahir | DW Steyn | DL Maddy | HH Streak | NM Carter | AC Thomas | TD Groenewald | AGR Loudon | AJ Shantry | AG Botha | PL Harris | IJL Trott | JO Troughton | IJ Westwood | CR Woakes | LM Daggett | LC Parker | SM Hole | Overs | Total | Byes/Leg-byes | Wickets | Run outs |
|---|---|---|---|---|---|---|---|---|---|---|---|---|---|---|---|---|---|---|---|---|---|---|---|---|
| v. Lancashire (Edgbaston) 18-21 April | 15.1-2-85-3 / 7-1-32-0 | 21-3-50-0 / 4-1-9-0 | 25-5-70-4 / 8-1-30-0 | 3-1-2-0 / 1-0-1-0 | 22-6-53-2 / 5-3-5-0 | | | 11-3-37-1 / 4-2-3-0 | 10-2-17-0 / 23-2-64-2 | | | | | 3-0-11-0 / 14-0-33-0 | | | | | | 110.1 / 66 | 333 / 189 | 8 / 12 | 10 / 3 | / 1 |
| v. Sussex (Edgbaston) 25-27 April | 9-1-41-2 / 17-4-55-4 | 5-3-11-0 / 14.3-5-47-4 | 10.5-2-36-3 / 14-3-31-0 | | 10-5-18-3 / 11-4-31-2 | | | 8-0-40-2 / 4-2-17-0 | | | | 4-1-13-0 | | | | | | | | 42.5 / 64.3 | 151 / 206 | 5 / 12 | 10 / 10 | |
| v. Worcestershire (Worcester) 2-5 May | 13-3-44-1 / 9-1-40-0 | 10-3-37-3 / 16-3-31-3 | 20.4-7-56-3 / 12-1-48-5 | 5-0-10-0 / 4-1-9-0 | 14-2-33-2 / 9.4-4-29-2 | | | 14-4-28-0 / 6-3-11-0 | 15-2-39-0 / 5-0-24-0 | | | | | 10-0-34-1 | | | | | | 101.4 / 61.4 | 288 / 209 | 7 / 16 | 10 / 10 | |
| v. Surrey (The Oval) 9-12 May | 24.3-4-111-0 | 19-5-35-0 | 24-6-75-1 | 7-4-6-0 | 16-1-68-0 | | | | 13-2-45-0 | | | | 10-3-27-0 | 4-1-11-0 | | | | | | 117.3 | 400 | 22 | 1 | |
| | | | | | | | | | | | | | | | | | | | | - | - | - | - | |
| v. Durham (Edgbaston) 16-19 May | 20.3-4-62-1 | | | | 21-1-85-3 | 8-3-19-1 | 18-5-43-0 | | 15-6-39-0 | 12-2-17-1 | | | | 2-1-5-0 | | | | | | 96.3 | 274 | 4 | 6 | |
| | | | | | | | | | | | | | | | | | | | | - | - | - | - | |
| v. Hampshire (Edgbaston) 30 May-2 June | 16-4-47-2 / 16-5-72-2 | 18.1-6-41-3 / 15.4-33-3 | 17-6-32-0 / 23-4-72-1 | | 2-1-8-1 / 5-1-22-1 | | | 12-5-26-3 / 13-3-37-0 | 2-0-5-0 / 12-3-37-0 | | | 2-0-23-0 | | 7-3-11-0 | | | | | | 67.1 / 93 | 169 / 312 | 10 / 5 | 10 / 7 | 1 |
| v. Worcestershire (Edgbaston) 15-18 June | 24.2-2-79-3 | 18-4-74-0 | 28-9-59-3 | | | | | 16-4-61-2 | 19-1-51-1 | | | 8-0-23-0 | | 10-2-38-1 | | | | | | 123.2 | 399 | 14 | 10 | |
| | | | | | | | | | | | | | | | | | | | | - | - | - | - | |
| v. Hampshire (Rose Bowl) 8-11 July | 17-4-69-1 | 4-0-13-0 | | | 7-1-25-1 | 25-7-63-0 | | 8.3-1-50-0 | 1-0-6-0 | | 29-3-96-1 | | | 1-0-14-0 | 0.5-0-9-1 | | | | | 1.5 / 91.3 | 23 / 331 | 0 / 9 | 1 / 5 | 2 |
| v. Yorkshire (Edgbaston) 13-16 July | | 25-6-102-1 / 29-7-93-4 | | | 7-2-30-0 | 30.4-4-105-3 | | | | | 27-6-44-0 | | | 4-1-5-0 | 6-1-17-0 | | | | | 128.4 | 400 | 4 | 9 | 1 |
| v. Kent (Canterbury) 20-23 July | | 26-5-78-2 | | 10-5-13-0 | | | 30-3-110-2 | | 21-4-81-1 | | 8-0-57-0 | 29-5-95-1 | 12-4-33-2 | | | 20-6-62-0 | | | | 156 | 550 | 21 | 9 | 1 |
| v. Durham (Riverside) 31 July-3 August | 30-6-108-0 / 4.1-0-34-1 | 27-7-63-1 / 1-0-17-0 | | | 27-5-63-5 / 2-0-12-0 | 27-7-59-1 / 5-0-38-0 | | | 5-0-23-0 / 5-0-32-0 | | 22.5-6-50-2 / 13-0-56-0 | 12-3-20-0 | | | | 17-3-61-1 | | | | 159.5 / 30.1 | 474 / 194 | 27 / 5 | 10 / 1 | |
| v. Sussex (Hove) 8-11 August | 17.3-3-62-4 / 19-4-37-0 | 9-0-42-2 / 6-1-20-0 | | | 6-1-12-0 / 19-4-48-1 | 15-3-29-0 | | | 4-1-10-0 / 49-8-123-4 | 16-8-31-4 / 13-3-48-0 | | 7-4-11-0 | 22-5-61-0 | | | | | | | 52.3 / 150 | 168 / 405 | 11 / 27 | 10 / 5 | |
| v. Kent (Edgbaston) 14-17 August | | | | | 25-9-44-0 | 21-5-53-1 | 30-10-74-3 | | 15.3-0-65-0 | 4-0-31-0 | | | | 12-1-48-0 | 4-0-24-0 | | | 8-0-31-0 | 2-0-16-0 | 121.3 | 400 | 14 | 4 | |
| v. Yorkshire (Scarborough) 22-24 August | 30-5-148-3 | | | 13-4-48-0 | 20-1-95-0 | | 32.1-5-109-4 | | 10-1-52-0 | | | | | 6-0-34-0 | | | | 15-4-65-0 | | 126.1 | 561 | 10 | 7 | |
| v. Surrey (Edgbaston) 6-9 September | 36-7-107-3 / 7-0-27-0 | | | | | 27-6-75-2 / 6-0-26-0 | 27.1-10-57-3 / 10-3-37-0 | | | | 34-11-73-2 / 15-2-44-0 | 3-1-6-0 | | | 12-3-48-0 / 7.4-0-42-1 | | | | | 139.1 / 45.4 | 373 / 179 | 7 / 3 | 10 / 1 | |
| v. Lancashire (Old Trafford) 11-13 September | 17-1-62-1 | | | | 14-2-67-2 / 11-3-37-0 | 17.4-2-62-5 / 5-3-10-1 | 25-9-75-0 / 5-0-15-0 | | | | 23-9-37-2 / 1.3-0-1-0 | 2-1-5-0 | | | | | | | | 98.4 / 22.3 | 311 / 71 | 3 / 8 | 10 / 1 | |
| **Overs** | 374.1 | 238.4 | 203.3 | 166 | 255.2 | 85.4 | 129.2 | 132.3 | 208.3 | 33 | 73.3 | 120.5 | 74 | 85 | 6.5 | 19.4 | 45 | 2 | 15 | | | | | |
| **Maidens** | 67 | 57 | 45 | 50 | 54 | 14 | 37 | 37 | 24 | 11 | 22 | 20 | 19 | 12 | 1 | 3 | 9 | 0 | 4 | | | | | |
| **Runs** | 1424 | 694 | 595 | 409 | 789 | 283 | 367 | 430 | 667 | 111 | 155 | 341 | 214 | 276 | 26 | 90 | 154 | 16 | 65 | | | | | |
| **Wickets** | 32 | 25 | 23 | 15 | 13 | 10 | 10 | 9 | 8 | 4 | 4 | 4 | 2 | 2 | 1 | 1 | 1 | 0 | 0 | | | | | |
| **Average** | 44.50 | 27.76 | 25.86 | 27.26 | 60.69 | 28.30 | 36.70 | 47.77 | 83.37 | 27.75 | 38.75 | 85.25 | 107.00 | 138.00 | 26.00 | 90.00 | 154.00 | - | - | | | | | |

## FIELDING

| | |
|---|---|
| 36 | TR Ambrose (36 ct) |
| 16 | IJL Trott |
| 14 | DL Maddy |
| 8 | AGR Loudon |
| 8 | IJ Westwood |
| 8 | TD Groenewald |
| 5 | MW Barnes |
| 4 | KC Sangakkara |
| 3 | LC Parker |
| 3 | JE Anyon |
| 2 | MJ Powell |
| 2 | AC Thomas |
| 1 | IR Bell |
| 1 | JO Troughton |
| 1 | NM Carter |
| 1 | AJ Shantry |
| 1 | AG Botha |
| 1 | CR Woakes |
| 0 | HH Streak |
| 0 | N Tahir |
| 0 | LM Daggett |
| 0 | DW Steyn |
| 0 | PL Harris |
| 0 | SM Hole |

### Final Division One Table

| | P | W | L | D | T | Ab | Bat | Bowl | Pens | Pts |
|---|---|---|---|---|---|---|---|---|---|---|
| Sussex | 16 | 7 | 3 | 5 | 0 | 1 | 37 | 43 | 0.00 | 202.00 |
| Durham | 16 | 7 | 5 | 4 | 0 | 0 | 38 | 47 | 1.50 | 197.50 |
| Lancashire | 16 | 5 | 2 | 8 | 0 | 1 | 40 | 44 | 0.00 | 190.00 |
| Surrey | 16 | 5 | 4 | 6 | 0 | 1 | 41 | 40 | 1.00 | 178.00 |
| Hampshire | 16 | 5 | 3 | 8 | 0 | 0 | 32 | 43 | 0.00 | 177.00 |
| Yorkshire | 16 | 4 | 4 | 8 | 0 | 0 | 49 | 38 | 0.00 | 175.00 |
| Kent | 16 | 3 | 5 | 7 | 0 | 1 | 43 | 36 | 0.00 | 153.00 |
| Warwickshire | 16 | 2 | 5 | 9 | 0 | 0 | 40 | 35 | 0.00 | 139.00 |
| Worcestershire | 16 | 1 | 8 | 5 | 0 | 2 | 18 | 35 | 0.00 | 95.00 |

**The Bears**

Limited overs nickname:
**THE BEARS**

# WORCESTERSHIRE CCC

## FIRST–CLASS MATCHES
### BATTING

| | GA Hick | SC Moore | SM Davies | BF Smith | GJ Batty | Kabir Ali | VS Solanki | MN Malik | PA Jaques | RJ Sillence | DE Bollinger | DKH Mitchell | JD Nel | Abdul Razzaq | MM Ali | RA Jones | KW Hogg | RW Price | MS Mason | JP Knappett | Extras | Total | Wickets | Result | Points |
|---|---|---|---|---|---|---|---|---|---|---|---|---|---|---|---|---|---|---|---|---|---|---|---|---|---|
| v. Durham (Worcester) 18-21 April | 15 | 46 | 14 | 0 | 20 | 2 | 24 | 13* | 19 | 0 | 21 | | | | | | | | | | 17 | 191 | 10 | | |
| | 35 | 0 | 6 | 2 | 47 | 19 | 67 | 5* | 97 | 6 | 2 | | | | | | | | | | 11 | 297 | 10 | L | 3 |
| v. Loughborough UCCE (Worcester) 25-27 April 2007 | 25 | 61 | 0 | 29 | | 0 | 11 | 2 | | 51* | | 112 | | | 12 | 24 | | | | | 25 | 352 | 10 | | |
| | | 36* | | | | | | | | | | 12* | | | | | | | | | 1 | 49 | 0 | W | |
| v. Warwickshire (Worcester) 2-5 May | 91 | 47 | 1 | 50 | 10 | 0 | 35 | 0 | 0 | 29* | | | | | | 1 | | | | | 24 | 288 | 10 | | |
| | 66 | 0 | 1 | 65 | 14 | 4 | 4 | 4 | 2 | 1 | | | | | | 11* | | | | | 37 | 209 | 10 | L | 3 |
| v. Yorkshire (Headingley) 9-12 May | 11 | 0 | 0 | 0 | 24 | 12 | 5 | 1* | 38 | 22 | | | 8 | | | | | | | | 8 | 129 | 10 | | |
| | 0 | 9 | 38 | 0 | 10 | 15 | 19 | 0 | 21 | 6 | | | 7* | | | | | | | | 7 | 132 | 10 | L | 2 |
| v. Lancashire (Old Trafford) 15-18 May | 110 | 29 | 43 | 1 | 1 | 39 | 54 | 3 | 21 | 0 | | | 0* | | | | | | | | 26 | 327 | 10 | D | 10 |
| v. Sussex (Worcester) 24-26 May | 15 | 47 | 0 | 0 | 0 | 9 | 13 | 1 | 5 | | 0 | | 2* | | | | | | | | 8 | 100 | 10 | | |
| | 108 | 22 | 40 | 5 | 64 | 6 | 17 | 6* | 0 | | 4 | | 4 | | | | | | | | 27 | 303 | 10 | L | 2 |
| v. Surrey (Worcester) 6-9 June | 15 | 143 | 81 | 65 | 9* | | 232 | | 124 | | | | | | | | 2* | | | | 30 | 701 | 6 | D | 12 |
| v. Warwickshire (Edgbaston) 15-18 June | 49 | 112 | 26 | 34 | 25 | 39 | 41 | 1* | 34 | | 3 | | | | | | 13 | | | | 22 | 399 | 10 | D | 11 |
| v. Surrey (Guildford) 25-28 July | 30 | 31 | 58 | 15 | 18 | 21 | 13 | | 3 | 6 | 8 | | 2* | | | | | | | | 12 | 217 | 10 | | |
| | 4 | 55 | 38* | 66 | 15* | | 11 | | 103 | | | | | | | | | | | | 15 | 307 | 5 | D | 8 |
| v. Hampshire (Rose Bowl) 8-10 August | 4 | 0 | 17 | 5 | 21 | 5 | 22 | | 0 | 6 | 0* | | | | | | | | 0 | | 6 | 86 | 10 | | |
| | 69 | 19 | 28 | 1 | 10 | 1 | 0 | | 10 | 28 | 0* | | | | | | | | 15 | | 6 | 187 | 10 | L | |
| v. Yorkshire (Kidderminster) 14-17 August | 69* | 10 | 22 | 36 | 7* | | 0 | | 20 | | | | | | | | | | | | 8 | 172 | 5 | | |
| | 31 | 65 | 26* | 98* | | | 44 | | 44 | | | | | | | | | | | | 29 | 337 | 4 | W | 17 |
| v. Kent (Canterbury) 21-24 August | | | 21 | 17* | | 0 | 42 | | | | | | | 22* | | | | | | | 8 | 110 | 3 | D | 4 |
| v. Durham (Riverside) 29-31 August | 64 | 27 | 26 | 0 | 0 | 8 | 6 | 4 | | | | 5 | 0* | 23 | | | | | | | 19 | 182 | 10 | | |
| | 66 | 9 | 87 | 60 | 72 | 4 | 0 | 4 | | | | 22 | 7* | 35 | | | | | | | 24 | 390 | 10 | L | |
| v. Hampshire (Kidderminster) 4-7 September | 29 | 24 | 84 | 10 | 5 | | | 20* | 11 | | | 0 | | 78 | 5 | | | 3 | | | 20 | 289 | 10 | | |
| | 19 | 37 | 2 | | 8 | | | 24* | 36 | | | 8 | | 14 | 77 | | | 6 | | | 6 | 237 | 9 | L | 5 |
| v. Sussex (Hove) 19-22 September | 16 | 48 | 31 | | 23 | 4 | | | 0 | | | 70* | | | 1 | 0 | | 0 | | 7 | 13 | 213 | 10 | | |
| | 22 | 5 | 0 | | 84 | 23 | | | 3 | | | 31 | | | 85 | 2 | | 15* | | 4 | 31 | 305 | 10 | L | 4 |
| Matches | 15 | 15 | 15 | 14 | 14 | 14 | 13 | 13 | 10 | 10 | 7 | 5 | 5 | 3 | 3 | 3 | 2 | 2 | 1 | 1 | | | | | |
| Innings | 24 | 25 | 25 | 22 | 22 | 19 | 21 | 17 | 17 | 13 | 8 | 8 | 8 | 5 | 5 | 5 | 2 | 4 | 2 | 2 | | | | | |
| Not Out | 1 | 1 | 2 | 2 | 3 | 0 | 0 | 7 | 0 | 2 | 2 | 2 | 6 | 1 | 0 | 1 | 1 | 1 | 0 | 0 | | | | | |
| Highest Score | 110 | 143 | 87 | 98* | 84 | 39 | 232 | 24* | 124 | 51* | 21 | 112 | 8 | 78 | 85 | 24 | 13 | 15* | 15 | 7 | | | | | |
| Runs | 963 | 882 | 690 | 559 | 487 | 211 | 660 | 91 | 541 | 202 | 38 | 260 | 30 | 172 | 180 | 38 | 15 | 24 | 15 | 11 | | | | | |
| Average | 41.86 | 36.75 | 30.00 | 27.95 | 25.63 | 11.10 | 31.42 | 9.10 | 31.82 | 18.36 | 6.33 | 43.33 | 15.00 | 43.00 | 36.00 | 9.50 | 15.00 | 8.00 | 7.50 | 5.50 | | | | | |
| 100s | 2 | 2 | 0 | 0 | 0 | 0 | 1 | 0 | 2 | 0 | 0 | 1 | 0 | 0 | 0 | 0 | 0 | 0 | 0 | 0 | | | | | |
| 50s | 6 | 3 | 4 | 6 | 3 | 0 | 2 | 0 | 1 | 1 | 0 | 1 | 0 | 1 | 2 | 0 | 1 | 0 | 0 | 0 | | | | | |
| Catches/Stumpings | 16/0 | 7/0 | 43/4 | 11/0 | 7/0 | 1/0 | 4/0 | 5/0 | 6/0 | 4/0 | 0/0 | 7/0 | 0/0 | 1/0 | 0/0 | 1/0 | 0/0 | 0/0 | 0/0 | 0/0 | | | | | |

**Home Ground:** New Road, Worcester
**Address:** County Ground, New Road, Worcester, WR2 4QQ
**Tel:** 01905 748474
**Fax:** 01905 748005
**Email:** info@wccc.co.uk
**Directions:** From the M5 Junction 7, follow the brown 'broken stumps' logos to WCCC.
**Capacity:** 4,500

**Other grounds used:** Edgbaston, Himley, Kidderminster, RGS Worcester, Taunton
**Year formed:** 1865

**Chief Executive:** Mark Newton
**Director of Cricket:** Steve Rhodes
**Captain:** Vikram Solanki
**County colours:** Green, black and white

**Honours**
County Championship
1964, 1965, 1974, 1988, 1989
Sunday League/NCL/Pro40
1971, 1987, 1988, 2007
Benson & Hedges Cup
1991
Gillette Cup/NatWest/C&G Trophy
1994

Website:
www.wccc.co.uk

## FIRST-CLASS MATCHES
# BOWLING

| | Kabir Ali | GJ Batty | MN Malik | DE Bollinger | RJ Sillence | RA Jones | JD Nel | DKH Mitchell | KW Hogg | Abdul Razzaq | RW Price | MS Mason | VS Solanki | BF Smith | MM Ali | SC Moore | Overs | Total | Byes/Leg-byes | Wickets | Run outs |
|---|---|---|---|---|---|---|---|---|---|---|---|---|---|---|---|---|---|---|---|---|---|
| v. Durham (Worcester) 18-21 April | 15-0-76-1 | 19.2-5-36-3 | 13-0-70-2 | 14-3-60-3 | 13-2-52-1 | | | | | | | | | | | | 74.2 | 313 | 19 | 10 | |
| | 19.3-5-65-3 | 37-7-123-4 | 15-0-56-0 | 19-2-94-1 | 18-6-54-1 | | | | | | | | 2-0-3-0 | | | | 110.3 | 416 | 21 | 10 | 1 |
| v. Loughborough UCCE (Worcester) 25-27 April | 5-2-16-5 | | 11-6-15-1 | | 5-2-10-1 | 12-2-37-3 | | 2-0-2-0 | | | | | | | 4-1-21-0 | | 39 | 104 | 3 | 10 | |
| | 15.4-4-39-6 | | 23-12-43-2 | | 15-2-59-0 | 12-1-51-1 | | 2-0-5-1 | | | | | 5-2-13-0 | | 12-0-71-0 | | 84.4 | 296 | 15 | 10 | |
| v. Warwickshire (Worcester) 2-5 May | 34-7-122-2 | 42-10-107-1 | 24-8-102-0 | | 31-4-130-1 | 15-2-82-1 | | | | | | | 17-4-54-1 | | | | 163 | 610 | 13 | 6 | |
| v. Yorkshire (Headingley) 9-12 May | 31-8-81-0 | 29-5-100-0 | 27-4-98-1 | | 34-7-120-2 | | 27-5-74-4 | | | | | | | | | 5-0-24-0 | 153 | 521 | 24 | 7 | |
| v. Lancashire (Old Trafford) 15-18 May | 16-3-50-8 | 4-1-6-0 | 11-2-30-0 | | 11-1-48-2 | | | 7-2-21-0 | | | | | | | | | 49 | 161 | 6 | 10 | |
| | 19-5-52-2 | 20-3-82-1 | 23-4-72-1 | | 14-3-53-2 | | | 11-3-27-1 | | | | | 1-0-5-0 | | | | 88 | 296 | 5 | 7 | |
| v. Sussex (Worcester) 24-26 May | 27-6-77-3 | 34.5-2-140-2 | 23-4-94-3 | 21-5-78-0 | | | 25-3-105-0 | | | | | | | | | | 130.5 | 512 | 18 | 8 | |
| v. Surrey (Worcester) 6-9 June | 23-1-84-2 | 34.2-6-100-3 | 17-2-70-2 | 24-8-68-0 | | | | | 15-4-44-3 | | | | | | | | 113.2 | 370 | 4 | 10 | |
| | 22-7-74-2 | 50-20-84-5 | 20-6-55-2 | 15-5-35-0 | | | | | 16-10-16-0 | | | | 5-3-8-0 | | | | 128 | 281 | 9 | 9 | |
| v. Warwickshire (Edgbaston) 15-18 June | 24-4-85-3 | 6-1-21-0 | 5-0-32-0 | 24-6-102-4 | | | | | 15-0-76-3 | | | | 7-0-18-0 | | | | 74 | 343 | 27 | 10 | |
| | | 9-2-25-0 | 2-0-5-0 | | | | | | | | | | | | | | 18 | 48 | 0 | 0 | |
| v. Surrey (Guildford) 25-28 July | 29.4-3-104-4 | 33-6-101-4 | | 22-7-57-0 | 9-1-37-1 | | 12-1-57-1 | | | | | | 1-0-5-0 | | | | 106.4 | 369 | 8 | 10 | |
| v. Hampshire (Rose Bowl) 8-10 August | 29-3-101-2 | 36-8-125-6 | | 20-0-83-0 | 18-4-50-0 | | | | | | | 21-7-51-1 | 2-0-18-0 | | | | 126 | 455 | 27 | 9 | |
| | 8-3-26-2 | 10-3-20-3 | | 7-2-21-3 | 7-0-22-0 | | | | | | | 3-1-11-0 | | | | | 35 | 103 | 3 | 8 | |
| v. Yorkshire (Kidderminster) 14-17 August | 24-7-69-3 | 9-2-28-0 | 18.5-2-85-2 | 16.5-1-82-4 | 5.1-0-29-1 | | | | | | | | | | | | 73.5 | 319 | 27 | 10 | |
| | 10-2-30-4 | 11-1-57-0 | 5.5-1-26-0 | 8.1-1-33-1 | 6.4-0-38-0 | | | | | | | | | | | | 41.4 | 188 | 4 | 5 | |
| v. Kent (Canterbury) 21-24 August | 10-1-41-0 | 6-1-24-0 | 12-3-62-1 | | 10-0-44-1 | | | 3-2-3-1 | | 10-2-37-0 | | | 3-0-14-0 | 7-1-49-0 | 4-1-18-0 | | 65 | 293 | 1 | 3 | |
| v. Durham (Riverside) 29-31 August | 12-0-52-0 | 24-8-106-6 | 18-2-88-2 | | | | | 2-0-12-0 | | 9.3-0-35-2 | | | 2-0-11-0 | | | | 69.3 | 297 | 4 | 10 | |
| | 8-0-46-1 | 17-6-37-0 | 11-2-58-1 | | | 14.1-3-61-1 | | 1-0-8-0 | | 16.4-5-54-2 | | | | | | | 69.1 | 279 | 4 | 5 | |
| v. Hampshire (Kidderminster) 4-7 September | | 16-5-54-0 | 27-2-109-1 | | 23-3-79-2 | | | 11-4-27-1 | 23-6-70-2 | 22.5-1-89-2 | | | 1-0-4-0 | | | | 123.5 | 444 | 12 | 10 | 2 |
| | | 12-0-64-0 | 11-1-57-0 | | 15-1-108-0 | | | 1-0-9-0 | 9-3-23-0 | 19-1-104-2 | | | | | | | 67 | 376 | 11 | 2 | |
| v. Sussex (Hove) 19-22 September | 17-4-79-3 | 26-6-83-0 | 23-1-103-2 | | | 24-5-125-2 | | 19.3-3-50-3 | | | | 17-4-63-0 | | | 4-1-10-0 | | 130.3 | 532 | 19 | 10 | |

| | Kabir Ali | GJ Batty | MN Malik | DE Bollinger | RJ Sillence | RA Jones | JD Nel | DKH Mitchell | KW Hogg | Abdul Razzaq | RW Price | MS Mason | VS Solanki | BF Smith | MM Ali | SC Moore |
|---|---|---|---|---|---|---|---|---|---|---|---|---|---|---|---|---|
| Overs | 398.5 | 489.3 | 340.4 | 191 | 234.5 | 63 | 96.1 | 41.3 | 46 | 67.3 | 58.5 | 24 | 45 | 7 | 21 | 9 |
| Maidens | 75 | 104 | 62 | 40 | 36 | 10 | 17 | 9 | 14 | 15 | 6 | 8 | 5 | 1 | 2 | 1 |
| Runs | 1369 | 1523 | 1330 | 713 | 932 | 295 | 345 | 116 | 136 | 219 | 256 | 62 | 149 | 49 | 106 | 42 |
| Wickets | 56 | 38 | 23 | 16 | 15 | 7 | 7 | 6 | 6 | 6 | 4 | 1 | 1 | 0 | 0 | 0 |
| Average | 24.44 | 40.07 | 57.82 | 44.56 | 62.13 | 42.14 | 49.28 | 19.33 | 22.66 | 36.50 | 64.00 | 62.00 | 149.00 | - | - | - |

## FIELDING

| | |
|---|---|
| 47 | SM Davies (43 ct, 4 st) |
| 16 | GA Hick |
| 11 | BF Smith |
| 7 | GJ Batty |
| 7 | SC Moore |
| 7 | DKH Mitchell |
| 6 | PA Jaques |
| 5 | MN Malik |
| 4 | VS Solanki |
| 4 | RJ Sillence |
| 1 | Abdul Razzaq |
| 1 | Kabir Ali |
| 1 | RA Jones |
| 0 | KW Hogg |
| 0 | MS Mason |
| 0 | MM Ali |
| 0 | RW Price |
| 0 | JP Knappett |
| 0 | JD Nel |
| 0 | DE Bollinger |

### Final Division One Table

| | P | W | L | D | T | Ab | Bat | Bowl | Pens | Pts |
|---|---|---|---|---|---|---|---|---|---|---|
| Sussex | 16 | 7 | 3 | 5 | 0 | 1 | 37 | 43 | 0.00 | 202.00 |
| Durham | 16 | 7 | 5 | 4 | 0 | 0 | 38 | 47 | 1.50 | 197.50 |
| Lancashire | 16 | 5 | 2 | 8 | 0 | 1 | 40 | 44 | 0.00 | 190.00 |
| Surrey | 16 | 5 | 4 | 6 | 0 | 1 | 41 | 40 | 1.00 | 178.00 |
| Hampshire | 16 | 5 | 3 | 8 | 0 | 0 | 32 | 43 | 0.00 | 177.00 |
| Yorkshire | 16 | 4 | 4 | 8 | 0 | 0 | 49 | 38 | 0.00 | 175.00 |
| Kent | 16 | 3 | 5 | 7 | 0 | 1 | 43 | 36 | 0.00 | 153.00 |
| Warwickshire | 16 | 2 | 5 | 9 | 0 | 0 | 40 | 35 | 0.00 | 139.00 |
| Worcestershire | 16 | 1 | 8 | 5 | 0 | 2 | 18 | 35 | 0.00 | 95.00 |

WORCESTERSHIRE ROYALS

Limited overs nickname:
WORCESTERSHIRE ROYALS

# YORKSHIRE CCC

## FIRST–CLASS MATCHES
## BATTING

| Match | JA Rudolph | AU Rashid | TT Bresnan | A McGrath | JJ Sayers | D Gough | Younus Khan | GL Brophy | JN Gillespie | C White | MJ Hoggard | MP Vaughan | AW Gale | A Shahzad | GJ Kruis | SM Guy | Inzamam-ul-Haq | MAK Lawson | RM Pyrah | CR Gilbert | A Lyth | MJ Wood | Imran Tahir | ND Thornicroft | SA Patterson | DJ Wainwright | Extras | Total | Wickets | Result | Points |
|---|---|---|---|---|---|---|---|---|---|---|---|---|---|---|---|---|---|---|---|---|---|---|---|---|---|---|---|---|---|---|---|
| v. Surrey (The Oval) 18-21 April | 122 | 86 | 116 | 20 | 26 | 23 | 4 | 22 | 123* | 7 | | | | | | | | | | | | | | | | | 45 | 594 | 9 | | |
| | 28 | 19 | 4* | 2 | 57 | | 12 | 12 | | 117 | | | | | | | | | | | | | | | | | 15 | 266 | 7 | W | 22 |
| v. Durham (Headingley) 25-27 April | 9 | 1 | 0 | | 149* | 50 | 42 | 80 | | 3 | 1 | | 36 | 2 | | | | | | | | | | | | | 41 | 414 | 10 | | |
| | 10* | | | | 10* | | | | | 8 | | | | | | | | | | | | | | | | | 2 | 30 | 1 | W | 21 |
| v. Hampshire (Rose Bowl) 2-5 May | 3 | 54 | 5 | 7 | 17 | 4 | 106 | 13 | 2 | | 4* | 72 | | | | | | | | | | | | | | | 12 | 299 | 10 | | |
| | 22 | | | 7 | 6 | | 202* | 100* | | | 61 | 16* | | | | | | | | | | | | | | | 25 | 439 | 4 | D | 9 |
| v. Worcestershire (Headingley) 9-12 May | 129* | 5 | 33 | 19 | 123 | 22* | 12 | 44 | | 97 | | | | | | | | | | | | | | | | | 37 | 521 | 7 | W | 22 |
| v. Loughborough UCCE (Headingley) 16-18 May | | | | | | | | | | | | | 68 | | | 37 | 4* | 106 | 64 | 31 | 23 | | | | | 46* | 4 | 383 | 6 | W | |
| v. Durham (Riverside) 23-26 May | 111 | 30 | 27 | 7 | 4 | 17 | 49 | | 15 | 64 | | | | | 0* | 25 | | | | | | | | | | | 44 | 393 | 10 | | |
| | 79 | 0 | 0 | 62 | 3 | 0 | 5 | | 23* | 0 | | | | | 7 | 28 | | | | | | | | | | | 11 | 218 | 10 | L | 7 |
| v. Kent (Tunbridge Wells) 6-9 June | 43 | 54 | 55* | 100 | 187 | 6 | 7 | | 13* | 21 | | | | | 25 | | | | | | | | | | | | 40 | 551 | 8 | D | 11 |
| v. Sussex (Headingley) 15-18 June | 0 | 22 | 4 | 9 | 2 | | 1 | 30 | 6 | 0 | | | | 32* | | 17 | | | | | | | | | | | 16 | 139 | 10 | | |
| | 46 | 49* | 27* | 58 | 3 | | 31 | 0 | | 49 | | | | | | | | | | | | | | | | | 21 | 284 | 6 | D | 9 |
| v. Lancashire (Old Trafford) 8-11 July | 25 | 28 | 28* | 56 | 0 | 0 | 6 | 73 | 13 | | 7 | 74 | | | | | | | | | | | | | | | 10 | 320 | 10 | D | 9 |
| v. Warwickshire (Edgbaston) 13-16 July | 82 | | | 188* | 16 | 10 | 49 | | 1 | 7 | 30 | 6 | | | 0* | | | | | | | | | | | | 11 | 400 | 9 | D | 9 |
| v. Surrey (Headingley) 20-23 July | 4 | 91* | 3 | 72 | 5 | 28 | 29 | 22 | 3 | 6 | | | | | 20 | | | | | | | | | | | | 24 | 307 | 10 | D | 12 |
| | | | | 0* | 0* | | | | | 2 | | | | | | | | | | | | | | | | | 0 | 2 | 1 | | |
| v. Kent (Scarborough) 25-28 July | 0 | 0 | 58 | 120 | 4 | 17 | 217* | 43 | 5* | 49 | | | | | | | | 5 | | | | | | | | | 32 | 550 | 9 | D | 12 |
| v. Lancashire (Headingley) 9-11 August | | 34 | 39 | 0 | 3 | 7 | 0 | 18 | 18* | 0 | | | | 15 | 0 | | | | | | | | | | | | 10 | 144 | 10 | | |
| | | 6 | 20* | 40 | 19 | 10 | 31 | 0 | | 44 | 16 | | | 16 | 15 | | | | | | | | | | | | 30 | 247 | 10 | L | 2 |
| v. Worcestershire (Kidderminster) 14-17 August | 29 | 108 | 13 | 55 | 4 | 0 | 15 | 41 | 4 | 0 | 2* | | | | | | | | | | | | | | | | 48 | 319 | 10 | L | 2 |
| | 92* | 73* | | 0 | 0 | | 6 | 13 | | 0 | | | | | | | | | | | | | | | | | 4 | 188 | 5 | L | |
| v. Warwickshire (Scarborough) 22-24 August | 220 | 52 | 101* | 58 | | | 38 | | | | 5 | 21 | 5* | | | 8 | | | | | | | | | | | 53 | 561 | 7 | W | 22 |
| v. Sussex (Hove) 5-7 September | 23 | 54* | 9 | 31 | | | 0 | | | 9 | 8 | 51 | 10 | | | | 8 | | | | | | 0 | | | | 44 | 247 | 10 | | |
| | 1 | 10 | 0 | 20 | | | 3 | | | 0 | 5 | 16 | 1* | | | | 22 | | | | | | 5 | | | | 6 | 89 | 10 | L | 3 |
| v. Hampshire (Headingley) 19-22 September | 0 | 14 | 11 | 6 | 25 | | 41 | | | | 7 | 26 | 0 | 0* | | | 51 | | | | | | | | | | 14 | 195 | 10 | D | 5 |
| | | | | | | | | | | | | | | | | | | | | | | | | | | | | | | | |
| Matches | 15 | 15 | 15 | 14 | 14 | 14 | 13 | 13 | 12 | 11 | 10 | 6 | 6 | 6 | 6 | 4 | 3 | 2 | 1 | 1 | 1 | 1 | 1 | 1 | 1 | 1 | | | | | |
| Innings | 22 | 21 | 20 | 22 | 22 | 15 | 19 | 19 | 13 | 18 | 9 | 8 | 8 | 7 | 6 | 5 | 4 | 2 | 1 | 1 | 1 | 1 | 2 | 0 | 0 | 1 | | | | | |
| Not Out | 3 | 4 | 6 | 2 | 3 | 1 | 2 | 1 | 5 | 0 | 2 | 1 | 0 | 3 | 3 | 0 | 0 | 1 | 0 | 0 | 0 | 0 | 0 | 0 | 0 | 1 | | | | | |
| Highest Score | 220 | 108 | 116 | 188* | 187 | 50 | 217* | 100* | 123* | 117 | 61 | 74 | 68 | 32* | 20 | 37 | 51 | 5 | 106 | 64 | 31 | 23 | 5 | 0 | 0 | 46* | | | | | |
| Runs | 1078 | 790 | 553 | 931 | 644 | 219 | 824 | 593 | 270 | 446 | 121 | 212 | 223 | 65 | 44 | 115 | 89 | 9 | 106 | 64 | 31 | 23 | 5 | 0 | 0 | 46 | | | | | |
| Average | 56.73 | 46.47 | 39.50 | 46.55 | 33.89 | 15.64 | 48.47 | 32.94 | 33.75 | 24.77 | 17.28 | 30.28 | 27.87 | 16.25 | 14.66 | 23.00 | 22.25 | 9.00 | 106.00 | 64.00 | 31.00 | 23.00 | 2.50 | - | - | - | | | | | |
| 100s | 4 | 1 | 2 | 3 | 3 | 0 | 3 | 1 | 1 | 1 | 0 | 0 | 0 | 0 | 0 | 0 | 0 | 0 | 0 | 0 | 1 | 0 | 0 | 0 | 0 | 0 | | | | | |
| 50s | 3 | 7 | 2 | 6 | 1 | 1 | 0 | 2 | 0 | 2 | 1 | 2 | 2 | 0 | 0 | 0 | 1 | 0 | 1 | 0 | 0 | 0 | 0 | 0 | 0 | 0 | | | | | |
| Catches/Stumpings | 19/0 | 8/0 | 6/0 | 11/0 | 5/0 | 2/0 | 11/0 | 35/3 | 3/0 | 4/0 | 2/0 | 0/0 | 5/0 | 0/0 | 0/0 | 11/0 | 5/0 | 0/0 | 1/0 | 0/0 | 0/0 | 1/0 | 0/0 | 0/0 | 1/0 | 1/0 | | | | | |

**Home Ground:** Headingley
**Address:** Headingley Cricket Ground, Leeds, LS6 3BU
**Tel:** 0870 4296774
**Fax:** 0113 2784099
**Email:** cricket@yorkshireccc.com
**Directions:** From M1 South leave at junction 43 to M621 as far as junction 2. From M62 West leave at junction 27 to take M621 as far as junction 2. From M62 East leave at junction 29 to join M1 northbound to junction 2 of M621. At junction 2 of the M621 follow the signs for Headingley stadium along A643. Follow Leeds Inner Ring Road (A58(M)) to A660 which is signposted to Headingley stadium. Signs along this route will indicate when you have reached the Headingley area and on Test match days additional temporary signing will direct you to the free Park & Ride car park to the north of Headingley at Beckett Park.
**Other grounds used:** Scarborough
**Year formed:** 1863

**Chief Executive:** Stewart Regan
**Operations Director:** Ian Dews
**Director of Cricket:** Martyn Moxon
**Captain:** Darren Gough
**County colours:** Blue and gold

Website:
**www.yorkshireccc.com**

**Honours**
County Championship
1867, 1869, 1870, 1893, 1896, 1898, 1901, 1902, 1905, 1908, 1912, 1919, 1922, 1923, 1924, 1925, 1931, 1932, 1933, 1935, 1937, 1938, 1939, 1946, 1949, 1959, 1960, 1962, 1963, 1966, 1967, 1968, 2001
Sunday League/NCL/Pro40
1983
Benson & Hedges Cup
1987
Gillette Cup/NatWest/C&G Trophy
1965, 1969, 2002

FIRST–CLASS MATCHES
# BOWLING

| | AU Rashid | D Gough | TT Bresnan | MJ Hoggard | JN Gillespie | A Shahzad | Younus Khan | GJ Kruis | ND Thornicroft | A McGrath | SA Patterson | DJ Wainwright | A Lyth | AW Gale | RM Pyrah | C White | MP Vaughan | MJ Wood | CR Gilbert | Imran Tahir | JA Rudolph | MAK Lawson | Overs | Total | Byes/Leg-byes | Wickets | Run outs |
|---|---|---|---|---|---|---|---|---|---|---|---|---|---|---|---|---|---|---|---|---|---|---|---|---|---|---|---|
| **v. Surrey** (The Oval) 18-21 April | 24-3-105-4 | 8-1-28-3 | 13-1-49-0 | 13-4-48-2 | 10-3-23-1 | | 9-2-41-0 | | | 2-0-15-0 | | | | | | | | | | | | 5-1-25-0 | 84 | 344 | 10 | 10 | |
| | 17.3-2-64-3 | 14-2-50-3 | 5-2-10-0 | 12-4-34-4 | 2-0-7-0 | | | | | | | | | | | | | | | | | | 50.3 | 170 | 5 | 10 | |
| **v. Durham** (Headingley) 25-27 April | 20.4-3-88-5 | 14-3-46-2 | 17-3-51-2 | 14-3-33-0 | | | 10-0-44-1 | | | | | | | | | | | | | | | | 75.4 | 274 | 12 | 10 | |
| | 4-0-39-1 | 12-2-34-1 | 5-1-36-2 | 11.1-2-32-5 | | | | | | | | | | | | | | | | | | | 39.1 | 169 | 6 | 10 | |
| **v. Hampshire** (Rose Bowl) 2-5 May | 26.3-2-79-2 | 9-2-40-0 | 22-6-65-4 | 19-2-52-1 | 14-4-40-3 | | 2-0-9-0 | | | | | | | | | | | | | 3-1-4-0 | | | 95.3 | 296 | 7 | 10 | |
| | 33-4-126-1 | 15-4-33-0 | 7-1-42-0 | 11-2-30-0 | 14-3-44-3 | | | | | 6-2-15-0 | | | | | | | | | | 1-0-8-0 | | | 105 | 366 | 16 | 8 | |
| **v. Worcestershire** (Headingley) 9-12 May | 8-2-14-1 | 7-2-19-1 | | | 14-5-34-5 | 13.5-2-56-3 | | | | | | | | | | | | | | | | | 42.5 | 129 | 6 | 10 | |
| | 17-4-47-4 | 9-2-27-1 | | 10-6-10-4 | 9-4-16-0 | 7-1-24-0 | 2-0-6-1 | | | 1-1-0-0 | | | | | | | | | | | | | 55 | 132 | 2 | 10 | |
| **v. Loughborough UCCE** (Headingley) 16-18 May | | | | | | 7-0-16-0 | | 5-2-12-0 | | 6-2-9-0 | 1-0-2-0 | 1-0-12-1 | 2-0-33-1 | 2-1-3-1 | | | | | | | | 2-0-4-0 | 26 | 93 | 2 | 3 | |
| | | | | | | 5-2-14-0 | | 6-2-60-6 | | 7-0-30-0 | 18-1-72-2 | | | 10-1-38-0 | | | 1-0-4-0 | 3-0-11-0 | | | | 13-1-53-0 | 73 | 289 | 7 | 6 | |
| **v. Durham** (Riverside) 23-26 May | 24-4-90-0 | 20.5-6-76-3 | 30-6-94-2 | 25-6-73-3 | | | 19-4-85-1 | | | 8-1-33-1 | | | | | | | | | | | | | 126.5 | 481 | 25 | 10 | |
| | 2.5-0-20-0 | 9-1-18-2 | 10-2-25-1 | 7-0-29-1 | | | 5-0-34-0 | | | | | | | | | | | | | | | | 33.5 | 131 | 5 | 4 | |
| **v. Kent** (Tunbridge Wells) 6-9 June | 11-1-55-0 | 16.2-6-47-6 | 16.3-4-34-1 | | 17-5-58-1 | 5-0-15-0 | 15-1-62-2 | | | 4-0-13-0 | | | | | | 5-0-9-0 | | | | | | | 84.5 | 292 | 8 | 10 | |
| | 35-4-77-0 | 6-1-12-1 | 22-3-82-2 | | 21-3-51-1 | 7-1-25-0 | 24-2-89-2 | | | 9-2-21-0 | | | | | | | | | | | | | 129 | 383 | 17 | 6 | |
| **v. Sussex** (Headingley) 15-18 June | 2-0-6-0 | | 9-2-14-2 | | 16-3-54-2 | 8.4-1-22-4 | 18-7-39-2 | | | 3-1-3-0 | | | | | | | | | | | | | 56.4 | 141 | 3 | 10 | |
| | 2-1-5-0 | | 2-1-2-0 | | 6-0-25-1 | 1-0-1-0 | 4-2-9-0 | | | 5-0-15-1 | | | | | | | | | | 2-2-0-0 | | | 22 | 57 | 0 | 2 | |
| **v. Lancashire** (Old Trafford) 8-11 July | 28-2-114-5 | | 13-4-29-0 | 4-1-22-0 | 6-2-6-0 | 5-2-17-0 | | | | 13-1-50-1 | | | | | | | | | | | | | 69 | 247 | 9 | 6 | |
| **v. Warwickshire** (Edgbaston) 13-16 July | | 6-4-12-0 | | 10-2-43-1 | 11-2-48-1 | | | | 7-0-36-0 | 13-3-59-0 | | | | | | 4-0-26-0 | 1-0-10-0 | | | 5-0-18-0 | | | 57 | 254 | 2 | 2 | |
| **v. Surrey** (Headingley) 20-23 July | 20.1-2-64-1 | 21-6-50-6 | 11-3-18-0 | | 16.4-4-52-1 | | | 1.2-0-5-0 | | | | | | | | 7-0-22-2 | | | | | | | 77.1 | 229 | 18 | 10 | |
| **v. Kent** (Scarborough) 25-28 July | 23.3-1-112-5 | 28-7-81-1 | 35-7-140-4 | | 20-5-55-0 | | | | | 4-0-21-0 | | | | | | 7-3-10-0 | | | | 7-0-54-0 | | | 124.3 | 486 | 13 | 10 | |
| | 5-3-5-0 | 3-2-1-0 | | | | | | | | | | | | | | | | | | 2-0-11-0 | | | 10 | 17 | 0 | 0 | |
| **v. Lancashire** (Headingley) 9-11 August | 33-2-109-3 | 21-4-74-1 | 26-7-98-2 | | 15-5-54-0 | 19-3-68-0 | 11.5-0-53-2 | | | 9-1-40-0 | | | | | | | 1-0-2-0 | | | | | | 135.5 | 517 | 19 | 10 | 2 |
| **v. Worcestershire** (Kidderminster) 14-17 August | 4-0-32-0 | 8-4-16-1 | 12-2-46-1 | 11-2-55-2 | 7-3-19-0 | | | | | | | | | | | | | | | | | | 42 | 172 | 4 | 5 | |
| | 13-0-75-0 | 9-2-55-0 | 12-1-45-1 | 9-1-49-1 | 11-2-74-2 | | 3-0-25-0 | | | | | | | | | | | | | | | | 57 | 337 | 14 | 4 | |
| **v. Warwickshire** (Scarborough) 22-24 August | | | 12-5-20-0 | 14-5-28-2 | 12.3-3-33-4 | | 10-4-31-2 | | | | | | | | | 10-5-12-2 | | | | | | | 58.3 | 129 | 5 | 10 | |
| | 14-2-66-2 | 14.3-3-52-5 | 9-3-39-0 | 12-2-28-3 | | | 6-0-33-0 | | | | | | | | | | | | | | | | 55.3 | 222 | 4 | 10 | |
| **v. Sussex** (Hove) 5-7 September | 35.1-3-136-3 | | 26-3-104-2 | 27-7-75-2 | | | 19-1-92-1 | | | 6-0-13-0 | | | | | | | | 7-0-19-0 | | | 37-2-141-0 | | 157.1 | 597 | 17 | 8 | |
| **v. Hampshire** (Headingley) 19-22 September | 9-1-50-0 | 12-2-56-0 | 14.3-4-36-1 | 15-2-76-2 | | | 10-4-21-0 | | | | | | | | | | | | | | | | 60.3 | 244 | 5 | 4 | 1 |

| | AU Rashid | D Gough | TT Bresnan | MJ Hoggard | JN Gillespie | A Shahzad | Younus Khan | GJ Kruis | ND Thornicroft | A McGrath | SA Patterson | DJ Wainwright | A Lyth | AW Gale | RM Pyrah | C White | MP Vaughan | MJ Wood | CR Gilbert | Imran Tahir | JA Rudolph | MAK Lawson |
|---|---|---|---|---|---|---|---|---|---|---|---|---|---|---|---|---|---|---|---|---|---|---|
| Overs | 412.2 | 287.4 | 332 | 205.4 | 238.3 | 92.4 | 85.5 | 110.2 | 21 | 76 | 13 | 19 | 1 | 2 | 12 | 6 | 8 | 1 | 3 | 37 | 16 | 24 |
| Maidens | 46 | 74 | 71 | 47 | 53 | 12 | 10 | 21 | 4 | 16 | 2 | 1 | 0 | 0 | 2 | 0 | 0 | 0 | 0 | 2 | 4 | 1 |
| Runs | 1578 | 876 | 1090 | 644 | 803 | 343 | 342 | 409 | 72 | 223 | 39 | 74 | 12 | 33 | 41 | 11 | 29 | 4 | 11 | 141 | 55 | 122 |
| Wickets | 40 | 37 | 34 | 32 | 23 | 9 | 8 | 6 | 5 | 2 | 2 | 1 | 1 | 0 | 0 | 0 | 0 | 0 | 0 | 0 | 0 | 0 |
| Average | 39.45 | 23.67 | 32.05 | 20.12 | 34.91 | 38.11 | 42.75 | 51.12 | 12.00 | 44.60 | 19.50 | 37.00 | 12.00 | - | 33.00 | - | 41.00 | - | - | - | - | - |

## FIELDING

| | |
|---|---|
| 38 | GL Brophy (35 ct, 3 st) |
| 19 | JA Rudolph |
| 11 | A McGrath |
| 11 | SM Guy |
| 11 | Younus Khan |
| 8 | AU Rashid |
| 6 | TT Bresnan |
| 5 | Inzamam-ul-Haq |
| 5 | AW Gale |
| 5 | JJ Sayers |
| 4 | C White |
| 3 | JN Gillespie |
| 2 | D Gough |
| 2 | MJ Hoggard |
| 1 | GJ Kruis |
| 1 | ND Thornicroft |
| 1 | CR Gilbert |
| 1 | MAK Lawson |
| 1 | DJ Wainwright |
| 0 | MP Vaughan |
| 0 | MJ Wood |
| 0 | RM Pyrah |
| 0 | SA Patterson |
| 0 | Imran Tahir |
| 0 | A Shahzad |
| 0 | A Lyth |

### Final Division One Table

| | P | W | L | D | T | Ab | Bat | Bowl | Pens | Pts |
|---|---|---|---|---|---|---|---|---|---|---|
| Sussex | 16 | 7 | 3 | 5 | 0 | 1 | 37 | 43 | 0.00 | 202.00 |
| Durham | 16 | 7 | 5 | 4 | 0 | 0 | 38 | 47 | 1.50 | 197.50 |
| Lancashire | 16 | 5 | 2 | 8 | 0 | 1 | 40 | 44 | 0.00 | 190.00 |
| Surrey | 16 | 5 | 4 | 6 | 0 | 1 | 41 | 40 | 1.00 | 178.00 |
| Hampshire | 16 | 5 | 3 | 8 | 0 | 0 | 32 | 43 | 0.00 | 177.00 |
| Yorkshire | 16 | 4 | 4 | 8 | 0 | 0 | 49 | 38 | 0.00 | 175.00 |
| Kent | 16 | 3 | 5 | 7 | 0 | 1 | 43 | 36 | 0.00 | 153.00 |
| Warwickshire | 16 | 2 | 5 | 9 | 0 | 0 | 40 | 35 | 0.00 | 139.00 |
| Worcestershire | 16 | 1 | 8 | 5 | 0 | 2 | 18 | 35 | 0.00 | 95.00 |

Limited overs nickname:
YORKSHIRE PHOENIX

# NATWEST PRO40 LEAGUE

## by Mark Baldwin

Ironically, at the start of what was to be a victorious campaign at the back end of a troubled, flood-ravaged season, Worcestershire's NatWest Pro40 League curtain-raiser against Hampshire Hawks on 13 July was merely the subject of yet more controversy.

Initially, Worcestershire had sought to safeguard the fixture at New Road, which was due to be televised live by Sky Sports and therefore one of their most lucrative events of the season, by deciding to go ahead with their LV County Championship match on their home ground against Kent from 8–11 July.

When that game could not be staged, due to the flood damage at Worcester, and leading in turn to the rumpus about whether it should be replayed or not, the club finally decided to move their Pro40 opener to Derby – at a cost, according to Worcestershire chief executive Mark Newton, of 'between £50,000 and £80,000'.

Despite all this manoeuvring, however, more rain in Derby meant that the match was washed out anyway.

That left Leicestershire to host the first action of the competition, but despite Paul Nixon's 82-ball 61 against his former county they went down by six wickets to Kent, for whom skipper Rob Key hit 63 with a six and six fours and Darren Stevens a 35-ball unbeaten 42 against his old county.

Another high-profile victim of the awful midsummer weather was the Cheltenham Festival, with Gloucestershire being forced to switch matches to Bristol after seeing both their scheduled Pro40 games against Northamptonshire and Lancashire called off there due to a combination of rain, a waterlogged outfield and the surrounding flooding which had caused the town's water supply to be turned off for safety reasons.

Two no results in their first three matches, however, helped both Gloucestershire and Lancashire become the early leaders of Division One. In Gloucestershire's first proper game, Ben Edmondson conceded only six runs from an excellent final over as Warwickshire were pipped by three runs at Bristol following a 74-ball 88 not out from Alex Gidman which featured four sixes.

---

### NatWest Pro40 Division One

**13 July**
at Derby
**Worcestershire** v. **Hampshire**
*Match abandoned (1pt each)*

**15 July**
at Old Trafford
**Lancashire** v. **Essex**
*Match abandoned (1pt each)*

**22 July**
at Cheltenham
**Gloucestershire** v. **Northamptonshire**
*Match abandoned (1pt each)*

**24 July**
at Edgbaston
**Warwickshire** 191 all out (39.2 overs)
(DL Maddy 56)
**Nottinghamshire** 194 for 4 (31.4 overs) (GP Swann 80,
MA Wagh 66)
*Nottinghamshire (2pts) won by 6 wickets*

at Cheltenham
**Gloucestershire** v. **Lancashire**
*Match abandoned (1pt each)*

**25 July**
at Northampton
**Northamptonshire** 185 for 6 (32 overs) (SD Peters 54)
**Lancashire** 189 for 5 (31.4 overs) (SG Law 89)
*Lancashire (2pts) won by 5 wickets*

**29 July**
at Edgbaston
**Sussex** 200 all out (40 overs) (RR Montgomerie 65,
MW Goodwin 52)
**Worcestershire** 204 for 3 (36 overs) (GA Hick 57*, VS Solanki 55)
*Worcestershire (2pts) won by 7 wickets*

at Bristol
**Gloucestershire** 212 for 5 (35 overs) (APR Gidman 88*)
**Warwickshire** 209 for 6 (35 overs) (DL Maddy 71,
KC Sangakkara 55)
*Gloucestershire (2pts) won by 3 runs*

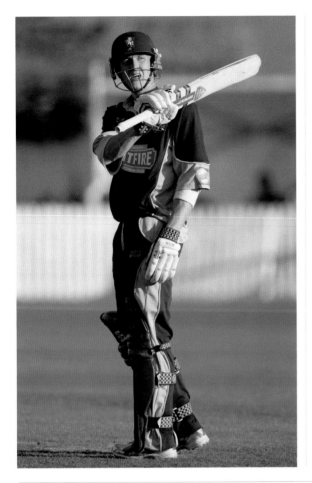

In Division Two, meanwhile, Kent and Durham both won their first two matches to set the early pace, with Key's 104 from100 balls helping to see off Derbyshire and Shivnarine Chanderpaul's unbeaten 80 from 68 balls, on his Durham debut, sweeping his side past Surrey's 248 for 6 after fine half-centuries too from Phil Mustard and former Scotland Under-19 captain Kyle Coetzer.

A superb hundred from Phil Jaques and a devastating opening burst from Kabir Ali, who took 4 for 19 in his first five overs, saw Worcestershire score a significant victory over Pro40 champions Essex at their Chelmsford headquarters and, three days later, they held off a spirited fightback from David Hussey and Chris Read who rallied Nottinghamshire from the depths of 46 for 5. Earlier Graeme Hick's 93 not out had included 43 runs from his last 20 balls.

Luke Wright's brutal 125 from a mere 73 balls was the perfect way to celebrate his England World Twenty20 squad call-up, and it also trumped Hamish Marshall's earlier 122 off 105 balls as Sussex chased down Gloucestershire's 266 for 7 at Hove. Two evenings later, under the Headingley lights, Yorkshire collapsed from 131 for 2 before ultimately scraping home breathlessly by one wicket against Middlesex – with Richard Pyrah hitting the fourth ball of the last over past mid on for four and then scuffing the next ball just past the bowler, Tim Murtagh, for a desperate winning single.

Joe Denly, the 21-year-old Kent batsman, grew in stature throughout the season after being given his chance to open the innings following the retirement of former county captain David Fulton at the end of the 2006 campaign.

## NatWest Pro40 Division Two

**14 July**
at Leicester
**Leicestershire** 175 all out (39.5 overs)
(PA Nixon 61)
**Kent** 179 for 4 (33.3 overs) (RWT Key 63)
*Kent (2pts) won by 6 wickets*

**16 July**
at Derby
**Glamorgan** 165 all out (40 overs)
**Derbyshire** 109 for 3 (16.5 overs)
*Derbyshire (2pts) won by 7 wickets – DL Method: target 109 from 22 overs*

**26 July**
at the Riverside
**Middlesex** 145 for 8 (19 overs) (EJG Morgan 52)
**Durham** 146 for 5 (18.3 overs)
*Durham (2pts) won by 5 wickets*

**29 July**
at Guildford
**Surrey** 248 for 6 (40 overs) (SA Newman 84, AD Brown 59)
**Durham** 249 for 3 (36 overs) (S Chanderpaul 80*, KJ Coetzer 76, P Mustard 63)
*Durham (2pts) won by 7 wickets*

at Derby
**Kent** 282 for 3 (40 overs) (RWT Key 104, M van Jaarsveld 62, JL Denly 52)
**Derbyshire** 272 for 9 (40 overs) (GM Smith 88)
*Kent (2pts) won by 10 runs*

at Ebbw Vale
**Middlesex** 183 for 5 (21 overs) (OA Shah 59, EC Joyce 55)
**Glamorgan** 94 all out (18.5 overs)
*Middlesex (2pts) won by 89 runs*

Essex's grip on the title was loosened irrevocably when Warwickshire won narrowly at Southend, while Hampshire's challenge also faltered when Sussex captain Chris Adams won a bristling personal duel with Shane Warne at Hove, hitting him for two sixes and five fours in a match-winning 70.

In the second division, Kent made it three wins out of three by beating previously undefeated Durham by three wickets at Canterbury as Darren Stevens led them home with a 59-ball 85 not out. And Scott Newman's 62 off just 33 balls, with nine fours and three sixes, saw Surrey out-hit Derbyshire in a rain-reduced match at The Oval. Yorkshire, however, displaced Kent at the top when fine batting from Gerard Brophy and Jacques Rudolph completed an eight-wicket drubbing of Glamorgan under the Sophia Gardens lights.

*Graeme Swann acknowledges the crowd's applause during a fine all-round performance for Nottinghamshire against Gloucestershire.*

## NatWest Pro40 Division One

**29 July (continued)**
at the Rose Bowl
**Hampshire** 224 for 6 (25 overs) (MJ Lumb 62, SM Ervine 57)
**Essex** 222 for 9 (25 overs) (JS Foster 61, GW Flower 54, DB Powell 4 for 30)
*Hampshire (2pts) won by 2 runs*

**1 August**
at the Rose Bowl
**Nottinghamshire** 214 for 8 (40 overs) (DJ Hussey 81)
**Hampshire** 218 for 4 (39.1 overs) (JP Crawley 97*, MJ Lumb 53)
*Hampshire (2pts) won by 6 wickets*

**2 August**
at Chelmsford
**Worcestershire** 225 (37.5 overs) (PA Jaques 101)
**Essex** 163 all out (32.2 overs) (Kabir Ali 4 for 34)
*Worcestershire (2pts) won by 62 runs*

**5 August**
at Trent Bridge
**Worcestershire** 225 for 5 (40 overs) (GA Hick 93*)
**Nottinghamshire** 216 for 9 (40 overs) (DJ Hussey 75, CMW Read 59, Kabir Ali 5 for 46)
*Worcestershire (2pts) won by 9 runs*

**6 August**
at Hove
**Gloucestershire** 266 for 7 (40 overs) (HJH Marshall 122, Kadeer Ali 76, RJ Kirtley 4 for 41)
**Sussex** 267 for 8 (38.3 overs) (LJ Wright 125, J Lewis 4 for 45)
*Sussex (2pts) won by 2 wickets*

**12 August**
at Trent Bridge
**Northamptonshire** 211 for 6 (40 overs) (CJL Rogers 58, DJG Sales 52)
**Nottinghamshire** 212 for 4 (29.4 overs) (SP Fleming 90)
*Nottinghamshire (2pts) won by 6 wickets*

at Hove
**Hampshire** 260 for 7 (40 overs) (MJ Lumb 108, JP Crawley 61, SM Ervine 56, RJ Kirtley 5 for 36)
**Sussex** 261 for 8 (38.5 overs) (CJ Adams 70, CD Nash 59)
*Sussex (2pts) won by 2 wickets*

at Southend
**Warwickshire** 188 for 6 (34 overs)
**Essex** 184 all out (34 overs) (GW Flower 53, HH Streak 4 for 39)
*Warwickshire (2pts) won by 6 runs*

**14 August**
at Old Trafford
**Lancashire** v. **Sussex**
*Match abandoned (1pt each)*

**15 August**
at Trent Bridge
**Nottinghamshire** v. **Essex**
*Match abandoned (1pt each)*

**19 August**
at Edgbaston
**Sussex** v. **Warwickshire**
*Match abandoned (1pt each)*

Steven Davies' 78-ball 83 spearheaded Worcestershire's excellent win over Lancashire, in a game played at Taunton due to the continued problems at New Road, but their lead at the top of the first division was cut to two points when Nottinghamshire crushed Gloucestershire by 116 runs at Trent Bridge, thanks in the main to Graeme Swann's 33-ball 59 and superb eight-over spell of 5 for 17.

Yorkshire's second division progress faltered with an inept batting display at Scarborough, and it was the same story at Lord's where Kent collapsed horribly from 100 for 2 to 151 all out just when it seemed Middlesex's 187 for 5 was going to prove inadequate. Those defeats were good news for Durham, though, for whom Phil Mustard belted a 21-ball fifty on his way to 78 from 40 balls in a buccaneering victory over Leicestershire at the Riverside.

Mustard was in equally eye-catching form on the same ground the following day, his unbeaten 66 from 31 balls racing Durham past Yorkshire's feeble 122 and putting the north-east county on top of Division Two, while Kent's slump continued with a nerve-shredding two-run defeat on home soil to Somerset. Peter Trego cut through the Kent top order to take 5 for 17 in 24 balls, but it was his diving catch at long off to dismiss James Tredwell for 51 off the last ball of the 39th over which was decisive.

Tredwell had dominated a seventh-wicket stand of 79 with Ryan McLaren, who had earlier revitalised the innings from 45 for 5 in company with Geraint Jones. But McLaren's all-round heroics cruelly did not stretch to the final ball of the match – a full toss from Steffan Jones – which he missed completely.

Somerset then moved to the top of Division Two by trouncing Leicestershire at Taunton, their third win in five days in the competition, while Hampshire kept their title hopes alive in Division One as Michael Lumb and Sean Ervine made short work of Warwickshire's 196 for 8. Sussex's emphatic win against Northamptonshire in front of a boisterous floodlit crowd at Hove also boosted their chances.

Warwickshire, meanwhile, were left facing up to relegation after losing two games in a weekend, at home to Lancashire and away at Northamptonshire, for whom Nicky Boje starred with bat and ball and both Riki Wessels and David Sales thumped half-centuries. Essex's first division status also came under threat as a result of defeat at home to Gloucestershire.

A breathless last ball win for Surrey at Canterbury, in a final over in which three wickets fell in successive balls, all but put paid to Kent's promotion ambitions while, on the same night in Chesterfield, fifties from Michael Di Venuto

## NatWest Pro40 Division Two

**29 July**
at Scarborough
**Yorkshire** 261 for 5 (40 overs) (JA Rudolph 127, AW Gale 53*)
**Somerset** 242 all out (37 overs) (ID Blackwell 97)
*Yorkshire (2pts) won by 9 runs – DL Method: target 252 from 38 overs*

**30 July**
at Lord's
**Leicestershire** 259 for 4 (40 overs) (J Allenby 91*, HD Ackerman 83)
**Middlesex** 232 all out (40 overs) (ET Smith 75, EC Joyce 69)
*Leicestershire (2pts) won by 27 runs*

**5 August**
at Taunton
**Somerset** 251 for 8 (40 overs) (JL Langer 59, ME Trescothick 56)
**Derbyshire** 219 all out (37.3 overs) (MG Dighton 55)
*Somerset (2pts) won by 32 runs*

at Lord's
**Surrey** 238 for 8 (40 overs) (MA Butcher 50)
**Middlesex** 239 for 4 (38.2 overs) (EJG Morgan 96, JWM Dalrymple 54*, OA Shah 50)
*Middlesex (2pts) won by 6 wickets*

**7 August**
at Derby
**Derbyshire** 175 for 9 (40 overs)
**Leicestershire** 152 for 9 (30.5 overs) (JN Snape 52*)
*Leicestershire (2pts) won by 1 wicket – DL Method: target 152 from 31 overs*

**8 August**
at Headingley
**Middlesex** 183 for 8 (40 overs) (BJM Scott 54*)
**Yorkshire** 184 for 8 (39.5 overs)
*Yorkshire (2pts) won by 2 wickets*

**12 August**
at Colwyn Bay
**Glamorgan** v. **Somerset**
*Match abandoned (1pt each)*

at Canterbury
**Durham** 203 all out (39.4 overs) (MJ Di Venuto 57)
**Kent** 204 for 7 (38.5 overs) (DI Stevens 85*)
*Kent (2pts) won by 3 wickets*

Marcus Trescothick hits another boundary on the way to his century during Somerset's narrow win against Surrey at The Oval.

and Kyle Coetzer further strengthened Durham's position at the top of the division.

Sunday 9 September was the day that Worcestershire got one hand on the Pro40 trophy, with 20-year-old Moeen Ali picking a fine time to score his first county hundred – off only 46 balls with a breathtaking six sixes and 14 fours – as Northamptonshire were brushed aside by a huge margin at Kidderminster. And they might have won the title, too, had Hampshire not squeezed past Gloucestershire, despite Moeen's brother Kadeer Ali's brave 114, at the Rose Bowl.

The evening of 10 September saw Lord's hosting a floodlit game for the first time, Middlesex marking that historic occasion by beating Derbyshire by four wickets, but it was under the Bristol lights three nights later that Worcestershire clinched their reward for all the pain and frustration of the 2007 season.

## NatWest Pro40 Division One

**25 August**
at Taunton
**Lancashire** 254 for 6 (40 overs) (VVS Laxman 85*)
**Worcestershire** 255 for 4 (37.4 overs) (SM Davies 83, GA Hick 50*)
*Worcestershire (2pts) won by 6 wickets*

**26 August**
at Trent Bridge
**Nottinghamshire** 270 for 6 (40 overs) (MA Wagh 65*, GP Swann 59, WI Jefferson 50)
**Gloucestershire** 154 (32.3 overs) (Kadeer Ali 56, GP Swann 5 for 17)
*Nottinghamshire (2pts) won by 116 runs*

at Colchester
**Essex** 177 all out (35.5 overs)
**Sussex** 151 all out (38 overs) (Danish Kaneria 5 for 22)
*Essex (2pts) won by 26 runs*

**27 August**
at Northampton
**Hampshire** 225 for 9 (40 overs) (MA Carberry 75*, RJ Logan 4 for 47)
**Northamptonshire** 228 for 5 (39 overs) (DJG Sales 92*, SD Peters 54)
*Northamptonshire (2pts) won by 5 wickets*

**29 August**
at the Rose Bowl
**Warwickshire** 196 for 8 (40 overs) (IJL Trott 90)
**Hampshire** 197 for 2 (29.2 overs) (MJ Lumb 82, SM Ervine 80*)
*Hampshire (2pts) won by 8 wickets*

**31 August**
at Hove
**Northamptonshire** 188 for 6 (40 overs) (RA White 56)
**Sussex** 192 for 4 (29.3 overs) (Naved-ul-Hasan 51)
*Sussex (2pts) won by 6 wickets*

**1 September**
at Edgbaston
**Warwickshire** 253 for 7 (40 overs) (NM Carter 92)
**Lancashire** 254 for 5 (39.5 overs) (GD Cross 76, VVS Laxman 50)
*Lancashire (2pts) won by 5 wickets*

**2 September**
at Old Trafford
**Lancashire** v. **Nottinghamshire**
*Match abandoned (1pt each)*

at Northampton
**Warwickshire** 230 for 8 (40 overs)
**Northamptonshire** 233 for 4 (36 overs) (N Boje 74*, DJG Sales 58, MH Wessels 52)
*Northamptonshire (2pts) won by 6 wickets*

**3 September**
at Chelmsford
**Gloucestershire** 245 for 8 (40 overs) (APR Gidman 80, CM Spearman 63)
**Essex** 174 all out (30.4 overs) (SP Kirby 4 for 29)
*Gloucestershire (2pts) won by 71 runs*

Gloucestershire's 270 for 9 was a fine score, but Worcestershire chased it down quite brilliantly as young openers Steven Davies and Moeen Ali sent them on their way with a stand of 151 from 17 overs. It was a performance worthy of champions.

All that remained in the final games of the competition was for Warwickshire and Essex to be confirmed as the relegated counties and for Northamptonshire to make a hash of their own first division survival.

After failing to score 40 from the last ten overs – an equation that then came down to just three from one – with wickets in hand against Essex in their final league fixture, Northants were then condemned to meet Middlesex in a play-off to decide which of the two teams would join Durham and Somerset in next year's Division One line-up. Middlesex, with a fifth successive win, duly sent Northants down, beating them by a convincing six wickets.

## NatWest Pro40 Division Two

**19 August**
at Leicester
**Leicestershire** 60 for 2 (20 overs)
**Yorkshire**
*Match abandoned (1pt each)*

at The Oval
**Derbyshire** 227 for 7 (35 overs) (WPC Weston 72)
**Surrey** 102 for 2 (13 overs) (SA Newman 62)
*Surrey (2pts) won by 24 runs – DL Method: target 79 from 13 overs*

**20 August**
at Cardiff
**Glamorgan** 129 for 8 (35 overs)
**Yorkshire** 131 for 2 (17.4 overs) (GL Brophy 66)
*Yorkshire (2pts) won by 8 wickets*

**23 August**
at Taunton
**Somerset** 289 for 6 (40 overs) (ME Trescothick 84, ND McKenzie 69, C Kieswetter 61)
**Durham** 258 all out (37.5 overs) (P Mustard 84, S Chanderpaul 68, AR Caddick 5 for 49)
*Somerset (2pts) won by 31 runs*

**26 August**
at the Riverside
**Leicestershire** 215 for 5 (40 overs) (HD Ackerman 72)
**Durham** 218 for 4 (30.1 overs) (P Mustard 78)
*Durham (2pts) won by 6 wickets*

at Lord's
**Middlesex** 187 for 5 (40 overs)
**Kent** 151 all out (36.4 overs) (RWT Key 72, TJ Murtagh 4 for 21)
*Middlesex (2pts) won by 36 runs*

at Scarborough
**Yorkshire** 145 all out (33.3 overs)
**Surrey** 147 for 5 (29.1 overs)
*Surrey (2pts) won by 5 wickets*

**27 August**
at the Riverside
**Yorkshire** 122 all out (39.5 overs) (A McGrath 50)
**Durham** 126 for 1 (15.4 overs) (P Mustard 66*)
*Durham (2pts) won by 9 wickets*

at The Oval
**Surrey** 280 for 8 (40 overs) (SA Newman 58, AD Brown 56, CP Schofield 51)
**Glamorgan** 227 all out (40 overs) (DL Hemp 59)
*Surrey (2pts) won by 53 runs*

at Canterbury
**Somerset** 214 for 8 (40 overs) (JL Langer 92, JC Hildreth 56, R McLaren 4 for 46)
**Kent** 212 for 7 (40 overs) (R McLaren 78*, JC Tredwell 51, PD Trego 5 for 44)
*Somerset (2pts) won by 2 runs*

**28 August**
at Taunton
**Somerset** 287 for 6 (40 overs) (ME Trescothick 54, JL Langer 53)
**Leicestershire** 177 (34.1 overs) (JL Sadler 54*)
*Somerset (2pts) won by 110 runs*

**4 September**
at Chesterfield
**Derbyshire** 195 for 9 (40 overs) (WPC Weston 51, Hassan Adnan 51)
**Durham** 201 for 3 (27.3 overs) (MJ Di Venuto 64, KJ Coetzer 54)
*Durham (2pts) won by 7 wickets*

at Canterbury
**Kent** 159 for 8 (40 overs)
**Surrey** 160 for 9 (40 overs) (SA Newman 92*)
*Surrey (2pts) won by 1 wicket*

**7 September**
at Cardiff
**Glamorgan** 178 for 8 (40 overs) (MJ Saggers 4 for 25)
**Kent** 179 for 2 (29.5 overs) (RWT Key 107*)
*Kent (2pts) won by 8 wickets*

## NatWest Pro40 Division One

**9 September**
at Kidderminster
**Worcestershire** 281 for 7 (40 overs) (MM Ali 100,
SM Davies 74)
**Northamptonshire** 130 all out (21.2 overs)
(MN Malik 4 for 60)
*Worcestershire (2pts) won by 151 runs*

at the Rose Bowl
**Hampshire** 274 for 5 (40 overs) (CC Benham 111,
SM Ervine 74)
**Gloucestershire** 260 for 6 (40 overs) (Kadeer Ali 114,
HJH Marshall 76)
*Hampshire (2pts) won by 14 runs*

**13 September**
at Bristol
**Gloucestershire** 270 for 9 (40 overs) (CM Spearman 71,
APR Gidman 63)
**Worcestershire** 271 for 4 (38.1 overs) (SM Davies 84,
MM Ali 72)
*Worcestershire (2pts) won by 6 wickets*

**16 September**
at Edgbaston
**Worcestershire** 175 all out (39.3 overs) (DKH Mitchell 53)
**Warwickshire** 176 for 3 (27.3 overs)
*Warwickshire (2pts) won by 7 wickets*

at Old Trafford
**Lancashire** 199 for 4 (40 overs) (MJ Chilton 77*)
**Hampshire** 122 for 7 (25.1 overs) (CC Benham 53)
*Lancashire (2pts) won by 32 runs – DL Method: target 155 from
25.1 overs*

at Northampton
**Essex** 204 all out (40 overs) (AN Cook 81*, L Klusener 4 for 40)
**Northamptonshire** 204 for 5 (40 overs) (DJG Sales 79)
*Match tied (1pt each)*

at Hove
**Nottinghamshire** 283 for 7 (40 overs) (MA Wagh 77,
SR Patel 72, SP Fleming 58)
**Sussex** 274 for 4 (40 overs) (CD Hopkinson 123*, RR Montgomerie 61)
*Nottinghamshire (2pts) won by 9 runs*

## NatWest Pro40 Division Two

**9 September**
at Leicester
**Leicestershire** 283 for 5 (40 overs) (J Allenby 70, PA Nixon 60)
**Glamorgan** 168 all out (33.2 overs) (DL Hemp 59)
*Leicestershire (2pts) won by 115 runs*

at Canterbury
**Kent** 228 for 9 (40 overs) (M van Jaarsveld 50)
**Yorkshire** 215 for 7 (40 overs) (JA Rudolph 86,
Inzamam-ul-Haq 53)
*Kent (2pts) won by 13 runs*

**10 September**
at Lord's
**Derbyshire** 196 for 9 (40 overs) (MG Dighton 67)
**Middlesex** 199 for 6 (38 overs) (EC Joyce 68)
*Middlesex (2pts) won by 4 wickets*

**11 September**
at The Oval
**Somerset** 258 for 9 (40 overs) (ME Trescothick 124,
JW Dernbach 5 for 44)
**Surrey** 253 for 9 (40 overs) (MR Ramprakash 115, MA Butcher 56)
*Somerset (2pts) won by 5 runs*

**15 September**
at Headingley
**Yorkshire** 236 for 5 (40 overs) (MP Vaughan 95)
**Derbyshire** 129 all out (24 overs) (GJ Kruis 4 for 17)
*Yorkshire (2pts) won by 107 runs*

at the Riverside
**Durham** 271 for 8 (40 overs) (DM Benkenstein 58*,
MJ Di Venuto 55)
**Glamorgan** 201 for 9 (40 overs) (GP Rees 63)
*Durham (2pts) won by 70 runs*

at Taunton
**Somerset** 211 for 9 (40 overs) (ND McKenzie 86,
JL Langer 54)
**Middlesex** 212 for 3 (37.1 overs) (ET Smith 80, EC Joyce 77)
*Middlesex (2pts) won by 7 wickets*

at Leicester
**Leicestershire** 231 for 8 (40 overs) (JL Sadler 62,
TJ New 51)
**Surrey** 236 for 9 (40 overs) (MR Ramprakash 72,
MA Butcher 62, MJ Nicholson 57*)
*Surrey (2pts) won by 1 wicket*

## Division One – Final Table

|  | P | W | L | T | NR | RR | Pts |
|---|---|---|---|---|---|---|---|
| Worcestershire | 8 | 6 | 1 | 0 | 1 | 0.75 | 13 |
| Nottinghamshire | 8 | 4 | 2 | 0 | 2 | 0.95 | 10 |
| Lancashire | 8 | 3 | 1 | 0 | 4 | 0.19 | 10 |
| Hampshire | 8 | 4 | 3 | 0 | 1 | 0.17 | 9 |
| Sussex | 8 | 3 | 3 | 0 | 2 | 0.09 | 8 |
| Gloucestershire | 8 | 2 | 4 | 0 | 2 | -0.33 | 6 |
| Northamptonshire | 8 | 2 | 4 | 1 | 1 | -0.95 | 6 |
| Warwickshire | 8 | 2 | 5 | 0 | 1 | -0.26 | 5 |
| Essex | 8 | 1 | 4 | 1 | 2 | -0.53 | 5 |

## Division Two – Final Table

|  | P | W | L | T | NR | RR | Pts |
|---|---|---|---|---|---|---|---|
| Durham | 8 | 6 | 2 | 0 | 0 | 1.31 | 12 |
| Somerset | 8 | 5 | 2 | 0 | 1 | 0.54 | 11 |
| Middlesex | 8 | 5 | 3 | 0 | 0 | 0.48 | 10 |
| Surrey | 8 | 5 | 3 | 0 | 0 | 0.38 | 10 |
| Kent | 8 | 5 | 3 | 0 | 0 | 0.26 | 10 |
| Yorkshire | 8 | 4 | 3 | 0 | 1 | 0.05 | 9 |
| Leicestershire | 8 | 3 | 4 | 0 | 1 | -0.26 | 7 |
| Derbyshire | 8 | 1 | 7 | 0 | 0 | -0.92 | 2 |
| Glamorgan | 8 | 0 | 7 | 0 | 1 | -2.35 | 1 |

## NatWest Pro40 Play-Off

**23 September**
at Southgate
**Northamptonshire** 148 all out (35.3 overs) (DJG Sales 70)
**Middlesex** 151 for 4 (36.2 overs)
*Middlesex won by 6 wickets*

## FEATURES OF NATWEST PRO40 LEAGUE 2007

### HIGHEST TOTAL

| 289 for 6 (40 overs) | Somerset v. Durham at Taunton | 23 August |
|---|---|---|

### HIGHEST TOTAL BATTING SECOND

| 274 for 4 (40 overs) | Sussex v. Nottinghamshire at Hove | 16 September |
|---|---|---|

### LOWEST TOTAL

| 94 (18.5 overs) | Glamorgan v. Middlesex at Ebbw Vale | 29 July |
|---|---|---|

### BEST INDIVIDUAL SCORE

| 127 | JA Rudolph | Yorkshire v. Somerset at Scarborough | 29 July |
|---|---|---|---|

*13 centuries were scored in the competition*

### FIVE WICKETS IN AN INNINGS

| 5-46 | Kabir Ali | Worcs v. Notts at Trent Bridge | 5 August |
|---|---|---|---|
| 5-36 | RJ Kirtley | Sussex v. Hampshire at Hove | 12 August |
| 5-49 | AR Caddick | Somerset v. Durham at Taunton | 23 August |
| 5-17 | GP Swann | Notts v. Glos at Trent Bridge | 26 August |
| 5-22 | Danish Kaneria | Essex v. Sussex at Colchester | 26 August |
| 5-44 | PD Trego | Somerset v. Kent at Canterbury | 27 August |
| 5-44 | JW Dernbach | Surrey v. Somerset at The Oval | 11 September |

*There were no instances of six wickets in an innings*

### TIED MATCHES

| Northamptonshire tied with Essex at Northampton | 16 September |
|---|---|

### WINNING BY ONE WICKET

| Leicestershire beat Derbyshire at Derby | 7 August |
|---|---|
| Surrey beat Kent at Canterbury | 4 September |
| Surrey beat Leicestershire at Leicester | 15 September |

### WINNING BY MORE THAN 150 RUNS

| 151 | Worcestershire beat Northamptonshire at Kidderminster | 9 September |
|---|---|---|

*There were five instances of a side winning by 100 runs or more*

### WINNING BY ONE RUN

*No team won by one run*

### NO PLAY POSSIBLE

| Worcestershire v. Hampshire at Derby | 13 July |
|---|---|
| Lancashire v. Essex at Old Trafford | 15 July |
| Gloucestershire v. Northamptonshire at Cheltenham | 22 July |
| Gloucestershire v. Lancashire at Cheltenham | 24 July |
| Glamorgan v. Somerset at Colwyn Bay | 12 August |
| Lancashire v. Sussex at Old Trafford | 14 August |
| Nottinghamshire v. Essex at Trent Bridge | 15 August |
| Warwickshire v. Sussex at Edgbaston | 19 August |
| Lancashire v. Nottinghamshire at Old Trafford | 2 September |

Steven Davies, the young Worcestershire wicketkeeper-batsman, was in sparkling form towards the end of his county's triumphant campaign.

## NATWEST PRO40: DIVISION ONE FEATURES 2007

### BATTING: LEADING AVERAGES

| | M | Inns | NO | Runs | HS | Av | 100 | 50 |
|---|---|---|---|---|---|---|---|---|
| GA Hick (Worcs) | 7 | 7 | 3 | 292 | 93* | 73.00 | - | 3 |
| DJG.Sales (Northants) | 6 | 6 | 1 | 314 | 92* | 62.80 | - | 4 |
| DJ Hussey (Notts) | 4 | 4 | 1 | 181 | 81 | 60.33 | - | 2 |
| MA Wagh (Notts) | 6 | 6 | 1 | 290 | 77 | 58.00 | - | 3 |
| JP Crawley (Hants) | 5 | 5 | 1 | 230 | 97* | 57.50 | - | 2 |
| CD Hopkinson (Sussex) | 5 | 4 | 1 | 170 | 123* | 56.66 | 1 | - |
| PA Jaques (Worcs) | 3 | 3 | 0 | 163 | 101 | 54.33 | 1 | - |
| L Klusener (Northants) | 7 | 7 | 4 | 161 | 36* | 53.66 | - | - |
| MJ Lumb (Hants) | 7 | 7 | 0 | 373 | 108 | 53.28 | 1 | 3 |
| Kadeer Ali (Glos) | 6 | 6 | 0 | 317 | 114 | 52.83 | 1 | 2 |
| APR Gidman (Glos) | 6 | 6 | 1 | 255 | 88* | 51.00 | - | 3 |
| CC Benham (Hants) | 4 | 4 | 0 | 200 | 111 | 50.00 | 1 | 1 |
| CMW Read (Notts) | 6 | 5 | 2 | 147 | 59 | 49.00 | - | 1 |
| SM Davies (Worcs) | 7 | 6 | 0 | 293 | 84 | 48.83 | - | 3 |
| LJ Wright (Sussex) | 5 | 4 | 0 | 195 | 125 | 48.75 | 1 | - |
| SM Ervine (Hants) | 7 | 7 | 1 | 269 | 80* | 44.83 | - | 4 |
| RR Montgomerie (Sussex) | 3 | 3 | 0 | 131 | 65 | 43.66 | - | 2 |
| DL Maddy (Warwicks) | 6 | 5 | 0 | 218 | 71 | 43.60 | - | 2 |
| TR Ambrose (Warwicks) | 8 | 7 | 2 | 213 | 43 | 42.60 | - | - |
| HJH Marshall (Glos) | 6 | 6 | 0 | 252 | 122 | 42.00 | 1 | 1 |
| CJ Adams (Sussex) | 6 | 4 | 0 | 162 | 70 | 40.50 | - | 1 |
| MA Carberry (Hants) | 7 | 7 | 3 | 152 | 75* | 38.00 | - | 1 |
| SR Patel (Notts) | 6 | 6 | 2 | 149 | 72 | 37.25 | - | 1 |
| NM Carter (Warwicks) | 4 | 4 | 0 | 146 | 92 | 36.50 | - | 1 |
| KC Sangakkara (Warwicks) | 6 | 5 | 0 | 177 | 55 | 35.40 | - | 1 |
| GD Cross (Lancs) | 3 | 3 | 0 | 106 | 76 | 35.33 | - | 1 |
| MM Ali (Worcs) | 6 | 6 | 0 | 207 | 100 | 34.50 | 1 | 1 |
| SD Peters (Northants) | 5 | 4 | 0 | 136 | 54 | 34.00 | - | 2 |
| AGR Loudon (Warwicks) | 8 | 7 | 2 | 164 | 39 | 32.80 | - | - |
| IJL Trott (Warwicks) | 8 | 7 | 1 | 196 | 90 | 32.66 | - | 1 |
| N Boje (Northants) | 5 | 5 | 1 | 130 | 74* | 32.50 | - | 1 |
| BF Smith (Worcs) | 4 | 4 | 1 | 96 | 43* | 32.00 | - | - |
| MW Goodwin (Sussex) | 6 | 5 | 1 | 126 | 52 | 31.50 | - | 1 |
| GP Swann (Notts) | 6 | 6 | 0 | 188 | 80 | 31.33 | - | 2 |
| AJ Hodd (Sussex) | 7 | 5 | 2 | 94 | 42 | 31.33 | - | - |
| VS Solanki (Worcs) | 4 | 4 | 0 | 121 | 55 | 30.25 | - | 1 |
| CM Spearman (Glos) | 6 | 6 | 0 | 181 | 71 | 30.16 | - | 2 |
| NJ O'Brien (Northants) | 5 | 4 | 1 | 88 | 43 | 29.33 | - | - |
| PJ Horton (Lancs) | 4 | 4 | 0 | 116 | 47 | 29.00 | - | - |
| SP Fleming (Notts) | 6 | 6 | 0 | 171 | 90 | 28.50 | - | 2 |
| CD Nash (Sussex) | 6 | 5 | 0 | 132 | 59 | 26.40 | - | 1 |

Qualification: averages 25 or above (minimum of three innings)

### LEADING RUN SCORERS – TOP 20

| Player | Runs | Inns |
|---|---|---|
| MJ Lumb (Hants) | 373 | 7 |
| Kadeer Ali (Glos) | 317 | 6 |
| DJG Sales (Northants) | 314 | 6 |
| SM Davies (Worcs) | 293 | 7 |
| GA Hick (Worcs) | 292 | 7 |
| MA Wagh (Notts) | 290 | 6 |
| SM Ervine (Hants) | 269 | 7 |
| APR Gidman (Glos) | 255 | 6 |
| HJH Marshall (Glos) | 252 | 6 |
| JP Crawley (Hants) | 230 | 5 |
| DL Maddy (Warwicks) | 218 | 6 |
| TR Ambrose (Warwicks) | 213 | 8 |
| MM Ali (Worcs) | 207 | 6 |
| CC Benham (Hants) | 200 | 4 |
| IJL Trott (Warwicks) | 196 | 8 |
| LJ Wright (Sussex) | 195 | 5 |
| GP Swann (Notts) | 188 | 6 |
| DJ Hussey (Notts) | 181 | 4 |
| CM Spearman (Glos) | 181 | 6 |
| KC Sangakkara (Warwicks) | 177 | 6 |

### BOWLING: LEADING AVERAGES

| Bowling | O | M | Runs | W | Av | Best | 4i | Econ |
|---|---|---|---|---|---|---|---|---|
| Danish Kaneria | 23 | 1 | 66 | 8 | 8.25 | 5-22 | 1 | 2.86 |
| RN ten Doeschate | 12 | 0 | 55 | 5 | 11.00 | 3-28 | - | 4.58 |
| GP Swann | 48 | 4 | 163 | 11 | 14.81 | 5-17 | 1 | 3.39 |
| Kabir Ali | 49 | 7 | 270 | 18 | 15.00 | 5-46 | 2 | 5.51 |
| RJ Kirtley | 26 | 0 | 168 | 11 | 15.27 | 5-36 | 2 | 6.46 |
| N Boje | 36 | 1 | 180 | 11 | 16.36 | 3-30 | - | 5.00 |
| G Keedy | 21 | 1 | 90 | 5 | 18.00 | 2-12 | - | 4.28 |
| RS Bopara | 11.5 | 0 | 91 | 5 | 18.20 | 3-27 | - | 7.69 |
| DB Powell | 34 | 2 | 201 | 11 | 18.27 | 4-30 | 1 | 5.91 |
| SP Kirby | 28.4 | 1 | 170 | 8 | 21.25 | 4-29 | 1 | 5.93 |
| J Lewis | 29 | 1 | 209 | 8 | 26.12 | 4-45 | 1 | 7.20 |
| RW Price | 41.2 | 1 | 210 | 8 | 26.25 | 3-27 | - | 5.08 |
| RJ Logan | 34 | 0 | 239 | 9 | 26.55 | 4-47 | 1 | 7.02 |
| AJ Bichel | 36 | 1 | 213 | 8 | 26.62 | 3-48 | - | 5.91 |
| L Klusener | 42 | 1 | 196 | 7 | 28.00 | 4-40 | 1 | 4.66 |
| TD Groenewald | 21 | 2 | 140 | 5 | 28.00 | 3-25 | - | 6.66 |
| NM Carter | 29.4 | 1 | 149 | 5 | 29.80 | 3-23 | - | 5.02 |
| SI Mahmood | 23.4 | 0 | 183 | 6 | 30.50 | 3-33 | - | 7.73 |
| RJ Sillence | 29 | 1 | 184 | 6 | 30.66 | 2-27 | - | 6.34 |
| JTA Bruce | 45 | 2 | 246 | 8 | 30.75 | 2-27 | - | 5.46 |
| Abdul Razzaq | 23 | 0 | 154 | 5 | 30.80 | 2-19 | - | 6.69 |
| BV Taylor | 28 | 1 | 156 | 5 | 31.20 | 3-33 | - | 5.57 |
| SD Udal | 44 | 0 | 223 | 7 | 31.85 | 2-30 | - | 5.06 |
| HH Streak | 32.3 | 0 | 192 | 6 | 32.00 | 4-39 | 1 | 5.90 |
| Naved-ul-Hasan | 37.5 | 2 | 225 | 7 | 32.14 | 3-54 | - | 5.94 |
| AJ Harris | 29 | 2 | 169 | 5 | 33.80 | 2-33 | - | 5.82 |
| AGR Loudon | 28 | 3 | 146 | 4 | 36.50 | 2-27 | - | 5.21 |
| MH Yardy | 31 | 0 | 149 | 4 | 37.25 | 2-28 | - | 4.80 |
| RS Ferley | 46 | 0 | 262 | 7 | 37.42 | 3-32 | - | 5.69 |
| AC Thomas | 25.5 | 2 | 161 | 4 | 40.25 | 2-49 | - | 6.23 |
| GJ Batty | 32.5 | 0 | 172 | 4 | 43.00 | 3-47 | - | 5.23 |
| AP Palladino | 29 | 0 | 175 | 4 | 43.75 | 1-19 | - | 6.03 |
| SM Ervine | 42.5 | 1 | 307 | 7 | 43.85 | 2-48 | - | 7.16 |

Qualification: averages 45 or less (minimum of four wickets)

### LEADING WICKET-TAKERS – TOP 20

| Player | W | O |
|---|---|---|
| Kabir Ali (Worcs) | 18 | 26 |
| N Boje (Northants) | 11 | 36 |
| DB Powell (Hants) | 11 | 34 |
| RJ Kirtley (Sussex) | 11 | 26 |
| GP Swann (Notts) | 11 | 48 |
| RJ Logan (Northants) | 9 | 34 |
| Danish Kaneria (Essex) | 8 | 23 |
| J Lewis (Glos) | 8 | 29 |
| SP Kirby (Glos) | 8 | 28.4 |
| AJ Bichel (Essex) | 8 | 36 |
| JTA Bruce (Hants) | 8 | 45 |
| RW Price (Worcs) | 8 | 41.2 |
| Naved-ul-Hasan (Sussex) | 7 | 37.5 |
| RS Ferley (Notts) | 7 | 46 |
| SD Udal (Hants) | 7 | 44 |
| L Klusener (Northants) | 7 | 42 |
| SM Ervine (Hants) | 7 | 42.5 |
| SI Mahmood (Lancs) | 6 | 23.4 |
| CG Greenidge (Glos) | 6 | 42.4 |
| RJ Sillence (Worcs) | 6 | 29 |

### FIELDING: LEADING DISMISSALS – TOP 20

SM Davies (Worcs) – 9 (6ct, 3st); N Pothas (Hants) – 8 (6ct, 2st); TR Ambrose (Warwicks) – 7 (5ct, 2 st); DJG Sales (Northants) – 7 (7ct); NJ O'Brien (Northants) – 6 (4ct, 2st); RJ Sillence (Worcs) – 6 (6ct); SJ Adshead (Glos) – 5 (5ct); N Boje (Northants) – 5 (5ct); LD Sutton (Lancs) – 4 (2ct, 2st); CMW Read (Notts) – 4 (3ct, 1st); JS Foster (Essex) – 4 (4ct); ML Pettini (Essex) – 4 (4ct); MA Carberry (Hants) – 4 (4ct); AGR Loudon (Warwicks) – 4 (4ct); AJ Hodd (Sussex) – 3 (3 ct); JP Crawley (Hants) – 3 (3ct); DKH Mitchell (Worcs) – 3 (3ct); V Chopra (Essex) – 3 (3ct); DL Maddy (Warwicks) – 3 (3ct); SP Fleming (Notts) – 3 (3ct)

# NATWEST PRO40: DIVISION TWO FEATURES 2007

## BATTING: LEADING AVERAGES

| | M | Inns | NO | Runs | HS | Av | 100 | 50 |
|---|---|---|---|---|---|---|---|---|
| MR Ramprakash (Surrey) | 4 | 4 | 1 | 215 | 115 | 71.66 | 1 | 1 |
| JA Rudolph (Yorks) | 7 | 6 | 1 | 304 | 127 | 60.80 | 1 | 1 |
| P Mustard (Durham) | 8 | 8 | 1 | 409 | 84 | 58.42 | - | 4 |
| RWT Key (Kent) | 8 | 8 | 1 | 408 | 107* | 58.28 | 2 | 2 |
| DI Stevens (Kent) | 7 | 6 | 3 | 172 | 85* | 57.33 | - | 1 |
| SA Newman (Surrey) | 8 | 8 | 1 | 378 | 92* | 54.00 | - | 4 |
| DM Benkenstein (Durham) | 8 | 7 | 3 | 215 | 58* | 53.75 | - | 1 |
| JL Langer (Somerset) | 7 | 7 | 1 | 304 | 92 | 50.66 | - | 4 |
| ME Trescothick (Somerset) | 7 | 7 | 0 | 329 | 124 | 47.00 | 1 | 3 |
| ND McKenzie (Somerset) | 5 | 5 | 0 | 233 | 86 | 46.60 | - | 2 |
| JL Sadler (Leics) | 7 | 7 | 2 | 222 | 62 | 44.40 | - | 2 |
| KJ Coetzer (Durham) | 8 | 8 | 1 | 310 | 76 | 44.28 | - | 2 |
| WPC Weston (Derbys) | 4 | 4 | 0 | 168 | 72 | 42.00 | - | 2 |
| JC Hildreth (Somerset) | 7 | 7 | 1 | 250 | 56 | 41.66 | - | 1 |
| GP Rees (Glam) | 3 | 3 | 0 | 125 | 63 | 41.66 | - | 1 |
| MA Butcher (Surrey) | 6 | 6 | 0 | 241 | 62 | 40.16 | - | 3 |
| EC Joyce (Middx) | 8 | 8 | 0 | 320 | 77 | 40.00 | - | 4 |
| PA Nixon (Leics) | 8 | 7 | 0 | 271 | 61 | 38.71 | - | 2 |
| ET Smith (Middx) | 8 | 8 | 0 | 301 | 80 | 37.62 | - | 2 |
| CP Schofield (Surrey) | 6 | 5 | 2 | 111 | 51 | 37.00 | - | 1 |
| M van Jaarsveld (Kent) | 8 | 8 | 1 | 250 | 62 | 35.71 | - | 2 |
| J Allenby (Leics) | 8 | 8 | 2 | 211 | 91* | 35.16 | - | 2 |
| AW Gale (Yorks) | 8 | 6 | 2 | 139 | 53* | 34.75 | - | 1 |
| OA Shah (Middx) | 5 | 5 | 0 | 172 | 59 | 34.40 | - | 2 |
| HD Ackerman (Leics) | 8 | 8 | 0 | 274 | 83 | 34.25 | - | 2 |
| GM Smith (Derbys) | 8 | 8 | 0 | 259 | 88 | 32.37 | - | 1 |
| TR Birt (Derbys) | 8 | 8 | 1 | 224 | 47 | 32.00 | - | - |
| JWM Dalrymple (Middx) | 8 | 8 | 3 | 155 | 54* | 31.00 | - | 1 |
| MJ Di Venuto (Durham) | 7 | 7 | 0 | 211 | 64 | 30.14 | - | 3 |
| MG Dighton (Derbys) | 6 | 6 | 0 | 175 | 67 | 29.16 | - | 2 |
| JC Tredwell (Kent) | 8 | 5 | 1 | 115 | 51 | 28.75 | - | 1 |
| GJ Muchall (Durham) | 7 | 5 | 2 | 82 | 41* | 27.33 | - | - |
| ID Blackwell (Somerset) | 7 | 7 | 0 | 187 | 97 | 26.71 | - | 1 |
| NRD Compton (Middx) | 6 | 5 | 2 | 79 | 48* | 26.33 | - | - |
| SM Katich (Derbys) | 7 | 7 | 1 | 157 | 46* | 26.16 | - | - |
| MA Wallace (Glam) | 7 | 7 | 2 | 127 | 37* | 25.40 | - | - |
| A McGrath (Yorks) | 8 | 7 | 1 | 152 | 50 | 25.33 | - | 1 |

**Qualification: averages 25 or above (minimum of three innings)**

## LEADING RUN SCORERS – TOP 20

| Player | Runs | Inns |
|---|---|---|
| P Mustard (Durham) | 409 | 8 |
| RWT Key (Kent) | 408 | 8 |
| SA Newman (Surrey) | 378 | 8 |
| ME Trescothick (Somerset) | 329 | 7 |
| EC Joyce (Middx) | 320 | 8 |
| KJ Coetzer (Durham) | 310 | 8 |
| JL Langer (Somerset) | 304 | 7 |
| JA Rudolph (Yorks) | 304 | 7 |
| ET Smith (Middx) | 301 | 8 |
| HD Ackerman (Leics) | 274 | 8 |
| PA Nixon (Leics) | 271 | 8 |
| GM Smith (Derbys) | 259 | 8 |
| JC Hildreth (Somerset) | 250 | 7 |
| M van Jaarsveld (Kent) | 250 | 8 |
| MA Butcher (Surrey) | 241 | 6 |
| ND McKenzie (Somerset) | 233 | 5 |
| TR Birt (Derbys) | 224 | 8 |
| JL Sadler (Leics) | 222 | 7 |
| MR Ramprakash (Surrey) | 215 | 4 |
| DM Benkenstein (Durham) | 215 | 8 |

## BOWLING: LEADING AVERAGES

| Bowling | O | M | Runs | W | Av | Best | 4i | Econ |
|---|---|---|---|---|---|---|---|---|
| GJ Kruis | 7 | 2 | 17 | 4 | 4.25 | 4-17 | 1 | 2.42 |
| TJ Murtagh | 52.4 | 6 | 253 | 21 | 12.04 | 4-21 | 1 | 4.80 |
| DI Stevens | 21 | 0 | 88 | 7 | 12.57 | 3-15 | - | 4.19 |
| PJ Wiseman | 22.5 | 0 | 114 | 9 | 12.66 | 3-18 | - | 4.99 |
| JKH Naik | 14.2 | 0 | 77 | 6 | 12.83 | 3-24 | - | 5.37 |
| JW Dernbach | 24 | 1 | 131 | 10 | 13.10 | 5-44 | 1 | 5.45 |
| SCJ Broad | 15 | 0 | 81 | 6 | 13.50 | 3-33 | - | 5.40 |
| Yasir Arafat | 15 | 2 | 69 | 5 | 13.80 | 3-25 | - | 4.60 |
| MJ Saggers | 45 | 8 | 153 | 11 | 13.90 | 4-25 | 1 | 3.40 |
| RM Pyrah | 43 | 3 | 223 | 13 | 17.15 | 3-22 | - | 5.18 |
| D Gough | 40 | 1 | 174 | 10 | 17.40 | 3-30 | - | 4.35 |
| T Lungley | 23 | 4 | 106 | 6 | 17.66 | 3-11 | - | 4.60 |
| JN Gillespie | 29 | 4 | 115 | 6 | 19.16 | 3-35 | - | 3.96 |
| RJ Hamilton-Brown | 24 | 1 | 118 | 6 | 19.66 | 3-28 | - | 4.91 |
| AR Caddick | 31.1 | 0 | 185 | 9 | 20.55 | 5-49 | 1 | 5.93 |
| M Kartik | 55 | 1 | 249 | 12 | 20.75 | 3-15 | - | 4.52 |
| DA Cosker | 31 | 1 | 149 | 7 | 21.28 | 3-30 | - | 4.80 |
| Mohammad Akram | 37.2 | 1 | 173 | 8 | 21.62 | 3-35 | - | 4.63 |
| Murtaza Hussain | 15 | 0 | 88 | 4 | 22.00 | 3-39 | - | 5.86 |
| ID Blackwell | 42.5 | 0 | 199 | 9 | 22.11 | 3-39 | - | 4.64 |
| DJ Wainwright | 33.4 | 2 | 157 | 7 | 22.42 | 2-30 | - | 4.66 |
| GM Smith | 33 | 2 | 162 | 7 | 23.14 | 2-32 | - | 4.90 |
| ST Finn | 23 | 1 | 122 | 5 | 24.40 | 3-23 | - | 5.30 |
| GR Breese | 59 | 1 | 303 | 12 | 25.25 | 3-31 | - | 5.13 |
| SJ Cook | 56 | 1 | 305 | 12 | 25.41 | 3-36 | - | 5.44 |
| RDB Croft | 32 | 0 | 185 | 7 | 26.42 | 2-29 | - | 5.78 |
| OD Gibson | 53.5 | 6 | 318 | 12 | 26.50 | 3-46 | - | 5.90 |
| CB Keegan | 14.3 | 0 | 108 | 4 | 27.00 | 3-13 | - | 7.44 |
| M van Jaarsveld | 23 | 1 | 108 | 4 | 27.00 | 2-26 | - | 4.69 |
| CJ Jordan | 53 | 3 | 272 | 10 | 27.20 | 3-28 | - | 5.13 |
| WPUJC Vaas | 32.4 | 4 | 138 | 5 | 27.60 | 2-17 | - | 4.22 |
| NJ Dexter | 25 | 1 | 112 | 4 | 28.00 | 3-27 | - | 4.48 |
| CW Henderson | 48.1 | 3 | 227 | 8 | 28.37 | 3-34 | - | 4.71 |
| JN Snape | 33.3 | 1 | 174 | 6 | 29.00 | 3-49 | - | 5.19 |
| PD Trego | 36.3 | 1 | 233 | 8 | 29.12 | 5-44 | 1 | 6.38 |
| JL Clare | 18 | 0 | 117 | 4 | 29.25 | 3-44 | - | 6.50 |
| GG Wagg | 34 | 2 | 236 | 8 | 29.50 | 3-37 | - | 6.94 |
| Harbhajan Singh | 38 | 1 | 177 | 6 | 29.50 | 2-34 | - | 4.65 |
| LE Plunkett | 60 | 2 | 306 | 10 | 30.60 | 3-54 | - | 5.10 |
| DD Masters | 41 | 0 | 248 | 8 | 31.00 | 2-32 | - | 6.04 |
| JWM Dalrymple | 40 | 1 | 221 | 7 | 31.57 | 3-36 | - | 5.52 |
| TT Bresnan | 44 | 2 | 228 | 7 | 32.57 | 2-27 | - | 5.18 |
| MJ Nicholson | 30 | 2 | 174 | 5 | 34.80 | 2-23 | - | 5.80 |
| JE Taylor | 36 | 5 | 210 | 6 | 35.00 | 3-33 | - | 5.83 |
| HT Waters | 24 | 2 | 178 | 5 | 35.60 | 3-47 | - | 7.41 |
| R McLaren | 31 | 1 | 179 | 5 | 35.80 | 4-46 | 1 | 5.77 |
| CM Willoughby | 43.1 | 2 | 234 | 6 | 39.00 | 3-32 | - | 5.42 |
| PS Jones | 49 | 2 | 295 | 7 | 42.14 | 2-30 | - | 6.02 |
| JC Tredwell | 61 | 3 | 301 | 7 | 43.00 | 2-20 | - | 4.93 |
| A Richardson | 32 | 1 | 174 | 4 | 43.50 | 2-57 | - | 5.43 |

**Qualification: averages 45 or less (minimum of four wickets)**

## LEADING WICKET-TAKERS – TOP 20

| Player | W | O |
|---|---|---|
| TJ Murtagh (Middx) | 21 | 52.4 |
| RM Pyrah (Yorks) | 13 | 43 |
| OD Gibson (Durham) | 12 | 53.5 |
| SJ Cook (Kent) | 12 | 56 |
| GR Breese (Durham) | 12 | 59 |
| M Kartik (Middx) | 12 | 55 |
| MJ Saggers (Kent) | 11 | 45 |
| JW Dernbach (Surrey) | 10 | 24 |
| D Gough (Yorks) | 10 | 40 |
| CJ Jordan (Surrey) | 10 | 53 |
| LE Plunkett (Durham) | 10 | 60 |
| AR Caddick (Somerset) | 9 | 31.1 |
| PJ Wiseman (Durham) | 9 | 22.5 |
| ID Blackwell (Somerset) | 9 | 42.5 |
| Mohammad Akram (Surrey) | 8 | 37.2 |
| GG Wagg (Derbys) | 8 | 34 |
| PD Trego (Somerset) | 8 | 36.3 |
| DD Masters (Leics) | 8 | 41 |
| CW Henderson (Leics) | 8 | 48.1 |
| DA Cosker (Glam) | 7 | 31 |

## FIELDING: LEADING DISMISSALS – TOP 20

JN Batty (Surrey) – 13 (12ct, 1st); PA Nixon (Leics) – 11 ( 7ct, 4st); GL Brophy (Yorks) – 10 (7ct, 3st); BJM Scott (Middx) – 10 (6ct, 4st); DJ Pipe (Derbys) – 8 (6ct, 2st); GO Jones (Kent) – 8 (6ct, 2st); NRD Compton (Middx) – 7 (7ct); GJ Muchall (Durham) – 7 (7ct); P Mustard (Durham) – 6 (4 ct, 2st); DL Hemp (Glam) – 6 (6ct); M van Jaarsveld (Kent) – 6 (6ct); MJ Walker (Kent) – 5 (5ct); JGE Benning (Surrey) – 5 (5ct); MA Wallace (Glam) – 4 (4ct); C Kieswetter (Somerset) – 4 (4ct); MP Vaughan (Yorks) – 4 (4ct); MG Dighton (Derbys) – 4 (4ct); HD Ackerman (Leics) – 4 (4ct); RWT Key (Kent) – 4 (4ct); EC Joyce (Middx) – 4 (4ct)

# WORCESTERSHIRE

Pat Gibson, of *The Times*, reports on how Worcestershire fought back from 'the worst disaster that any county club has suffered in the history of the game…'

It was a scene of utter desolation. New Road, Worcester, one of the most cherished cricket grounds in the world and so quintessentially English that the tea ladies have their own designated parking spaces, looked like a disaster area in the aftermath of the floods that engulfed it twice in rain-hit July.

Where Sir Donald Bradman used to sniff the new-mown grass and linseed oil and launch himself into an Ashes tour with a double-century, there was an all-pervading stench from the silt and slurry that had been swept in from the nearby meadows to overwhelm the square and outfield. The famous view across the ground from the picturesque, gabled pavilion towards the towering cathedral resembled a mudflat with not a blade of grass to be seen.

Inside, chairs, tables and a newly laid carpet were beyond salvation. Outside, cookers, refrigerators and other kitchen equipment lay in ruins. There was no possibility of Worcestershire playing any more cricket there for the rest of the season. All they could do, once the mud had been cleared away, was re-seed the entire ground, give the new grass the rest of the summer to grow and hope for a decent pitch in 2008.

Worcestershire had experienced plenty of floods before, 137 of them, in fact, since the club was formed in 1899. The worst was in 1947, when the water reached three and a half feet above the floor of the pavilion, which is itself several feet above the ground, but that was during the winter. The last time they were flooded in the summer was in 1969 and never as late as July. Now the waters had swept across the fields from the River Teme, one of the tributaries of the Severn, twice in a fortnight, depositing all that muck on the ground.

'Clearing up after the winter floods is relatively easy,' Mark Newton, the Worcestershire chief executive, said. 'This was infinitely worse than any of them because of the depth of the water, the amount of residue that was left and the fact that our cellars, kitchens and marquees were fully stocked for the height of the season and we lost the lot. I firmly believe that this was the worst disaster that any county club has suffered in the history of the game and I would not wish it on anybody else. It was such a prolonged crisis that from a professional point of view we were pushed very close to the limit.'

Clean-up costs, replacement of equipment and reinstatement of the outfield and practice area added up to £343,000 and lost revenue, including refunds of £63,000 to Twenty20 Cup ticket-holders, £90,000 to sponsors and advertisers and £100,000 in hospitality, amounted to £474,000, taking the grand total to a gulp-inducing £817,000.

What happened after that defied belief. The team, already in a hopeless position at the bottom of the LV County Championship first division, rallied to win the NatWest Pro40 title without playing a game at home, the outfield

was lush and green again within three months and Worcestershire were so confident about their future that they took the enormous gamble of signing Simon Jones, England's injury plagued fast bowler, from Glamorgan on a two-year contract.

'When you are in a situation like we were, it is amazing how many doors are opened by various people to help you,' Newton said. 'I cannot praise the ECB too highly for their support. They were very conscious of our situation and within what was fair and reasonable they were very helpful on all fronts. The Clydesdale Bank have also been very helpful and so have HM Revenue, who have agreed that all businesses affected by floods can have payments delayed for an agreed period, which will help us in cash-flow terms. Our balance sheet will show a huge loss for the year but we intend to recover that over the next two or three years, starting with a programme of fund-raising events and donations from local businesses and other cricket-loving benefactors.

'What it has done is concentrate the mind even more. The most encouraging thing is that everybody who works here is pulling together. Morale is very high and that really

came about through winning the Pro40, which was our first title for 13 years and a fantastic achievement. It created a great feeling at all levels within the club and, ironically, out of all this, we will be a much more efficient club. It will take a disastrous winter of floods for us not to be ready for the start of the 2008 season.'

Whatever happens, there is no question of Worcestershire leaving their wonderfully evocative ground. 'We feel very strongly about that,' Newton said. 'Recently, we were voted one of the top ten grounds in the world that people most wanted to visit to watch cricket. If we contemplated moving, it would go down very badly with a lot of people and I would probably be strung from the Severn Bridge. We all know how lovely this ground can be and when our new £10m development, which we are still hoping to start in the next year or two, is completed all the buildings will be above the flood level. All that would happen in future is that the field itself would be flooded and that would save us much of the grief that we have gone through this season. We would still suffer if we were flooded again in the summer but that last happened 38 years ago. If it doesn't happen again for another 38 years we can live with that.'

**Far left** It is 26 June and supposedly high summer, but New Road is completely submerged by the first of two devastating floods.

**Left** Out of misery comes joy for Worcestershire and their supporters as the players celebrate the winning runs in their victory over Gloucestershire that confirmed them as Pro40 Champions.

# TWENTY20 CUP

## By Mark Baldwin

Frantic, dramatic and utterly compelling to the very last over, before 21,000 at Edgbaston, the fifth finals day in Twenty20 Cup history will go down as one of the best yet.

For Rob Key's Kent, it was especially memorable. Key, at 28 one of the younger English county captains, had spoken beforehand of how winning the Twenty20 Cup would be one of the greatest days even in Kent's proud legacy of one-day cricket success. Afterwards, he said the day 'was the biggest in the domestic calendar' and that the competition as a whole – watched as it is by huge audiences right around the country – gave aspiring county players an exciting taste of life at a higher level.

Indeed, in a day packed with current England and world stars like Lancashire's Andrew Flintoff, Muttiah Muralitharan, Brad Hodge and James Anderson, Sussex's Matt Prior, Mushtaq Ahmed and Naved-ul-Hasan, Gloucestershire's Jon Lewis and Hamish Marshall and Kent's own Lasith Malinga, it was noticeable how many of the players of lesser profile made a grab for centre stage.

Key himself, with 15 Test matches in his locker but hungry for more England recognition in both forms of the game, showcased his lesser-known talents as an imaginative and destructive shot-maker at the top of the order. His unbeaten 68 from 54 balls in the semi-final against Sussex contained two sixes off Mushtaq and provided his side both with initial momentum and finishing power.

Joe Denly, his opening partner and at 21 one of the fastest-emerging batting talents in the game, also did his senior representative claims no harm with flashing innings of 31 from 20 balls in the semi-final and 28 from 26 balls in the final.

And, while 25-year-old James Tredwell backed up Key's view that he is the best young English one-day spinner in the land, two more senior but equally talented Englishmen – Darren Stevens and Matthew Walker – mocked those who continue to suggest that county cricket is merely full of washed-up has-beens and young never-will-bes.

Stevens, at 31, has developed into one of the best limited-overs all-rounders in the domestic game since his move from Leicestershire to Kent in 2005. After helping

Tredwell to slow up the Sussex innings in the semi-final with four overs costing just 13 runs – and the wicket of the much-vaunted Luke Wright – Stevens proceeded to bowl just as vital a mid-innings spell of four overs for 22 runs in the final and then play the match-winning innings of 30 not out from 21 balls.

If Ryan McLaren, the 24-year-old South African, had not earlier taken a magnificent hat-trick, which began by halting Hamish Marshall's superb 49-ball 65, then Stevens would have been a shoo-in for the final's man-of-the-match award. Arriving at the crease with Kent at 96 for 3 and seemingly struggling to get over the line in the face of some tenacious Gloucestershire outcricket, Stevens held his nerve as further wickets tumbled and the asking rate climbed alarmingly. And then, with 13 required off Carl Greenidge's final over – or, more realistically, 12 if Kent lost only one more wicket – Stevens struck two telling boundaries, the second off a no-ball, to take his team resoundingly to their first trophy in six years.

Walker's 35-ball 45 had also been vital to Kentish hopes, while another unsung Englishman – Mark Hardinges – made massive contributions to Gloucestershire's effort with figures of 2 for 24 from four overs and an unbeaten 39 earlier which included a tremendous last-over six off the fearsome Malinga high over long on.

Hardinges, too, had produced a four-over analysis of 2 for 16 in the day's first semi-final as Gloucestershire trounced pre-tournament favourites Lancashire by following up a great display in the field with a batting effort led by Craig Spearman's five sixes and eight fours.

Gloucestershire had seen off Worcestershire in the quarter-finals, while Kent almost misjudged their chase at Nottinghamshire, Sussex eased past Yorkshire at a packed Hove and Muralitharan flew in from Colombo early that same morning before taking 4 for 18 to help Lancashire pip Warwickshire by six runs.

Sadly, however, much of the initial group stages of the Twenty20 Cup were ravaged by the awful midsummer weather. Leicestershire, the defending champions and still the only county to have won this competition twice, were particularly badly hit.

Moreover, the Foxes' remarkable record of reaching every finals day during the first four years of the Cup was ended in the most unfortunate of circumstances as torrential rain in Manchester caused the last match of their group against Lancashire to be washed out. It was their fifth no result in eight group games.

A sad but all-too-familiar sight during the 2007 Twenty20 Cup: the rain pelts down, this time at Derby on a wintry 5 July, and another match has to be abandoned.

To compound their misery, just over the Pennines at Headingley they were devastated to see Yorkshire managing to play their last game – against Derbyshire – and winning it by four wickets to pip Leicestershire for one of the two best third-place qualification spots. That Leicestershire had won two of the only three games they managed to play only added to their sense of grievance, plus the fact that Lancashire's point for the washout (their fourth) also enabled them to reach the lucrative knockout stages.

The North Division was the worst hit by the weather, with ten matches called off, but there were also six washouts in the Midland/West/Wales Division and four in the South group. Indeed, the only two counties not to have any no-results were Somerset and Surrey – and neither of them qualified for the quarter-finals.

Ironically, Surrey were miffed when rain reduced their match against Sussex at The Oval to a mere five overs per side, when a complete washout would have suited them more. But their frustration was even more acute when, in front of a record 23,000 crowd for a domestic match at The Oval, Kent then beat them for the first time in eight Twenty20 contests to earn the one remaining quarter-final spot.

Elsewhere, Luke Wright enhanced his growing reputation by opening the Sussex innings to such good (and violent) effect that he scored more runs than anyone, 346 at 43.25, in the competition but also hit an astonishing 33 fours and

19 sixes from his nine innings. His strike rate too, 177.43, was bettered only by the ageless Graeme Hick (183.80).

Other seasoned hitters such as Marcus Trescothick, Lance Klusener, Craig White and Azhar Mahmood also figured in the top ten strike rates, and yet it was instructive again to see spinners being highly successful in curbing even the most powerful of batsmen in this most explosive of formats.

Six spinners – Gareth Breese, David Wainwright, Gary Keedy, Murali Kartik, Claude Henderson and Chris Schofield – were in the top ten of bowlers' economy rates, with Graeme Swann in 11th place, and born-again leg-spinner Schofield was joint leading wicket-taker on 17 (at just 8.82 runs apiece) alongside Kent seamer Simon Cook.

## North Division

**22 June**
at Old Trafford
**Durham** 149 for 5 (20 overs)
**Lancashire** 152 for 4 (19.3 overs) (MB Loye 80*)
*Lancashire (2pts) won by 6 wickets*

at Leicester
**Leicestershire** 154 for 5 (16 overs)
**Yorkshire** 141 for 9 (16 overs)
*Leicestershire (2pts) won by 13 runs*

at Derby
**Derbyshire** 148 all out (18.3 overs)
(GD Clough 4 for 24)
**Nottinghamshire** 149 for 4 (18.2 overs) (SR Patel 55*)
*Nottinghamshire (2pts) won by 6 wickets*

**23 June**
at Trent Bridge
**Lancashire** 163 for 7 (20 overs)
**Nottinghamshire** 167 for 4 (19.3 overs) (SR Patel 84*)
*Nottinghamshire (2pts) won by 6 wickets*

**25 June**
at Derby
**Derbyshire** v. **Durham**
*Match abandoned (1pt each)*

at Headingley
**Yorkshire** v. **Lancashire**
*Match abandoned (1pt each)*

at Trent Bridge
**Nottinghamshire** v. **Leicestershire**
*Match abandoned (1pt each)*

**27 June**
at Trent Bridge
**Nottinghamshire** 203 for 8 (20 overs) (GP Swann 61,
AG Botha 4 for 29)

**Derbyshire** 150 all out (19.5 overs)
*Nottinghamshire (2pts) won by 53 runs*

at Old Trafford
**Lancashire** 143 for 9 (20 overs) (BJ Hodge 57)
**Yorkshire** 113 all out (18.4 overs)
*Lancashire (2pts) won by 30 runs*

at the Riverside
**Leicestershire** 98 for 6 (13 overs)
**Durham** 104 for 2 (11 overs) (P Mustard 52*)
*Durham (2pts) won by 8 wickets*

**29 June**
at Trent Bridge
**Nottinghamshire** 149 for 9 (20 overs)
**Yorkshire** 145 for 5 (20 overs) (A McGrath 55)
*Nottinghamshire (2pts) won by 4 runs*

at the Riverside
**Lancashire** 180 for 4 (20 overs) (MB Loye 89)
**Durham** 141 for 9 (16.5 overs)
(ST Jayasuriya 4 for 24)
*Lancashire (2pts) won by 39 runs*

at Derby
**Derbyshire** 176 for 6 (20 overs) (GM Smith 79)
**Leicestershire** 177 for 4 (19.4 overs) (HD Ackerman 66, PA Nixon 65)
*Leicestershire (2pts) won by 6 wickets*

**30 June**
at Leicester
**Leicestershire** v.
**Nottinghamshire**
*Match abandoned
(1pt each)*

Nottinghamshire's
Samit Patel plays another
extravagant stroke on
the way to a match-
winning 84 not out
against Lancashire at
Trent Bridge.

at Headingley
**Durham** 65 for 9 (9 overs)
**Yorkshire** 66 for 1 (6.5 overs)
*Yorkshire (2pts) won by 9 wickets*

**1 July**
at Old Trafford
**Lancashire** v. **Derbyshire**
*Match abandoned (1pt each)*

**2 July**
at Leicester
**Derbyshire** 50 for 2 (7.3 overs)
**Leicestershire** 28 for 2 (4.3 overs)
*Match abandoned (1pt each)*

**3 July**
at the Riverside
**Durham** 133 for 5 (20 overs)
**Yorkshire** 134 for 4 (19.4 overs)
(AW Gale 56)
*Yorkshire (2pts) won by 6 wickets*

**4 July**
at Leicester
**Leicestershire** 41 for 3 (4.4 overs)
**Durham**
*Match abandoned (1pt each)*

at Headingley
**Nottinghamshire** 61 for 3 (5 overs)
**Yorkshire** 65 for 2 (4.4 overs)
*Yorkshire (2pts) won by 8 wickets*

**5 July**
at Derby
**Derbyshire** v. **Lancashire**
*Match abandoned (1pt each)*

**6 July**
at Old Trafford
**Lancashire** v. **Leicestershire**
*Match abandoned (1pt each)*

at the Riverside
**Durham** v. **Nottinghamshire**
*Match abandoned (1pt each)*

at Headingley
**Derbyshire** 119 for 7 (20 overs)
**Yorkshire** 122 for 6 (18.3 overs)
*Yorkshire (2pts) won by 4 wickets*

## North Division – Final Table

|  | P | W | L | T | NR | RR | Pts |
|---|---|---|---|---|---|---|---|
| Nottinghamshire | 8 | 4 | 1 | 0 | 3 | 0.89 | 11 |
| Lancashire | 8 | 3 | 1 | 0 | 4 | 0.84 | 10 |
| Yorkshire | 8 | 4 | 3 | 0 | 1 | -0.05 | 9 |
| Leicestershire | 8 | 2 | 1 | 0 | 5 | -0.14 | 9 |
| Durham | 8 | 1 | 4 | 0 | 3 | -0.57 | 5 |
| Derbyshire | 8 | 0 | 4 | 0 | 4 | -1.09 | 4 |

## South Division

**22 June**
at The Oval
**Middlesex** 163 for 6 (20 overs) (JWM Dalrymple 61)
**Surrey** 168 for 4 (19.2 overs) (MR Ramprakash 85*)
*Surrey (2pts) won by 6 wickets*

at Chelmsford
**Sussex** 165 for 5 (20 overs) (MW Goodwin 102*)
**Essex** 171 for 4 (17.1 overs)
*Essex (2pts) won by 6 wickets*

at the Rose Bowl
**Kent** 153 for 6 (20 overs) (RWT Key 59)
**Hampshire** 153 for 7 (20 overs)
*Match tied (1pt each)*

**23 June**
at Canterbury
**Kent** 44 for 1 (5.1 overs)
**Essex** 46 for 6 (5 overs)
*Kent (2pts) won by 3 runs – DL Method: target 50 from 5 overs*

**24 June**
at Hove
**Sussex** v. **Middlesex**
*Match abandoned (1pt each)*

at The Oval
**Hampshire** 72 for 8 (10 overs)
**Surrey** 75 for 4 (8.5 overs)
*Surrey (2pts) won by 6 wickets*

**25 June**
at Southgate
**Middlesex** 73 for 7 (12 overs)
**Hampshire** 68 for 8 (12 overs)
*Middlesex (2pts) won by 5 runs*

**26 June**
at Canterbury
**Kent** 181 for 3 (20 overs) (RWT Key 62)

**Sussex** 182 for 3 (17.1 overs) (LJ Wright 103)
*Sussex (2pts) won by 7 wickets*

**27 June**
at Uxbridge
**Middlesex** 146 for 7 (20 overs) (ET Smith 66)
**Kent**
*Match abandoned (1pt each)*

at the Rose Bowl
**Hampshire** 103 for 2 (13 overs) (AC Voges 66*)
**Sussex** 108 for 1 (10 overs) (CJ Adams 56*)
*Sussex (2pts) won by 9 wickets*

**28 June**
at Chelmsford
**Surrey** 174 for 4 (20 overs) (MR Ramprakash 74*, JGE Benning 69)
**Essex** 175 for 7 (18.5 overs) (JS Foster 52)
*Essex (2pts) won by 3 wickets*

**29 June**
at the Rose Bowl
**Hampshire** v. **Middlesex**
*Match abandoned (1pt each)*

at Chelmsford
**Kent** 141 for 7 (20 overs)
**Essex** 99 all out (14.5 overs) (DI Stevens 4 for 14)
*Kent (2pts) won by 42 runs*

at Hove
**Surrey** 168 for 6 (20 overs)
**Sussex** 68 all out (16.5 overs) (CP Schofield 4 for 12)
*Surrey (2pts) won by 100 runs*

**1 July**
at the Rose Bowl
**Essex** 99 for 8 (15 overs)
**Hampshire** 100 for 3 (12.2 overs) (SM Ervine 50*)
*Hampshire (2pts) won by 7 wickets*

**2 July**
at Beckenham
**Kent** 131 for 8 (20 overs)
**Surrey** 132 for 4 (17.4 overs)
*Surrey (2pts) won by 6 wickets*

**3 July**
at Lord's
**Surrey** 85 for 5 (13.3 overs)
**Middlesex** 73 for 2 (7.4 overs)
*Middlesex (2pts) won by 8 wickets – DL Method: target 73 from 10 overs*

at Hove
**Sussex** 163 for 6 (20 overs)
**Essex** 146 for 5 (20 overs) (RS Bopara 55)
*Sussex (2pts) won by 17 runs*

**4 July**
at Beckenham
**Kent** 146 for 4 (20 overs)
**Middlesex** 120 all out (18.4 overs)
*Kent (2pts) won by 26 runs*

**5 July**
at The Oval
**Sussex** 65 for 3 (5 overs)
**Surrey** 60 for 6 (5 overs)
*Sussex (2pts) won by 5 runs*

at Chelmsford
**Hampshire** 107 for 5 (16 overs)
**Essex**
*Match abandoned (1pt each)*

Chris Schofield was one of the success stories of the competition with his exotic mix of leg breaks, googlies and top spinners. He took 4 for 12 as Surrey bowled out Sussex for 68 at Hove.

**6 July**
at The Oval
**Surrey** 145 all out (19.5 overs)
**Kent** 148 for 4 (19.1 overs)
*Kent (2pts) won by 6 wickets*

at Lord's
**Middlesex** 126 for 9 (20 overs)
**Essex** 128 for 7 (19.5 overs) (M Kartik 5 for 13)
*Essex (2pts) won by 3 wickets*

at Hove
**Sussex** 205 for 5 (20 overs) (LJ Wright 98)
**Hampshire** 132 for 8 (20 overs) (RJ Kirtley 4 for 22)
*Sussex (2pts) won by 73 runs*

## South Division – Final Table

| | P | W | L | T | NR | RR | Pts |
|---|---|---|---|---|---|---|---|
| Sussex | 8 | 5 | 2 | 0 | 1 | 0.17 | 11 |
| Kent | 8 | 4 | 2 | 1 | 1 | 0.32 | 10 |
| Surrey | 8 | 4 | 4 | 0 | 0 | 0.80 | 8 |
| Essex | 8 | 3 | 4 | 0 | 1 | -0.36 | 7 |
| Middlesex | 8 | 2 | 3 | 0 | 3 | -0.20 | 7 |
| Hampshire | 8 | 1 | 4 | 1 | 2 | -1.11 | 5 |

## Midlands/Wales/West Division

**22 June**
at Cardiff
**Glamorgan** v. **Gloucestershire**
*Match abandoned (1pt each)*

at Northampton
**Northamptonshire** v. **Worcestershire**
*Match abandoned (1pt each)*

at Edgbaston
**Warwickshire** 161 for 6 (20 overs)
**Somerset** 154 for 8 (20 overs)
*Warwickshire (2pts) won by 7 runs*

**24 June**
at Taunton
**Somerset** 200 for 7 (20 overs) (ME Trescothick 76)
**Northamptonshire** 92 for 1 (7 overs) (U Afzaal 54)
*Northamptonshire (2pts) won by 24 runs – DL Method: target 69 from 7 overs*

at Edgbaston
**Warwickshire** 173 for 5 (20 overs)
**Glamorgan** 170 for 7 (20 overs)
*Warwickshire (2pts) won by 3 runs*

**25 June**
at Bristol
**Worcestershire** 101 for 7 (10 overs)
**Gloucestershire** 103 for 1 (8.4 overs)
*Gloucestershire (2pts) won by 9 wickets*

**26 June**
at Edgbaston
**Warwickshire** 174 for 7 (20 overs) (DL Maddy 51)
**Northamptonshire** 162 for 7 (20 overs)
*Warwickshire (2pts) won by 12 runs*

at Cardiff
**Somerset** 142 for 8 (20 overs)
**Glamorgan** 143 for 5 (19.2 overs)
*Glamorgan (2pts) won by 5 wickets*

**27 June**
at Taunton
**Somerset** 104 all out (19.2 overs)
**Gloucestershire** 109 for 2 (12.3 overs)
*Gloucestershire (2pts) won by 8 wickets*

at Worcester
**Worcestershire** v. **Warwickshire**
*Match abandoned (1pt each)*

**28 June**
at Cardiff
**Glamorgan** v. **Northamptonshire**
*Match abandoned (1pt each)*

**29 June**
at Bristol
**Warwickshire** 149 for 8 (20 overs) (TR Ambrose 77)
**Gloucestershire** 122 (19.4 overs)
*Warwickshire (2pts) won by 27 runs*

at Kidderminster
**Worcestershire** 227 for 6 (20 overs) (GA Hick 110, VS Solanki 58)
**Northamptonshire** 222 for 3 (20 overs) (L Klusener 111*, DJG Sales 52)
*Worcestershire (2pts) won by 5 runs*

at Taunton
**Somerset** 202 for 6 (20 overs) (MJ Wood 88, CL White 68)
**Glamorgan** 174 for 5 (20 overs) (DL Hemp 68*)
*Somerset (2pts) won by 28 runs*

**1 July**
at Kidderminster
**Gloucestershire** 198 for 7 (20 overs) (HJH Marshall 100)
**Worcestershire** 137 all out (16.3 overs)
*Gloucestershire (2pts) won by 61 runs*

**2 July**
at Campbell Park
**Northamptonshire** v. **Gloucestershire**
*Match abandoned (1pt each)*

at Cardiff
**Warwickshire** 94 for 3 (11 overs)
**Glamorgan** 73 for 6 (9 overs)
*Warwickshire (2pts) won by 9 runs – DL Method: target 83 from 9 overs*

**3 July**
at Taunton
**Somerset** 148 for 7 (20 overs)
**Worcestershire** 149 for 7 (19.4 overs) (PA Jaques 59)
*Worcestershire (2pts) won by 3 wickets*

**4 July**
at Bristol
**Gloucestershire** 100 for 9 (20 overs)
**Somerset** 102 for 4 (16.5 overs)
*Somerset (2pts) won by 6 wickets*

at Northampton
**Warwickshire** 100 for 7 (18 overs)

**Northamptonshire** 101 for 6 (16 overs)
*Northamptonshire (2pts) won by 4 wickets*

**5 July**
at Himley
**Worcestershire** v. **Glamorgan**
*Match abandoned (1pt each)*

**6 July**
at Bristol
**Glamorgan** 114 for 6 (20 overs)
**Gloucestershire** 117 for 4 (17.2 overs)
*Gloucestershire (2pts) won by 6 wickets*

at Northampton
**Northamptonshire** 137 for 7 (20 overs)
(DJG Sales 61*)
**Somerset** 139 for 2 (17.5 overs)
(CL White 50*)
*Somerset (2pts) won by 8 wickets*

at Edgbaston
**Worcestershire** 143 for 5 (20 overs)
**Warwickshire** 130 for 8 (20 overs)
*Worcestershire (2pts) won by 13 runs*

## Midlands/Wales/West Division – Final Table

|  | P | W | L | T | NR | RR | Pts |
|---|---|---|---|---|---|---|---|
| Warwickshire | 8 | 5 | 2 | 0 | 1 | 0.23 | 11 |
| Gloucestershire | 8 | 4 | 2 | 0 | 2 | 0.98 | 10 |
| Worcestershire | 8 | 3 | 2 | 0 | 3 | -0.59 | 9 |
| Northamptonshire | 8 | 2 | 3 | 0 | 3 | 0.06 | 7 |
| Somerset | 8 | 3 | 5 | 0 | 0 | -0.22 | 6 |
| Glamorgan | 8 | 1 | 4 | 0 | 3 | -0.67 | 5 |

## Quarter-Finals

**17 July**
at Bristol
**Worcestershire** 123 for 6 (17 overs)
**Gloucestershire** 131 for 3 (14.1 overs)
*Gloucestershire won by 7 wickets – DL Method: target 129 from 17 overs*

**18 July**
at Hove
**Sussex** 193 for 5 (20 overs) (MW Goodwin 57)
**Yorkshire** 155 all out (19.5 overs)
*Sussex won by 38 runs*

at Trent Bridge
**Nottinghamshire** 138 all out (20 overs)
**Kent** 139 for 1 (19.5 overs) (JL Denly 63*, RWT Key 54)
*Kent won by 9 wickets*

at Edgbaston
**Lancashire** 193 for 5 (20 overs) (GD Cross 62)
**Warwickshire** 187 for 7 (20 overs) (NM Carter 58, M Muralitharan 4 for 18)
*Lancashire won by 6 runs*

## Semi-Finals

**4 August**
at Edgbaston
**Lancashire** 148 for 6 (20 overs)
**Gloucestershire** 152 for 2 (16.5 overs) (CM Spearman 86)
*Gloucestershire won by 8 wickets*

at Edgbaston
**Sussex** 140 all out (19.4 overs)
**Kent** 141 for 5 (19.2 overs) (RWT Key 68*)
*Kent won by 5 wickets*

**Opposite** Kent captain Rob Key is surrounded by his jubilant team as the winners of the 2007 Twenty20 Cup celebrate their thrilling final victory against Gloucestershire.

## FINAL – GLOUCESTERSHIRE v. KENT
4 August 2007 at Edgbaston

### GLOUCESTERSHIRE

| | | |
|---|---|---|
| HJH Marshall | b McLaren | 65 |
| CM Spearman | c van Jaarsveld b Yasir Arafat | 2 |
| Kadeer Ali | c Tredwell b Yasir Arafat | 6 |
| CG Taylor | lbw b Cook | 1 |
| APR Gidman | run out | 5 |
| MA Hardinges | not out | 39 |
| *SJ Adshead | b McLaren | 0 |
| ID Fisher | lbw b McLaren | 0 |
| J Lewis (capt) | lbw b Malinga | 17 |
| CG Greenidge | not out | 1 |
| BM Edmondson | | |
| Extras | lb 7, w 3 | 10 |
| | (8 wkts 20 overs) | **146** |

| | O | M | R | W |
|---|---|---|---|---|
| Malinga | 4 | 0 | 44 | 1 |
| Yasir Arafat | 2 | 0 | 13 | 2 |
| Cook | 4 | 0 | 16 | 1 |
| McLaren | 4 | 0 | 22 | 3 |
| Stevens | 4 | 0 | 22 | 0 |
| Tredwell | 2 | 0 | 22 | 0 |

**Fall of Wickets**
1-16, 2-36, 3-42, 4-62, 5-111, 6-111, 7-111, 8-137

### KENT

| | | |
|---|---|---|
| JL Denly | c Marshall b Hardinges | 28 |
| RWT Key (capt) | c Marshall b Greenidge | 18 |
| MJ Walker | c Fisher b Lewis | 45 |
| M van Jaarsveld | b Hardinges | 9 |
| DI Stevens | not out | 30 |
| R McLaren | b Lewis | 5 |
| *GO Jones | run out | 4 |
| Yasir Arafat | not out | 3 |
| JC Tredwell | | |
| SJ Cook | | |
| SL Malinga | | |
| Extras | lb 1, w 2, nb 2 | 5 |
| | (6 wkts 19.3 overs) | **147** |

| | O | M | R | W |
|---|---|---|---|---|
| Lewis | 4 | 0 | 28 | 2 |
| Greenidge | 3.3 | 0 | 47 | 1 |
| Edmondson | 4 | 0 | 26 | 0 |
| Hardinges | 4 | 0 | 24 | 2 |
| Gidman | 4 | 0 | 21 | 0 |

**Fall of Wickets**
1-32, 2-78, 3-96, 4-109, 5-123, 6-127

Umpires: NA Mallender & P Willey
Toss: Kent
Man of the Match: R McClaren

## Kent won by 4 wickets

# KENT

Mark Pennell, who covers Kent cricket for the *Kent Messenger*, offers a personal account of the county's triumph in the Twenty20 Cup.

With all four previous winners eliminated a new name was sure to be engraved on the Twenty20 Cup come 10.00 pm on Saturday 4 August. In the build-up to Edgbaston finals day, however, very few pundits made Kent favourites to lift their first knockout title in 29 years.

After all, this was the 'misfiring Spitfires' who had made it through the Twenty20 qualifying rounds only once previously, and the team whose sole game plan during the formative years of this shortest form of cricket was something akin to 'hit and giggle'. Kent had experimented with five captains in the first four years of the competition, and here was a team with one of the worst playing records in the land having won only ten times from 27 starts in the competition through to the 2007 campaign. So it was probably understandable that Kent, playing in their first knockout final in a decade, were the unfancied dark horses out of the four counties to qualify.

In reality, though, under the strong and level-headed leadership of Rob Key and the management of coaching triumvirate Graham Ford, Simon Willis and Paul Farbrace, Kent had fashioned a new, powerful and self-confident Spitfires side. Of the team which started Kent's Twenty20 Cup quarter-final against Leicestershire in July 2006, only Key, Darren Stevens, James Tredwell, Matthew Walker and Martin van Jaarsveld survived, and of them only Tredwell retained the same berth in a revamped batting order for 2007. With Ryan McLaren, Yasir Arafat, Lasith Malinga and a fully fit Simon Cook to strengthen his seam options and compliment the hugely underrated Tredwell and Stevens, Key selected young England Lions batsman Joe Denly to help to give the Spitfires flying starts. Key also moved strokemakers like Walker, Stevens and Geraint Jones to the middle of a flexible yet dangerous batting order.

But it was the misfortune of losing three successive tosses that ultimately helped Key to decide upon a cup-winning game plan for his new-look team. When forced into batting second, Kent had landed their first ever Twenty20 Cup win over Surrey by six wickets in front of a sell-out crowd at The Oval to qualify from the group stages. Then, when chasing for a second time, they beat quarter-final opponents Nottinghamshire by nine wickets in a tense, penultimate-ball finish at Trent Bridge. Come finals day, Kent's batsmen again showed their penchant for the run chase by hitting 141 for 5 to beat Sussex by five wickets in a thrilling second semi-final.

Having lost the toss again, Key had steered his side into their first Twenty20 final with four balls to spare with an immaculately timed unbeaten 68 against a Sussex bowling attack perceived as one of the best in limited-overs cricket. While the likes of Rana Naved and James Kirtley lost their nerve to send down late no-balls and wides, so Key held his, hammering out his team's intent with eight fours and a brace of sixes in his man-of-the-match-winning knock. The consensus in the press box was that Kent had deserved their semi-final triumph. After a racing, 10-an-over start, Sussex had been pegged back by shrewd bowling, canny field-placing and exemplary fielding. The Spitfires had caught everything and fashioned three run outs, the best of them a flying, backhanded flick from McLaren at cover point that accounted for Chris Adams.

By 7.15 pm the floodlights were on and the omens for a Kent cup final win were starting to look good. After all, this was also my own 47th birthday and Bomber the Spitfire, aka Kent Academy assistant Andy Bennett, had won the annual mascots' race by a short head. At the toss Key this time called correctly against Gloucestershire's Jonathan Lewis, yet he still backed his instinct to bowl first against a Gladiators side who had successfully out-muscled favourites Lancashire to win the first semi-final by eight wickets when batting second earlier in the day. When Malinga and Arafat proved expensive with the new ball, Key must have questioned his strategy as mop-haired Hamish Marshall got Gloucestershire off to a flying start, until Key's introduction of Cook and Stevens applied a partial brake.

With four overs remaining and Marshall well set with 65 from 49 balls, the Gladiators looked capable of posting a total beyond Kent's reach. But, with their score on 111 for 4, McLaren's third over and the 17th of the innings provided the first ever Twenty20 Cup final hat-trick. Marshall dragged the ball onto his stumps while attempting to cut, Steven Adshead played inside the line to lose his off stump and then left-hander Ian Fisher was leg before to a near yorker. McLaren, who spent the summer of 2005 at Edgbaston working on the Warwickshire ground staff, had made himself into a Kentish hero and restored the Spitfires' self-belief all in the space of three deliveries.

Mark Hardinges' late flurry of 39 runs helped set an asking rate of 7.35 an over, a target that stiffened following the loss of Key to a controversial low catch at mid wicket by Marshall, who then leapt to his right to take another, unquestionable, flying chance to dismiss Denly.

Walker's punchy 45, full of cuts and pulls, eased Kent back into contention but once Lewis returned to deceive the left-hander with a slower-ball bouncer, so the pressure and the asking rate mounted. Lewis, having opted against using any spin bowlers, entrusted the final over to Carl Greenidge and, with 13 required, Gloucestershire appeared slight favourites in spite of the tension.

But Stevens, a previous cup-winner with Leicestershire, clattered the first ball to the mid wicket rope for four, and then happily shouldered arms as Greenidge sent down a leg-side wide despite coming in off a short run. Two scrambled singles left Kent needing six from three balls; the time had come for Stevens and the Spitfires to prove their new-found mettle.

As Stevens latched onto the next ball, a low full toss from Greenidge, most spectators missed Peter Willey's no-ball call as all eyes followed the ball to the boundary rope at extra cover. Confusion reigned for a couple of seconds before Willey confirmed his call for overstepping which, together with the boundary, gave Kent their historic win with three balls and four wickets to spare and sent Stevens and Arafat into a jig of delight. Having been showered with champagne and presented with Stevens's match shirt as a treasured memento, I left the press conference and the ground with barely half-an-hour of my birthday left to celebrate. But who cares, for this had been a momentous day for Kent... and a birthday to remember.

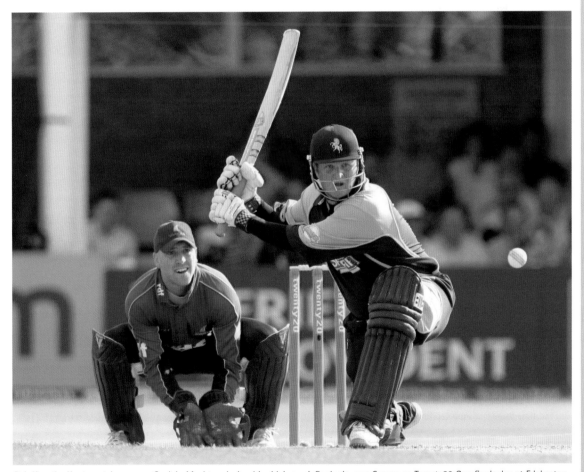

Rob Key, the Kent captain, sweeps Saqlain Mushtaq during his side's semi-final win over Sussex on Twenty20 Cup finals day at Edgbaston.

# FRIENDS PROVIDENT TROPHY

**by Mark Baldwin**

An impressive campaign in the North Conference meant that Durham were already assured of a semi-final place before losing to Warwickshire in an unsatisfactory rain-ruined match.

When the weather intervened, they were 77 for 3 from 16.2 overs in reply to Warwickshire's huge 314 for 5, in which Tim Ambrose had plundered 135 from a mere 82 balls – with five sixes and 14 fours – and Jonathan Trott had also scored 107.

It was enough, however, to propel Warwickshire into their own ill-fated semi-final, against Hampshire, but Durham didn't care: they were already through, and had earned themselves a precious home tie, too.

Yet if Durham's bowlers were hit around by Ambrose and Trott in this last match, for the rest of the group stages they were a mightily potent force. This theme was established right at the beginning, when Leicestershire were bundled out for just 138 at Grace Road with Callum Thorp taking 4 for 30 and Ottis Gibson 3 for 21 at the start of what was to become such a memorable season for him.

A hiccup in the second match, in which Simon Katich's 81 and a 59-ball unbeaten 60 from Ian Harvey guided Derbyshire to their target, was followed by six straight wins. It was a streak which meant Durham were sure to go one better than in 2006, when they finished second to Lancashire in the North Conference table but didn't go further due to the inexplicable absence that year of semi-finals.

Confidence soared in the ranks when they easily defended their total of 220 for 9, in which Paul Collingwood hit 74 from 85 balls, against a Lancashire side boasting the presence of Andrew Flintoff, Jimmy Anderson and Saj Mahmood as well as a powerful batting line-up centred around Brad Hodge and Mal Loye.

Then came a succession of fine all-round performances, and the only tight finish was in the game against Nottinghamshire, which clinched them top spot in the group.

A breezy 71 from 75 balls by Phil Mustard – a real success at the head of the order throughout the campaign – looked like setting up a comfortable enough chase of Notts' 238 for 8 but a collapse left Gareth Breese holding his side's hopes in his hands.

Breese was equal to the challenge, scoring a run-a-ball 68, with eight fours, and at the death being joined by last man Neil Killeen in an unbroken tenth-wicket stand of 24 –of which Killeen made three – to clinch the game with an over to spare. Killeen had earlier taken 3 for 28 from his ten overs.

Other highlights of Durham's group campaign were Mustard's 108 against Northants and 94-ball 77 against Yorkshire, and Will Smith's brilliant 105-

Gareth Breese was Durham's hero in their crucial group stage victory against Nottinghamshire at the Riverside.

ball 103 against Worcestershire which followed his 62 not out from 73 balls in the win over Scotland.

The semi-final was a remarkable match, and was won by Liam Plunkett with a vital 30 not out to add to his competition-best of 4 for 15 during Essex's plunge to 71 all out earlier in a short but action-packed day.

Durham were themselves teetering on the very edge of doom at 38 for 7 in reply – with Ottis Gibson being badly missed at mid on by Danish Kaneria one run later – before Plunkett eased nerves by smashing a free hit for six following a Graham Napier no-ball.

Plunkett showed nerve and the batting ability which has long marked him down as an international-class all-rounder of the future to deny Andy Bichel (4 for 22) and the rest of the Essex seamers.

**Durham's Friends Provident Trophy North Conference results:**

22 April (Leicester): beat Leicestershire by 8 wickets
29 April (the Riverside): lost to Derbyshire by 4 wickets
 7 May (the Riverside): beat Lancashire by 57 runs
20 May (Northampton): beat Northants by 4 wickets
28 May (the Riverside): beat Scotland by 5 wickets
 1 June (the Riverside): beat Worcestershire by 143 runs
 3 June (Headingley): beat Yorkshire by 53 runs
10 June (the Riverside): beat Nottinghamshire by 1 wicket
13 June (Edgbaston): lost to Warwickshire by 39 runs
    (DL Method)

**Semi-Final:**
20 June (the Riverside): beat Essex by 3 wickets

# NORTH CONFERENCE

**22 April**
at Old Trafford
**Worcestershire** 182 for 4 (42 overs) (SC Moore 66)
**Lancashire** 90 all out (25.1 overs)
*Worcestershire (2pts) won by 122 runs*

at Edgbaston
**Northamptonshire** 297 for 6 (50 overs) (U Afzaal 87, DJG Sales 56)
**Warwickshire** 298 for 4 (49.5 overs) (IJL Trott 125*, TR Ambrose 111*)
*Warwickshire (2pts) won by 6 wickets*

at Trent Bridge
**Yorkshire** 280 for 4 (50 overs) (Younus Khan 100, AW Gale 69*, GL Brophy 53)
**Nottinghamshire** 243 all out (47.5 overs) (CMW Read 68, MA Wagh 56)
*Yorkshire (2pts) won by 37 runs*

at Leicester
**Leicestershire** 138 all out (37.3 overs) (JK Maunders 72*, CD Thorp 4 for 30)
**Durham** 139 for 2 (28.1 overs) (P Mustard 66)
*Durham (2pts) won by 8 wickets*

**29 April**
at the Riverside
**Durham** 212 for 9 (50 overs)
**Derbyshire** 213 for 6 (48.2 overs) (SM Katich 81, IJ Harvey 60*)
*Derbyshire (2pts) won by 4 wickets*

at Old Trafford
**Lancashire** 183 all out (42.2 overs) (G Chapple 66, HH Streak 4 for 37)
**Warwickshire** 187 for 8 (48 overs) (TR Ambrose 55*)
*Warwickshire (2pts) won by 2 wickets*

at the Grange
**Yorkshire** 259 for 8 (50 overs) (A McGrath 66)
**Scotland** 217 all out (49.3 overs) (CM Wright 59)
*Yorkshire (2pts) won by 42 runs*

at Worcester
**Leicestershire** 231 all out (49 overs)
**Worcestershire** 189 all out (44.3 overs)
*Leicestershire (2pts) won by 42 runs*

at Northampton
**Nottinghamshire** 328 for 5 (50 overs) (BM Shafayat 104, JER Gallian 68, MA Wagh 66)
**Northamptonshire** 206 for 9 (39.3 overs) (DJG Sales 116*)
*Nottinghamshire (2pts) won by 122 runs*

**6 May**
at Worcester
**Worcestershire** 234 for 8 (50 overs) (PA Jaques 113)
**Nottinghamshire** 235 for 3 (48.3 overs) (DJ Hussey 88, MA Wagh 68*)
*Nottinghamshire (2pts) won by 7 wickets*

at Old Trafford
**Lancashire** 289 for 3 (50 overs) (BJ Hodge 130*, A Flintoff 66)
**Northamptonshire** 100 for 3 (21 overs)
*Lancashire (2pts) won by 20 runs – DL Method: target 121 from 21 overs*

at Leicester
**Scotland** 255 for 6 (50 overs) (GJ Bailey 76*, DF Watts 56)
**Leicestershire** 256 for 6 (50 overs) (PA Nixon 60, HD Ackerman 51)
*Leicestershire (2pts) won by 4 wickets*

**7 May**
at Headingley
**Yorkshire** 282 for 8 (50 overs) (JA Rudolph 100)
**Leicestershire** 284 for 4 (47.2 overs) (J Allenby 84,
HD Ackerman 66, JL Sadler 59*)
*Leicestershire (2pts) won by 6 wickets*

at the Riverside
**Durham** 220 for 9 (50 overs) (PD Collingwood 74)
**Lancashire** 163 all out (45.2 overs)
*Durham (2pts) won by 57 runs*

at Derby
**Warwickshire** 244 for 6 (37 overs) (DL Maddy 117)
**Derbyshire** 218 for 9 (34.1 overs) (GM Smith 56)
*Warwickshire (2pts) won by 26 runs – DL Method: target 245
from 34.1 overs*

at Northampton
**Scotland** 191 for 6 (34 overs)
**Northamptonshire** 197 for 4 (34 overs) (DJ Jacobs 88)
*Northamptonshire (2pts) won by 6 wickets – DL Method: target
197 from 34 overs*

13 May
at Derby
**Derbyshire** v. **Northamptonshire**
*Match abandoned (1pt each)*

at Trent Bridge
**Nottinghamshire** v. **Warwickshire**
*Match abandoned (1pt each)*

at Headingley
**Worcestershire** 215 for 7 (50 overs) (GA Hick 86*)
**Yorkshire** 6 for 0 (1.4 overs)
*Match abandoned (1pt each)*

**20 May**
at Worcester
**Derbyshire** 199 for 6 (50 overs) (WPC Weston 78)
**Worcestershire** 201 for 3 (39 overs) (BF Smith 66*,
GA Hick 65*)
*Worcestershire (2pts) won by 7 wickets*

at the Grange
**Nottinghamshire** 293 for 6 (50 overs) (JER Gallian 97,
CMW Read 58)
**Scotland** 216 all out (50 overs)
*Nottinghamshire (2pts) won by 77 runs*

at Old Trafford
**Yorkshire** 250 for 8 (50 overs) (A McGrath 135*)

**Lancashire** 251 for 3 (45.4 overs) (BJ Hodge 141*,
MB Loye 55)
*Lancashire (2pts) won by 7 wickets*

at Edgbaston
**Warwickshire** 265 for 7 (50 overs) (TR Ambrose 58,
DL Maddy 50)
**Leicestershire** 206 all out (48.2 overs) (PA Nixon 59,
JN Snape 58, DW Steyn 5 for 29)
*Warwickshire (2pts) won by 59 runs*

at Northampton
**Northamptonshire** 251 for 6 (50 overs) (DJ Jacobs 69,
DJG Sales 53)
**Durham** 252 for 6 (50 overs) (P Mustard 108,
DM Benkenstein 97*, JJ van der Wath 4 for 40)
*Durham (2pts) won by 4 wickets*

**27 May**
at Northampton
**Northamptonshire** v. **Leicestershire**
*Match abandoned (1pt each)*

at Old Trafford
**Scotland** 142 for 7 (22 overs)
**Lancashire** 132 all out (22 overs)
*Scotland (2pts) won by 10 runs*

**28 May**
at Leicester
**Leicestershire** v. **Lancashire**
*Match abandoned (1pt each)*

at Edgbaston
**Warwickshire** v. **Yorkshire**
*Match abandoned (1pt each)*

at the Riverside
**Scotland** 205 all out (47.4 overs) (GJ Bailey 92)
**Durham** 208 for 5 (44 overs) (WR Smith 62*)
*Durham (2pts) won by 5 wickets*

at Trent Bridge
**Nottinghamshire** 170 for 6 (13 overs) (DJ Hussey 56)
**Derbyshire** 120 for 9 (13 overs)
*Nottinghamshire (2pts) won by 50 runs*

**31 May**
at Derby
**Yorkshire** 253 for 4 (50 overs) (JA Rudolph 81)
**Derbyshire** 195 all out (40.2 overs) (AG Botha 50)
*Yorkshire (2pts) won by 39 runs – DL Method: target 235 from
42 overs*

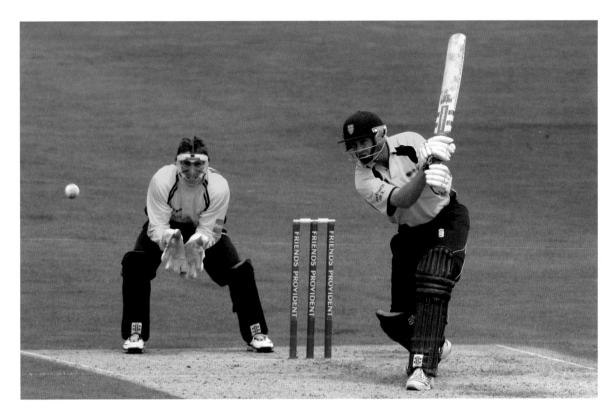

Durham captain Dale Benkenstein always led from the front during his side's successful campaign. Notice how Yorkshire wicketkeeper Simon Guy wears a protective face mask in a design adapted from a hockey goalkeeper's grille.

**1 June**
at the Riverside
**Durham** 332 for 4 (50 overs) (WR Smith 103, DM Benkenstein 94*)
**Worcestershire** 189 all out (33.5 overs) (MM Ali 86, GR Breese 5 for 49)
*Durham (2pts) won by 143 runs*

**3 June**
at the Grange
**Scotland** 102 all out (34.1 overs) (GG Wagg 4 for 36)
**Derbyshire** 103 for 4 (24.4 overs)
*Derbyshire (2pts) won by 6 wickets*

at Headingley
**Durham** 266 for 8 (50 overs) (SB Styris 98, P Mustard 77)
**Yorkshire** 213 all out (45.4 overs) (A McGrath 100)
*Durham (2pts) won by 53 runs*

at Worcester
**Warwickshire** 303 for 6 (50 overs) (KC Sangakkara 115, DL Maddy 106)
**Worcestershire** 307 for 2 (46 overs) (VS Solanki 144*, PA Jaques 102)
*Worcestershire (2pts) won by 8 wickets*

at Oakham School
**Nottinghamshire** 299 for 5 (50 overs) (SP Fleming 107, MA Wagh 81)
**Leicestershire** 275 for 7 (50 overs) (HD Ackerman 72, PA Nixon 57*, GD Clough 4 for 43)
*Nottinghamshire (2pts) won by 24 runs*

**10 June**
at Derby
**Derbyshire** 232 all out (48.4 overs) (DJ Birch 60, SD Stubbings 57)
**Lancashire** 235 for 4 (48.1 overs) (BJ Hodge 119*)
*Lancashire (2pts) won by 6 wickets*

at the Riverside
**Nottinghamshire** 238 for 8 (50 overs) (SP Fleming 98)
**Durham** 242 for 9 (49 overs) (P Mustard 71, GR Breese 68*)
*Durham (2pts) won by 1 wicket*

at Northampton
**Worcestershire** 302 for 6 (50 overs) (GA Hick 120)
**Northamptonshire** 246 for 9 (50 overs) (DJG Sales 64)
*Worcestershire (2pts) won by 56 runs*

**10 June**
at the Grange
**Warwickshire** 242 for 6 (50 overs) (IJL Trott 88*, AGR Loudon 53*)
**Scotland** 146 all out (46.3 overs)
*Warwickshire (2pts) won by 96 runs*

**13 June**
at Edgbaston
**Warwickshire** 314 for 5 (50 overs) (TR Ambrose 135, IJL Trott 107*)
**Durham** 77 for 3 (16.2 overs)
*Warwickshire (2pts) won by 39 runs – DL Method: target 117 from 16.2 overs*

at Trent Bridge
**Lancashire** 219 for 9 (50 overs) (SJ Croft 63)
**Nottinghamshire** 134 for 2 (28.1 overs) (WI Jefferson 60*, DJ Hussey 51*)
*Nottinghamshire (2pts) won by 37 runs – DL Method: target 98 from 28.1 overs*

at Headingley
**Northamptonshire** 314 for 4 (50 overs) (U Afzaal 132, SD Peters 107)
**Yorkshire** 119 for 2 (21 overs) (A McGrath 62*)
*Yorkshire (2pts) won by 1 run – DL Method: target 119 from 21 overs*

at Leicester
**Derbyshire** 246 for 7 (50 overs) (DJ Pipe 83, AG Botha 54*, J Allenby 5 for 43)
**Leicestershire** 239 for 1 (42.1 overs) (JL Sadler 113*, JK Maunders 109*)
*Leicestershire (2pts) won by 9 wickets – DL Method: target 239 from 48 overs*

at Worcester
**Worcestershire** 365 for 7 (50 overs) (VS Solanki 132, PA Jaques 69, BF Smith 59)
**Scotland** 20 for 3 (8 overs)
*Match abandoned (1pt each)*

## North Conference – Final Table

|                    | P | W | L | T | NR | RR    | Pts |
|--------------------|---|---|---|---|----|-------|-----|
| Durham             | 9 | 7 | 2 | 0 | 0  | 0.86  | 14  |
| Warwickshire       | 9 | 6 | 1 | 0 | 2  | 0.70  | 14  |
| Nottinghamshire    | 9 | 6 | 2 | 0 | 1  | 0.80  | 13  |
| Worcestershire     | 9 | 4 | 3 | 0 | 2  | 0.20  | 10  |
| Yorkshire          | 9 | 4 | 3 | 0 | 2  | 0.08  | 10  |
| Leicestershire     | 9 | 4 | 3 | 0 | 2  | -0.31 | 10  |
| Lancashire         | 9 | 3 | 5 | 0 | 1  | -0.63 | 7   |
| Derbyshire         | 9 | 2 | 6 | 0 | 1  | -0.24 | 5   |
| Northamptonshire   | 9 | 1 | 6 | 0 | 2  | -0.72 | 4   |
| Scotland           | 9 | 1 | 7 | 0 | 1  | -1.05 | 3   |

When Hampshire turned up at Kent's lovely Nevill Ground in Tunbridge Wells on a rare sunny Sunday in June, they knew that defeat would virtually end their semi-final qualification hopes. What followed was one of the most exciting one-day contests of the summer, see-sawing first one way and then another until Shane Warne's men finally triumphed in a nerve-jangling finish.

Kent, at that stage top of the South Conference and favourites to reach the last four, initially made Hampshire struggle for runs, but Nic Pothas and Dimitri Mascarenhas revived them with 46 and 50 respectively. Then, however, the last five wickets fell for 15 runs, and 220 all out – with two balls unused – looked suspiciously like under-achievement.

Warne, though, as ever had other ideas. Rallying his men, he went back on to the attack with the new ball and suddenly Kent were 47 for 4 after ten overs in reply. Warne himself also cranked up the pressure with a masterly display of leg-spin bowling in which every ball seemed an event.

From 136 for 8, however, Kent were themselves dramatically revived when Ryan McLaren joined Matthew Walker in a stand which eventually realised 69.

With 21 required from four overs, Warne brought himself back for his final over: it cost only two and gave the maestro figures of 3 for 30. Then, McLaren fell for a 48-ball 43 to Shaun Udal with 16 needed.

Walker kept Kentish hopes alive with a six off Sean Ervine which Michael Lumb, leaping at long on, could only get his fingertips to – but, with three runs needed from four balls, Walker fell lbw for 83 trying to whip Chris Tremlett through mid wicket.

A scrappy win three days later at home to Surrey (who recovered from 32 for 6 to reach 181), in which Stuart Clark's 6 for 27 and an opening partnership of 90 between John Crawley and Michael Carberry were the standout features, was then enough to see Hampshire not only qualify but top the South Conference table itself.

It was a magnificent achievement, especially following the early defeat to Essex in which they had been tumbled out for just 75, the abandonment of the scheduled match at Gloucestershire and the thrilling tied game against Somerset at the Rose Bowl.

Other group stage highlights included Pothas's 114 as an opener in the first game against Middlesex, unbeaten innings of 67 and 66 from Sean Ervine and Kevin Pietersen which saw Hampshire home against Ireland, and Mascarenhas's 56-ball 74 – with four sixes and four fours – which allied to half-centuries from both Pothas and Lumb and Clark's 4 for 25 overwhelmed Glamorgan.

The build-up to the semi-final was dominated by Warwickshire's unfathomable decision to omit Ian Bell after England's management had made him available. Kevin Pietersen, in contrast, was in the Hampshire line-up and had been flown south from England's Test match at Durham, which ended the evening before, in the same helicopter that Bell could have used.

In the match itself, Hampshire's collective nous seemed too much for their visitors, who were never in the hunt. John Crawley's well-judged 65 was the basis of a solid Hampshire total in the conditions of 206 for 7, and Stuart Clark again impressed with 3 for 38 as Warwickshire were bowled out for 166.

Nic Pothas hits out for Hampshire during their semi-final win against Warwickshire at the Rose Bowl.

## Hampshire Friends Provident Trophy South Conference results:

22 April (the Rose Bowl): beat Middlesex by 91 runs
29 April (Chelmsford): lost to Essex by 135 runs
7 May (the Rose Bowl): beat Ireland by 8 wickets
13 May (Bristol): match abandoned v Gloucestershire
18 May (the Rose Bowl): tied with Somerset
20 May (the Rose Bowl): beat Sussex by 6 wickets
3 June (Swansea): beat Glamorgan by 137 runs
10 June (Tunbridge Wells): beat Kent by 2 runs
13 June (the Rose Bowl): beat Surrey by 3 wickets

### Semi-Final:

20 June (the Rose Bowl): beat Warwickshire by 40 runs

## SOUTH CONFERENCE

**22 April**
at the Rose Bowl
**Hampshire** 294 for 6 (50 overs) (N Pothas 114, MJ Lumb 59)
**Middlesex** 203 all out (44.3 overs) (ET Smith 59)
*Hampshire (2pts) won by 91 runs*

at The Oval
**Kent** 271 all out (46.2 overs) (RWT Key 108, JC Tredwell 88, SJ Magoffin 4 for 58)
**Surrey** 274 for 7 (48.5 overs) (SA Newman 73, Azhar Mahmood 63, JN Batty 52*)
*Surrey (2pts) won by 3 wickets*

at Taunton
**Somerset** 310 for 9 (50 overs) (C Kieswetter 69*, CL White 54)
**Glamorgan** 286 for 8 (50 overs) (MJ Powell 69, PD Trego 4 for 54)
*Somerset (2pts) won by 24 runs*

**29 April**
at Chelmsford
**Essex** 210 for 7 (50 overs) (JS Foster 69*)
**Hampshire** 75 all out (24.5 overs)
*Essex (2pts) won by 135 runs*

at Belfast
**Kent** 231 for 7 (50 overs) (JL Denly 102*)
**Ireland** 173 all out (43.5 overs)
*Kent (2pts) won by 58 runs*

at Lord's
**Middlesex** 262 for 8 (50 overs) (JWM Dalrymple 68*, OA Shah 56)
**Glamorgan** 256 for 9 (50 overs) (MTG Elliott 87, BJ Wright 61)
*Middlesex (2pts) won by 6 runs*

**29 April (continued)**
at Taunton
**Sussex** 287 for 5 (50 overs) (RR Montgomerie 125, MW Goodwin 88)
**Somerset** 249 all out (44.2 overs) (ME Trescothick 58, CL White 51, RSC Martin-Jenkins 4 for 50)
*Sussex (2pts) won by 38 runs*

at The Oval
**Surrey** 496 for 4 (50 overs) (AD Brown 176, JGE Benning 152, R Clarke 82*)
**Gloucestershire** 239 all out (34.1 overs) (MA Hardinges 57, SJ Adshead 54, Mohammad Akram 4 for 36)
*Surrey (2pts) won by 257 runs*

**6 May**
at Taunton
**Somerset** 341 for 8 (50 overs) (JL Langer 132, CL White 65)
**Ireland** 213 for 9 (41 overs) (GC Wilson 51, CM Willoughby 5 for 33)
*Somerset (2pts) won by 128 runs*

at Lord's
**Gloucestershire** 221 (50 overs) (MA Hardinges 50)
**Middlesex** 222 for 9 (47.5 overs) (AJ Strauss 70, SP Kirby 5 for 36)
*Middlesex (2pts) won by 1 wicket*

at Chelmsford
**Essex** 234 all out (47.5 overs) (RC Irani 81, RS Bopara 56)
**Kent** 237 for 7 (49.4 overs) (DI Stevens 61, MJ Walker 58)
*Kent (2pts) won by 3 wickets*

Surrey's team are pictured for posterity after their one-day world record 496 for 4 against battered and bruised Gloucestershire at The Oval.

**7 May**
at the Rose Bowl
**Ireland** 221 for 6 (48 overs) (PG Gillespie 55, DT Johnston 52*)
**Hampshire** 178 for 2 (28.2 overs) (SM Ervine 67*, KP Pietersen 66*)
*Hampshire (2pts) won by 8 wickets – DL Method: target 175 from 29 overs*

at Bristol
**Sussex** 193 for 5 (31 overs)
(RR Montgomerie 100)
**Gloucestershire** 196 for 9 (30.5 overs)
*Gloucestershire (2pts) won by 1 wicket – DL Method: target 194 from 31 overs*

at Canterbury
**Middlesex** 233 for 5 (41 overs) (OA Shah 95*)
**Kent** 202 for 5 (29.2 overs) (M van Jaarsveld 86*)
*Kent (2pts) won by 5 wickets – DL Method: target 200 from 32 overs*

**10 May**
at Dublin
**Gloucestershire** 248 all out (50 overs) (MJ North 77, MA Hardinges 70, DT Johnston 4 for 13)
**Ireland** 63 all out (21 overs) (CG Greenidge 4 for 15)
*Gloucestershire (2pts) won by 185 runs*

**11 May**
at Hove
**Sussex** 81 for 2 (19.4 overs)
**Glamorgan**
*Match abandoned (1pt each)*

**13 May**
at Bristol
**Gloucestershire** v. **Hampshire**
*Match abandoned (1pt each)*

at The Oval
**Surrey** v. **Middlesex**
*Match abandoned (1pt each)*

at Dublin
**Ireland** 227 for 5 (50 overs) (WTS Porterfield 88)
**Essex** 228 for 3 (41.3 overs) (RS Bopara 101, RC Irani 90*)
*Essex (2pts) won by 7 wickets*

**18 May**
at the Rose Bowl
**Somerset** 220 for 6 (50 overs) (ID Blackwell 55)
**Hampshire** 220 for 9 (50 overs) (MA Carberry 65)
*Match tied (1pt each)*

**20 May**
at Canterbury
**Glamorgan** 85 all out (31.5 overs) (SJ Cook 4 for 25, R McLaren 4 for 29)
**Kent** 87 for 1 (11.4 overs)
*Kent (2pts) won by 9 wickets*

at Bristol
**Gloucestershire** 259 for 7 (50 overs) (Kadeer Ali 89, GP Hodnett 50)
**Somerset** 201 all out (43.5 overs)
(ID Blackwell 72)
*Gloucestershire (2pts) won by 58 runs*

at Chelmsford
**Middlesex** 277 for 7 (50 overs) (EJG Morgan 100, DC Nash 51, Danish Kaneria 4 for 49)
**Essex** 278 for 1 (45.2 overs) (ML Pettini 103*, V Chopra 102, RS Bopara 56*)
*Essex (2pts) won by 9 wickets*

at the Rose Bowl
**Sussex** 201 all out (49.4 overs)
(RR Montgomerie 89)
**Hampshire** 202 for 4 (48.1 overs) (MJ Lumb 66, SM Ervine 57*)
*Hampshire (2pts) won by 6 wickets*

**22 May**
at Hove
**Surrey** 281 for 7 (50 overs) (MR Ramprakash 142*)
**Sussex** 265 all out (49 overs) (MW Goodwin 86, CD Nash 52, CP Schofield 4 for 32)
*Surrey (2pts) won by 16 runs*

**26 May**
at Taunton
**Somerset** v. **Kent**
*Match abandoned (1pt each)*

**27 May**
at Swansea
**Glamorgan** v. **Essex**
*Match abandoned (1pt each)*

at The Oval
**Surrey** v. **Ireland**
*Match abandoned (1pt each)*

**28 May**
at Hove
**Sussex** v. **Ireland**
*Match abandoned (1pt each)*

Shane Warne appeals successfully for Rob Key's wicket during his superb performance for Hampshire against Kent at Tunbridge Wells.

at Bristol
**Gloucestershire** 222 for 7 (33 overs) (APR Gidman 65,
MJ North 55, RN ten Doeschate 5 for 50)
**Essex** 200 all out (31.2 overs) (RC Irani 60, V Chopra 51)
*Gloucestershire (2pts) won by 22 runs*

at Cresselly
**Glamorgan** 203 for 8 (39 overs) (JP Maher 76)
**Surrey** 206 for 7 (37 overs) (MA Butcher 72*, AG Wharf 4 for 45)
*Surrey (2pts) won by 3 wickets*

**3 June**
at Hove
**Kent** 264 for 9 (50 overs) (AJ Hall 123, RJ Kirtley 5 for 41)
**Sussex** 152 all out (33.4 overs) (MJ Prior 76)
*Kent (2pts) won by 112 runs*

at Swansea
**Hampshire** 283 for 6 (50 overs) (AD Mascarenhas 74,
MJ Lumb 66, N Pothas 62*)
**Glamorgan** 146 all out (38.5 overs) (SR Clark 4 for 25)
*Hampshire (2pts) won by 137 runs*

at Lord's
**Somerset** 332 for 5 (50 overs) (JL Langer 145, PD Trego 78,
CL White 61)
**Middlesex** 245 (40.4 overs) (EJG Morgan 76,
PD Trego 4 for 61)
*Somerset (2pts) won by 87 runs*

at Whitgift School
**Essex** 248 all out (47.3 overs) (AN Cook 125,
Azhar Mahmood 4 for 39)
**Surrey** 240 all out (49.4 overs) (MR Ramprakash 77,
MA Butcher 53, Danish Kaneria 4 for 44)
*Essex (2pts) won by 8 runs*

**10 June**
at Colwyn Bay
**Gloucestershire** 283 for 9 (50 overs) (Kadeer Ali 101)
**Glamorgan** 277 for 9 (50 overs) (TL Maynard 71)
*Gloucestershire (2pts) won by 6 runs*

at Dublin
**Ireland** 175 all out (47 overs) (WTS Porterfield 68,
JWM Dalrymple 4 for 39)
**Middlesex** 179 for 4 (37.1 overs)
*Middlesex (2pts) won by 6 wickets*

at Tunbridge Wells
**Hampshire** 220 all out (49.4 overs) (AD Mascarenhas 50)
**Kent** 218 all out (49.3 overs) (MJ Walker 83)
*Hampshire (2pts) won by 2 runs*

at Bath
**Surrey** 214 for 9 (50 overs) (JN Batty 50)
**Somerset** 218 for 7 (47.5 overs) (ME Trescothick 52)
*Somerset (2pts) won by 3 wickets*

at Arundel
**Essex** 256 for 9 (50 overs) (GW Flower 55)
**Sussex** 124 all out (40.1 overs)
*Essex (2pts) won by 132 runs*

**13 June**
at Belfast
**Ireland** v. **Glamorgan**
*Match abandoned (1pt each)*

at Chelmsford
**Somerset** 193 all out (49.4 overs) (JL Langer 82,
Danish Kaneria 5 for 32)
**Essex** 194 for 3 (34.2 overs) (ML Pettini 87, RS Bopara 51*)
*Essex (2pts) won by 7 wickets*

at Tunbridge Wells
**Gloucestershire** 275 for 6 (50 overs) (HJH Marshall 63,
APR Gidman 62)
**Kent** 235 all out (46.2 overs) (AJ Hall 55)
*Gloucestershire (2pts) won by 40 runs*

at Lord's
**Sussex** 271 for 9 (50 overs) (MW Goodwin 111,
RR Montgomerie 82)
**Middlesex** 262 for 8 (50 overs) (NRD Compton 110*,
OA Shah 88)
*Sussex (2pts) won by 9 runs*

at the Rose Bowl
**Surrey** 181 all out (49.5 overs) (CP Schofield 75*,
R Clarke 55, SR Clark 6 for 27)
**Hampshire** 182 for 7 (48.2 overs) (JP Crawley 55)
*Hampshire (2pts) won by 3 wickets*

## South Conference – Final Table

| | P | W | L | T | NR | RR | Pts |
|---|---|---|---|---|---|---|---|
| Hampshire | 9 | 6 | 1 | 1 | 1 | 0.31 | 14 |
| Essex | 9 | 6 | 2 | 0 | 1 | 1.04 | 13 |
| Gloucestershire | 9 | 6 | 2 | 0 | 1 | 0.12 | 13 |
| Kent | 9 | 5 | 3 | 0 | 1 | 0.88 | 11 |
| Surrey | 9 | 4 | 3 | 0 | 2 | 0.78 | 10 |
| Somerset | 9 | 4 | 3 | 1 | 1 | 0.19 | 10 |
| Middlesex | 9 | 3 | 5 | 0 | 1 | -0.37 | 7 |
| Sussex | 9 | 2 | 5 | 0 | 2 | -0.68 | 6 |
| Glamorgan | 9 | 0 | 6 | 0 | 3 | -1.41 | 3 |
| Ireland | 9 | 0 | 6 | 0 | 3 | -1.79 | 3 |

## SEMI-FINALS

**20 June**
at the Riverside
**Essex** 71 all out (22.1 overs)
(LE Plunkett 4 for 15)
**Durham** 72 for 7 (19 overs)
(AJ Bichel 4 for 22)
*Durham won by 3 wickets*

at the Rose Bowl
**Hampshire** 206 for 7 (50 overs)
(JP Crawley 65)
**Warwickshire** 166 all out (43.3 overs)
*Hampshire won by 40 runs*

## FRIENDS PROVIDENT TROPHY FINAL
### 18–19 August

An odd failure to use the tried and (by now, universally) trusted Duckworth/Lewis method for deciding weather-affected one-day matches in, well, one day meant that Durham could not officially celebrate the first trophy of their short life as a first-class county until all but a handful of their travelling 6,500 fans from the north-east had returned home.

As it was, only 38 minutes and 51 balls were necessary, after play had resumed after more rain at 12.30 pm on Sunday's reserve day, for Durham to wrap up an emphatic victory by 125 runs against a Hampshire side which never got into the game.

This was mainly because Phil Mustard, the young wicketkeeper-batsman, capped his fine competition form by blazing 49 early on Saturday morning and because Kyle Coetzer, Shivnarine Chanderpaul and Dale Benkenstein, the dependable Durham captain, also batted superbly in their differing ways.

Shane Warne, the Hampshire captain, tried all he could but remained wicketless, as Chanderpaul especially played classily against him, and then Hampshire's bid to score 313 was immediately undermined by Ottis Gibson's dramatic two wickets from the first two balls of their reply.

Michael Lumb and Sean Ervine both fell to fine slip catches by Michael Di Venuto, as Gibson found just enough movement against the two left-handers, and when the 38-year-old fast bowler later returned to

*Liam Plunkett jumps for joy – and relief – after hitting the winning runs in Durham's extraordinary semi-final victory over Essex.*

Phil Mustard, the exciting Durham wicketkeeper-batsman, sets the tone from the top of the order during his quickfire 49 in the Lord's final.

pin Kevin Pietersen lbw for 12 the Hampshire race had almost been run.

John Crawley batted defiantly but Hampshire's innings could not recover and when the weather closed in they still required another 155 from 105 balls with five wickets left.

Just as unsatisfactory as the reserve day finish was the experiment, during the whole of the competition, to allow captain and batsman a minimum of two appeals per innings to the third umpire if they felt a mistake had been made by the standing umpires in the middle.

Fine in theory, it was half-baked in practice and many players virtually ignored its presence. In the final itself, Warne failed to appeal when an lbw that could well have been given was turned down against

Chanderpaul, and Trevor Jesty, the third umpire, also ruled against an appeal for the run out of Crawley when Gibson fingertipped a Pietersen straight drive into the bowlers' stumps.

Television replays were inconclusive, even though Gibson insisted he had touched the ball, and Jesty quite rightly decided he could not undermine the on-field officials. The player's word sadly does not come into it anymore.

Otherwise, the competition was excellent, less affected by the summer's poor weather in the early stages and benefiting hugely from the decision to restore semi-finals. Only the further restoration of quarter-finals, thankfully planned for 2008, will make the structure even better.

The history-makers: Durham's players celebrate their county's first trophy since the club achieved first-class status in 1992.

On the field, too, there were some memorable performances – none more so than on the last Sunday of a sun-soaked April when Alistair Brown and James Benning put on 294 for the first wicket as Surrey totalled a world record 496 for 4 from their 50 overs – beating Sri Lanka's 443 for 9 against Holland in 2006 – against a shell-shocked Gloucestershire at The Oval.

Brown hit eight sixes and 20 fours in an astonishing 176 from 97 balls, while a positively pedestrian Benning included four sixes and 15 fours in his own 134-ball 152. Rikki Clarke then came in to thrash 82 not out from a mere 28 balls, studded with six sixes and nine fours. Mark Ramprakash and Mark Butcher didn't even get a bat.

## FINAL – DURHAM v. HAMPSHIRE
### 18-19 August 2007 at Lord's

### DURHAM

| | | |
|---|---|---|
| MJ Di Venuto | c Carberry b Powell | 12 |
| *P Mustard | lbw b Bruce | 49 |
| KJ Coetzer | c Warne b Ervine | 61 |
| S Chanderpaul | run out | 78 |
| PD Collingwood | c Mascarenhas b Powell | 22 |
| DM Benkenstein (capt) | not out | 61 |
| OD Gibson | not out | 15 |
| GR Breese | | |
| LE Plunkett | | |
| G Onions | | |
| N Killeen | | |
| Extras | lb 4, w 8, nb 2 | 14 |
| | (5 wkts 50 overs) | **312** |

| | O | M | R | W |
|---|---|---|---|---|
| Powell | 10 | 0 | 80 | 2 |
| Bruce | 9 | 0 | 43 | 1 |
| Mascarenhas | 6 | 0 | 45 | 0 |
| Ervine | 6 | 0 | 34 | 1 |
| Tremlett | 9 | 0 | 60 | 0 |
| Warne | 10 | 1 | 46 | 0 |

**Fall of Wickets**
1-44, 2-69, 3-180, 4-220, 5-278

### HAMPSHIRE

| | | |
|---|---|---|
| MJ Lumb | c Di Venuto b Gibson | 0 |
| JP Crawley | b Collingwood | 68 |
| SM Ervine | c Di Venuto b Gibson | 0 |
| KP Pietersen | lbw b Gibson | 12 |
| MA Carberry | b Onions | 23 |
| *N Pothas | c Onions b Collingwood | 47 |
| AD Mascarenhas | b Plunkett | 12 |
| SK Warne (capt) | b Plunkett | 5 |
| CT Tremlett | c Di Venuto b Collingwood | 0 |
| DB Powell | c Collingwood b Plunkett | 1 |
| JTA Bruce | not out | 4 |
| Extras | lb 10, w 3, nb 2 | 15 |
| | (all out 41 overs) | **187** |

| | O | M | R | W |
|---|---|---|---|---|
| Gibson | 8 | 1 | 24 | 3 |
| Killeen | 8 | 0 | 29 | 0 |
| Onions | 6 | 0 | 28 | 1 |
| Plunkett | 9 | 1 | 42 | 3 |
| Breese | 3 | 0 | 21 | 0 |
| Collingwood | 7 | 0 | 33 | 3 |

**Fall of Wickets**
1-0, 2-0, 3-17, 4-75, 5-142, 6-174, 7-177, 8-178, 9-182

Umpires: IJ Gould & PJ Hartley
Toss: Hampshire
Man of the Match: OD Gibson

### Durham won by 125 runs

# DURHAM

Tim Wellock, who writes regularly on Durham cricket for both the *Daily Telegraph* and the *Northern Echo*, gives his end-of-season report on the achievements in 2007 of English cricket's youngest first-class county... and their oldest player.

The crop failures so often witnessed during Durham's 15-year wait for the seeds of first-class cricket to germinate were quickly forgotten as this year's spectacular blossoming proved an enthralling experience.

The summer of 2007 ended with the Professional Cricketers' Association Player of the Year, 38-year-old Ottis Gibson, observing, 'It's great to be champions for a day'. After completing their seventh win at Canterbury, Durham were top of the LV County Championship for 24 hours until Sussex overhauled them by 4.5 points.

Second place was an improvement of five places on their previous best, achieved in 2006 when Gibson hit his career-best 155 in the final game at Headingley to help them hang on to Division One status by half a point.

Yet, while he scored 578 runs at a respectable 27.52, it was with the ball that Gibson really amazed everyone. Initially upstaged by Steve Harmison, he had only taken 23 wickets in the first eight games; Gibson then claimed 57 in the final seven. Only Mushtaq Ahmed surpassed his total of 80 wickets, which was 11 more than the previous Durham record.

Among the many instances of high drama in Durham's season, which included a bizarre yet gripping Friends Provident Trophy semi-final at home to Essex, there were two other surreal moments involving Gibson. One was when he took wickets with the first two balls of Hampshire's innings on his way to earning the Man of the Match award as Durham landed their first silverware by winning the Friends Provident Trophy final by 125 runs. The other came at the Riverside on a rainy day in July when he claimed Hampshire's final wicket to go with the other nine he had already taken.

Gibson was the first bowler to achieve the feat in England since Richard Johnson for Middlesex against Derbyshire in 1994, and it was a classic case of using experience to exploit conditions. After the second day was washed out, Durham lost their remaining three wickets for seven runs before Gibson got to work. He had 5 for 31 from 12 overs at lunch and 8 for 47 from 17 overs before a 90-minute break for rain, after which he took the last two in three balls to finish with 10 for 47.

Relying more on swing than seam, Gibson showed he could move it either way to the left-handers. Michael Carberry was the first victim, edging to first slip, and then Michael Lumb decided at the last second to withdraw his bat and was lbw. Four batsmen offered regulation catches to Phil Mustard and

last man James Bruce went first ball, groping forward to a perfectly pitched delivery that left him to clip off stump. It was a moment of pure joy as the crowd rose and Gibson raced away, arms wheeling, somewhere in the direction of point with his ecstatic team-mates in hot pursuit.

He barely seemed to come down from cloud nine for the rest of the season, but showed rare restraint with the bat in the Friends Provident Trophy semi-final when he was joined by Liam Plunkett with Durham on 38 for 7 in reply to Essex's 71 all out.

Plunkett scored 30 of the 34 needed while Gibson made the most valuable 5 not out of his life. It was in complete contrast to the unbeaten 15 he bludgeoned off seven balls at Lord's to lift Durham to 312 for 5, the highest total in a domestic 50-over final. Then, after removing Lumb and Sean Ervine with the first two balls of the reply, Gibson also had Kevin Pietersen lbw for 12 to finish with 3 for 24.

He felt his metamorphosis owed something to being dropped for the third championship game against Kent, the only match he missed all season apart from a Friends Provident Trophy group game against Lancashire. 'I felt I bowled well in the first two games, but then Liam Plunkett became available and I was left out against Kent,' he said. 'I was disappointed but adopted the adage, "Don't get bitter, get better" and every time I went on the field I tried to do everything that was required for the team. People appreciate that, and if the other players see your efforts they raise their game too. I had some fantastic catches taken off my bowling.'

Gibson's success is also the end product of putting everything into practice that he has learnt as a coach over the last six years, which includes fitness. 'There were times when I was in at 8.00 am for a massage to get ready to bowl. That's the mindset I adopted and perhaps it's one reason for my success.'

Durham also won the Division Two title in the NatWest Pro40 League after being relegated last year. The transformation, however, was by no means entirely down to Gibson. The signing of Michael Di Venuto, plus the early season form of Harmison, and in one-day cricket the promotion of Phil Mustard to open the innings, were all big factors.

Di Venuto carried his bat in his first innings at Worcester, and repeated the feat in the third match at home to Kent, making 204. Harmison, available for the first three games following his retirement from one-day internationals, took 24 wickets in those contests. Harmison's desire to be part of Durham's success was best illustrated by his strenuous efforts to get fit for the Friends Provident Trophy final a month after a hernia operation, but he was cruelly denied when a back problem flared up and ended his season.

When Harmison first went away on Test duty, Graham Onions came to the fore, and at the time his 8 for 101 at Edgbaston was the second-best innings analysis in Durham's first-class history.

Others making a notch in the county's record book were the redoubtable captain, Dale Benkenstein, who became the first to score 1,000 Championship runs in three successive seasons, and wicketkeeper Mustard, whose 65 Championship victims helped him to gain selection for England's one-day series in Sri Lanka. He also scored the county's fastest one-day 50 off 21 balls in the Pro40 match against Leicestershire and was the Friends Provident Trophy's top scorer with 484 runs at 44.0 and a strike rate of 88.48.

There were maiden Championship centuries by three Durham academy products, meanwhile – 20-year-old left-handed opener Mark Stoneman, Aberdonian Kyle Coetzer and Ben Harmison.

Shivnarine Chanderpaul arrived in early August and impressed sufficiently to be invited back for the 2008 season, although his brief sojourn at the World Twenty20 Championship is unlikely to have whetted his appetite for what remains Durham's Achilles heel. Although three Twenty20 Cup ties were washed out, they won only one out of eight games and still have the worst record of all the counties.

Traditionalists might say they should wear that as a badge of honour to go with their hard-earned trophies.

At 38, Ottis Gibson had the season of his life and played a huge part in Durham's emergence as a trophy-winning county before retiring to become England's full-time fast-bowling coach.

# AUSTRALIA

## ENGLAND IN AUSTRALIA
### by Jonathan Agnew

In the week before the opening Test match of the most eagerly-awaited Ashes series of recent times – especially in Australia – Mike Selvey, of the *Guardian*, and I went out to dinner with Duncan Fletcher, the England head coach.

We took only ten minutes from sitting down around the table before the subject which was to become the tour's main hot potato was raised, 'Come on then,' said Duncan, 'Who would you pick – Giles or Panesar?'

Both Selv and I said that Ashley Giles would be our choice. And, before you all throw down this book in disgust, let me explain. Monty Panesar was playing in the match that was then going on, against South Australia at Adelaide, but had not bowled well. In addition, a longish England tail had been exposed. Giles had not played, mainly because of a niggling injury, but I was still firmly of the opinion – which I subsequently went on the record about – that Giles should get the nod for the First Test at Brisbane. But only for the First Test.

For the Second Test I would have left out Jimmy Anderson, and gone with two spinners as part of a five-man attack. That is not hindsight, either, because I said it during the build-up to a match England simply could not afford to lose after the terrible hammering at Brisbane.

Ricky Ponting flicks a ball from Matthew Hoggard away for four during his brilliant innings of 196 at the Gabba.

When Panesar did eventually play, of course, he immediately took five wickets in the first innings at Perth as England – 2-0 down by that stage after the disintegration at Adelaide on the final day – briefly threatened to make a belated game of it. But then England's own first innings at Perth failed to take advantage of Australia's below-par score, and suddenly the Ashes were back in Aussie hands.

And how they celebrated, and how they had desired the prize. The Australian players had thought of nothing else but this from the day England had taken the urn from their grasp at The Oval in September 2005, and for Ricky Ponting in particular it was redemption.

Ponting could not bear being labelled as the captain who, after 18 years, had allowed the Ashes to slip back into English possession and how he made England pay for their poor preparation leading up to the series and the selection errors at Brisbane and Adelaide.

His 196 at Brisbane, when Australia came out of the traps like snarling dogs in an atmosphere at the Gabba which can only be described as Colosseum-like, was just the start of his personal crusade first to get the Ashes back and then to bury England under a 5-0 whitewash.

England's own players must realise, right now, that Australians will always be pumped up in the extreme for every Ashes contest – and it is therefore of some comfort to hear younger players like Alastair Cook saying that they never want to experience the feelings and emotions they endured in the 2006–07 series.

If England are to win again in 2009, when at least they won't have to worry about Glenn McGrath and Shane Warne for the first time in more than a decade, they will need to be clinical in their preparations and highly aggressive in their game plans. Australia will not give up the Ashes quite as limply as England did.

At the start of the series Duncan Fletcher told me that this was the best-prepared side that England had ever put into the field. He was happy that key players were rested, and with the preparations which had involved some one-day cricket in India during the ICC Champions Trophy.

I would, however, take issue with this – not least because Steve Harmison, the main strike weapon, was clearly not properly match fit until the series was all but over. I'm afraid that Harmison's first ball at Brisbane will go down as one of the Ashes moments to make Englishmen cringe and Australians crow. It was beyond belief, really, and the most awful statement.

I can still recall how I described it on air for *Test Match Special*, and how I felt when I witnessed it. '…and Harmison bowls, and it's gone to second slip,' is what I said, and I remember not quite believing what had happened even as I said it.

When I came off commentary 20 minutes later I was still half-thinking that perhaps I'd got it wrong. And,

## FIRST TEST – AUSTRALIA v. ENGLAND
### 23–27 November 2006 at Brisbane

### AUSTRALIA

| | First Innings | | Second Innings | |
|---|---|---|---|---|
| JL Langer | c Pietersen b Flintoff | 82 | not out | 100 |
| ML Hayden | c Collingwood b Flintoff | 21 | run out | 37 |
| RT Ponting (capt) | lbw b Hoggard | 196 | not out | 60 |
| DR Martyn | c Collingwood b Giles | 29 | | |
| MEK Hussey | b Flintoff | 86 | | |
| MJ Clarke | c Strauss b Anderson | 56 | | |
| *AC Gilchrist | lbw b Hoggard | 0 | | |
| SK Warne | c Jones b Harmison | 17 | | |
| B Lee | not out | 43 | | |
| SR Clark | b Flintoff | 39 | | |
| GD McGrath | not out | 8 | | |
| Extras | b 2, lb 8, w 8, nb 7 | 25 | lb 4, nb 1 | 5 |
| | (9 wkts dec 155 overs) | 602 | (1 wkt dec 45.1 overs) | 202 |

| | First Innings | | | | Second Innings | | | |
|---|---|---|---|---|---|---|---|---|
| | O | M | R | W | O | M | R | W |
| Harmison | 30 | 4 | 123 | 1 | 12.1 | 1 | 54 | 0 |
| Hoggard | 31 | 5 | 98 | 2 | 11 | 2 | 43 | 0 |
| Anderson | 29 | 6 | 141 | 1 | 9 | 1 | 54 | 0 |
| Flintoff | 30 | 4 | 99 | 4 | 5 | 2 | 11 | 0 |
| Giles | 25 | 2 | 91 | 1 | 5 | 0 | 22 | 0 |
| Bell | 1 | 0 | 12 | 0 | - | - | - | - |
| Pietersen | 9 | 1 | 28 | 0 | 3 | 0 | 14 | 0 |

**Fall of Wickets**
1-79, 2-141, 3-198, 4-407, 5-467, 6-467, 7-500, 8-528, 9-578
1-68

### ENGLAND

| | First Innings | | Second Innings | |
|---|---|---|---|---|
| AJ Strauss | c Hussey b McGrath | 12 | c sub b Clark | 11 |
| AN Cook | c Warne b McGrath | 11 | c Hussey b Warne | 43 |
| IR Bell | c Ponting b Clark | 50 | lbw b Warne | 0 |
| PD Collingwood | c Gilchrist b Clark | 5 | st Gilchrist b Warne | 96 |
| KP Pietersen | lbw b McGrath | 16 | c Martyn b Lee | 92 |
| A Flintoff (capt) | c Gilchrist b Lee | 0 | c Langer b Warne | 16 |
| *GO Jones | lbw b McGrath | 19 | b McGrath | 33 |
| AF Giles | c Hayden b Warne | 24 | c Warne b Clark | 23 |
| MJ Hoggard | c Gilchrist b Clark | 0 | c Warne b Clark | 8 |
| SJ Harmison | c Gilchrist b McGrath | 0 | c McGrath b Clark | 13 |
| JM Anderson | not out | 2 | not out | 4 |
| Extras | b 2, lb 8, w 2, nb 6 | 18 | b 8, lb 10, w 2, nb 11 | 31 |
| | (all out 61.1 overs) | 157 | (all out 100.1 overs) | 370 |

| | First Innings | | | | Second Innings | | | |
|---|---|---|---|---|---|---|---|---|
| | O | M | R | W | O | M | R | W |
| Lee | 15 | 3 | 51 | 1 | 22 | 1 | 98 | 1 |
| McGrath | 23.1 | 8 | 50 | 6 | 19 | 3 | 53 | 1 |
| Clark | 14 | 5 | 21 | 3 | 24.1 | 6 | 72 | 4 |
| Warne | 9 | 0 | 25 | 0 | 34 | 7 | 124 | 4 |
| Hussey | - | - | - | - | 1 | 0 | 5 | 0 |

**Fall of Wickets**
1-28, 2-28, 3-42, 4-78, 5-79, 6-126, 7-149, 8-153, 9-154
1-29, 2-36, 3-91, 4-244, 5-271, 6-293, 7-326, 8-346, 9-361

Umpires: BF Bowden (New Zealand) & SA Bucknor (West Indies)
Toss: Australia
Man of the Match: RT Ponting

## Australia won by 277 runs

funnily enough, one of the first emails that we received that morning from listeners back in England was from a lad who told us he was walking home from the pub with one ear on his portable and, when I said it had gone to second slip, had started to jump up and down in the street because he thought Harmison had got Justin Langer out first ball.

How I wish he had. Soon, though, you could hear the Aussies beginning to mock and by the end of that opening day you knew that England were seriously undercooked and that Australia were right up for it.

England's problems had begun when Marcus Trescothick, so important at the top of the order, had announced during the warm-up game against New South Wales at Sydney that he was not mentally fit for the tour. His sudden departure created a big hole to fill, and although Cook did manfully in his first Ashes series to move up from No. 3, it left England very dependent on Andrew Strauss. Sadly, Strauss did not have a good series. Any chance England had of stopping Australia's runaway train came at Adelaide where both Paul Collingwood and Kevin Pietersen batted beautifully to make sure an important toss was not wasted.

Yet, from the small matter of 468 for 3, England managed to lose this match too. They simply should not have declared at 551, but gone on until Australia had no sniff whatsoever. This would also have meant Warne and McGrath bowling more and more overs on a flat pitch, and even if England had not forced a victory there they would at least have had a toehold in the series.

Panesar had again been left out, meaning England only had Giles to back up their seamers as Australia themselves worked their way up past 500. In addition poor Giles had the cruel misfortune to drop Ponting on 35 at deep mid wicket, although it was not as straightforward a catch as some have since claimed. It was hit hard and flat and it came at Giles head-high as he came in off the boundary. And, as anyone who has played cricket knows, any catches at that height are difficult to take.

But it was a let-off for Ponting, and it would have been 78 for 4 if Giles had held it. As it was, Ponting went on to score 142 and with runs too from Michael Hussey, Michael Clarke and Adam Gilchrist, England had missed their greatest single opportunity to make scoreboard pressure count.

What happened in England's second innings, though, was the most depressing part of their slide to Ashes humiliation. Warne was in his pantomime dame mode, in his element as England panicked and he raised himself yet again to get in amongst things. Both theatrically and

## SECOND TEST – AUSTRALIA v. ENGLAND
1–5 December 2006 at Adelaide

### ENGLAND

| | First Innings | | Second Innings | |
|---|---|---|---|---|
| AJ Strauss | c Martyn b Clark | 14 | c Hussey b Warne | 34 |
| AN Cook | c Gilchrist b Clark | 27 | c Gilchrist b Clark | 9 |
| IR Bell | c & b Lee | 60 | run out | 26 |
| PD Collingwood | c Gilchrist b Clark | 206 | not out | 22 |
| KP Pietersen | run out | 158 | b Warne | 2 |
| A Flintoff (capt) | not out | 38 | c Gilchrist b Lee | 2 |
| *GO Jones | c Martyn b Warne | 1 | c Hayden b Lee | 10 |
| AF Giles | not out | 27 | c Hayden b Warne | 0 |
| MJ Hoggard | | | b Warne | 4 |
| SJ Harmison | | | lbw b McGrath | 8 |
| JM Anderson | | | lbw b McGrath | 1 |
| Extras | lb 10, w 2, nb 8 | 20 | b 3, lb 5, w 1, nb 2 | 11 |
| | (6 wkts dec 168 overs) | 551 | (all out 73 overs) | 129 |

| | First Innings | | | | Second Innings | | | |
|---|---|---|---|---|---|---|---|---|
| | O | M | R | W | O | M | R | W |
| Lee | 34 | 1 | 139 | 1 | 18 | 3 | 35 | 2 |
| McGrath | 30 | 5 | 107 | 0 | 10 | 6 | 15 | 2 |
| Clark | 34 | 6 | 75 | 3 | 13 | 4 | 22 | 1 |
| Warne | 53 | 9 | 167 | 1 | 32 | 12 | 49 | 4 |
| Clarke | 17 | 2 | 53 | 0 | - | - | - | - |

**Fall of Wickets**
1-32, 2-45, 3-158, 4-468, 5-489, 6-491
1-31, 2-69, 3-70, 4-73, 5-77, 6-94, 7-97, 8-105, 9-119

### AUSTRALIA

| | First Innings | | Second Innings | |
|---|---|---|---|---|
| JL Langer | c Pietersen b Flintoff | 4 | c Bell b Hoggard | 7 |
| ML Hayden | c Jones b Hoggard | 12 | c Collingwood b Flintoff | 18 |
| RT Ponting (capt) | c Jones b Hoggard | 142 | c Strauss b Giles | 49 |
| DR Martyn | c Bell b Hoggard | 11 | (5) c Strauss b Flintoff | 5 |
| MEK Hussey | b Hoggard | 91 | (4) not out | 61 |
| MJ Clarke | c Giles b Hoggard | 124 | not out | 21 |
| *AC Gilchrist | c Bell b Giles | 64 | | |
| SK Warne | lbw b Hoggard | 43 | | |
| B Lee | not out | 7 | | |
| SR Clark | b Hoggard | 0 | | |
| GD McGrath | c Jones b Anderson | 14 | b 2, lb 2, w 1, nb 2 | 7 |
| Extras | b 4, lb 2, w 1, nb 7 | 14 | | |
| | (all out 165.3 overs) | 513 | (4 wkts 32.5 overs) | 168 |

| | First Innings | | | | Second Innings | | | |
|---|---|---|---|---|---|---|---|---|
| | O | M | R | W | O | M | R | W |
| Hoggard | 42 | 6 | 109 | 7 | 4 | 0 | 29 | 1 |
| Flintoff | 26 | 5 | 82 | 1 | 9 | 0 | 44 | 2 |
| Harmison | 25 | 5 | 96 | 0 | 4 | 0 | 15 | 0 |
| Anderson | 21.3 | 3 | 85 | 1 | 3.5 | 0 | 23 | 0 |
| Giles | 42 | 7 | 103 | 1 | 10 | 0 | 46 | 1 |
| Pietersen | 9 | 0 | 32 | 0 | 2 | 0 | 7 | 0 |

**Fall of Wickets**
1-8, 2-35, 3-65, 4-257, 5-286, 6-384, 7-502, 8-505, 9-507
1-14, 2-33, 3-116, 4-121

Umpires: SA Bucknor (West Indies) & RE Koertzen (South Africa)
Toss: England
Man of the Match: RT Ponting

## Australia won by 6 wickets

Paul Collingwood led England's initially thrilling fightback at Adelaide with a Test-best 206, but it was all to turn to dust on a fateful final afternoon.

in terms of his skill, he was on top form, and successive England batsmen – most obviously Pietersen, Flintoff and Jones – played poor shots just when their country needed them to hang on grimly in partnership with Collingwood, who remained not out at the end when sickeningly he ran out of partners.

Even then, Australia had a reasonably tough run chase to go two-up, but you knew they would do it after the way England had slumped. How Collingwood and Pietersen must have felt at the end after their heroics with the bat, and Matthew Hoggard whose first-innings 7 for 109 on a seriously flat pitch was truly remarkable, doesn't bear thinking about.

I bumped into Duncan Fletcher at breakfast the next morning in the team hotel. He looked ashen. Duncan claimed he had wanted to play both spinners at Adelaide, but had bowed to Flintoff's wishes. That rather undermined his captain, I thought, but it was too late anyway. At 2-0 down, and the stuffing knocked right out of them, England were gone as Ashes contenders.

So, what about Flintoff as captain? Well, I supported that decision at the time, and I think it was generally accepted that his appointment was partly to make sure that England got the best out of his mate Harmison. The other players too, wanted to play for Freddie, as we saw in the one-day series that followed the Tests.

## THIRD TEST – AUSTRALIA v. ENGLAND
### 14–18 December 2006 at Perth

### AUSTRALIA

| | First Innings | | | Second Innings | | |
|---|---|---|---|---|---|---|
| JL Langer | b Panesar | 37 | | b Hoggard | 0 | |
| ML Hayden | c Jones b Hoggard | 24 | | c Collingwood b Panesar | 92 | |
| RT Ponting (capt) | lbw b Harmison | 2 | | c Jones b Harmison | 75 | |
| MEK Hussey | not out | 74 | | c Jones b Panesar | 103 | |
| MJ Clarke | c & b Harmison | 37 | | not out | 135 | |
| A Symonds | c Jones b Panesar | 26 | | c Collingwood b Panesar | 2 | |
| *AC Gilchrist | c Bell b Panesar | 0 | | not out | 102 | |
| SK Warne | c Jones b Panesar | 25 | | | | |
| B Lee | lbw b Panesar | 10 | | | | |
| SR Clark | b Harmison | 3 | | | | |
| GD McGrath | c Cook b Harmison | 1 | | | | |
| Extras | w 1, nb 4 | 5 | | lb 15, w 2, nb 1 | 18 | |
| | (all out 71 overs) | 244 | | (5 wkts dec 112 overs) | 527 | |

| | First Innings | | | | Second Innings | | | |
|---|---|---|---|---|---|---|---|---|
| | O | M | R | W | O | M | R | W |
| Hoggard | 12 | 2 | 40 | 1 | 20 | 4 | 85 | 1 |
| Flintoff | 9 | 2 | 36 | 0 | 19 | 2 | 76 | 0 |
| Harmison | 19 | 4 | 48 | 4 | 24 | 3 | 116 | 1 |
| Panesar | 24 | 4 | 92 | 5 | 34 | 3 | 145 | 3 |
| Mahmood | 7 | 2 | 28 | 0 | 10 | 0 | 59 | 0 |
| Pietersen | – | – | – | – | 5 | 1 | 31 | 0 |

**Fall of Wickets**
1-47, 2-54, 3-69, 4-121, 5-172, 6-172, 7-214, 8-234, 9-242
1-0, 2-144, 3-206, 4-357, 5-365

### ENGLAND

| | First Innings | | | Second Innings | | |
|---|---|---|---|---|---|---|
| AJ Strauss | c Gilchrist b Clark | 42 | | lbw b Lee | 0 | |
| AN Cook | c Langer b McGrath | 15 | | c Gilchrist b McGrath | 116 | |
| IR Bell | c Gilchrist b Lee | 0 | | c Langer b Warne | 87 | |
| PD Collingwood | c Hayden b McGrath | 11 | | c Gilchrist b Clark | 5 | |
| KP Pietersen | c Symonds b Lee | 70 | | not out | 60 | |
| A Flintoff (capt) | c Warne b Symonds | 13 | | (7) b Warne | 51 | |
| *GO Jones | c Langer b Symonds | 0 | | (8) run out | 0 | |
| SI Mahmood | c Gilchrist b Clark | 10 | | (9) lbw b Clark | 4 | |
| MJ Hoggard | c Hayden b Warne | 4 | | (6) b McGrath | 0 | |
| SJ Harmison | c Lee b Clark | 23 | | lbw b Warne | 0 | |
| MS Panesar | not out | 16 | | b Warne | 1 | |
| Extras | w 1, nb 10 | 11 | | b 11, lb 4, w 6, nb 5 | 26 | |
| | (all out 64.1 overs) | 215 | | (all out 122.2 overs) | 350 | |

| | First Innings | | | | Second Innings | | | |
|---|---|---|---|---|---|---|---|---|
| | O | M | R | W | O | M | R | W |
| Lee | 18 | 1 | 69 | 2 | 22 | 3 | 75 | 1 |
| McGrath | 18 | 5 | 48 | 2 | 27 | 9 | 61 | 2 |
| Clark | 15.1 | 3 | 49 | 3 | 25 | 7 | 56 | 2 |
| Warne | 9 | 0 | 41 | 1 | 39.2 | 6 | 115 | 4 |
| Symonds | 4 | 1 | 8 | 2 | 9 | 1 | 28 | 0 |

**Fall of Wickets**
1-36, 2-37, 3-55, 4-82, 5-107, 6-114, 7-128, 8-155, 9-175
1-0, 2-170, 3-185, 4-261, 5-261, 6-336, 7-336, 8-345, 9-346

Umpires: Aleem Dar (Pakistan) & RE Koertzen (South Africa)
Toss: Australia
Man of the Match: MEK Hussey

### Australia won by 206 runs

## FOURTH TEST – AUSTRALIA v. ENGLAND
### 26–28 December 2006 at Melbourne

### ENGLAND

| | First Innings | | | Second Innings | | |
|---|---|---|---|---|---|---|
| AJ Strauss | b Warne | 50 | | c Gilchrist b Lee | 31 | |
| AN Cook | c Gilchrist b Lee | 11 | | b Clark | 20 | |
| IR Bell | lbw b Clark | 7 | | lbw b McGrath | 2 | |
| PD Collingwood | c Ponting b Lee | 28 | | (5) c Langer b Lee | 16 | |
| KP Pietersen | c Symonds b Warne | 21 | | (4) b Clark | 1 | |
| A Flintoff (capt) | c Warne b Clark | 13 | | lbw b Clark | 25 | |
| *CMW Read | c Ponting b Warne | 3 | | not out | 26 | |
| SI Mahmood | c Gilchrist b McGrath | 0 | | lbw b Warne | 0 | |
| SJ Harmison | c Clarke b Warne | 7 | | lbw b Warne | 4 | |
| MS Panesar | c Symonds b Warne | 4 | | c Clarke b Lee | 14 | |
| MJ Hoggard | not out | 9 | | b Lee | 5 | |
| Extras | b 2, lb 1, nb 3 | 6 | | lb 12, w 1, nb 4 | 17 | |
| | (all out 74.2 overs) | 159 | | (all out 65.5 overs) | 161 | |

| | First Innings | | | | Second Innings | | | |
|---|---|---|---|---|---|---|---|---|
| | O | M | R | W | O | M | R | W |
| Lee | 13 | 4 | 36 | 2 | 18.5 | 6 | 47 | 4 |
| McGrath | 20 | 8 | 37 | 1 | 12 | 2 | 26 | 1 |
| Clark | 17 | 6 | 27 | 2 | 16 | 6 | 30 | 3 |
| Symonds | 7 | 2 | 17 | 0 | – | – | – | – |
| Warne | 17.2 | 4 | 39 | 5 | 19 | 3 | 46 | 2 |

**Fall of Wickets**
1-23, 2-44, 3-101, 4-101, 5-122, 6-135, 7-136, 8-145, 9-146
1-41, 2-48, 3-49, 4-75, 5-90, 6-108, 7-109, 8-127, 9-146

### AUSTRALIA

| | First Innings | | |
|---|---|---|---|
| JL Langer | c Read b Flintoff | 27 | |
| ML Hayden | c Read b Mahmood | 153 | |
| B Lee | c Read b Flintoff | 0 | |
| RT Ponting (capt) | c Cook b Flintoff | 7 | |
| MEK Hussey | b Hoggard | 6 | |
| MJ Clarke | c Read b Harmison | 5 | |
| A Symonds | c Read b Harmison | 156 | |
| *AC Gilchrist | c Collingwood b Mahmood | 1 | |
| SK Warne | not out | 40 | |
| SR Clark | c Read b Mahmood | 8 | |
| GD McGrath | c Bell b Mahmood | 0 | |
| Extras | lb 6, w 1, nb 9 | 16 | |
| | (all out 108.3 overs) | 419 | |

| | First Innings | | | |
|---|---|---|---|---|
| | O | M | R | W |
| Hoggard | 21 | 6 | 82 | 1 |
| Flintoff | 22 | 1 | 77 | 3 |
| Harmison | 28 | 6 | 69 | 2 |
| Mahmood | 21.3 | 1 | 100 | 4 |
| Panesar | 12 | 1 | 52 | 0 |
| Collingwood | 3 | 0 | 20 | 0 |
| Pietersen | 1 | 0 | 13 | 0 |

**Fall of Wickets**
1-44, 2-44, 3-62, 4-79, 5-84, 6-363, 7-365, 8-383, 9-417

Umpires: Aleem Dar (Pakistan) & RE Koertzen (South Africa)
Toss: England
Man of the Match: SK Warne

### Australia won by an innings and 99 runs

**Opposite** Glenn McGrath and Shane Warne, two true greats of the game, leave a Test match field for the final time together at Sydney... with Australia about to finish the Ashes series with their coveted 5-0 whitewash of England as revenge for 2005.

## FIFTH TEST – AUSTRALIA v. ENGLAND
2–5 January 2007 at Sydney

## SERIES AVERAGES
Australia v. England

### ENGLAND

| | First Innings | | Second Innings | |
|---|---|---|---|---|
| AJ Strauss | c Gilchrist b Lee | 29 | lbw b Clark | 24 |
| AN Cook | c Gilchrist b Clark | 20 | c Gilchrist b Lee | 4 |
| IR Bell | b McGrath | 71 | c Gilchrist b Lee | 28 |
| KP Pietersen | c Hussey b McGrath | 41 | c Gilchrist b McGrath | 29 |
| PD Collingwood | c Gilchrist b McGrath | 27 | c Hayden b Clark | 17 |
| A Flintoff (capt) | c Gilchrist b Clark | 89 | st Gilchrist b Warne | 7 |
| *CMW Read | c Gilchrist b Lee | 2 | (8) c Ponting b Lee | 4 |
| SI Mahmood | c Hayden b Lee | 0 | (9) b McGrath | 4 |
| SJ Harmison | lbw b Clark | 2 | (10) not out | 16 |
| MS Panesar | lbw b Warne | 0 | (7) run out | 0 |
| JM Anderson | not out | 0 | c Hussey b McGrath | 5 |
| Extras | lb 5, w 3, nb 2 | 10 | b 2, lb 3, w 1, nb 3 | 9 |
| | (all out 103.4 overs) | 291 | (all out 58 overs) | 147 |

| | First Innings | | | | Second Innings | | | |
|---|---|---|---|---|---|---|---|---|
| | O | M | R | W | O | M | R | W |
| McGrath | 29 | 8 | 67 | 3 | 21 | 11 | 38 | 3 |
| Lee | 22 | 5 | 75 | 3 | 14 | 5 | 39 | 3 |
| Clark | 24 | 6 | 62 | 3 | 12 | 4 | 29 | 2 |
| Warne | 22.4 | 1 | 69 | 1 | 6 | 1 | 23 | 1 |
| Symonds | 6 | 2 | 13 | 0 | 5 | 2 | 13 | 0 |

Fall of Wickets
1-45, 2-58, 3-166, 4-167, 5-245, 6-258, 7-258, 8-282, 9-291
1-5, 2-55, 3-64, 4-98, 5-113, 6-114, 7-114, 8-122, 9-123

### AUSTRALIA

| | First Innings | | Second Innings | |
|---|---|---|---|---|
| JL Langer | c Read b Anderson | 26 | not out | 20 |
| ML Hayden | c Collingwood b Harmison | 33 | not out | 23 |
| RT Ponting (capt) | run out | 45 | | |
| MEK Hussey | c Read b Anderson | 37 | | |
| MJ Clarke | c Read b Harmison | 11 | | |
| A Symonds | b Panesar | 48 | | |
| *AC Gilchrist | c Read b Anderson | 62 | | |
| SK Warne | st Read b Panesar | 71 | | |
| B Lee | c Read b Flintoff | 5 | | |
| SR Clark | c Pietersen b Mahmood | 35 | | |
| GD McGrath | not out | 0 | | |
| Extras | lb 10, w 4, nb 6 | 20 | lb 3 | 3 |
| | (all out 96.3 overs) | 393 | (0 wkts 10.5 overs) | 46 |

| | First Innings | | | | Second Innings | | | |
|---|---|---|---|---|---|---|---|---|
| | O | M | R | W | O | M | R | W |
| Flintoff | 17 | 2 | 56 | 1 | - | - | - | - |
| Anderson | 26 | 8 | 98 | 3 | 4 | 0 | 12 | 0 |
| Harmison | 23 | 5 | 80 | 2 | 5 | 1 | 13 | 0 |
| Mahmood | 11 | 1 | 59 | 1 | 1.5 | 0 | 18 | 0 |
| Panesar | 19.3 | 0 | 90 | 2 | - | - | - | - |

Fall of Wickets
1-34, 2-100, 3-118, 4-155, 5-190, 6-260, 7-318, 8-325, 9-393

Umpires: Aleem Dar (Pakistan) & BF Bowden (New Zealand)
Toss: England
Man of the Match: SR Clark
Man of the Series: RT Ponting

### AUSTRALIA

| Batting | M | Inns | NO | Runs | HS | Av | 100 | 50 | c/st |
|---|---|---|---|---|---|---|---|---|---|
| MEK Hussey | 5 | 7 | 2 | 458 | 103 | 91.60 | 1 | 4 | 5/- |
| RT Ponting | 5 | 8 | 1 | 576 | 196 | 82.28 | 2 | 2 | 4/- |
| MJ Clarke | 5 | 7 | 2 | 389 | 135* | 77.80 | 2 | 1 | 2/- |
| A Symonds | 3 | 4 | 0 | 232 | 156 | 58.00 | 1 | - | 3/- |
| ML Hayden | 5 | 9 | 1 | 413 | 153 | 51.62 | 1 | 1 | 7/- |
| SK Warne | 5 | 5 | 1 | 196 | 71 | 49.00 | - | 1 | 5/- |
| AC Gilchrist | 5 | 6 | 1 | 229 | 102* | 45.80 | 1 | 2 | 24/2 |
| JL Langer | 5 | 9 | 2 | 303 | 100* | 43.28 | 1 | 1 | 5/- |
| B Lee | 5 | 5 | 2 | 65 | 43* | 21.66 | - | - | 2/- |
| SR Clark | 5 | 5 | 0 | 85 | 39 | 17.00 | - | - | -/- |
| DR Martyn | 2 | 3 | 0 | 45 | 29 | 15.00 | - | - | 3/- |
| GD McGrath | 5 | 5 | 2 | 10 | 8* | 3.33 | - | - | -/- |

| Bowling | Overs | Mds | Runs | Wkts | Av | Best | 5/inn | 10m |
|---|---|---|---|---|---|---|---|---|
| SR Clark | 194.2 | 53 | 443 | 26 | 17.03 | 4-72 | - | - |
| GD McGrath | 209.1 | 65 | 502 | 21 | 23.90 | 6-50 | 1 | - |
| SK Warne | 241.2 | 44 | 698 | 23 | 30.34 | 5-39 | 1 | - |
| B Lee | 196.5 | 32 | 664 | 20 | 33.20 | 4-47 | - | - |
| A Symonds | 31 | 8 | 79 | 2 | 39.50 | 2-8 | - | - |

Also bowled: MEK Hussey 1-0-5-0, MJ Clarke 17-2-53-0.

### ENGLAND

| Batting | M | Inns | NO | Runs | HS | Av | 100 | 50 | c/st |
|---|---|---|---|---|---|---|---|---|---|
| KP Pietersen | 5 | 10 | 1 | 490 | 158 | 54.44 | 1 | 3 | 3/- |
| PD Collingwood | 5 | 10 | 1 | 433 | 206 | 48.11 | 1 | 1 | 7/- |
| IR Bell | 5 | 10 | 0 | 331 | 87 | 33.10 | - | 4 | 5/- |
| A Flintoff | 5 | 10 | 1 | 254 | 89 | 28.22 | - | 2 | -/- |
| AN Cook | 5 | 10 | 0 | 276 | 116 | 27.60 | 1 | - | 2/- |
| AJ Strauss | 5 | 10 | 0 | 247 | 50 | 24.70 | - | 1 | 3/- |
| AF Giles | 2 | 4 | 1 | 74 | 27* | 24.66 | - | - | 1/- |
| CMW Read | 2 | 4 | 1 | 35 | 26* | 11.66 | - | - | 11/1 |
| GO Jones | 3 | 6 | 0 | 63 | 33 | 10.50 | - | - | 9/- |
| SJ Harmison | 5 | 9 | 1 | 73 | 23 | 9.12 | - | - | 1/- |
| MS Panesar | 3 | 6 | 1 | 35 | 16* | 7.00 | - | - | -/- |
| JM Anderson | 3 | 5 | 3 | 12 | 5 | 6.00 | - | - | -/- |
| MJ Hoggard | 4 | 7 | 1 | 30 | 9* | 5.00 | - | - | -/- |
| SI Mahmood | 3 | 6 | 0 | 18 | 10 | 3.00 | - | - | -/- |

| Bowling | Overs | Mds | Runs | Wkts | Av | Best | 5/inn | 10m |
|---|---|---|---|---|---|---|---|---|
| MJ Hoggard | 141 | 25 | 486 | 13 | 37.38 | 7-109 | 1 | - |
| MS Panesar | 89.3 | 8 | 379 | 10 | 37.90 | 5-92 | 1 | - |
| A Flintoff | 137 | 18 | 481 | 11 | 43.72 | 4-99 | - | - |
| SI Mahmood | 51.2 | 4 | 264 | 5 | 52.80 | 4-100 | - | - |
| SJ Harmison | 170.1 | 29 | 614 | 10 | 61.40 | 4-48 | - | - |
| JM Anderson | 93.2 | 18 | 413 | 5 | 82.60 | 3-98 | - | - |
| AF Giles | 82 | 9 | 262 | 3 | 87.33 | 1-46 | - | - |

Also bowled: IR Bell 1-0-12-0, PD Collingwood 3-0-20-0, KP Pietersen 29-2-125-0.

## Australia won by 10 wickets

England might have gone with Andrew Strauss, but his problems at the top of the order probably made it a good thing that they didn't.

The bottom line, as I see it, was that England were not well prepared – for all Fletcher's cries to the contrary – and they put in some absolutely wretched performances at Brisbane, and in the second innings at Adelaide, to lose the Ashes almost before they had started. Australia were superb, but England brought a lot of it upon themselves.

After a false dawn in Australia's first innings at Perth, and some worthy resistance from Cook and the much-improved Ian Bell in England's second innings, it was 3-0. Then came a horrible, bleak experience in the unseasonal cold at Melbourne in the Fourth Test, which lasted all of three days as Australia won by an innings and Warne said his triumphant farewell to his home ground.

But, in a way, I was glad that England were beaten again at the MCG, because it at least made the final Test at Sydney a little bit more interesting. Sure, McGrath and Warne were now saying their farewells to Test cricket, which made the occasion a real bittersweet one, but over and above all that, could Australia win 5-0?

They could, and it was a sensational achievement. Warne even scored 71 as well, as Australia completed a ten-wicket victory that said everything about their superiority. It was hugely fitting for McGrath and Warne to leave the Test stage with an Ashes whitewash to savour, but what will the quality of Australia's bowling be by 2009? On that could hang the next Ashes tale... if England get their act together next time.

## COMMONWEALTH BANK SERIES

The one-day series that followed the disastrous Test series turned out to be Duncan Fletcher's last success as England coach, and a fine achievement it was to beat both Australia and New Zealand after all the grief and pain of the Ashes thrashing.

Andrew Flintoff also deserves praise for the way he led and inspired the side, while Paul Collingwood once

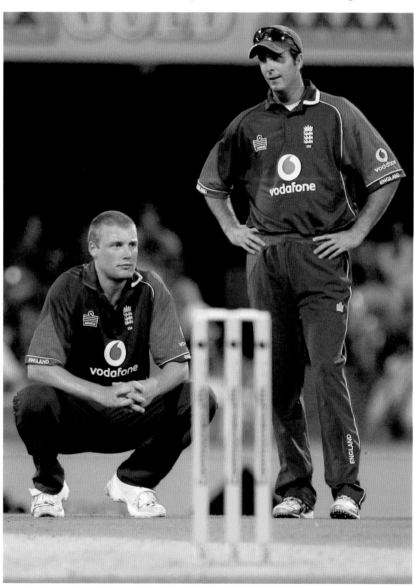

England's two captains in the Commonwealth Bank Series, Andrew Flintoff and Michael Vaughan, pictured at the Gabba during the fourth match.

again showed he could step up a level when it was least expected. Following his magnificent double-hundred in the Adelaide Test, the first by an England batsman in Australia since Wally Hammond 70 years earlier, Collingwood had somewhat fallen away.

But after a poor start to the one-day series, he ended it by hitting successive scores of 106, 120 not out and 70. His first century came as England first qualified for the final by beating New Zealand at Brisbane. His other big scores helping England to see off Australia by four wickets and 34 runs (on the Duckworth-Lewis calculations) in Melbourne and Sydney respectively to lift the CB trophy by a 2-0 margin.

Jimmy Anderson and Liam Plunkett also made some significant contributions with the ball, while Flintoff and Monty Panesar always commanded respect in the field and Collingwood's all-round abilities shone out brightly.

At the World Cup, however, which came hard on the heels of the Ashes winter Down Under, it was again Australia and not England who made the impression when it mattered most.

**Match One**
12 January 2007 Day/Night at Melbourne (MCG)
**England** 242 for 8 (50 overs) (KP Pietersen 82)
**Australia** 246 for 2 (45.2 overs) (RT Ponting 82*, AC Gilchrist 60, MJ Clarke 57*)
*Australia won by 8 wickets*

**Match Two**
14 January 2007 at Hobart
**Australia** 289 for 8 (50 overs) (A Symonds 69, AC Gilchrist 61, SE Bond 4 for 61)
**New Zealand** 184 all out (38.3 overs) (RL Taylor 84)
*Australia won by 105 runs*

**Match Three**
16 January 2007 at Hobart
**New Zealand** 205 for 9 (50 overs) (JM Anderson 4 for 42)
**England** 206 for 7 (49.5 overs) (A Flintoff 72*)
*England won by 3 wickets*

**Match Four**
19 January 2007 Day/Night at Brisbane
**England** 155 all out (42 overs)
**Australia** 156 for 6 (38.4 overs) (J Lewis 4 for 36)
*Australia won by 4 wickets*

**Match Five**
21 January 2007 Day/Night at Sydney
**New Zealand** 218 all out (47.4 overs) (CD McMillan 89, SR Clark 4 for 54)

**Australia** 224 for 8 (48.4 overs) (MJ Clarke 75, MEK Hussey 65*)
*Australia won by 2 wickets*

**Match Six**
23 January 2007 Day/Night at Adelaide
**New Zealand** 210 all out (50 overs) (JDP Oram 86, A Flintoff 4 for 21)
**England** 120 (37.5 overs) (DL Vettori 4 for 24)
*New Zealand won by 90 runs*

**Match Seven**
26 January 2007 Day/Night at Adelaide
**England** 110 all out (34.3 overs) (MG Johnson 4 for 45)
**Australia** 111 for 1 (24.3 overs) (RT Ponting 51*)
*Australia won by 9 wickets*

**Match Eight**
28 January 2007 Day/Night at Perth
**Australia** 343 for 5 (50 overs) (ML Hayden 117, RT Ponting 111)
**New Zealand** 335 for 5 (50 overs) (JDP Oram 101*, L Vincent 66)
*Australia won by 8 runs*

**Match Nine**
30 January 2007 Day/Night at Perth
**New Zealand** 318 for 7 (50 overs) (L Vincent 76, RL Taylor 71, JDP Oram 54*)
**England** 260 for 8 (50 overs) (EC Joyce 66)
*New Zealand won by 58 runs*

**Match Ten**
2 February 2007 Day/Night at Sydney
**England** 292 for 7 (50 overs) (EC Joyce 107, IR Bell 51)
**Australia** 200 for 9 (38.5 overs) (ML Hayden 51)
*England won by 92 runs*

**Match Eleven**
4 February 2007 Day/Night at Melbourne (MCG)
**New Zealand** 290 for 7 (50 overs) (L Vincent 90, PG Fulton 60)
**Australia** 291 for 5 (48.2 overs) (RT Ponting 104, BJ Hodge 99*)
*Australia won by 5 wickets*

**Match Twelve**
6 February 2007 Day/Night at Brisbane
**England** 270 for 7 (50 overs) (PD Collingwood 106, AJ Strauss 55, SE Bond 4 for 46)
**New Zealand** 256 for 8 (50 overs) (SP Fleming 106)
*England won by 14 runs*

## Points Table

| | P | W | L | T | NR | RR | Pts |
|---|---|---|---|---|---|---|---|
| Australia | 8 | 7 | 1 | 0 | 0 | 0.67 | 31 |
| England | 8 | 3 | 5 | 0 | 0 | -0.61 | 13 |
| New Zealand | 8 | 2 | 6 | 0 | 0 | -0.01 | 9 |

## First Final

9 February 2007 at Melbourne (MCG)
**Australia** 252 all out (48.3 overs) (ML Hayden 82, RT Ponting 75)
**England** 253 for 6 (49.3 overs) (PD Collingwood 120*, IR Bell 65)
*England won by 4 wickets*

## Second Final

11 February 2007 Day/Night at Sydney
**England** 246 for 8 (50 overs) (PD Collingwood 70)
**Australia** 152 for 8 (27 overs)
*England won by 34 runs – DL Method: target 187 from 27 overs*

## TWENTY20 INTERNATIONAL

9 January 2007 Day/Night at Sydney
**Australia** 221 for 5 (20 overs)
**England** 144 for 9 (20 overs)
*Australia won by 77 runs*

Andrew Flintoff is surrounded by delighted England players after dismissing Australian batsman Michael Hussey during the Commonwealth Bank Series second final at Sydney.

## AUSTRALIA REPORT
### by Jim Maxwell

Australia's emphatic win in the 2006 Champions Trophy final flagged a momentum that turned Ricky Ponting's team into a juggernaut. It was no surprise, six months or so later, when Australia produced another powerful performance to win a record third consecutive World Cup.

Ponting's peerless batting reinforced his confidence and authority in charge of a team he described as 'the best one-day team I have ever played in', prior to their decisive win over Sri Lanka in the World Cup final itself.

Like his predecessors Steve Waugh, Mark Taylor and Allan Border, however, Ponting has relied on the supreme wicket-taking skills of Shane Warne and Glenn McGrath.

However, it is also important to appreciate how well Australia have played without Warne in the limited-overs arena in more recent times. The sense of a committed team ethic has been overwhelming in the last two World Cup campaigns. The numbers are emphatic: 21 matches, 21 wins.

Australia's depth and resilience have been tested, too, first in overcoming Warne's absence and then with regards to Brett Lee's withdrawal through injury in the 2007 tournament. Matthew Hayden's remarkable return to form inspired the batting, while Brad Hogg and Nathan Bracken expertly supported McGrath's gleaming valedictory tour.

The top order was so commanding, indeed, that Mike Hussey, who had been rated number one in the rankings before the World Cup, was a supernumerary. Adam Gilchrist showed why he has been the most destructive wicketkeeper-batsman of all time with his astonishing, match-winning century in the final. McGrath, meanwhile, capped off his memorable career with a Man of the Series award, demonstrating that experience can outwit and outsmart those that dare to underestimate a veteran's composure.

His ambition to finish with 1,000 international wickets is 51 shy of the target, but post-retirement forays into the frolic of Twenty20 cricket as a superannuated star could still tip him over the mark.

Overcoming injuries and coping with his wife's serious illness, McGrath has played out the twilight years with distinction, determined to finish on his terms. Has there ever been a better length bowler than this raw-boned country kid, who switched from basketball to cricket and became the scourge of opening batsmen?

For the record, McGrath and Warne combined for 70 Test victories. Statistically, McGrath marginally bettered his illustrious spin-bowling partner, playing in 84 winning teams over 124 Tests, against Warne's 92 from 145.

Warne, *Wisden*'s Cricketer of the Century, was a freak. He mastered the skill of wrist spin bowling, combining remarkable control with mesmerising variations. His

Ricky Ponting takes more runs off England during the World Cup in the Caribbean.

competitive personality also meant he was always threatening batsmen, chiding and tempting, then bamboozling them with a huge leg break or the deadly skidding flipper.

Prior to his shoulder injury in 1996, he bowled an explosive variety of deliveries, none better than the flipper that wrecked Alec Stewart's stumps at the Gabba in the 1994–95 Ashes series. Warne's mental strength sustained him over the last decade, and he would have retired in 2005 had his magnificent bowling retained the Ashes.

The expression 'he's in' drew thousands of fans to watch the legendary Don Bradman bat, and Warne's unique talent excited the same response, providing hours of phenomenal entertainment and artistry, drawing new audiences to the game.

Justin Langer (left), Glenn McGrath and Shane Warne pose with their children for the world's cameras after marking their retirements from Test cricket. Australia had just won the final Ashes Test at the Sydney Cricket Ground that gave Australia a 5-0 whitewash of England.

His exceptional control strangled England in the 2006–07 Ashes series, highlighted by a fifth-day demolition of England's batting in Adelaide and then the finale in front of a home crowd at the MCG, where he bowled Andrew Strauss to claim his 700th Test wicket.

Rival teams, though, must be hoping that Australia will become more vulnerable following the retirements of these two bowling linchpins, Warne and McGrath.

Stuart MacGill will at last get the chance to parade his talent more regularly, adding to his 198 Test wickets taken at a better strike rate than Warne. And, although there is a dearth of spin successors behind the 36-year-old MacGill, there should be enough pace and swing to be imposing.

Stuart Clark's accurate attack was prominent in Australia's regaining of the Ashes. Alongside the experienced Brett Lee, the emerging abilities of Mitchell Johnson, Ben Hilfenhaus and the raw speed of Shaun Tait, mean there is currently plenty of fast bowling ammunition.

Justin Langer, recast as an opener in 2001, also ended his distinguished career in the fifth Ashes Test at Sydney. His combination with Hayden created one of the most productive partnerships in Test history, and Langer's determination is the model for all aspiring Test cricketers.

One of his mentors, the departing coach John Buchanan, was regaled as a great visionary. Under his charge Australia racked up 69 wins in 90 Tests, plus a swag of World Cups and one-day trophies. Buchanan expanded the support structure for the team, another factor that contributed to their outstanding Caribbean campaign.

Australia's only hiccup occurred at the end of home Tri-Series, when their dominant form evaporated in a shock loss to England in the finals. New Zealand then won the Chappell/Hadlee Trophy by a 3-0 margin, with Mike Hussey leading a team weakened by the absence of Ponting and Gilchrist.

Managing the workload for key personnel has become a major issue for this powerful team, and the busy schedule over the next two years must incorporate a resting policy to avoid burn-out.

# BANGLADESH

In a year in which tangible progress was made in the one-day international arena, Bangladesh claimed the major World Cup scalps of India and South Africa and also sent West Indies packing by six wickets during the ICC World Twenty20 tournament.

Mohammad Ashraful, the prodigiously talented 22-year-old batsman, succeeded to the captaincy in June 2007 and several other promising young cricketers made significant strides forward in world terms.

Ashraful's appointment was greeted excitedly by Bangladeshis who see him as the man to take their national side to the next level. He was still a day short of his 17th birthday when he made an astonishing century on Test debut, against Sri Lanka, in September 2001, and he went into the captaincy with the experience of 35 Tests and 101 ODIs despite his tender years.

Habibul Bashar, the previous captain, did a fine job for his country but it is the likes of Ashraful, fast bowlers Mashrafe bin Mortaza and Syed Rasel, wicketkeeper Mushfiqur Rahim, left-arm spinner Enamul Haque junior and opening batsmen Tamim Iqbal and Shahriar Nafees who represent the future.

Bangladesh, however, remain inconsistent. Outside of their World Cup and World Twenty20 exploits, they only had ODI series wins against Zimbabwe and Scotland to shout about. India visited and defeated them 1-0 in a two-match Test series and 2-0 in ODIs, while a tour of Sri Lanka ended with an emphatic 3-0 beating in the Tests and another 3-0 reversal in the ODI series which followed.

There was also an unexpected defeat against Ireland in the Super Eight stage of the World Cup, which was as dispiriting as the group win against India and the later victory against South Africa in Guyana, in which Ashraful scored a brilliant 87, were thrilling.

Former Zimbabwe captain and coach David Houghton, meanwhile, turned down the opportunity to succeed Dav Whatmore as head coach, and Bangladesh were in danger of drifting during the lengthy void which followed Whatmore's departure after the World Cup.

The year also contained the sad death in a road accident, at the age of just 22, of slow left-arm spinner Manjural Islam.

Bangladesh captain Mohammad Ashraful dives for the crease during his side's memorable ICC World Twenty20 win against the West Indies.

## TWENTY20 INTERNATIONAL

28 November 2006 at Khulna
**Bangladesh** 166 all out (19.5 overs)
**Zimbabwe** 123 for 9 (20 overs)
*Bangladesh won by 43 runs*

## ONE–DAY INTERNATIONALS
## v. Zimbabwe

**Match One**
30 November 2006 at Khulna
**Zimbabwe** 184 for 9 (50 overs)
(Abdur Razzak 4 for 33)
**Bangladesh** 186 for 1 (45.3 overs)
(Shahriar Nafees 105*, Aftab Ahmed 60*)
*Bangladesh won by 9 wickets*

**Match Two**
3 December 2006 Day/Night at Bogra
**Zimbabwe** 217 for 7 (50 overs) (SC Williams 61)
**Bangladesh** 218 for 4 (42.4 overs)
(Shahriar Nafees 67, Mehrab Hossain jnr 54)
*Bangladesh won by 6 wickets*

## Match Three

5 December 2006 Day/Night at Bogra
**Bangladesh** 220 all out (49.2 overs) (CB Mpofu 4 for 42)
**Zimbabwe** 194 all out (49 overs) (SC Williams 68, Abdur Razzak 5 for 33)
*Bangladesh won by 26 runs*

## Match Four

8 December 2006 at Mirpur
**Zimbabwe** 146 all out (47.2 overs)
**Bangladesh** 147 for 2 (32.2 overs) (Aftab Ahmed 58*)
*Bangladesh won by 8 wickets*

## Match Five

9 December 2006 at Mirpur
**Zimbabwe** 193 for 8 (50 overs) (S Matsikenyeri 75)
**Bangladesh** 194 for 7 (49 overs) (GB Brent 4 for 22)
*Bangladesh won by 3 wickets*
**Bangladesh won the series 5–0**

# ONE-DAY INTERNATIONALS v. Scotland

## Match One

15 December 2006 at Chittagong
**Scotland** 153 all out (45.1 overs)
**Bangladesh** 154 for 4 (29.1 overs) (Aftab Ahmed 66)
*Bangladesh won by 6 wickets*

## Match Two

17 December 2006 at Mirpur
**Bangladesh** 278 for 6 (50 overs) (Aftab Ahmed 52,
Mashrafe bin Mortaza 51*)
**Scotland** 132 all out (41.3 overs) (Abdur Razzak 4 for 23)
*Bangladesh won by 146 runs*
**Bangladesh won the series 2–0**

# ONE-DAY INTERNATIONALS v. India

## Match One

10 May 2007 at Dhaka
**Bangladesh** 250 for 7 (47 overs) (Javed Omar 80, Shakib Al Hasan 50)
**India** 251 for 5 (46 overs) (MS Dhoni 91*, KD Karthik 58*)
*India won by 5 wickets*

## Match Two

12 May 2007 at Dhaka
**India** 284 for 8 (49 overs) (G Gambhir 101)
**Bangladesh** 238 for 9 (49 overs)
*India won by 46 runs*

## Match Three

14 May 2007 at Chittagong
*Match abandoned – no result*
**India won the series 2–0**

---

## FIRST TEST – BANGLADESH v. INDIA
### 18–22 May 2007 at Chittagong

### INDIA

| | First Innings | | Second Innings | |
|---|---|---|---|---|
| W Jaffer | b Mashrafe bin Mortaza | 0 | c Habibul Bashar b S Hossain | 0 |
| KD Karthik | c M Ashraful b M bin Mortaza | 56 | c Nafees b M bin Mortaza | 22 |
| R Dravid (capt) | c Khaled Mashud b S Hossain | 61 | c Rajin Saleh b Shahadat Hossain | 2 |
| SR Tendulkar | c M Ashraful b Shahadat Hossain | 101 | b Mohammad Rafique | 31 |
| SC Ganguly | c M Rafique b M bin Mortaza | 100 | c Nafees b Mohammad Rafique | 13 |
| *MS Dhoni | c Javed Omar b M bin Mortaza | 36 | not out | 17 |
| RR Powar | b Mohammad Rafique | 7 | st Khaled Mashud b M Rafique | 6 |
| A Kumble | retired hurt | 1 | | |
| Z Khan | c Khaled Mashud b S Hossain | 0 | (8) not out | 2 |
| VR Singh | not out | 1 | | |
| RP Singh | | | | |
| Extras | b 1, lb 9, w 2, nb 12 | 24 | lb 1, w 2, nb 4 | 7 |
| | (8 wkts dec 98.5 overs) | 387 | (6 wkts dec 24 overs) | 100 |

| | First Innings | | | | Second Innings | | | |
|---|---|---|---|---|---|---|---|---|
| | O | M | R | W | O | M | R | W |
| Mashrafe bin Mortaza | 24.5 | 5 | 97 | 4 | 8 | 1 | 36 | 1 |
| Shahadat Hossain | 18 | 1 | 76 | 3 | 7 | 3 | 30 | 2 |
| Mohammad Rafique | 24 | 3 | 99 | 1 | 8 | 0 | 27 | 3 |
| Enamul Haque jnr | 15 | 0 | 59 | 0 | 1 | 0 | 6 | 0 |
| Shakib Al Hasan | 13 | 2 | 29 | 0 | - | - | - | - |
| Mohammad Ashraful | 1 | 0 | 5 | 0 | - | - | - | - |
| Rajin Saleh | 3 | 1 | 12 | 0 | - | - | - | - |

**Fall of Wickets**
1-0, 2-124, 3-132, 4-321, 5-366, 6-381, 7-384, 8-387
1-0, 2-6, 3-60, 4-64, 5-78, 6-93

### BANGLADESH

| | First Innings | | Second Innings | |
|---|---|---|---|---|
| Javed Omar | lbw b Singh RP | 7 | not out | 52 |
| Shahriar Nafees | c Tendulkar b Khan | 32 | c Dhoni b Singh RP | 1 |
| Habibul Bashar (capt) | c Tendulkar b Singh RP | 0 | c Singh RP b Powar | 37 |
| Rajin Saleh | c Ganguly b Powar | 41 | not out | 7 |
| Mohammad Ashraful | c Karthik b Singh RP | 5 | | |
| Shakib Al Hasan | b Singh VR | 27 | | |
| *Khaled Mashud | lbw b Singh VR | 2 | | |
| Mashrafe bin Mortaza | b Singh VR | 79 | | |
| Mohammad Rafique | st Dhoni b Powar | 9 | | |
| Shahadat Hossain | b Tendulkar | 31 | | |
| Enamul Haque jnr | not out | 0 | | |
| Extras | lb 1, w 3, nb 1 | 5 | lb 6, nb 1 | 7 |
| | (all out 68.2 overs) | 238 | (2 wkts 28 overs) | 104 |

| | First Innings | | | | Second Innings | | | |
|---|---|---|---|---|---|---|---|---|
| | O | M | R | W | O | M | R | W |
| Khan | 15 | 1 | 63 | 1 | 7 | 0 | 24 | 0 |
| Singh RP | 17 | 2 | 45 | 3 | 6 | 0 | 29 | 1 |
| Singh VR | 15.2 | 5 | 48 | 3 | 5 | 1 | 22 | 0 |
| Powar | 17 | 1 | 66 | 2 | 7 | 2 | 16 | 1 |
| Tendulkar | 4 | 0 | 15 | 1 | 3 | 0 | 7 | 0 |

**Fall of Wickets**
1-20, 2-20, 3-47, 4-58, 5-114, 6-116, 7-122, 8-149, 9-226
1-12, 2-82

Umpires: BR Doctrove (West Indies) & DJ Harper (Australia)
Toss: India
Test debuts: Shakib Al Hasan, RR Powar
Man of the Match: Mashrafe bin Mortaza

## Match drawn

## SECOND TEST – BANGLADESH v. INDIA
### 25–27 May 2007 at Dhaka

### INDIA

| | First Innings | |
|---|---|---|
| KD Karthik | c H Bashar b M bin Mortaza | 129 |
| W Jaffer | retired hurt | 138 |
| R Dravid (capt) | c Javed Omar b M Rafique | 129 |
| SR Tendulkar | not out | 122 |
| SC Ganguly | c Khaled Mashud b M Rafique | 15 |
| *MS Dhoni | not out | 51 |
| RR Powar | | |
| Z Khan | | |
| A Kumble | | |
| RP Singh | | |
| I Sharma | | |
| Extras | b 7, lb 7, w 5, nb 7 | 26 |
| | (3 wkts dec 153 overs) | **610** |

| | First Innings | | |
|---|---|---|---|
| | O | M | R | W |
| Mashrafe bin Mortaza | 31.4 | 4 | 100 | 1 |
| Syed Rasel | 23.4 | 0 | 109 | 0 |
| Mohammad Sharif | 25.4 | 2 | 109 | 0 |
| Mohammad Rafique | 45 | 4 | 181 | 2 |
| Shakib Al Hasan | 19 | 1 | 62 | 0 |
| Mohammad Ashraful | 8 | 0 | 35 | 0 |

**Fall of Wickets**
1-408, 2-493, 3-525

### BANGLADESH

| | First Innings | | Second Innings (following on) | |
|---|---|---|---|---|
| Javed Omar | c Karthik b Khan | 0 | c Dhoni b Khan | 0 |
| Shahriar Nafees | b Khan | 2 | c Dhoni b Singh | 4 |
| Habibul Bashar (capt) | c Dhoni b Singh | 4 | c Dravid b Khan | 5 |
| Rajin Saleh | c Jaffer b Kumble | 20 | c Ganguly b Powar | 42 |
| Mohammad Ashraful | lbw b Khan | 0 | c Tendulkar b Kumble | 67 |
| Shakib Al Hasan | lbw b Khan | 30 | c Dravid b Powar | 15 |
| Mohammad Sharif | lbw b Kumble | 13 | (9) c & b Kumble | 17 |
| *Khaled Mashud | c Dhoni b Kumble | 25 | (7) c Tendulkar b Powar | 8 |
| Mashrafe bin Mortaza | c Kumble b Sharma | 2 | (8) c Dhoni b Tendulkar | 70 |
| Mohammad Rafique | b Khan | 12 | lbw b Tendulkar | 11 |
| Syed Rasel | not out | 2 | not out | 1 |
| Extras | lb 2, nb 6 | 8 | lb 1, w 3, nb 9 | 13 |
| | (all out 37.2 overs) | **118** | (all out 57.3 overs) | **253** |

| | First Innings | | | | Second Innings | | | |
|---|---|---|---|---|---|---|---|---|
| | O | M | R | W | O | M | R | W |
| Khan | 10 | 1 | 34 | 5 | 8 | 1 | 54 | 2 |
| Singh | 9 | 2 | 28 | 1 | 6 | 2 | 28 | 1 |
| Kumble | 9.2 | 3 | 32 | 3 | 15 | 1 | 72 | 2 |
| Sharma | 7 | 1 | 19 | 1 | 6 | 1 | 30 | 0 |
| Powar | 2 | 1 | 3 | 0 | 16 | 4 | 33 | 3 |
| Tendulkar | - | - | - | - | 6.3 | 1 | 35 | 2 |

**Fall of Wickets**
1-0, 2-5, 3-7, 4-7, 5-40, 6-58, 7-85, 8-93, 9-110
1-0, 2-10, 3-10, 4-91, 5-135, 6-148, 7-152, 8-206, 9-221

Umpires: BR Doctrove (West Indies) & DJ Harper (Australia)
Toss: Bangladesh
Test debut: I Sharma
Man of the Match: Z Khan
Man of the Series: SR Tendulkar

## India won by an innings and 239 runs

## SERIES AVERAGES
### Bangladesh v. India

### BANGLADESH

| Batting | M | Inns | NO | Runs | HS | Av | 100 | 50 | c/st |
|---|---|---|---|---|---|---|---|---|---|
| Mashrafe bin Mortaza | 2 | 3 | 0 | 151 | 79 | 50.33 | - | 2 | -/- |
| Rajin Saleh | 2 | 4 | 1 | 110 | 42 | 36.66 | - | - | 1/- |
| Shahadat Hossain | 1 | 1 | 0 | 31 | 31 | 31.00 | - | - | -/- |
| Mohammad Ashraful | 2 | 3 | 0 | 72 | 67 | 24.00 | - | 1 | 2/- |
| Shakib Al Hasan | 2 | 3 | 0 | 72 | 30 | 24.00 | - | - | -/- |
| Javed Omar | 2 | 4 | 1 | 59 | 52* | 19.66 | - | 1 | 2/- |
| Mohammad Sharif | 1 | 2 | 0 | 30 | 17 | 15.00 | - | - | -/- |
| Khaled Mashud | 2 | 3 | 0 | 35 | 25 | 11.66 | - | - | 3/1 |
| Habibul Bashar | 2 | 4 | 0 | 46 | 37 | 11.50 | - | - | 2/- |
| Mohammad Rafique | 2 | 3 | 0 | 32 | 12 | 10.66 | - | - | 1/- |
| Shahriar Nafees | 2 | 4 | 0 | 39 | 32 | 9.75 | - | - | 2/- |
| Syed Rasel | 1 | 2 | 2 | 3 | 2* | - | - | - | -/- |
| Enamul Haque jnr | 1 | 1 | 1 | 0 | 0* | - | - | - | -/- |

| Bowling | Overs | Mds | Runs | Wkts | Av | Best | 5/inn | 10m |
|---|---|---|---|---|---|---|---|---|
| Shahadat Hossain | 25 | 4 | 106 | 5 | 21.20 | 3-76 | - | - |
| Mashrafe bin Mortaza | 64.3 | 10 | 233 | 6 | 38.83 | 4-97 | - | - |
| Mohammad Rafique | 77 | 7 | 307 | 6 | 51.16 | 3-27 | - | - |

Also bowled: Rajin Saleh 3-1-12-0, Mohammad Ashraful 9-0-40-0, Enamul Haque jnr 16-0-65-0, Shakib Al Hasan 32-3-91-0, Mohammad Sharif 25.4-2-109-0, Syed Rasel 23.4-0-109-0.

### INDIA

| Batting | M | Inns | NO | Runs | HS | Av | 100 | 50 | c/st |
|---|---|---|---|---|---|---|---|---|---|
| SR Tendulkar | 2 | 3 | 1 | 254 | 122* | 127.00 | 2 | - | 4/- |
| MS Dhoni | 2 | 3 | 2 | 104 | 51* | 104.00 | - | 1 | 6/1 |
| W Jaffer | 2 | 3 | 1 | 138 | 138* | 69.00 | 1 | - | 1/- |
| KD Karthik | 2 | 3 | 0 | 207 | 129 | 69.00 | 1 | 1 | 2/- |
| R Dravid | 2 | 3 | 0 | 192 | 129 | 64.00 | 1 | 1 | 2/- |
| SC Ganguly | 2 | 3 | 0 | 128 | 100 | 42.66 | 1 | - | 2/- |
| RR Powar | 2 | 2 | 0 | 13 | 7 | 6.50 | - | - | -/- |
| Z Khan | 2 | 2 | 1 | 2 | 2* | 2.00 | - | - | -/- |
| A Kumble | 2 | 1 | 1 | 1 | 1* | - | - | - | 2/- |
| VR Singh | 1 | 1 | 1 | 1 | 1* | - | - | - | -/- |
| RP Singh | 2 | 0 | 0 | 0 | 0 | - | - | - | 1/- |
| I Sharma | 1 | 0 | 0 | 0 | 0 | - | - | - | -/- |

| Bowling | Overs | Mds | Runs | Wkts | Av | Best | 5/inn | 10m |
|---|---|---|---|---|---|---|---|---|
| SR Tendulkar | 13.3 | 1 | 57 | 3 | 19.00 | 2-35 | - | - |
| RR Powar | 42 | 8 | 118 | 6 | 19.66 | 3-33 | - | - |
| A Kumble | 24.2 | 4 | 104 | 5 | 20.80 | 3-32 | - | - |
| RP Singh | 38 | 6 | 130 | 6 | 21.66 | 3-45 | - | - |
| Z Khan | 40 | 3 | 175 | 8 | 21.87 | 5-34 | 1 | - |
| VR Singh | 20.2 | 6 | 70 | 3 | 23.33 | 3-48 | - | - |
| I Sharma | 13 | 2 | 49 | 1 | 49.00 | 1-19 | - | - |

# INDIA

### by Gulu Ezekiel

Even by the roller-coaster standards of Indian cricket, nothing could match the crazy swing in fortunes witnessed in the six-month period between the World Cup in the West Indies and the inaugural ICC World Twenty20 in South Africa.

In the opening week of the World Cup, India were stunned by Bangladesh, then crushed Bermuda and were finally outplayed by Sri Lanka. It meant that the 2003 runners-up were eliminated at the first stage and it appeared as if the whole nation had erupted in fury.

Indian cricketers – used to being feted like movie stars – were now running for cover. Protests broke out on the streets, players' homes were attacked, editorials mocking Indian cricket were written and the Board of Control for Cricket in India suddenly decided their boys were pampered and over-paid and needed some disciplining.

The first casualty was coach Greg Chappell, who after a stormy two years in the job decided not to ask for an extension to his contract and stepped down. Captain Rahul Dravid, the darling of Indian cricket fans for half a decade, was now everyone's favourite whipping boy. It is a wonder he, too, did not walk away from the job there and then.

That would happen six months later after a successful tour of England, and while there was shock all round at the sudden decision, there is no doubt the World Cup fall-out was the beginning of the end.

The announcement came on the morning of India's group game against Pakistan in the World Twenty20 and sent shockwaves through a team being led for the first time by wicketkeeper Mahendra Singh Dhoni. The match ended in a tie, India being declared winners on the 'bowl-out'. And, just ten days later, they had beaten Pakistan in another cliff-hanger, this time in the final to return home as conquering heroes.

The contrast could not have been starker – in March their effigies were being burnt and mock funerals conducted by disgruntled fans. In September, Dhoni and his triumphant team were given an open-topped bus parade through the streets of Mumbai that brought

Posters of Indian players are burnt by disappointed fans back home after their team was beaten by Sri Lanka in the World Cup. Police also had to protect the homes of leading players in the wake of India's shock early exit from the tournament.

the metropolis to a grinding halt as millions turned out to greet them. And the same BCCI officials who were threatening pay-cuts after the 50-over debacle were now lining up to hand over massive bonuses to the Twenty20 heroes.

Dhoni, in the eyes of the public and media, had emulated Kapil Dev who in 1983 equally shocked the cricket world by lifting the Prudential World Cup. The Twenty20 may be a watered-down version but the world champions tag was good enough 24 years later. And following Dravid's resignation, Dhoni was given charge of the ODI team as well – a remarkable achievement for someone who had made his international debut less than three years ago.

Despite the World Cup disaster, Dravid's two years in charge had much to commend it. He took over under controversial circumstances from Sourav Ganguly and

Six months later, and ecstatic India fans crowd the streets of Mumbai to welcome their heroes home after Mahendra Singh Dhoni's team had won the inaugural ICC World Twenty20 tournament in South Africa.

guided India to their first Test series victory in the West Indies since 1971 and in England since 1986, plus a maiden Test win on South African soil.

The pressures of the job – considered the most publicly scrutinised after that of the Indian Prime Minister – had, however, got to a man who liked to keep his own counsel and stick to the long shadows cast by the likes of Sachin Tendulkar and Ganguly. That has become a hopeless task in the pressure-cooker atmosphere that surrounds the job in recent years, with the hyperactive electronic media in particular snatching away all vestiges of privacy and family time.

After being routed 4-0 in the ODI series in South Africa late in 2006, India salvaged some pride when they clinched their first-ever Twenty20 international by six wickets with a ball to spare in Johannesburg, in a sign of things to come. They also began the Test series in grand fashion. Having failed to win a Test match in

South Africa on three previous tours since 1992, they outplayed the hosts in the First Test at Johannesburg by 123 runs.

In the process India appeared to have uncovered a new fast-bowling talent – and character to boot – in Sri Sreesanth, who took the Man of the Match award with eight wickets. The Test also marked yet another comeback by Ganguly, who showed great character in top scoring for India in the first innings with 51 not out. He would end up as India's top run scorer in the series and thereby cement his place in the side.

The victory celebrations got out of hand, though, and the team were handed a hefty bill for a damaged dressing room at the New Wanderers Stadium. It was also all a bit premature. South Africa came back strongly to win the Second Test at Durban by 174 runs and the third at Cape Town by five wickets to burst India's bubble in their last campaign before the World Cup.

Shortly after the World Cup, Dravid also led the team to a 2-0 Test series victory in Bangladesh. In summer 2007, despite losing the NatWest ODI series to England in a cliff-hanger, Dravid delighted India cricket fans by winning the Second Test at Trent Bridge and holding on for a 1-0 victory to lift the inaugural Pataudi Trophy.

The positive balance sheet of his captaincy showed three Test series wins abroad and two defeats (in Pakistan and South Africa).

But even after Dravid's departure India's swing in fortunes continued. In October world champions Australia showed they were still the kings of the 50-over game by soundly beating India 4-2 in an ODI series that was sadly overshadowed by bad blood between the teams and allegations of racism levelled by Andrew Symonds against Indian crowds.

For India, and new captain Dhoni in particular, it was a tough lesson in the stark differences between the two formats of the game.

## ONE-DAY INTERNATIONALS v. West Indies

**Match One**
21 January 2007 at Nagpur
**India** 338 for 3 (50 overs) (SC Ganguly 98, G Gambhir 69, MS Dhoni 62*, R Dravid 54*)
**West Indies** 324 for 8 (50 overs) (S Chanderpaul 149*, CH Gayle 52)
*India won by 14 runs*

**Match Two**
24 January 2007 Day/Night at Cuttack
**India** 189 all out (48.2 overs) (KD Karthik 63, DB Powell 4 for 27)
**West Indies** 169 (48.2 overs) (S Chanderpaul 66)
*India won by 20 runs*

**Match Three**
27 January 2007 Day/Night at Chennai
**India** 268 all out (48 overs) (AR Uthappa 70, SR Tendulkar 60, R Dravid 57, DJ Bravo 4 for 39)
**West Indies** 270 for 7 (43.4 overs) (MN Samuels 98, BC Lara 83)
*West Indies won by 3 wickets*

**Match Four**
31 January 2007 at Vadodara
**India** 341 for 3 (50 overs) (SR Tendulkar 100*, R Dravid 78, SC Ganguly 68)
**West Indies** 181 all out (41.4 overs) (MN Samuels 55)
*India won by 160 runs*

**India won the series 3–1**

## ONE-DAY INTERNATIONALS v. Sri Lanka

**Match One**
8 February 2007 Day/Night at Kolkata
**Sri Lanka** 102 for 3 (18.2 overs) (ST Jayasuriya 63*)
**India**
*Match abandoned – no result*

**Match Two**
11 February 2007 at Rajkot
**Sri Lanka** 257 for 8 (50 overs) (KC Sangakkara 110, TM Dilshan 56, MM Patel 4 for 49)
**India** 252 for 9 (50 overs) (SC Ganguly 62, SR Tendulkar 54)
*Sri Lanka won by 5 runs*

**Match Three**
14 February 2007 at Margoa
**Sri Lanka** 230 for 8 (50 overs) (RP Arnold 66*, Z Khan 5 for 42)
**India** 233 for 5 (46.3 overs) (MS Dhoni 67*, R Dravid 66)
*India won by 5 wickets*

**Match Four**
17 February 2007 at Visakhapatnam
**Sri Lanka** 259 for 7 (47 overs) (LPC Silva 107*)
**India** 263 for 3 (41 overs) (Yuvraj Singh 95*, SC Ganguly 58*, AR Uthappa 52)
*India won by 7 wickets*

**India won the series 2–1**

## ONE-DAY INTERNATIONALS v. South Africa in Ireland

**Match One**
26 June 2007 at Belfast
**India** 242 for 8 (50 overs) (SR Tendulkar 99, R Dravid 74)
**South Africa** 245 for 6 (49.3 overs) (JH Kallis 91*)
*South Africa won by 4 wickets*

**Match Two**
29 June 2007 at Belfast
**South Africa** 226 for 6 (50 overs) (MN van Wyk 82, MV Boucher 55*)
**India** 227 for 4 (49.1 overs) (SR Tendulkar 93)
*India won by 6 wickets*

**Match Three**
1 July 2007 at Belfast
**South Africa** 148 for 7 (31 overs) (JM Kemp 61, HH Gibbs 56)
**India** 152 for 4 (30.2 overs) (Yuvraj Singh 61*)
*India won by 6 wickets*

**India won the series 2–1**

# NEW ZEALAND

Stephen Fleming's long and highly creditable reign as New Zealand captain came to an end following yet another World Cup semi-final defeat. His successor, Daniel Vettori, then experienced exactly the same disappointment in his own first big tournament in charge, the ICC World Twenty20.

Fleming decided to play on as a Test batsman, but retired from one-day internationals following the Black Caps' exit from the World Cup at the hands of Sri Lanka. He would, no doubt, have wanted to go out on a high – especially as the New Zealanders had warmed up for the World Cup by thrashing favourites and subsequent winners Australia 3-0 in the Chappell/Hadlee Trophy immediately before it – but Fleming can still hold his head high.

He had more than ten years at the helm, having become the youngest captain in New Zealand's history when at 23 he succeeded the sacked Lee Germon in February 1997. He captained his country in a record 80 Tests, winning 28 of them and enjoying some notable results along the way. The 1999 series win in England, when his team triumphed 2-1, was one of the obvious highlights but there was also a Test series victory in the West Indies and two hard-fought away draws in Australia and India.

Fleming, who had scored 6,620 runs at 39.64 from 104 Tests before departing for New Zealand's short tour of South Africa (his first as the

Stephen Fleming, New Zealand's fine captain from 1997 to 2007, is pictured playing one of his favourite square cuts.

former captain), rightly gained a considerable reputation for being one of the most tactically astute captains in world cricket.

Boosting his Test average above 40 was one of the reasons he gave for wanting to continue on at least until after New Zealand's back-to-back home and away series with England in the first half of 2008, and there is no doubt that his record as a batsman – good though it is – might have been even better if he had not worn the cares of captaincy for so long.

Vettori, meanwhile, is expected to be an equally committed and canny leader. Coincidentally, he had just turned 18 when he made his Test debut one match before Fleming took over from Germon, and so has played a leading role in the Fleming era with 73 Test appearances during that time.

New Zealand lost to Pakistan, under Vettori, in the World Twenty20 semi-final, but it is still in the one-day arena that they seem more capable of punching above their weight.

Shane Bond, the fast bowler, was named Player of the Year, but fitness worries are his constant companion. Chris Martin and Peter Gillespie are dependable, but Vettori will be hoping that the likes of Daryl Tuffey, Kyle Mills and Ian Butler can also shake off injury problems to boost the seam-bowling department.

There were draws, 1-1 and 2-2 respectively, in the Test and ODI series played at home to Sri Lanka, and Vettori can look forward to working alongside John Bracewell for the foreseeable future after the coach signed a new two-year contract. John Wright, the former New Zealand opener and India coach, has also joined New Zealand Cricket in a high-performance role.

The decision by Hamish Marshall, the talented batsman, to quit international cricket so that he could earn 'four times the money' playing regular county cricket for Gloucestershire on a Kolpak registration, was a blow but the re-emergence of Craig McMillan can be chalked up on the other side of the ledger. It was McMillan's magnificent 117, indeed, together with a buccaneering unbeaten 86 from Brendon McCullum, which swept New Zealand to their whitewash of Australia in the Chappell/Hadlee Trophy's third and final match at Hamilton despite having to chase the Aussies' intimidating 50-over total of 346 for 5.

Nathan Astle's retirement, at the start of 2007, also robbed them of a talented strokemaker but the batting generally, with Ross Taylor especially promising, is combative and deep.

Under Fleming, the Black Caps have many times lived up to their traditional reputation for being the most dangerous of underdogs. With Vettori in charge, expect more of the same.

## TWENTY20 INTERNATIONALS
## v. Sri Lanka

**Match One**
22 December 2006 Day/Night at Wellington
**New Zealand** 162 for 8 (20 overs)
**Sri Lanka** 62 for 1 (5.5 overs) (ST Jayasuriya 51*)
*Sri Lanka won by 18 runs – DL Method: target 44 from 5.5 overs*

**Match Two**
26 December 2006 at Auckland
**Sri Lanka** 115 all out (18.2 overs)
**New Zealand** 116 for 5 (18.3 overs)
*New Zealand won by 5 wickets*

**Series drawn**

## ONE-DAY INTERNATIONALS

**Match One**
28 December 2006 at Napier
**New Zealand** 285 for 8 (50 overs) (RL Taylor 128*, NJ Astle 83)
**Sri Lanka** 286 for 3 (40 overs) (ST Jayasuriya 111, WU Tharanga 68)
*Sri Lanka won by 7 wickets*

**Match Two**
31 December 2006 at Queenstown
**Sri Lanka** 224 for 7 (50 overs) (KC Sangakkara 89)
**New Zealand** 228 for 9 (50 overs) (JAH Marshall 50)
*New Zealand won by 1 wicket*

**Match Three**
2 January 2007 at Christchurch
**Sri Lanka** 112 all out (35.2 overs) (MJ Mason 4 for 24)
**New Zealand** 110 for 6 (24.3 overs)
*New Zealand won by 4 wickets – DL Method: target 110 from 46 overs*

**Match Four**
6 January 2007 at Auckland
**Sri Lanka** 262 for 6 (50 overs) (KC Sangakkara 79, ST Jayasuriya 70)
**New Zealand** 73 all out (26.3 overs)
*Sri Lanka won by 189 runs*

**Match Five**
9 January 2007 at Hamilton
*Match abandoned – no result*

**Series drawn**

## FIRST TEST – NEW ZEALAND v. SRI LANKA
### 7–9 December 2006 at Christchurch

### SRI LANKA

| | First Innings | | Second Innings | |
|---|---|---|---|---|
| WU Tharanga | c How b Franklin | 33 | c Fleming b Bond | 24 |
| ST Jayasuriya | c Fleming b Bond | 5 | run out | 10 |
| KC Sangakkara | c Sinclair b Bond | 4 | not out | 100 |
| DPMD J'wardene (capt) | c Franklin b Bond | 8 | c Fleming b Franklin | 0 |
| CK Kapugedera | lbw b Franklin | 37 | c Oram b Bond | 1 |
| LPC Silva | b Franklin | 0 | c Vettori b Bond | 0 |
| *HAPW Jayawardene | c How b Martin | 7 | run out | 11 |
| WPUJC Vaas | c McCullum b Oram | 4 | c McCullum b Oram | 0 |
| MF Maharoof | c Fleming b Oram | 15 | c McCullum b Bond | 7 |
| SL Malinga | not out | 7 | c McCullum b Franklin | 0 |
| M Muralitharan | c Astle b Martin | 14 | run out | 8 |
| Extras | lb 13, w 1, nb 6 | 20 | lb 5, nb 4 | 9 |
| | (all out 52.4 overs) | 154 | (all out 53.1 overs) | 170 |

| | First Innings | | | | Second Innings | | | |
|---|---|---|---|---|---|---|---|---|
| | O | M | R | W | O | M | R | W |
| Bond | 13 | 2 | 43 | 3 | 19.1 | 5 | 63 | 4 |
| Martin | 16.4 | 2 | 37 | 2 | 11 | 2 | 38 | 0 |
| Franklin | 12 | 0 | 30 | 3 | 13 | 1 | 34 | 2 |
| Oram | 10 | 5 | 30 | 2 | 7 | 1 | 19 | 1 |
| Astle | 1 | 0 | 1 | 0 | 1 | 0 | 1 | 0 |
| Vettori | – | – | – | – | 2 | 0 | 10 | 0 |

**Fall of Wickets**
1-11, 2-17, 3-37, 4-87, 5-87, 6-106, 7-110, 8-121, 9-132
1-18, 2-44, 3-45, 4-46, 5-46, 6-74, 7-80, 8-99, 9-143

### NEW ZEALAND

| | First Innings | | Second Innings | |
|---|---|---|---|---|
| CD Cumming | b Muralitharan | 43 | c Jayawardene HAPW b Vaas | 43 |
| JM How | lbw b Malinga | 0 | lbw b Muralitharan | 11 |
| MS Sinclair | c Jayawardene HAPW b Vaas | 36 | c Sangakkara b Muralitharan | 4 |
| SP Fleming (capt) | c Sangakkara b Maharoof | 48 | lbw b Vaas | 0 |
| NJ Astle | lbw b Muralitharan | 2 | lbw b Muralitharan | 24 |
| JDP Oram | c Silva b Vaas | 1 | not out | 12 |
| *BB McCullum | b Vaas | 0 | not out | 14 |
| DL Vettori | c Jayawardene DPMD b Malinga | 63 | | |
| JEC Franklin | lbw b Muralitharan | 0 | | |
| SE Bond | lbw b Muralitharan | 1 | | |
| CS Martin | not out | 0 | | |
| Extras | lb 5, nb 7 | 12 | b 1, lb 1, w 5, nb 4 | 11 |
| | (all out 85.4 overs) | 206 | (5 wkts 33 overs) | 119 |

| | First Innings | | | | Second Innings | | | |
|---|---|---|---|---|---|---|---|---|
| | O | M | R | W | O | M | R | W |
| Vaas | 18 | 4 | 49 | 3 | 12 | 3 | 33 | 2 |
| Malinga | 19.4 | 2 | 43 | 2 | 4 | 1 | 35 | 0 |
| Maharoof | 14 | 3 | 44 | 1 | 3 | 0 | 15 | 0 |
| Muralitharan | 34 | 7 | 65 | 4 | 14 | 5 | 34 | 3 |

**Fall of Wickets**
1-3, 2-73, 3-106, 4-108, 5-113, 6-113, 7-188, 8-190, 9-206
1-58, 2-66, 3-66, 4-68, 5-103

Umpires: BG Jerling (South Africa) & SJA Taufel (Australia)
Toss: Sri Lanka
Test debut: LPC Silva
Man of the Match: SE Bond

## New Zealand won by 5 wickets

## SECOND TEST – NEW ZEALAND v. SRI LANKA
### 15–18 December 2006 at Wellington

### SRI LANKA

| | First Innings | | Second Innings | |
|---|---|---|---|---|
| WU Tharanga | c McCullum b Martin | 7 | lbw b Martin | 20 |
| ST Jayasuriya | c Fleming b Martin | 0 | c Fleming b Vettori | 31 |
| KC Sangakkara | not out | 156 | c Franklin b Bond | 8 |
| DPMD J'wardene (capt) | b Martin | 0 | c Sinclair b Vettori | 31 |
| CK Kapugedera | c Sinclair b Oram | 5 | b Vettori | 27 |
| LPC Silva | c Fleming b Franklin | 61 | not out | 152 |
| *HAPW Jayawardene | lbw b Vettori | 25 | c sub b Martin | 37 |
| WPUJC Vaas | c McCullum b Bond | 0 | c McCullum b Vettori | 47 |
| MF Maharoof | c McCullum b Vettori | 4 | lbw b Vettori | 1 |
| SL Malinga | c Sinclair b Vettori | 0 | lbw b Vettori | 0 |
| M Muralitharan | c & b Bond | 0 | st McCullum b Vettori | 0 |
| Extras | b 1, lb 1, nb 8 | 10 | lb 7, nb 4 | 11 |
| | (all out 65 overs) | 268 | (all out 109.3 overs) | 365 |

| | First Innings | | | | Second Innings | | | |
|---|---|---|---|---|---|---|---|---|
| | O | M | R | W | O | M | R | W |
| Bond | 16 | 2 | 84 | 2 | 19 | 3 | 67 | 1 |
| Martin | 13 | 2 | 51 | 3 | 23 | 1 | 98 | 2 |
| Franklin | 12 | 2 | 46 | 1 | 25 | 8 | 63 | 0 |
| Oram | 3 | 0 | 10 | 1 | – | – | – | – |
| Vettori | 14 | 1 | 53 | 3 | 42.3 | 6 | 130 | 7 |
| Astle | 7 | 2 | 22 | 0 | – | – | – | – |

**Fall of Wickets**
1-0, 2-27, 3-41, 4-81, 5-201, 6-239, 7-240, 8-251, 9-259
1-44, 2-62, 3-62, 4-100, 5-168, 6-261, 7-349, 8-355, 9-364

### NEW ZEALAND

| | First Innings | | Second Innings | |
|---|---|---|---|---|
| CD Cumming | b Maharoof | 13 | c J'wardene HAPW b Muralitharan | 20 |
| JM How | lbw b Malinga | 26 | lbw b Malinga | 33 |
| MS Sinclair | b Malinga | 6 | c J'wardene DPMD b Muralitharan | 37 |
| SP Fleming (capt) | c Jayawardene HAPW b Malinga | 0 | c Sangakkara b Malinga | 27 |
| NJ Astle | b Malinga | 17 | lbw b Muralitharan | 9 |
| *BB McCullum | b Muralitharan | 43 | b Muralitharan | 17 |
| DL Vettori | b Malinga | 0 | (8) lbw b Muralitharan | 51 |
| JDP Oram | lbw b Muralitharan | 1 | (7) lbw b Vaas | 4 |
| JEC Franklin | lbw b Muralitharan | 1 | c Silva b Muralitharan | 44 |
| SE Bond | lbw b Muralitharan | 8 | c Sangakkara b Maharoof | 6 |
| CS Martin | not out | 0 | not out | 4 |
| Extras | b 7, lb 6, nb 2 | 15 | b 9, lb 7, w 11, nb 7 | 34 |
| | (all out 39.1 overs) | 130 | (all out 85.1 overs) | 286 |

| | First Innings | | | | Second Innings | | | |
|---|---|---|---|---|---|---|---|---|
| | O | M | R | W | O | M | R | W |
| Vaas | 4 | 0 | 8 | 0 | 18 | 2 | 64 | 1 |
| Malinga | 18 | 4 | 68 | 5 | 16 | 1 | 62 | 2 |
| Maharoof | 5 | 2 | 10 | 1 | 11 | 1 | 47 | 1 |
| Muralitharan | 12.1 | 3 | 31 | 4 | 34.1 | 9 | 87 | 6 |
| Jayasuriya | – | – | – | – | 6 | 3 | 10 | 0 |

**Fall of Wickets**
1-30, 2-40, 3-40, 4-66, 5-75, 6-85, 7-90, 8-98, 9-116
1-56, 2-60, 3-115, 4-139, 5-156, 6-161, 7-163, 8-259, 9-278

Umpires: BG Jerling (South Africa) & SJA Taufel (Australia)
Toss: Sri Lanka
Man of the Match: LPC Silva

## Sri Lanka won by 217 runs

## SERIES AVERAGES
### New Zealand v. Sri Lanka

### NEW ZEALAND

| Batting | M | Inns | NO | Runs | HS | Av | 100 | 50 | c/st |
|---|---|---|---|---|---|---|---|---|---|
| DL Vettori | 2 | 3 | 0 | 114 | 63 | 38.00 | - | 2 | 1/- |
| CD Cumming | 2 | 4 | 0 | 119 | 43 | 29.75 | - | - | -/- |
| BB McCullum | 2 | 4 | 1 | 74 | 43 | 24.66 | - | - | 8/1 |
| MS Sinclair | 2 | 4 | 0 | 83 | 37 | 20.75 | - | - | 4/- |
| SP Fleming | 2 | 4 | 0 | 75 | 48 | 18.75 | - | - | 7/- |
| JM How | 2 | 4 | 0 | 70 | 33 | 17.50 | - | - | 2/- |
| JEC Franklin | 2 | 3 | 0 | 45 | 44 | 15.00 | - | - | 2/- |
| NJ Astle | 2 | 4 | 0 | 52 | 24 | 13.00 | - | - | 1/- |
| JDP Oram | 2 | 4 | 1 | 18 | 12* | 6.00 | - | - | 1/- |
| SE Bond | 2 | 3 | 0 | 15 | 8 | 5.00 | - | - | 1/- |
| CS Martin | 2 | 3 | 3 | 4 | 4* | - | - | - | -/- |

| Bowling | Overs | Mds | Runs | Wkts | Av | Best | 5/inn | 10m |
|---|---|---|---|---|---|---|---|---|
| JDP Oram | 20 | 6 | 59 | 4 | 14.75 | 2-30 | - | - |
| DL Vettori | 58.3 | 7 | 193 | 10 | 19.30 | 7-130 | 1 | 1 |
| SE Bond | 67.1 | 12 | 257 | 10 | 25.70 | 4-63 | - | - |
| JEC Franklin | 62 | 11 | 173 | 6 | 28.83 | 3-30 | - | - |
| CS Martin | 63.4 | 7 | 224 | 7 | 32.00 | 3-51 | - | - |

Also bowled: NJ Astle 9-2-24-0.

### SRI LANKA

| Batting | M | Inns | NO | Runs | HS | Av | 100 | 50 | c/st |
|---|---|---|---|---|---|---|---|---|---|
| KC Sangakkara | 2 | 4 | 2 | 268 | 156* | 134.00 | 2 | - | 4/- |
| LPC Silva | 2 | 4 | 1 | 213 | 152* | 71.00 | 1 | 1 | 2/- |
| WU Tharanga | 2 | 4 | 0 | 84 | 33 | 21.00 | - | - | -/- |
| HAPW Jayawardene | 2 | 4 | 0 | 80 | 37 | 20.00 | - | - | 4/- |
| CK Kapugedera | 2 | 4 | 0 | 70 | 37 | 17.50 | - | - | -/- |
| WPUJC Vaas | 2 | 4 | 0 | 51 | 47 | 12.75 | - | - | -/- |
| ST Jayasuriya | 2 | 4 | 0 | 46 | 31 | 11.50 | - | - | -/- |
| DPMD Jayawardene | 2 | 4 | 0 | 39 | 31 | 9.75 | - | - | 2/- |
| MF Maharoof | 2 | 4 | 0 | 27 | 15 | 6.75 | - | - | -/- |
| M Muralitharan | 2 | 4 | 0 | 22 | 14 | 5.50 | - | - | -/- |
| SL Malinga | 2 | 4 | 1 | 7 | 7* | 2.33 | - | - | -/- |

| Bowling | Overs | Mds | Runs | Wkts | Av | Best | 5/inn | 10m |
|---|---|---|---|---|---|---|---|---|
| M Muralitharan | 94.2 | 24 | 217 | 17 | 12.76 | 6-87 | 1 | 1 |
| SL Malinga | 57.4 | 8 | 208 | 9 | 23.11 | 5-68 | 1 | - |
| WPUJC Vaas | 52 | 9 | 154 | 6 | 25.66 | 3-49 | - | - |
| MF Maharoof | 33 | 6 | 116 | 3 | 38.66 | 1-10 | - | - |

Also bowled: ST Jayasuriya 6-3-10-0.

## CHAPPELL/HADLEE TROPHY

### Match One
16 February 2007 Day/Night at Wellington
**Australia** 148 all out (49.3 overs) (SE Bond 5 for 23)
**New Zealand** 149 for 0 (27 overs) (L Vincent 73*,
SP Fleming 70*)
*New Zealand won by 10 wickets*

### Match Two
18 February 2007 at Auckland
**Australia** 336 for 4 (50 overs) (MEK Hussey 105,
BJ Hodge 97*)
**New Zealand** 337 for 5 (48.4 overs) (RL Taylor 117,
PG Fulton 76*, CD McMillan 52)
*New Zealand won by 5 wickets*

### Match Three
20 February 2007 Day/Night at Hamilton
**Australia** 346 for 5 (50 overs) (ML Hayden 181*,
SR Watson 68)
**New Zealand** 350 for 9 (49.3 overs) (CD McMillan 117,
BB McCullum 86*, PG Fulton 51)
*New Zealand won by 1 wicket*

### New Zealand won the series 3–0

Fast bowler Shane Bond was named New Zealand's Player of the Year.

# PAKISTAN

Even by Pakistan's standards, the past year has witnessed extraordinary trials and tribulations, joy and sadness. But the death of Bob Woolmer, then Pakistan coach, in the immediate aftermath of their astonishing World Cup defeat and exit at the hands of Ireland, overshadows everything else.

In particular, the bungling of the inquiry into Woolmer's death, with the initial shocking allegations that it had been murder, still remains hard to accept, suffice to say that the whole cricket world was hugely relieved (though no less desperately sad) when it was confirmed three months later that former England batsman Woolmer had died of natural causes.

Yet a cricket year that began with the ball-tampering allegations of umpire Darrell Hair at The Oval in August 2006 fresh in the memory also contained yet more controversy. Shoaib Akhtar, the combustible but charismatic fast bowler, was found guilty of drug-taking and banned for two years, while fellow paceman Mohammad Asif was indicted, too, and banned for one year.

Later, the Pakistan Cricket Board overturned the bans following their own inquiry, yet the 12-month span to October 2007 was to end in tragi-comedy surrounding the two men, rather than farce, when Shoaib got into a dressing-room fight with Asif shortly before the ICC World Twenty20 event in South Africa and was immediately sent home. Shoaib was eventually banned for 13 weeks by the PCB, when a number of other related offences were taken into account, though he was planning on a Test comeback – against India of all people – when this book went to press.

In theory, with wonderful fast bowlers like Shoaib, Asif, Umar Gul, Rana Naved-ul-Hasan and the raw but exciting Tanvir Sohail unveiled during the World Twenty20, to choose from – plus the leg-spin talents of Danish Kaneria, top-quality batsmen and the unpredictable but gifted Shahid Afridi – Pakistan should be up with the world's leading teams and perhaps even beating them.

In practice, however, as so often with Pakistan cricket, the very opposite is often

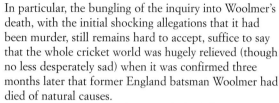

The management alliance between Inzamam-ul-Haq and Bob Woolmer, as Pakistan captain and coach, was for the most part highly successful.

true. For instance, when South Africa won their first Test series in the subcontinent for seven years by taking a two-match series 1-0 in early October 2007, Pakistan had dropped to seventh in the ICC Test rankings with only the West Indies and Bangladesh below them.

That short series followed soon after the massive disappointment of losing to India by just five runs in a thrilling World Twenty20 final in Johannesburg. Yet, up to the moment that the otherwise heroic Misbah-ul-Haq fatally tried to scoop a ball up and over short fine leg, when clean straight hitting might have been the best option with most of the final over still to be bowled, Pakistan looked destined to become inaugural World Twenty20 champions themselves after a magnificent campaign bursting with natural talent and flair.

Their year had begun with Test and ODI series victories over the West Indies, with Mohammad Yousuf setting a new world record mark in 2006 of 1,788 Test runs in a calendar year. But then came Test and ODI series defeats in South Africa, followed by the World Cup debacle, and Inzamam-ul-Haq's immediate retirement as Pakistan's one-day captain. Shoaib Malik took over, and he and new coach Geoff Lawson almost won instant immortality in that World Twenty20 final after New Zealand had been brushed aside in the semi-final.

But it was not to be, and a turbulent year ended in typically dramatic fashion with Inzamam announcing his full retirement once the home Tests against South Africa were finished. Scoring 14 in his penultimate innings meant that he began his last innings, in which Pakistan were to find a stiff second innings target too much for them in Lahore, needing just six runs to eclipse Javed Miandad as the highest run-getter in Pakistan's Test history.

'Inzy' clipped his first ball for three through mid wicket, but then shuffled down the pitch to his second – from the slow left-arm spinner Paul Harris – and was stumped, two runs short of Miandad's mark.

He had scored 8,830 runs from 120 Tests, at an average of 49.60, and one of his 25 hundreds was made on his 100th Test appearance. Like 16 others, it was also made in a winning cause.

Inzamam, who first sprang to prominence in the 1992 World Cup, which he helped Pakistan to win so memorably with vital and swift runs in both the semi-final and final, scored more than 20,000 international runs in all. In partnership with Woolmer, moreover, he enjoyed a largely successful and highly satisfying stint as Pakistan captain – before it all ended in tears at the World Cup.

'Bowling to Inzy was almost like bowling to a brick wall,' said Allan Donald, the great South African speedster, in tribute. 'He was very difficult to bowl at, and when he was playing well he had all the shots and all the time in the world.'

## FIRST TEST – PAKISTAN v. WEST INDIES
### 11–14 November 2006 at Lahore

### WEST INDIES

| | First Innings | | Second Innings | |
|---|---|---|---|---|
| CH Gayle | lbw b Shahid Nazir | 34 | c Kamran Akmal b Umar Gul | 11 |
| D Ganga | c Younis Khan b Umar Gul | 3 | run out | 5 |
| RR Sarwan | c Younis Khan b Shahid Nazir | 3 | lbw b Umar Gul | 23 |
| BC Lara (capt) | c Kamran Akmal b Umar Gul | 61 | lbw b Mohammad Hafeez | 122 |
| S Chanderpaul | lbw b Shahid Nazir | 5 | (6) c M Yousuf b Shahid Nazir | 81 |
| DJ Bravo | c Shahid Nazir b Danish Kaneria | 32 | (7) lbw b Umar Gul | 2 |
| *D Ramdin | c M Hafeez b Danish Kaneria | 12 | (8) c Imran Farhat b Danish Kaneria | 1 |
| D Mohammed | c Kamran Akmal b Umar Gul | 35 | (9) c Abdul Razzaq b Shahid Nazir | 15 |
| JE Taylor | lbw b Umar Gul | 8 | (10) c Kamran Akmal b Umar Gul | 8 |
| FH Edwards | c Shoaib Malik b Umar Gul | 2 | (5) c Younis Khan b Shahid Nazir | 10 |
| CD Collymore | not out | 1 | not out | 1 |
| Extras | lb 8, nb 2 | 10 | lb 7, nb 5 | 12 |
| | (all out 56.1 overs) | 206 | (all out 94 overs) | 291 |

| | First Innings | | | | Second Innings | | | |
|---|---|---|---|---|---|---|---|---|
| | O | M | R | W | O | M | R | W |
| Umar Gul | 15.1 | 2 | 65 | 5 | 29 | 6 | 99 | 4 |
| Shahid Nazir | 14 | 4 | 42 | 3 | 20 | 8 | 63 | 3 |
| Abdul Razzaq | 7 | 2 | 22 | 0 | 7 | 2 | 19 | 0 |
| Danish Kaneria | 18 | 3 | 58 | 2 | 29 | 7 | 78 | 1 |
| Shoaib Malik | 2 | 0 | 11 | 0 | 5 | 1 | 14 | 0 |
| Mohammad Hafeez | - | - | - | - | 4 | 0 | 11 | 1 |

**Fall of Wickets**
1-41, 2-41, 3-46, 4-52, 5-96, 6-122, 7-174, 8-202, 9-203
1-16, 2-20, 3-56, 4-101, 5-238, 6-248, 7-251, 8-278, 9-288

### PAKISTAN

| | First Innings | | Second Innings | |
|---|---|---|---|---|
| Mohammad Hafeez | lbw b Taylor | 57 | lbw b Collymore | 1 |
| Imran Farhat | lbw b Taylor | 9 | not out | 8 |
| Younis Khan | c Sarwan b Edwards | 11 | not out | 0 |
| Mohammad Yousuf | st Ramdin b Gayle | 192 | | |
| Inzamam-ul-Haq (capt) | b Mohammed | 0 | | |
| Shoaib Malik | c Mohammed b Taylor | 69 | | |
| Abdul Razzaq | c Ramdin b Taylor | 5 | | |
| *Kamran Akmal | c Lara b Gayle | 78 | | |
| Shahid Nazir | c Collymore b Mohammed | 0 | | |
| Umar Gul | not out | 16 | | |
| Danish Kaneria | c Ramdin b Mohammed | 23 | | |
| Extras | b 4, lb 7, w 6, nb 8 | 25 | lb 4 | 4 |
| | (all out 146 overs) | 485 | (1 wkt 5.1 overs) | 13 |

| | First Innings | | | | Second Innings | | | |
|---|---|---|---|---|---|---|---|---|
| | O | M | R | W | O | M | R | W |
| Edwards | 26 | 3 | 109 | 1 | 2.1 | 1 | 7 | 0 |
| Taylor | 33 | 7 | 115 | 4 | - | - | - | - |
| Collymore | 25 | 6 | 63 | 0 | 3 | 2 | 2 | 1 |
| Bravo | 20 | 3 | 63 | 0 | - | - | - | - |
| Mohammed | 31 | 4 | 98 | 3 | - | - | - | - |
| Gayle | 10 | 3 | 24 | 2 | - | - | - | - |
| Sarwan | 1 | 0 | 2 | 0 | - | - | - | - |

**Fall of Wickets**
1-16, 2-45, 3-133, 4-140, 5-279, 6-285, 7-433, 8-444, 9-446
1-2

Umpires: EAR de Silva (Sri Lanka) & SJA Taufel (Australia)
Toss: West Indies
Man of the Match: Umar Gul

## Pakistan won by 9 wickets

## SECOND TEST – PAKISTAN v. WEST INDIES
### 19–23 November 2006 at Multan

### PAKISTAN

| | First Innings | | Second Innings | |
|---|---|---|---|---|
| Mohammad Hafeez | c Ramdin b Taylor | 36 | b Taylor | 18 |
| Imran Farhat | c Lara b Bravo | 74 | run out | 76 |
| Younis Khan | c Morton b Taylor | 56 | c Ramdin b Mohammed | 56 |
| Mohammad Yousuf | c Lara b Gayle | 56 | c Chanderpaul b Mohammed | 191 |
| Inzamam-ul-Haq (capt) | lbw b Taylor | 31 | lbw b Taylor | 10 |
| Shoaib Malik | c Bravo b Collymore | 42 | b Powell | 4 |
| Abdul Razzaq | not out | 16 | c Chanderpaul b Mohammed | 80 |
| *Kamran Akmal | c Bravo b Collymore | 17 | not out | 2 |
| Shahid Nazir | lbw b Taylor | 7 | | |
| Umar Gul | c Bravo b Taylor | 7 | | |
| Danish Kaneria | run out | 0 | | |
| Extras | b 9, lb 4, nb 2 | 15 | b 8, lb 10, w 3, nb 3 | 24 |
| | (all out 124 overs) | 357 | (7 wkts 147.4 overs) | 461 |

| | First Innings | | | | Second Innings | | | |
|---|---|---|---|---|---|---|---|---|
| | O | M | R | W | O | M | R | W |
| Taylor | 26 | 6 | 91 | 5 | 25 | 4 | 75 | 2 |
| Collymore | 31 | 9 | 67 | 2 | 28 | 9 | 66 | 0 |
| Powell | 14 | 4 | 50 | 0 | 20 | 6 | 47 | 1 |
| Gayle | 22 | 6 | 52 | 1 | 29 | 5 | 85 | 0 |
| Bravo | 19 | 6 | 41 | 1 | 13 | 3 | 40 | 0 |
| Mohammed | 11 | 1 | 39 | 0 | 27.4 | 4 | 101 | 3 |
| Morton | 1 | 0 | 4 | 0 | 3 | 0 | 20 | 0 |
| Chanderpaul | - | - | - | - | 2 | 0 | 9 | 0 |

**Fall of Wickets**
1-83, 2-125, 3-212, 4-250, 5-269, 6-315, 7-333, 8-346, 9-357
1-24, 2-124, 3-243, 4-284, 5-306, 6-451, 7-454

### WEST INDIES

| | First Innings | |
|---|---|---|
| CH Gayle | lbw b Danish Kaneria | 93 |
| D Ganga | lbw b Danish Kaneria | 82 |
| BC Lara (capt) | c Shoaib Malik b Danish Kaneria | 216 |
| RS Morton | lbw b Umar Gul | 5 |
| S Chanderpaul | c Abdul Razzaq b Shahid Nazir | 14 |
| DJ Bravo | c Younis Khan b Danish Kaneria | 89 |
| *D Ramdin | c Kamran Akmal b Shahid Nazir | 11 |
| D Mohammed | st Kamran Akmal b Danish Kaneria | 36 |
| DB Powell | lbw b Abdul Razzaq | 9 |
| JE Taylor | lbw b Abdul Razzaq | 1 |
| CD Collymore | not out | 1 |
| Extras | b 9, lb 18, nb 7 | 34 |
| | (all out 167.4 overs) | 591 |

| | First Innings | | | |
|---|---|---|---|---|
| | O | M | R | W |
| Umar Gul | 38 | 13 | 96 | 1 |
| Shahid Nazir | 29 | 2 | 103 | 2 |
| Danish Kaneria | 46 | 7 | 181 | 5 |
| Abdul Razzaq | 17.4 | 4 | 65 | 2 |
| Mohammad Hafeez | 24 | 2 | 72 | 0 |
| Shoaib Malik | 13 | 1 | 47 | 0 |

**Fall of Wickets**
1-162, 2-220, 3-281, 4-302, 5-502, 6-523, 7-563, 8-583, 9-590

Umpires: MR Benson (England) & DJ Harper (Australia)
Toss: Pakistan
Man of the Match: Mohammad Yousuf

## Match drawn

---

## THIRD TEST – PAKISTAN v. WEST INDIES
### 27 November – 1 December 2006 at Karachi

### PAKISTAN

| | First Innings | | Second Innings | |
|---|---|---|---|---|
| Mohammad Hafeez | b Collymore | 18 | c Ramdin b Taylor | 104 |
| Imran Farhat | c Ramdin b Bravo | 47 | c Ramdin b Powell | 20 |
| Younis Khan | run out | 20 | lbw b Gayle | 38 |
| Mohammad Yousuf | lbw b Collymore | 102 | b Sarwan | 124 |
| Inzamam-ul-Haq (capt) | c Chanderpaul b Ganga | 18 | not out | 58 |
| Shoaib Malik | lbw b Taylor | 18 | b Collymore | 10 |
| Abdul Razzaq | c Ramdin b Bravo | 7 | c Gayle b Sarwan | 10 |
| *Kamran Akmal | b Collymore | 31 | | |
| Shahid Nazir | b Powell | 0 | | |
| Umar Gul | b Powell | 26 | | |
| Danish Kaneria | not out | 7 | | |
| Extras | b 1, lb 7, nb 2 | 10 | b 13, lb 21, w 1 | 35 |
| | (all out 100.5 overs) | 304 | (6 wkts dec 123.5 overs) | 399 |

| | First Innings | | | | Second Innings | | | |
|---|---|---|---|---|---|---|---|---|
| | O | M | R | W | O | M | R | W |
| Taylor | 22 | 3 | 76 | 1 | 24 | 8 | 60 | 1 |
| Collymore | 21 | 6 | 57 | 3 | 22 | 10 | 52 | 1 |
| Gayle | 16 | 3 | 27 | 0 | 15 | 2 | 38 | 1 |
| Powell | 23.5 | 5 | 83 | 2 | 24 | 6 | 70 | 1 |
| Bravo | 14 | 6 | 33 | 2 | 19 | 1 | 68 | 0 |
| Ganga | 4 | 0 | 20 | 1 | - | - | - | - |
| Sarwan | - | - | - | - | 17.5 | 0 | 70 | 2 |
| Chanderpaul | - | - | - | - | 2 | 0 | 7 | 0 |

**Fall of Wickets**
1-26, 2-72, 3-112, 4-178, 5-222, 6-239, 7-248, 8-265, 9-272
1-43, 2-122, 3-271, 4-365, 5-384, 6-399

### WEST INDIES

| | First Innings | | Second Innings | |
|---|---|---|---|---|
| CH Gayle | c Abdul Razzaq b Umar Gul | 40 | b Umar Gul | 2 |
| D Ganga | c Kamran Akmal b Abdul Razzaq | 81 | lbw b Shahid Nazir | 2 |
| BC Lara (capt) | b Umar Gul | 0 | c Shoaib Malik b Umar Gul | 49 |
| RR Sarwan | b Umar Gul | 0 | retired hurt | 35 |
| S Chanderpaul | c Imran Farhat b Danish Kaneria | 36 | lbw b Danish Kaneria | 69 |
| RS Morton | c Imran Farhat b Danish Kaneria | 21 | c & b Danish Kaneria | 16 |
| DJ Bravo | c Kamran Akmal b Danish Kaneria | 8 | c Younis Khan b Shahid Nazir | 26 |
| *D Ramdin | run out | 50 | not out | 25 |
| DB Powell | b Umar Gul | 1 | c Younis Khan b Danish Kaneria | 4 |
| JE Taylor | c Kamran Akmal b Shahid Nazir | 1 | lbw b Abdul Razzaq | 1 |
| CD Collymore | not out | 1 | lbw b Abdul Razzaq | 0 |
| Extras | b 4, lb 3, nb 7 | 14 | b 9, lb 5, nb 5 | 19 |
| | (all out 96 overs) | 260 | (all out 76 overs) | 244 |

| | First Innings | | | | Second Innings | | | |
|---|---|---|---|---|---|---|---|---|
| | O | M | R | W | O | M | R | W |
| Umar Gul | 24 | 5 | 79 | 4 | 19 | 2 | 89 | 2 |
| Shahid Nazir | 17 | 3 | 58 | 1 | 18 | 6 | 49 | 2 |
| Danish Kaneria | 35 | 12 | 62 | 3 | 26 | 6 | 69 | 3 |
| Abdul Razzaq | 16 | 5 | 44 | 1 | 12 | 5 | 23 | 2 |
| Mohammad Hafeez | 4 | 1 | 10 | 0 | - | - | - | - |
| Shoaib Malik | - | - | - | - | 1 | 1 | 0 | 0 |

**Fall of Wickets**
1-51, 2-51, 3-51, 4-114, 5-153, 6-190, 7-204, 8-213, 9-216
1-2, 2-17, 3-97, 4-126, 5-183, 6-227, 7-227, 8-236, 9-244

Umpires: MR Benson (England) & DJ Harper (Australia)
Toss: Pakistan
Man of the Match: Mohammad Yousuf
Man of the Series: Mohammad Yousuf

## Pakistan won by 199 runs

## SERIES AVERAGES
Pakistan v. West Indies

### PAKISTAN

| Batting | M | Inns | NO | Runs | HS | Av | 100 | 50 | c/st |
|---|---|---|---|---|---|---|---|---|---|
| Mohammad Yousuf | 3 | 5 | 0 | 665 | 192 | 133.00 | 4 | 1 | 1/- |
| Imran Farhat | 3 | 6 | 1 | 234 | 76 | 46.80 | - | 2 | 3/- |
| Kamran Akmal | 3 | 4 | 1 | 128 | 78 | 42.66 | - | 1 | 8/1 |
| Mohammad Hafeez | 3 | 6 | 0 | 234 | 104 | 39.00 | 1 | 1 | 1/- |
| Younis Khan | 3 | 6 | 1 | 181 | 56 | 36.20 | - | 2 | 6/- |
| Abdul Razzaq | 3 | 5 | 1 | 118 | 80 | 29.50 | - | 1 | 3/- |
| Inzamam-ul-Haq | 3 | 5 | 1 | 117 | 58* | 29.25 | - | 1 | -/- |
| Shoaib Malik | 3 | 5 | 0 | 143 | 69 | 28.60 | - | 1 | 3/- |
| Umar Gul | 3 | 3 | 1 | 49 | 26 | 24.50 | - | - | -/- |
| Danish Kaneria | 3 | 3 | 1 | 30 | 23 | 15.00 | - | - | 1/- |
| Shahid Nazir | 3 | 3 | 0 | 7 | 7 | 2.33 | - | - | 1/- |

| Bowling | Overs | Mds | Runs | Wkts | Av | Best | 5/inn | 10m |
|---|---|---|---|---|---|---|---|---|
| Umar Gul | 125.1 | 28 | 428 | 16 | 26.75 | 5-65 | 1 | - |
| Shahid Nazir | 98 | 23 | 315 | 11 | 28.63 | 3-42 | - | - |
| Danish Kaneria | 154 | 35 | 448 | 14 | 32.00 | 5-181 | 1 | - |
| Abdul Razzaq | 59.4 | 18 | 173 | 5 | 34.60 | 2-23 | - | - |
| Mohammad Hafeez | 32 | 3 | 93 | 1 | 93.00 | 1-11 | - | - |

Also bowled: Shoaib Malik 21-3-72-0.

### WEST INDIES

| Batting | M | Inns | NO | Runs | HS | Av | 100 | 50 | c/st |
|---|---|---|---|---|---|---|---|---|---|
| BC Lara | 3 | 5 | 0 | 448 | 216 | 89.60 | 2 | 1 | 3/- |
| S Chanderpaul | 3 | 5 | 0 | 205 | 81 | 41.00 | - | 2 | 3/- |
| CH Gayle | 3 | 5 | 0 | 180 | 93 | 36.00 | - | 1 | 1/- |
| D Ganga | 3 | 5 | 0 | 173 | 82 | 34.60 | - | 2 | -/- |
| DJ Bravo | 3 | 5 | 0 | 157 | 89 | 31.40 | - | 1 | 3/- |
| D Mohammed | 2 | 3 | 0 | 86 | 36 | 28.66 | - | - | 1/- |
| D Ramdin | 3 | 5 | 1 | 99 | 50 | 24.75 | - | 1 | 9/1 |
| RR Sarwan | 2 | 4 | 1 | 61 | 35* | 20.33 | - | - | 1/- |
| RS Morton | 2 | 3 | 0 | 42 | 21 | 14.00 | - | - | 1/- |
| CD Collymore | 3 | 5 | 4 | 11 | 8* | 11.00 | - | - | 1/- |
| FH Edwards | 1 | 2 | 0 | 12 | 10 | 6.00 | - | - | -/- |
| JE Taylor | 3 | 5 | 0 | 19 | 8 | 3.80 | - | - | 1/- |
| DB Powell | 2 | 3 | 0 | 10 | 9 | 3.33 | - | - | -/- |

| Bowling | Overs | Mds | Runs | Wkts | Av | Best | 5/inn | 10m |
|---|---|---|---|---|---|---|---|---|
| D Ganga | 4 | 0 | 20 | 1 | 20.00 | 1-20 | - | - |
| JE Taylor | 130 | 28 | 417 | 13 | 32.07 | 5-91 | 1 | - |
| RR Sarwan | 18.5 | 0 | 72 | 2 | 36.00 | 2-70 | - | - |
| D Mohammed | 69.4 | 9 | 238 | 6 | 39.66 | 3-98 | - | - |
| CD Collymore | 130 | 42 | 307 | 7 | 43.85 | 3-57 | - | - |
| CH Gayle | 92 | 19 | 226 | 4 | 56.50 | 2-24 | - | - |
| DB Powell | 81.5 | 21 | 250 | 4 | 62.50 | 2-83 | - | - |
| DJ Bravo | 85 | 19 | 245 | 3 | 81.66 | 2-33 | - | - |
| FH Edwards | 28.1 | 4 | 116 | 1 | 116.00 | 1-109 | - | - |

Also bowled: S Chanderpaul 4-0-16-0, RS Morton 4-0-24-0.

## ONE-DAY INTERNATIONALS v. West Indies

**Match One**
5 December 2006 at Rawalpindi
**Pakistan** v. **West Indies**
*Match abandoned – no result*

**Match Two**
7 December 2006 Day/Night at Faisalabad
**West Indies** 151 all out (49.5 overs)
**Pakistan** 154 for 8 (48.2 overs)
*Pakistan won by 2 wickets*

**Match Three**
10 December 2006 at Lahore
**West Indies** 207 for 7 (46.3 overs) (LMP Simmons 70)
**Pakistan** 192 for 3 (33.4 overs) (Imran Farhat 58)
*Pakistan won by 7 wickets – DL Method: target 191 from 35 overs*

**Match Four**
13 December 2006 at Multan
**Pakistan** 209 all out (49.5 overs) (Yasir Hameed 71)
**West Indies** 212 for 3 (34.5 overs) (MN Samuels 100*,
S Chanderpaul 60)
*West Indies won by 7 wickets*

**Match Five**
16 December 2006 Day/Night at Karachi
**West Indies** 238 for 7 (50 overs) (S Chanderpaul 101,
Naved-ul-Hasan 4 for 43)
**Pakistan** 239 for 3 (46.5 overs) (Mohammad Hafeez 92,
Kamran Akmal 56)
*Pakistan won by 7 wickets*
**Pakistan won the series 3–1**

## ONE-DAY INTERNATIONALS v. Sri Lanka

18 May 2007 Day/Night at Abu Dhabi
**Sri Lanka** 235 for 9 (50 overs) (MF Maharoof 69*)
**Pakistan** 239 for 5 (42 overs) (Shahid Afridi 73*,
Kamran Akmal 51*)
*Pakistan won by 5 wickets*

20 May 2007 Day/Night at Abu Dhabi
**Pakistan** 313 for 9 (50 overs) (Salman Butt 74, Yasir Hameed 50)
**Sri Lanka** 215 all out (39.5 overs) (DPMD Jayawardene 61)
*Pakistan won by 98 runs*

22 May 2007 Day/Night at Abu Dhabi
**Sri Lanka** 296 for 9 (50 overs) (DPMD Jayawardene 83, LPC Silva 64)
**Pakistan** 181 all out (42.5 overs) (Shoaib Malik 79*)
*Sri Lanka won by 115 runs*
**Pakistan won the series 2–1**

# SOUTH AFRICA

**D**espite much that was good, the past cricket year will be remembered around the world – sadly – as yet another instance of South Africa choking in sight of a big prize.

It was a year to remember for Mark Boucher, South Africa's wicketkeeper, who set a new Test record when he made his 396th dismissal.

It happened not once, but twice (or even three times if you count their ICC Champions Trophy semi-final defeat against the West Indies back in October 2006). And if a World Cup semi-final thrashing by Australia in St Lucia (by seven wickets with 111 balls remaining) wasn't bad enough, then losing their way in the last group match of the inaugural ICC World Twenty20 – in a tournament they had hosted so brilliantly – really stuck in the South African craw.

Graeme Smith's team were inconsolable after being beaten by India by such a big margin that they didn't even sneak into the semi-finals on run rate. It was nothing less than stage fright.

Yet at least the first Twenty20 world championship was seen as a success; especially as no one really knew what to expect. In hindsight, that success should help Smith and his players get over at least part of that disappointment. The World Cup, however, was different. This was a deadly serious affair, especially with South Africa pushing Australia in the ICC rankings for the right to call themselves the best one-day international side in the world.

But, once again, the South Africans folded in all-too-familiar fashion as Australia romped to a seven-wicket semi-final victory. It was embarrassingly one-sided and, somewhere along the line, a South Africa team is somehow going to have to come to terms with the demands of such high-profile, high-pressure contests.

Continuity was quite impressively maintained, however, following the

shattering World Cup blow, when both Smith and
Mickey Arthur, the coach, signed further contracts to
keep them in their jobs. And Shaun Pollock, despite a
moderate World Cup by his world-class standards, had
the compensation soon afterwards of being named as
South Africa's Cricketer of the Year.

Herschelle Gibbs' six sixes in an over bowled by Daan
van Bunge, Holland's occasional leg spinner, was one of
the highlights of a generally forgettable World Cup all
round, but South Africans were soon also mourning the
loss of their ICC President, Percy Sonn, who died
following an operation in May.

In their home season leading up to the World Cup,
meanwhile, there had been only success for South Africa
in series against both India and Pakistan.

First India were trounced 4-0 in a one-day series,
before Smith's team bounced back from the severe
handicap of losing the opening Test against the same
opponents to take the three-match series 2-1.

Pollock reached a memorable personal landmark as
the first South African to join the elite 400-wicket club
and, during the Test series that followed against
Pakistan, it was the turn of Makhaya Ntini to celebrate
as he became only the third bowler from his country to
take 300 Test wickets. The Pakistanis were beaten 2-1 in
the Tests and 3-1 in the ODI series but then came the
World Cup to dampen South African spirits.

What raised them again, following the World
Twenty20 disappointment, was the renewed and majestic
form of Jacques Kallis – controversially omitted from the
Twenty20 plans – and another magnificent personal
achievement for Mark Boucher, the wicketkeeper.

Kallis, who had resigned the vice-captaincy in protest
at being left out of the Twenty20 side, hit three centuries
in four innings (totalling 421 runs for an average of
210.50) as Pakistan were beaten 1-0 in a two-match Test
series in Pakistan. 'The break has done me the world of
good', he said.

And Boucher, early in the series, received a generous
tribute from Ian Healy after breaking the former
Australia wicketkeeper's world record dismissals mark of
395. Still only 30, the combative Boucher can surely go
on to raise the new Test record mark to rarified levels.

The big question for South Africa's team, however,
even with the emergence of fresh fast bowling talent in
the form of the blistering Morne Morkel and the
impressive Dale Steyn, still remains whether they have
the bottle to become world champions themselves in the
foreseeable future.

One of the new breed of South African quicks is the distinctly sharp
Morne Morkel, who also impressed during a short spell in English
county cricket with Kent.

## ONE-DAY INTERNATIONALS
## v. India

### Match One
19 November 2006 Day/Night at Johannesburg
**South Africa** v. **India**
*Match abandoned – no result*

### Match Two
22 November 2006 Day/Night at Durban
**South Africa** 248 for 8 (50 overs) (JH Kallis 119*)
**India** 91 all out (29.1 overs) (A Nel 4 for 13)
*South Africa won by 157 runs*

### Match Three
26 November 2006 at Cape Town
**South Africa** 274 for 7 (50 overs) (JM Kemp 100*,
AJ Hall 56*)
**India** 168 all out (41.3 overs) (R Dravid 63, MS Dhoni 55,
SM Pollock 4 for 26)
*South Africa won by 106 runs*

### Match Four
29 November 2006 Day/Night at Port Elizabeth
**South Africa** 243 for 8 (50 overs) (HH Gibbs 93*)
**India** 163 all out (38.1 overs)
*South Africa won by 80 runs*

### Match Five
3 December 2006 at Centurion
**India** 200 for 9 (50 overs) (SR Tendulkar 55)
**South Africa** 201 for 1 (31.2 overs) (AB de Villiers 92*,
GC Smith 79)
*South Africa won by 9 wickets*

**South Africa won the series 4–0**

## TWENTY20 INTERNATIONAL

1 December 2006 Day/Night at Johannesburg
**South Africa** 126 for 9 (20 overs)
**India** 127 for 4 (19.5 overs)
*India won by 6 wickets*

## FIRST TEST – SOUTH AFRICA v. INDIA
### 15–18 December 2006 at Johannesburg

### INDIA

| | First Innings | | | Second Innings | | |
|---|---|---|---|---|---|---|
| W Jaffer | lbw b Ntini | 9 | | c Smith b Nel | | 4 |
| V Sehwag | c Boucher b Pollock | 4 | | c Gibbs b Nel | | 33 |
| R Dravid (capt) | c Smith b Kallis | 32 | | c Boucher b Pollock | | 1 |
| SR Tendulkar | c de Villiers b Kallis | 44 | | b Pollock | | 14 |
| VVS Laxman | c Boucher b Ntini | 28 | | c Smith b Ntini | | 73 |
| SC Ganguly | not out | 51 | | c Boucher b Ntini | | 25 |
| *MS Dhoni | c Pollock b Ntini | 5 | | c Boucher b Pollock | | 18 |
| A Kumble | c Kallis b Nel | 6 | | c Prince b Nel | | 1 |
| Z Khan | lbw b Pollock | 9 | | c Boucher b Ntini | | 37 |
| S Sreesanth | c Amla b Pollock | 0 | | not out | | 6 |
| VR Singh | c & b Pollock | 29 | | run out | | 11 |
| Extras | lb 15, w 11, nb 6 | 32 | | b 2, lb 10, w 1 | | 13 |
| | (all out 79.5 overs) | **249** | | (all out 64.4 overs) | | **236** |

| | First Innings | | | | Second Innings | | | |
|---|---|---|---|---|---|---|---|---|
| | O | M | R | W | O | M | R | W |
| Steyn | 10.1 | 3 | 26 | 0 | - | - | - | - |
| Ntini | 18 | 1 | 57 | 3 | 15.4 | 2 | 77 | 3 |
| Pollock | 17.5 | 7 | 39 | 4 | 16 | 4 | 33 | 3 |
| Nel | 18.5 | 5 | 45 | 1 | 19 | 4 | 58 | 3 |
| Kallis | 15 | 0 | 67 | 2 | 11 | 2 | 30 | 0 |
| Smith | - | - | - | - | 3 | 0 | 26 | 0 |

**Fall of Wickets**
1-14, 2-14, 3-83, 4-110, 5-156, 6-167, 7-188, 8-205, 9-205
1-20, 2-37, 3-41, 4-61, 5-119, 6-147, 7-148, 8-218, 9-219

### SOUTH AFRICA

| | First Innings | | | Second Innings | | |
|---|---|---|---|---|---|---|
| GC Smith (capt) | lbw b Sreesanth | 5 | | (2) c Sehwag b Sreesanth | | 10 |
| HH Gibbs | c Sehwag b Khan | 0 | | (1) c Tendulkar b Khan | | 0 |
| HM Amla | c Laxman b Sreesanth | 0 | | c Dhoni b Sreesanth | | 17 |
| JH Kallis | c Laxman b Sreesanth | 12 | | c Ganguly b Sreesanth | | 27 |
| AG Prince | c Dhoni b Kumble | 24 | | b Kumble | | 97 |
| AB de Villiers | c Sehwag b Khan | 6 | | run out | | 17 |
| *MV Boucher | b Sreesanth | 5 | | lbw b Khan | | 23 |
| SM Pollock | lbw b Sreesanth | 5 | | b Kumble | | 40 |
| A Nel | c Khan b Singh | 21 | | lbw b Kumble | | 6 |
| M Ntini | b Kumble | 0 | | (11) c Sehwag b Khan | | 8 |
| DW Steyn | not out | 0 | | (10) not out | | 6 |
| Extras | b 2, w 3, nb 1 | 6 | | lb 8, nb 19 | | 27 |
| | (all out 25.1 overs) | **84** | | (all out 86.5 overs) | | **278** |

| | First Innings | | | | Second Innings | | | |
|---|---|---|---|---|---|---|---|---|
| | O | M | R | W | O | M | R | W |
| Khan | 10 | 3 | 32 | 2 | 22.5 | 5 | 79 | 3 |
| Sreesanth | 10 | 3 | 40 | 5 | 25 | 8 | 59 | 3 |
| Singh | 3.1 | 0 | 8 | 1 | 18 | 4 | 67 | 0 |
| Kumble | 2 | 1 | 2 | 2 | 20 | 4 | 54 | 3 |
| Ganguly | - | - | - | - | 1 | 0 | 11 | 0 |

**Fall of Wickets**
1-5, 2-5, 3-5, 4-21, 5-33, 6-38, 7-45, 8-84, 9-84
1-0, 2-22, 3-34, 4-84, 5-120, 6-164, 7-231, 8-245, 9-264

Umpires: MR Benson (England) & DJ Harper (Australia)
Toss: India
Man of the Match: S Sreesanth

## India won by 123 runs

## SECOND TEST – SOUTH AFRICA v. INDIA
### 26–30 December 2006 at Durban

### SOUTH AFRICA

| | First Innings | | Second Innings | |
|---|---|---|---|---|
| GC Smith (capt) | c Tendulkar b Khan | 5 | (2) b Sreesanth | 59 |
| AB de Villiers | c Tendulkar b Sreesanth | 9 | (1) c Laxman b Singh | 47 |
| HM Amla | lbw b Khan | 1 | lbw b Sreesanth | 0 |
| HH Gibbs | c Dhoni b Sreesanth | 63 | c sub b Kumble | 9 |
| AG Prince | c Laxman b Sreesanth | 121 | c Ganguly b Sreesanth | 0 |
| *MV Boucher | b Sreesanth | 53 | lbw b Khan | 8 |
| SM Pollock | c Sehwag b Singh | 11 | not out | 63 |
| AJ Hall | lbw b Kumble | 0 | lbw b Sreesanth | 21 |
| A Nel | b Kumble | 0 | | |
| M Morkel | not out | 31 | (9) c Singh b Sehwag | 27 |
| M Ntini | lbw b Kumble | 16 | | |
| Extras | lb 3, w 1, nb 14 | 18 | b 5, lb 7, w 7, nb 12 | 31 |
| | (all out 91.3 overs) | 328 | (8 wkts dec 67.4 overs) | 265 |

| | First Innings | | | | Second Innings | | | |
|---|---|---|---|---|---|---|---|---|
| | O | M | R | W | O | M | R | W |
| Khan | 23 | 7 | 83 | 2 | 20 | 5 | 65 | 1 |
| Sreesanth | 24 | 4 | 109 | 4 | 19 | 4 | 80 | 4 |
| Singh | 13 | 1 | 60 | 1 | 10 | 2 | 64 | 1 |
| Kumble | 28.3 | 1 | 62 | 3 | 16 | 4 | 37 | 1 |
| Ganguly | 3 | 1 | 11 | 0 | – | – | – | – |
| Sehwag | – | – | – | – | 2.4 | 1 | 7 | 1 |

**Fall of Wickets**
1-8, 2-13, 3-28, 4-122, 5-222, 6-256, 7-257, 8-257, 9-296
1-99, 2-108, 3-121, 4-121, 5-140, 6-143, 7-213, 8-265

### INDIA

| | First Innings | | Second Innings | |
|---|---|---|---|---|
| W Jaffer | c de Villiers b Ntini | 26 | c Nel b Ntini | 28 |
| V Sehwag | c de Villiers b Nel | 0 | c Smith b Ntini | 8 |
| R Dravid (capt) | lbw b Nel | 11 | c Boucher b Ntini | 5 |
| SR Tendulkar | c Boucher b Ntini | 63 | lbw b Ntini | 0 |
| VVS Laxman | not out | 50 | b Nel | 15 |
| SC Ganguly | c Gibbs b Ntini | 0 | c Gibbs b Ntini | 26 |
| *MS Dhoni | c de Villiers b Morkel | 34 | c Boucher b Nel | 47 |
| A Kumble | c Boucher b Morkel | 0 | c Amla b Hall | 11 |
| Z Khan | c Amla b Morkel | 2 | c Hall b Nel | 21 |
| S Sreesanth | c Boucher b Hall | 28 | c Boucher b Hall | 10 |
| VR Singh | c Boucher b Pollock | 4 | not out | 0 |
| Extras | b 1, lb 7, w 2, nb 12 | 22 | b 2, lb 1, w 1, nb 4 | 8 |
| | (all out 77.5 overs) | 240 | (all out 55.1 overs) | 179 |

| | First Innings | | | | Second Innings | | | |
|---|---|---|---|---|---|---|---|---|
| | O | M | R | W | O | M | R | W |
| Nel | 23 | 5 | 60 | 2 | 16 | 4 | 57 | 3 |
| Ntini | 15 | 4 | 41 | 3 | 19 | 6 | 48 | 5 |
| Morkel | 18 | 1 | 86 | 3 | 6 | 0 | 24 | 0 |
| Pollock | 14.5 | 10 | 17 | 1 | 9 | 4 | 21 | 0 |
| Hall | 7 | 0 | 28 | 1 | 5.1 | 1 | 26 | 2 |

**Fall of Wickets**
1-5, 2-35, 3-61, 4-125, 5-125, 6-179, 7-179, 8-183, 9-235
1-14, 2-34, 3-38, 4-45, 5-83, 6-85, 7-101, 8-160, 9-179

Umpires: Asad Rauf (Pakistan), MR Benson (England) & IL Howell
Toss: South Africa
Test debut: M Morkel
Man of the Match: M Ntini

## South Africa won by 174 runs

## THIRD TEST – SOUTH AFRICA v. INDIA
### 2–6 January 2007 at Cape Town

### INDIA

| | First Innings | | Second Innings | |
|---|---|---|---|---|
| W Jaffer | c Kallis b Steyn | 116 | c de Villiers b Ntini | 2 |
| *KD Karthik | c Amla b Harris | 63 | (7) not out | 38 |
| R Dravid (capt) | c Boucher b Pollock | 29 | c & b Harris | 47 |
| SR Tendulkar | c Kallis b Harris | 64 | (5) lbw b Pollock | 14 |
| VVS Laxman | b Steyn | 13 | (6) run out | 1 |
| SC Ganguly | c Amla b Pollock | 66 | (4) c Gibbs b Kallis | 46 |
| V Sehwag | c Ntini b Harris | 40 | (2) c Boucher b Steyn | 4 |
| A Kumble | lbw b Pollock | 0 | c Gibbs b Steyn | 6 |
| Z Khan | st Boucher b Harris | 1 | run out | 1 |
| S Sreesanth | c Gibbs b Pollock | 3 | c Kallis b Steyn | 4 |
| MM Patel | not out | 0 | c Pollock b Steyn | 0 |
| Extras | b 5, lb 4, w 2, nb 8 | 19 | lb 5, nb 1 | 6 |
| | (all out 131.1 overs) | 414 | (all out 64 overs) | 169 |

| | First Innings | | | | Second Innings | | | |
|---|---|---|---|---|---|---|---|---|
| | O | M | R | W | O | M | R | W |
| Steyn | 27 | 12 | 58 | 2 | 7 | 0 | 30 | 4 |
| Ntini | 26 | 4 | 107 | 0 | 8 | 1 | 29 | 1 |
| Pollock | 29.1 | 9 | 75 | 4 | 15 | 5 | 24 | 1 |
| Kallis | 12 | 4 | 36 | 0 | 12 | 0 | 31 | 1 |
| Harris | 37 | 3 | 129 | 4 | 22 | 6 | 50 | 1 |

**Fall of Wickets**
1-153, 2-202, 3-240, 4-269, 5-337, 6-395, 7-395, 8-398, 9-407
1-6, 2-6, 3-90, 4-114, 5-115, 6-121, 7-147, 8-165, 9-169

### SOUTH AFRICA

| | First Innings | | Second Innings | |
|---|---|---|---|---|
| GC Smith (capt) | c Sehwag b Kumble | 94 | (2) c Karthik b Khan | 55 |
| AB de Villiers | c Karthik b Sreesanth | 1 | (1) c Karthik b Khan | 22 |
| HM Amla | c Karthik b Sreesanth | 63 | lbw b Kumble | 10 |
| JH Kallis | c Patel b Tendulkar | 54 | (5) c Dravid b Khan | 32 |
| AG Prince | b Kumble | 26 | (6) not out | 38 |
| HH Gibbs | c Jaffer b Sehwag | 7 | (7) not out | 0 |
| *MV Boucher | c Karthik b Patel | 50 | | |
| SM Pollock | c Ganguly b Khan | 31 | (4) c Laxman b Khan | 37 |
| PL Harris | not out | 11 | | |
| DW Steyn | b Kumble | 1 | | |
| M Ntini | lbw b Kumble | 0 | b 10, lb 2, nb 5 | 17 |
| Extras | b 10, lb 10, w 1, nb 14 | 35 | | |
| | (all out 128.3 overs) | 373 | (5 wkts 64.1 overs) | 211 |

| | First Innings | | | | Second Innings | | | |
|---|---|---|---|---|---|---|---|---|
| | O | M | R | W | O | M | R | W |
| Khan | 20 | 3 | 74 | 1 | 21 | 2 | 62 | 4 |
| Sreesanth | 24 | 9 | 58 | 2 | 13 | 2 | 50 | 0 |
| Kumble | 42.3 | 6 | 117 | 4 | 25 | 4 | 74 | 1 |
| Patel | 20 | 5 | 43 | 1 | 1 | 0 | 2 | 0 |
| Sehwag | 12 | 0 | 31 | 1 | 1 | 0 | 8 | 0 |
| Tendulkar | 10 | 2 | 30 | 1 | 3.1 | 2 | 3 | 0 |

**Fall of Wickets**
1-14, 2-173, 3-177, 4-260, 5-260, 6-281, 7-350, 8-371, 9-372
1-36, 2-55, 3-127, 4-132, 5-209

Umpires: Asad Rauf (Pakistan) & DJ Harper (Australia)
Toss: India
Man of the Match: GC Smith
Man of the Series: SM Pollock

## South Africa won by 5 wickets

## SERIES AVERAGES
South Africa v. India

### SOUTH AFRICA

| Batting | M | Inns | NO | Runs | HS | Av | 100 | 50 | c/st |
|---|---|---|---|---|---|---|---|---|---|
| AG Prince | 3 | 6 | 1 | 306 | 121 | 61.20 | 1 | 1 | 1/- |
| M Morkel | 1 | 2 | 1 | 58 | 31* | 58.00 | - | - | -/- |
| GC Smith | 3 | 6 | 0 | 228 | 94 | 38.00 | - | 3 | 4/- |
| SM Pollock | 3 | 6 | 1 | 187 | 63* | 37.40 | - | 1 | 3/- |
| JH Kallis | 2 | 4 | 0 | 125 | 54 | 31.25 | - | 1 | 4/- |
| MV Boucher | 3 | 5 | 0 | 139 | 53 | 27.80 | - | 2 | 15/1 |
| AB de Villiers | 3 | 6 | 0 | 102 | 47 | 17.00 | - | - | 5/- |
| HH Gibbs | 3 | 6 | 1 | 79 | 63 | 15.80 | - | 1 | 6/- |
| HM Amla | 3 | 6 | 0 | 91 | 63 | 15.16 | - | 1 | 5/- |
| AJ Hall | 1 | 2 | 0 | 21 | 21 | 10.50 | - | - | 1/- |
| A Nel | 2 | 3 | 0 | 27 | 21 | 9.00 | - | - | 1/- |
| DW Steyn | 2 | 3 | 2 | 7 | 6* | 7.00 | - | - | -/- |
| M Ntini | 3 | 4 | 0 | 24 | 16 | 6.00 | - | - | 1/- |
| PL Harris | 1 | 1 | 1 | 11 | 11* | - | - | - | 1/- |

| Bowling | Overs | Mds | Runs | Wkts | Av | Best | 5/inn | 10m |
|---|---|---|---|---|---|---|---|---|
| SM Pollock | 101.5 | 39 | 209 | 13 | 16.07 | 4-39 | - | - |
| AJ Hall | 12.1 | 1 | 54 | 3 | 18.00 | 2-26 | - | - |
| DW Steyn | 44.1 | 6 | 114 | 6 | 19.00 | 4-30 | - | - |
| M Ntini | 101.4 | 18 | 359 | 15 | 23.93 | 5-48 | 1 | - |
| A Nel | 76.5 | 18 | 220 | 9 | 24.44 | 3-57 | - | - |
| PL Harris | 59 | 9 | 179 | 5 | 35.80 | 4-129 | - | - |
| M Morkel | 24 | 1 | 110 | 3 | 36.66 | 3-86 | - | - |
| JH Kallis | 50 | 6 | 164 | 3 | 54.66 | 2-67 | - | - |

Also bowled: GC Smith 3-0-26-0.

### INDIA

| Batting | M | Inns | NO | Runs | HS | Av | 100 | 50 | c/st |
|---|---|---|---|---|---|---|---|---|---|
| KD Karthik | 1 | 2 | 1 | 101 | 63 | 101.00 | - | 1 | 5/- |
| SC Ganguly | 3 | 6 | 1 | 214 | 66 | 42.80 | - | 2 | 3/- |
| VVS Laxman | 3 | 6 | 1 | 180 | 73 | 36.00 | - | 2 | 5/- |
| SR Tendulkar | 3 | 6 | 0 | 199 | 64 | 33.16 | - | 2 | 3/- |
| W Jaffer | 3 | 6 | 0 | 185 | 116 | 30.83 | 1 | - | 1/- |
| MS Dhoni | 2 | 4 | 0 | 104 | 47 | 26.00 | - | - | 3/- |
| R Dravid | 3 | 6 | 0 | 125 | 47 | 20.83 | - | - | 1/- |
| V Sehwag | 3 | 6 | 0 | 89 | 40 | 14.83 | - | - | 6/- |
| VR Singh | 2 | 4 | 1 | 44 | 29 | 14.66 | - | - | 1/- |
| Z Khan | 3 | 6 | 0 | 71 | 37 | 11.83 | - | - | 1/- |
| S Sreesanth | 3 | 6 | 1 | 51 | 28 | 10.20 | - | - | -/- |
| A Kumble | 3 | 6 | 0 | 24 | 11 | 4.00 | - | - | -/- |
| MM Patel | 1 | 2 | 1 | 0 | 0* | 0.00 | - | - | 1/- |

| Bowling | Overs | Mds | Runs | Wkts | Av | Best | 5/inn | 10m |
|---|---|---|---|---|---|---|---|---|
| S Sreesanth | 115 | 30 | 396 | 18 | 22.00 | 5-40 | 1 | - |
| V Sehwag | 15.4 | 1 | 46 | 2 | 23.00 | 1-7 | - | - |
| A Kumble | 134 | 20 | 346 | 14 | 24.71 | 4-117 | - | - |
| Z Khan | 116.5 | 25 | 395 | 13 | 30.38 | 4-62 | - | - |
| SR Tendulkar | 13.1 | 4 | 33 | 1 | 33.00 | 1-30 | - | - |
| MM Patel | 21 | 5 | 45 | 1 | 45.00 | 1-43 | - | - |
| VR Singh | 44.1 | 7 | 199 | 3 | 66.33 | 1-8 | - | - |

Also bowled: SC Ganguly 4-1-22-0.

## FIRST TEST – SOUTH AFRICA v. PAKISTAN
11–15 January 2007 at Centurion

### PAKISTAN

| | First Innings | | Second Innings | |
|---|---|---|---|---|
| Mohammad Hafeez | c Boucher b Ntini | 19 | c Smith b Kallis | 15 |
| Imran Farhat | c Amla b Ntini | 26 | c de Villiers b Harris | 68 |
| Yasir Hameed | c Ntini b Nel | 65 | c Boucher b Kallis | 9 |
| Younis Khan | c Nel b Pollock | 68 | lbw b Pollock | 38 |
| Inzamam-ul-Haq (capt) | c Amla b Ntini | 42 | c de Villiers b Pollock | 35 |
| Faisal Iqbal | c Boucher b Kallis | 1 | c Gibbs b Harris | 9 |
| *Kamran Akmal | c Pollock b Nel | 29 | c Gibbs b Harris | 15 |
| Naved-ul-Hasan | c & b Nel | 30 | c Prince b Pollock | 33 |
| Shahid Nazir | c Gibbs b Ntini | 15 | b Ntini | 40 |
| Danish Kaneria | c Kallis b Ntini | 0 | c Gibbs b Harris | 23 |
| Mohammad Asif | not out | 1 | not out | 8 |
| Extras | b 6, lb 6, w 2, nb 3 | 17 | lb 5, nb 4 | 9 |
| | (all out 96.5 overs) | 313 | (all out 96.2 overs) | 302 |

| | First Innings | | | | Second Innings | | | |
|---|---|---|---|---|---|---|---|---|
| | O | M | R | W | O | M | R | W |
| Ntini | 24 | 3 | 83 | 5 | 16 | 2 | 78 | 1 |
| Nel | 26.5 | 3 | 100 | 3 | 22 | 6 | 69 | 0 |
| Pollock | 18 | 5 | 38 | 1 | 22 | 7 | 60 | 3 |
| Kallis | 15 | 3 | 55 | 1 | 16 | 0 | 44 | 2 |
| Harris | 13 | 2 | 25 | 0 | 20.2 | 6 | 46 | 4 |

**Fall of Wickets**
1-48, 2-50, 3-183, 4-193, 5-204, 6-256, 7-276, 8-300, 9-311
1-41, 2-58, 3-115, 4-154, 5-175, 6-187, 7-199, 8-255, 9-283

### SOUTH AFRICA

| | First Innings | | Second Innings | |
|---|---|---|---|---|
| AB de Villiers | c Younis Khan b Mohammad Asif | 4 | (2) c Younis Khan b M Asif | 12 |
| GC Smith (capt) | c Kamran Akmal b M Asif | 0 | (1) lbw b Mohammad Hafeez | 32 |
| HM Amla | c Kamran Akmal b M Asif | 71 | not out | 64 |
| JH Kallis | c Younis Khan b M Asif | 18 | (5) not out | 60 |
| AG Prince | st Kamran Akmal b D Kaneria | 138 | | |
| HH Gibbs | lbw b Naved-ul-Hasan | 94 | | |
| *MV Boucher | c & b Danish Kaneria | 2 | | |
| SM Pollock | not out | 39 | | |
| PL Harris | b Danish Kaneria | 3 | (4) c Faisal Iqbal b M Asif | 7 |
| A Nel | b Naved-ul-Hasan | 5 | | |
| M Ntini | c Younis Khan b Mohammad Asif | 5 | | |
| Extras | lb 13, nb 25 | 38 | b 8, lb 4, nb 12 | 24 |
| | (all out 117.5 overs) | 417 | (3 wkts 60.5 overs) | 199 |

| | First Innings | | | | Second Innings | | | |
|---|---|---|---|---|---|---|---|---|
| | O | M | R | W | O | M | R | W |
| Mohammad Asif | 27.5 | 4 | 89 | 5 | 14 | 2 | 56 | 2 |
| Naved-ul-Hasan | 17 | 2 | 92 | 2 | 7 | 3 | 21 | 0 |
| Shahid Nazir | 20 | 1 | 96 | 0 | 3 | 1 | 13 | 0 |
| Danish Kaneria | 41 | 8 | 97 | 3 | 24.5 | 5 | 61 | 0 |
| Mohammad Hafeez | 11 | 1 | 24 | 0 | 12 | 2 | 36 | 1 |
| Imran Farhat | 1 | 0 | 6 | 0 | - | - | - | - |

**Fall of Wickets**
1-3, 2-8, 3-53, 4-143, 5-356, 6-358, 7-383, 8-386, 9-391
1-20, 2-67, 3-80

Umpires: SA Bucknor (West Indies) & BR Doctrove (West Indies)
Toss: Pakistan
Man of the Match: HM Amla

## South Africa won by 7 wickets

## SECOND TEST – SOUTH AFRICA v. PAKISTAN
### 19–22 January 2007 at Port Elizabeth

### SOUTH AFRICA

| | First Innings | | | | Second Innings | | | |
|---|---|---|---|---|---|---|---|---|
| AB de Villiers | c Kamran Akmal b Shoaib Akhtar | | | 2 | (2) b Mohammad Asif | | | 15 |
| GC Smith (capt) | c Younis Khan b Danish Kaneria | | | 28 | (1) c Inzamam-ul-Haq b M Asif | | | 10 |
| HM Amla | c Kamran Akmal b Shoaib Akhtar | | | 5 | b Mohammad Sami | | | 16 |
| JH Kallis | c Kamran Akmal b Shoaib Akhtar | | | 24 | lbw b Mohammad Asif | | | 91 |
| AG Prince | c Imran Farhat b M Sami | | | 2 | lbw b Danish Kaneria | | | 22 |
| HH Gibbs | lbw b Danish Kaneria | | | 2 | c Younis Khan b M Asif | | | 40 |
| *MV Boucher | c Younis Khan b Danish Kaneria | | | 35 | c Younis Khan b M Asif | | | 46 |
| SM Pollock | c M Sami b Shoaib Akhtar | | | 4 | c & b Danish Kaneria | | | 36 |
| A Nel | c Danish Kaneria b M Asif | | | 10 | not out | | | 23 |
| M Ntini | not out | | | 0 | (11) c Yasir Hameed b D Kaneria | | | 18 |
| PL Harris | c Yasir Hameed b Mohammad Asif | | | 4 | (10) c sub b Danish Kaneria | | | 0 |
| Extras | lb 3, nb 5 | | | 8 | b 3, lb 5, nb 6 | | | 14 |
| | (all out 40 overs) | | | **124** | (all out 133.2 overs) | | | **331** |

| | First Innings | | | | Second Innings | | | |
|---|---|---|---|---|---|---|---|---|
| | O | M | R | W | O | M | R | W |
| Shoaib Akhtar | 11 | 2 | 36 | 4 | – | – | – | – |
| Mohammad Asif | 9 | 2 | 34 | 2 | 38 | 16 | 76 | 5 |
| Danish Kaneria | 14 | 3 | 36 | 3 | 51.2 | 14 | 105 | 4 |
| Mohammad Sami | 6 | 1 | 15 | 1 | 29 | 5 | 90 | 1 |
| Imran Farhat | – | – | – | – | 7 | 0 | 20 | 0 |
| Mohammad Hafeez | – | – | – | – | 8 | 0 | 32 | 0 |

**Fall of Wickets**
1-9, 2-27, 3-40, 4-49, 5-58, 6-83, 7-89, 8-120, 9-120
1-18, 2-30, 3-61, 4-117, 5-195, 6-205, 7-285, 8-289, 9-290

### PAKISTAN

| | First Innings | | | | Second Innings | | | |
|---|---|---|---|---|---|---|---|---|
| Mohammad Hafeez | c Amla b Ntini | | | 13 | lbw b Pollock | | | 32 |
| Imran Farhat | c de Villiers b Ntini | | | 0 | c Kallis b Ntini | | | 7 |
| Younis Khan | c Gibbs b Ntini | | | 45 | (4) not out | | | 67 |
| Yasir Hameed | c de Villiers b Ntini | | | 2 | (3) run out | | | 6 |
| Mohammad Yousuf | lbw b Pollock | | | 32 | c Gibbs b Pollock | | | 18 |
| *Kamran Akmal | c Prince b Nel | | | 33 | (7) not out | | | 57 |
| Mohammad Sami | c Boucher b Ntini | | | 10 | | | | |
| Inzamam-ul-Haq (capt) | not out | | | 92 | (6) lbw b Ntini | | | 1 |
| Shoaib Akhtar | c Boucher b Kallis | | | 4 | | | | |
| Danish Kaneria | c Gibbs b Pollock | | | 1 | | | | |
| Mohammad Asif | b Ntini | | | 7 | | | | |
| Extras | b 4, lb 11, w 5, nb 1, p 5 | | | 26 | lb 1, w 1, nb 1 | | | 3 |
| | (all out 76 overs) | | | **265** | (5 wkts 57.3 overs) | | | **191** |

| | First Innings | | | | Second Innings | | | |
|---|---|---|---|---|---|---|---|---|
| | O | M | R | W | O | M | R | W |
| Nel | 23 | 3 | 68 | 1 | 14 | 2 | 63 | 0 |
| Ntini | 21 | 6 | 59 | 6 | 19 | 6 | 50 | 2 |
| Kallis | 13 | 0 | 56 | 1 | 6 | 0 | 17 | 0 |
| Pollock | 14 | 2 | 42 | 2 | 13 | 4 | 47 | 2 |
| Harris | 5 | 1 | 20 | 0 | 5.3 | 0 | 13 | 0 |

**Fall of Wickets**
1-0, 2-17, 3-19, 4-79, 5-135, 6-135, 7-165, 8-183, 9-190
1-29, 2-35, 3-48, 4-87, 5-92

Umpires: BR Doctrove (West Indies) & PD Parker (Australia)
Toss: South Africa
Man of the Match: Inzamam-ul-Haq

## Pakistan won by 5 wickets

---

## THIRD TEST – SOUTH AFRICA v. PAKISTAN
### 26–28 January 2007 at Cape Town

### PAKISTAN

| | First Innings | | | | Second Innings | | | |
|---|---|---|---|---|---|---|---|---|
| Mohammad Hafeez | c de Villiers b Ntini | | | 10 | c Prince b Steyn | | | 10 |
| Imran Farhat | c Smith b Kallis | | | 20 | lbw b Steyn | | | 13 |
| Yasir Hameed | c Kallis b Ntini | | | 7 | c Prince b Hall | | | 35 |
| Younis Khan | c de Villiers b Kallis | | | 8 | c Boucher b Ntini | | | 0 |
| Mohammad Yousuf | c Prince b Ntini | | | 83 | b Hall | | | 18 |
| Inzamam-ul-Haq (capt) | c Boucher b Hall | | | 6 | c Boucher b Steyn | | | 22 |
| *Kamran Akmal | c de Villiers b Steyn | | | 0 | st Boucher b Harris | | | 6 |
| Mohammad Sami | c Boucher b Kallis | | | 4 | c Amla b Kallis | | | 31 |
| Shahid Nazir | c Harris b Ntini | | | 3 | c Boucher b Kallis | | | 27 |
| Danish Kaneria | c Boucher b Kallis | | | 0 | not out | | | 1 |
| Mohammad Asif | not out | | | 0 | c Prince b Harris | | | 6 |
| Extras | lb 2, w 6, nb 8 | | | 16 | b 6, lb 2, w 5, nb 4 | | | 17 |
| | (all out 43.1 overs) | | | **157** | (all out 51.2 overs) | | | **186** |

| | First Innings | | | | Second Innings | | | |
|---|---|---|---|---|---|---|---|---|
| | O | M | R | W | O | M | R | W |
| Steyn | 11 | 3 | 40 | 1 | 13 | 3 | 47 | 3 |
| Ntini | 13.1 | 2 | 44 | 4 | 10 | 2 | 41 | 1 |
| Kallis | 11 | 1 | 42 | 4 | 7 | 0 | 36 | 2 |
| Hall | 8 | 2 | 29 | 1 | 7 | 1 | 23 | 2 |
| Harris | – | – | – | – | 14.2 | 2 | 31 | 2 |

**Fall of Wickets**
1-13, 2-27, 3-47, 4-54, 5-81, 6-90, 7-151, 8-154, 9-156
1-17, 2-28, 3-44, 4-83, 5-92, 6-111, 7-121, 8-176, 9-179

### SOUTH AFRICA

| | First Innings | | | | Second Innings | | | |
|---|---|---|---|---|---|---|---|---|
| HH Dippenaar | lbw b Mohammad Asif | | | 0 | (2) c Kamran Akmal b D Kaneria | | | 3 |
| GC Smith (capt) | c Inzamam-ul-Haq b Shahid Nazir | | | 64 | (1) lbw b Mohammad Asif | | | 33 |
| HM Amla | c Kamran Akmal b M Asif | | | 2 | (4) c Kamran Akmal b M Asif | | | 3 |
| JH Kallis | c Kamran Akmal b M Sami | | | 28 | (5) b Shahid Nazir | | | 51 |
| AG Prince | c Yasir Hameed b Danish Kaneria | | | 19 | (6) not out | | | 59 |
| AB de Villiers | b Danish Kaneria | | | 11 | (7) not out | | | 4 |
| PL Harris | c Younis Khan b Mohammad Asif | | | 1 | (3) lbw b Danish Kaneria | | | 0 |
| *MV Boucher | not out | | | 40 | | | | |
| AJ Hall | c Kamran Akmal b Danish Kaneria | | | 4 | | | | |
| DW Steyn | run out | | | 3 | | | | |
| M Ntini | lbw b Mohammad Sami | | | 0 | | | | |
| Extras | b 4, lb 4, w 1, nb 2 | | | 11 | b 4, lb 4 | | | 8 |
| | (all out 53 overs) | | | **183** | (5 wkts 64 overs) | | | **161** |

| | First Innings | | | | Second Innings | | | |
|---|---|---|---|---|---|---|---|---|
| | O | M | R | W | O | M | R | W |
| Mohammad Asif | 16 | 2 | 53 | 3 | 21 | 8 | 43 | 2 |
| Mohammad Sami | 9 | 1 | 41 | 2 | 1 | 0 | 9 | 0 |
| Shahid Nazir | 8 | 0 | 37 | 1 | 9 | 1 | 42 | 1 |
| Danish Kaneria | 20 | 6 | 44 | 3 | 28 | 9 | 52 | 2 |
| Mohammad Hafeez | – | – | – | – | 5 | 1 | 7 | 0 |

**Fall of Wickets**
1-0, 2-12, 3-92, 4-107, 5-128, 6-133, 7-133, 8-140, 9-183
1-30, 2-36, 3-36, 4-39, 5-156

Umpires: SA Bucknor (West Indies) & PD Parker (Australia)
Toss: South Africa
Man of the Match: JH Kallis
Man of the Series: JH Kallis

## South Africa won by 5 wickets

## SERIES AVERAGES
### South Africa v. Pakistan

### SOUTH AFRICA

| Batting | M | Inns | NO | Runs | HS | Av | 100 | 50 | c/st |
|---|---|---|---|---|---|---|---|---|---|
| AG Prince | 3 | 5 | 1 | 240 | 138 | 60.00 | 1 | 1 | 6/- |
| JH Kallis | 3 | 6 | 1 | 272 | 91 | 54.40 | - | 3 | 3/- |
| HH Gibbs | 2 | 3 | 0 | 136 | 94 | 45.33 | - | 1 | 7/- |
| MV Boucher | 3 | 4 | 1 | 123 | 46 | 41.00 | - | - | 11/1 |
| SM Pollock | 2 | 3 | 1 | 79 | 39* | 39.50 | - | - | 1/- |
| HM Amla | 3 | 6 | 1 | 161 | 71 | 32.20 | - | 2 | 4/- |
| GC Smith | 3 | 6 | 0 | 167 | 64 | 27.83 | - | 1 | 2/- |
| A Nel | 2 | 3 | 1 | 38 | 23* | 19.00 | - | - | 2/- |
| AB de Villiers | 3 | 6 | 1 | 48 | 15 | 9.60 | - | - | 7/- |
| M Ntini | 3 | 4 | 1 | 23 | 18 | 7.66 | - | - | 1/- |
| AJ Hall | 1 | 1 | 0 | 4 | 4 | 4.00 | - | - | -/- |
| DW Steyn | 1 | 1 | 0 | 3 | 3 | 3.00 | - | - | -/- |
| PL Harris | 3 | 6 | 0 | 15 | 7 | 2.50 | - | - | 1/- |
| HH Dippenaar | 1 | 2 | 0 | 3 | 3 | 1.50 | - | - | -/- |

| Bowling | Overs | Mds | Runs | Wkts | Av | Best | 5/inn | 10m |
|---|---|---|---|---|---|---|---|---|
| AJ Hall | 15 | 3 | 52 | 3 | 17.33 | 2-23 | - | - |
| M Ntini | 103.1 | 21 | 355 | 19 | 18.68 | 6-59 | 2 | - |
| DW Steyn | 24 | 6 | 87 | 4 | 21.75 | 3-47 | - | - |
| PL Harris | 58.1 | 11 | 135 | 6 | 22.50 | 4-46 | - | - |
| SM Pollock | 67 | 18 | 187 | 8 | 23.37 | 3-60 | - | - |
| JH Kallis | 68 | 4 | 250 | 10 | 25.00 | 4-42 | - | - |
| A Nel | 85.5 | 14 | 300 | 4 | 75.00 | 3-100 | - | - |

### PAKISTAN

| Batting | M | Inns | NO | Runs | HS | Av | 100 | 50 | c/st |
|---|---|---|---|---|---|---|---|---|---|
| Younis Khan | 3 | 6 | 1 | 226 | 68 | 45.20 | - | 2 | 9/- |
| Inzamam-ul-Haq | 3 | 6 | 1 | 198 | 92* | 39.60 | - | 1 | 2/- |
| Mohammad Yousuf | 2 | 4 | 0 | 151 | 83 | 37.75 | - | 1 | -/- |
| Naved-ul-Hasan | 1 | 2 | 0 | 63 | 33 | 31.50 | - | - | -/- |
| Kamran Akmal | 3 | 6 | 1 | 140 | 57* | 28.00 | - | 1 | 10/1 |
| Imran Farhat | 3 | 6 | 0 | 134 | 68 | 22.33 | - | 1 | 1/- |
| Shahid Nazir | 2 | 4 | 0 | 85 | 40 | 21.25 | - | - | -/- |
| Yasir Hameed | 3 | 6 | 0 | 124 | 65 | 20.66 | - | 1 | 3/- |
| Mohammad Hafeez | 3 | 6 | 0 | 99 | 32 | 16.50 | - | - | -/- |
| Mohammad Sami | 2 | 3 | 0 | 45 | 31 | 15.00 | - | - | 1/- |
| Mohammad Asif | 3 | 5 | 3 | 22 | 8* | 11.00 | - | - | -/- |
| Danish Kaneria | 3 | 5 | 1 | 25 | 23 | 6.25 | - | - | 3/- |
| Faisal Iqbal | 1 | 2 | 0 | 10 | 9 | 5.00 | - | - | 1/- |
| Shoaib Akhtar | 1 | 1 | 0 | 4 | 4 | 4.00 | - | - | -/- |

| Bowling | Overs | Mds | Runs | Wkts | Av | Best | 5/inn | 10m |
|---|---|---|---|---|---|---|---|---|
| Shoaib Akhtar | 11 | 2 | 36 | 4 | 9.00 | 4-36 | - | - |
| Mohammad Asif | 125.5 | 34 | 351 | 19 | 18.47 | 5-76 | 2 | - |
| Danish Kaneria | 179.1 | 45 | 395 | 15 | 26.33 | 4-105 | - | - |
| Mohammad Sami | 45 | 7 | 155 | 4 | 38.75 | 2-41 | - | - |
| Naved-ul-Hasan | 24 | 5 | 113 | 2 | 56.50 | 2-92 | - | - |
| Shahid Nazir | 40 | 3 | 188 | 2 | 94.00 | 1-37 | - | - |
| Mohammad Hafeez | 36 | 4 | 99 | 1 | 99.00 | 1-36 | - | - |

Also bowled: Imran Farhat 8-0-26-0.

## TWENTY20 INTERNATIONAL
## v. Pakistan

2 February 2007 Day/Night at Johannesburg
**Pakistan** 129 for 8 (20 overs)
**South Africa** 132 for 0 (11.3 overs) (GC Smith 71*,
LL Bosman 53*)
*South Africa won by 10 wickets*

## ONE-DAY INTERNATIONALS

### Match One
4 February 2007 at Centurion
**South Africa** 392 for 6 (50 overs) (JH Kallis 88*,
MV Boucher 78, GC Smith 72, AB de Villiers 67)
**Pakistan** 228 all out (46.4 overs) (Shoaib Malik 52*)
*South Africa won by 164 runs*

### Match Two
7 February 2007 Day/Night at Durban
**Pakistan** 351 for 4 (50 overs) (Mohammad Yousuf 101*,
Younis Khan 93, Shahid Afridi 77*, Imran Nazir 57)
**South Africa** 210 all out (40 overs)
*Pakistan won by 141 runs*

### Match Three
9 February 2007 Day/Night at Port Elizabeth
**Pakistan** 245 for 8 (49.5 overs) (Mohammad Yousuf 79,
AJ Hall 4 for 35)
**South Africa**
*Match abandoned – no result*

### Match Four
11 February 2007 at Cape Town
**Pakistan** 107 all out (45.4 overs)
**South Africa** 113 for 0 (14 overs) (GC Smith 56*,
AB de Villiers 50*)
*South Africa won by 10 wickets*

### Match Five
14 February 2007 Day/Night at Johannesburg
**Pakistan** 153 all out (40.5 overs) (SM Pollock 5 for 23)
**South Africa** 156 for 1 (28.2 overs) (AB de Villiers 71*,
JH Kallis 71*)
*South Africa won by 9 wickets*

**South Africa won the series 3–1**

# SRI LANKA

Sri Lanka Cricket

Falling at the final hurdle of the 2007 World Cup made it a bitter-sweet year for Sri Lanka. On the one hand, a genuinely exciting team is emerging from the teardrop isle; on the other, a lack of tangible success is proving a frustratingly familiar tale.

There was no doubt that the Sri Lankans were the second-best team at the World Cup, but Australia were still some distance ahead of them when the pressure was on. Sri Lanka's big guns were themselves outpounded as Adam Gilchrist and company showed them that they still have a way to go.

Yet get there they might. With Glenn McGrath following Shane Warne into retirement, and the likes of Shaun Pollock, Andrew Flintoff and Anil Kumble all either facing up to retirement or reduced effectiveness themselves, it is Muttiah Muralitharan who now stands unchallenged as the outstanding all-conditions bowler in world cricket. What is more, Murali was hinting at playing on for another four years – especially on the Test match stage where he is set to grab Warne's world record 708-wicket mark and drag it into the realms of fantasy.

With 700 wickets already in his first 16 years of Tests, the rubber-wristed 'Kandy man' could even get close to a barely-believable 900 if he remains as good as his word. What is more, Chaminda Vaas, for so long Murali's one world-class support act in the Sri Lankan attack, has also voiced his determination to stay around until the next World Cup is held in the subcontinent… also in 2011.

With Lasith Malinga and Dilhara Fernando both now established as bowlers of genuine pace and threat, and with Farvez Maharoof to provide back-up, Sri Lanka look capable of fielding perhaps the world game's best all-round bowling attack in the next few years.

Under Mahela Jayawardene's maturing captaincy, and with a deep and strong batting line-up centred around Kumar Sangakkara and Upul Tharanga, the new coaching team assembled by Trevor Bayliss, who succeeded his fellow Australian Tom Moody as head coach following the World Cup, has much to work with.

Such is Sri Lanka's array of batting talent, indeed, and the numbers of youthful prodigies emerging, that even the sad freezing out of former captain Marvan Atapattu – due to a stand-off between him and Asantha de Mel, the chairman of selectors – did not seem to cost the national side too many runs. The form of the seemingly ageless Sanath Jayasuriya had much to do with that, of course, but the bottom line after a year dominated by one-day international cricket is that Sri Lanka still have much to prove.

A short Test series and one-day rubber were drawn in New Zealand, but Sri Lanka were beaten by India and Pakistan in one-day tournaments either side of the World Cup. Then England beat them 3-2 on home soil in a series which followed on from their disappointing performance at the inaugural world Twenty20 championship in South Africa for which they were one of the highly fancied teams. The ICC Champions Trophy campaign in India proved a similar story.

There was, in compensation, a 3-0 Test series trouncing of Bangladesh, during which Sangakkara completed record successive double-hundreds, while a one-day series against the same opponents was also won. Sri Lanka, however, should be doing very much better than that.

The exciting Lasith Malinga launches himself into another of his extraordinary slinging deliveries. Genuinely fast, he is a key member of Sri Lanka's world-class attack.

## FIRST TEST – SRI LANKA v. BANGLADESH
### 25–28 June 2007 at Colombo (SSC)

### BANGLADESH

| | First Innings | | Second Innings | |
|---|---|---|---|---|
| Javed Omar | c Jayawardene HAPW b Vaas | 8 | lbw b Malinga | 62 |
| Shahriar Nafees | c Jayawardene HAPW b Malinga | 15 | c & b Muralitharan | 38 |
| Rajin Saleh | lbw b Muralitharan | 3 | c Jayawardene DPMD b Dilshan | 51 |
| Habibul Bashar | lbw b Fernando | 2 | c Jayawardene HAPW b Vaas | 17 |
| M Ashraful (capt) | c Warnapura b Fernando | 7 | c Vaas b Muralitharan | 37 |
| Shakib Al Hasan | lbw b Muralitharan | 16 | c Warnapura b Malinga | 8 |
| *Khaled Mashud | not out | 12 | b Malinga | 1 |
| Shahadat Hossain | c Muralitharan b Fernando | 1 | (10) st J'wardene HAPW b M'tharan | 1 |
| Mashrafe bin Mortaza | st J'wardene HAPW b M'tharan | 1 | (8) lbw b Muralitharan | 9 |
| Mohammad Rafique | lbw b Muralitharan | 11 | (9) b Malinga | 0 |
| Abdur Razzak | st J'wardene HAPW b M'tharan | 4 | not out | 0 |
| Extras | lb 2, nb 7 | 9 | b 2, lb 10, w 1, nb 17 | 30 |
| | (all out 32.3 overs) | 89 | (all out 87.1 overs) | 254 |

| | First Innings | | | | Second Innings | | | |
|---|---|---|---|---|---|---|---|---|
| | O | M | R | W | O | M | R | W |
| Vaas | 7 | 3 | 8 | 1 | 12 | 3 | 36 | 1 |
| Malinga | 7 | 0 | 31 | 1 | 17 | 2 | 80 | 4 |
| Fernando | 11 | 2 | 33 | 3 | 15 | 5 | 28 | 0 |
| Muralitharan | 7.3 | 3 | 15 | 5 | 36.1 | 12 | 87 | 4 |
| Dilshan | - | - | - | - | 7 | 3 | 11 | 1 |

**Fall of Wickets**
1-28, 2-28, 3-32, 4-43, 5-50, 6-61, 7-64, 8-69, 9-85
1-86, 2-126, 3-160, 4-227, 5-231, 6-238, 7-250, 8-252, 9-253

### SRI LANKA

| | First Innings | |
|---|---|---|
| MG Vandort | c Nafees b Mohammad Rafique | 117 |
| BSM Warnapura | lbw b Shahadat Hossain | 0 |
| KC Sangakkara | c Khaled Mashud b S Hossain | 6 |
| DPMD J'wardene (capt) | c Razzak b M bin Mortaza | 127 |
| LPC Silva | c M bin Mortaza b A Razzak | 1 |
| TM Dilshan | run out | 79 |
| *HAPW Jayawardene | not out | 120 |
| WPUJC Vaas | not out | 100 |
| SL Malinga | | |
| M Muralitharan | | |
| CRD Fernando | | |
| Extras | b 6, lb 7, w 2, nb 12 | 27 |
| | (6 wkts dec 135.5 overs) | 577 |

| | First Innings | | | |
|---|---|---|---|---|
| | O | M | R | W |
| Mashrafe bin Mortaza | 19 | 2 | 72 | 1 |
| Shahadat Hossain | 18 | 0 | 102 | 2 |
| Abdur Razzak | 30 | 2 | 109 | 1 |
| Mohammad Rafique | 28.5 | 1 | 138 | 1 |
| Shakib Al Hasan | 16 | 0 | 57 | 0 |
| Mohammad Ashraful | 13 | 0 | 52 | 0 |
| Rajin Saleh | 3 | 0 | 12 | 0 |
| Habibul Bashar | 8 | 0 | 22 | 0 |

**Fall of Wickets**
1-1, 2-14, 3-187, 4-304, 5-321, 6-354

Umpires: Asad Rauf (Pakistan) & SL Shastri (India)
Toss: Sri Lanka
Test debut: BSM Warnapura
Man of the Match: M Muralitharan

### Sri Lanka won by an innings and 234 runs

## SECOND TEST – SRI LANKA v. BANGLADESH
### 3–5 July 2007 at Colombo (PSS)

### BANGLADESH

| | First Innings | | Second Innings | |
|---|---|---|---|---|
| Javed Omar | c Jayawardene HAPW b Malinga | 8 | lbw b Vaas | 28 |
| Shahriar Nafees | lbw b Malinga | 0 | c Jayawardene HAPW b Vaas | 20 |
| Rajin Saleh | c J'wardene DPMD b M'tharan | 21 | c J'wardene DPMD b Fernando | 0 |
| Habibul Bashar | c Jayawardene DPMD b Malinga | 5 | (5) b Fernando | 12 |
| M Ashraful (capt) | c Warnapura b Malinga | 0 | (6) not out | 129 |
| Mehrab Hossain | b Fernando | 6 | (4) b Fernando | 8 |
| *Mushfiqur Rahim | c J'wardene HAPW b M'tharan | 9 | c & b Muralitharan | 80 |
| Mashrafe bin Mortaza | c J'wardene DPMD b Fernando | 0 | (9) lbw b Vaas | 0 |
| Mohammad Rafique | c Vaas b Muralitharan | 2 | (10) run out | 3 |
| Mohammad Sharif | not out | 4 | (8) lbw b Vaas | 2 |
| Shahadat Hossain | b Muralitharan | 1 | run out | 2 |
| Extras | lb 1, w 1, nb 4 | 6 | b 2, lb 2, w 2, nb 9 | 15 |
| | (all out 25.2 overs) | 62 | (all out 86.2 overs) | 299 |

| | First Innings | | | | Second Innings | | | |
|---|---|---|---|---|---|---|---|---|
| | O | M | R | W | O | M | R | W |
| Vaas | 5 | 1 | 6 | 0 | 20.2 | 8 | 55 | 4 |
| Malinga | 9 | 1 | 25 | 4 | 15 | 1 | 86 | 0 |
| Fernando | 6 | 1 | 16 | 2 | 17 | 2 | 60 | 3 |
| Muralitharan | 5.2 | 1 | 14 | 4 | 28 | 6 | 84 | 1 |
| Dilshan | - | - | - | - | 6 | 1 | 10 | 0 |

**Fall of Wickets**
1-3, 2-14, 3-22, 4-22, 5-33, 6-45, 7-48, 8-51, 9-59
1-48, 2-51, 3-55, 4-59, 5-78, 6-269, 7-276, 8-276, 9-286

### SRI LANKA

| | First Innings | |
|---|---|---|
| MG Vandort | b Mashrafe bin Mortaza | 14 |
| BSM Warnapura | c Nafees b Shahadat Hossain | 82 |
| KC Sangakkara | not out | 200 |
| DPMD J'wardene (capt) | c Nafees b Shahadat Hossain | 49 |
| LPC Silva | c M bin Mortaza b M Hossain | 33 |
| TM Dilshan | b Mehrab Hossain | 0 |
| *HAPW Jayawardene | c Javed Omar b M bin Mortaza | 14 |
| WPUJC Vaas | not out | 30 |
| SL Malinga | | |
| M Muralitharan | | |
| CRD Fernando | | |
| Extras | b 6, lb 7, w 3, nb 13 | 29 |
| | (6 wkts dec 124.5 overs) | 451 |

| | First Innings | | | |
|---|---|---|---|---|
| | O | M | R | W |
| Mashrafe bin Mortaza | 30 | 7 | 77 | 2 |
| Shahadat Hossain | 21 | 3 | 81 | 2 |
| Mohammad Sharif | 24 | 4 | 86 | 0 |
| Mohammad Rafique | 35 | 3 | 134 | 0 |
| Mohammad Ashraful | 7 | 0 | 31 | 0 |
| Mehrab Hossain | 7.5 | 0 | 29 | 2 |

**Fall of Wickets**
1-41, 2-169, 3-267, 4-359, 5-359, 6-395

Umpires: Asad Rauf (Pakistan) & RE Koertzen (South Africa)
Toss: Sri Lanka
Test debut: Mehrab Hossain
Man of the Match: KC Sangakkara

### Sri Lanka won by an innings and 90 runs

## THIRD TEST – SRI LANKA v. BANGLADESH
### 11–14 July 2007 at Kandy

### BANGLADESH

| | First Innings | | Second Innings | |
|---|---|---|---|---|
| Javed Omar | lbw b Malinga | 8 | c Sangakkara b Malinga | 22 |
| Shahriar Nafees | c de Silva b Muralitharan | 29 | c J'wardene DPMD b M'tharan | 64 |
| Habibul Bashar | c J'wardene HAPW b Maharoof | 18 | b Muralitharan | 15 |
| Rajin Saleh | c J'wardene DPMD b M'tharan | 0 | (7) c J'wardene HAPW b de Silva | 0 |
| M Ashraful (capt) | c Jayawardene HAPW b de Silva | 26 | (4) lbw b Muralitharan | 19 |
| Tushar Imran | c Jayawardene DPMD b de Silva | 17 | c J'wardene DPMD b Malinga | 17 |
| *Mushfiqur Rahim | not out | 11 | (5) c Tharanga b de Silva | 1 |
| Mashrafe bin Mortaza | c & b Muralitharan | 5 | c sub b Muralitharan | 8 |
| Mohammad Rafique | c & b Muralitharan | 5 | not out | 0 |
| Shahadat Hossain | c Dilshan b Muralitharan | 0 | b Muralitharan | 5 |
| Syed Rasel | c Silva b Muralitharan | 0 | c Maharoof b Muralitharan | 4 |
| Extras | b 4, lb 2, w 1, nb 5 | 12 | b 4, lb 1, w 3, nb 13 | 21 |
| | (all out 48.5 overs) | 131 | (all out 59 overs) | 176 |

| | First Innings | | | | Second Innings | | | |
|---|---|---|---|---|---|---|---|---|
| | O | M | R | W | O | M | R | W |
| Malinga | 10 | 2 | 41 | 1 | 10 | 0 | 46 | 2 |
| de Silva | 12 | 3 | 29 | 2 | 12 | 4 | 34 | 2 |
| Maharoof | 8 | 4 | 21 | 1 | 16 | 7 | 37 | 0 |
| Muralitharan | 14.5 | 6 | 28 | 6 | 21 | 5 | 54 | 6 |
| Dilshan | 4 | 1 | 6 | 0 | – | – | – | – |

**Fall of Wickets**
1-10, 2-50, 3-61, 4-64, 5-98, 6-111, 7-118, 8-130, 9-131
1-47, 2-98, 3-123, 4-138, 5-138, 6-142, 7-166, 8-167, 9-172

### SRI LANKA

| | First Innings | |
|---|---|---|
| MG Vandort | b Syed Rasel | 43 |
| WU Tharanga | lbw b Syed Rasel | 12 |
| KC Sangakkara | not out | 222 |
| DPMD J'wardene (capt) | c Mohammad Ashraful b S Rasel | 165 |
| LPC Silva | run out | 25 |
| TM Dilshan | not out | 17 |
| *HAPW Jayawardene | | |
| MF Maharoof | | |
| WRS de Silva | | |
| M Muralitharan | | |
| SL Malinga | | |
| Extras | b 4, lb 2, w 2, nb 8 | 16 |
| | (4 wkts dec 107 overs) | 500 |

| | First Innings | | | |
|---|---|---|---|---|
| | O | M | R | W |
| Mashrafe bin Mortaza | 24 | 2 | 125 | 0 |
| Syed Rasel | 31 | 1 | 104 | 3 |
| Shahadat Hossain | 16 | 1 | 71 | 0 |
| Mohammad Rafique | 14 | 1 | 72 | 0 |
| Mohammad Ashraful | 12 | 0 | 74 | 0 |
| Tushar Imran | 10 | 0 | 48 | 0 |

**Fall of Wickets**
1-47, 2-74, 3-385, 4-445

Umpires: RE Koertzen (South Africa) & SL Shastri (India)
Toss: Sri Lanka
Man of the Match: M Muralitharan
Man of the Series: M Muralitharan

### Sri Lanka won by an innings and 193 runs

## SERIES AVERAGES
### Sri Lanka v. Bangladesh

### SRI LANKA

| Batting | M | Inns | NO | Runs | HS | Av | 100 | 50 | c/st |
|---|---|---|---|---|---|---|---|---|---|
| KC Sangakkara | 3 | 3 | 2 | 428 | 222* | 428.00 | 2 | – | 1/- |
| HAPW Jayawardene | 3 | 2 | 1 | 134 | 120* | 134.00 | 1 | – | 9/3 |
| DPMD Jayawardene | 3 | 3 | 0 | 341 | 165 | 113.66 | 2 | – | 9/- |
| MG Vandort | 3 | 3 | 0 | 174 | 117 | 58.00 | 1 | – | 1/- |
| TM Dilshan | 3 | 3 | 0 | 96 | 79 | 48.00 | – | 1 | 1/- |
| BSM Warnapura | 2 | 2 | 0 | 82 | 82 | 41.00 | – | 1 | 3/- |
| LPC Silva | 3 | 3 | 0 | 59 | 33 | 19.66 | – | – | 1/- |
| WU Tharanga | 1 | 1 | 0 | 12 | 12 | 12.00 | – | – | 1/- |
| WPUJC Vaas | 2 | 2 | 2 | 130 | 100* | – | – | 1 | 2/- |
| M Muralitharan | 3 | 0 | 0 | 0 | 0 | – | – | – | 5/- |
| CRD Fernando | 2 | 0 | 0 | 0 | 0 | – | – | – | -/- |
| WRS de Silva | 1 | 0 | 0 | 0 | 0 | – | – | – | 1/- |
| MF Maharoof | 1 | 0 | 0 | 0 | 0 | – | – | – | 1/- |
| SL Malinga | 3 | 0 | 0 | 0 | 0 | – | – | – | -/- |

| Bowling | Overs | Mds | Runs | Wkts | Av | Best | 5/inn | 10m |
|---|---|---|---|---|---|---|---|---|
| M Muralitharan | 112.5 | 33 | 282 | 26 | 10.84 | 6-28 | 3 | 1 |
| WRS de Silva | 24 | 7 | 63 | 4 | 15.75 | 2-29 | – | – |
| CRD Fernando | 49 | 10 | 137 | 8 | 17.12 | 3-33 | – | – |
| WPUJC Vaas | 44.2 | 15 | 105 | 6 | 17.50 | 4-55 | – | – |
| SL Malinga | 68 | 6 | 309 | 12 | 25.75 | 4-25 | – | – |
| TM Dilshan | 17 | 5 | 27 | 1 | 27.00 | 1-11 | – | – |
| MF Maharoof | 24 | 11 | 58 | 1 | 58.00 | 1-21 | – | – |

### BANGLADESH

| Batting | M | Inns | NO | Runs | HS | Av | 100 | 50 | c/st |
|---|---|---|---|---|---|---|---|---|---|
| Mohammad Ashraful | 3 | 6 | 1 | 218 | 129* | 43.60 | 1 | – | 1/- |
| Mushfiqur Rahim | 2 | 4 | 1 | 101 | 80 | 33.66 | – | 1 | 1/- |
| Shahriar Nafees | 3 | 6 | 0 | 166 | 64 | 27.66 | – | 1 | 3/- |
| Javed Omar | 3 | 6 | 0 | 136 | 62 | 22.66 | – | 1 | 1/- |
| Tushar Imran | 1 | 2 | 0 | 34 | 17 | 17.00 | – | – | -/- |
| Khaled Mashud | 1 | 2 | 0 | 13 | 12* | 13.00 | – | – | 1/- |
| Rajin Saleh | 3 | 6 | 0 | 75 | 51 | 12.50 | – | 1 | -/- |
| Shakib Al Hasan | 1 | 2 | 0 | 24 | 16 | 12.00 | – | – | -/- |
| Habibul Bashar | 3 | 6 | 0 | 69 | 18 | 11.50 | – | – | 1/- |
| Mehrab Hossain | 1 | 2 | 0 | 14 | 8 | 7.00 | – | – | -/- |
| Mohammad Sharif | 1 | 2 | 1 | 6 | 4* | 6.00 | – | – | -/- |
| Mohammad Rafique | 3 | 6 | 1 | 21 | 11 | 4.20 | – | – | -/- |
| Abdur Razzak | 1 | 2 | 1 | 4 | 4 | 4.00 | – | – | 1/- |
| Mashrafe bin Mortaza | 3 | 6 | 0 | 23 | 9 | 3.83 | – | – | 2/- |
| Syed Rasel | 1 | 2 | 0 | 4 | 4 | 2.00 | – | – | -/- |
| Shahadat Hossain | 3 | 6 | 0 | 10 | 5 | 1.66 | – | – | -/- |

| Bowling | Overs | Mds | Runs | Wkts | Av | Best | 5/inn | 10m |
|---|---|---|---|---|---|---|---|---|
| Mehrab Hossain | 7.5 | 0 | 29 | 2 | 14.50 | 2-29 | – | – |
| Syed Rasel | 31 | 1 | 104 | 3 | 34.66 | 3-104 | – | – |
| Shahadat Hossain | 55 | 4 | 254 | 4 | 63.50 | 2-81 | – | – |
| Mashrafe bin Mortaza | 73 | 11 | 274 | 3 | 91.33 | 2-77 | – | – |
| Abdur Razzak | 30 | 2 | 109 | 1 | 109.00 | 1-109 | – | – |
| Mohammad Rafique | 77.5 | 5 | 344 | 1 | 344.00 | 1-138 | – | – |

Also bowled: Rajin Saleh 3-0-12-0, Habibul Bashar 8-0-22-0, Tushar Imran 10-0-48-0,
Shakib Al Hasan 16-0-57-0, Mohammad Sharif 24-4-86-0, Mohammad Ashraful 32-0-157-0.

## ONE–DAY INTERNATIONALS v. Bangladesh

**Match One**
20 July 2007 at Colombo (PSS)
**Sri Lanka** 234 for 6 (50 overs) (LPC Silva 65, WU Tharanga 57)
**Bangladesh** 164 all out (40.3 overs) (CRD Fernando 4 for 24)
*Sri Lanka won by 70 runs*

**Match Two**
23 July 2007 at Colombo (RPS)
**Bangladesh** 137 all out (46.5 overs) (ST Jayasuriya 4 for 31)
**Sri Lanka** 141 for 5 (31.1 overs)
*Sri Lanka won by 5 wickets*

**Match Three**
25 July 2007 at Colombo (RPS)
**Sri Lanka** 196 all out (39.5 overs) (J Mubarak 72)
**Bangladesh** 157 all out (37.1 overs) (T Iqbal 54, ST Jayasuriya 4 for 14)
*Sri Lanka won by 39 runs*
**Sri Lanka won the series 3-0**

# ICC WORLD CUP

**by Haydn Gill**

The Cricket World Cup (CWC) 2007, the first to be staged in the West Indies, elicited mixed reactions. For some, there was a sense of accomplishment. Others described it as the worst ever, plagued by disaster after disaster, none more distressing than the death of widely admired Pakistan coach Bob Woolmer within the first fortnight and the subsequent confusion over whether or not he had been murdered.

A day after the tournament, while International Cricket Council (ICC) chief executive Malcolm Speed was labelling the event a success, critics were branding it a fiasco. A more middle-of-the-road assessment recognised that there was the good, the bad and the ugly, in varying degrees. The frequently stated dream of Chris Dehring, head of the company set up by the West Indies Cricket Board (WICB) to plan and run it all, was to stage 'the best World Cup ever'. Ultimately, there were more negatives than positives.

The upside included a collection of modern stadiums, either completely new or extensively refurbished, state-of-the-art facilities second to none that will prove one of the legacies of what was the biggest sporting extravaganza ever undertaken in the scattered cricketing mini-states of the Caribbean. Moreover, in spite of the stunning elimination of India and Pakistan at the group stage – and most of the thousands of their supporters as a consequence – officials were able to report record ticket revenue, surpassing the receipts from the World Cup in South Africa four years earlier.

From the moment the Caribbean was awarded the event, sceptics doubted the region's capabilities to handle such challenges as logistics, accommodation, transportation, security and event management. While there were issues on each count, the general consensus was a pass mark.

On the field of play, you had to admire the way mighty Australia achieved an unprecedented hat-trick of titles, creating an aura of invincibility and a record of phenomenal achievement in maintaining a 100 per cent winning streak, as they had done in South Africa. The champions blasted totals in excess of 300 on five occasions, won three matches by margins of better than 200 runs, one by ten wickets and another by nine. They also produced both the tournament's leading run-scorer, the muscular left-hander Matthew Hayden, and top wicket-taker, the remarkable Glenn McGrath who immediately proceeded into retirement.

The eight previous World Cups had each unearthed a host of astounding individual performances but few matched some of the displays on show in the Caribbean. No one had ever blazed to a CWC hundred as fast as Hayden, who rushed to the landmark off 66 balls against South Africa in the group stage clash of the two most-favoured teams. No one in any previous one-day international had clouted six sixes in an over as South Africa's Herschelle Gibbs did against the

Ireland's promising young opening bowler, Boyd Rankin, celebrates the prized wicket of Younis Khan as Pakistan slip to a shock defeat, and exit, in the group stage.

Habibul Bashar, the Bangladesh captain, hits out during the other major upset of the initial group stage: his side's memorable victory against India.

Netherlands leg spinner Daan van Bunge, like Hayden taking advantage of the short boundaries at the new Warner Park in St Kitts. No one in any previous World Cup match had snatched four wickets in four balls as exciting Sri Lankan fast bowler Lasith Malinga did with his slingshot action against South Africa. And Adam Gilchrist's amazing 149 off 104 balls off the worthy finalists, Sri Lanka, was more than simply the highest individual score in any World Cup final. It was an unforgettable exhibition of power hitting.

While such feats will long be remembered, so too will the fact that the tournament contained too few close, thrilling contests, in spite of a format that was designed to make things interesting from the Super Eights stage.

In too many matches, results were obvious from early on, removing the element of excitement that is fundamental to one-day cricket. Among the exceptions were a dramatic tie between Zimbabwe and Ireland at the group stage. And, in the Super Eights, South Africa's win by one wicket over Sri Lanka and last-over clinchers by Sri Lanka, by two runs over England, and by England, by one wicket over the West Indies in a match that marked an emotional send-off for retiring West Indies captain Brian Lara.

There was also a touching, teary-eyed farewell for Pakistan's Inzamam-ul-Haq who quit the captaincy and announced his retirement from one-day internationals a day after his team suffered a shock loss in the group stage to spirited Ireland, the day of Woolmer's death.

Competing at the World Cup for the first time, the part-timers of Ireland made a name for themselves by earning their dramatic tie against Zimbabwe in their opener and following up with their upset of Pakistan two days later at Kingston's Sabina Park on St Patrick's Day, the same day that Bangladesh upstaged India by five wickets at the Queen's Park Oval in Port of Spain.

They were results that virtually sealed the fate of the two Asian powerhouses, putting Ireland and Bangladesh deservedly through to the Super Eights but denying the tournament the presence of two of the more exciting teams. It also led to several cancellations from their multitude of supporters, especially India, significantly reducing attendances for their anticipated later appearances.

Some matches did attract near-capacity crowds, including the final, which was watched by close to 27,000 spectators at the transformed Kensington Oval. Organisers reported that more than 400,000 fans came through the turnstiles during the tournament.

Among the negatives, observers questioned the stringent restrictions placed on spectators, lamenting the lack of traditional Caribbean flavour. The list of prohibited items in stadiums included alcohol, cans, plastic bottles and gas-operated horns, while fans had to seek written permission to bring in musical instruments. Once some of the limitations were eased in the latter half of the tournament, the stands took on more of the typical West Indian flair. The prolonged duration, however, was another issue. The 16 teams (a record number) took 47

Adam Gilchrist played one of the finest innings even of his explosive career to set Australia racing towards another World Cup final triumph, this time against Sri Lanka.

The victorious Australia team gather around the World Cup trophy itself, held between captain Ricky Ponting and Man of the Match Adam Gilchrist, and celebrate their remarkable third success in a row following tournament wins in both 1999 and 2003.

days to complete the 51 matches, due in some part to the decision to allocate reserve days for every match.

Woolmer's death cast a pall of gloom not only over the tournament but also over the game itself. The former England batsman was found unconscious in his Kingston hotel room and the sense of shock intensified when the Jamaican police initially stated they were treating it as murder. Three months later, they changed their conclusion, deeming it death by natural causes after all. Still, doubt remained up to an inquest in October and November, almost six months later.

The tournament will also be remembered for the farcical ending to the final that overshadowed Gilchrist's amazing effort. It was inconceivable that experienced match officials, all members of the ICC's so-called elite panel, should have made the elementary error that forced a bizarre finish in darkness to a match already shortened by rain, the first such occurrence in nine finals.

When Sri Lanka accepted an offer go off for bad light and concede the match with 35 overs completed, standing umpires Steve Bucknor and Aleem Dar and off-field officials Rudi Koertzen, Billy Bowden and match referee Jeff Crowe incorrectly advised the captains they would have to return to the ground the following day to complete the remaining three overs. In the end, the teams sensibly returned to the middle to finish off the match in near complete darkness, an anti-climax that typified some of the overall shortcomings.

At the presentation ceremony that followed, Speed, Dehring and WICB president Ken Gordon were roundly booed by spectators expressing their discontent for those they held responsible for the disappointment of an event that held so much promise.

*Haydn Gill is cricket correspondent for the* Nation *newspaper in Barbados for which he covered the World Cup.*

## Group A

14 March at St Kitts
**Australia** 334 for 6 (50 overs) (RT Ponting 113,
ML Hayden 60)
**Scotland** 131 for 9 (40.1 overs) (CJO Smith 51)
*Australia won by 203 runs*

16 March at St Kitts
**South Africa** 353 for 3 (40 overs) (JH Kallis 128*,
MV Boucher 75*, HH Gibbs 72, GC Smith 67)
**Holland** 132 for 9 (40 overs) (RN ten Doeschate 57)
*South Africa won by 221 runs*

18 March at St Kitts
**Australia** 358 for 5 (50 overs) (BJ Hodge 123, MJ Clarke 93*,
AC Gilchrist 57)
**Holland** 129 all out (26.5 overs) (GB Hogg 4 for 27)
*Australia won by 229 runs*

20 March at St Kitts
**Scotland** 186 for 8 (50 overs)
**South Africa** 188 for 3 (23.2 overs) (GC Smith 91,
AB de Villiers 62)
*South Africa won by 7 wickets*

22 March at St Kitts
**Scotland** 136 all out (34.1 overs)
**Holland** 140 for 2 (23.5 overs) (RN ten Doeschate 70*)
*Holland won by 8 wickets*

24 March at St Kitts
**Australia** 377 for 6 (50 overs) (ML Hayden 101, MJ Clarke 92,
RT Ponting 91)
**South Africa** 294 all out (48 overs) (AB de Villiers 92,
GC Smith 74)
*Australia won by 83 runs*

| | P | W | L | T | NR | RR | Pts |
|---|---|---|---|---|---|---|---|
| **Australia** | 3 | 3 | 0 | 0 | 0 | +3.43 | 6 |
| **South Africa** | 3 | 2 | 1 | 0 | 0 | +2.40 | 4 |
| **Holland** | 3 | 1 | 2 | 0 | 0 | -2.53 | 2 |
| **Scotland** | 3 | 0 | 3 | 0 | 0 | -3.79 | 0 |

## Group B

15 March at Trinidad
**Sri Lanka** 321 for 6 (50 overs) (DPMD Jayawardene 85,
KC Sangakkara 76, LPC Silva 55*)
**Bermuda** 78 all out (24.4 overs) (MF Maharoof 4 for 23)
*Sri Lanka won by 243 runs*

17 March at Trinidad
**India** 191 all out (49.3 overs) (SC Ganguly 66,
Mashrafe bin Mortaza 4 for 38)
**Bangladesh** 192 for 5 (48.3 overs) (Mushfiqur Rahim 56*,
Shakib Al Hasan 53, Tamim Iqbal 51)
*Bangladesh won by 5 wickets*

19 March at Trinidad
**India** 413 for 5 (50 overs) (V Sehwag 114, SC Ganguly 89,
Yuvraj Singh 83, SR Tendulkar 57*)
**Bermuda** 156 all out (43.1 overs) (DL Hemp 76*)
*India won by 257 runs*

21 March at Trinidad
**Sri Lanka** 318 for 4 (50 overs) (ST Jayasuriya 109,
KC Sangakkara 56, LPC Silva 52*)
**Bangladesh** 112 all out (37 overs)
*Sri Lanka won by 198 runs – DL Method: target: 311 from
46 overs*

23 March at Trinidad
**Sri Lanka** 254 for 6 (50 overs) (WU Tharanga 64, LPC Silva 59)
**India** 185 all out (43.3 overs) (R Dravid 60)
*Sri Lanka won by 69 runs*

25 March at Trinidad
**Bermuda** 94 for 9 (21 overs)
**Bangladesh** 96 for 3 (17.3 overs)
*Bangladesh won by 7 wickets – DL Method: target: 96 from 21 overs*

| | P | W | L | T | NR | RR | Pts |
|---|---|---|---|---|---|---|---|
| **Sri Lanka** | 3 | 3 | 0 | 0 | 0 | +3.18 | 6 |
| **Bangladesh** | 3 | 2 | 1 | 0 | 0 | -0.25 | 4 |
| **India** | 3 | 1 | 2 | 0 | 0 | +1.21 | 2 |
| **Bermuda** | 3 | 0 | 3 | 0 | 0 | -4.72 | 0 |

## Group C

14 March at St Lucia
**Canada** 199 all out (50 overs)
**Kenya** 203 for 3 (43.2 overs) (SO Tikolo 72*, MA Ouma 58)
*Kenya won by 7 wickets*

16 March at St Lucia
**England** 209 for 7 (50 overs) (KP Pietersen 60)
**New Zealand** 210 for 4 (41 overs) (SB Styris 87*, JDP Oram 63*)
*New Zealand won by 6 wickets*

18 March at St Lucia
**England** 279 for 6 (50 overs) (EC Joyce 66, PD Collingwood 62*)
**Canada** 228 for 7 (50 overs) (AA Mulla 58)
*England won by 51 runs*

20 March at St Lucia
**New Zealand** 331 for 7 (50 overs) (RL Taylor 85,
CD McMillan 71, SB Styris 63, SP Fleming 60)
**Kenya** 183 all out (49.2 overs) (RD Shah 71)
*New Zealand won by 148 runs*

22 March at St Lucia
**New Zealand** 363 for 5 (50 overs) (L Vincent 101,
SP Fleming 66, BB McCullum 52*)
**Canada** 249 for 9 (49.2 overs) (JM Davison 52, IS Billcliff 50)
*New Zealand won by 114 runs*

24 March at St Lucia
**Kenya** 177 all out (43 overs) (SO Tikolo 76)
**England** 178 for 3 (33 overs) (EC Joyce 75, KP Pietersen 56*)
*England won by 7 wickets*

|              | P | W | L | T | NR | RR    | Pts |
|--------------|---|---|---|---|----|-------|-----|
| New Zealand  | 3 | 3 | 0 | 0 | 0  | +2.14 | 6   |
| England      | 3 | 2 | 1 | 0 | 0  | +0.42 | 4   |
| Kenya        | 3 | 1 | 2 | 0 | 0  | -1.19 | 2   |
| Canada       | 3 | 0 | 3 | 0 | 0  | -1.39 | 0   |

## Group D

13 March at Jamaica
**West Indies** 241 for 9 (50 overs) (MN Samuels 63)
**Pakistan** 187 all out (47.2 overs) (Shoaib Malik 62)
*West Indies won by 54 runs*

15 March at Jamaica
**Ireland** 221 for 9 (50 overs) (JP Bray 115*)
**Zimbabwe** 221 all out (50 overs) (S Matsikenyeri 73*,
V Sibanda 67)
*Match tied*

17 March at Jamaica
**Pakistan** 132 all out (45.4 overs)
**Ireland** 133 for 7 (41.4 overs) (NJ O'Brien 72)
*Ireland won by 3 wickets*

19 March at Jamaica
**Zimbabwe** 202 for 5 (50 overs) (SC Williams 70*,
BRM Taylor 50)
**West Indies** 204 for 4 (47.5 overs)
*West Indies won by 6 wickets*

21 March at Jamaica
**Pakistan** 349 all out (49.5 overs) (Imran Nazir 160)
**Zimbabwe** 99 all out (19.1 overs)
*Pakistan won by 93 runs – DL Method: target 193 from 20 overs*

23 March at Jamaica
**Ireland** 183 for 8 (48 overs)
**West Indies** 190 for 2 (38.1 overs) (S Chanderpaul 102*)
*West Indies won by 8 wickets – DL Method: target 190 from
48 overs*

|             | P | W | L | T | NR | RR    | Pts |
|-------------|---|---|---|---|----|-------|-----|
| West Indies | 3 | 3 | 0 | 0 | 0  | +0.78 | 6   |
| Ireland     | 3 | 1 | 1 | 1 | 0  | -0.80 | 3   |
| Pakistan    | 3 | 1 | 2 | 0 | 0  | -0.50 | 2   |
| Zimbabwe    | 3 | 0 | 2 | 1 | 0  | +0.01 | 1   |

## Super Eights

27–28 March at Antigua
**Australia** 322 for 6 (50 overs) (ML Hayden 158)
**West Indies** 219 all out (45.3 overs) (BC Lara 77,
D Ramdin 52)
*Australia won by 103 runs*

28 March at Guyana
**Sri Lanka** 209 all out (49.3 overs) (TM Dilshan 58,
RP Arnold 50, CK Langeveldt 5 for 39)
**South Africa** 212 for 9 (48.2 overs) (JH Kallis 86,
GC Smith 59, SL Malinga 4 for 54)
*South Africa won by 1 wicket*

29 March at Antigua
**West Indies** 177 all out (44.4 overs)
**New Zealand** 179 for 3 (39.2 overs) (SB Styris 80*)
*New Zealand won by 7 wickets*

30 March at Guyana
**England** 266 for 7 (50 overs) (PD Collingwood 90)
**Ireland** 218 all out (48.1 overs) (NJ O'Brien 63,
A Flintoff 4 for 43)
*England won by 48 runs*

31 March at Antigua
**Bangladesh** 104 for 6 (22 overs)
**Australia** 106 for 0 (13.5 overs) (AC Gilchrist 59*)
*Australia won by 10 wickets – DL Method: target 105 from
22 overs*

1 April at Guyana
**Sri Lanka** 303 for 5 (50 overs) (ST Jayasuriya 115,
DPMD Jayawardene 82)
**West Indies** 190 all out (44.3 overs)
(S Chanderpaul 76)
*Sri Lanka won by 113 runs*

Lasith Malinga's express slingshots brought him an astonishing four wickets in four balls against South Africa.

2 April at Antigua
**Bangladesh** 174 all out (48.3 overs) (SB Styris 4 for 43)
**New Zealand** 178 for 1 (29.2 overs) (SP Fleming 102*, HJH Marshall 50*)
*New Zealand won by 9 wickets*

3 April at Guyana
**Ireland** 152 for 8 (35 overs)
**South Africa** 165 for 3 (31.3 overs) (JH Kallis 66*)
*South Africa won by 7 wickets – DL Method: target 160 from 35 overs)*

4 April at Antigua
**Sri Lanka** 235 all out (50 overs) (WU Tharanga 62, DPMD Jayawardene 56, SI Mahmood 4 for 50)
**England** 233 for 8 (50 overs) (KP Pietersen 58, RS Bopara 52)
*Sri Lanka won by 2 runs*

7 April at Guyana
**Bangladesh** 251 for 8 (50 overs) (Mohammad Ashraful 87, A Nel 5 for 45)
**South Africa** 184 all out (48.4 overs) (HH Gibbs 56*)
*Bangladesh won by 67 runs*

8 April at Antigua
**England** 247 all out (49.5 overs) (KP Pietersen 104, IR Bell 77)
**Australia** 248 for 3 (47.2 overs) (RT Ponting 86, MJ Clarke 55*)
*Australia won by 7 wickets*

9 April at Guyana
**New Zealand** 263 for 8 (50 overs)
(PG Fulton 83)
**Ireland** 134 all out (37.4 overs)
(DL Vettori 4 for 23)
*New Zealand won by 129 runs*

10 April at Grenada
**South Africa** 356 for 4 (50 overs)
(AB de Villiers 146, JH Kallis 81, HH Gibbs 61*, MV Boucher 52)
**West Indies** 289 for 9 (50 overs)
(RR Sarwan 92)
*South Africa won by 67 runs*

11 April at Barbados
**Bangladesh** 143 all out (37.2 overs) (Shakib Al Hasan 57*)
**England** 147 for 6 (44.5 overs)
*England won by 4 wickets*

12 April at Grenada
**New Zealand** 219 for 7 (50 overs) (SB Styris 111*)
**Sri Lanka** 222 for 4 (45.1 overs) (KC Sangakkara 69*, ST Jayasuriya 64)
*Sri Lanka won by 6 wickets*

13 April at Barbados
**Ireland** 91 all out (30 overs)
**Australia** 92 for 1 (12.2 overs)
*Australia won by 9 wickets*

14 April at Grenada
**South Africa** 193 for 7 (50 overs) (HH Gibbs 60)
**New Zealand** 196 for 5 (48.2 overs) (SB Styris 56, SP Fleming 50)
*New Zealand won by 5 wickets*

15 April at Barbados
**Ireland** 243 for 7 (50 overs) (WTS Porterfield 85)
**Bangladesh** 169 all out (41.2 overs)
*Ireland won by 74 runs*

16 April at Grenada
**Sri Lanka** 226 all out (49.4 overs) (DPMD Jayawardene 72, LPC Silva 64, NW Bracken 4 for 19)
**Australia** 232 for 3 (42.4 overs) (RT Ponting 66*, A Symonds 63*)
*Australia won by 7 wickets*

17 April at Barbados
**England** 154 all out (48 overs) (AJ Hall 5 for 18)
**South Africa** 157 for 1 (19.2 overs) (GC Smith 89*)
*South Africa won by 9 wickets*

18 April at Grenada
**Ireland** 77 all out (27.4 overs) (M Muralitharan 4 for 19,
MF Maharoof 4 for 25)
**Sri Lanka** 81 for 2 (10 overs)
*Sri Lanka won by 8 wickets*

19 April at Barbados
**West Indies** 230 for 5 (50 overs) (RR Sarwan 91*,
S Chanderpaul 50)
**Bangladesh** 131 all out (43.5 overs)
*West Indies won by 99 runs*

20 April at Grenada
**Australia** 348 for 6 (50 overs) (ML Hayden 103, RT Ponting 66,
SR Watson 65*)
**New Zealand** 133 all out (25.5 overs) (PG Fulton 62,
GB Hogg 4 for 29)
*Australia won by 215 runs*

21 April at Barbados
**West Indies** 300 all out (49.5 overs) (CH Gayle 79,
DS Smith 61, MN Samuels 51)
**England** 301 for 9 (49.5 overs) (KP Pietersen 100,
MP Vaughan 79)
*England won by 1 wicket*

| | P | W | L | T | NR | RR | Pts |
|---|---|---|---|---|---|---|---|
| **Australia** | 7 | 7 | 0 | 0 | 0 | +2.40 | 14 |
| **Sri Lanka** | 7 | 5 | 2 | 0 | 0 | +1.22 | 10 |
| **New Zealand** | 7 | 5 | 2 | 0 | 0 | +0.25 | 10 |
| **South Africa** | 7 | 4 | 3 | 0 | 0 | +0.27 | 8 |
| **England** | 7 | 3 | 4 | 0 | 0 | -0.39 | 6 |
| **West Indies** | 7 | 2 | 5 | 0 | 0 | -0.79 | 4 |
| **Bangladesh** | 7 | 1 | 6 | 0 | 0 | -1.16 | 2 |
| **Ireland** | 7 | 1 | 6 | 0 | 0 | -2.01 | 2 |

## Semi-Finals

24 April at Jamaica
**Sri Lanka** 289 for 5 (50 overs) (DPMD Jayawardene 115*,
WU Tharanga 73)
**New Zealand** 208 all out (41.4 overs) (M Muralitharan 4 for 31)
*Sri Lanka won by 81 runs*

25 April at St Lucia
**South Africa** 149 all out (43.5 overs) (SW Tait 4 for 39)
**Australia** 153 for 3 (31.3 overs) (MJ Clarke 60*)
*Australia won by 7 wickets*

## FINAL – SRI LANKA v. AUSTRALIA
### 28 April 2007 at Bridgetown, Barbados

### AUSTRALIA

| | | |
|---|---|---|
| *AC Gilchrist | c Silva b Fernando | 149 |
| ML Hayden | c Jayawardene b Malinga | 38 |
| RT Ponting (capt) | run out | 37 |
| A Symonds | not out | 23 |
| SR Watson | b Malinga | 3 |
| MJ Clarke | not out | 8 |
| MEK Hussey | | |
| GB Hogg | | |
| SW Tait | | |
| GD McGrath | | |
| NW Bracken | | |
| Extras | lb 4, w 16, nb 3 | 23 |
| | (4 wkts 38 overs) | **281** |

| | O | M | R | W |
|---|---|---|---|---|
| Vaas | 8 | 0 | 54 | 0 |
| Malinga | 8 | 1 | 49 | 2 |
| Fernando | 8 | 0 | 74 | 1 |
| Muralitharan | 7 | 0 | 44 | 0 |
| Dilshan | 2 | 0 | 23 | 0 |
| Jayasuriya | 5 | 0 | 33 | 0 |

Fall of Wickets:
1-172, 2-224, 3-261, 4-266

### SRI LANKA

| | | |
|---|---|---|
| WU Tharanga | c Gilchrist b Bracken | 6 |
| ST Jayasuriya | b Clarke | 63 |
| *KC Sangakkara | c Ponting b Hogg | 54 |
| DPMD J'wardene (capt) | lbw b Watson | 19 |
| LPC Silva | b Clarke | 21 |
| TM Dilshan | run out | 14 |
| RP Arnold | c Gilchrist b McGrath | 1 |
| WPUJC Vaas | not out | 11 |
| SL Malinga | st Gilchrist b Symonds | 10 |
| CRD Fernando | not out | 1 |
| M Muralitharan | | |
| Extras | lb 1, w 14 | 15 |
| | (8 wkts 36 overs) | **215** |

| | O | M | R | W |
|---|---|---|---|---|
| Bracken | 6 | 1 | 34 | 1 |
| Tait | 6 | 0 | 42 | 0 |
| McGrath | 7 | 0 | 31 | 1 |
| Watson | 7 | 0 | 49 | 1 |
| Hogg | 3 | 0 | 19 | 1 |
| Clarke | 5 | 0 | 33 | 2 |
| Symonds | 2 | 0 | 6 | 1 |

Fall of Wickets:
1-7, 2-123, 3-145, 4-156, 5-188, 6-190, 7-194, 8-211

Umpires: SA Bucknor (West Indies) & Aleem Dar (Pakistan)
Toss: Australia
Man of the Match: AC Gilchrist
Man of the Tournament: GD McGrath

## Australia won by 53 runs –
### DL Method: target 269 from 36 overs

# WEST INDIES

## by Tony Cozier

Another harrowing year for West Indies cricket was typified by defeats on the field and upheavals off it, none more traumatic than the failure of the first World Cup ever staged in the Caribbean to live up to confident expectations that it would be the 'best ever' and the retirement of the iconic captain Brian Lara at the end of it. The two were closely connected.

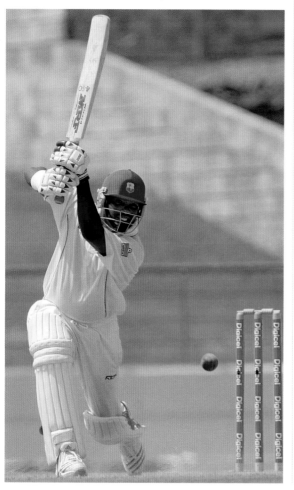

If several of the myriad problems that marred the tournament were unpredictable and no fault of the organisers, the overall sense of disappointment reflected poorly on the West Indies. So did the appalling performance of the team for which Lara paid the price. Inevitably, Lara's departure attracted the largest crowd to the remade Kensington Oval for his final match, the last of the Super Eight round, fittingly against England.

Only a day earlier, one of the most compelling players of his time had unexpectedly declared that it would be the farewell appearance of a career in which he repeatedly rewrote the game's record books with rare style and panache. It ended in the anti-climax of a run out but there were many tears among the thousands who rose to acclaim him.

In light of his team's failed campaign and amid certified reports of general indiscipline, the selectors decided a new beginning was needed and turned to Ramnaresh Sarwan as the sixth captain in ten years. At such a time, in any sport, the inescapable cliché is that it is the end of an era. In this case, the expression is entirely appropriate. Since he first took over the mantle as the team's standard-bearer in 1992, on the retirement of Viv Richards, Lara utterly dominated West Indies cricket like no other. Without him, they now blatantly lack a genuine star batsman for the first time since the formative years of the 1930s when the great George Headley carried the same heavy run-scoring load.

It is a sad paradox that his time should have coincided with the turbulence that continues to undermine West Indies cricket. A lot of it, however, was of his own making and it eventually meant a premature end. But, as batsman supreme and a fair-minded competitor, Lara left a distinctive legacy that helped sustain waning interest during a prolonged period of decline. Even at the height of Lara's powers, as the West Indies endured loss after loss, there was concern for the very future of the game in a region that once basked in the glory of their magnificent players and teams.

It reached the point that a committee of three, headed by retired Jamaica Prime Minister PJ Patterson, was commissioned by then West Indies Cricket Board (WICB) president Ken Gordon 'to consider the composition and structure of the WICB and to make recommendations which will improve its overall operations, governance

Brian Lara, the batting genius, had all the shots in the world (plus a few of his own) and all the time in the world in which to play them.

Brian Lara, the sporting superstar, was always the centre of attention for adoring cricket crowds all over the world.

effectiveness, team performance and strengthen its credibility and public support'. By the time it presented its final report in October, Gordon had resigned after two difficult years. As he left he declared that the profit from the World Cup, although still to be finalised, would eliminate the WICB's debt of approximately US$15 million.

These were welcome boosts for Gordon's successor, Julian Hunte, 67, a former finance minister and ambassador to the United Nations for St Lucia. He had been a WICB director for 28 years up to 1998, latterly as vice-president, so it was very much back to the future. One of his first moves was to appoint Dinanath Ramnarine, head of the West Indies Players Association (WIPA), as a board director. Ramnarine, the former Test leg spinner, had fought running battles with the Board since taking up the post in 2003 and won most of them. But the repeated confrontation was clearly damaging and Hunte saw his decision as giving the WIPA 'the opportunity to be part of the solution instead of continuing to be perceived as part of the problem'.

Against such an uncertain background, Sir Allen Stanford, the Texan billionaire who has located part of his global financial organisation in Antigua for more than 20 years, announced plans for an expansion of his successful, inaugural Twenty20 tournament in 2006. Inaugurated with an estimated US$38 million to cover operational expenses, prize money and grants of US$280,000 to the governing bodies of the 19 participating teams, it would include the Turks and Caicos Islands and Cuba in 2008. Importantly, Stanford gained the WICB's recognition at

an annual cost of US$1 million over the next three years, a sort of franchise arrangement.

Preparations for the World Cup, and the WICB's tight financial position, inevitably had a negative impact on the 2007 domestic season. The Carib Beer Series and the limited-over Kentucky Fried Chicken (KFC) Cup were each limited to one round, with the Carib Challenge reduced from semi-finals between the top four Cup finishers to a straight final between the two top teams.

The Carib titles were straight fights between Barbados and Trinidad & Tobago. Guyana and Jamaica only won one of their five matches, the Leeward Islands and the Windward Islands none. Barbados's fiercely contested, victory over Trinidad & Tobago by three wickets at home in the opening match of the season proved decisive in securing the Cup from the round-robin league. Trinidad & Tobago, though, improved consistently and compensated for failing to retain the Carib Cup by claiming the one-day KFC Cup with victory over the Windwards one weekend and the Carib Challenge in the final over Barbados the next, a repeat of the 2006 result. The Challenge final was such an ill-tempered affair that Deryck Murray, the former Test wicketkeeper, now president of the Trinidad & Tobago Cricket Board (TTCB) and a director of the WICB, noted that he had 'never played in or been a spectator at a game where the umpires' job had been so difficult'. Yet no player was disciplined.

Such behaviour matched the overall standard of the cricket that, once more, offered little hope for a swift revival of West Indies cricket.

# ZIMBABWE

There is no doubting the highlight of Zimbabwe's year, and no one in cricket can have begrudged their long-suffering players the moment when Australia were beaten at the start of the ICC World Twenty20.

Yes, the Australians were ring-rusty, but this was a triumph for the spirit and the ability of a predominantly youthful Zimbabwean side, in which 21-year-old wicketkeeper-batsman Brendan Taylor was the star of the show with a brilliant 60 not out.

Taylor was on the field for the entire 40 overs of the match, having earlier kept beautifully as Elton Chigumbura's three wickets and some magnificent fielding had held Australia's stellar batting line-up in check. He then initially played second string to the powerful Vusi Sibanda as Zimbabwe's run-chase was built on a flying start from their openers, and paced his own innings to perfection by hitting Brad Hodge for two sixes in an ultimately significant 15th over.

With 12 runs needed off the last over, Taylor swept Nathan Bracken's first ball daringly for four and Zimbabwe's ecstatic players were already streaming on to the field in celebration as the penultimate ball evaded Stuart Clark – via Taylor's pads – to end up as a match-clinching boundary to fine leg.

Either side of this happy moment, however, there was not much for Zimbabwean cricket to cheer about as their exile from Tests continues. In July 2007 they were dropped from the ICC Test rankings list as they had played only eight Test matches in the previous three years.

Wicketkeeper Brendan Taylor celebrates the dismissal of Andrew Symonds in Zimbabwe's astonishing ICC World Twenty20 victory against Australia. Taylor later played a match-winning innings with the bat.

Tatenda Taibu, their former captain, did return to the international scene after a self-imposed absence of almost two years – following threats to his family – and his magnificent 107 in the third ODI against South Africa in Harare, just before the World Twenty20, showed that he had lost none of his precocious talent.

It could not prevent Zimbabwe losing the three-match series 3-0, however, even though they finished only 28 runs shy of South Africa's 323 for 9. Eight months earlier, a rare victory in a series lost 3-1 at home to Bangladesh was their first in 14 ODIs. Zimbabwe's showing in the World Cup was poor, with defeats to West Indies and Pakistan following a nervy tie against Ireland.

But there remains fine young talent in Zimbabwe, and it is a wonder that it is still being nurtured amid the country's terrible economic plight. Genuine international-class prospects such as Taylor, Taibu and Sean Williams, the left-hand batsman and slow left-arm spinner, deserve so much better.

Prosper Utseya, the youthful off-spinning captain, has been re-appointed until August 2008, and former Zimbabwe captain Robin Brown has taken over as head coach from Kevin Curran, who is now heading up the Zimbabwe Cricket Academy.

But talent, heartbreakingly for those who remember Zimbabwe's high promise in the 1980s and 1990s, is still draining away. Gavin Ewing and Dion Ebrahim are the latest former internationals to quit the country, to ply their trade in club cricket around the world, and Anthony Ireland, the 22-year-old fast bowler, walked out after the World Cup to join Gloucestershire on a two-year Kolpak registration.

## ONE-DAY INTERNATIONALS
## v. Bangladesh

**Match One**
4 February 2007 at Harare
**Bangladesh** 260 for 9 (50 overs) (Habibul Bashar 78, Shakib Al Hasan 68)
**Zimbabwe** 215 all out (48 overs) (CJ Chibhabha 57, Mashrafe bin Mortaza 4 for 31)
*Bangladesh won by 45 runs*

**Match Two**
6 February 2007 at Harare
**Bangladesh** 153 all out (46 overs)
(GB Brent 4 for 30)
**Zimbabwe** 156 for 2 (35.2 overs) (V Sibanda 93*)
*Zimbabwe won by 8 wickets*

**Match Three**
9 February 2007 at Harare
**Bangladesh** 228 for 9 (50 overs) (Shahriar Nafees 69)
**Zimbabwe** 214 all out (49.4 overs) (V Sibanda 64)
*Bangladesh won by 14 runs*

**Match Four**
10 February 2007 at Harare
**Zimbabwe** 244 for 8 (50 overs) (E Chigumbura 77*, CJ Chibhabha 54, SC Williams 51)
**Bangladesh** 246 for 9 (47.2 overs) (Aftab Ahmed 92, Mushfiqur Rahim 57)
*Bangladesh won by 1 wicket*

**Bangladesh won the series 3–1**

## ONE-DAY INTERNATIONALS
## v. South Africa

**Match One**
22 August 2007 at Bulawayo
**Zimbabwe** 206 all out (50 overs) (E Chigumbura 59, GB Brent 59*)
**South Africa** 210 for 5 (46.5 overs) (AB de Villiers 63, GH Bodi 51, GC Smith 50)
*South Africa won by 5 wickets*

**Match Two**
25 August 2007 at Harare
**Zimbabwe** 247 for 7 (50 overs) (SC Williams 54, S Matsikenyeri 52)
**South Africa** 251 for 2 (39.1 overs) (HH Gibbs 111, GC Smith 96)
*South Africa won by 8 wickets*

**Match Three**
26 August 2007 at Harare
**South Africa** 323 for 9 (50 overs) (AB de Villiers 107, JA Morkel 97)
**Zimbabwe** 295 for 7 (50 overs) (T Taibu 107*)
*South Africa won by 28 runs*

**South Africa won the series 3–0**

# OTHER INTERNATIONAL MATCHES

## ICC CHAMPIONS TROPHY 2006

### Qualifying Group

7 October 2006 Day/Night at Mohali
**Sri Lanka** 302 for 8 (50 overs) (WU Tharanga 105)
**Bangladesh** 265 for 9 (50 overs) (Farhad Reza 67*)
*Sri Lanka won by 37 runs*

8 October 2006 Day/Night at Ahmedabad
**Zimbabwe** 85 all out (30.1 overs)
**West Indies** 90 for 1 (14.2 overs)
*West Indies won by 9 wickets*

10 October 2006 Day/Night at Ahmedabad
**Sri Lanka** 285 for 7 (50 overs) (WU Tharanga 110, KC Sangakkara 80)
**Zimbabwe** 141 all out (42.3 overs)
*Sri Lanka won by 144 runs*

11 October 2006 Day/Night at Jaipur
**Bangladesh** 161 all out (46.3 overs) (Aftab Ahmed 59)
**West Indies** 164 for 0 (36.4 overs) (CH Gayle 104*, S Chanderpaul 52*)
*West Indies won by 10 wickets*

13 October 2006 Day/Night at Jaipur
**Bangladesh** 231 for 6 (50 overs) (Shahriar Nafees 123*)
**Zimbabwe** 130 all out (44.4 overs) (BRM Taylor 52)
*Bangladesh won by 101 runs*

14 October 2006 Day/Night at Mumbai
**West Indies** 80 all out (30.4 overs) (MF Maharoof 6 for 14)
**Sri Lanka** 83 for 1 (13.2 overs)
*Sri Lanka won by 9 wickets*

|  | P | W | L | T | NR | RR | Pts |
|---|---|---|---|---|---|---|---|
| **Sri Lanka** | 3 | 3 | 0 | 0 | 0 | +2.67 | 6 |
| **West Indies** | 3 | 2 | 1 | 0 | 0 | +0.40 | 4 |
| **Bangladesh** | 3 | 1 | 2 | 0 | 0 | +0.02 | 2 |
| **Zimbabwe** | 3 | 0 | 3 | 0 | 0 | -2.93 | 0 |

### Group A

15 October 2006 Day/Night at Jaipur
**England** 125 all out (37 overs)
**India** 126 for 6 (29.3 overs)
*India won by 4 wickets*

18 October 2006 Day/Night at Mumbai
**West Indies** 234 for 6 (50 overs) (RS Morton 90*, BC Lara 71)

**Australia** 224 for 9 (50 overs) (AC Gilchrist 92, JE Taylor 4 for 49)
*West Indies won by 10 runs*

21 October 2006 at Jaipur
**England** 169 all out (45 overs) (AJ Strauss 56)
**Australia** 170 for 4 (36.5 overs) (DR Martyn 78)
*Australia won by 6 wickets*

26 October 2006 Day/Night at Ahmedabad
**India** 223 for 9 (50 overs) (MS Dhoni 51)
**West Indies** 224 for 7 (49.4 overs) (RR Sarwan 53, S Chanderpaul 51)
*West Indies won by 3 wickets*

28 October 2006 Day/Night at Ahmedabad
**West Indies** 272 for 4 (50 overs) (DJ Bravo 112*, CH Gayle 101)
**England** 276 for 7 (48.3 overs) (KP Pietersen 90*, AJ Strauss 50, IR Bell 50)
*England won by 3 wickets*

29 October 2006 Day/Night at Mohali
**India** 249 for 8 (50 overs) (V Sehwag 65, R Dravid 52)
**Australia** 252 for 4 (45.4 overs) (DR Martyn 73*, RT Ponting 58, SR Watson 50)
*Australia won by 6 wickets*

|  | P | W | L | T | NR | RR | Pts |
|---|---|---|---|---|---|---|---|
| **Australia** | 3 | 2 | 1 | 0 | 0 | +0.53 | 4 |
| **West Indies** | 3 | 2 | 1 | 0 | 0 | +0.01 | 4 |
| **India** | 3 | 1 | 2 | 0 | 0 | +0.48 | 2 |
| **England** | 3 | 1 | 2 | 0 | 0 | -1.04 | 2 |

### Group B

16 October 2006 Day/Night at Mumbai
**New Zealand** 195 all out (45.4 overs) (SP Fleming 89)
**South Africa** 108 all out (34.1 overs)
*New Zealand won by 87 runs*

17 October 2006 Day/Night at Jaipur
**Sri Lanka** 253 all out (49.2 overs) (Abdul Razzaq 4 for 50)
**Pakistan** 255 for 6 (48.1 overs) (Imran Farhat 53)
*Pakistan won by 4 wickets*

20 October 2006 Day/Night at Mumbai
**New Zealand** 165 all out (49.2 overs) (M Muralitharan 4 for 23)
**Sri Lanka** 166 for 3 (36 overs) (WU Tharanga 56)
*Sri Lanka won by 7 wickets*

24 October 2006 Day/Night at Ahmedabad
**South Africa** 219 for 9 (50 overs) (AB de Villiers 54, SL Malinga 4 for 53)

**Sri Lanka** 141 all out (39.1 overs)
*South Africa won by 78 runs*

25 October 2006 Day/Night at Mohali
**New Zealand** 274 for 7 (50 overs) (SB Styris 86, SP Fleming 80)
**Pakistan** 223 all out (46.3 overs) (Mohammad Yousuf 71,
Shoaib Malik 52)
*New Zealand won by 51 runs*

27 October 2006 Day/Night at Mohali
**South Africa** 213 for 8 (50 overs) (MV Boucher 69, JM Kemp 64)
**Pakistan** 89 all out (25 overs) (M Ntini 5 for 21)
*South Africa won by 124 runs*

| | P | W | L | T | NR | RR | Pts |
|---|---|---|---|---|---|---|---|
| **South Africa** | 3 | 2 | 1 | 0 | 0 | +0.77 | 4 |
| **New Zealand** | 3 | 2 | 1 | 0 | 0 | +0.57 | 4 |
| **Sri Lanka** | 3 | 1 | 2 | 0 | 0 | -0.20 | 2 |
| **Pakistan** | 3 | 1 | 2 | 0 | 0 | -1.11 | 2 |

### Semi-Finals

1 November 2006 Day/Night at Mohali
**Australia** 240 for 9 (50 overs) (RT Ponting 58,
A Symonds 58, KD Mills 4 for 38)
**New Zealand** 206 all out (46 overs) (DL Vettori 79)
*Australia won by 34 runs*

2 November 2006 Day/Night at Jaipur
**South Africa** 258 for 8 (50 overs) (HH Gibbs 77)
**West Indies** 262 for 4 (44 overs) (CH Gayle 133*,
S Chanderpaul 57*)
*West Indies won by 6 wickets*

### Final

5 November 2006 Day/Night at Mumbai
**West Indies** 138 all out (30.4 overs)
**Australia** 116 for 2 (28.1 overs) (SR Watson 57*)
*Australia won by 8 wickets – DL Method: target 116 runs from 35 overs*

## ONE-DAY INTERNATIONALS
## Kenya v. Bermuda

### Match One
11 November 2006 at Mombasa
**Kenya** 224 for 8 (50 overs)
**Bermuda** 145 all out (45 overs)
*Kenya won by 79 runs*

### Match Two
12 November 2006 at Mombasa
**Bermuda** 184 for 8 (42 overs) (JJ Tucker 52, TM Odoyo 4 for 25)
**Kenya** 186 for 3 (37.5 overs) (T Mishra 64*, SO Tikolo 60*)
*Kenya won by 7 wickets*

### Match Three
14 November 2006 at Mombasa
**Kenya** 305 for 8 (50 overs) (SO Tikolo 111, RDM Leverock 5 for 53)
**Bermuda** 201 for 6 (50 overs) (DA Minors 68)
*Kenya won by 104 runs*
**Kenya won the series 3–0**

## ICC TRI SERIES in South Africa
### (Bermuda, Canada and Holland)

### Match One
26 November 2006 at Potchefstroom
**Holland** 271 for 8 (50 overs)
**Canada** 254 for 8 (50 overs) (DES Maxwell 59, A Bagai 53)
*Holland won by 17 runs*

### Match Two
27 November 2006 at Potchefstroom
**Bermuda** 235 for 8 (50 overs) (DL Hemp 55)
**Canada** 239 for 5 (47.5 overs) (S Dhaniram 63, A Bagai 58*)
*Canada won by 5 wickets*

### Match Three
28 November 2006 at Potchefstroom
**Bermuda** 177 all out (46 overs)
**Holland** 180 for 2 (37.5 overs) (RN ten Doeschate 65,
B Zuiderent 63*)
*Holland won by 8 wickets*

### Match Four
30 November 2006 at Benoni
**Bermuda** 178 for 9 (50 overs) (S Mukuddem 57,
GR Codrington 4 for 33)
**Canada** 179 for 7 (39.4 overs)
*Canada won by 3 wickets*

### Match Five
1 December 2006 at Benoni
**Canada** 223 for 8 (50 overs)
**Holland** 205 for 9 (41.4 overs) (DLS van Bunge 52)
*Holland won by 1 wicket – DL Method: target 205 from 42 overs*

### Match Six
2 December 2006 at Benoni
**Holland** 91 all out (26.4 overs) (S Mukuddem 4 for 40)
**Bermuda** 94 for 4 (17 overs)
*Bermuda won by 6 wickets*

| | P | W | L | T/NR | BP | RR | Pts |
|---|---|---|---|---|---|---|---|
| **Holland** | 4 | 3 | 1 | -/- | 1 | -0.42 | 13 |
| **Canada** | 4 | 2 | 2 | -/- | 1 | +0.24 | 9 |
| **Bermuda** | 4 | 1 | 3 | -/- | 1 | +0.17 | 5 |

## ICC TRI SERIES in Kenya
### (Canada, Kenya and Scotland)

**Match One**
17 January 2007 at Mombasa
**Kenya** 328 for 5 (50 overs) (DO Obuya 73, CO Obuya 68*,
T Mishra 66, RD Shah 54)
**Scotland** 138 all out (36.2 overs)
*Kenya won by 190 runs*

**Match Two**
18 January 2007 at Mombasa
**Canada** 292 for 5 (50 overs) (Q Ali 70, A Bagai 64*,
S Dhaniram 51*)
**Scotland** 293 for 8 (49.5 overs) (RR Watson 117*, NS Poonia 73)
*Scotland won by 2 wickets*

**Match Three**
20 January 2007 at Mombasa
**Kenya** v. **Canada**
*Kenya won – Canada forfeited due to player illness*

**Match Four**
21 January 2007 at Mombasa
**Kenya** 259 for 9 (50 overs) (RD Shah 113)
**Scotland** 253 for 8 (50 overs) (DF Watts 59, RM Haq 59,
SO Tikolo 4 for 41)
*Kenya won by 6 runs*

**Match Five**
23 January 2007 at Mombasa
**Canada** 208 all out (44.3 overs) (CM Wright 4 for 29)
**Scotland** 209 for 8 (47.2 overs)
*Scotland won by 2 wickets*

**Match Six**
24 January 2007 at Mombasa
**Canada** 213 for 9 (50 overs) (AM Samad 50)
**Kenya** 144 all out (35.1 overs)
*Canada won by 69 runs*

| | P | W | L | T/NR | BP | RR | Pts |
|---|---|---|---|---|---|---|---|
| **Kenya** | 4 | 3 | 1 | -/- | 1 | +0.85 | 13 |
| **Scotland** | 4 | 2 | 2 | -/- | 0 | -0.91 | 8 |
| **Canada** | 4 | 1 | 3 | -/- | 1 | +0.36 | 5 |

## ICC WORLD CRICKET LEAGUE – Division One

**Match One**
29 January 2007 at Nairobi
**Bermuda** 133 all out (39.3 overs) (DA Minors 52)
**Kenya** 137 for 0 (18.1 overs) (DO Obuya 74*, MA Ouma 57*)
*Kenya won by 10 wickets*

**Match Two**
30 January 2007 at Nairobi
**Canada** 200 all out (44 overs) (A Bagai 74,
RN ten Doeschate 4 for 31)
**Holland** 201 for 2 (35 overs) (B Zuiderent 77*)
*Holland won by 8 wickets*

**Match Three**
30 January 2007 at Nairobi
**Ireland** 280 for 7 (50 overs) (JP Bray 116)
**Scotland** 284 for 7 (50 overs) (NFI McCullum 100,
RM Haq 52)
*Scotland won by 3 wickets*

**Match Four**
31 January 2007 at Nairobi
**Scotland** 276 for 4 (50 overs) (DF Watts 70, GM Hamilton 64*,
DR Brown 50*)
**Canada** 269 for 9 (50 overs) (A Bagai 137*)
*Scotland won by 7 runs*

**Match Five**
31 January 2007 at Nairobi
**Holland** 131 all out (46.2 overs)
**Kenya** 133 for 3 (32.1 overs)
*Kenya won by 7 wickets*

**Match Six**
31 January 2007 at Nairobi
**Bermuda** 275 for 8 (50 overs) (CJ Smith 52, DA Minors 51)
**Ireland** 276 for 6 (48.4 overs) (WTS Porterfield 112*,
KJ O'Brien 54)
*Ireland won by 4 wickets*

**Match Seven**
2 February 2007 at Nairobi
**Ireland** 284 for 4 (50 overs) (KJ O'Brien 143,
WTS Porterfield 104*)
**Kenya** 286 for 9 (49 overs) (NO Odhiambo 66, TM Odoyo 61*,
WK McCallan 4 for 36, AC Botha 4 for 42)
*Kenya won by 1 wicket*

**Match Eight**
2 February 2007 at Nairobi
**Scotland** 207 for 8 (37 overs) (DF Watts 58)
**Holland** 205 all out (36.5 overs)
*Scotland won by 2 runs*

**Match Nine**
2 February 2007 at Nairobi
**Canada** 162 for 8 (21 overs) (JM Davison 69*)
**Bermuda** 106 all out (15.5 overs) (S Dhaniram 4 for 10)
*Canada won by 56 runs*

## Match Ten
4 February 2007 at Nairobi
**Scotland** 254 for 8 (50 overs) (RM Haq 71, DF Watts 58, GM Hamilton 58)
**Kenya** 177 all out (46 overs) (TM Odoyo 53)
*Scotland won by 77 runs*

## Match Eleven
4 February 2007 at Nairobi
**Ireland** 308 for 7 (50 overs) (EJG Morgan 115, KJ O'Brien 52)
**Canada** 312 for 4 (49.4 overs) (A Bagai 122, Q Ali 60*, JM Davison 57)
*Canada won by 6 wickets*

## Match Twelve
4 February 2007 at Nairobi
**Bermuda** 194 all out (46.3 overs) (DL Hemp 58)
**Holland** 198 for 2 (43.1 overs) (RN ten Doeschate 109*, B Zuiderent 71)
*Holland won by 8 wickets*

## Match Thirteen
5 February 2007 at Nairobi
**Scotland** 268 for 9 (50 overs) (GM Hamilton 58, RR Watson 57)
**Bermuda** 269 for 5 (49 overs) (IH Romaine 85*)
*Bermuda won by 5 wickets*

## Match Fourteen
5 February 2007 at Nairobi
**Kenya** 250 for 9 (50 overs) (T Mishra 62, H Osinde 4 for 33)
**Canada** 92 all out (14.5 overs) (PJ Ongondo 5 for 51, TM Odoyo 4 for 39)
*Kenya won by 158 runs*

## Match Fifteen
5 February 2007 at Nairobi
**Holland** 260 for 7 (46 overs) (DJ Reekers 104, ES Szwarczynski 56*)
**Ireland** 254 for 8 (46 overs) (EJG Morgan 94, WTS Porterfield 84, RN ten Doeschate 4 for 57)
*Holland won by 6 runs*

| | P | W | L | T | NR | RR | Pts |
|---|---|---|---|---|---|---|---|
| Kenya | 5 | 4 | 1 | 0 | 0 | +1.36 | 8 |
| Scotland | 5 | 4 | 1 | 0 | 0 | +0.35 | 8 |
| Holland | 5 | 3 | 2 | 0 | 0 | +0.12 | 6 |
| Canada | 5 | 2 | 3 | 0 | 0 | -0.85 | 4 |
| Ireland | 5 | 1 | 4 | 0 | 0 | -0.06 | 2 |
| Bermuda | 5 | 1 | 4 | 0 | 0 | -1.31 | 2 |

## Final
7 February 2007 at Nairobi
**Scotland** 155 all out (47 overs)
**Kenya** 158 for 2 (37.5 overs) (DO Obuya 93)
*Kenya won by 8 wickets*

## ICC TRI SERIES in Antigua
**(Bangladesh, Bermuda and Canada)**

## Match One
25 February 2007 at St John's
**Bermuda** 205 for 8 (50 overs)
**Bangladesh** 206 for 2 (37.3 overs) (Shahriar Nafees 104*)
*Bangladesh won by 8 wickets*

## Match Two
26 February 2007 at St John's
**Bermuda** 206 for 8 (50 overs) (U Bhatti 4 for 45)
**Canada** 207 for 7 (44.1 overs) (AM Samad 83, DC Borden 4 for 30)
*Canada won by 3 wickets*

## Match Three
28 February 2007 at St John's
**Bangladesh** 278 for 5 (50 overs) (Shakib Al Hasan 134*, Mohammad Ashraful 60, Habibul Bashar 57)
**Canada** 265 for 7 (50 overs) (IS Billcliff 93, GEF Barnett 77)
*Bangladesh won by 13 runs*

| | P | W | L | T/NR | BP | RR | Pts |
|---|---|---|---|---|---|---|---|
| Bangladesh | 2 | 2 | 0 | -/- | 1 | +0.83 | 9 |
| Canada | 2 | 1 | 1 | -/- | 0 | +0.18 | 4 |
| Bermuda | 2 | 0 | 2 | -/- | 0 | -0.96 | 0 |

## AFRO-ASIAN CUP

## Match One
6 June 2007 at Bangalore
**Asia** 317 for 9 (50 overs) (Mohammad Yousuf 66, DPMD Jayawardene 65)
**Africa** 283 all out (47.5 overs) (SM Pollock 130)
*Asia won by 34 runs*

## Match Two
9 June 2007 at Chennai
**Asia** 337 for 7 (50 overs) (SC Ganguly 88, V Sehwag 52, Mohammad Yousuf 51)
**Africa** 306 all out (49.5 overs) (MV Boucher 73, HH Dippenaar 67, CRD Fernando 4 for 36)
*Asia won by 31 runs*

## Match Three
10 June 2007 at Chennai
**Asia** 331 for 8 (50 overs) (MS Dhoni 139*, DPMD Jayawardene 107)
**Africa** 318 for 7 (50 overs) (JM Kemp 86, AB de Villiers 70, SM Pollock 58*, Mohammad Rafique 4 for 65)
*Asia won by 13 runs*
**Asia won the series 3–0**

## ONE-DAY INTERNATIONALS

### Ireland v. India
23 June 2007 at Belfast
**Ireland** 193 all out (50 overs) (NJ O'Brien 52)
**India** 172 for 1 (35 overs) (G Gambhir 80*, SC Ganguly 74*)
*India won by 9 wickets – DL Method: target 171 from 39 overs*

### Ireland v. South Africa
24 June 2007 at Belfast
**South Africa** 173 for 4 (31 overs) (MN van Wyk 52)
**Ireland** 131 all out (30.5 overs) (VD Philander 4 for 12)
*South Africa won by 42 runs*

### Scotland v. Pakistan
1 July 2007 at Edinburgh
*Match abandoned – no result*

### India v. Pakistan
3 July 2007 at Glasgow
*Match abandoned – no result*

### Canada v. Holland
**Match One**
3 July 2007 at Toronto
**Holland** 289 for 7 (50 overs) (PW Borren 96, ES Szwarczynski 51)
**Canada** 172 all out (43 overs) (S Dhaniram 55)
*Holland won by 117 runs*

**Match Two**
4 July 2007 at Toronto
*Match abandoned – no result*

## IRELAND QUADRANGULAR SERIES
(Holland, Ireland, Scotland and West Indies)

**Match One**
10 July 2007 at Dublin
**Holland** 80 all out (31.2 overs) (DR Smith 4 for 8)
**West Indies** 82 for 0 (14.3 overs) (CH Gayle 51*)
*West Indies won by 10 wickets*

**Match Two**
11 July 2007 at Dublin
**Ireland** 210 for 8 (50 overs) (EJG Morgan 51)
**Holland** 209 for 6 (50 overs) (Mudassar Bukhari 71)
*Ireland won by 1 run*

**Match Three**
12 July 2007 at Dublin
**Scotland** 152 for 7 (30 overs)
**West Indies** 165 for 6 (29.5 overs) (CH Gayle 85*, RM Haq 4 for 28)
*West Indies won by 4 wickets – DL Method: target 165 from 30 overs*

**Match Four**
13 July 2007 at Belfast
**Scotland** 71 for 5 (22.2 overs)
**Holland**
*Match abandoned – no result*

**Match Five**
14 July 2007 at Dublin
**Ireland** 84 for 4 (17.2 overs)
**West Indies**
*Match abandoned – no result*

**Match Six**
15 July 2007 at Belfast
**Ireland** 222 for 7 (50 overs) (NJ O'Brien 72)
**Scotland** 199 all out (49.3 overs) (RR Watson 83, NFI McCullum 54)
*Ireland won by 23 runs*

| | P | W | L | T | NR | RR | Pts |
|---|---|---|---|---|---|---|---|
| West Indies | 3 | 2 | 0 | 0 | 1 | +3.97 | 11 |
| Ireland | 3 | 2 | 0 | 0 | 1 | +0.24 | 10 |
| Scotland | 3 | 0 | 2 | 0 | 1 | -0.87 | 2 |
| Holland | 3 | 0 | 2 | 0 | 1 | -1.64 | 2 |

## ONE-DAY INTERNATIONAL
### Scotland v. India
16 Aug 2007 at Glasgow
**Scotland** 203 for 9 (46 overs)
**India** 212 for 3 (39.5 overs) (G Gambhir 85*, AR Uthappa 55)
*India won by 7 wickets – DL Method: target 209 from 46 overs*

## ICC TRI SERIES
(Bangladesh, Kenya and Pakistan)

**Match One**
1 September 2007 at Nairobi
**Kenya** 138 for 7 (20 overs)
**Bangladesh** 139 for 5 (17.4 overs)
*Bangladesh won by 5 wickets*

**Match Two**
2 September 2007 at Nairobi
**Pakistan** 191 for 7 (20 overs)
**Bangladesh** 161 for 7 (20 overs) (Mohammed Nazimuddin 81)
*Pakistan won by 30 runs*

**Match Three**
4 September 2007 at Nairobi
**Kenya** 92 all out (19.4 overs)
**Pakistan** 93 for 2 (14 overs)
*Pakistan won by 8 wickets*
**Pakistan won the series**

The English First-Class Form Charts are on pages 98–133.